Plant Production and Protection Series   *No. 34*

GRASSLANDS
of the
WORLD

Edited by
J.M. Suttie, S.G. Reynolds and **C. Batello**

FOOD AND AGRICULTURE ORGANIZATION OF THE UNITED NATIONS
Rome, 2005

ISBN 92-5-105337-5

CONTENTS

Chapter 3 – Grasslands of South Africa   77
Anthony R. Palmer and Andrew M. Ainslie

Chapter 4 – GRASSLANDS OF PATAGONIA   121
Andrés F. Cibils and Pablo R. Borrelli

FOREWORD

The Food and Agriculture Organization of the United Nations has long been concerned with grasslands, forage crops and pastoral development issues, which have been the focus of various field-based activities and Regular Programme work of the Grassland and Pasture Crops Group within the Crop and Grassland Service.

Grasslands cover a very large portion of the earth's surface and are important as a feed source for livestock, as a habitat for wildlife, for environmental protection and for the *in situ* conservation of plant genetic resources. In both developed and developing countries, many millions of livestock farmers, ranchers and pastoralists depend on grasslands and conserved products such as hay and silage and on a range of fodder crops for their livelihoods. Rapid increases in human and livestock populations have contributed to increased pressures on the world's grasslands, particularly in arid and semi-arid environments. Now more than ever, information is needed on the status of the world's grasslands.

FAO, through the Grassland and Pasture Crops Group, has endeavoured over many years to make available information on grassland themes to a range of audiences. Earlier books included those of Whyte, Nillson-Leissner and Trumble (1969) on *Legumes in Agriculture* and Whyte, Moir and Cooper (1975) on *Grasses in Agriculture*, *Tropical Grasses* by Skerman & Riveros (1990) and *Tropical Forage Legumes* by Skerman, Cameron and Riveros (1988), *Pasture - cattle - coconut systems* by Reynolds (1995), with *Managing Mobility in African Grasslands* by Niamir-Fuller (1999). More recent publications have included studies on: *Hay and Straw Conservation* (Suttie, 2000); *Silage in the Tropics* (t'Mannetje, 2000); *Grassland Resource Assessment* (Harris, 2001); *Transhumant Grazing Systems in Temperate Asia* (Suttie & Reynolds, 2003); *Know to Move, Move to Know* (Schareika, 2003); *Site-Specific Grasses and Herbs* (Krautzer, Peratoner and Bozzo, 2004); *Wild and Sown Grasses* (Peeters, 2004); *Fodder Oats: a world overview* (Suttie & Reynolds, 2004); *Forage Legumes for Temperate Grasslands* (Frame, 2005); and *Grasslands: Developments, Opportunities, Perspectives* (Reynolds & Frame, 2005). The publications are complemented by detailed information on grassland species and extensive *Country Pasture Resource Profiles* to be found on the FAO Grassland Web site at <http://www.fao.org/ag/grassland.htm>.

The present book provides an overview of a range of grassland systems worldwide, with contributions by experts from many regions, and in a final chapter briefly assesses the state of the grasslands, their management, various grassland resources, the complementary roles of sown pastures, fodder crops and natural grasslands and concludes by looking at various social, economic and environmental factors. Researchers, grassland scientists and policy-makers will find the material useful and the book will contribute towards the accumulated knowledge on the world's grasslands. The contributions of authors are much appreciated by FAO in its efforts to disseminate information on grasslands and pastoral systems. The considerable input made by the editors is particularly acknowledged – retired staff member James Suttie, and Stephen Reynolds and Caterina Batello of the Grassland and Pasture Crops Group of the Crop and Grassland Service – both for their personal contributions and Stephen Reynolds for ensuring that the book was brought to publication.

Mahmoud Solh
Director
Plant Production and Protection Division
FAO Agriculture Department

ACKNOWLEDGEMENTS

This publication is based on a number of regional and country studies written by various authors, who are acknowledged in the text. Particular thanks to Dr Wolfgang Bayer, who assisted with the early review of some of the chapters. In locating and contacting authors to prepare papers, the following provided much appreciated assistance: Prof. Klaus Kellner, School of Environmental Sciences and Development, Potchefstroom University, South Africa; Drs Dennis Cash and Bok Sowell, Montana State University, and Professor Denis Child, Colorado State University, United States of America; and Dr Rod Heitschmidt, ARS, Miles City, Montana, United States of America.

The authors of Chapter 2 have dedicated their chapter to Jim Ellis and Peter de Leeuw. Both made an important contribution to rangeland science in East Africa and are referred to in the chapter. Jim was killed in a skiing accident in 2002 and Peter passed away in 2003.

Paulo César de Faccio Carvalho, Faculdade de Agronomia – UFRGS, Porto Alegre, Brazil helped to locate photographs from Brazil for Chapter 5. Pablo Borrelli assisted with Spanish translations of the manuscripts from which Chapter 5 was prepared and the authors of Chapter 5 acknowledge the assistance of Ing. Ag. Oscar Pittaluga, who provided comments on early drafts. The author of Chapter 7 acknowledges the inputs of B. Erdenebaatar and N. Batjargal. Thanks also to Dr Jonathan Robinson for comments and to Petra Staberg for assistance with the FAO Grassland Web site, and in particular with the finalization and layout of the Country Pasture/Forage Resource Profiles. Mary Reynolds assisted with proofreading.

Dr J. Boonman died tragically after preparing the draft of Chapter 10 with Professor Sergey Mikhalev, but indicated while preparing the paper that he wished to dedicate it to the memory of Dr David Pratt and his early work on the grasslands of East Africa.

Thanks are due to the authors – M.A. Al-Jaloudy, O. Berkat, M. Tazi, A. Coulibally, M. Dost, A.R. Fitzherbert, M.F. Garbulsky, V.A. Deregibus, D. Geesing, H. Djibo, Z. Hu, D. Zhang, H. Kagone, A. Karagöz, C. Kayouli, M. Makhmudovich, A. Masri, B.K. Misri, D. Nedjraoui, K. Oppong-Anane, D. Pariyar, J.H Rasambainarivo, N. Ranaivoarivelo, O. Thieme, R.R. Vera and K. Wangdi – of a number of Country Pasture/Forage Resource Profiles on the FAO Grassland Web site <http://www.fao.org/ag/grassland.htm>, from which information has been drawn, particularly in the preparation of Chapter 11.

Photographs, unless otherwise acknowledged, are by the authors of each chapter or by the editors. Stephen Reynolds selected and located photographs in the text. Cathleen J. Wilson generously agreed to three of her photographs being used in Chapter 2 on the understanding that they are not used elsewhere or copied without her permission, as did Marzio Marzot in several chapters. Peter Harris kindly provided a number of photographs, as did Dr Jeff Printz, USDA-NRCS, and Alice Carloni of TCIP, FAO. Dr Mae Elsinger, Rangeland Biologist, Agriculture and Agri-Food Canada (AAFC)-Prairie Farm Rehabilitation (PFRA) Range and Biodiversity Division, Manitoba, Canada, provided a number of photographs by various authors from AAFC-PFRA files, which are identified with her name in Chapter 6. Other photographs used were provided by SARDI (South Australian Research and Development Institute), Dr M. Halling, Dr Martín Garbulsky, Dr V. Alejandro Deregibus, Prof. Alain Peeters and Duane McCartney, Lacombe Research Centre, Agriculture and Agri-Food Canada. Mr Constantin Melidis and Elena Palazzani provided assistance with the scanning of a number of photographs. Several of the grassland maps were prepared by Christopher Aurich. Lucie Herzigova, FAO, assisted with the finalization of a number of the figures. Cover design was by Studio Bartoleschi, Rome. Cover photographs are by Daniel Miller, Stephen Reynolds and Marzio Marzot. Final editing for consistency of language and style, and preparation for publication, was by Thorgeir Lawrence.

CONTRIBUTORS

Ainslie, Andrew M., ARC-Range & Forage Institute, Grahamstown, South Africa.

Batello, Caterina, Grassland and Pasture Crops Group, FAO Crop and Grassland Service.

Berretta, Elbio J., Director, Regional INIA Tacuarembó Ruta 5, km 386, 45000 Tacuarembó, Uruguay.

Boonman, Joseph G.† (deceased), Boma Consult, The Hague, Netherlands.

Borrelli, Pablo R., OVIS XXI, Santa Fe 2843 10°B, 1425-Buenos Aires, Argentina.

Cibils, Andrés F., Dept. of Animal and Range Sciences, New Mexico State University, Las Cruces, NM 88003, United States of America.

Hanson, Jean, International Livestock Research Institute, Addis Ababa, Ethiopia.

McIvor, John G., CSIRO Sustainable Ecosystems, Queensland Bioscience Precinct, 306 Carmody Road, St Lucia, Qld 4067, Australia.

Maraschin, Gerzy E., Professor, Faculdade de Agronomía – UFRGS, RS – Brazil.

Mikhalyov, Sergey S., Professor of Grassland Science, Agronomy Faculty, Moscow Timiryazev Agricultural Academy, Moscow, Russian Federation.

Miller, Daniel J., United States Agency for International Development, 1300 Pennsylvania Ave. NW, Washington, DC 20523, United States of America.

Nyabenge, M., International Livestock Research Institute, Nairobi, Kenya.

Palmer, Anthony R., ARC-Range & Forage Institute, Grahamstown, South Africa.

Pieper, Rex D., New Mexico State University, Las Cruces, New Mexico.

Reid, Robin S., International Livestock Research Institute, Nairobi, Kenya.

Reynolds, Stephen G., Senior Officer, Grassland and Pasture Crops Group, FAO Crop and Grassland Service.

Royo Pallarés, Olegario, Belgrano 841, 3470 Mercedes, Provincia Corrientes, Argentina.

Serneels, S., International Livestock Research Institute, Nairobi, Kenya.

Suttie, James M., FAO Grassland and Pasture Group Staff Member (retired).

Glossary of technical terms and abbreviations used in the text

ABARE	Australian Bureau of Agricultural and Resource Economics
AFLP	amplified fragment length polymorphism
aimag	largest Mongolian rural administrative unit, ≈ province, comprising several *sum*
airag	fermented mares milk, mildly alcoholic
AMBA	Argentine Merino Breeder Association
ANPP	annual above ground primary productivity
AR	accumulation rate
ARC	Agricultural Research Council (South Africa)
ARC-RFI	Range and Forage Institute (South Africa)
ARC-ISCW	Institute for Soil Climate and Water (South Africa)
ARS	Agricultural Research Service (United States of America)
AUM	animal unit month
AUY	animal unit year
AVHRR	advanced very high resolution radiometer
bag	smallest Mongolian administrative unit below *sum*, replacing the former soviet-type brigade
badia	semi-desert grazing land (Arabic)
bod	traditional large livestock unit in Mongolia
brigalow	*Acacia harpophylla* forest and woodlands
BSE	bovine spongiform encephalopathy (mad cow disease)
CAM	Crassulacean acid metabolism
camp	paddock (South Africa)
CCD	[United Nations] Convention to Combat Desertification in those Countries Experiencing Serious Drought and/or Desertification, particularly in Africa
CEC	cation exchange capacity
CIS	Confederation of Independent States
CISNR	Commission for Integrated Survey of National Resources (China)
CONICET	Consejo Nacional de Investigaciones Científicas y Técnicas (Argentina)
CP	crude protein
CRP	Conservation Reserve Program (United States of America)

CRSP	Collaborative Research Support Program (United States of America)
CSIRO	Commonwealth Scientific and Industrial Research Organization
CYE	comparative yield estimate
DGR	daily growth rates
DLWG	daily liveweight gain
DSS	decision support system
DWR	dry weight rank
EEA/EEPRI	Ethiopian Economic Association/Ethiopian Economic Policy Research Institute
ENSO	El Niño-Southern Oscillation
ephemeroids	Russian term denoting perennials whose vegetative parts die down annually (*e.g. Poa bulbosa*)
foggage	reserved standing herbage for grazing after the growing season
FO	forage offer
FSAU	Food Security Analysis Unit (Somalia)
FSU	former Soviet Union
garrigue	low growing secondary vegetation with aromatic herbs and prickly dwarf shrubs in the Mediterranean basin
GEF	Global Environment Facility
ger	Mongolian herders mobile felt dwelling (Russian *yurt*)
GIS	geographical information system
GLASOD	Global Assessment of Soil Degradation (global study published in 1990 by the UNEP and the International Soil Reference and Information Centre in cooperation with the Winand Staring Centre, the International Society of Soil Science, FAO and the International Institute for Aerospace Survey and Earth Sciences)
GSSA	Grassland Society of Southern Africa
GTZ	Deutsche Gesellschaft für Technische Zusammenarbeit
HPG	high performance grazing
HUG	high utilization grazing
IBP	International Biological Program
IEA	Instituto Ecologia Applicata, Rome, Italy
IGAD	Intergovernmental Authority on Development
IGBP	International Geosphere-Biosphere Programme
INIA	Instituto Nacional de Investigación Agropecuaria
INTA	Instituto Nacional de Tecnología Agropecuaria [National Institute for Agricultural Technology, Argentina]
IFEVA-UBA	Instituto de Investicaciones Fisiológicas y Ecológicas – Universidad de Buenos Aires (Argentina)

IUCN	The World Conservation Union
khainag	yak × cattle hybrid (Mongolia)
khot ail	traditional herding unit of households camping and working together (Mongolia)
Kolkhoz	a collective or cooperative farm in the soviet system
Kray	territory (Russian Federation)
LADA	land degradation assessment in drylands
LAI	leaf area index
Landsat TM	land remote-sensing satellite – thematic mapper
LAR	leaf appearance rate
LER	leaf expansion rate
LEWS	Livestock Early Warning System
LFA	landscape function analysis
liman	flood meadow (Russian Federation)
LLS	leaf life span
LSU	livestock unit
LTER	Long-Term Ecological Research (this is a Network/Program in the United States of America)
LWG	liveweight gain
malezales	marshy, low-lying wetlands – South America
masl	metres above sea level
matorral	drought-resistant Mediterranean scrub, taller than garrigue (= French *maquis*)
MAP	mean annual precipitation
negdel	Mongolian former cooperative — replaced by *sum*
NDVI	normalized difference vegetation index
NIRS	near infra-red spectroscopy
NOAA	National Oceanic and Atmospheric Administration (United States of America)
nomadism	generally used of pastoral groups thought to have no fixed base, but follow entirely erratic rain storms
Oblast	region (Russian Federation)
OM	organic matter
otor	movement of livestock to distant pasture to improve condition
PAGE	policy analysis of the greenhouse effect
PAR	photosynthetically active radiation
PAP	primary aerial productivity
ppm	parts per million
PROLANA	El Programa para Mejorar la Calidad de la Lana Argentina
rakhi	alcoholic drink distilled from *airag*
RAPD	random amplified polymorphic DNA

RASHN	Russian Academy of Agricultural Sciences
RCE	regional centre of endemism
SAGPyA	Secretaría de Agricultura Ganadería, Pesca y Alimentos, (Argentina)
SETCIP	Secretaría de Ciencía, Tecnología e Innovación Productiva
Sovkhozy	state-operated agricultural estate in the former USSR for specialized large-scale production
SP	secondary production
SPOT	Satellite probatoire d'observation de la Terre (Experimental Earth Observation System)
SPUR2	Simulation of Production and Utilization of Rangelands (software)
sum	Mongolian administrative unit, below *aimag*
transhumance	pastoral systems where people with their animals move between distinct seasonal pastures, usually at considerable distance or altitude from each other
tugrik or togrog	Mongolian national currency
UFRGS	Universidade Federal do Rio Grande do Sul [Federal University of Rio Grande del Sul, Brazil]
UNEP	United Nations Environment Programme
USGS/EDC	United States Geological Survey/EROS Data Center
UVB	ultraviolet B
veldt	extensive grasslands in South Africa
WWF	World Wide Fund for Nature
zud	climatic disaster that affects livestock – usually deep frozen snow which denies access to grazing, but may be lack of snow to drink, unusual cold, or drought (Mongolian)

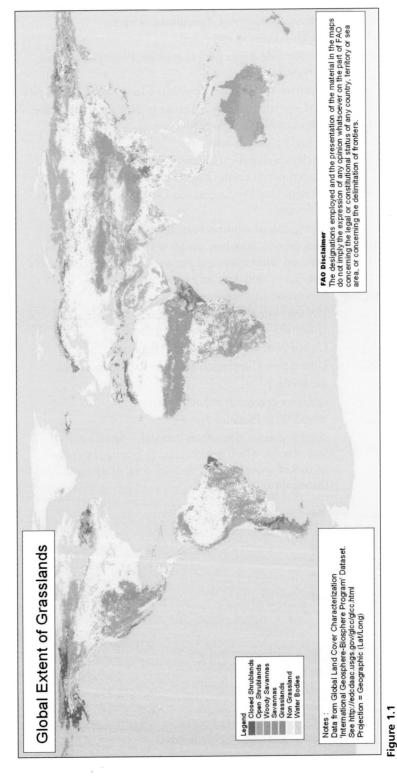

Figure 1.1
Extent of the world's grasslands.

Chapter 1
Introduction

Grasslands in the wider sense are among the largest ecosystems in the world (Figure 1.1); their area is estimated at 52.5 million square kilometres, or 40.5 percent of the terrestrial area excluding Greenland and Antarctica (World Resources Institute, 2000, based on IGBP data). In contrast, 13.8 percent of the global land area (excluding Greenland and Antarctica) is woody savannah and savannah; 12.7 percent is open and closed shrub; 8.3 percent is non-woody grassland; and 5.7 percent is tundra.

In its narrow sense, "grassland" may be defined as ground covered by vegetation dominated by grasses, with little or no tree cover; UNESCO defines grassland as "land covered with herbaceous plants with less than 10 percent tree and shrub cover" and wooded grassland as 10–40 percent tree and shrub cover (White, 1983). In this study, grassland is used in its wider sense of "grazing land". Definitions of grassland and the associated term "range" are multitude, many with specific local legal connotations; the Second Expert Meeting on Harmonizing Forest-related Definitions for use by Various Stakeholders (FAO, 2000) gives eleven pages of them. The Oxford Dictionary of Plant Sciences (Allaby, 1998) gives a succinct definition:

"Grassland occurs where there is sufficient moisture for grass growth, but where environmental conditions, both climatic and anthropogenic, prevent tree growth. Its occurrence, therefore, correlates with a rainfall intensity between that of desert and forest and is extended by grazing and/or fire to form a plagioclimax in many areas that were previously forested."

S.G. REYNOLDS

Plate 1.1
Grasslands – sheep on spring grazing.

S.G. REYNOLDS

Plate 1.2
Mosaic of cultivated cropland and grassland.

This study has been undertaken by the Grassland and Pasture Crops Group of FAO and grassland is taken to be grazing land. The emphasis is on extensive grazing lands (Plate 1.1) since these form large, identifiable units. Unsown grassland that occurs as a mosaic of uncultivated patches within farming land (Plate 1.2) is not dealt with here, but it is nevertheless important in smallholder systems as a source of livestock feed; in commercial systems it is more important as a wildlife habitat and a refuge for biodiversity.

No grassland is entirely natural, and there are many degrees of interference: fire, whether spontaneous or lit by man, has influenced, and continues to influence, large areas; and grazing by livestock and, in some continents, by large herds of wild herbivores. More invasive interventions have been clearing of woody vegetation either to give better grazing or originally for cropping; subdivision with or without fencing; provision of water points to extend the grazing area or season; and various "improvement" techniques such as oversowing with pasture grass and legume seeds – with or without surface scarification and fertilizer. In the early days of FAO, Semple (1956) summarized much of the available techniques and problems, and most are relevant today, although some technologies have progressed in detail. In general, grassland is said to be natural if it is not the result of full ploughing and sowing – the composition of much old sown pasture has, of course, little to do with the seed mixture used at its establishment.

The better-watered parts of many of the world's great grassland zones have been developed for arable farming, notably in the North American Prairie, the South American Pampas, and the East European Steppe, and grazing is now often relegated to the more marginal lands, unfit for cropping, where

J.M. SUTTIE

Plate 1.3
Milking at a transit camp on the way to summer pastures in Tarialan, Mongolia.

the population is often totally dependent on livestock for its livelihood. In Africa also there is little extensive grassland uncultivated in regions where the rainfall permits the production of even meagre subsistence crops. The effect of developing the best land for crops has several negative effects on the use of the remaining land for grazing, including obstructing traditional migration routes in zones of transhumance and denying access to water points.

The terms "nomadism" and "transhumance" are sometimes used indiscriminately when applied to mobile livestock production systems. Transhumance describes those pastoral systems where people with their animals moved between two distinct seasonal pasture areas, usually at considerable distance or altitude from each other (Plate 1.3). Nomadism is used for pastoral groups that have no fixed base, but follow erratic rain storms.

Great grazing lands still exist, however. Among the most important are the steppes that stretch from Mongolia (Plate 1.4) and northern China to Europe; the Tibet-Qinghai Plateau (Plates 1.5 and 1.6) and the adjacent mountain grazing of the Himalaya-Hindu Kush (Plate 1.7); the North American prairies; in South America – the Pampas, the Chaco, Campos (Plate 1.8), Llanos and Cerrados pastures, the cold lands of Patagonia (Plate 1.9) and the Altiplanos; the Australian grasslands; in the Mediterranean Region and western Asia there are large areas of semi-arid grazed land; south of the Sahara there are the vast Sahelian and Sudano-Sahelian zones, as well as most of the eastern part of Africa from the Horn to the Cape.

Two fairly important types of grassland are not dealt with. Very large areas in the tropics are covered by *Imperata cylindrica,* often in nearly pure stand; this relatively unpalatable, strongly rhizomatous grass is hard to eradicate,

S.G. REYNOLDS

Plate 1.4
Horse herd on grasslands near Arkhangai, Mongolia.

PETER HARRIS

Plate 1.5
Grasslands on the Qinghai Plateau, China.

burns easily and thus makes the re-establishment of forest cover difficult. It usually establishes itself when forest has been cleared, often for crop production. It occurs throughout the tropics; the total area has not been established, but Garrity *et al.* (1997) estimate that the area of *Imperata* is 35 million hectares in Asia alone. There are also large areas of potential grazing in the herbage under tree crops (Plate 1.10), mainly in the tropics; some is used, but much is not yet exploited for livestock production; this is dealt with in detail in another FAO publication, *Pasture – cattle – coconut systems* (Reynolds, 1995).

Extensive grazing is usually the exploitation of managed natural ecosystems on which human activities may have had a considerable impact to facilitate or

S.G. REYNOLDS

Plate 1.6
The high plateau near Lake Namtso, Tibet Autonomous Region, China.

S.G. REYNOLDS

Plate 1.7
Subalpine pastures at Suri Paya, Kaghan Valley, Pakistan.

improve livestock production; it is a land use, not a specific crop, and must, for example, compete with crops, wildlife, forestry and recreation. The choice of use is not fixed and depends on economic factors as well as soil and climate. It is usually on land unsuitable for intensive cultivation because of topography, poor soil or a short growing season – the season may be limited by moisture availability or temperature. Exploitation by the grazing animal is, in many countries, the principal practical method of exploiting the natural vegetation of arid, stony, flooded, montane or remote areas. It follows, therefore, that all discussion of grassland must be in the context of animal production and of the human communities that gain their livelihood thereby (Riveros, 1993).

ELBIO BERRETTA

Plate 1.8
The Campos – winter scene on the Basaltic Campos in the north of Uruguay.

PABLO BORELLI

Plate 1.9
Patagonia – sheep being herded on the Magellan steppe, near the Coyle river.

Sown pasture (Plate 1.11) is important within commercial arable farming systems, and, since it competes with other crops for land and inputs, must be economically viable compared with other crops at the farm-system level. In well-watered areas it may replace natural grassland, often in association with crop production. Sown pastures are usually most productive in their early years and yields fall off thereafter; to remain productive they require careful management and inputs, with or without periodic resowing; they usually

S.G. REYNOLDS

Plate 1.10
Cattle grazing under coconuts.

S.G. REYNOLDS

Plate 1.11
Improved pastures – Brazil.

also need fencing and water reticulation. Since grazing requires fairly large, enclosed areas to be managed effectively, sown pasture is not really suited to smallholder farms.

Sown fodder, often irrigated in semi-arid areas, can provide conserved fodder for winter use, and examples are given in the chapters on North America, Patagonia, Russia and the Campos. Fodder growing is traditional in some smallholder areas, but, unlike sown pasture, fodder can be used on any size of farm, not only large ones, whether for use green or conserved; how it has

S.G. REYNOLDS

Plate 1.12
Inner Mongolia – meadow hay prepared by herders for winter feeding.

S.G. REYNOLDS

Plate 1.13
Straw stacked for use as winter feed – Muzaffarabad, Pakistan.

become very important economically in the Pakistan Punjab is described by
Dost (2004). Hay from natural meadows has been used by herders (Plate 1.12)
for a very long time, but traditional pastoralists do not usually sow fodder;
Wang (2003) describes an interesting scheme in the Altai region of Xinjiang
in China, wherein Kazakh herders produce alfalfa (*Medicago sativa*) hay for
winter feed on irrigated lowlands while maintaining their spring to autumn
transhumant migration.

Crop residues, especially straws and stovers (Plate 1.13), are very important
as livestock feed in both commercial and traditional systems; in commercial
farming they are usually part of the roughage ration and supplemented with

other fodders and concentrates; in traditional subsistence systems they may be the main feed when grazing is not available. In the irrigated lands of southern Asia, crop residues are often the main feed of large ruminants year-round. Residues are not discussed in detail in most of the studies, but their conservation and use is described in a recent FAO Grassland Group publication (Suttie, 2000). In some extensive grazing systems with adjacent cropping zones, crop residues may also figure as lean-season feed. Lean seasons vary: in some areas it is winter; in tropical areas it is the dry season; and in Mediterranean zones it is the hot, dry summer. It is, of course, much more important in agricultural and mixed farming areas. Crop residues and stubbles are important in West African transhumance systems and there is a complementarity between cropping and stock rearing communities: herders move north into the desert fringe during the rains (and the season when the crops are on the ground) and move back to the agricultural areas after harvest, in the dry season; traditionally the farmers did not keep livestock.

Some studies reported here, notably those on the Campos, North America and Australia, describe how exotic pasture plants have been introduced to grassland, often with fertilizer application and varying degrees of scarification of the surface and checks to the native vegetation, and have become naturalized. With an increasing interest in maintaining biodiversity and protecting native vegetation, attitudes to introduced "improving" plants may be changing. A primary quality of an improving plant is its ability to spread and colonize natural vegetation; now such qualities may cause a plant to be listed as an invasive alien.

Grazing systems can be roughly divided into two main types – commercial and traditional, with the traditional type often mainly aimed at subsistence.

Commercial grazing of natural pasture is very often large-scale and commonly involves a single species, usually beef cattle or sheep, which would mainly be for wool production. Some of the largest areas of extensive commercial grazing developed in the nineteenth century on land which had not previously been heavily grazed by ruminants; these grazing industries were mainly developed by immigrant communities in the Americas and Australasia, and to a much less degree in southern and eastern Africa.

Traditional livestock production systems are very varied according to climate and the overall farming systems of the area. They also use a wider range of livestock, since buffaloes, asses, goats, yak and camels are predominantly raised in the traditional sector. All species are discussed in the various chapters, but buffalo, of which there are 170 million worldwide (FAOSTAT, 2004), are little mentioned since most are kept in agricultural or agropastoral systems in tropical and sub-tropical Asia (only Egypt and Brazil have significant numbers elsewhere), and are fed largely on crop residues, not on grasslands. In traditional farming systems livestock are often mainly kept for subsistence and savings, and are frequently multi-purpose, providing

Plate 1.14
Mongolia – the higher altitude summer pastures of Turgen are used to avoid the insects in the lower Uvs lake basin.

meat, milk, draught, fibres and frequently fuel in the form of dung-cakes. In many cultures the number of livestock is associated with social standing.

Many traditional systems are sedentary, and these are usually agropastoral, combining crop production with livestock that can utilize crop residues and by-products and make use of land unsuitable for crops. Extensive grasslands, however, are frequently exploited by mobile systems, transhumant or nomadic, where herds move between grazing areas according to season; some move according to temperature, others follow feed availability. Other factors may affect migratory movements: in the Great Lakes Basins region of Mongolia, herders have to leave the low grazing lands near Uvs lake and go to the mountains in June because of plagues of biting insects (Plate 1.14), returning to the lakeside in autumn, but having to move to the mountains in winter to avoid the very low temperatures of the basin (Erdenebaatar, 2003). Two areas of mobile herding are described in the chapters on Mongolia and the Tibet Plateau. Mobile herders often keep mixed flocks, as this helps reduce herding risk as well as making a fuller use of the vegetation on offer – the various species may be herded separately.

Political and economic changes over the past 150 years have had a marked effect on the distribution, condition and use of grasslands and these are described in most of the chapters. Settlement, ranching and the inroads of cropping into former grassland have been mentioned above. Former colonies have gained their independence and states that had been under absolute rulers have become democracies; this has often led to the breakdown of traditional authorities and grazing rights, raising the problems of privately owned livestock on public land. The great grazing lands of Central Asia, China and the Russian Federation have gone from feudal systems to collective management and then, in the past twenty years, to decollectivization and privately owned stock – approaches to management and grazing rights have varied from country to country and some are described in the chapters on the Russian Federation, Mongolia and Tibet Autonomous Region, China.

The herbaceous layer of grazing lands is usually, but not always, grasses; several other plant types cover large grazed areas. Cyperaceae, especially *Kobresia* spp., dominate many of the better-watered, hard-grazed yak pastures, especially those of the alpine meadow type. Halophytes, notably Chenopodiaceae, both herbaceous and shrubby, are important on alkaline and saline soils in many arid and semi-arid grazing lands. In tundra, lichens, especially *Cladonia rangifer*, and mosses provide reindeer feed. Sub-shrubs are important: various species of *Artemisia* are important in steppic regions of the old world from North Africa to the northern limit of the steppe, and also occur in North America. Ericaceous sub-shrubs (species of *Calluna*, *Erica* and *Vaccinium*) are very important grazing for sheep and deer on UK moorland.

Browse is frequently mentioned as a significant feed source, often consumed in the lean season and in some cases fruits are also eaten. Tree fodder is especially important in tropical and sub-tropical situations with alternating wet and dry seasons and is discussed in the chapters on Africa and Australia (where it may be referred to as "top feed"). Various mixed shrub formations (garrigue, maquis) are grazed in the Mediterranean zone. Trees and shrubs, notably *Salix* spp., are also winter feed in some cold areas.

Extensive grasslands have multiple uses in addition to being a very important source of livestock feed and of livelihoods for stock raisers and herders. Most grasslands are important catchment areas and the management of their vegetation is of primordial importance for the water resources of downstream lands; mismanagement of the grazing not only damages the pasture, but, since it increases erosion and run-off, can cause serious damage to agricultural land and infrastructure lower in the catchment and cause siltation of irrigation systems and reservoirs. The main benefits of good catchment management mainly accrue to communities outside the grasslands, but the maintenance efforts have to be made by herders or ranchers. These grasslands are major reserves of biodiversity, providing important wildlife habitat and *in situ* conservation of genetic resources. In some regions, grasslands are important for tourism and leisure, and may have sites of religious significance (Plate 1.15); in other areas, wild foods, medicines and other useful products are collected (Plate 1.16).

Grasslands are a very large carbon sink at world level. Minahi *et al.* (1993) state that they are almost as important as forests in the recycling of greenhouse gasses and that soil organic matter under grassland is of the same magnitude as in tree biomass; the carbon storage capacity under grassland can be increased by avoiding tillage.

S. G. REYNOLDS

Plate 1.15
Stupas (Mane in Nepali) at Sailung in Ramechap district, Nepal, at about 3 000 m
altitude, used by Buddhists to offer prayers for peace.

PETER HARRIS

Plate 1.16
Drying herbs at the summer camp, Qinghai.

PURPOSE OF THE BOOK

This book is primarily aimed at agricultural scientists, educationalists, extensionists and decision-makers with interests in the grassland and land-use fields. It brings together information on the characteristics, condition, present use and problems of the world's main natural grasslands. Since grassland is commercialized through grazing livestock, particular attention is paid to the livestock production systems associated with each main type. Grazing resources do not, of course, consist solely of the edible herbage – many other factors have to be taken into account, notably water in all areas and shelter in winter-cold climates. Seasonality of forage supply is a characteristic of almost all grazing lands so the strategies for dealing with lean seasons are described. The main problems of each type are described and possible strategies for their sustainable management discussed – taking into account their multiple functions beyond simply livestock production.

STRUCTURE OF THE BOOK

Nine area or country studies are presented as full chapters.

Chapter 2 covers eastern Africa in its wider sense from Eritrea and southern Sudan to Rwanda and Burundi. These comprise extensive semi-arid to arid grasslands, savannah, bushlands and woodlands, but also include the natural grazing areas of the extensive highland areas of the region, which are also pastoral rangelands. Stock rearing is traditional and has been a major land use for a very long time. The population is very varied; pastoral groups tend to be of different ethnicities from agricultural or agropastoral groups. Most pastoral systems are in the semi-arid areas, with small areas in hyper-arid and sub-humid zones. Access to resources are under national laws, but frequently traditional land use rights are granted by local communities. National land tenure systems, introduced after independence, are unrelated to traditional ones. Planted fodder is becoming important in farming systems as free grazing becomes scarce.

Chapter 3 covers South Africa, which has a range of climates from winter rainfall in the extreme south to summer rainfall in the lower latitudes. Much is semi-arid extensive grazing, especially towards the west. Grassland is mainly in the central, high regions. Sour-veldt occurs under high-rainfall on acid soils, and sweet-veldt on fertile soils in semi-arid zones. Savannah occurs in the north and east, and arid savannah extends to the Kalahari. Production systems in communal areas, based on pastoralism and agro-pastoralism, are subsistence-based and labour intensive; crop land is allocated to households, grazing areas are shared by a community. Commercial areas are fenced ranches. Much of the better-watered grassland has been converted to crops; in communal areas this gives a patchwork with thicket. Sown pasture is not of major importance, except on dairy farms.

Chapter 4 covers Patagonia, which is treeless semi-arid grass and shrub steppes that have only been grazed by domestic livestock for a little over a century. Temperatures decrease from north to south. Most vegetation has been seriously modified by sheep, particularly in the past 40–50 years, with palatable grasses being replaced by unpalatable woody plants. European settlement began at the end of the nineteenth century, with commercial sheep farming. Sheep farming is almost a monoculture in the steppes. Overstocking and poor grazing management have led to serious pastoral degradation, which, coupled with poor prices for livestock products, has caused serious economic problems for stock owners.

Chapter 5 deals with the Campos, grassland with few trees or shrubs, which includes parts of Brazil, Paraguay and Argentina, and all of Uruguay. Grassland-based livestock production is very important, exploiting the natural grassland that covers most of the area. Stock rearing is on large, delimited holdings and is commercial. Poor herbage quality is a major limiting factor to livestock production, as is usual in moist sub-tropical grasslands. Fattening off grass can take up to four years. Intensive fattening of younger stock uses some sown pasture. Exotic temperate legumes can be grown and may be over-sown into native swards after land preparation; once established, legumes encourage the development of winter grasses.

Chapter 6 deals with the grasslands of Central North America. At the time of settlement from Europe, there was extensive grassland from the prairies of Canada to the Gulf of Mexico, on mainly level topography. Great Plains grassland is in three bands running north-south: tall-grass; mixed grass; and short-grass with the tall-grass in the better watered west. About half of the beef cattle in the United States of America (USA) are in the great plains. Woody vegetation types are embedded, with the trees varying according to latitude. C_4 species comprise more than 80 percent from 30° to 42°N, while C_3 species increase dramatically north of 42°N. Cattle predominate, sheep are far fewer and declining. Most land is privately owned, much in small farms. In dry areas, there is extensive ranching. Grazing is seasonal, especially in the north, with supplemental feed in winter. Many small operations are no longer economically viable so are being abandoned.

Chapter 7 deals with Mongolia, where 80 percent of the country is extensive grazing and a further ten percent is forest or forest scrub, which is also grazed. Its climate is arid to semi-arid and the frost-free period of most of the steppe is one hundred days; transhumant herding on natural pasture is the only sustainable way of using such land. Cattle, with yak in the higher areas, horses, camels, sheep and goats are raised; local breeds are used. During the past century, management has changed from traditional transhumance, to collectives that retained herd mobility from the 1950s, to private herding from 1992. Mixed herds are kept, with herd composition varying according to region. Herding is based on using different pastures for the four seasons of the year. While livestock are now privately owned, grazing rights have not yet been allocated; this causes problems for maintenance of pastoral infrastructure and respect of good grazing practice.

Chapter 8 deals with the Tibetan Steppe, another cold, arid zone of mobile herding. Its high, cold grazing lands vary from cold deserts to semi-arid steppe and shrublands, to alpine steppe and moist alpine meadows. Much is above 4 000 m; some camps are as high as 5 100 m. It is traditionally an area of transhumant herding, which has undergone vast changes in the past half century – from feudalism, through a collective period, to privatized livestock and individual grazing rights, which are circumscribing the mobility necessary for herding risk avoidance in such a climate. The steppe contains the headwaters of many of the major rivers of Asia and has a very rich flora and fauna with many endemic species, so grazing management is not only important for herders' livelihoods but also for catchment maintenance and *in situ* preservation of genetic resources and biodiversity.

Chapter 9 deals with Australia's grasslands. Australia has a latitudinal range of 11°S to 44°S, which, coupled with annual precipitation from 100 mm to 4 000 mm, generates a wide range of grassland environments. Native herbage remains the base of a significant portion of the grazing industry. Most farms rely on animal products from grasslands, and most grasslands products are exported. Arid and semi-arid tropical areas are used for extensive cattle grazing; water from artesian wells and bores is necessary. Pasture growth is very seasonal and stock lose weight in the dry season. In the intermediate rainfall zones, crops are combined with sheep rearing; ley farming systems, where a legume-based pasture phase of two to five years is alternated with crops for one to three years, were widely adopted in southern areas. Sown pasture technology is well developed in the temperate zone, based on the use of selected, exotic species, with emphasis on legumes. Development of sown pastures was slower in the tropical areas and suffered a setback when disease affected *Stylosanthes* stands.

Chapter 10 deals with the Russian steppe, which is described with a view to its rehabilitation as a natural resource. The vast plains formerly provided a formidable grazing resource, due more to their extent than to their productivity. In the 1950s, the lion's share of the virgin steppe was ploughed not just for cereal but, ironically as it turned out, largely for fodder production. Large-scale stall-feeding operations based on maize silage and cereals were typical, but proved unsustainable, and livestock numbers have dwindled to less than half in the past decade. In the current transition to family-based livestock farming, however informal as yet, direct grazing has regained terrain. Fortunately, the succession from fallow land to "typical" steppe vegetation is quite rapid and passes through seral stages dominated by *Agropyron* spp., which provide a more powerful herbage resource than the climax *Stipa* spp. and *Festuca sulcata* steppe. Ecological monitoring of the steppe as a natural resource is paramount in order to assist in rehabilitating the fallow grasslands to the preferred botanical composition.

The above coverage leaves some obvious gaps, but it is not possible in a book of normal size to cover all grasslands in similar detail. Chapter 11 gives summarized information on many of the large grazing areas not covered in the nine studies, with sections on: (i) Africa – North Africa; West Africa; and Madagascar; (ii) Latin America – the Llanos; and the Gran Chaco; (iii) Western Asia – Turkey; Iran; the Syrian Arab Republic; and Jordan; (iii) Central Asia – Uzbekistan; and Kyrgyzstan; (iv) The Himalaya-Hindu Kush zone; and (v) China other than the Tibet-Qinghai Plateau. Much of the information for the minor studies comes from the FAO "Country Pasture Profiles", studies that provide information on the pasture and forage resources of countries, and usually drafted by national scientists. They are available on the FAO Web site, as described in Chapter 11. Much information for temperate Asia is available in the FAO Grassland Group publication *Transhumant Grazing Systems in Temperate Asia* (Suttie and Reynolds, 2003).

A final chapter discusses grassland perspectives.

COMPLEMENTARY INFORMATION RESOURCES

Four recent FAO Grassland Group publications deal with extensive grasslands: *Grassland Resource Assessment* (Harris, 2001); *Managing Mobility in African Rangelands* (in conjunction with IT Publications and Beijer Institute of Agricultural Economics) (Niamir-Fuller, 1999); *Grasslands: Developments Opportunities Perspectives* (Reynolds and Frame, 2005); and *Transhumant Grazing Systems in Temperate Asia* (Suttie and Reynolds, 2003). The FAO Grassland Web site contains a series of Country Pasture Profiles that give country-by-country descriptions of grassland-based production systems. To date, 80 countries have been described – see: http://www.fao.org/ag/AGP/AGPC/doc/pasture/forage.htm. These profiles provide the basis for Chapter 11 and are described therein. The interrelation of grassland, crops, livestock and other grassland resources is analysed in *The Future is an Ancient Lake. Traditional knowledge, biodiversity and genetic resources for food and agriculture in Lake Chad Basin ecosystems* (Batello, Marzot and Touré, 2004).

Sown pasture and fodder and their conservation are discussed in a number of FAO publications, including: *Hay and Straw Conservation* (Suttie, 2000), which also deals with fodder cultivation; *Silage making in the tropics with particular emphasis on smallholders* (t'Mannetje, 2000); *Wild and Sown Grasses* (Peeters, 2004); *Site-Specific Grasses and Herbs. Seed production and use for restoration of mountain environments* (Krautzer, Peratoner and Bozzo, 2004); *Forage Legumes for Temperate Grasslands* (Frame, 2005); *Fodder Oats: a World Overview* (Suttie and Reynolds, 2004). Tropical forages are dealt with in *Tropical Grasses* (Skerman and Riveros, 1989) and *Tropical Forage Legumes* (Skerman, Cameron and Riveros, 1988).

The FAO-AGP Grassland Index gives descriptions of and agronomic information on a wide range of forages – see <http://www.fao.org/ag/AGP/AGPC/doc/GBASE/Default.htm>.

REFERENCES

Allaby, M. 1998. *Oxford Dictionary of Plant Sciences.* Oxford, UK: Oxford University Press.

Batello, C., Marzot, M. & Touré, A.H. 2004. *The Future is an Ancient Lake. Traditional knowledge, biodiversity and genetic resources for food and agriculture in Lake Chad Basin ecosystems.* Rome, Italy: FAO. 309 p.

Dost, M. 2004. Fodder Oats in Pakistan. pp. 71–91, *in:* J.M. Suttie and S.G. Reynolds (eds). *Fodder oats, a world overview. FAO Plant Production and Protection Series,* No. 33.

Erdenebaatar, B. 2003. Studies on long-distance transhumant grazing systems in Uvs and Khuvsgul aimags of Mongolia, 1999–2000. pp. 31–68, *in:* J.M. Suttie and S.G. Reynolds (eds). *Transhumant grazing systems in temperate Asia. FAO Plant Production and Protection Series,* No. 31.

FAO. 2000. Second expert meeting on harmonizing forest-related definitions for use by various stakeholders. See: http://www.fao.org/DOCREP/005/Y4171E/Y4171E37.htm

FAOSTAT. 2004. Agriculture data. Agricultural production – Live animals. Data downloaded from http://faostat.fao.org

Frame, J. 2005. *Forage Legumes for Temperate Grasslands.* Rome, Italy, and Enfield, USA: FAO, and Science Publishers Inc. 309 p.

Garrity, D.P., Soekardi, M., van Noordwijk, M., de la Cruz, R., Pathak, P.S., Gunasena, H.P.M., Van So, N., Huijun, G. & Majid, N.M. 1997. The *Imperata* grassland of tropical Asia: Area, distribution and typology. pp. 3–29, *in:* D.P. Garrity (ed). *Agroforestry innovations to rehabilitate Imperata grasslands. Agroforestry Systems (Special Issue),* **36**(1–3).

Harris, P.S. 2001. Grassland resource assessment for pastoral systems. *FAO Plant Production and Protection Paper,* No. 162. 150 p.

Krautzer, B., Peratoner, G. & Bozzo, F. 2004. *Site-Specific Grasses and herbs. Seed production and use for restoration of mountain environments. FAO Plant Production and Protection Series,* No. 32. 111 p.

Minahi, K., Goudriaan, J., Lantinga, E.A. & Kimura, T. 1993. Significance of grasslands in emission and absorption of greenhouse grasses. *In:* M.J. Barker (ed). *Grasslands for Our World.* Wellington, New Zealand: SIR Publishing.

Niamir-Fuller, M. (ed). 1999. *Managing mobility in African Rangelands. The legitimization of transhumance.* London: Intermediate Technology Publications, for FAO and Beijer International Institute of Ecological Economics.

Peeters, A. 2004. *Wild and Sown Grasses. Profiles of a temperate species selection: ecology, biodiversity and use.* London: Blackwell Publishing, for FAO. 311 p.

Reynolds, S.G. 1995. *Pasture-cattle-coconut systems.* FAO-RAPA Publication, Bangkok. 668 p.

Reynolds, S.G. & Frame, J. 2005. *Grasslands: Developments Opportunities Perspectives.* Rome, Italy, and Enfield, USA: FAO, and Science Publishers Inc. 565 p.

Riveros, F. 1993. Grasslands for our world. *In:* M.J. Barker (ed). *Grasslands for Our World.* Wellington, New Zealand: SIR Publishing.

Semple, A.T. 1956. *Improving the World's Grasslands. FAO Agricultural Studies,* No. 16.

Skerman, P.J. & Riveros, F. 1989/90. *Tropical grasses. FAO Plant Production and Protection Series,* No. 23.

Skerman, P.J., Cameron, D.G. & Riveros, F. 1988. *Tropical forage legumes.* (2nd edition, revised and expanded). *FAO Plant Production and Protection Series,* No. 2. 692 p.

Suttie J.M. 2000. *Hay and straw conservation for small-scale and pastoral conditions. FAO Plant Production and Protection Series,* No. 29. 303 p. Available online – see http://www.fao.org/documents/show_cdr.asp?url_file=/docrep/005/X7660E/X7660E00.htm

Suttie J.M. & Reynolds, S.G. 2004. *Fodder Oats: a World Overview. FAO Plant Production and Protection Series,* No. 33. 251 p.

Suttie J.M. & Reynolds, S.G. 2003. *Transhumant grazing systems in temperate Asia. FAO Plant Production and Protection Series,* No. 31. 331 pp.

t'Mannetje, L. (ed). 2000. *Silage making in the tropics with particular emphasis on smallholders. FAO Plant Production and Protection Paper,* No. 161. 180 p.

Wang, W.L. 2003. Studies on traditional transhumance and a system where herders return to settled winter bases in Burjin county, Altai Prefecture, Xinjiang, China. pp. 115–141, *in:* J.M. Suttie and S.G. Reynolds (eds). *Transhumant grazing systems in temperate Asia. FAO Plant Production and Protection Series,* No. 31.

White, F. 1983. *The Vegetation of Africa; a descriptive memoir to accompany the Unesco/AETFAT/UNSO vegetation map of Africa.* Natural Resources Research Series, XX. Paris, France: UNESCO. 356 p.

World Resources Institute - PAGE. 2000. Downloaded from http://earthtrends. wri.org/text/forests-grasslands-drylands/map-229.htm

Chapter 2
The changing face of pastoral systems in grass-dominated ecosystems of eastern Africa

R.S. Reid, S. Serneels, M. Nyabenge and J. Hanson

SUMMARY

All eastern Africa is in the tropics, but its grasslands cover a very wide range of altitudes. Extensive grasslands are mostly in arid and semi-arid zones. The area is subject to droughts and a high degree of pastoral risk. Potential vegetation is largely desert and semi-desert, bush and woodland, with only a small area of pure grassland, but the grass-dominated herbaceous layer of the other formations is very important for wildlife and livestock; 75 percent of eastern Africa is dominated by grasslands, often with a varying amount of woody vegetation. The grasslands have been grazed by livestock and game for millennia. Eastern Africa is a centre of genetic diversity for grasses. Six to eleven main grassland zones have been described. Grasslands are either under government control, are open access or are common property resources. Access to resources are under national laws but frequently traditional land use rights are granted by local communities. National land tenure systems are unrelated to traditional ones. Governments supported cropping and reduction of communal grazing land; contraction of pastoral systems reduces the scale of resource use by pastoral peoples. The population is very varied – pastoral groups tend to be of different ethnicities from agricultural or agropastoral groups. Most pastoral systems are in the semi-arid areas, with small areas in hyper-arid and subhumid zones. Traditionally, livestock and their products were for subsistence and wealth, but now many are marketed. Grasslands are increasingly being integrated into farming as pastoral systems evolve. Sown forages are widely used in agricultural areas. Cattle, like people, are mostly in the non-pastoral areas (70 percent), except in countries with little high-potential land. Cattle, camels, sheep, goats and donkeys are the main livestock kept by the pastoralists for subsistence; most herds are mixed. Indigenous breeds are the majority, although exotic cattle are kept for dairying in high altitude zones. Wildlife are widespread in the grazing lands and are important for tourism. Agricultural development along watercourses limits access by wildlife and pastoral stock.

SCOPE

This chapter focuses on the grazing lands or rangelands of Burundi, Eritrea, Ethiopia, Kenya, Rwanda, Somalia, the Sudan, the United Republic of Tanzania (Tanzania) and Uganda (Figure 2.1). These comprise extensive semi-

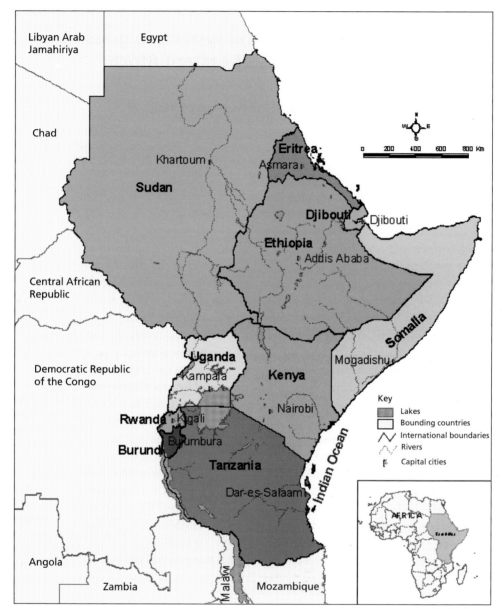

Figure 2.1
Countries in eastern Africa as defined for this chapter.

arid to arid grasslands, savannah, bushlands and woodlands, and also cover the
natural grazing areas of the extensive highland areas of the region. These are
also the pastoral rangelands that Holechek, Pieper and Herbel (1989) defined as
"uncultivated land that will support grazing or browsing animals".

Pastoral management systems in eastern Africa have developed over
the last three to four thousand years by the indigenous groups of pastoral

peoples living in the region, whose livelihoods depend on livestock. These traditional and often sustainable ways are now being threatened by agricultural development, the need to produce more food from marginal lands, population growth and global climate change. Fluctuations in rainfall and drought are recurring problems in the rangelands of the region and 70 million people in the Horn of Africa, many of whom are pastoralists, suffer from long-term chronic food insecurity (FAO, 2000). Poverty levels are high, with more than half of the people in the region surviving on less than US$ 1 per day (Thornton *et al.,* 2002). The population of the region has doubled since 1974, and it is predicted to increase another 40 percent by 2015 (FAO, 2000). Against this background, the traditional ways of pastoralists continue to change, and many are settling (or are settled) and diversifying their income-generating activities into crop production, wage labour and other activities, while other family members continue to herd the family stock and move to follow the availability of forage.

This chapter examines the changes in pastoral rangeland systems in eastern Africa over recent years and estimates future changes in the rangelands of the region due to global climate change, human population growth and market opportunities.

Mapping rangelands, livestock and pastoral peoples

The productive potential of the eastern African region varies enormously from place to place, as shown by the differences in the growing season across the region (Figure 2.2; Fischer, Velthuizen and Nachtergaele, 2000). On this map, areas coloured brown and yellow have less than 60 growing days[1] and thus rarely support crops (= arid, according to White, 1998); areas adequate for short-season crops with 60–120 growing days are shown in light green (= semi-arid); areas with 121–180 days, shaded in medium green, can support longer-season crops (= dry subhumid); and areas with >180 growing days are in dark green, and have few production constraints (= wet subhumid). Over the region, about 37 percent of the land surface (or 2.3×10^6 km²) is only agriculturally suitable for grazing by wildlife and livestock (= arid and semi-arid areas), while the other 63 percent (3.9×10^6 km²) is additionally suitable for crop cultivation, forestry and other types of land use. Of these arid and semi-arid areas principally suitable for grazing, about 1.6×10^6 km² (or about 70 percent of the grazing land) is arid and completely unsuitable for crop production (zero growing days) and thus is probably only available for grazing during the rare high rainfall years or during a

---

[1] Growing days are defined as "the period (in days) during the year when precipitation (P) exceeds half the potential evapotranspiration (PET) plus a period required to evapotranspire up to 100 mm of water from excess precipitation assumed stored in the soil profile" (FAO, 1978). The mean daily temperature during the growing period has to exceed 5°C (Fischer, Velthuizen and Nachtergaele, 2000).

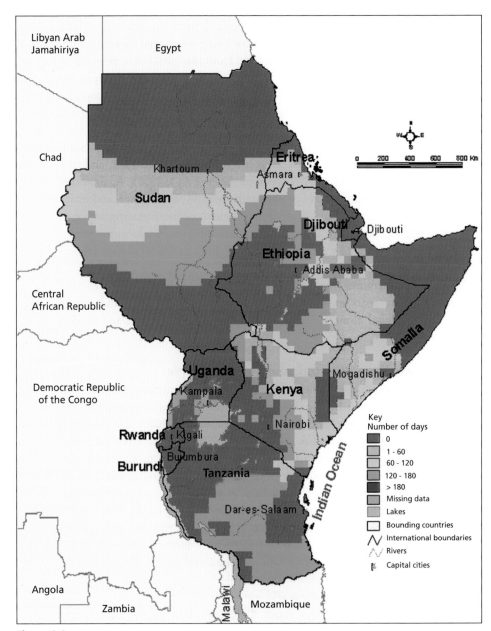

Figure 2.2
Length of growing period (days) with sufficient soils and water to grow crops. Re-classified from Fischer, Velthuizen and Nachtergaele, 2000.

few weeks or months in normal or low rainfall years. Significant drylands cover northern Sudan, eastern Ethiopia, much of Eritrea and Somalia and northern Kenya, while most of Tanzania, Rwanda, Burundi and Uganda are relatively wet. These four high-rainfall countries and southern Kenya, the highlands of

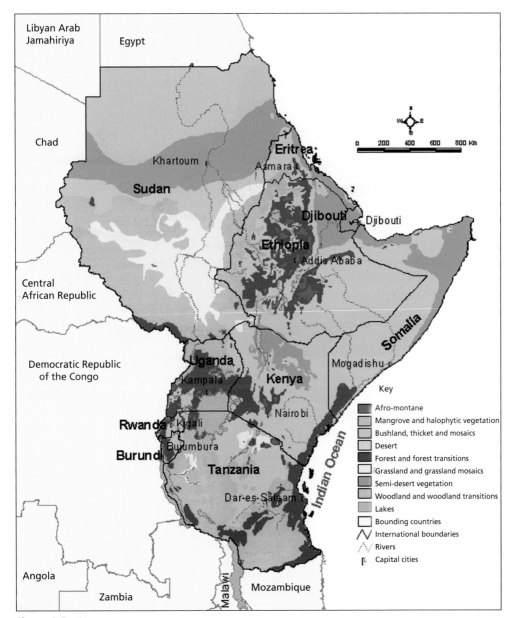

Figure 2.3
Potential vegetation in eastern Africa. Re-classified from White, 1983.

Ethiopia and southern Sudan have the highest potential for intensive crop-livestock production. Much of this is now already under cropland, with the exception of southern Sudan (for cropland, see Figure 2.7).

The potential vegetation of eastern Africa is largely desert and semi-desert (26 percent of the land surface), bushland (33 percent) and woodland

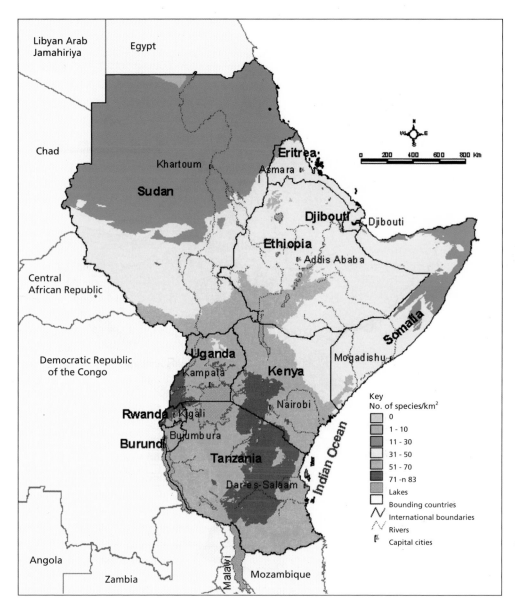

Figure 2.4
Density of large mammal species in eastern Africa, based on data from IEA, 1998.

(21 percent) (from Figure 2.3; White, 1983). Only 12 percent of the region is naturally forested, and even less is pure grassland (7 percent). Afromontane vegetation, much of it potential grazing land, is rare (0.5 percent) and mostly restricted to Ethiopia, with very small amounts on volcanic mountains in Kenya, Uganda, Rwanda and Tanzania. Although pure grassland is found only in central

J.M. SUTTIE

Plate 2.1
Predator harvesting game. Cheetah among Harpachne schimperi *– Athi plains, Kenya.*

and south-eastern Sudan, northern and western Tanzania and northwest Kenya, the herbaceous layer of semi-deserts, bushlands and woodlands are dominated by grasses, so they are included here as part of the "grass-dominated areas" of eastern Africa because of their importance for livestock and wildlife. This means that 75 percent of eastern Africa is dominated by either pure grasslands or grasslands with varying amounts of woody vegetation within or above the grass layer. Significant woodlands exist only in southern Sudan, Tanzania and Eritrea, and in northern Uganda and western Ethiopia.

Eastern Africa is renowned for the diversity and number of its large grazing and browsing wildlife (Plates 2.1, 2.2 and 2.3). A map of the density (number per km²) of species of medium and large mammals in eastern Africa was developed by a simultaneous overlay of 281 individual species distribution maps (see Figure 2.4, developed by Reid *et al.* (1998) based on analysis of databases from IEA (1998)). The highest diversity of medium to large mammal species is found in two large, contiguous patches: one in the Rift Valley of south-central Kenya and central Tanzania, and the other in and east of the Ruwenzori Mountains in southwestern Uganda and northern Rwanda. This is the richest diversity of mammals of this size in all of Africa (Reid *et al.*, 1998) and probably the world. Most of Burundi, Kenya, Rwanda, Tanzania and Uganda support diverse groups of large mammals, with fewer in most of Djibouti, Eritrea, Ethiopia and Somalia. This map does not account for the rarity or endemism of large mammals, which can be distributed quite differently from overall diversity.

Plate 2.2
Large non-ruminant herbivores – zebra herd – Athi plains, Kenya.

Plate 2.3
Gerenuk - dry area browsers – Tsavo East, Kenya.

As expected, most of the people in eastern Africa live in the wetter and highland areas (Figure 2.5; Deichmann, 1996; Thornton *et al.*, 2002). High population levels are found in the Ethiopian highlands, the Lake Victoria Basin and the southern Tanzanian highlands. Significant clusters of people

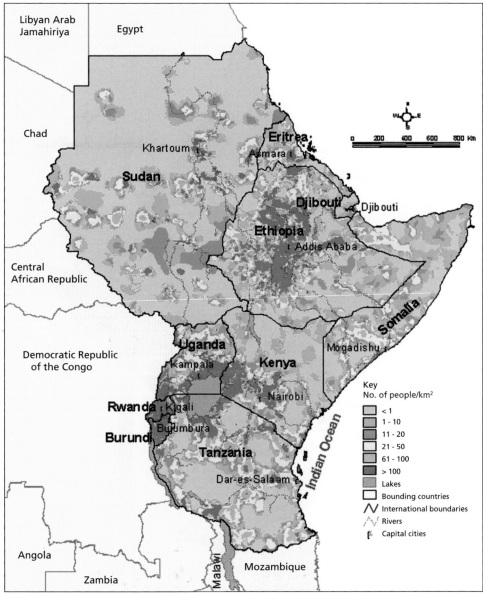

Figure 2.5
Human population density in eastern Africa in 2001. From Deichmann, 1996; Thornton et al., 2002.

live in areas marginally suitable for cultivation in Eritrea around Asmara, in central Sudan and along the coasts of Kenya, Tanzania and Somalia. The only places where many people live in drylands are along the Nile in northern Sudan, around Mogadishu in Somalia and in western Somaliland of northern Somalia. Few people live in most of the drylands of eastern Africa and in the

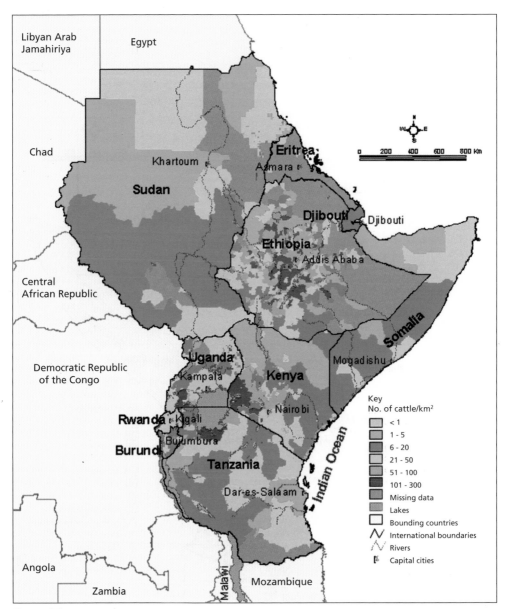

Figure 2.6
Cattle population densities in eastern Africa in the late 1990s, from Kruska, 2002.

wetter areas of the Sudd in southern Sudan, in the tsetse belts of Tanzania and in protected areas.

Cattle are largely distributed in a pattern similar to the human population distribution in eastern Africa (Figure 2.6; Kruska, 2002), with high concentrations around Lake Victoria and in the Ethiopian highlands. Few cattle are found in the driest areas of northern Sudan, eastern and northern Ethiopia, Eritrea and northeastern Somalia. There are also few cattle in wet, southern Sudan (the Sudd) and northern Uganda, and in the subhumid, *miombo* woodland regions of southern Tanzania. Most of the cattle are in non-pastoral areas across the region: 70 percent are in cropland and urban areas, while 30 percent are in pastoral lands. These proportions vary strongly from country to country, partly because of differences in amounts of high-potential land. For example, about 35 percent of Kenya is high potential and 80 percent of the nation's cattle herd resides there. In contrast, there is very little high-potential land in Somalia and Djibouti and thus all the cattle live in drylands in those countries.

A previous global analysis of pastoral systems (from Reid *et al.*, 2003) has been used to estimate the extent of grass-dominated pastoral systems in eastern Africa. This pastoral systems map (Figure 2.7) was created using four Geographical Information System (GIS) data layers: land cover (USGS/EDC, 1999; Loveland *et al.*, 2000), length of growing period (Fischer, Velthuizen and Nachtergaele, 2000), rainfall (IWMI, 2001; Jones and Thornton, 2003) and human population density for Africa (Deichmann, 1996).

Initially, land cover, length of growing period and human population maps were used to establish the location of all cultivatable land (>60 growing days), all land cover currently under crops in the USGS coverage (dryland cropland and pasture; irrigated cropland and pasture; mixed dryland and irrigated cropland and pasture; cropland and grassland mosaic; and cropland and woodland mosaic) and any other areas with sufficient human population (>20 people/km²) to exclude extensive rangeland use (for details, see Reid *et al.*, 2000a; Thornton *et al.*, 2002). This classification thus joined all but the most extensive agropastoral systems with cropland, and maps about 9 percent more cropland than is in the USGS database. "Urban" included all areas with more than 450 people/km². The remaining areas (not cultivatable, low human population density) were discriminated into pastoral system classes by mean annual rainfall as follows: areas receiving less than 50 mm of rainfall were classified as hyper-arid; areas with 51–300 mm were arid; and areas with 301–600 mm were semi-arid. Highland areas were those with temperatures of more than 5°C but less than 20°C during the growing season, or less than 20°C for one month a year.

Most of eastern Africa's pastoral systems are semi-arid (34 percent), with much smaller areas of arid (12 percent), hyper-arid (8 percent), humid to sub-humid (9 percent), and temperate and highland (1 percent) pastoral systems (Figure 2.7). Cropland and urban areas cover 27 percent of the region. Only Sudan has the driest (hyper-arid) pastoral systems, while eastern Eritrea, northern Ethiopia, Djibouti, Somalia and northern Kenya support extensive arid pastoral systems. The most common land cover type in Kenya, Somalia, Ethiopia and Sudan is semi-arid rangeland. Tanzania, Uganda and Sudan have the most extensive wet pastoral systems.

By comparing potential vegetation (Figure 2.3) and pastoral and cropland systems (Figure 2.7), we can see what types of vegetation farmers have pre-

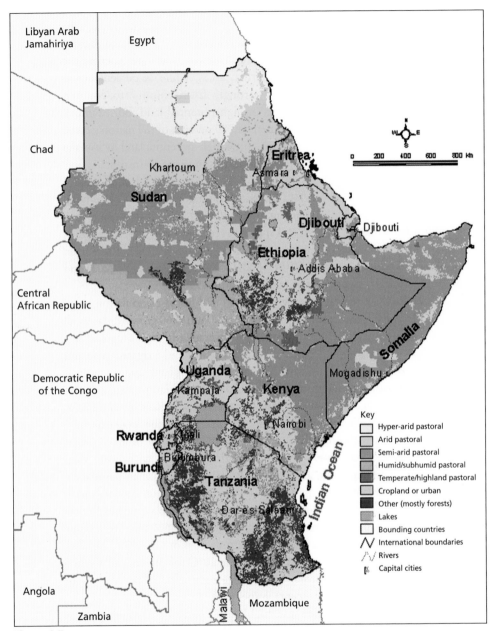

Figure 2.7
Pastoral system areas and cropland and urban areas of eastern Africa in 2001, based on Thornton et al. *(2002) and Reid* et al. *(2003).*

ferred to use for cropland. On average, 27 percent of the region is cropped, but this is disproportionately found in afromontane vegetation (74 percent converted to cropland), forest (62 percent converted), woodland (34 percent converted) and bushland (31 percent converted). Farmers have ploughed lesser areas of pure grassland (23 percent converted), semi-deserts (3 percent) and deserts (1 percent). These land use choices have pushed pastoral use from the wetter to the drier areas in eastern Africa over time.

PLANT COMMUNITIES IN GRASSLANDS AND RANGELANDS

The grasslands of eastern Africa are very diverse, with a range of dominant species dependent on rainfall, soil type and management or grazing system. Eastern Africa is renowned as a centre of genetic diversity of tropical grasses and the centre of greatest diversity of cultivated grass species (Boonman, 1993). Over 90 percent of the major cultivated forage grasses have their centre of origin in sub-Saharan Africa and are indigenous to the extensive grasslands of eastern Africa. There are an estimated 1 000 species of grass indigenous to the region, with more than 600 species found in Kenya alone (Boonman, 1993). The wide distribution and adaptability of many of these species across a range of environments and management systems indicates the presence of considerable genetic diversity within the region. This diversity has been exploited to select superior ecotypes for use in many other parts of the world. *Brachiaria* species, originating from eastern Africa, are the most widely planted forage grass, with estimates of areas under *Brachiaria* pastures in Brazil ranging from 30 to 70 million hectares in 1996 (Fisher and Kerridge, 1996).

To aid description and study of the rangeland, many attempts have been made to classify the vegetation into types that cover large areas of the region. Rattray (1960) identified 12 types of grassland in eastern Africa, based on the genera of the dominant grass in the grassland. These include *Aristida, Chloris, Cenchrus, Chrysopogon, Exotheca, Hyparrhenia, Heteropogon, Loudetia, Pennisetum, Panicum, Setaria* and *Themeda*. Pratt and Gwynne (1977) described six eco-climatic zones based on climate, vegetation and land use. These are described as the afro-alpine area of upland grasslands; the equatorial humid to dry sub-humid area of forests and bushlands (Plates 2.4 and 2.5); the dry subhumid to semi-arid area of savannah, shrub and woodland; the semi-arid areas of dry woodland and savannah (such as the *Acacia-Themeda* association); the arid area of *Commiphora, Acacia, Cenchrus ciliaris* and *Chloris roxburghiana*; and the very arid area of dwarf shrub grassland of *Chrysopogon*. A more recent classification, based primarily on the dominant grass, is described as vegetation type or region by Herlocker (1999). He described eleven vegetation regions in eastern Africa as *Pennisetum* mid-grass; *Pennisetum* giant grass; *Panicum-Hyparrhenia* tall-grass; *Hyparrhenia* tall-grass; *Hyparrhenia-Hyperthelia* tall-grass; *Themeda* mid-grass; *Chrysopogon* mid-grass; *Leptothrium* mid-grass; *Cenchrus-Schoenefeldia* annual mid-grass; *Panicum*-annual; *Aristida* mid- and short-grass region; and *Aristida* short-grass region.

Themeda triandra (Plate 2.6) is one of the most widespread grass species in sub-Saharan Africa but it is only the dominant grassland type in central and northern Tanzania. The species is very variable and shows wide adaptation to

Plate 2.4
Acacia bushlands cover much of the rich volcanic soils of eastern Africa.

Plate 2.5
Farmers use many of the trees in bushlands and woodlands to manufacture charcoal for market.

Plate 2.6
Maasai sheep grazing in a Themeda *grassland, southwestern Kenya.*

growth in both the highland regions and the lowland savannahs. *Themeda, Bothriochloa, Digitaria* and *Heteropogon* mixtures are common in the open dry savannah areas of Tanzania, such as the Serengeti plains. Short tufted ecotypes of *Themeda triandra* are found at high altitudes and taller more woody types are found in the open lowland savannahs (Rattray, 1960). These vary in palatability, but all types quickly lose palatability with age. *Themeda triandra* can tolerate light to moderate grazing, and productivity can reach 400 kg/ha/day in the wet season in the Serengeti plains, making them among the most productive grasslands in the world (Herlocker, 1999). Plant biomass, quality and species numbers decline in the absence of grazing, are at a peak under moderate to high grazing (McNaughton, 1976, 1979, 1984) and can decline under very high grazing. In the Mara region in Kenya, to the north, which is a continuation of the grassland ecosystem of the Serengeti Plains, *Themeda* makes up about 50 percent of the grass cover in lightly to moderately grazed sites, dropping to 1–5 percent cover near settlements where Maasai corral their livestock each night (Vuorio, Muchiru and Reid, in prep.).

The dominant grass species in the drylands of eastern Africa include *Aristida, Cenchrus, Chrysopogon* and *Heteropogon*. These are often found growing as an association, the dominant species determined by the environment and soil type. *Aristida* grassland is widely distributed in the dry pastoral areas of Kenya, Ethiopia and the Sudan. Although many species are tough and have low palatability, they have wide adaptability to a broad range of environments. *Cenchrus* grassland is often found associated with *Aristida,* or in Somalia with *Leptothrium* (Herlocker, 1999), and has higher palatability and better adaptation to hot dry areas with high evapotranspiration. *Cenchrus* is one of the few grass genera that has been characterized for agronomic attributes. Over 300 ecotypes, mostly collected from Tanzania and Kenya, were characterized for 12 agronomic attributes (Pengelly, Hacker and Eagles, 1992). The ecotypes showed wide variability in their agronomic traits and were clustered into six groups (Pengelly, Hacker and Eagles, 1992). The annual *C. biflorus,* which is adapted to dryland areas, is also found in eastern Africa associated with *Schoenefeldia* sp. and is typical of one dry area south of the Sahara in western Eritrea (Herlocker, 1999).

Chrysopogon plumulosus is the most widespread species found in the semi-desert grasslands and bushlands of the Horn of Africa (Herlocker, 1999) and is avidly grazed, especially in Somalia and Sudan, where it is burnt to stimulate regrowth for grazing. *Chrysopogon* is very sensitive to grazing. Overgrazing results in elimination of the species and a change in species composition to annuals such as *Aristida* spp. (Herlocker, 1999). This harsh management regime in low rainfall areas has resulted in reduced stands of this grassland in recent years (IBPGR, 1984). Herlocker (1999) recognized three zones in the *Chrysopogon* region according to the associated woody vegetation. These include *Commiphora-Acacia* bushland and *Acacia etbaica* open woodland, which occur across the region, and the *Acacia bussei* open woodland in Somalia and Ethiopia. He also recognized two subregions: the *Cenchrus-Chloris* subregion in the wetter areas and the *Sporobolus* subregion in the drier areas. Rattray (1960) recognized the *Chloris* areas as a vegetation type in its own right, and included the *Sporobolus* as an associated grass in a *Chrysopogon* vegetation type in very dry semi-desert areas of Somalia and Ethiopia.

Although not a vegetation type recognized by Herlocker (1999), *Heteropogon* grassland is found in open woodland or grassland in the semi-arid and arid rangelands in Somalia (Box, 1968), Kenya and Ethiopia. It is represented mostly by *H. contortus,* which is commonly called spear grass due to its awns and needle-sharp tips on the grass florets. It is a persistent species, which is indigenous to the region, spreads rapidly through seed and grows in lowland or middle altitudes with poor, stony, well drained soils. It is commonly found with annual species of *Aristida* and *Digitaria* (Rattray, 1960). The species does not have good palatability and is only useful when young.

Chloris roxburghiana is a dominant species in dryland areas of Kenya, Ethiopia, Tanzania, Somalia and Uganda, and is usually found growing in association with *Chrysopogon aucheri* and *Cenchrus ciliaris* in *Commiphora* and *Acacia* woodland (Rattray, 1960). Despite its wide distribution, Herlocker (1999) treats this vegetation type as a subtype of the *Chrysopogon* mid-grass region. *Chloris roxburghiana* is widespread throughout the entire region and is an important species for livestock and wildlife. This species contributes up to 50 percent of the diet of wild herbivores in eastern Kenya (IBPGR, 1984) but is in danger of disappearing due to overgrazing and land degradation[2]. The species is very variable. A recent study using random amplified polymorphic DNA (RAPD) markers to study diversity among four populations from ecologically distinct sites in eastern Kenya showed significant variation among the populations (W.N. Mnene, KARI, Nairobi, pers. comm.).

Chloris gayana is an important native species and a component of the *Hyparrhenia* type of grassland (Rattray, 1960) in open steppe and wooded grassland vegetation or flooded valleys in the higher rainfall areas of Kenya, Ethiopia, Tanzania, Somalia and Uganda. Herlocker (1999) considers this vegetation type part of the *Hyparrhenia-Hyperthelia* tall-grass region of miombo woodland. The miombo woodland is an important vegetation type covering the southern two thirds of Tanzania. *Chloris gayana*, or Rhodes grass, is not an important grass ecologically in the vegetation of the region, but is important commercially as a forage grass. It shows wide adaptability with high palatability, and is a fast-growing, persistent, frost- and drought-tolerant species valued for grazing (Skerman and Riveros, 1990). Commercial cultivars of Rhodes grass have been developed from genotypes collected in Kenya and grown in the region since the 1930s (Boonman, 1997). An analysis of genetic diversity in *Chloris gayana* using amplified fragment length polymorphisms (AFLPs) revealed considerable variation between the diploid and tetraploid cultivars, with genetic similarity ranging between 66 and 89 percent in the diploids and 63 and 87 percent in the tetraploids (Ubi, Komatsu and Fujimori, 2000).

Hyparrhenia is one of the most widespread grassland types in eastern Africa, and this grassland region, which is characterized by woodlands and wooded grasslands dominated by *H. rufa,* covers parts of Uganda, Kenya and Ethiopia (Herlocker, 1999). Several other species of *Hyparrhenia* are found in the region, of which the most important are *H. hirta, H. diplandra* and *H. filipendula.* These tough perennial grasses are usually found growing in combination with other grasses in woodland or open grassland, from the lowland to mid-altitude areas. They are fast growing, and grazed while young, but become tough and unpalatable as they mature and lose nutritive value (Skerman and Riveros, 1990). Crude protein levels of *H. dissoluta* in Kenya can decrease from over 14 percent to less than 3 percent after flowering (Dougall, 1960). After flowering, these grasses are much valued and used as thatching for traditional rural housing, and mature grasses have commercial value, being sold as standing grass to be cut for roofing in some rural areas. This and burning ensure young regrowth with higher value for grazing in many areas. Grazing

---

[2] In this chapter, we consider degraded land to be land that due to natural processes or human activity is no longer able to sustain an economic function or the original ecological function, or both (GLASOD, 1990).

is important to encourage growth of other more palatable and valuable forage grasses, such as *Cynodon dactylon*, *Panicum maximum* and *Setaria sphacelata* (Herlocker, 1999).

Loudetia species are often found mixed with *Hyparrhenia* spp. and *Themeda triandra* in open grassland on shallow, rocky, sandy soils. They provide late-season grazing for livestock (Rattray, 1960) but have low palatability (Skerman and Riveros, 1990). Although Herlocker (1999) did not consider this a vegetation type *per se*, and Rattray (1960) only considered this as a grassland type for Uganda, *Loudetia* is widely distributed in rangeland ecosystems in Tanzania, Kenya and Ethiopia, but is never the dominant species. The most common species in the region is *Loudetia simplex*, which shows considerable variability in morphology in Ethiopia (Phillips, 1995). However, the genus has not been widely studied due to its low economic importance.

The highland areas of eastern Africa cover about 80 million hectares of Ethiopia, Kenya and Uganda. *Exotheca abyssinica* grassland is common on poor waterlogged soils in high altitude areas of eastern Africa, especially on the seasonally waterlogged vertisols, of which there are 12.6 million hectares alone in Ethiopia (Srivastava *et al.*, 1993). This species is closely related to *Hyparrhenia* and is often found growing in association with *Themeda triandra*. *E. abyssinica* has tough leaves and low nutritive value (Dougall, 1960), providing good grazing while young but quickly becoming tough and unpalatable. *Setaria incrassata* and *S. sphacelata* are also common grassland species found in *Acacia* woodland up to 2 600 m altitude on the vertisols of Uganda, Sudan and Ethiopia (Rattray, 1960). *S. incrassata* is a very variable species, with morphotypes varying in plant robustness, bristles, and number and density of spikelets (Phillips, 1995). It is closely related to *S. sphacelata*, which is also a very variable species, allowing selection of a range of cultivars from Kenyan ecotypes that vary in frost tolerance, maturity, pigmentation and nutritive value (Skerman and Riveros, 1990). Both *S. sphacelata* and *S. incrassata* are palatable grasses that withstand heavy grazing.

Pennisetum grassland areas can be classified as two types: high altitude grasslands of *P. clandestinum* and savannah grassland of *P. purpureum* (Rattray, 1960; Herlocker, 1999). Although belonging to the same genus, these species are morphologically and ecotypically very distinct, and have very different distribution and ecological niches. Both species are indigenous to eastern Africa, with high economic importance, and are cultivated in many other parts of the world.

P. clandestinum is a prostrate stoloniferous perennial that is widely distributed in areas from 1 400 m to over 3 000 m in Kenya, Ethiopia, Tanzania and Uganda. Its common name, Kikuyu grass, derives from the highlands of Kenya, where it is abundant, being named after the Kikuyu ethnic group of central Kenya. It shows wide adaptability to drought, waterlogging and occasional frosts (Skerman and Riveros, 1990). It is highly digestible, palatable, persistent and withstands severe defoliation and grazing. It is the dominant species in natural pastures in many parts of the eastern African highlands. It is an invasive secondary species, which can quickly colonize disturbed soil in cropping areas and fallow land, spreading by seeds or stolons, and may become a serious weed in cropland (Boonman, 1993). It shows wide variability, with three distinct ecotypes classified on leaf width and length, stolon size and floral structure (Skerman and Riveros, 1990). Several ecotypes have been selected as commercial cultivars, which have been widely introduced into tropical highland and subtropical areas. It is now widely grown outside its native distribution and is commonly cultivated in the Americas. Studies in the USA using starch gel electrophoresis to describe the distribution of genetic variation within and among introduced populations found a relatively high proportion of polymorphic loci across populations, indicating fixed heterozygosity due to polyploidy (Wilen *et al.*, 1995). The highland grazing areas of *P. clandestinum* are often mixed with *P. sphacelatum* and *Eleusine floccifolia*. These two grasses are frequent in overgrazed pastures in the highlands and mid-altitudes in the Rift Valley, but are not palatable (Sisay and Baars, 2002) and are important for traditional basket making. Cattle avoid these grasses, which have the potential to become major weeds on upland pastures unless collected for basket making. Basket making is an important activity and source of income for rural women and collection of these weedy grasses also maintains the quality of the communal grazing areas and grasslands in the highlands.

Pennisetum purpureum is a tall, erect, vigorous perennial species that grows in damp grasslands and forest areas up to 2 400 m in Kenya, Tanzania, Uganda and Sudan. Herlocker (1999) recognized this as a vegetation region in Kenya and Uganda, around the shores of Lake Victoria. *Pennisetum purpureum* is widely distributed through sub-Saharan Africa and is commonly called elephant grass or Napier grass, named after Colonel Napier of Bulawayo in Zimbabwe, who promoted its use at the start of the century. It is now widely used for cut-and-carry (where grass is collected by hand and carried to stall-fed cattle) for the smallholder dairy industry in eastern Africa and frequently produces up to 10–12 t/ha dry matter in rainfed conditions (Boonman, 1993). Elephant grass is palatable when young and leafy. It is fast growing and should be cut often to avoid its becoming tough and unpalatable with a high proportion of stem. Due to its importance in the region, considerable research has been done on elephant grass, including studies on its diversity. Tcacenco and Lance (1992) studied 89 morphological characters on 9 genotypes of elephant grass to determine which characters were most useful for description of the variation in the species, and concluded that variation existed from plant to plant, even within the same accession. A larger collection of 53 accessions was characterized for 20 morphological and 8 agronomic characters (Van de Wouw, Hanson and Leuthi, 1999). Again the germplasm was found to be very variable, but accessions could be clustered into six groups with similar morphology. More recently, molecular techniques using RAPD markers were applied to study the genetic diversity in the same collection, and also among farm clones in Kenya (Lowe *et al.,* 2003). This technique was able to separate out hybrids between *P. purpureum* and *P. glaucum* from pure elephant grass accessions. Despite being clonally propagated, genetic diversity (Magguran, 1988) across all accessions was found to be fairly high, with a Shannon's diversity index of 0.306.

Panicum maximum is another tall, fast growing species that is often found associated with *Pennisetum* in eastern African grasslands or associated with *Cenchrus* and *Bothriochloa* in *Acacia* woodland in the dry savannah areas (Rattray, 1960). Herlocker (1999) recognized the *Panicum-Hyparrhenia* region along the coast northwards from Tanzania, through Kenya into Somalia. *Panicum maximum* is more widely distributed in Kenya, Ethiopia and Tanzania and is typical of shady places in the foothills of mountain ranges up to 2 000 m. *P. maximum* is a pioneer grass that comes in after clearing and cultivation of the lowland forest. There is a wide variation in plant habit, robustness of culms and pubescence (Phillips, 1995), and ecotypes with good agronomic characters have been selected as commercial cultivars. *P. maximum* is fast growing and palatable, and its wide adaptation and variability make it an excellent grazing species in the savannahs. A collection of 426 ecotypes of *P. maximum* collected from Tanzania and Kenya were evaluated for morphological and agronomic traits in Brazil (Jank *et al.,* 1997). Twenty-one morphological descriptors were found to discriminate among accessions and were used to cluster the collection. Considerable variation was found among the ecotypes and some with wide adaptation were selected for establishment of a breeding programme. Other locally well-adapted ecotypes are also being developed for use within the region of adaptation.

POLITICAL AND SOCIAL SYSTEMS IN PASTORAL LANDS OF EASTERN AFRICA

Most dry grasslands of eastern Africa are characterized by frequent droughts and high levels of risk of production for pastoral peoples (Little, [2000]). Livestock are one of the few ways to convert sunlight into nutritious food in these drylands (wildlife are also important). Pastoralists traditionally manage risk by moving their livestock on a daily and seasonal basis to follow changes in the quality and quantity of pasture (IFAD, 1995). Cattle, camels, sheep, goats and donkeys are the main livestock species and are kept by the pastoralists for subsistence for their milk, meat and traction. Most herds are mixed as a means of adaptation to a changing environment, to supply food for the family and to act as a cash reserve in times of shortage, during droughts or disease-pandemics (Niamir, 1991).

Although sale of livestock is a major source of income for pastoralists today, widespread sale (or commoditization) of livestock only became common in the last century, with colonialism (Hodgson, 2000). Settled crop-livestock farmers are particularly oriented toward marketing: selling animals, milk and hides regularly. Herds are managed in a way that minimizes sales because of the traditional social and economic functions of livestock other than income generation (Coppock, 1994). In most pastoral areas, livestock are used as a social "safety net", with livestock exchange cementing mutual obligations to help each other in times of need. Like many other pastoral areas, cattle are also of particular significance in the Borana area of Ethiopia as a symbol of wealth and prestige, and owners are reluctant to sell. Sheep and goats are usually sold to raise cash for household needs. Although marketing of livestock products (milk, meat, hides) in pastoral systems is a relatively new phenomenon, pastoral peoples who live near markets and roads are increasingly selling products.

Traditionally, herders consume a large part of the milk produced; any surplus is shared with neighbours, exchanged in barter or sold in urban areas. In Somalia, a commercial milk chain through a cooperative has been established by the pastoralists for marketing camel milk in Mogadishu as a source of income to buy sugar, clothes and medicines (Herren, 1990). An EU-funded project, *Strengthening food security through decentralized cooperation,* active from 1996 to 2002, also supported establishment of a small processing plant for pasteurizing camel milk and marketing the resulting products in suitable packaging for the Somali market (EC, 2000). The 2001–2 drought had a considerable effect on camel calving intervals and milk sales. In some parts of Somalia, there was virtually no income from milk sales following the drought. Milk formerly provided approximately 40 percent of a household's income and the return on livestock sales, which typically provide an additional 40 percent of income, was halved after the drought (FSAU, 2003). Maasai in Kenya and Tanzania living close to main roads or towns sell fresh milk, butter or fermented milk. The Borana in southern Ethiopia sour cow's milk and process it into butter for sale in local markets or for transport to large cities (Holden and Coppock, 1992). Distance to market, season and wealth of the household (which is directly related to the number of livestock owned) influence marketing of dairy products in the southern rangelands of Ethiopia (Coppock, 1994).

Most of the extensive grasslands in the region are either under the control of the government and designated as wildlife and conservation areas for national parks (about 10 percent of the land area) or are open access or common property resources. Access to these resources and the conditions under which they can be used are under national laws, but frequently traditional land use rights are granted by local communities. Traditionally, long-term sustainability of these rangelands has been ensured by agreed management norms, but these are increasingly breaking down as lands privatize, crop farmers migrate to pastoral areas and human needs grow. Governments are also reducing support to pastoral peoples, who are often marginalized in national affairs (IFAD, 1995). Options for income generation and alternative land uses for extensive grasslands for pastoralists are limited and can lead to overutilization and land degradation if none of the users take responsibility for the management and sustainability of the system.

Common property and traditional access regimes with sustainable range management institutions and resource sharing arrangements were practiced in the region until the colonial era (IFAD, 1995) and continue in some areas today. These were and are based on a transhumance grazing system developed over many years to exploit the ecological heterogeneity and make optimal use of the scarce resources of grazing and water throughout the year. These traditional management practices include grazing rotation strategies and establishment of grazing preserves for the dry season. Drought is the most serious challenge facing pastoralists in the region and access to land and water are often the cause of conflict between pastoralists, ranchers and crop-livestock farmers (Mkutu, 2001). Traditional systems of access to water are common in most countries in the region. The pastoralists of northern Somalia and southern Ethiopia also have a complex and well-regulated system of well management to regulate water use, as well as traditional informal and formal social controls on use of common property and open property resources to ensure sustainable use of the grassland and water resources (Niamir, 1991). This is exemplified by herder response to drought and conflict in southern Somalia, where herders move camels and cattle great distances to good pastures in times of drought, while they graze small stock closer to home (Little, [2000]).

Over the last century, these indigenous range management institutions have been weakened by demographic, political and social change in the region. The greatest threat to the traditional pastoralist system comes from the rapid population growth of the last twenty years and conversion of communal grassland to open access state property or private land, which has led to more grassland being used for smallholder crop-livestock farming. Policies have constrained the movement of pastoralists and promoted sedentarization and many permanent settlements have been established in the rangelands; with many pastoralists choosing to shift their production systems to include crop-livestock farming (Galaty, 1994; Campbell *et al.,* 2000). In S.E. Kajiado District, Kenya, land use conflict reflects ongoing competition over access to scarce land and water resources between herders, farmers and wildlife – competition that has intensified strongly over the last 40 years, after the district became open to outside migrants.

Today, farming extends into the wetter margins of the rangelands, along rivers and around swamps. This has reduced the area available for grazing and the ease of access to water for both domestic stock and wildlife. Political alliances have emerged among land managers to gain or maintain control of critical land and water resources and to influence policy on agriculture, wildlife and tourism and land tenure (Campbell *et al.,* 2000). Another well-documented example of this is from the Beja pastoralists in northeastern Sudan, who, as a result of drought, are changing their nomadic way of life as camel and smallstock herders to more settled, smallholder farming and rearing of small ruminants. Like other pastoralists in the region, they find that small ruminants are easy to manage near the homestead, cost less, are more easily sold and breed more quickly than camels (Pantuliano, 2002). Government policies have supported cropping and reduction of communal grazing land and, more recently, mobility patterns and access to key resources have been constrained by conflict and civil insecurity. Many Beja now move very little or not at all, reducing their capacity to make effective use of the rangeland from the perspective of livestock production. As Beja settle, vegetation around settlements has changed, with the disappearance of seven palatable species and an increase in unpalatable species (Pantuliano, 2002). These changes are typical of those faced by pastoralists across the region. Even so, many families (or parts of families) still send the younger family members for transhumance in the dry season while the women and older family members remain on the farm to take care of the crops and smallstock.

The national land tenure systems of the region are unrelated to the traditional land tenure and access regimes of the pastoralist groups. In Ethiopia, the Sudan and Somalia, all land is state owned and cropping land can be leased from or allocated by the government. In Somalia, land tenure is under a mixture of traditional and modern legal systems (Amadi, 1997). The 1975 Land Reform Act of Somalia gave land for state enterprises and mechanized agriculture (Unruh, 1995); pastoralists only had rights as part of government-sponsored cooperatives and associations, and were forced to move from their traditional lands to more marginal lands with open access. All land belonged to the state and 50-year leases were provided to users, although many enclosures were not legally leased and ownership was respected by local communities under traditional systems (Amadi, 1997). Following the conflict and the absence of a central government, the deregulation of land tenure and unauthorized enclosure of pastoral land for grass production by entrepreneurs for export livestock production to Kenya left poor herders and agropastoralists with little livelihood security (de Waal, 1996). For the Sudan, the government recognizes rights of possession over land but also reserves the right to acquire land from local owners for the state (Amadi, 1997). In Ethiopia, land is allocated through the land administration, and redistribution occurs, so people do not have secure rights over their land (EEA/EEPRI, 2002), resulting in inter-ethnic and inter-communal conflict over resources. In neighbouring Eritrea, land is owned by the community, and land tenure is governed by traditional laws and administered under traditional village administrative bodies (Amadi, 1997).

Land tenure in Uganda is very complex, reflecting the rich history of the country. *Mailo* tenure is particular to the Buganda area of the country and dates back to 1900 when the king (*kabaka*) of the Buganda people shared land among the chiefs to own in perpetuity. In 1975, the Land Reform Decree made all land public with title vested in the Uganda Land Commission, and allowed leasehold tenure (Busingye, 2002). Although the mailo system was officially abolished, it continued until the late 1990s, when the 1995 Constitution and the Land Act of 1998 were implemented. Freehold tenure was also granted by the state and later by the Land Commission, mostly to institutions for religious and educational purposes (Busingye, 2002). The 1995 Constitution and 1998 Land Act also identified a new land tenure system called customary tenure. The land is held, used and disposed of following the customary regulation of the community, and people using the land have some rights. Customary tenure is the most common system in the rangelands (Amadi, 1997). The emphasis is on use, which is controlled by the family, who distribute land to male family members for their use rather than ownership. Customary tenure also includes the communal land, where users have rights to grazing, farming, fuelwood, access to water and land for traditional uses and burial grounds (Busingye, 2002). Ownership is through the family or community, and there are no individual ownership rights. Traditional authorities allocate the land and resolve disputes. In addition some land was declared Crown Lands in 1900, and areas are still held by the state under the Uganda Land Commission as protected areas, some of which are now open access.

The land tenure system in the United Republic of Tanzania is a legacy of colonial rule, with all lands being public land and remain vested in the President as a trustee for and on behalf of all citizens of Tanzania (Nyongeza, 1995; Shivji, 1999). The state grants rights of occupancy and tolerates customary occupation and use of land. All public land is categorized under three types: General, Reserved or Village land, which are each managed and administered by ministry officials. The Commissioner for Lands has the power to allocate land on the general, and even reserved, lands. When a village registers its land, the title deeds are held in trust for the whole village by the Village Chairman and Council. Numerous land-related conflicts exist in Tanzania, partly caused by conflicting land use policies. The Villagization Programme (1974–76) concentrated people together, displacing some and allocating them land that was taken from others. Some of the villages were relocated into reserved land, thus creating pockets of habitation and cultivation in protected areas. With the economic liberalization in the mid 1980s, large-scale land alienation occurred, in particularly in the Arusha region, where vast parts of rangelands were leased out to large-scale farmers (Igoe and Brockington, 1999). Village land can also be allocated by the government, if it is not registered or its use can not be demonstrated. To secure their title deeds, many pastoralists started cultivating. Much of the rangeland areas in Tanzania have been categorized as reserved lands, having been set aside as national parks, game reserves or game controlled areas, thus making them inaccessible for herders and their livestock (Brockington, 2002).

Land tenure in Kenyan pastoral systems has evolved rapidly over the last half century. About the 1940s, Kenyan colonial authorities introduced an entirely new type of land use to rangeland ecosystems: wildlife-only protected land. In subsequent years, the Kenya Game Department transferred the management of game reserves in Maasailand to local District Councils. After independence in 1963, these reserves were designated "County Council Reserves"[3] (Lamprey and Waller, 1990). Most of these conservation areas were established in the dry season grazing reserve for pastoral people, livestock and wildlife. This change in land tenure appropriated these critical resources for use by wildlife alone for the first time.

Also in the mid-1960s, the Kenya Government gave pastoral groups title deeds to large tracts of grazing land that they had used traditionally over a long period (Lawrance Report, 1966). Each member shared ownership of the entire ranch under the Group Representatives Act, 1968, but the livestock were owned by individual members (Lamprey and Waller, 1990). Although these ranches were large (Koyake Group Ranch in the Mara area is 971 km²) and group ranch boundaries were relatively porous to livestock and wildlife movement, these group ranches started to circumscribe who could live where in the ecosystem. The group ranch system was instituted more strongly in the wetter rangelands in the south and just north of Mt. Kenya; arid rangelands further northwest and northeast were largely unaffected by this change in tenure.

Since the early 1980s, group ranches have been adjudicated and are becoming privatized (Galaty, 1994). Areas near towns and roads were the first to be privatized. For example, the rangeland nearest to Nairobi was privatized in the early 1980s, while other group ranches in drier areas are currently undergoing subdivision. Pastoral land owners are struggling to balance the trade-offs of private tenure: even though secure ownership is a boon, lack of access to wider grazing lands and loss of wildlife are not. Groups and families are trying to address these problems with reciprocal grazing arrangements and establishment of community wildlife reserves. This process has partly been driven by pastoral peoples throughout Kenya beginning to settle permanently to have access to schools, health care and other business opportunities in the higher potential areas. At the same time, pastoral people want to secure their ownership rights as they see large tracts of communal land leased to outsiders for mechanized agriculture.

Privatization of land in pastoral areas robs pastoral peoples of one of their greatest assets: communal access to land. In the 1960s, Hardin (1968) decried communal access to land, describing it as the "tragedy of the commons", assuming that communal access meant free and unregulated access leading to overuse. This has been used as an argument in favour of privatization.

---

[3] Intitially established in the late 1940s as 'National Reserves' under Kenya Royal National Parks, these areas were once again redesignated as national reserves under the 1976 Wildlife (Conservation and Management) Act. However, they continued to be managed by county councils.

However, most communal access to pastoral land and water is not unregulated, rather it is governed by traditional rules of access controlling who uses the land and water, where and when. These rules were designed to sustain grassland productivity for the use of all in communally shared lands. Privatization of land is now causing the "tragedy of privatization", where pastoral people are impoverished because land holdings are too small to support their livelihoods in dry grazing lands. This is what Rutten (1992) nicely coined as "selling land to buy poverty". The overgrazing issue is discussed below, applicable to both communal and privatized land.

INTEGRATION OF GRASSLANDS INTO SMALLHOLDER FARMING SYSTEMS

As pastoral systems evolve and herders avoid drought and disasters through diversification and risk management, sedentarization and settlement to improve income-earning capacity is occurring in northern Kenya and southern Ethiopia (Little *et al.*, 2001). There continues to be an expansion of cropping in areas where agriculture is feasible, to allow herders to better manage risk and respond to drought (Little *et al.*, 2001). As cropping expands into the rangelands of the region, grasslands have become an integral part of crop-livestock systems.

Nearly all grassland areas in developing countries are grazed (CAST, 1999). One viable alternative for settled crop-livestock farmers in the region is to use cultivated forage grasses to support livestock production and reduce the pressure on the natural grassland. Cultivated forages have received less attention from breeders than other crops (CAST, 1999). However, recent expansion in dairying, especially around urban areas in eastern Africa, and the anticipated increased demand for livestock production proposed by Delgado *et al.* (1999) has led smallholder farmers to pay more attention to increased use of cultivated grasses. Inclusion of grasses into a crop-livestock system can also have positive environmental benefits. Vegetation cover can be improved through transfer of seeds and trampling and breaking soil crusts and fertility improved by manure deposited during grazing (Steinfeld, de Haan and Blackburn, 1997). Fallow and grassland rotations improve soil fertility and minimize soil erosion, while reduced nutrient losses from manure from livestock fed on grasses in a cut-and-carry system double the effective availability of nitrogen and phosphorus and can be put back into the system to maintain nutrient balances (de Haan, Steinfeld and Blackburn, 1997).

Rhodes grass and elephant grass are among the earliest tropical grasses grown in eastern Africa, since the start of the twentieth century. They have been widely planted for livestock production in Kenya and Uganda since the 1930s (Boonman, 1993) and are an important part of crop-livestock systems in higher-potential areas. Grass rotations and fallowing of crop lands were common practices to provide soil cover and restore organic matter some 50 years ago, but this practice has reduced due to increasing population pressure and demand for crop land (Boonman, 1993). Due to scarcity of land, most dairy farmers in the heavily populated highlands of eastern Africa now practice a cut-and-carry zero grazing system. Currently, elephant grass is the most important forage crop in dairy systems in the Central Kenya Highlands (Staal *et al.,* 1997) and has been shown to constitute between 40 to 80 percent of the forage for the smallholder dairy farms. In Kenya alone, more than 0.3 million smallholder dairy producers (53 percent) rely on elephant grass as a major source of feed. The demand is so high that landless farmers plant along highway verges and on communal land to cut and sell to stock owners.

Rhodes grass has also been widely used for improved pastures due to its wide adaptation and vigorous root system, which confers reasonable tolerance to drought and persistence under grazing and makes it suitable for erosion control, and of value for hay making (Boonman, 1993). It shows some cold tolerance, and several commercial varieties have been developed in Kenya. It ranks second only to elephant grass in yield and drought tolerance, producing up to 18 t DM/ha in suitable environments (Boonman, 1993).

Another cultivated grass with wide adaptability that is being grown in eastern Africa is setaria (*Setaria sphacelata*). Herbage yield can equal Rhodes grass and it is more persistent at higher altitudes, up to about 3 000 m above sea level, and can tolerate frost and seasonal waterlogging (Boonman, 1993). However, it is not as drought tolerant as Rhodes grass and has a tendency to invade agricultural land, and can become weedy and difficult to eradicate. Although its use reduced in Kenya during the 1980s, it is still a useful grass in wetter and higher-altitude areas, and it is now gaining importance for use in soil stabilization and erosion control along bunds in Tanzania and central Kenya (Boonman, 1993). Unfortunately, none of these options for improved forage production are available to settled pastoralists across the vast dryland areas of the region.

CASE STUDIES OF THE EVOLUTION OF EXTENSIVE RANGE SYSTEMS OVER THE LAST 40 YEARS
General
Expansion of cropland, intensification of livestock production and changes in land tenure are common forces for change in pastoral systems around the world (Niamir-Fuller, 1999; Blench, 2000). Across Africa, colonial and post-colonial policies favoured crop cultivation over livestock production, thus giving agriculturalists the economic "upper hand" compared to pastoralists (Niamir-Fuller, 1999). As described earlier, pastoralists are thus either pushed onto more marginal lands for grazing or they begin to take up crop agriculture themselves, becoming agropastoralists (vide Campbell *et al.,* 2000). In most cases, customary political and management systems are becoming weaker (Niamir-Fuller, 1999). Livestock development projects are also driving change in pastoral lands by opening up remote pastures with the spread of borehole

technology and fragmentation of rangelands by veterinary cordon fences; this is true in eastern Africa, but particularly in southern Africa. Conflicts have resulted in changes in land tenure, with restricted access to traditional grazing lands as well as reduced mobility of pastoralists in insecure areas (Mkutu, 2001).

This "contraction" of pastoral grazing systems reduces the scale of resource use by pastoral peoples. Pastoral success depends largely on tracking patchy resources through time. In most traditional systems, this requires an opportunistic strategy of movement from daily and weekly changes in grazing orbits, to seasonal migrations over large landscapes. Many of the forces driving change in pastoral systems curtail the ability of pastoralists to move: sedentarization limits the maximal grazing distance achievable from a fixed homestead; privatization of land tenure limits access to many pastures; and gazetting of protected areas prevents pastoralists from reaching some pastures.

Evolution of land use changes in the semi-arid rangelands surrounding the Serengeti-Mara Ecosystem, straddling the Kenyan–Tanzanian border

Maasailand in southern Kenya and northern Tanzania has been subject to considerable vegetation changes since the beginning of the twentieth century. Over the past century, the area has passed through successive stages of transformation as the result of the interaction between four distinct, and probably cyclical, processes of change: change in vegetation; climate; tsetse and tick infection; and pastoral occupation and management. At the end of the nineteenth century, Maasai pastoralists had access to extensive grasslands (Waller, 1990). During and following the great rinderpest epidemic of 1890, cattle populations in eastern Africa succumbed rapidly: by 1892, 95 percent had died. Famine and epidemics of endemic diseases such as smallpox reduced human populations to negligible numbers in Maasailand. Wild ruminants also died in great numbers due to rinderpest, but gradually developed immunity. By 1910, wildlife numbers rose, with the exception of wildebeest and buffalo, whose numbers were kept low from yearling mortality. These natural disasters disrupted the grazing patterns and reduced intensity. Dense woodlands and thickets established in the Mara Plains and northern Serengeti (Dublin, 1995) because fires were less frequent, since population decreased with the famine and there were fewer people to light fires, so fuel loads grew with less grazing offtake. This dense, woody vegetation was a habitat for tsetse flies, which fed on the abundant wildlife and prevented significant human re-settlement. Until the 1950s, Maasai chose to settle and graze away from the Mara Plains (Waller, 1990). At that time, the human population in the area was rapidly increasing and Maasai herdsmen used fire to improve grazing pastures (Plate 2.7) and to clear tsetse-infested bush. Increased elephant densities further maintained the woodland decline in the Maasai Mara and Serengeti as the animals moved to the

R.S. REID

Plate 2.7
Large areas of eastern African grasslands burn every year, providing short green regrowth for many species of livestock and wildlife in these ecosystems.

protected areas from the surrounding, more densely inhabited areas. Between 1957 and 1973, woodlands in the Mara decreased from about 30 percent to about 5 percent cover (Lamprey and Waller, 1990). By the mid-1970s the wildebeest population had increased to about 1.5 million, and currently fluctuates around 1 million (Dublin, 1995).

Over the past 25 years, considerable changes in land cover and land use have taken place in the Serengeti-Mara ecosystem and in the rangelands surrounding the protected core of the ecosystem (Serneels, Said and Lambin, 2001). The ecosystem is made up of protected land (Serengeti National Park, Ngorongoro Conservation Area (NCA) and several Game Controlled Areas in Tanzania, and Maasai Mara National Reserve in Kenya), surrounded by semi-arid rangelands that are largely inhabited by Maasai agropastoralists. Land cover changes leading to a contraction of the rangelands were most pronounced in the Kenyan part of the ecosystem, surrounding the Maasai Mara. About 45 000 ha of rangelands were converted to large-scale mechanized farming after 1975. Expansion of the wheat farms reached a maximum extent in 1997–8, at 60 000 ha. By 2000, about half of the wheat fields had been abandoned, mostly because the yields in the drier areas were too uncertain to make cultivation viable. The abandoned areas once more became available to livestock and wildlife. Permanent settlements have spread from the north to the south in the last 50 years, with significant settlement areas now on the northern border of the Mara Reserve (Lamprey and Waller, 1990). In the rangelands, most attempts at subsistence cultivation were abandoned after a few years, due to crop destruction by wildlife and highly variable yields linked with climate variability. In the Tanzanian part of the ecosystem, land cover changes were less pronounced. No conversion for large-scale farming occurred; most land cover changes were either expansion of smallholder cultivation or natural succession in rangelands. Extensive areas of cultivated land (subsistence to medium-scale agriculture) were found in the unprotected lands, right up to the border with the protected areas west of Serengeti and southeast of NCA. In the NCA and the Loliondo Game Controlled Area, about 2 percent of land cover changes were attributed to smallholder impact over the past 20 years. In the NCA, cultivation is regulated: only hand-hoe cultivation is allowed and fields are small and scattered. In the Loliondo, no such restrictions are in place, but the area is very inaccessible, so the lack of opportunities to export the crops outside the area effectively controls the extent of cultivation.

The conversion of rangelands to agriculture has had a serious impact on the wildebeest population in the Kenyan part of the Serengeti-Mara ecosystem. The population declined drastically over the past twenty years and is currently fluctuating around an estimated population of 31 300 animals, which is about 25 percent of the population size at the end of the 1970s. Fluctuations in the wildebeest population in the Kenyan part of the Serengeti-Mara ecosystem, over the last decades, have been correlated strongly with the availability of forage during the dry and the wet seasons (Serneels and Lambin, 2001). Expansion of large-scale mechanized wheat farming in Kenya since the early 1980s has drastically reduced the wildebeest wet-season range, forcing the wildebeest population to use drier rangelands or to move to areas where competition with cattle is greater. The expansion of the farming area has not influenced the size of the total cattle population in the Kenyan part of the study area, nor its spatial distribution. The much larger migratory wildebeest population of the Serengeti, in Tanzania, did not decline at the same time as the Kenyan population but is also regulated by food supply in the dry season (Mduma, Sinclair and Hilborn, 1999). Around the Serengeti, in Tanzania, land use changes are much less widespread, occur at a lower rate and affect a much smaller area compared with the Kenyan part of the ecosystem. Moreover, land use changes around the Serengeti have taken place away from the main migration routes of wildebeest.

Protected areas and local land use: source of conflict in Tanzania

Savannah ecosystems are well represented in African protected area networks (Davis, Heywood and Hamilton, 1994). In Tanzania, very large tracts of savannah have been set aside for conservation, partly because these rangelands support the most diverse assemblage of migrating ungulates on earth (Sinclair, 1995). However, there are few resources to manage these conservation areas effectively and the rural populations surrounding them are among the poorest in the world. Thus, conflict and complementarity between conservation and development have become major issues in Ngorongoro (Homewood and Rodgers, 1991), Mkomazi (Rogers *et al.*, 1999), Selous (Neumann, 1997) and Tarangire (Igoe and Brockington, 1999).

Mkomazi Game Reserve in Northern Tanzania is a 3 200 km² savannah area stretching from the Kenya-Tanzania border to the northeastern slopes of the Pare and Usambara mountains. Mkomazi lies within the Somali-Maasai regional centre of endemism (RCE) (White, 1983), where the dominant vegetation is *Acacia-Commiphora* bush, woodland and wooded grassland. Mkomazi borders the Afromontane RCE, with the lowland and montane forests of the Usambaras recognized as an outstanding centre of plant diversity (Davis *et al.*, 1994), an endemic bird area (Stattersfield *et al.*, 1998) and a centre of endemism for many other taxa (Rodgers and Homewood, 1982). This "dry border" ecotone position means that Mkomazi species richness may be enhanced not only by the presence of species primarily associated with the adjacent ecosystems, but also by divergent selection driving the evolution of new forms (cf. Smith *et al.*, 1997). This diversity makes Mkomazi particularly valuable to opportunistic land users like pastoralists, but also for conservation of its rich species and landscape diversity. Based on the perceived species richness and concerns by the conservationists about the impacts on Mkomazi's vegetation of large numbers of cattle grazing in the western part of the reserve and large mammal populations, the resident pastoralists were evicted from the park in 1988 and use of its resources by the neighbouring communities was prohibited.

Mkomazi has been widely presented as undergoing ecological degradation prior to the 1988 evictions and recovery since then (e.g. Mangubuli, 1991; Watson, 1991). Data to confirm or refute that claim are as yet unavailable (Homewood and Brockington, 1999), but eviction was viewed as a risk-averse decision from a conservation point of view. However, from a pastoral point of view, the eviction did have serious impacts on the livelihoods of those who were evicted. Besides pastoral people, a large number of non-pastoral people also depended on the reserve for their livelihoods and used the reserve for beekeeping, collection of wild foods to supplement their diets or for sale at the local markets, and collection of fuelwood. Since the eviction, an estimated 25 percent of the livestock population have been restricted to a narrow and insufficient grazing area between Mkomazi reserve and the mountains bordering it to the south. Others have moved away from the reserve onto the increasingly crowded rangelands. Options for long-distance migration were greatly reduced, as the evictions occurred three years after the proliferation of large-scale commercial agriculture in northeastern Tanzania (Igoe and Brockington, 1999).

The impact of the evictions from Tarangire National Park, north-central Tanzania, shortly after its creation in 1968 was not felt immediately. There was no large-scale farming in the region at that time and pastoral Maasai were able to develop alternative, if less optimal, subsistence strategies. The effects became visible more than 20 years later, during the 1993/4 drought. By this time, some of the best wet-season pastures in Simanjiro District had been lost to large-scale commercial agriculture and more livestock were forced onto the dry-season grazing grounds in the early grazing season, depleting the season's grass growth sooner. The Maasai of Simanjiro found previous drought-coping strategies precluded by loss of access to drought reserve areas which had been enclosed inside the Tarangire National Park or allocated to large-scale commercial farms (Igoe and Brockington, 1999).

The examples of Mkomazi and Tarangire clearly point to costs and benefits in conservation decisions, with conflicts likely to intensify as human needs grow.

Control of the tsetse fly and evolution of a subhumid-grassland in southwestern Ethiopia: Ghibe Valley

Wetter grasslands and woodlands have also evolved rapidly in the last century. One cause of that change is the control of trypanosomiasis, the disease transmitted to livestock and people by the tsetse fly, which allowed farmers to use animal traction more extensively (greater numbers and more healthy oxen) and thus to expand the amount of land they cultivated at the household level (Jordan, 1986). Despite the logic of this progression, Ghibe Valley in Ethiopia is one of the few places in Africa where these changes have been seen clearly (Reid, 1999; Bourn *et al.*, 2001)

Ghibe Valley is located about 180 km to the southwest of Addis Ababa, where the main road to Jimma descends from the Ethiopian highland massif. Tsetse flies were first controlled in this area in 1991, using pesticide-drenched targets and pesticide poured on the cattle themselves. Within this landscape in 1993, just after the control, the majority of the arable land was wooded grassland used by wildlife and the few livestock herded by agropastoral peoples. Smallholder farms covered about a quarter of the arable land, while large-holder farms covered less than 1 percent (Reid *et al.*, 1997). About 90 percent of this landscape supports soils that are moderately to highly suitable for agriculture. Smallholder farmers grow a diversity of crop types, including maize, sorghum, tef, noug or niger seed (*Guizotia abyssinica*), false banana (*Ensete ventricosum*), groundnuts, wheat, beans and hot peppers, while large-holders grow a number of crops for market (citrus, onions, maize, spices). People use the large uncultivated tracts of grassland and woodland for settlements, hunting, wild plant gathering, beekeeping, livestock grazing, firewood collection, charcoal making and woodlot cultivation.

Rapid land use and land cover change was caused by the combined effects of drought and migration, changes in settlement and land tenure policy, and changes in the severity of trypanosomiasis (Reid *et al.*, 2000b; Reid, Thornton and Kruska, 2001). Each cause affected the location and pattern of land use and land cover in different ways. Previous to the control, a strong increase in the severity of the trypanosomiasis caused massive loss of livestock, farmers were unable to plough as effectively and the area of cropland contracted by 25 percent. Changes after tsetse control were slow to appear on the land itself, with nearly a five-year delay in impact on land use, although there was a more immediate impact on livestock health and populations. Changes were bi-directional and varied in speed, with both intensification and dis-intensification (Conelly, 1994; Snyder, 1996) occurring within the same landscape, sometimes slowly and sometimes rapidly.

These changes in land use caused profound changes in ecological properties and the structure of the valley's ecosystems (Reid *et al.*, 2000b). When land use expanded, large areas of woodland were cleared for cultivation and firewood became more scarce. As human populations grew, plants with medicinal value became more rare and the large herds of grazing herbivores were decimated. Most of the biodiversity in the valley is limited to the narrow ribbons of woodland along the rivers; it is these rich woodlands that farmers began to clear after successful tsetse control (Reid *et al.*, 1997; Wilson *et al.*, 1997).

CURRENT RESEARCH IN PASTORAL SYSTEMS OF EASTERN AFRICA
Management of grasslands

Management regimes for the grasslands of eastern Africa generally fall into three types: (1) state-managed for tourism and ranching; (2) commercial use for livestock or crop production; or (3) traditional management by pastoral and agropastoral groups. Livestock production, particularly cattle, is the major use for rangelands, with over 100 million head of livestock in the rangelands of eastern Africa (Herlocker, 1999). There is also a growing market for meat from wildlife, which is being met through commercial ranching and culling in the region. Grassland management is linked to use by livestock and wildlife, and there is often conflict between their exploitation for commercial income generation and the more sustainable management regimes of traditional groups. Wildlife-based tourism is of particular importance for generation of state, private and community income in the rangelands of Kenya (Plate 2.8) and Tanzania (Myers, 1972) and to a lesser extent in Uganda and Ethiopia. Recent efforts to privatize land and introduce more livestock are also changing the way people interact with wildlife.

Government development projects have focused on improving the productivity of the rangelands and increased livestock production from common property resources. The World Bank has sponsored several projects on rangeland management, including in Somalia, Kenya and Ethiopia. Earlier projects focused on increasing the productivity of rangelands for livestock production and several included formation of pastoral associations, which dealt with grazing rights and policies. These projects had disappointing results due to the parastatal organizational form, inappropriate technologies and poor apprecia-

Plate 2.8
Acacia bushland near Nakuru, Kenya, supports endangered Rothchild's giraffe.

tion of traditional systems and people. Only recently have issues of integrated natural resource management and full involvement of stakeholders been given attention, although there remain problems in reaching the local people through public sector organizations (de Haan and Gilles, 1994).

Traditional management systems by pastoralists recognized the need for controlled access to conserve the biodiversity and allow the rangeland to recover. Traditional grazing systems are more effective for sustainable resource use and maintenance of rangeland condition (Pratt and Gwynne, 1977). However, the traditional systems are under threat from increased livestock populations and decreased grazing lands, resulting in increased grazing pressure. This is already being recognized by Boran pastoralists in Ethiopia, who perceive that the condition of the rangelands is poor compared to 30 to 40 years ago (Angassa and Beyene, 2003) and consider the rangelands degraded and their livestock production declining.

Annual variation in amount and distribution of rainfall, together with grazing, fire and human activities, results in wide variation in grassland productivity (Walker, 1993). Rangeland ecosystems are very resilient and recover well when there is sufficient rainfall and controlled use of the resources. Range condition is dependent on both the grazing system, considered as timing and frequency of grazing, and grazing intensity, defined as the cumulative effects grazing animals have on rangelands during a particular period (Holechek *et al.*, 1998). Grazing intensity is closely associated with livestock productivity, trends in ecological conditions, forage production, catchment status and soil

C.J. WILSON

Plate 2.9
Heavily grazed grassland in the highlands near Bule, Ethiopia.

stability. It is considered as a primary tool in range management, and flexibility of grazing intensity is critical to rangeland ecosystem health. Grazing intensity has a major impact on range condition (Plate 2.9). In a recent study in Ethiopia, range condition, based on the herbaceous layer, basal cover, litter cover, relative number of seedlings, age distribution of grasses, soil erosion and soil compaction, was higher in lightly grazed areas in the Rift Valley than in the heavily grazed communal lands (Sisay and Baars, 2002). In Serengeti and Maasai Mara, grazing was found to stimulate net primary productivity at most locations, with maximum stimulation at intermediate grazing intensities and declines at high levels of grazing. Stimulation was dependent upon soil moisture status at the time of grazing (McNaughton, 1985).

There are many examples in the literature of the impact of management on species composition and diversity (Herlocker, 1999). In a study in the rangelands of southern Ethiopia, perennial grasses were relatively resilient in terms of cover and productivity in response to grazing, while continuous grazing encouraged forbs with lower grazing value for cattle (Coppock, 1994). Grazing affects species diversity and richness in grasslands (Oba, Vetaas and Stenseth, 2001). Optimal conservation of plant species richness was found at intermediate levels of biomass production and was found to decline if biomass increased in ungrazed areas of arid-zone grazing lands in northern Kenya. These intermediate levels can be achieved by manipulating management and grazing pressure, although there will be seasonal fluctuations due to environment. In the Serengeti Plains in Tanzania, elimination of grazing led to dominance by tall vegetatively propagated grass species, while the short sexually reproduced species disappeared (Belsky, 1986). This implies that even though the greatest number of species are found at intermediate grazing intensities, some species are always lost when ungrazed pastures are grazed. Although there are more species at intermediate levels of grazing, it is possible that any grazing negatively affects rare plant species that are sensitive to grazing.

Desertification: driven by climate or overgrazing by livestock?

One of the most controversial and debated aspects of research about pastoral systems is the existence and extent of overgrazing, desertification and land degradation[4] in pastoral lands, particularly in Africa. Global assessments of drylands maintain that much of the earth's land surface is degraded (GLASOD, 1990) and that livestock are the principal global cause of desertification (Mabbutt, 1984). Analysts suggest that African pastures are 50 percent more degraded than those in Asia or Latin America (GLASOD, 1990). However, other analyses show that livestock numbers only exceed likely carrying capacities of arid and semi-arid rangelands in about 3–19 percent[5] of Africa (Ellis *et al.*, 1999). In addition, there is no sustained evidence for a reduction in productivity, as measured by no change in the water-use efficiency of the Sahelian vegetation over 16 years, suggesting that the extent of the Sahara is more strongly influenced by drought than grazing (Tucker, Dregne and Newcomb, 1991; Nicholson, Tucker and Ba, 1998).

However, these broad assessments are only correlative and can not assess cause and effect rigorously, and can not measure the relative impacts of different causative agents. Certainly, at more local scales, livestock impacts are highly visible and persistent around towns, water points and along cattle tracks (e.g. Georgiadis, 1987; Hiernaux, 1996). More illuminating – but much more difficult to acquire – are two types of evidence: (1) remote sensing studies at the landscape scale, tracking the extent of degradation or desertification and of sufficient duration to cover drought and non-drought periods; and

---

[4] Definitions of desertification, overgrazing and degradation are controversial and
    problematic. We use the term desertification here to refer to the concepts used by the cited
    global assessment (GLASOD, 1990). We use degradation to mean an irreversible change in
    ecosystem state or function. We agree with de Queiroz (1993) that "degradation" has been
    defined relative to human management objectives and thus is relative; for example, a change
    from grassland to bushland is "degradation" to a cattle-keeper but may be "aggradation"
    from the perspective of carbon sequestration. We would prefer a set of quantitative measures
    that can assess the state of a particular piece of land and be used by land managers to assess
    the desirability of different changes from the context of their own management objectives.
    We define overgrazing here as any level of herbivore grazing that induces either temporary
    or permanent changes in the species composition or function of a grassland.

[5] Carrying capacity is exceeded in 19% of areas receiving 0–200 mm rainfall per annum, 15%
    of the 200–400 mm zone, 3% of the 400–600 mm zone and 8.5% of the 600–800 mm zone
    (Ellis *et al.*, 1999).

(2) either long-term experiments or observational studies at the pasture scale that assess the relative impacts of drought, livestock and other agents on ecosystem dynamics. Most of the research on land degradation and desertification in Africa has been focused on the Sahel, which has been intensively studied since the first droughts in the 1970s. Some landscape-scale studies based on a combination of fine-resolution satellite data and field measurements have been carried out in different parts of Africa and demonstrated the existence of local-scale degradation of rangelands in Ferlo, Senegal (Diouf and Lambin, 2001) and Turkana, Kenya, where highly affected areas covered only 5 percent of the land surface (Reid and Ellis, 1995). The importance of studying land degradation and desertification problems over a sufficiently long period is illustrated by studies conducted in Burkina Faso by Lindqvist and Tengberg (1993) and later by Rasmussen, Fog and Madsen (2001). The first group of scientists studied the amount of woody vegetation cover in three sites in northern Burkina Faso (1955–89). They found that important loss in woody vegetation cover occurred during the first of a series of droughts that started in the late 1960s, when large areas of bare soil developed. The authors found little evidence of vegetation recovery until 1989, despite increasing rainfall since 1985. Rasmussen, Fog and Madsen (2001) revisited the area, adding 10 years of satellite data. They found a decrease in albedo and thus increase in vegetation cover over the period 1986–1996, which was confirmed by fieldwork, thus showing the recovery of vegetation after drought. Interviews with local people indicated that the species composition of the regenerating herbaceous vegetation has changed considerably since the late 1970s. Land degradation caused by heavy grazing pressure was mostly found in the proximity of important water resources, which probably cover only a small proportion of the landscape in total. Schlesinger and Gramenopoulos (1996) also used the amount of woody vegetation cover as an indicator of desertification in western Sudan, but studied sites that were devoid of human use over the period 1943–1994. They analysed a time series of aerial photographs and Corona satellite images and did not find a significant decline in woody vegetation for the study period, despite several droughts having occurred during that period. Thus, at least in this area, they showed that the Sahara is not expanding and that drought had little effect on woody vegetation. In another part of the Sudan, the concentration of livestock around water points and settlements led to local loss of vegetative cover and accelerated erosion (Ayoub, 1998). In contrast, others have found that heavy livestock grazing around pastoral settlements in arid areas had minor impacts on woody vegetation and biodiversity, with impacts confined within the settlements themselves (Sullivan, 1999). Woody vegetation can replace palatable grass species in heavily grazed areas, caused by grazing pressure rather than climate (Skarpe, 1990; Perkins, 1991).

At the pasture or field level, the picture is more complex. Generally, livestock grazing, browsing and trampling causes loss of vegetation, competition with wildlife and sometimes a change in soils when use is prolonged and heavy. The impacts depend to some degree on the level and variability of rainfall (Ellis and Swift, 1988). In areas of southern Ethiopia with more and reliable rainfall supporting perennial vegetation (an equilibrium grazing system), the impacts of grazing in one season can reduce vegetative cover and production in the next (Coppock, 1994). In systems on the edge of perennial grass production, heavy grazing, especially in combination with drought, can reduce vegetative cover and production, even during subsequent wet years when more lightly grazed areas recover fully (de Queiroz, 1993). In systems with low and erratic rainfall (non-equilibrium systems), heavy grazing may (Milchunas and Laurenroth, 1993) or may not (Hiernaux, 1996) strongly influence production in subsequent seasons. Heavy grazing in annual grasslands changes the species composition of grassland vegetation, with more species in areas protected from grazing and fewer in heavily grazed areas (Hiernaux, 1998).

The nature of interrelationships and thresholds between biophysical, socio-economic, institutional and policy factors at different spatial scales and temporal dimensions influencing land degradation and desertification are still poorly understood. A recent initiative on land degradation assessment in drylands (LADA project), executed by FAO, responds to the need for an accurate assessment of land degradation in drylands at a flexible scale and to strengthen support to plan actions and investments to reverse land degradation, improve socio-economic livelihoods, conserve dryland ecosystems and their unique biological diversity (see: http:/www.fao.org/ag/agl/agll/lada/home.stm). Besides developing a set of tools and methods to assess and quantify the nature, extent, severity and impacts of land degradation on ecosystems, catchments, river basins and carbon storage in drylands at a range of spatial and temporal scales, the project also aims to build national, regional and global assessment capacities to enable the design and planning of interventions to mitigate land degradation and establish sustainable land use and management practices (Nachtergaele, 2002).

Another useful livestock evaluation tool to enhance early warning systems to detect changes in livestock condition is being developed under the USAID Global Livestock Collaborative Research Support Program (CRSP) by Texas A&M University (Corbett *et al.*, 1998). The Livestock Early Warning System (LEWS) integrates advanced crop and grazing models, based on empirical relationships between weather, vegetation, regrowth potential, soil and climate dynamics, with near infra-red spectroscopy (NIRS) for faecal analysis to detect changes in diet of free ranging livestock. These changes are linked to changes in vegetation patterns and can be used to predict drought and feed shortages for livestock some 6 to 8 weeks before pastoralists begin to see changes in the condition of the rangelands and their livestock. This allows them to better prepare for the coming feed shortages and nutritional crises in a timely manner by transhumance, as well as avoiding overgrazing of the rangeland resources.

HOW HAVE PASTORAL ECOSYSTEMS CHANGED IN RESPONSE TO LIVESTOCK AND HUMAN-USE CHANGES?

Overgrazing

A discussion of the impacts of grazing is provided in the preceding section and will not be considered further here, but grazing is without doubt one of the major forces effecting change in pastoral systems.

Competition between livestock and wildlife

Livestock can and do compete with several species of wildlife for forage in eastern Africa, but this may vary according to rainfall. Wildlife appear to avoid heavily grazed areas completely in arid northern Kenya (De Leeuw *et al.*, 2001), but mix more closely with livestock in semi-arid rangelands in southern Kenya (Waweru and Reid, unpub. data).

Wildlife probably avoid areas close to settlements because livestock remove most of the forage. Around Samburu pastoral settlements in northern Kenya, Grevy's zebra graze away from the settlements during the day, but move close to them during the night (Williams, 1998). Samburu build their settlements along riverine areas, within walking distance of streambeds where Samburu dig wells. After livestock are put into their corrals for the night, zebra come down to the streambeds to drink and leave by the next morning. They may also come close to the settlements at night for better predator protection as well.

In the group ranches around the Maasai Mara game reserve, wildlife avoid areas very close to settlements, but cluster at intermediate distances from settlements (Reid *et al.*, 2001). Wildlife may cluster around settlements to have access to moderately grazed grasslands, where their access to energy and nutrients is very high. They may also graze close by for protection from predators. Current settlements tend to be built on areas that have been settled for a long time and contain numerous old settlement scars where nutrient enrichment in the soils below old livestock corrals can last for a century or more (Muchiru, Western and Reid, submitted).

Changes in rangeland burning regimes

Livestock grazing and less frequent rangeland burning can strongly affect the state of the vegetation in rangeland systems. Wildlife and livestock systems, when side-by-side, often are of two different vegetative states: wildlife systems remain grasslands if elephants and fire are present (e.g. Dublin, 1995), while neighbouring livestock systems are much more woody (Western, 1989). Traditional rangeland burning is an essential practice to maintain the grassland state critical to grazers, but may reduce the amount of carbon sequestered in these ecosystems.

Rangeland fragmentation and loss of wildlife habitat

Fragmentation can also occur when fence lines are built to prevent the spread of disease or to prevent wildlife from foraging in enclosed pastures. This fragmentation prevents both livestock and wildlife from reaching parts of the landscape; often the fenced parts contain key resources like swamps and riverine areas. Impacts on wildlife are not entirely known, but decreases in population sizes and viability can be expected. Eventually, fragmentation can completely exclude species from an area.

Impacts of expansion of cultivation and settlement

Recent evidence suggests that the impact of cultivation on vegetation, wildlife and soils in pastoral ecosystems is greater than that of livestock. Expansion of cultivation fragments rangeland landscapes when farmers convert rangeland into cropland (Hiernaux, 2000). Land degradation through crop cultivation has been documented (Niamir-Fuller, 1999), but the impacts of livestock use and crop cultivation (or any other land uses) has rarely been compared. The conversion of savannah to cultivation in parts of the Mara ecosystem of Kenya, along with poaching and drought, has caused more than a 60 percent loss in resident wildlife populations in the Mara ecosystem in the last 20 years (Ottichilo *et al.*, 2000; Homewood *et al.*, 2001; Serneels, Said and Lambin, 2001).

In non-cultivated areas, mixed livestock-wildlife systems may be more productive than either wildlife-only or livestock-only systems (Western, 1989). These mixed systems, when maintained at moderate livestock grazing levels, coupled with pastoral rangeland burning, may support higher levels of plant and animal biodiversity than livestock-only or wildlife-only systems, analogous to the increase in plant diversity seen at the edge of wildlife reserves frequented by pastoralists and their livestock (Western and Gichohi, 1993). Further, it is hypothesized that when livestock populations are moderate in size or mobile, pastoralism produces significant global benefits in the form of biodiversity conservation, carbon sequestration, soil retention, soil fertility maintenance and catchment protection.

Estimates of how the expansion of cultivation will affect pastoral systems over the next half century are based on scenarios of human population growth and climate change for the year 2050 from Reid *et al.* (2000a) and Thornton *et al.* (2002). Surprisingly, these changes may bring about an absolute expansion of cultivation of only 4 percent, or a relative increase of about 15 percent (Figures 2.8 and 2.9). Most of the change will probably occur around the edges of currently cultivated land in areas with the most rainfall. Thus pastoral areas are expected to continue to contract further in the future and pastoral peoples to either continue to adopt agropastoralism or become restricted to drier and drier land.

Carbon sequestration

It is not clear whether current changes in the eastern African rangelands (land use change, overgrazing, fragmentation) are causing a net release or net accumulation of carbon, either above or below ground. Expansion of cultivation into rangelands probably strongly reduces carbon below ground, but may

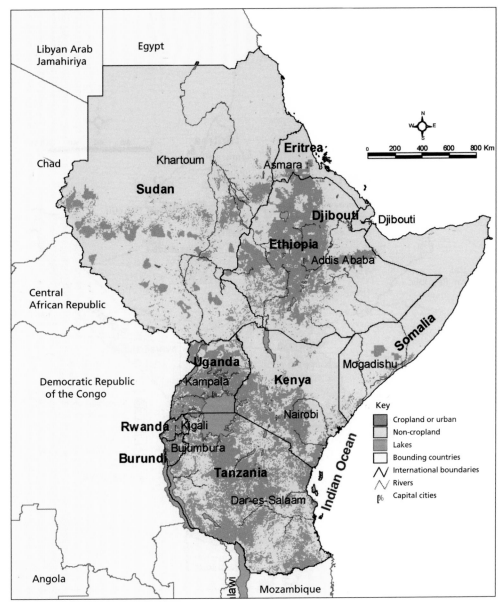

Figure 2.8
Estimated extent of cropland and urban areas in eastern Africa in 2000. From Thornton et al., 2002.

increase carbon above ground if farmers plant significant numbers of trees (the success of which depends on rainfall). If overgrazing converts grassland to bushland, then above-ground carbon will increase, but below-ground effects are unknown. In addition, rangelands are a significant carbon sink (IPCC, 2000), but the potential of these areas for further sequestration is not clear.

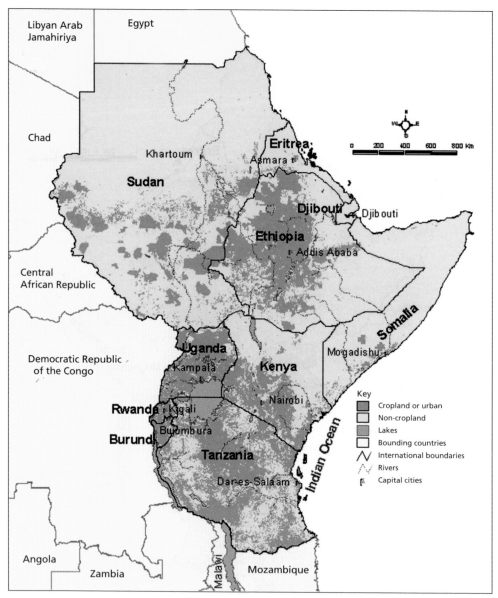

Figure 2.9
Projected extent of cropland and urban areas in eastern Africa in 2050. From Thornton et al., 2002.

Bush encroachment

Although grazing effects can be difficult to disentangle from the effects of climate, those that have attempted to do so show that livestock grazing can drive grassland systems into bushland (Archer, Scimel and Holland, 1995). Heavy livestock grazing can convert grassland to bushland in eastern

Africa, analogous to that observed in southern Africa (Ringrose *et al.*, 1990). Sometimes this conversion forms a monospecific stand of persistent woody species, which greatly reduces biodiversity (de Queiroz, 1993).

Rehabilitation of grasslands

Rehabilitation of grasslands usually involves use of exclosures and restricted access to allow the vegetation to recover and natural species to re-establish from the seed bank in the soil or from spread of plants by vegetative means. Grime (1979) recognized a variety of mechanisms of regeneration, with different types of revegetative strategies based on disturbance, vegetative cover and management, and proposed a model of vegetative succession and vegetation dynamics. Vegetative expansion is associated with undisturbed habitats with few seedlings and relies on rhizomes and stolons of perennial grasses. Seasonal regeneration of gaps involves synchronous germination of seeds from abundant seeders. Regeneration from persistent seed banks and wind dispersed seeds is associated with spatially unpredictable disturbances. Woody species also have persistent seed and seedling banks but opportunities for recruitment are infrequent. Disturbances alter ecosystem processes and may alter the equilibrium balance of the system (Chapin, 2003). Disturbances are usually revegetated by species of the original community and return to the previous species composition within a few years (Belsky, 1986). Introduction of new species through colonization and recruitment following disturbances may result in system change, and plant traits may be important indicators to predict the consequences of global change (Chapin, 2003).

Many previous attempts at rehabilitation have not been successful due to lack of consultation and involvement of local communities and their customs, and a perception that traditional systems need changes. Many technological interventions have been tested in the rangelands of southern Ethiopia but lack of development impact is linked to unrealistic expectations of development planners and poor appreciation of social values and production rationale of pastoralists (Coppock, 1994). Community participation in rehabilitation of degraded rangelands is an important step in promoting the success of current projects. A system in Samburu District in Kenya built on local knowledge and traditions to work in partnership with local people on local problems is having some success (Herlocker, 1999).

Rehabilitation offers an opportunity to sequester carbon through forestation, grass and shrub establishment. This is particularly important because pastoral lands are so extensive and they sequester large amounts of carbon. Rangelands are only second to tropical forests in the amount of carbon they sequester, although most of this sequestration is unseen below ground in rangelands, in contrast to carbon above ground in rain forests (IPCC, 2000). Poor use of range-lands can cause up to a 50 percent loss in soil carbon, so the potential gains from rehabilitation are substantial (Cole *et al.*, 1989; IPCC, 2000; Reid *et al.*, 2003).

Reseeding has been tried, with limited success, using thirty-two different species of grasses in Kenya (Bogdan and Pratt, 1967), although disturbance with subsequent colonization and regrowth was found to be successful for revegetation in the Serengeti Plains of Tanzania (Belsky, 1986). Options to improve success in Kenya were identified as selection of appropriate species for the ecosystem, good quality seeds, integration of reseeding with overall land management policy, adequate seedbed preparation, reasonable rain and a complete rest from grazing during the establishment period (Bogdan and Pratt, 1967). *Chloris roxburghiana* was difficult to establish in the south Kenya rangelands using seeds collected from natural stands (Mnene, Wandera and Lebbie, 2000). While there is the opportunity to introduce more productive exotic species into the system, these may often not be as well suited to the environment as the indigenous species and may not establish well. The study by Mnene indicated that ecotypes of the same species from different areas also showed poor establishment compared with seeds collected from populations in the same area.

Seed supply to support reseeding is a major constraint in eastern Africa and most species have to be collected from the wild (Bogdan and Pratt, 1967), a situation that has changed little over the past 30 years. Most succession in pastoral areas is through natural means, such as wind dispersal, although some projects are collecting seeds from natural stands for revegetation purposes. A limited number of cultivars of Rhodes grass, setaria, coloured guinea grass (*Panicum coloratum*) and signal grass (*Urochloa decumbens*) are available in Kenya from the Kenya Seed Company. These are useful for pasture establishment but have limited use for reseeding rangelands, except for revegetation of the *Hyparrhenia* tall-grass region as described by Herlocker (1999) and other areas where these grasses are an important part of the natural ecosystem. These species can also be used for range improvement due to their high palatability and nutritive value, but establishment is often poor due to low rainfall and competition, as well as open grazing during the establishment phase (Bogdan and Pratt, 1967).

PRIORITIES FOR RESEARCH AND DEVELOPMENT PROGRAMMES IN PASTORAL LANDS
Some history
In the late 1970s, the World Bank withdrew 98 percent of its funding to pastoral research and development because there had been little progress in improving the intensity of production in livestock-dominated systems (de Haan, 1999). The pressure to intensify existed despite the fact that crop cultivation often failed in these systems and often was unsustainable over the long term (Niamir-Fuller, 1999). Intensification of production has had such success in higher potential land that policy-makers assumed it was appropriate for pastoral lands, particularly because most policy-makers have

received their training in cropping systems for wet areas, with no personal experience in extensive rangelands (Horowitz and Little, 1987). It might be that the "intensification paradigm" is inappropriate for pastoral lands and that the success and sustainability of production depends on extensification rather than intensification, maintaining mobility and flexibility for opportunistic production (e.g. Sandford, 1983; Scoones, 1995).

In addition, recent re-evaluations have recognized that livestock production is not the sole value of pastoral lands; rather, the focus might be more appropriately placed on improving pastoral livelihoods and maintaining ecosystem health in these vast lands (de Haan, 1999; Niamir-Fuller, 1999). A consensus is emerging that pastoral lifestyles are more compatible with maintenance of rangeland integrity than are other types of land use.

Rapidly changing systems with changing needs

Pastoral systems in eastern Africa are rapidly evolving, driven by a combination of policy changes, drought, migration and human population pressure. Research and development efforts need to recognize such change and develop ways to understand and mitigate the effects of these changes.

Focus generally on human welfare and maintaining environmental goods and services

Eventually, if major constraints are removed, it may be possible for pastoralists to herd more productive livestock breeds in eastern African pastoral ecosystems. Until that happens, the focus should be less on production increases *per se* and more on diversifying livelihoods and maintaining environmental goods and services in pastoral lands (de Haan, 1999). There is good potential for alternative sources of income within pastoral areas from plant products (resins, medicinal plants), pastoral ecotourism and wildlife tourism (de Haan, 1999). There is some suggestion that income from ecotourism will surpass income from beef production in these lands in the developed world over the next decade (de Haan, 1999). Analogous to the Clean Development Mechanism of the Kyoto Protocol, it eventually may be possible to pay pastoralists (through biodiversity credits, for example) for maintaining ecosystem goods and services that have global benefits.

More emphasis on providing pastoral people with high quality information

Recent reviews of pastoral development emphasize the probable failure of many technical interventions in pastoral ecosystems. Blench (2000) suggests that the best way forward is better provision of high quality information to pastoralists, by asking the question: "What will pastoralists do if they have access to more and better information?" Pastoralists, because of their mobility and loose connections to national economies, are likely to be some of the last to have access to information in any form, particularly high technology information.

Restoring pastoral access to key resources, increasing mobility and flexibility, and ensuring security

In many parts of eastern Africa, pastoralism is the only way to convert sunlight into food. In these systems, new policies and management practices can still learn from the wisdom of Stephen Sanford (1983): opportunistic management of widely varying forage resources will be essential to reducing pastoral vulnerability. This means that maintenance of mobility and flexibility in grazing management strategies will remain particularly important. Another issue in eastern Africa is security – pastoral livelihood will hardly improve in areas where there is armed conflict. Asset and income diversification and improved access to information and external resources will also help. Improved risk management will enable pastoralists to take action to reduce the chance of losing assets, income or other aspects of well-being (Little *et al.*, 2001).

Addressing gaps in our knowledge about how pastoral systems work in eastern Africa

We conclude this chapter with a number of questions that remain either unanswered or partly answered, but that must be addressed fully in eastern African rangelands. How many pastoralists are there in eastern Africa? How poor are pastoralists compared with people in crop-livestock systems? What is the evidence that eastern African rangelands are degraded (Niamir-Fuller, 1999)? Does the magnitude and variability of rainfall modify the effect of the driving forces of change in pastoral ecosystems? How does extensification of pastoral systems in eastern Africa affect ecosystem goods and services? What are the ecological and economic costs and benefits of different land use practices and land use change in these systems? How do pastoral land use practices (adoption of cultivation, abandonment of nomadism, permanent settlement, landscape fragmentation) affect the distribution, diversity and viability of nutrients, vegetation, biodiversity and landscapes in pastoral ecosystems in eastern Africa? How do changes in land tenure and economic policy affect pastoral ecosystem structure and function? How do changes in pastoral ecosystems affect household incomes and nutrition? What are the economic, social and ecological values of global ecosystem goods and services provided by pastoral ecosystems in eastern Africa (Homewood, 1993; Niamir-Fuller, 1999)? What are the most reliable and broadly comparative indicators of ecosystem change across eastern African pastoral systems (e.g. microbes, soil crusts)? What forces serve to enhance or maintain complexity in pastoral ecosystems and livelihoods, and what decreases complexity? How do we establish benchmarks for ecosystem and livelihood change in pastoral systems that are already heavily used?

Addressing gaps in our knowledge about how these systems can be improved

Does the addition of livestock to wildlife-only systems in eastern Africa improve biodiversity and nutrient cycling? What social institutions best promote mobility and flexibility of land use among pastoralists and what policy alternatives can strengthen these institutions (de Haan, 1999)? What information is most useful to pastoralists and policy-makers, and in what form is it most easily accessible to each group? What types of incentive encourage extensification rather than intensification of pastoral ecosystems? How can pastoralists be compensated for protecting environmental goods and services of benefit to the globe? Will carbon credits work for pastoral lands? How can pastoralists take advantage of global conventions and funders (UN Convention to Combat Desertification (CCD); Global Environment Facility (GEF))? How can pastoralism be better integrated with crop cultivation in areas where such integration would be beneficial? How and when is co-conservation (integration of pastoral production and biodiversity conservation) most successful in eastern Africa?

REFERENCES

Amadi, R. 1997. Land tenure in the IGAD area – what next? The IGAD experience. *in:* Sub-regional workshop on land tenure issues in natural resources management in the Anglophone East Africa with a focus on the IGAD region. Sahara and Sahel Observatory/United Nations Economic Commission for Africa (OSS/UNECA).

Angassa, A. & Beyene, F. 2003. Current range conditions in southern Ethiopia in relation to traditional management strategies: The perception of Borana pastoralists. *Tropical Grasslands*, **37**: 53–59.

Archer, S., Schimel, D.S. & Holland, E.A. 1995. Mechanism of shrubland expansion: land use, climate or CO_2. *Climatic Change*, **29**: 91–99.

Ayoub, A.T. 1998. Extent, severity and causative factors of land degradation in the Sudan. *Journal of Arid Environments*, **38**: 397–409.

Belsky, A.J. 1986. Revegetation of artificial disturbances in grasslands of the Serengeti National Park, Tanzania. II. Five years of successional change. *Journal of Ecology*, **74**: 937–951.

Blench, R. 2000. *'You can't go home again.'* Extensive pastoral livestock systems: issues and options for the future. ODI/FAO, London, UK.

Bogdan, A.V. & Pratt, D.J. 1967. Reseeding denuded pastoral land in Kenya. Kenya Ministry of Agriculture and Animal Husbandry, Nairobi, Kenya.

Boonman, J.G. 1993. *East Africa's grasses and fodders: Their ecology and husbandry.* Dordrecht, The Netherlands: Kluwer Academic Publishers.

Boonman, J.G. 1997. Farmer's success with tropical grasses: Crop-pasture rotations in mixed farming in East Africa. Ministry of Foreign Affairs, The Hague, The Netherlands.

Bourn, D., Reid, R., Rogers, D., Snow, B. & Wint, W. 2001. Environmental change and the autonomous control of tsetse and trypanosomosis in sub-Saharan Africa. Environmental Research Group Oxford Ltd., Oxford, UK.

Box, T.W. 1968. Range resources of Somalia. *Journal of Range Management,* **21**: 388–392.

Brockington, D. 2002. *Fortress Conservation: The Preservation of the Mkomazi Game Reserve, Tanzania.* Oxford, UK: James Currey.

Busingye, H. 2002. Customary land tenure reform in Uganda: Lessons for South Africa. *in:* International Symposium on Communal Tenure Reform, Johannesburg, South Africa, 12–13 August 2002.

Campbell, D.J., Gichohi, H., Mwangi, A. & Chege, L. 2000. Land use conflicts in S.E. Kajiado District, Kenya. *Land Use Policy,* **17**: 338–348.

CAST [Council for Agricultural Science and Technology]. 1999. Animal agriculture and global food supply. Task force report 135. Council for Agricultural Science and Technology, USA. 92 p.

Chapin, F.S. 2003. Effects of plant traits on ecosystem and regional processes: a conceptual framework for predicting the consequences of global change. *Annals of Botany,* **91**: 455–463.

Cole, C.V., Stewart, J.W.B., Ojima, D.S., Parton, W.J. & Schimel, D.S. 1989. Modeling land use effects on soil organic matter dynamics in the North America Great Plains. pp. 89–98, *in:* L. Bergstrom (ed). *Ecology of Arable Land – Perspectives and Challenges: Developments in Plant and Soil Sciences.* Dordrecht, The Netherlands: Kluwer Academic Publishers.

Conelly, W.T. 1994. Population pressure, labour availability and agricultural disintensification: The decline of farming on Rusinga Island, Kenya. *Human Ecology,* **22**: 145–170.

Coppock, D.L. 1994. The Borana plateau of southern Ethiopia: Synthesis of pastoral research, development and change, 1980–91. International Livestock Centre for Africa, Addis Ababa, Ethiopia.

Corbett, J.D., Stuth, J., Dyke, P. & Jama, A. 1998. New tools for the characterization of agricultural (crop and livestock) environments: the identification of pastoral ecosystems as a preliminary structure for use in sample site identification. Presented at National Workshop on Early Warning System for Monitoring Livestock Nutrition and Health. Addis Ababa, Ethiopia, 4 February 1998. Sponsored by the Small Ruminant Collaborative Research Support Program (SR-GL/CRSP) in collaboration with the Ethiopian Agricultural Research Organization (EARO).

Davis, S.D., Heywood, V. & Hamilton, A. (eds). 1994. *Centres of plant diversity. A guide and strategy for their conservation. Volume 1. Europe and Africa.* Cambridge, UK: IUCN.

de Haan, C. 1999. Future challenges to international funding agencies in pastoral development: an overview. pp. 153–155, *in:* D. Eldridge and D. Freudenberger (eds). *Proceedings of the 6th International Rangeland Congress,* Townsville, Australia, 17–23 July 1999.

de Haan, C. & Gilles, J.L. 1994. An overview of the World Bank's involvement in pastoral development. Recent trends in World Bank pastoral development projects: A review of 13 bank projects in light of the "New Pastoral Ecology". Overseas Development Institute (ODI), London, UK.

de Haan, C., Steinfeld, H. & Blackburn, H. 1997. *Livestock and the environment: Finding a balance.* FAO, Rome, Italy. 115 p.

de Leeuw, J., Waweru, M.N., Okello, O.O., Maloba, M., Nguru, P., Said, M.Y., Aligula, H.M., Heitkonig, I.M. & Reid, R.S. 2001. Distribution and diversity of wildlife in northern Kenya in relation to livestock and permanent water points. *Biological Conservation,* **100**: 297–306.

Delgado, C., Rosegrant, M., Steinfeld, H., Ehui, S. & Courbois, C. 1999. Livestock to 2020: The next food revolution. *Food, Agriculture and the Environment Discussion Paper*, No. 28. International Food Policy Research Institute (IFPRI), Food and Agriculture Organization of the United Nations (FAO) and the International Livestock Research Institute (ILRI). Washington, D.C. 72 pp.

de Queiroz, J.S. 1993. Range degradation in Botswana. *Pastoral Development Network Paper*, No. 35b. Overseas Development Institute (ODI), London, UK.

de Waal, A. 1996. Class and power in a stateless Somalia. A Discussion Paper. Published on the Justice Africa Web site. See: http://www.justiceafrica.org/clas-somalia.html.

Deichmann, U. 1996. *Africa Population Database.* 3rd version. University of California, Santa Barbara, California, USA, as a cooperative activity between National Center for Geographic Information and Analysis (NCGIA), Consultative Group on International Agricultural Research (CGIAR), United Nations Environment Programme/Global Resource Information Database (UNEP/GRID) and World Resources Institute (WRI).

Diouf, A. & Lambin, E.F. 2001. Monitoring land-cover changes in semi-arid regions: remote sensing data and field observations in the Ferlo, Senegal. *Climate Research,* **17**: 195–208.

Dougall, H.W. 1960. Average nutritive values of Kenya feeding stuffs for ruminants. *East Africa Agriculture and Forestry Journal,* **26**: 119–128.

Dublin, H.T. 1995. Vegetation dynamics in the Serengeti-Mara ecosystem: the role of elephants, fire and other factors. pp. 71–90, *in:* A.R.E. Sinclair and P. Arcese (eds). *Serengeti II: Dynamics, Management and Conservation of an Ecosystem.* Chicago, Illinois, USA: University of Chicago Press.

EEA/EEPRI [Ethiopian Economic Association/Ethiopian Economic Policy Research Institute]. 2002. A research report on land tenure and agricultural development in Ethiopia. Addis Ababa, Ethiopia: United Printers, for Ethiopian Economic Association/Ethiopian Economic Policy Research Institute.

EC [European Commission]. 2000. EU Food aid and food security programme Towards recipient country ownership of food security. Bi-annual report 1998–9. ECSC-EEC-EAEC. Brussels, Belgium. 41 p

Ellis, J., Reid, R.S., Thornton, P.K. & Kruska, R. 1999. Population growth and land use change among pastoral people: local processes and continental patterns. Poster. pp. 168–169, *in:* D. Eldridge and D. Freudenberger (eds). *Proceedings of the 6th International Rangeland Congress*, Townsville, Australia, 17–23 July 1999.

Ellis, J. & Swift, D.M. 1988. Stability of African pastoral ecosystems: Alternative paradigms and implications for development. *Journal of Range Management*, **41**: 450–459.

FAO. 1978. Reports of the agro-ecological zones project. *FAO World Soils Resources Reports.* No. 48.

FAO. 2000. *The elimination of food insecurity in the Horn of Africa. A strategy for concerted government and UN agency action.* Summary report of the Inter-agency Task Force on the UN Response to Long-term Food Security, Agricultural Development and Related Aspects in the Horn of Africa. FAO, Rome, Italy. 13 p. See: http://www.gm-unccd.org/FIELD/Multi/FAO/FAO9.pdf

Fischer, G., Velthuizen, A. & Nachtergaele, F.O. 2000. Global agro-ecological zones assessment: methodology and results. Interim report. International Institute for Applied Systems Analysis (IIASA), Laxenburg, Austria.

Fisher, M.J. & Kerridge, P.C. 1996. The agronomy and physiology of *Brachiaria* species. pp. 43–52, *in:* J.W. Miles, B. L. Maass and C.B. do Valle (eds). Brachiaria: *Biology, Agronomy and Improvement.* CIAT, Cali, Colombia.

FSAU [Food Security Assessment Unit Somalia]. 2003. *Annual Post Gu 2003 Food Security Outlook.* Food Security Assessment Unit Somalia, Nairobi, Kenya. 28 p. See: http://www.unsomalia.net/unsoma/FSAU/FOCUS.htm

Galaty, J.G. 1994. Rangeland tenure and pastoralism in Africa. pp. 185–204, *in:* E. Fratkin, K.A. Galvin and E.A. Roth (eds). *African Pastoralist Systems: An Integrated Approach.* Boulder, Colorado, USA: Lynne Reiner Publishers.

Georgiadis, N.J. 1987. Responses of savanna grasslands to extreme use by pastoralist livestock. PhD Thesis. Syracuse University, NY, USA.

GLASOD. 1990. *Global Assessment of Soil Degradation.* International Soil Reference and Information Centre, Wageningen, The Netherlands, and United Nations Environment Programme, Nairobi, Kenya.

Grime, J.P. 1979. *Plant strategies and vegetation processes.* New York, NY, USA: Wiley.

Hardin, G. 1968. The tragedy of the commons. *Science*, **162**: 1243–1248.

Herlocker, D. (ed). 1999. *Rangeland ecology and resource development in Eastern Africa.* GTZ, Nairobi, Kenya.

Herren, U.J. 1990. The commercial sale of camel milk from pastoral herds in the Mogadishu hinterland, Somalia. *ODI Pastoral Development Network*, Paper 30a. Overseas Development Institute (ODI), London, UK.

Hiernaux, P. 1996. The crisis of Sahelian pastoralism: ecological or economic? *Pastoral Development Network Paper*, No. 39a. Overseas Development Institute (ODI), London, UK.

Hiernaux, P. 1998. Effects of grazing on plant species composition and spatial distribution in rangelands of the Sahel. *Plant Ecology,* **138**: 191–202.

Hiernaux, P. 2000. Implications of the "new rangeland paradigm" for natural resource management. pp. 113–142, *in:* H. Adriansen, A. Reenberg and I. Nielsen (eds). *The Sahel. Energy Supply, Economic pillars of Rural Sahelian Communities, Need for Revised Development Strategies.* Proceedings from the 12th Danish Sahel Workshop, 3–5 January 2000. *SEREIN [Sahel-Sudan Environmental Research Initiative] Occasional Papers,* No. 11. 212 p.

Hodgson, D.L. 2000. Pastoralism, patriarchy and history among Maasai in Tanganyika, 1890–1940. pp. 97–120, *in:* D.L. Hodgson (ed). *Rethinking pastoralism in Africa.* Oxford, UK: James Currey Publ., and Athens, Ohio, USA: Ohio University Press.

Holden, S.J. & Coppock, D.L. 1992. Effects of distance to market, season and family wealth on pastoral dairy marketing in Ethiopia. *Journal of Arid Environments,* **23**: 321–334.

Holechek, J.L., de Souza Gomes, H., Molinar, F. & Galt, D. 1998. Grazing intensity: critique and approach. *Rangelands,* **20**: 15–18.

Holechek, J.L., Pieper, R.D. & Herbel, C.H. 1989. *Range management: principles and practices.* New Jersey, USA: Prentice Hall.

Homewood, K. & Brockington, D. 1999. Biodiversity, conservation and development in Mkomazi Game Reserve, Tanzania. *Global Ecology and Biogeography,* **8**: 301–313.

Homewood, K., Lambin, E.F., Coast, E., Kariuki, A., Kikula, I., Kivelia, J., Said, M., Serneels, S. & Thompson, M. 2001. Long-term changes in Serengeti-Mara wildebeest and land cover: Pastoralism, population, or policies? *Proceedings of the National Academy of Sciences of the United States of America,* **98**: 12544–12549.

Homewood, K.M. 1993. Livestock economy and ecology in El Kala, Algeria: Evaluating ecological and economic costs and benefits in pastoralist systems. *Pastoral Development Network Paper,* No. 35a. Overseas Development Institute, London, UK.

Homewood, K.M. & Rodgers, W.A. 1991. *Maasailand Ecology: pastoralist development and wildlife conservation in Ngorongoro, Tanzania.* Cambridge, UK: Cambridge University Press.

Horowitz, M.M. & Little, P.D. 1987. African pastoralism and poverty: some implications for drought and famine. pp. 59–82, *in:* M. Glantz (ed). *Drought and Famine in Africa: Denying Drought a Future.* Cambridge, UK: Cambridge University Press.

IBPGR [International Board for Plant Genetic Resources]. 1984. *Forage and browse plants for arid and semi-arid Africa.* IBPGR, Rome, Italy.

IEA [Instituto Ecologia Applicata]. 1998. AMD African Mammals Databank – A Databank for the Conservation and Management of the African Mammals Vols 1 and 2. Report to the Directorate-General for Development (DGVIII/A/1) of the European Commission. Project No. B7-6200/94-15/VIII/ENV. Instituto Ecologia Applicata, Rome, Italy.

IFAD [International Fund for Agricultural Development]. 1995. Common property resources and the rural poor in sub-Saharan Africa. IFAD, Rome, Italy.

Igoe, J. & Brockington, D. 1999. Pastoral Land Tenure and Community Conservation: A Case Study from North-East Tanzania. Doc. 7385IIED. *IIED Pastoral land tenure series,* No. 11. 103 pp. IIED, London, UK.

IPCC [Intergovernmental Panel on Climate Change]. 2000. *Land use, land-use change and forestry.* Cambridge, UK: Cambridge University Press.

ISO [International Organization for Standardization]. **1996.** *Requirements for characterization of excavated soil and other soils materials for re-use. CD 15176 ISO/TC 190/SC 7/* Soil and site assessment/ WG1/N2. rev.3.

IWMI [International Water Management Institute]. 2001. *World Water and Climate Atlas.* International Water Management Institute, Colombo, Sri Lanka.

Jank, L., Calixto, S., Costa, J.C.G., Savidan, Y.H. & Curvo, J.B.E. 1997. Catalogo de caracterizacao e avaliacao de germoplasma de *Panicum maximum*: descricao morfologica e comportamento agronomico. Centro Nacional de Pesquisa de Gado de Corte, Campo Grande, Brazil.

Jones, P.G. & Thornton, P.K. 2003. The potential impact of climate change on maize production in Africa and Latin America in 2055. *Global Environmental Change,* **13**: 51–59.

Jordan, A.M. 1986. *Trypanosomiasis Control and African Rural Development.* London, UK: Longman.

Kruska, R. 2002. GIS database of cattle population density for Africa. International Livestock Research Institute, Nairobi, Kenya.

Lamprey, R. & Waller, R. 1990. The Loita-Mara region in historical times: patterns of subsistence, settlement and ecological change. pp. 16–35, *in:* P. Robertshaw (ed). *Early Pastoralists of South-western Kenya.* British Institute in Eastern Africa, Nairobi, Kenya.

Lawrance Report. 1966. *Report of the Mission on Land Consolidation and Registration in Kenya, 1965-66.* Government Printer, Nairobi.

Lindqvist, S. & Tengberg, A. 1993. New evidence of desertification from case studies in Northern Burkina Faso. *Geografiska Annaler,* **75A**: 127–135.

Little, P.D. [2000]. Living in risky environments: the political ecology of pastoralism in East Africa. *In:* S. Taylor, G. White and E. Fratkin (eds). *African Development in the 21st Century.* Rochester, NY, USA: University of Rochester Press. Forthcoming. See: http://www.cnr.usu.edu/research/crsp/politic-ecol.pdf

Little, P.D., Smith, K., Cellarius, B.A. Coppock, D.L. & Barrett, C.B. 2001. Avoiding disaster: Diversification and risk management among east African herders. *Development and Change,* **32**: 401–433.

Loveland, T.R., Reed, B.C., Brown, J.F., Ohlen, D.O., Zhu, Z., Yang, L. & Merchant, J. 2000. Development of global land cover characteristics database and IGBP DISCover from 1-km AVHRR data. *International Journal of Remote Sensing*, **21**: 1303–1330.

Lowe, A.J., Thorpe, W., Teale, A. & Hanson, J. 2003. Characterisation of germ-plasm accessions of Napier grass (*Pennisetum purpureum* and *P. purpureum* × *P. glaucum* hybrids) and comparison with farm clones using RAPD. *Genetic Resources and Crop Evolution*, **50**: 121–132.

Mabbutt, J.A. 1984. A new global assessment of the status and trends of desertification. *Environmental Conservation*, **11**: 100–113.

Magguran, A.E. 1988. *Ecological diversity and its measurement*. Princeton, New Jersey, USA: Princeton University Press.

Mangubuli, M.J. 1991. Mkomazi Game Reserve – a recovered pearl. *Kakakuona*, **4**: 11–13.

McNaughton, S.J. 1976. Serengeti migratory wildebeest: facilitation of energy flow by grazing. *Science*, **199**: 92–94.

McNaughton, S.J. 1979. Grassland-herbivore dynamics. pp. 46–81, *in:* A.R.E. Sinclair and M. Norton-Griffiths (eds). *Serengeti: Dynamics of an Ecosystem.* Chicago, Illinois, USA: University of Chicago Press.

McNaughton, S.J. 1984. Grazing lawns: Animals in herds, plant form and co-evolution. *American Naturalist*, **124**: 863–886.

McNaughton, S.J. 1985. Ecology of a grazing ecosystem: the Serengeti. *Ecological Monographs*, **55**: 259–294.

Mduma, S.A.R., Sinclair, A.R.E. & Hilborn, R. 1999. Food regulates the Serengeti wildebeest: a 40-year record. *Journal of Animal Ecology*, **68**: 1101–1122.

Milchunas, D.G. & Laurenroth, W. K. 1993. Quantitative effects of grazing on vegetation and soils over a global range of environments. *Ecological Monographs*, **63**: 327–366.

Mkutu, K. 2001. Pastoralism and conflict in the Horn of Africa. Report, Africa Peace Forum and Saferworld. Department of Peace Studies, University of Bradford. 35 p.

Mnene, W.N., Wandera, F.P. & Lebbie, S.H. 2000. Arresting environmental degradation through accelerated on-site soil sedimentation and revegetation using micro-catchment and re-seeding. Paper presented at the 3rd All-Africa Conference on Animal Agriculture, Alexandria, Egypt, 6–9 November 2000.

Muchiru, A.N., Western, D.J. & Reid, R.S. submitted. The role of abandoned Maasai settlements in restructuring savanna herbivore communities, Amboseli, Kenya. *Journal of Applied Ecology.*

Myers, N. 1972. National parks in savanna Africa. *Science*, **78**: 1255–1263.

Nachtergaele, F. 2002. Land degradation assessment in drylands (LADA project). *LUCC Newsletter*, No. 8 (Dec. 2002): 15. See: http://www.indiana.edu/~act/focus1/LUCCnews8.pdf

Neumann, R.N. 1997. Primitive ideas. Protected area buffer zones and the politics of land in Africa. *Development and Change*, **27**: 559–582.

Niamir, M. 1991. Traditional African range management techniques: Implications for rangeland management. Overseas Development Institute (ODI), London, UK.

Niamir-Fuller, M. 1999. International aid for rangeland development: trends and challenges. pp. 147–152, *in:* D. Eldridge and D. Freudenberger (eds). *Proceedings of the 6th International Rangeland Congress,* Townsville, Australia, 17–23 July 1999.

Nicholson, S.E., Tucker, C.J. & Ba, M.B. 1998. Desertification, drought and surface vegetation: an example from the West African Sahel. *Bulletin of the American Meteorological Society,* **79**: 815–830.

Nyongeza, A. 1995. National Land Policy. The Ministry of Lands, Housing and Urban Development, Dar es Salaam, Kenya.

Oba, G., Vetaas, O.R. & Stenseth, N.C. 2001. Relationships between biomass and plant species richness in arid-zone grazing lands. *Journal of Applied Ecology,* **38**: 836–845.

Ottichilo, W.K., de Leeuw, J., Skidmore, A.K., Prins, H.H.T. & Said, M.Y. 2000. Population trends of large non-migratory wild herbivores and livestock in the Masai Mara ecosystem, Kenya, between 1977 and 1997. *African Journal of Ecology,* **38**: 202–216.

Pantuliano, S. 2002. Sustaining livelihoods across the rural-urban divide: Changes and challenges facing the Beja pastoralists of North Eastern Sudan. International Institute for Environment and Development (IIED), London, UK.

Pengelly, B.C., Hacker, J.B. & Eagles, D.A. 1992. The classification of a collection of buffel grasses and related species. *Tropical Grasslands,* **26**: 1–6.

Perkins, J.S. 1991. The impact of borehole-dependent cattle grazing on the environment and society of the eastern Kalahari sandveld, Central District, Botswana. PhD Thesis, University of Sheffield, Sheffield, UK.

Phillips, S. 1995. *Flora of Ethiopia and Eritrea – Poaceae (Gramineae).* Addis Ababa, Ethiopia, and Uppsala, Sweden: Addis Ababa University, and Science Faculty, Uppsala University.

Pratt, D.J. & Gwynne, M.D. 1977. *Rangeland management and ecology in East Africa.* London, UK: Hodder and Stoughton.

Rasmussen, K., Fog, B. & Madsen, J.E. 2001. Desertification in reverse? Observations from northern Burkina Faso. *Global Environmental Change,* **11**: 271–282.

Rattray, J.M. 1960. *The grass cover of Africa.* FAO, Rome, Italy.

Reid, R.S. 1999. Impacts of trypanosomosis on land-use and the environment in Africa: state of our knowledge and future directions. pp. 500–514, *in:* OAU, Nairobi (Kenya). International Scientific Council for Trypanosomiasis Research and Control. Proceedings of the 24th meeting of the International Scientific Council for Trypanosomiasis Research and Control. OAU/STRC Publication, no. 119. Nairobi, Kenya: OAU/STRC.

Reid, R.S. & Ellis, J.E. 1995. Impacts of pastoralists on woodlands in south Turkana, Kenya: livestock-mediated tree recruitment. *Ecological Applications,* **5**: 978–992.

Reid, R.S., Thornton P.K. & Kruska, R.L. 2001. Predicting agricultural expansion: livestock disease control and changing landscapes in southwestern Ethiopia. pp. 271–290, *in:* A. Arildsen and D. Kaimowitz (eds). *Agricultural Technologies and Tropical Deforestation*. Wallingford, UK: CAB International.

Reid, R.S., Wilson, C.J., Kruska, R.L. & Mulatu, W. 1997. Impacts of tsetse control and land-use on vegetative structure and tree species composition in southwestern Ethiopia. *Journal of Applied Ecology*, **34**: 731–747.

Reid, R.S., Kruska, R.L., Wilson, C.J. & Thornton P.K. 1998. Conservation crises of the 21st century: tension zones among wildlife, people and livestock across Africa in 2050. pp. 353, *in:* A. Farina, J. Kennedy and V. Bossu (eds). International Congress of Ecology. Firma Effe, Reggio Emilia, Italy, 12–16 July, 1998.

Reid, R.S., Kruska, R.L., Deichmann, U., Thornton, P.K. & Leak, S.G.A. 2000a. Human population growth and extinction of the tsetse fly. *Agricultural Ecosystems and Environment*, **77**: 227–236.

Reid, R.S., Kruska, R.L., Muthui, N., Taye, A., Wotton, S., Wilson, C.J. & Mulatu, W. [Andualem Taye; Woudyalew Mulatu]. 2000b. Land-use and land-cover dynamics in response to changes in climatic, biological and socio-political forces: the case of southwestern Ethiopia. *Landscape Ecology*, **15**(4): 339–355.

Reid, R.S., Rainy, M.E., Wilson, C.J., Harris, E., Kruska, R.L., Waweru, M., Macmillan, S.A. & Worden, J.S. 2001. *Wildlife cluster around pastoral settlements in Africa. 2,* PLE Science Series, International Livestock Research Institute, Nairobi, Kenya.

Reid, R.S., Thornton, P.K., McCrabb, G.J., Kruska, R.L., Atieno, F. & Jones, P.G. 2003. Is it possible to mitigate greenhouse gas emissions in pastoral ecosystems of the tropics? *Environment, Development and Sustainability*, **6**: 91–109.

Ringrose, S., Matheson, W., Tempest, F. & Boyle, T. 1990. The development and causes of range degradation features in southeast Botswana using multitemporal Landsat MSS imagery. *Photogrammetric Engineering and Remote Sensing*, **56**: 1253–1262.

Rodgers, W. & Homewood, K. 1982. Species richness and endemism in the Usambara Mountain forests. Tanzania. *Biological Journal of the Linnean Society*, **18**: 197–224.

Rogers, P., Brockington, D., Kiwasila, H. & Homewood, K. 1999. Environmental awareness and conflict genesis. People versus parks in Mkomazi Game Reserve. pp. 26–51. *in:* T. Granfelt (ed). *Managing the globalised environment*. London, UK: Intermediate Technology Publications.

Rutten, M.M.E.M. 1992. *Selling Wealth to Buy Poverty. The Process of the Individualization of Land Ownership among the Maasai pastoralists of Kajiado District, Kenya, 1890–1990*. Saarbrücken, Germany: Verlag Breitenbach Publishers.

Sandford, S. 1983. *Management of Pastoral Development in the Third World*. Chichester, UK: John Wiley & Sons.

Schlesinger, W.H. & Gramenopoulos, N. 1996. Archival photographs show no climate-induced changes in woody vegetation in the Sudan, 1943–1994. *Global Change Biology,* **2**: 137–141.

Scoones, I. 1995. New directions in pastoral development in Africa. pp. 1–36, *in:* I. Scoones (ed). *Living with Uncertainty: New Directions in Pastoral Development in Africa.* London, UK: Intermediate Technology Publications.

Serneels, S. & Lambin, E.F. 2001. Impact of land-use changes on the wildebeest migration in the northern part of the Serengeti-Mara ecosystem. *Journal of Biogeography,* **28**: 391–407.

Serneels, S., Said, M.Y. & Lambin, E.F. 2001. Land-cover changes around a major East African wildlife reserve: the Mara Ecosystem (Kenya). *International Journal of Remote Sensing,* **22**: 3397–3420.

Shivji, I.G. 1999. The Lands Act 1999: a cause for celebration or a celebration of a cause? Keynote address to the Workshop on Land, held at Morogoro, 19–20 February 1999.

Sinclair, A.R.E. 1995. Serengeti past and present. pp. 3–30, *in:* A.R.E. Sinclair and P. Arcese (eds). *Serengeti II: Dynamics, Management and Conservation of an Ecosystem.* Chicago, Illinois, USA: University of Chicago Press.

Sisay, A. & Baars, R.M.T. 2002. Grass composition and rangeland condition of the major grazing areas in the mid-Rift Valley, Ethiopia. *African Journal of Range and Forage Science,* **19**: 167–173.

Skarpe, C. 1990. Shrub layer dynamics under different herbivore densities in an arid savanna, Botswana. *Journal of Applied Ecology,* **27**: 873–885.

Skerman, P.J. & Riveros, F. 1990. *Tropical grasses. FAO Plant Production and Protection Series,* No. 23. 832 p. FAO, Rome, Italy.

Smith, T.B., Wayne, R.K., Girman, D.J. & Bruford, M.W. 1997. A role for ecotones in generating rainforest biodiversity. *Science,* **276**: 1855–1857.

Snyder, K.A. 1996. Agrarian change and land-use strategies among Iraqw farmers in northern Tanzania. *Human Ecology,* **24**: 315–340.

Srivastava, K.L., Abebe, M., Astatke, A., Haile, M. & Regassa, H. 1993. Distribution and importance of Ethiopian vertisols and location of study sites. pp. 13–27, *in: Improved management of Vertisols for sustainable crop-livestock production in the Ethiopian highlands: Synthesis report 1986–92.* Technical Committee of the Joint Vertisol Project, Addis Ababa, Ethiopia.

Staal, S., Chege, L., Kenyanjui, M., Kimari, A., Lukuyu, B., Njumbi, D., Owango, M., Tanner, J.C., Thorpe, W. & Wambugu, M. 1997. *Characterisation of dairy systems supplying the Nairobi milk market.* International Livestock Research Institute, Nairobi, Kenya.

Stattersfield, A.J., Crosby, M.J., Long, A.J. & Wedge, D.C. 1998. *Endemic bird areas of the world. Priorities for biodiversity conservation.* Cambridge, UK: Birdlife International.

Steinfeld, H., de Haan, C. & Blackburn, H. 1997. *Livestock-environment interactions: Issues and options.* Fressingfield, UK: WRENmedia. 56 p.

Sullivan, S. 1999. The impacts of people and livestock on topographically diverse open wood- and shrublands in arid north-west Namibia. *Global Ecology and Biogeography Letters*, **8**: 257–277.

Tcacenco, F.A. & Lance, G.N. 1992. Selection of morphological traits for characterization of elephant grass accessions. *Tropical Grasslands*, **26**: 145–155.

Thornton, P.K., Kruska, R.L., Henninger, N., Kristjanson, P.M., Reid, R.S., Atieno, F., Odero, A. & Ndegwa, T. 2002. *Mapping Poverty and Livestock in the Developing World*. International Livestock Research Institute, Nairobi, Kenya.

Tucker, C.J., Dregne, H.E. & Newcomb, W.W. 1991. Expansion and contraction of the Sahara Desert from 1980 to 1990. *Science*, **253**: 299–301.

Ubi, B.E., Komatsu, T. & Fujimori, M. 2000. AFLP-based analysis of genetic diversity in diploid and tetraploid cultivars of rhodesgrass (*Chloris gayana* Kunth). *In: VIII International Plant and Animal Genome Conference*, San Diego, California, USA, 9–12 January 2000. See: http://www.intl-pag.org/8/abstracts/pag8905.html

Unruh, J.D. 1995. The relationship between the indigenous pastoralist resource tenure and state tenure in Somalia. *GeoJournal*, **36**: 19–26.

USGS/EDC [U.S. Geological Survey – Earth Resources Observation Systems Data Center]. 1999. 1-km Land Cover Characterization Database, with revisions for Latin America. U.S. Geological Survey – Earth Resources Observation Systems (EROS) Data Center (EDC), Sioux Falls, South Dakota, USA.

Van de Wouw, M., Hanson, J. & Luethi, S. 1999. Morphological and agonomic characterization of a collection of napier grass (*Pennisetum purpureum*) and *P. purpureum* × *P. glaucum*. *Tropical Grasslands*, **33**: 150–158.

Vuorio, V., Muchiru, A.N. & Reid, R.S. In prep. Abandoned Maasai settlements facilitate changes in plant diversity in the Mara ecosystem, southwestern Kenya.

Walker, B.H. 1993. Rangeland ecology: understanding and managing change. *Ambio*, **22**: 80–87.

Waller, R.D. 1990. Tsetse fly in western Narok, Kenya. *Journal of African History*, **31**: 81–101.

Watson, R.M. 1991. Mkomazi – restoring Africa. *Swara*, **14**: 14–16.

Western, D. 1989. Conservation without parks: wildlife in the rural landscape. pp. 158–165, *in:* D. Western and M.C. Pearl (eds). *Conservation for the Twenty-first Century*. Oxford, UK: Oxford University Press.

Western, D. & Gichohi, H. 1993. Segregation effects and the impoverishment of savanna parks: the case for ecosystem viability analysis. *African Journal of Ecology*, **31**: 269–281.

White, D.H. 1998. Livestock commodities: a global agro-climatic analysis. *Economic Evaluation Unit Working Paper*, No. 30. Australian Centre for International Agricultural Research (ACIAR), Canberra, Australia.

White, F. 1983. *The Vegetation of Africa; a descriptive memoir to accompany the Unesco/AETFAT/UNSO vegetation map of Africa*. Natural Resources Research Series, XX. Paris, France: UNESCO. 356 p.

Wilen, C.A., Holt, J.S., Ellstrand, N.C. & Shaw, R.G. 1995. Genotypic diversity of Kikuyu grass (*Pennisetum clandestinum*) populations in California. *Weed Science*, **43**: 209–214.

Williams, S.D. 1998. Grevy's zebra: ecology in a heterogeneous environment. PhD thesis. University College, London, UK.

Wilson, C.J., Reid, R.S., Stanton, N.L. & Perry, B.D. 1997. Ecological consequences of controlling the tsetse fly in southwestern Ethiopia: effects of land-use on bird species diversity. *Conservation Biology*, **11**: 435–447.

Chapter 3
Grasslands of South Africa

Anthony R. Palmer and Andrew M. Ainslie

SUMMARY

South Africa is subtropical, with temperatures modified by altitude. The interior, where the bulk of grasslands are found, is semi-arid to arid, with rainfall decreasing westwards. The south and southwest have winter rainfall; the eastern Cape is bimodal; and Kwa-Zulu Natal has summer rainfall. Grassland is mainly in the central, high regions: sour-veldt occurs under high-rainfall on acid soils, and sweet-veldt on fertile soils in semi-arid zones. Savannah occurs in the north and east; arid savannah extends to the Kalahari. The Nama-karoo, a vast area of steppe in the centre and west, is mostly used for sheep and goats. There are three categories of land tenure: 70 percent is freehold and managed commercially; 14 percent is communally managed without clear individual boundaries and managed for subsistence; 16 percent is reserves or freehold industrial and urban. South Africa is multi-ethnic with a majority indigenous population and a minority of descendants of colonists who own much of the commercial farm land. Natural pasture is the main feed source for grazing livestock. Production systems in communal areas, based on pastoralism and agropastoralism, are subsistence-based and labour intensive; cropland is allocated to households, grazing areas are shared by a community. Commercial areas are fenced ranches and further subdivided into paddocks; rotational grazing is normally practised. Stock rearing is very ancient; cattle predominate but sheep and goats are very important. In subsistence systems, traditional breeds predominate; in commercial farming, exotic and locally-created improved breeds prevail. Sheep are mainly commercial, and goats are for subsistence. Cattle predominate in the east, and sheep in the drier west and southeast. Goats are widely distributed. The region is home to large numbers of grazing and other wildlife, which are common on large-scale ranches and are increasing in importance as a managed resource. Low profits from domestic stock have led to an increase in game farming and ecotourism. Much of the better-watered grassland has been converted to crops; in communal areas this gives a patchwork with thicket. Fire and browsing has reduced woody vegetation, but bush encroachment remains a problem. Sown pasture is not of major importance, except on dairy farms. Over-seeding of degraded range is of limited use. Strategies for maintaining pastoral production include rotation, resting, bush control and provision of winter pasture in cool areas.

INTRODUCTION

The Republic of South Africa is situated at the southern tip of Africa. It is bordered to the north by Namibia, Botswana, Zimbabwe and Mozambique; in the west by the Atlantic Ocean; and in the south and east by the Indian Ocean (Figure 3.1). The total land area is 1 223 201 km² (excluding Lesotho and Swaziland). The enclaves of Lesotho and Swaziland are sovereign states. South Africa's population is estimated at 40.6 million (Stats SA, 1996), of which approximately 46 percent is rural and 54 percent is urban. Agriculture accounts for 3.2 percent of GDP and 7 percent (R 14.57 billion in 2000[1]) of exports and supports, directly or indirectly, 15 percent of the population (National Department of Agriculture and Land Affairs, 2001).

In its position at the southern end of the African continent, South Africa is the gateway to the subcontinent, providing and maintaining ports and road, rail and telecommunication links between southern Africa and the rest of the world. With a long history of trade and scientific exchange with Europe and North America, South Africa has developed opportunities for marketing its agricultural products within these economies. Many of these products (beef, mutton, fleece and hides) have been derived directly from grasslands. The national science programmes and those associated with resource management and agriculture have been linked through government and tertiary education initiatives to explore trends in resource condition and production. These initiatives have focused on three primary research areas: (1) describing the biodiversity of rangelands and their associated resources; (2) developing an understanding of the impact of herbivory on the resource; and (3) developing methods for improving production. In addition, research programmes have endeavoured to understand the relationships between herbivory by domestic livestock and the sustained use of the resource for agricultural production.

South Africa has a unique combination of natural resources, climatic environments and ethnic groups, making it an interesting and challenging country. Grasslands are a major component of the natural vegetation, with the biome comprising some 295 233 km² of the central regions of the country, and adjoining and extending into most of the major biomes (forest, savannah, thicket, Nama-karoo) in the region. This interface between grasslands and other biomes contributes substantially to their floristic and faunal diversity and to the important role they play in the agricultural economy. The grasslands of South Africa are also the home to most of the human population, with the mining and other industrial complexes of Gauteng (formerly the Witwatersrand) being located on the high-veldt grasslands. This proximity to large human populations and their associated markets, as well the climatic environment, which favours commercial, rainfed agriculture, has had a large impact on the native grasslands. Millions of hectares have been ploughed and converted into

---

[1] ZA Rand 6.4475 = US$ 1 (mid-October 2004).

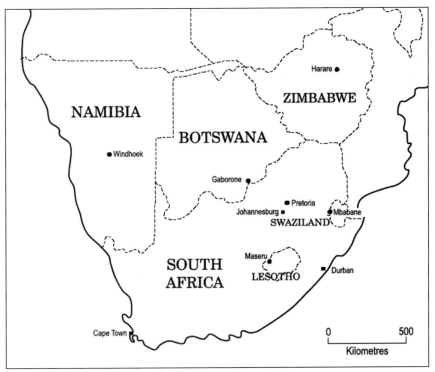

Figure 3.1
The Republic of South Africa, showing its position in southern Africa.

dryland cultivation for the production of maize, oilseed, millet and other commercial rainfed crops. Commercial ranching of cattle and sheep for the markets
in Gauteng, Mpumalanga and the Free State has placed pressure on the grasslands, resulting in changes in species composition and production potential.
However these trends are not ubiquitous, and millions of hectares of native
grassland still occur.

Grasslands are also the most important resource available to the graziers in
developing regions of South Africa. The former homelands of Transkei, Ciskei
and KwaZulu Natal, situated on the eastern seaboard, are predominantly grassland. The inhabitants of these regions are dependant upon this resource for the
production of meat, milk, hides and fleeces, and for the provision of draught
power, as well as other traditional uses of livestock. Although these products
are not produced in conventional commercial systems, they contribute substantially to the economy and food security of these regions. In this chapter,
we will introduce the role of grasslands in this economy based on communal
land tenure systems.

The grasslands (see Figure 3.2) adjoin a number of other economically
important biomes (savannah, thicket and Nama-karoo) and grassland patches
are found within these biomes. It is important to include these biomes in this

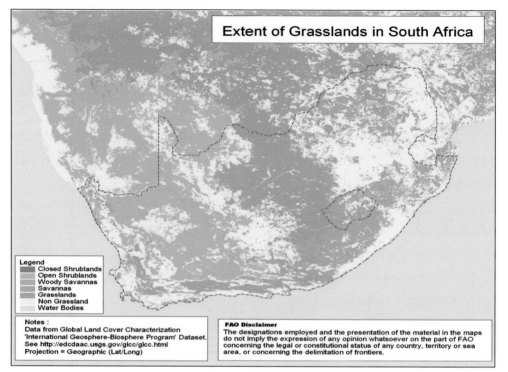

Figure 3.2
The extent of grasslands in South Africa.

chapter, as their ecology is strongly interlinked, and to consider the role that all grasslands and their associated biota play in the economy of South Africa. In this chapter, grasslands in South Africa will have a wider definition than at the biome level.

The grassland resources of South Africa have been extensively reported, with four important publications appearing recently (Cowling, Richardson and Pierce, 1997; Dean and Milton 1999; Tainton, 1999, 2000). These provide exhaustive information on types of rangeland resources; their general ecology, including history, biodiversity, species composition and associated environmental conditions; dynamics; productivity; and land-use and management options available to their peoples.

In addition, information applicable to the management of grasslands in southern Africa is provided in the approximately 980 research publications that have appeared since 1966 in the *African Journal of Range and Forage Science* and its predecessors. Other peer-reviewed scientific journals that provide exhaustive information on the natural resources of South Africa include the *South African Journal of Botany, South African Journal of Science, Memoirs of the Botanical Survey of South Africa, South African Journal of Wildlife Research,* and *Bothalia.* Researchers are strongly encouraged to publish in the wider international literature and many important research articles appear in peer-reviewed journals published elsewhere. This chapter does not attempt to synthesize or review all this available information, but provides a brief summary of the current status of our understanding of southern African grassland ecosystems.

PHYSICAL FEATURES

The Great Escarpment and the Drakensberg mountains provide the physical barriers that largely determine the climate and vegetation of much of the livestock growing regions of South Africa. The combination of moderate to high rainfall and high elevation associated with these features means that the largest area of native grasslands occurs here. In geological time, several phases of uplifting, erosion and deposition have created complex landforms determined by the underlying geology. The country has five main physiographical regions at differing elevations (Figure 3.3).

- The southwestern fold mountains, which influence the climate and vegetation patterns of the southern Cape.
- The coastal plain, which extends from the Namibian border on the west, all along the coast to southern Mozambique on the east. This narrow plain between the Ocean and the Great Escarpment is the region with the most fertile soils, moderate to high rainfall, and where most intensive livestock production occurs.
- The Great Escarpment, which forms the major barrier to moisture reaching the interior, together with the central high-veldt, contain most of the high elevation

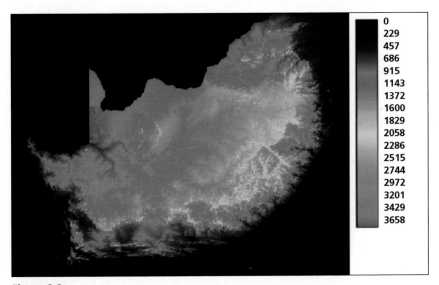

0
229
457
686
915
1143
1372
1600
1829
2058
2286
2515
2744
2972
3201
3429
3658

Figure 3.3
Elevational map (in metres) for South Africa.
Source: Dent, Lynch and Schulze, 1987.

A.R. PALMER

Plate 3.1
*Kalahari: The arid savannah occurs in the northwestern portions of South Africa
and southern Botswana, and is associated with the sands of the Kalahari system.
The vegetation comprises a woody layer of mainly single-stemmed deciduous
shrubs, and a ground layer of grasses and forbs.*

grasslands. The major urban, mining and agricultural activities take place
in the central high-veldt, which lies at 1 600–1 700 m above sea level.

- The great Karoo basin lies at 1 400–1 600 m and contains the steppe-type
  vegetation associated with fertile aridosols of a semi-arid region.
- The Kalahari region, bordering on Namibia and Botswana, also represents
  a very important extensive livestock producing area. The region is the
  southern part of the continental-scale basin, which is covered by sands of
  varying depth (sometimes >200 m). Deep boring technology has enabled
  commercial graziers to become permanently established in the region and
  to optimize livestock production off arid grasslands. The vegetation is an
  arid savannah (Plate 3.1), with a carrying capacity of 30 to 40 ha per Livestock Unit (LSU).

South Africa is thus characterized by a high interior plateau, surrounded
on three sides by the Great Escarpment and the Drakensberg mountains,
which provide the physical barriers that largely determine the climate and
vegetation. The plateau is intruded by several mountain massifs, with the
highlands of Lesotho exceeding 3 000 m in places. The northern and western
sections of the plateau contain two large basins, namely the Kalahari and the
Transvaal Bushveldt (Partridge, 1997). Adjacent to the Great Escarpment lies
a coastal plinth that varies in width from 50 to 200 km. This plinth is incised
by deep riverine gorges.

CLIMATE
Rainfall
With a mean annual rainfall of approximately 450 mm, South Africa is regarded as semi-arid. There is wide regional variation in annual rainfall (Figure 3.4), from <50 mm in the Richtersveldt on the border with Namibia, to >3 000 mm in the mountains of the southwestern Cape. However, only 28 percent of the country receives more than 600 mm (Table 3.1).

The uncertainty of the rainfall is best expressed by the coefficient of variation in annual rainfall (Figure 3.5). The low rainfall regions have the highest coefficient of variation and drought is common. Annual rainfall distribution is skewed such that there are more below-average than above-average rainfall years, and the median is more meaningful than the mean. The high seasonal variations are accompanied by high spatial variability, and the annual potential evapotranspiration (PET) may exceed annual precipitation by ratios of up to 20:1, hence drought conditions are a common phenomenon (Schulze, 1997). The declaration of drought status to a magisterial district has historically been used by the Department of Agriculture and Land Affairs to intervene in

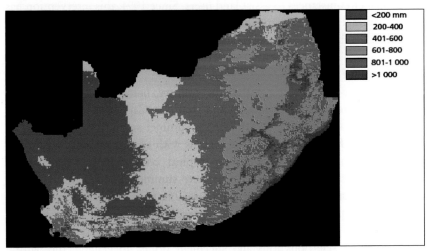

	<200 mm
	200-400
	401-600
	601-800
	801-1 000
	>1 000

Figure 3.4
The median annual rainfall for South Africa.
Source: Dent, Lynch and Schulze, 1987.

TABLE 3.1
Annual rainfall distribution and climatic classification in South Africa

Rainfall (mm)	Classification	Percentage of land surface
<200	Desert	22.8
201-400	Arid	24.6
401-600	Semi-arid	24.6
601-800	Subhumid	18.5
801-1000	Humid	6.7
<1000	Super-humid	2.8

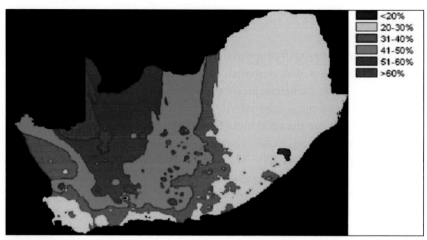

	<20%
	20-30%
	31-40%
	41-50%
	51-60%
	>60%

Figure 3.5
The coefficient of variation in annual rainfall for South Africa. Derived from the long-term rainfall records (50 years or more data) from 1015 stations.

exceptional circumstances to assist land users. Since 1994, this intervention has been discouraged; instead, graziers are encouraged to plan their production system within the long-term expectations of their farms.

Seasonality of rainfall

There are three major zones within the country, namely the winter rainfall region of the western, southwestern and southern Cape; the bimodal rainfall region of the Eastern Cape; and the strong summer seasonality of the central high-veldt and KwaZulu Natal. The regions with strong summer seasonality are strongly influenced by the inter-tropical convergence, which moves southwards during the southern hemisphere summer. The season of rainfall in the southwestern and southern coastal regions is influenced by the frontal systems developing in the southern Oceans. These frontal systems bring cool, moist air during the winter season (June–August) and promote the development of sclerophyllous and succulent floras. In general, the natural vegetation of these regions is less useful for livestock production. Because of the varying rainfall seasonality, growing periods vary throughout the country. In the north, east and along the coastal belt, summer seasonality encourages C_4 grass production and the main focus is on cattle and sheep production. In the semi-arid central and western regions, C_3 grasses and shrubs predominate, and this favours sheep and goat production.

Temperatures

Temperatures in South Africa are strongly determined by elevation and distance from the sea. The high elevation (1 500–1 700 m) inland regions experience a warm summer (January) with mean daily maximum temperatures of 26–28°C and cool winter (July) mean daily minima of 0–2°C), with frost during the coolest months (Schulze 1997). These conditions favour the development and maintenance of grassland. This region experiences occasional snow. The warm Mozambique current on the east coast plays a strong role in ameliorating temperatures along the coastal zone between East London and Mozambique. The northern parts of the coastal zone experience warm winter daily minima (8–10°C) and warm summer maxima (32°C) and the climate is strongly subtropical. The vast interior, represented by the Kalahari basin and the Nama-karoo, experiences a more extreme climate, with low winter mean daily minima (0–2°C) and high mean daily summer maxima (32–34°C). The southern and southwestern coastal zone experiences moderate winter mean daily minima (6–8°C) as a result of the circumpolar Westerlies that bring moist, cold air from the southern Oceans during June, July and August (winter). The temperatures on the west coast, from Cape Town to Port Nolloth, are influenced by the cold Benguela current. This arid region experiences July mean daily minima of 6–8°C, but little or no frost, and is able to support a rich succulent flora. The cold ocean current favours the development of fog during the winter months, bringing cold, moist air onto the coastal plain.

Soils

The relatively young South African geology gives rise to soils of high nutrient status. The Nama-karoo biome of the central regions comprise predominantly mudstones and sandstones of the Karoo Supergroup, which give rise to shallow (<30 cm) aridosols, typically with a calcareous hardpan layer in the profile. During the Jurassic age, these sedimentary rocks were intruded by dolerites, which criss-cross the landscape in characteristic dykes. The dolerites contain plagioclase, which give rise to soils of high clay content, and these features contain many grasses and associated phreatophytic woody shrubs and represent refugia for many desirable (to the herbivore) plant species. The dolerite sills and dykes provide summer grazing, whereas the nutrient-rich, calcareous plains provide abundant, high quality winter forage.

The savannahs of the Mpumalanga Lowveldt are associated with the gab-bros and granites of the Bushveldt igneous complex. The latter give rise to sandy soils of moderate nutrient status. The gabbros give rise to a nutrient-rich Mispah rock complex.

In geological time, several phases of uplifting, erosion and deposition have created complex landforms determined by the underlying geology. The Cape Fold Mountains and the Lesotho Highlands are the largest surfaces that intrude above the African plane. The Cape Fold Mountains are siliceous rocks, giving rise to immature, litholic soils. The Lesotho Highlands, in con-trast, are basaltic, giving rise to mollisols (Partridge, 1997). The grasslands of the high-veldt are associated with soils of basalt and andesitic origin, with high nutrient status.

PEOPLE

Hominids have occupied southern Africa for three million years (Volman, 1984), and although the ancestral forms used fire (Thackeray *et al.*, 1990), there are no artefacts that enable us to quantify the extent of their impact. They undoubtedly burnt large tracts of land in the interior, thereby promoting the development of grasslands, and early hominids must be regarded as a significant agent in the evolution of grasslands in South Africa.

Contemporary South Africa is a multicultural nation, with many ethnic groups and colonial nations represented in its populations. It is this wide variation in the origins of its people that make understanding the management of its natural resources so challenging. The remaining San people of the southern Kalahari represent the oldest traditional users of natural vegetation for survival. San people are still able to subsist as hunter-gatherers in the most arid regions of the country, providing some evidence of how it is possible to sustain small human populations in this region. San exhibit a strong understanding of resource limitations and probably follow the principles embodied in the disequilibrium theory (Ellis and Swift, 1988) the closest of all southern African people. Until the end of the nineteenth century, San also survived in the mountainous regions of the Drakensberg and along the Great Escarpment. The evidence of their history is found in the numerous rock paintings and other artefacts that occur in caves along the Great Escarpment. They hunted on the grasslands of the mountainous interior.

The Nguni people of the eastern seaboard are graziers with a long (>10 000 years) history of maintaining domestic livestock. These people comprise the Seswati, AmaZulu and AmaXhosa nations, and occupy the leasehold lands in the former homelands of Gazankulu, KwaZulu Natal, Transkei and Ciskei. The society is organized around a village, comprising dwelling units, cultivated lands and grazing lands. Their early cattle were of *Bos indicus* stock and this line is being developed and protected in recent years with the establishment of an Nguni studbook. Situated on the eastern escarpment and in the Drakensberg is the mountain kingdom of Lesotho, the home of the Basotho people. Lesotho falls entirely within the grassland biome and the Basotho people are cattle and sheep farmers, depending largely on the natural grassland for production. Almost all of Lesotho is communally managed and the challenges to managing the grasslands sustainably remain the same as those of communal rangeland in South Africa.

Europeans of Dutch descent first arrived in South Africa in 1652, and settled initially at the supply station in Cape Town. These settlers were joined by French Huguenots, who brought with them a knowledge of viticulture and animal husbandry (mainly sheep). Descendants of the early Dutch settlers began moving into the interior of the country with the abolition of slavery, and developed the extensive cattle and sheep farming enterprises that currently occupy land in the Kalahari, central Free State and the North West Province. It was only in 1820 that settlers of British origin arrived and settled on the eastern seaboard. They developed mixed-farming operations in the Eastern Cape and Kwa-Zulu Natal, including cattle and wool-sheep enterprises.

LIVESTOCK

South Africa's national commercial cattle herd is estimated to number 13.8 million, including not only various international dairy and beef-cattle breeds, but also indigenous breeds such as the Afrikaner (or Afrikander). Locally developed breeds include the Drakensberger and Bonsmara. These breeds are systematically and scientifically improved through breeding programmes, performance testing and the evaluation of functional efficiency. Almost 590 000 t of beef was produced in 2000. Owing to relatively low carrying capacity on the natural pastures, extensive cattle ranching is practised in the lower rainfall regions.

In addition to the cattle, in 1999 there were about 25.8 million sheep and 6.3 million goats in the country, in addition to smaller numbers of pigs, poultry and farmed ostriches. The numbers of cattle and small stock fluctuate in response to high and low rainfall years. The 1999 census data shows the distribution between the freehold and communal sectors (Table 3.2). Beef production is the most important livestock-related activity, followed by small-stock (sheep and goat) production. The combined livestock sector contributes 75 percent of total agricultural output (National Department of Agriculture, 1999). Livestock numbers and production for the period 1995–2003 are shown in Table 3.3).

TABLE 3.2
National livestock census 1999.

Tenure	Cattle	Sheep	Goats
Freehold	6 275 000	19 300 000	2 070 000
Communal	6 825 000	9 300 000	4 230 000
TOTAL	13 100 000	28 600 000	6 300 000

SOURCE: National Department of Agriculture, 1999.

TABLE 3.3
Production (×1000 t) in the period 1995–2003 of beef and veal; chicken; mutton and lamb; goat; game; wool; and milk.

Commodity	1995	1996	1997	1998	1999	2000	2001	2002	2003
Beef and Veal	508	508	503	496	513	622	532	576	590
Chicken meat	600	649	692	665	706	817	813	820	820
Mutton and lamb	110	98	91	91	112	118	104	100	104
Goat meat	36	37	37	37	36	36	36	36	36
Game meat	10	11	13	14	15	16	16	17	17
Total meat	1 397	1 437	1 467	1 428	1 511	1 719	1 618	1 667	1 686
Wool (greasy)	67	62	57	53	56	53	57	57	57
Milk (total)	2 794	2 638	2 851	2 968	2 667	2 540	2 700	2 750	2 750

SOURCE: FAO database 2004.

The grasslands support a high proportion (70–80 percent) of the total sheep and wool produced. The main breeds of sheep are fine-wool Merino, the South African mutton Merino, Dohne Merino, Dormer, Dorper (the last-named two are locally developed breeds) and the Karakul. The Nama-karoo, a steppe like vegetation of the central and western regions, supports both sheep and goat enterprises. The Karakul industry is limited to the dry northwestern regions of Northern Cape Province.

WILDLIFE

South Africa possesses a rich and diverse wildlife resource, with many unique and interesting mammals, birds, reptiles and amphibians, providing a wide range of products, including tourism opportunities, meat, hides, curios, recreation and trophy hunting. There are 338 large and small mammal species (Smithers, 1983) and 920 bird species (Maclean, 1993). Four families (Elephantidae, Equidae, Bovidae and Suidae) contribute most of the large mammal taxa and represent the largest biomass of primary consumers. During the last thirty years, the large mammal fauna has begun to make a significant contribution to the economy of rangeland through increasing ecotourism and the development of private game farms and nature reserves. About 10 percent of the country is designated as National Parks and formal conservation areas, but a considerable proportion of the wildlife exists outside formally proclaimed conservation areas. Many livestock farmers derive some or all of their income from hunting or ecotourism. In 1997, approximately 8 000 private game ranches, covering some 15 million hectares, had been established (Grossman, Holden and Collinson, 1999). This figure has continued to increase rapidly since then, with many farms being enclosed by game-proof fencing. The issuing of a certificate of adequate enclosure by the various provincial nature conservation authorities permits the landowner to exercise rights over the wild herbivores that would otherwise only exist during the so-called "hunting season" in May–July each year. Individual landowners are now able to capture, transport, hunt and introduce any wild animal for which a permit has been provided and for which there is a certificate of adequate enclosure. Although this has had some positive consequences for the protection of certain rare species (e.g. mountain zebra, blesbok), where the last remaining populations were on private land, it has had some negative impacts. These include the large-scale introduction of common and freely available native species (e.g. impala, nyala, warthog) to regions where there is no record of their historical occurrence. The full consequences of these introductions on other species (e.g. nyala on kudu; impala on bushbuck) are not properly understood and further research is required. Conservation agencies have themselves been guilty of transgressions of this nature, re-introducing species such as warthog in the Eastern Cape Province, which have proliferated and are now regarded as a problem animal by graziers.

The natural flora, comprising some 24 000 taxa, is one of the richest floras in the world and creates many opportunities for developing the ecotourism industry. Regions of particular significance include Namaqualand, which attracts visitors to its unique floral displays during September of each year. The diverse Cape floral kingdom, with its estimated 8 000 taxa and associated avifauna, also provides the visitor with a glimpse of unique evolutionary forces driving speciation in the region. The southern Cape and its "garden route", with a high structural diversity (Afromontane forests, coastal thicket, lowland *fynbos* and mountain *fynbos*), attracts many international visitors.

LAND TENURE

There are four broad categories of land use in South Africa that are relevant to agricultural production, representing various land tenure regimes. Approximately 70 percent of the country is "commercial" farmland under freehold tenure, 14 percent is state land that is communally managed, 10 percent is formally conserved by the State as National and other parks, and the remaining 6 percent is freehold land used for mining, urban and industrial development. The communal areas are situated mainly in the former homelands of Transkei, Ciskei, Bophutatswana, Lebowa, Kwa-Zulu, Venda and Gazankulu in the north and east of the country, while the commercial areas occupy most of the western, central and southern regions.

There are two widely disparate types of land tenure systems (Table 3.4). On the freehold farms there are clear boundaries, exclusive rights for the individual properties, and commercial farming objectives. These landowners are able to trade with their properties and use their title as collateral security against loans. In contrast, in the communal areas, there are often unclear boundaries, generally open access rights to grazing areas and farmers are subsistence oriented.

TABLE 3.4
A comparison between communal and freehold tenure systems in a similar area (approximately 15 000 ha) of the Peddie district, Eastern Cape, South Africa.

Tenure system	Communal		Commercial (Freehold)	
Economic orientation	Multiple use but essentially subsistence		Profit (commercial)	
Human population density (persons per km²)	56		3–6	
Livestock	Cattle	3 548	Cattle	2 028
	Sheep	5 120	Goats	3 000
	Goats	14 488		
Ability to maintain natural resources	Poor		Economics and strong peer pressure to achieve desired conservation state	
Livestock owners	Approx 3 000		10–12	
Infrastructure	Poor		Road system, power network, fencing and water provision	
Access to formal markets	Poor		Good – commodity-based marketing	
Historical access to subsidies and loans	Weak		Good	

Source: Palmer, Novellie and Lloyd, 1999.

Here, land tenure issues considerably hamper the introduction and adoption of improved management practices.

Freehold and commercial sector

The commercial farming sector is well developed, capital-intensive and largely export oriented. Commercial-area livestock production accounts for 75 percent of national agricultural output and comes from 52 percent of the farming and grazing land (Table 3.5). The freehold area in the rural Western Cape, with its associated cropping economy, comprises 53 072 land parcels with an average size of 243 ha. In the Eastern Cape, where land parcels can be regarded as individual ranches or enterprises, there are 37 823 land parcels with an average size of 451 ha. There are approximately 50 000 large-scale commercial farmers, who are predominantly, but not exclusively, drawn from the white population. In 2000, they exported products worth about R 16 billion, or nearly 10 percent of South Africa's total exports.

Cattle are predominant in the eastern parts of the country where the range-lands generally have a higher carrying capacity. Beef-cattle ranching is the largest contributor to commercial farming income and the major breeds are Brahman, Afrikaner and Simmentaler. Sheep are largely concentrated in the drier west, and also in the southeast. Goats are more widely distributed and the main breeds are the Boergoat and the Angora. Grazing livestock are raised under extensive ranching conditions, relying on natural pasture, occasionally supplemented by protein and mineral licks. Ostriches are farmed in the southern parts of the country, and also utilize natural vegetation, supplemented by fodders and concentrates.

The commercial areas are divided into fenced ranches (farms) and then further subdivided into a number of paddocks (camps). Rotational grazing is normally practised. Compared with the communal areas, stocking rates tend to be more conservative and are adjusted by the rancher to track production.

Communal and subsistence sector

The communal areas occupy about 13 percent of the total farming area of South Africa and hold approximately 52 percent of the total cattle population, 72 percent of the goats and 17 percent of the sheep (see Table 3.2). They differ markedly from the freehold areas in their production systems, objectives and

TABLE 3.5
Land areas (million hectares) of the major land use types in South Africa.

	Total area	Farm land	Potential arable	Arable land used	Grazing land	Nature conservation	Forestry	Other
Developing agriculture	17	14.4	2.5	N/A	11.9	0.78	0.25	1.5
Commercial agriculture	105	86.0	14.1	12.9	71.9	11.0	1.2	6.8

NOTE: N/A = not available.
SOURCE: Development Bank of Southern Africa, 1991.

property rights; only the cropping areas are normally allocated to individual households, while the grazing areas tend to be shared by members of a community. The communal sector has a substantially higher human population per unit area than the freehold sector, and has suffered from lower levels of state intervention. Investments in infrastructure (access roads, fences, water provision, power supply, dipping facilities) have not kept pace with those in freehold areas, where regional authorities have orchestrated the maintenance of roads and fences. The production systems in the communal areas are based on pastoralism and agropastoralism, and the majority of households are subsistence-based and labour intensive, with limited use of technology and external inputs. The outputs and objectives of livestock ownership are more diverse than in commercial livestock production, and include draught power, milk, dung, meat, cash income and capital storage, as well as sociocultural factors. The combination of objectives tends to be met by a policy of herd maximization rather than turnover; hence even the large herd owners tend to sell only to meet cash needs, leading to higher stocking rates than in the freehold system. The mean land parcel size (612 ha) in the former homelands of Ciskei and Transkei is greater than that of the freehold areas of the Western (243 ha) or Eastern Cape (451 ha), reflecting the free-ranging nature of livestock.

Communal area livestock production contributes 5–6 percent of formal agricultural output and is mainly confined to the eastern and northern part of the country. However, herd sizes vary considerably between and within regions, and livestock ownership is strongly skewed, with a small number of people owning large herds and the majority owning few animals or none at all.

Stock numbers tend to be unevenly distributed across the landscape in communal areas. There is a tendency for high concentrations of people and livestock near to permanent water, while other areas remain potentially underutilized due to a lack of water. In the rugged terrain of Ciskei, Transkei and Kwa-Zulu Natal, livestock spend the longest part of the day on the inter-fluvial ridges. Animal numbers tend to be geared more to the quantity of reliable water than to the reliable quantity of forage, hence drought effects tend to be more severe in communal than in commercial areas.

Mixed livestock ownership is more common in communal than freehold areas. Cattle are the generally preferred livestock species, but economic and ecological conditions often limit the possibilities for cattle ownership. Ownership of livestock is skewed, with 5 percent of residents owning 10 or more cattle in rural villages in the former Ciskei (Ainslie *et al.*, 1997), while 67 percent of households own no cattle. In the case of sheep, 7 percent of households own 10 or more, with 82 percent owning none. For goats, 18 percent of households own 10 or more, while 43 percent own none.

Cattle, sheep and goats are herded during the cropping season in cropping areas, and where there are predator or theft risks in other areas, but herding tends to be relaxed during the dry season, during which animals have access to crop residues. In the northern communal areas, many larger herdowners have "cattle posts" away from the village and crop lands and maintain most of their animals there, keeping only the milk and draught animals at the village during the wet season. Pigs and poultry in the communal areas are generally free ranging and scavenging, although some owners practise housing and feeding.

The exclusion of fire from the savannah regions under communal management has encouraged bush encroachment. In the semi-arid regions of Mpumalanga, the Northern Province and the North West province, fire has generally been excluded. Cutting large trees for fuel or building material has resulted in coppice growth (sprouting) and has stimulated shrubbiness. Consequently, large areas of the medium-rainfall savannahs have become severely bush infested, to the detriment of the grazing potential for cattle and sheep. In the subhumid communal areas of Kwa-Zulu Natal and the Transkei, fire is used to stimulate grass production during the early summer, and this maintains a grassland state along the coastal region (Shackleton, 1991).

AUTHORITIES RESPONSIBLE FOR MANAGEMENT

The National Department of Agriculture within the Ministry of Agriculture and Land Affairs is the key institution dealing with forage resources. The National Department of Agriculture is divided into five directorates, one of which deals directly with rangeland and pasture resources. The Land and Resource Management Directorate is responsible for the implementation of the Conservation of Agricultural Resources, Act No. 43 of 1984. This act empowers the head of the Directorate to intervene when the grassland resources of the country are perceived to be threatened by herbivory, alien infestation or cultivation. In addition, each of the nine provinces has a division or directorate that provides research and management advice on rangeland and pasture resources. These sections provide support to extension services and planners, establish standards, develop capacity, and conduct research appropriate to the needs of that province.

Market systems

Marketing of grassland products is conducted through a commodity-based marketing system. Since 1994, the so-called Control Boards of the single-channel marketing system have been disbanded, and a free market system prevails. Each commodity has had to develop its own competitive marketing framework. For example, wool is marketed through numerous brokers, including Cape Mohair & Wool and BKB. Brokers are able to buy direct from the producer and offer the product for sale at auction. Generally, auction prices are determined by the international wool price and local markets have little influence. Negative changes in the exchange rate (Rand against US$) advantages those farmers who produce export-quality wool. In 2000, the greasy wool clip was 52 671 t and South Africa produced 25 percent of Africa's wool crop. Approximately 80 percent of the South African wool crop is processed locally to "tops" level, making it suitable for export to the European market. Beef and mutton marketing has also recently been released from the controlled marketing environment of the previous regime. In 2000, South Africa's mutton production amounted to 114 000 t, most of which was consumed locally.

Landforms and agro-ecological zones
The country has five main physiographic regions, as discussed earlier.

Based on bioclimatic and growth form information, Rutherford and Westfall (1986) defined six biomes in South Africa. An improvement has been suggested by Low and Rebelo (1996), who further subdivided the savannah biome to include the category "Thicket", which occurs predominantly in the river valleys of the eastern and southeastern coastal region (Figure 3.6).

BIOMES
The areas of the various biomes are given in Table 3.6.

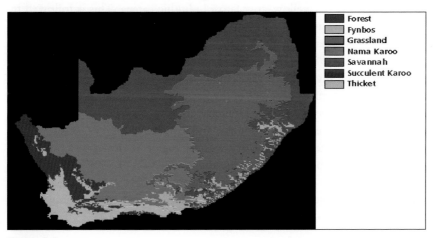

Figure 3.6
The biomes of South Africa.
Source: After Rutherford and Westfall, 1986; Low and Rebelo, 1996.

TABLE 3.6
Area occupied by each of the biomes in South Africa (excluding Lesotho and Swaziland).

Biome	Area (km²)	As a percentage
Grassland	295 233	24.27
Savannah	419 009	34.44
Nama-karoo	297 836	24.48
Succulent Karoo	82 589	6.79
Thicket	41 818	3.44
Fynbos	78 570	6.46
Forest	1 479	0.12
Total	1 216 536	100

Grassland

The grassland biome is situated mainly in the central, high lying regions of South Africa (Figure 3.6) (O'Connor and Bredenkamp, 1997). The biome spans a precipitation gradient from ca. 400 to >1 200 mm/yr, a temperature gradient from frost-free to snow-bound in winter, ranges in altitude from sea level to >3 300 metres and occurs on a spectrum of soil types, from humic clays to poorly structured sands (O'Connor and Bredenkamp, 1997). Although the general structure is fairly uniform, there is a wide range in floristic composition, associated environmental variables, dynamics and management options. There is a strong dominance of hemicryptophytes of the Poaceae. Standing biomass is moisture dependant and decreases with the rainfall gradient. Herbivory from domestic and wild herbivores has a decisive impact on standing biomass and species composition.

The biome was originally defined on climatic factors and is limited to summer and strong summer rainfall areas, with a summer aridity index between 2.0 and 3.9 (Rutherford and Westfall, 1986). Frost is common, occurring for 30–180 days/yr. The most common soil in the biome, accounting for 50 percent of the area, is the red-yellow-grey latosol plinthic catena. This is followed by black and red clays and solonetzic soils, freely drained latosols and black clays (Rutherford and Westfall, 1986).

Acocks (1953, 1988) defined thirteen pure grassland types and six "false" or anthropogenically-induced grasslands, ranging from the so-called "sweet" grasslands of the semi-arid regions of the Eastern Cape, to the "sour" grasslands of the high-rainfall regions of the Drakensberg. There are now six recognizable grassland floristic regions (O'Connor and Bredenkamp, 1997), reflecting a topo-moisture gradient from the dry western region to the eastern mountains and escarpment (Table 3.7). Following the completion of a revised vegetation map of South Africa (National Botanical Institute, 2004), sixty-seven grassland units have been described on the basis of floristic and climatic uniqueness, including, for example, the Bedford Dry Grassland (Plate 3.2).

TABLE 3.7
Regions within the grassland biome.

Region Name	Dominant taxa	Geology	Soil type	Altitude (m) and Precipitation (mm)
Central inland plateau	*Themeda triandra, Eragrostis curvula.*	sandstone, shale	deep red, yellow, eutrophic	1 400–1 600 m 600–700 mm
Dry western region (see Plate 3.3)	*Eragrostis lehmanniana, E. obtusa, Stipagrostis obtusa.*	mudstone, shale	shallow aridosols	1 200–1 400 m 450–600 mm
Northern areas	*Trachypogon spicatus, Diheteropogon amplectans.*	quartzites, shale, andesitic lava	shallow, lithosols	1 500–1 600 m 650–750 mm
Eastern inland plateau	*Themeda triandra, Aristida junciformis, Eragrostis plana.*	sandstones and shales	deep sand loam	1 600–1 800 m 700–950 mm
Eastern mountains and escarpment	*Hyparrhenia hirta, Aristida diffusa.*	Drakensberg complex	shallow lithosols	1 650–3 480 m >1 000 mm
Eastern lowlands	*Hyparrhenia hirta, Sporobolus pyramidalis.*	dolerite	shallow lithosols	1 200–1 400 m 850 mm

SOURCE: O'Connor and Bredenkamp, 1997.

A.R. PALMER

Plate 3.2
The Bedford Dry Grassland Unit.

The concepts "sweet" and "sour" refer to the palatability of the grasses, dwarf shrubs and trees to domestic livestock. Although difficult to define in a strict scientific sense, these terms have retained their use throughout the farming community, being applied to both individual species and to components of the landscape. Sweet-veldt usually occurs on high nutrient status soils under arid and semi-arid conditions. These soils are generally derived from the shales, mudstones and sandstones of the Karoo Supergroup. Sour-veldt is associated with acid soils of quartzite and andesitic origin, and occurs in higher (>600 mm) precipitation and high elevation (>1 400 mm) areas. Ellery, Scholes and Scholes (1995) have suggested that the concept is driven by the C:N ratios of the grasses and that the sweet-veldt has a lower C:N ratio than sour-veldt.

Savannah

Vegetation dynamics in the African savannah are driven by a number of variables, including rainfall amount, rainfall uncertainty, frost, fire, herbivory, ambient CO_2 levels and soil moisture. Depending on the seasonal environmental conditions and management history, a grassland at the boundary of the savannah biome can change from a monolithic physiognomy, to one dominated by shrubs and trees. O'Connor and Bredenkamp (1997) summarize five hypotheses to account for the possible exclusion of woody elements from grasslands. In this dynamic environment, where the grasslands abut the savannah, it is necessary to provide some information on the savannah biome.

A.R. PALMER

Plate 3.3
Arid grasslands of southern Africa occur in southern Namibia and the northwestern portions of South Africa. Dominant genera include Stipagrostis, Eragrostis *and* Enneapogon.

The savannah biome comprises the northern and eastern portions of South Africa, with the arid savannah extending into the southern Kalahari. The savannah biome is the region where large portions of the national beef production occur under extensive rangeland conditions. The flora comprises a woody layer (mainly single-stemmed, seasonally deciduous, trees and shrubs), with a ground layer of grasses and forbs. The standing biomass of shrubs and trees is 16–20 t/ha (Rutherford, 1982). The dominant grasses are C_4 and form the important production component for domestic livestock. A strong summer seasonality in the rainfall encourages woody shrub production. There is strong evidence of woody shrub encroachment throughout this and other biomes (Hoffman and O'Connor, 1999). A number of explanations have been suggested for the increase in woody shrub biomass, including (1) a reduction in fire frequency (Trollope, 1980); (2) the removal of grass biomass by domestic herbivory, with the resultant success of woody shrubs (du Toit, 1967); and (3) the C_3 shrubs having a competitive advantage over C_4 grasses under elevated CO_2 conditions (Bond and van Wilgen, 1996). Graziers attempt to control the woody encroachment using a number of approaches, including clear felling; burning followed by intensive browsing by goats; and chemical control. The last-named seems to be the favoured approach, with an estimated R 10 million spent annually on herbicides. The biome is utilized by both commercial and communal graziers. In general, the woody encroachment problems are more severe in land under communal tenure, although multiple use ensures that wood is used for fuel, construction and traditional purposes.

Nama-karoo

The Nama-karoo biome covers much of the central and western regions of the country. The biome is dominated by a steppe-type vegetation, comprising a mixture of shrubs, dwarf shrubs and annual and perennial grasses. The biome is associated with the moderate rainfall regions (250-450 mm per annum) and is suited to commercial sheep and goat production. The summer seasonality of the rainfall in the eastern parts of the biome means that there is often abundant grass production during the growing season. Graziers attempt to optimize production by sparing or resting grassy dwarf shrubland in the wet season. Herbivory by domestic livestock during the growing season has been shown to reduce grass cover and promote the growth of larger shrubs (species of *Rhus, Acacia* and *Euclea*) and dwarf shrubs. In the winter months, the dwarf shrubs maintain their crude protein at around 8 percent, providing excellent forage. The nutrient-rich substrata provided by the mudstones, sandstones and dolerites mean that this production can be considered sustainable. There were earlier suggestions that large-scale structural transformations were taking place in this biome (Acocks, 1964), with the dwarf shrubs supposedly spreading into the adjoining grasslands of central Free State. This process has not continued in the manner envisaged and the relatively high rainfall of the 1990s has promoted grass production in the eastern portions of the biome. In the western portions of the biome, there is alarming evidence of woody encroachment, with two species in particular (*Acacia mellifera* and *Rhigozum trichotomum*) increasing in density and cover in regions with a long history of domestic herbivory. Production of mutton and fibre continues to thrive in the Nama-karoo. During the recent past there has also been an increase in the area of land set aside for informal conservation, with many farmers capitalizing on the unique landscapes and indigenous fauna of the biome to develop ecotourism operations. Important indigenous herbivores, which contribute to red meat production, include springbok, blesbok, kudu, gemsbok and wildebeest.

Thicket

The thicket biome occurs in the drainage lines and ridges of the southeastern coastal region and inland to the Great Escarpment. The thicket comprises a dense cover of succulent shrubs, woody shrubs and small trees, with a height of 1.5–3.0 m. The woody shrubs are multistemmed, seasonally-deciduous, C_3 plants. In the xeric portions of the thicket biome (300–450 mm/yr precipitation), there is a large component of crassulacean acid metabolism (CAM)-type leaf succulents (e.g. *Portulacaria afra*), stem succulents (*Euphorbia* spp.) and many species of small succulent shrubs (e.g. species of *Aloe* and *Crassula*). Important grass species that contribute significantly to cattle production include *Panicum maximum, P. deustum, Digitaria eriantha* and *Setaria sphacelata*. Although the thicket biome does not contain extensive grasslands, clearing of thicket is carried out by both freehold and communal graziers to promote grasslands.

These grasslands provide high quality, year-round grazing, as the shale-derived soils associated with thicket are rich in nutrients.

Two important thicket types are recognized: succulent thicket and mesic thicket. Succulent thicket occurs under semi-arid conditions (300–450 mm/ yr) and is dominated by leaf- and stem-succulent shrubs (*Portulacaria afra, Euphorbia bothae, E. ledienii, E. coerulescens, E. tetragona, E. triangularis*, numerous *Crassula* spp. and *Aloe* spp.). Mesic thicket contains fewer succulents and occurs under higher rainfall (>450 mm/yr) conditions. The cover by woody shrubs is usually continuous, but they seldom exceed 4 m in height.

Short succulent thicket occurs in the low elevation (300–350 m) inland river valleys of the Great Fish, Bushmans, Sundays and Gamtoos rivers. Here the Ecca series mudstones provide a nutrient-rich substratum. The soils are shallow, comprising arid lithosols derived from the basement rock. The valley climate is hot and dry, with extremely high summer maximum temperatures (45°C) and low winter minimum temperatures. In the Great Fish river valley, the structure and composition of the "pristine" form of short succulent thicket is dominated by *Portulacaria afra, Rhigozum obovatum* and *Euphorbia bothae*, in small (3–4 m diameter) clumps. The vegetation in the clumps may contain emergent shrubs (e.g. *Boscia oleoides*), but they are usually <1.5 m in height. The clumps are interspersed by karroid shrubs (*Becium burchellianum, Walafrida geniculata* and *Pentzia incana*) and grasses (*Cymbopogon plurinodis, Aristida congesta* and *Eustachys mutica*). Further west, *Euphorbia bothae* is replaced by either *E. ledienii* (Sundays River) or *E. coerulescens* (Jansenville and the Noorsveldt).

Degradation of the succulent thicket type takes a number of forms, including a decline in the abundance of *Portulacaria afra*, which is susceptible to excessive browsing by goats and cattle. There are some alien species present (e.g. *Opuntia ficus-indica* or *O. aurantiaca*), but there remains a structure akin to the short succulent thicket. Clumps are still an important feature, but the vegetation has been opened up by livestock. In the severely degraded state, clumps no longer exist. *Portulacaria afra* and other palatable species (e.g. *Rhigozum obovatum* and *Boscia oleoides*) have been removed, exposing the Ecca shales.

The structure and composition of the "pristine" form of the medium succulent thicket comprises *Portulacaria afra, Rhigozum obovatum, Ptaeroxylon obliquum* and *Cussonia spicata* in larger (10–12 m diameter) clumps, often associated with the nests or mounds of the wood-eating harvester termite (*Microhodotermes viator*). The vegetation in the clumps may be up to 2.5 m in height, with inter-clump areas covered by dwarf shrubs (*Becium burchellianum, Walafrida geniculata* and *Pentzia incana*) and grasses (*Cymbopogon plurinodis, Aristida congesta* and *Eustachys mutica*) with Nama-karoo affinity.

Tall succulent thicket is associated with the steep slopes of the incised river valleys. Emerging tree succulents, which are a distinctive feature of this form, include *Euphorbia triangularis* and *E. tetragona*. These shrubs, which can reach 8–10 m in height, are eaten by domestic herbivores only when short. When the endangered black rhinoceros were recently re-introduced to this region, adult animals knocked the tall succulents down to eat the new leaves at the tops of the shrubs.

The mesic thicket type contains far fewer leaf and stem succulents and is composed primarily of multistemmed woody shrubs such as *Scutia myrtina, Olea europea* var. *africana, Rhus longispina, R. incisa* and *R. undulata.* Succulent taxa include numerous species of the genera *Aloe, Euphorbia, Gasteria* and *Crassula,* although these growth forms do not represent a major component of the standing biomass.

Succulent karoo

The succulent karoo biome occurs in the winter rainfall regions of the southern and southwestern portions of South Africa. The flora of the biome comprises mainly shrubs (0.5–1.5 m) and dwarf shrubs (<0.5 m), with succulent leaves and stems. The climate of the region is arid to semi-arid (100–350 mm/yr), with a strong winter seasonality. The succulent karoo is well known for its high floristic diversity, part of which is a function of its proximity to the adjacent floristically-rich fynbos biome, but also the unique climatic environment (low, seasonal (winter) rainfall with relatively low uncertainty (coefficient of variation = 30–45 percent) (Cowling and Hilton-Taylor, 1999). Some of the areas with

A.R. PALMER

Plate 3.4
Succulent karoo occurs in the winter-rainfall region of the southern and southwestern portions of South Africa. The vegetation comprises shrubs (0.5–1.5 m) and dwarf shrubs (<0.5 m) with succulent stems and leaves.

high floristic diversity, such as Richtersveldt and Namaqualand, receive a large portion of their precipitation in the form of coastal advective fog during the coolest months of the year. There are many species in two succulent families (Crassulaceae and Mesembryanthecaceae), numerous endemic taxa (e.g. several species of the genus *Pachypodium*) and distinctive growth forms (leaf and stem succulents). This diversity has made the biome ideal for the development of an ecotourism industry that promotes the unique floristic character of the region. The arid conditions mean that the region is most suited to extensive livestock production and the flora of the biome has been subjected to herbivory from domestic goats and ostriches. These herbivores form the main suite of animals responsible for much of the direct impact on the vegetation of the biome. In recent times there have been known changes in the species composition, with some landscapes currently dominated by species unpalatable (to domestic livestock), such as *Pteronia incana* and *P. pallens*. The productivity of the biome has been significantly affected by these changes and many graziers now depend on irrigated pastures to sustain livestock production.

Fynbos

The fynbos biome occurs in the winter rainfall regions of the southern and southwestern portions of South Africa, being associated with the moderate to high rainfall (450–1 000 mm) region. The vegetation of the biome is dominated by sclerophyllous shrubs and trees, with rich floristic diversity, but has little or no forage value. Much of the natural vegetation has been cleared to enable wheat, oats, rye, barley, canola and lupin production. The crop residues provide large areas of post-harvesting stubble for sheep production during the dry summer months. Within the biome, irrigated pastures are also major contributors to sheep production.

Forest

Forest occurs in patches along the southern coastal zone, in the cooler southern facing slopes of the Great Escarpment and in the high-rainfall regions of the Drakensberg. Forest is not significant in livestock production in South Africa.

PASTORAL AND AGRICULTURAL SYSTEMS

The main forage resource for livestock in South Africa is rangeland grazing, with 68.6 percent of the area being used for livestock grazing and a further 9.6 percent used by wild herbivores. In the higher-rainfall zones, crop residues are a very important feed supplement in both freehold and communal areas during the dry season, when range grazing is scarce. In freehold areas, many livestock farmers plant fodder species as dryland pasture. Irrigated fodder production is important in freehold areas, but varies from season to season, as cash crops are more favoured. In 1980, 468 000 ha were under irrigated cultivation with alfalfa, but this had declined to 214 000 ha in 1987. In times of drought, South Africa imports maize from the international market. There are some zero-grazing dairy operations near large cities, and three large commercial feedlots are found on the high-veldt.

Veldt grazing

The principal agro-ecological units within South Africa are illustrated in the generalized image of the Acocks (1953) map of the Veldt Types of South Africa (Figure 3.7). Acocks (1953) provided a unique perspective on the classification and distribution of the agro-economic divisions of vegetation in South Africa. This map serves to illustrate the broad floristic diversity of the vegetation and continues to remain an important classification for graziers. There are 70 Veldt Types, with a primary focus on those types most useful for livestock production. As this diversity is reflected in composition, structure, phenology and production, it is extremely difficult to provide broad generalizations concerning the management options for each veldt type, most of which have received some research attention, with the mesic grass-veldt – with its higher

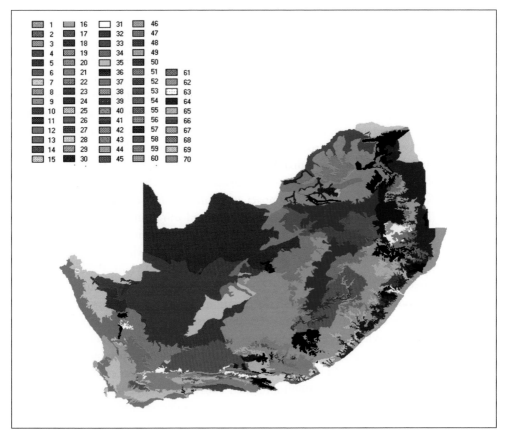

Figure 3.7
Veldt types of South Africa, as described in Acocks, 1953.

production potential and greater economic importance – being given the greatest attention. The research focus has been on supporting government intervention in three major areas.

The first area receiving government research support is the estimation of sustainable production (carrying capacity), which was deemed important, as government attempted to enforce restrictions on the numbers of livestock on freehold properties. Grazing trials (mainly on-station), attempted to determine sustainable production levels, using a number of ecological and animal performance indices. Ecological indices that were measured to assess livestock impact on the rangeland included plant species composition, plant vigour and biomass production. In general, on-station trials did not permit the application of extreme treatments that would be appropriate to test the ecosystem. Researchers were reluctant to be perceived to be degrading a state-owned resource and trials were frequently terminated within the time-frames of system run-down. Conclusions for each veldt type vary enormously, but we would like to elaborate on those delivered for the semi-arid grasslands of the Eastern Cape.

It is well recognized that rainfall is the primary determinant of forage production and a number of production models have been developed for predicting the aboveground primary production in natural rangeland in southern Africa. Coe, Cumming and Phillipson (1976) demonstrate a linear relationship between annual rainfall and primary production for conservation areas in southern Africa. These predictions are regarded as conservative by commercial graziers, many of whom suggest that production for livestock can be optimized by rotational grazing (Danckwerts and Teague, 1989). In an effort to assess the sustainable production of grasslands in the Eastern Cape Province, a grazing trial was established on a freehold ranch (the so-called Kroomie Trial) to test the impact of animal type (cattle or sheep), number (light, moderate or heavy stocking rate) and duration (rotation versus continuous) on rangeland condition and animal production. Preliminary results suggest that continuous grazing under moderate stocking rate (that recommended by the National Department of Agriculture) yields the best livestock mass gain. However, in the Kroomie trial, no significant changes in species composition are obvious and the duration of the trial (10 years) is insufficient to make conclusive assertions regarding system run-down. Even in situations like this, where the questions have been clearly defined and the treatments meticulously applied, no clear answers to "sustainable" production levels are available. Using SPUR2 (Wight and Skiles, 1987; Hanson *et al* 1994), Palmer, Ainslie and Hoffman (1999) simulated a 50-year beef operation under continuous grazing for a site receiving 500 mm/yr (similar in elevation and rainfall to the conditions at Kroomie). The "recommended stocking rate", determined by the National Department of Agriculture and Land Affairs, was 6 ha/LSU. When running another simulation at 4 ha/LSU, with ambient CO_2 at 330 ppm,

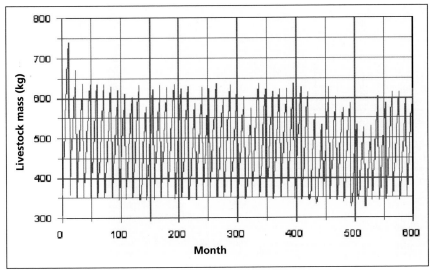

Figure 3.8
Simulated carrying capacity for Grahamstown using SPUR2, with stocking rate set at that recommended by the Department of Agriculture (4 ha/LSU) under a continuous grazing system.

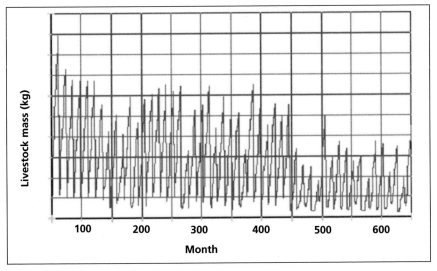

Figure 3.9
Simulated carrying capacity for Grahamstown using SPUR2, with stocking rate set at 2 ha/LSU under a continuous grazing system. System shows signs of run-down after 300 months.

the system remained sustainable (Figure 3.8). Only when the stocking rate was increased dramatically, doubled to 2 ha/LSU, did the system run down within the 50-year simulation period (Figure 3.9). These results suggest that the recommended stocking rates for grassland systems are well below those that are

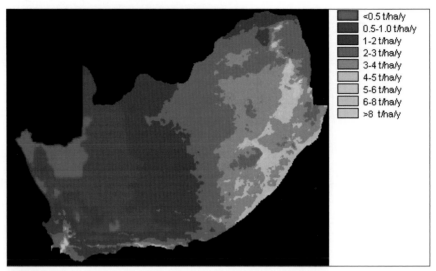

Figure 3.10
Rangeland production in South Africa using the model of Le Houérou, Bingham and Skerbek (1988) and median annual rainfall (Dent, Lynch and Schulze, 1987).

likely to lead to system run-down. In the communal areas of the Eastern Cape, livestock numbers at the district level reflect the fact that stocking rates are substantially higher than those applied by freehold graziers and recommended by the Department of Agriculture. This presents a problem for administrators, who are unable to reduce livestock numbers in areas where graziers are unresponsive to regulation.

Production relationships can be simplified to straightforward expressions of kilograms of annual dry matter production of forage per millimetre of annual rainfall (Le Houérou, 1984). An aboveground biomass production model based on the concept of rain-use-efficiency has been developed (Palmer, 1998) and applied to rangeland. The resultant map for commercial production is shown as Figure 3.10. Production may be converted to carrying capacity for cattle by assuming a daily requirement of 11.25 kg DM/LSU and a use factor of 0.4 (Le Houérou, pers. comm.). The use factor may decline to 0.2 in mesic, "sour" grasslands with high C:N ratios.

The second focus of research to receive substantial government funding in support of intervention policies was assessment of grazing systems. During 1950–1990 it was expedient for government to provide support for fencing, water points and stock management infrastructure. Field trials were designed to assess the advantages of rotational versus continuous grazing. Rotational grazing requires that the pasture allocated to a group or groups of animals be subdivided into one enclosure more than the number of groups (Booysen, 1967). According to Tainton, Aucamp and Danckwerts (1999), the primary objectives of rotational grazing are to:

- control the frequency at which plants are grazed by controlling the frequency with which each camp in the system is grazed;
- control the intensity at which plants are grazed by controlling the number of animals that graze each camp and their period of occupation; and
- reduce the extent to which veldt is selectively grazed by confining a relatively large number of animals to a small proportion of the veldt so as to offer them little opportunity to select.

The published results of many grazing trials (Department of Agriculture [South Africa], 1951) suggest that while animal performance in continuous grazing systems was superior to that of various rotational grazing ones, continuous grazing was condemned. After the contribution of Booysen (1969), who maintained that retaining sufficient active green biomass was essential to optimize regrowth, further research continued into the advantages of variations in rotational grazing. The concepts of Booysen (1969) are encompassed in the term High Performance Grazing (HPG), with the alternative, intensive-use, approach being High Utilization Grazing (HUG) (Tainton, Aucamp and Danckwerts, 1999). The HPG approach is thought to perform better in the semi-arid grasslands and savannahs, whereas HUG is more appropriate in the fire-induced grasslands of the humid regions. The inappropriate application of HUG, encompassed by the protagonists of Holistic Resource Management (Savory, 1988), to the more fragile, semi-arid systems, has been controversial and is discouraged.

The third area receiving research attention funded by the Department of Agriculture was veldt condition assessment. In this work, floristic composition was regarded as an indicator of the impact of management and stocking rates. Gradient studies, which explored changes in species composition along grazing gradients, were popular. Within this research area, it was difficult to attribute the floristic variation along gradients directly to herbivory. Differences in species composition were often a consequence of enrichment, trampling and associated changes in soil structure and chemistry.

LEGUME AND FODDER INTRODUCTION

A number of subtropical pasture legumes and fodders have been screened at sites with from 100–700 mm annual rainfall. Range reinforcement is done on a large scale in commercial dairy regions. Favoured grasses include *Pennisetum clandestinum* (Kikuyu grass), *Panicum maximum* and *Digitaria eriantha*, while legumes such as silver leaf *Desmodium* are over-sown into natural vegetation.

Foggage (Plate 3.5) is important in commercial beef and dairy production systems in South Africa. Graziers use a wide range of commercially available grasses and legumes. The performance of growing beef steers grazing foggaged dryland Kikuyu grass pastures and given limited access (3 hours daily) to leucaena (*Leucaena leucocephala* cv. Cunningham) was better than

S.G. REYNOLDS

Plate 3.5
Foggage Kikuyu for winter grazing.

that of steers grazing only Kikuyu foggage during autumn and early winter (Zacharias, Clayton and Tainton, 1991). Animals grazing leucaena performed better and gained 24.8 kg per animal more, over 90 days, than those on Kikuyu alone. There is concern about the risk of leucaena becoming invasive in the humid coast and its use, and that of other potentially aggressive species (e.g. *Lespedeza sericea*), has been discouraged until further evaluation has been carried out.

Investigations to determine whether frosted Kikuyu provides better quality foggage than natural pasturage in the sour-veldt area during the winter months revealed that this grass had a crude protein content of 8–10 percent in winter. The performance of animals grazing such frosted Kikuyu was highly satisfactory (Rethman and Gouws, 1973). Sheep performance and patterns of herbage utilization were determined in two grazing trials involving different amounts and quality of Kikuyu foggage. In two grazing trials involving different quantity and quality of Kikuyu foggage, wether lambs maintained live mass in one, whereas dry ewes and wether lambs both lost 8–10 percent of their initial mass in the other. This suggests that Kikuyu foggage alone does not provide a viable source of fodder. Grazing capacity was proportional to the yield of foggage and some 50 percent of the total herbage was utilized. The estimates of quality indicated that a higher level of utilization would have resulted in poorer sheep performance (Barnes and Dempsey, 1993).

DRYLAND FODDER

Dryland fodder production is only possible in the higher-rainfall regions of the country. The principal form of dryland fodder is cereal crop residues, which make an important contribution to livestock diets in communal areas during the dry season. Some communal area farmers collect and store at least part of their residues to feed to selected animals, such as milch cows and draught oxen, but most is utilized *in situ*.

Cultivation of rainfed crops in South Africa is widespread in both freehold and communal land use systems. The most significant commercial grain producing areas are the maize triangle of the central high-veldt, the wheat growing region of the southwestern Cape and the maize growing regions of central Kwa-Zulu Natal. Maize is widely preferred as the staple food in the communal areas, but millet and sorghum are more reliable crops apart from in the highest-rainfall zones. National cereal production (roughly 80 percent maize, 16 percent wheat and 4 percent others, including millet and sorghum) fluctuates considerably from year to year according to rainfall. Production has varied from a low of 5 044 000 t in the drought year of 1991/92 to a record high of 15 966 000 t in 1993/94 (Table 3.8). It is difficult to assess what proportion crop residues contribute to national production as no research has been published, but it is thought to be considerable in areas of commercial rainfed cultivation (>600 mm mean annual rainfall).

In drier central and western zones, farmers commonly have small areas of drought-tolerant fodders (e.g. *Agave americana*, *Opuntia* spp. or *Atriplex nummalaria*) as a drought reserve.

IRRIGATED FODDER

Irrigation has two main functions in the humid summer rainfall regions. In winter it is used for temperate pasture species such as ryegrass and in summer it is used to supplement rainfall. In winter, the temperate species are completely dependant upon irrigation for survival and it can only be justified in intensive production systems such as dairy or the production of fat lambs.

TABLE 3.8
Commercial field crop production for South Africa from 1992 to 2000 (×1000 t).

Crop	1992	1993	1994	1995	1996	1997	1998	1999	2000
Maize	3 277	9 997	13 275	4 866	10 171	10 136	7 693	7 946	10 584
Wheat	1 324	1 983	1 840	1 977	2 711	2 428	1 787	1 725	2 122
Green corn	266	262	278	279	280	290	292	299	300
Barley	265	230	275	300	176	182	215	90	142
Groundnuts	132	150	174	117	215	157	108	163	169
Sorghum	118	515	520	290	535	433	358	223	352
Soybeans	62	68	67	58	80	120	200	174	148
Oats	45	47	37	38	33	30	25	22	25
Total crops	5 044	12 727	15 966	7 491	13 647	13 229	10 098	10 024	13 244

Source: FAO database.

Plate 3.6
*Dairy cows on irrigated ryegrass pastures (*Lolium multiflorum*) near Fort Nottingham, KwaZulu-Natal.*

Dryland pasture production may be improved by irrigation. Where irrigation is available, despite the relative advantages of using water for other more lucrative crops, some farmers may choose to grow irrigated pasture. Alfalfa (*Medicago sativa*) is the main purpose-grown irrigated fodder, and is grown throughout the country. In 1980, 468 000 ha were under irrigated alfalfa, but this declined to 214 000 ha in 1987. This may show a preference amongst farmers with water rights to grow cash crops. New legislation (Water Act of 1998), which separates water rights from property rights and increases the cost of abstracting water from rivers, will reinforce this trend. In high-performance production systems (e.g. dairy – Plate 3.6), Kikuyu grass (*Pennisetum clandestinum*), cocksfoot (*Dactylis glomerata*), tall fescue (*Festuca arundinacea*) and ryegrasses (*Lolium multiflorum* and *L. perenne*) are cultivated. Some other legumes (*Trifolium pratense* and *T. repens*) respond well to irrigation. Many other species and numerous cultivars are available commercially (Bartholomew, 2000).

EXCEPTIONAL CIRCUMSTANCES FODDER
In times of drought, South Africa has provided fodder at subsidized rates to farmers. According to the new drought policy (National Department of Agriculture, 1995), the fodder subsidies have been terminated in order to encourage farmers to build up their own forage reserves and to discourage them from retaining excessive stock numbers. Nonetheless, it is likely that some commercial farmers, and probably the government, will continue

TABLE 3.9
Plants used for fodder during exceptional circumstances.

Botanical name	Common name	Uses
Agave americana	American aloe	Drought fodder in arid and semi-arid regions
Anthephora pubescens	Wool grass	Spring and summer grazing
Atriplex mueleri	Australian saltbush	Drought fodder
Atriplex nummalaria	Old Man Saltbush	Drought fodder
Atriplex semibaccata	Creeping saltbush	Drought fodder
Cenchrus ciliaris	Blue buffalo grass	Tufted perennial; spring, summer and autumn grazing
Opuntia spp.	Spineless cactus	Drought fodder
Opuntia ficus-indica	Prickly pear	Drought fodder
Vigna unguiculata	Cowpea	Undersowing maize, millet or sorghum

to import fodder in extreme drought conditions. In the arid and semi-arid regions, farmers are encouraged to plant suitable drought-tolerant fodder crops (Table 3.9). Since 1994, there have been no magisterial districts declared as drought stricken, and so these new policies have not been tested.

CONSTRAINTS TO PASTURE AND FODDER PRODUCTION AND IMPROVEMENT

Low and uncertain rainfall throughout most of the country are the main constraints to the productivity of natural pastures and to the establishment of exotic pasture crops. Concern about exotics becoming problematic limits the introduction and testing of hardy species considered suited to the environmental and utilization rigours of the communal areas (e.g. *Leucaena* spp. and *Lespedeza sericea*). The availability and price of seeds for fodder or for pasture improvement are major constraints to communal area farmers. Considerable portions of the savannah vegetation on the freehold farms are severely bush infested, but the cost of thinning or clearing generally outweighs the benefits in terms of increased carrying capacity. Open access to grazing, at least within communities, in the communal areas necessitates broad collective agreement and cooperation in any pasture improvement venture – something most communities, socially fragmented as they are, seem unable to attain. Traditionally, communal area farmers do not retain exclusive use of their unfenced croplands for their own livestock after harvest, which blocks opportunities and incentives for undersowing or alley cropping.

Commercial ranchers find it increasingly difficult to maintain production in the western and central regions, which receive low and uncertain rainfall and where there are increases in undesirable woody species. Low profit margins and higher production costs discourage many landowners from maintaining commercial herds. There has been a decline in sheep and wool production from the Nama-karoo region (Dean and MacDonald, 1994), which has been attributed to a decline in resource condition. There appears to be an increase in the number of uninhabited freehold farms in the arid and semi-arid regions, suggesting that farms are being abandoned or managed as larger units. Reflecting de-agrarianization trends throughout the developed world, South African rangelands under freehold tenure are becoming depopulated. The children of freehold farmers do not regard farming as an exciting career option, and leave the farm for training in more lucrative career paths. When freehold land is converted from livestock ranching to game farming, the staff complement required to manage the farm is reduced and labour is encouraged to move to the smaller towns, with better education, health and municipal services.

In contrast to freehold land, the population in communal areas has increased since the initiation of re-location policies by the previous regime. This trend has continued since the advent of the new democracy, with rural land being used for the construction of dwellings, roads, clinics, schools and stores. Many residents have access to a piece of cultivated dryland, either close to their dwelling or at an allocation some distance away, but within the administrative region of the village. This allocation is generally used for maize, millet or cash crops, and is seldom planted to pasture crops. Crop residues may be available to livestock at the end of the harvest. Access to irrigation is limited to a very few villagers, who are usually part of government schemes.

EVOLUTION OF GRASSLANDS OVER THE LAST 40 YEARS

There is clear evidence of changes in the structure and specific composition of grasslands in southern Africa in the recent past. In a comprehensive review of the impact of recent human occupation of the eastern seaboard, Hoffman (1997) reports that "crop farmers first entered southern Africa along the northeastern coastal margins", where they practised slash-and-burn agriculture and small-stock farming. At first, only the vegetation around the coastal forest margins was cleared. These early farmers moved westwards, clearing cropland in woodland and forest, creating a mosaic of open grassland and thicket patches. The expansion of grassland brought about a shift in herd composition and there was an increase in cattle-based economy. In the communal rangelands of Kwa-Zulu Natal, Transkei and Ciskei, grasslands are maintained by the continued removal of shrubs and trees for firewood, annual burning (Plate 3.7) and the use of goats to control woody encroachment. However, the encroachment of woody plants into grassland remains a constant threat elsewhere. During a project to re-photograph, from the same viewpoint, historical photographs taken in natural rangeland, M.T. Hoffman of the University of Cape Town (pers. comm.) has shown that woody encroachment is a feature of almost every photograph that has been re-taken. Published examples of this are available in Hoffman (1997) and Hoffman and O'Connor (1999). Urbanization and cultivation has played an important role in transforming grasslands. Rural villages and abandoned cultivated land have replaced natural grassland in the former homelands of Transkei, Ciskei, Qwa-Qwa, Venda, Lebowa, Bophutatswana and Kwa-Zulu. In rural villages, free-ranging livestock use the entire landscape without restriction, concentrating nutrients around the

Plate 3.7
Grass regrowth after the annual burn in Kwa-Zulu Natal.

homesteads and kraal where they are held overnight. The areas near homesteads have a lower standing biomass, but are extremely photosynthetically active and provide short, nutritious grazing during the growing season. However photosynthetic activity in other components of the landscape and in abandoned cultivated land is low, suggesting suboptimal production of natural rangeland (Palmer *et al.*, 2001).

RESEARCH

Range and botanical sciences in South Africa have a very active research community, with funding and leadership in a number of ministries. The primary research agency for rangeland is the Agricultural Research Council (ARC), which supports two institutes dealing with understanding the processes (Range and Forage Institute – ARC-RFI) and condition assessment (Institute for Soil Climate and Water – ARC-ISCW) of rangeland. These institutes receive most of their core funding (approximately R 45 million in 2001) from the Ministry of Arts, Culture, Science and Technology. They also receive direct, project-orientated funding from the National Department of Agriculture and Land Affairs. Research direction is driven largely by the needs of directorates within the Department, which at present has five primary programmes: (1) Monitoring; (2) Problem organisms; (3) Rangeland resources; (4) Geographical Information Systems (GIS); and (5) Decision Support Systems (DSS). In the monitoring programme, research efforts of ARC-RFI and ARC-ISCW are directed towards resource evaluation using remote sensing and GIS modelling techniques. There is a strong emphasis on using satellite imagery to explore the extent of and trends in soil erosion, bush encroachment and rangeland degradation. The directorate has supported the calibration of NOAA AVHRR data for use in assessing trends since the launch of these satellites in 1980, and is now funding research into using high resolution infra-red instruments (digital cameras and other high resolution sensors) to assess range and landscape degradation at the farm and village scale. The problem organism division continues to show interest in brown locusts, quelea control, woody weed encroachment (especially alien taxa such as *Prosopis* spp.) and alien weed control. The list of alien weeds is extensive, with some 197 taxa being listed as declared weeds and invader plants (Henderson, 2001) and a further 60 taxa being considered as proposed weeds (Henderson, 2001) and a threat to range and water resources. The rangeland resources division funds projects that assess the impact of different grazing management approaches (e.g. continuous versus rotational grazing) on rangeland. This is being carried out in a network of replicated grazing trials throughout the country.

The Grassland Society of Southern Africa (GSSA) is the professional organization representing the discipline. GSSA maintains a full-time secretariat for its members, organizes annual congresses at localities around the subcontinent and publishes a peer-reviewed journal (*African Journal of Range and Forage Science*). The journal has been published since 1966, and about a thousand peer-reviewed articles have appeared.

Botanical research relating to rangeland is conducted by the National Botanical Institute (NBI) of the Ministry of Environmental Affairs and Tourism. NBI has focused on exploring the natural patterns and processes driving vegetation status in the arid and semi-arid regions of the Nama-karoo and succulent karoo biomes.

MANAGEMENT OF GRASSLANDS

In response to a decline in profit margins and negative sentiments associated with domestic livestock production, there has been a marked increase in game farming and ecotourism on commercial ranching areas. This is manifested in the large numbers of game-proof fences erected on farm boundaries and the removal of internal fences and stock watering points. This change has an impact on the management of rangeland, as livestock can no longer be manipulated and it is more difficult to apply rotational grazing. In commercial farming operations, fire is used on many high-elevation rangelands to provide grazing during the early growing season. Fire is used primarily by commercial ranchers to remove low quality material remaining after winter and to encourage a flush of short green grass in spring (see Plate 3.7).

Development of techniques for the rehabilitation of grasslands

The processes of degradation in arid and semi-arid rangelands are poorly understood and only recently have some researchers provided a conceptual framework for exploring rehabilitation within the context of an understanding of landscape function. Ludwig *et al.* (1997) suggest that the landscape comprises a series of inter-connected patches, with resource control being a key feature in the maintenance of the integrity of the landscape. Nutrients and moisture move from one patch to another, mainly though water flow patterns. The obstructions or patches in the landscape prevent nutrients from being lost, with run-on areas acting as sites of nutrient and moisture accumulation. Run-on areas are connected to one another by runoff zones or fetches. In a degrading landscape, it is suggested that these runoff areas increase in size and the run-on areas can no longer capture and accumulate nutrients, and so nutrients are lost to rivers and transported away from the landscape. In order to quantify these processes and relate them to South African landscapes, landscape function analysis (LFA) (Ludwig *et al.*, 1997) was applied to two contrasting land use types (Palmer *et al.*, 2001). The results showed that landscape with a long history of communal management has surface accumulations of C and N, which may not have been processed efficiently. Although Palmer *et al.* (2001) did not investigate nutrient loss, there were significant differences between landscape-scale organizations, with communal landscape having a lower landscape functionality index than the freehold grassland. There was greater patchiness in the communal landscape, with longer fetches than the landscape with a long history of commercial management. In accordance with Ludwig *et al.* (1997), it is recommended that rehabilitation of degraded rangelands in South Africa should strive to reduce the extent of runoff zones and increase the resource control exercised by patches.

Spatially explicit diversity indices (moving standard deviation index) have been applied to near-infrared (NIR) imagery (Landsat TM and SPOT) (Tanser and Palmer, 1999) recorded over land with different management histories and condition classes. Degraded grasslands, located in areas with a long history of communal management, had higher spatial diversity of selected growth indices than healthy grassland. Grasslands, savannahs and thicket with a high standing biomass and a long history of conservative land management, showed low spatial diversity indices. Rehabilitation techniques should attempt to reduce landscape photosynthetic heterogeneity.

Over-seeding with commercially available seeds has long been regarded as a solution to rehabilitation of degraded rangeland. In the thicket biome, re-vegetation of former cultivated lands has been successful when lime-coated seed (a mixture of seven local species, including *Panicum maximum, Cenchrus ciliaris* and *Eragrostis curvula*) was broadcast over the cultivated land and a long (three-year) rest applied. However, there has been limited success reported elsewhere, where commercial seeds generally require irrigation after planting and any early effect is usually discounted within a few years.

Using the principles embodied in the LFA theory, Van Rooyen (2000) has shown that it is possible to rehabilitate degraded biospheres in the southern

Kalahari using brush packing with *Rhigozum trichotomum*. In this highly mobile sand-dune environment, brush packing results in sand stabilization and enables seedling establishment.

Sustainable management of the environment and maintenance of biodiversity

South Africa has ratified the United Nations Conventions that strive to maintain biodiversity and improve sustainable management of rangelands, specifically the Convention on Biological Diversity (CBD) and the United Nations Convention to Combat Desertification (UNCCD). These conventions are administered by the Ministry of Environmental Affairs and Tourism, which supports the assessment of the state of resources. The most recent product of this programme has been an assessment of degradation and desertification at a national scale (Hoffman and Ashwell, 2001), which defines the nature and extent of rangeland transformation.

Seed production

There is formal certification of pasture and fodder seed in South Africa. South African seed merchants produce approximately 200 t of seed per annum for sale locally and for export. With the long-term goal of preserving germplasm (in most cases, as seed) of the entire South African flora, the ARC-Plant Genetic Resources Division in Pretoria focuses at present on preservation of seeds of plant species of economic importance. A wide variety of South African pasture grasses are included in the current accessions, such as species of the genera *Anthephora*, *Brachiaria*, *Cenchrus*, *Cynodon*, *Panicum*, *Pennisetum*, *Setaria* and *Stipagrostis*.

RECOMMENDATIONS AND LESSONS LEARNED CONCERNING SUSTAINABLE GRASSLAND MANAGEMENT

Many of the wild herbivores in South Africa (e.g. blesbok, bontebok, black wildebeest, blue wildebeest, springbok, Burchell's zebra and red hartebeest) create enriched patches which provide highly nutritious fodder throughout the year (Palmer, Novellie and Lloyd, 1999). These patches form a relatively small portion of the landscape (Lutge, Hardy and Hatch, 1996) and researchers (Booysen, 1969) recognized that the remainder of the rangeland was not used. It was suggested that in order to prevent this "area-selective grazing" in livestock production systems, ranchers should fence numerous paddocks and rotate the domestic animals in a system that maximized the use of the aboveground primary production. This principle was built into the legislation to permit government intervention in the primarily white-owned ranches. This intervention, which provided subsidies to farmers for fencing, dam construction and the erection of water points, encouraged ranchers to develop their farms. In the process, the government provided the rancher with the tools to efficiently remove large quantities of aboveground standing biomass. This approach may have been useful in the grasslands where research had been carried out to show that grass species composition could be changed by applying rotational grazing. However, this has had some very serious consequences in the thicket biome, where succulent shrubs such as *Portulacaria afra* have been completely removed from the landscape and do not regenerate after severe defoliation (Stuart-Hill and Aucamp, 1993). In the savannah biome, there is clear evidence of continuing woody encroachment by a wide range of shrub species, including *Acacia karroo, A. mellifera, Dichrostachys cinerea, Rhus undulata* and *Rhigozum trichotomum*. Researchers suggest that this is largely due to the removal of competitive grass species by herbivory, although alternative hypotheses are suggested.

Maintenance of production and productivity

Following on the thinking of J.C. Smuts, who spear-headed rangeland conservation initiatives in South Africa, Davies (1968) suggested that a holistic approach is needed whereby plant, soil and animal influences are studied as controllable parts of the environment. Savory (1988) further embellished on this approach, coining the term Holistic Resource Management, which embodied principles that were contrary to the conventional thinking amongst range scientists (Clayton and Hurt, 1998). Savory (1988) encouraged ranchers to employ non-selective grazing by maintaining large, mixed species – herds that would intensively use a restricted area until the standing biomass had been severely reduced, thereby eliminating competition among species. This area would then receive a long rest, whereupon herbivores would return. Numerous commercial graziers in South Africa have been encouraged to follow this thinking, with no formal scientific debate being entertained on the success of the approach. Vorster (1999) provides a convincing argument for discouraging ranchers from pursuing this approach without careful assessment of the rangeland resource.

Strategies for maintaining and optimizing aboveground grass production include rotational grazing and resting; control of woody encroachment; provision of winter pastures in the cool, mesic regions where forage quality declines in winter; and supplementary feeding on cultivated lands. In beef production systems, livestock are finished in feedlots where maize provides the major feed element. In these systems, production costs are determined by the international maize price.

Priorities for the development of programmes and research

The National Department of Agriculture, in cooperation with ARC-RFI, ARC-ISCW and CSIRO-Environmentek, is the key institution dealing with forage resources. The Directorate of Land and Resource Management in the National Department of Agriculture and Land Affairs is responsible for the implementation of the Conservation of Agricultural Resources, Act No. 43 of 1984. This act empowers the Directorate to intervene when the agricultural resources of the country are threatened by soil erosion, alien infestation or woody encroachment. Prior to 1994, this act was used to subsidize the provision of fencing; the erection of new water provision points; the purchase and transport of supplementary fodder during exceptional circumstances; the construction of soil erosion works; the clearing of all weeds (alien and indigenous); and to support rangeland research. Since 1994, intervention from the Directorate has concentrated on supporting research in the focus areas mentioned above and to intervene at community level though the Landcare programme. In addition, each of the nine Provinces has a section that deals with rangeland and pasture research. These sections conduct research appropriate to the needs of that Province. South Africa's National Agricultural Policy states that the main objective is improvement of research in natural resource management (National Department of Agriculture, 1995). On a project basis, pasture science-related programmes deal with the characterization of rangeland, production modelling, rangeland reclamation, agroforestry and rangeland management systems. Examples of individual projects related to rangeland and pasture science can be found on the ARC Web site.

The National Department of Education maintains eleven agricultural colleges, and carries out topic-oriented, formal training courses. All courses are certified by one of the tertiary training institutions.

REFERENCES

Acocks, J.P.H. 1953. Veld types of South Africa. *Memoir of the Botanical Survey of South Africa,* No. 28.

Acocks, J.P.H. 1964. Karoo vegetation in relation to the development of deserts. pp. 100–112, *in:* D.H.S. Davis (ed). *Ecological Studies of Southern Africa.* The Hague, The Netherlands: W. Junk.

Acocks, J.P.H. 1988. Veld types of South Africa. 3rd edition. *Memoirs of the Botanical Survey of South Africa,* **57**: 1–146.

Ainslie, A., Cinderby, S., Petse, T., Ntshona, Z., Bradley, P.N., Deshingkar, P. & Fakir, S. 1997. Rural livelihoods and local level natural resource management in Peddie district. Stockholm Environment Institute Technical Report.

Barnes, D.L. & Dempsey, C.P. 1993. Grazing trials with sheep on kikuyu (*Pennisetum clandestinum* Chiov.) foggage in the eastern Transvaal highveld. *African Journal of Range and Forage Science,* **10**: 66–71.

Bartholomew, P.E. 2000. Establishment of pastures. *In:* N.M. Tainton (ed). *Pasture Management in South Africa.* Pietermaritzburg, South Africa: Natal University Press.

Bond, W.J. & van Wilgen, B. 1996. *Fire and Plants.* London, UK: Chapman and Hall.

Booysen, P. DeV. 1967. Grazing and grazing management terminology in southern Africa. *Proceedings of the Grassland Society of Southern Africa*, **2**: 45–57

Booysen, P. DeV. 1969. An evaluation of the fundamentals of grazing management systems. *Proceedings of the Grassland Society of Southern Africa*, **4**: 84–91

Coe, M.J., Cumming, D.M. & Phillipson, J. 1976. Biomass production of large African herbivores in relation to rainfall and primary production. *Oecologia*, **22**: 341–354.

Cowling, R.M. & Hilton-Taylor, C. 1997. Plant biogeography, endemism and diversity. pp. 42–56, *in:* Dean and Milton, 1999, q.v.

Cowling, R.M., Richardson, D.M. & Pierce, S.M. (eds). 1997. *Vegetation of South Africa*. Cambridge, UK: Cambridge University Press.

Danckwerts, J.E. & Teague, W.R. 1989. *Veld management in the Eastern Cape*. Government Printer, Pretoria, South Africa.

Davies, W. 1968. Pasture problems in South Africa. *Proceedings of the Grassland Society of Southern Africa*, **3**: 135–140.

Dean, W.R.J. & Macdonald, I.A.W. 1994. Historical changes in stocking rates of domestic livestock as a measure of semi-arid and arid rangeland degradation in the Cape Province, South Africa. *Journal of Arid Environments*, **26**: 281–298.

Dean, W.R.J. & Milton, S.J. (eds). 1999. *The karoo. Ecological patterns and processes*. Cambridge, UK: Cambridge University Press.

Dent, M., Lynch, S.D. & Schulze, R.E. 1987. *Mapping mean annual and other rainfall statistics over southern Africa*. Water Research Commission., Pretoria, South Africa. Report No. 109/1/89

Department of Agriculture [South Africa]. 1951. *Pasture research in South Africa. Progress Report*. Division of Agricultural Education & Extension, Pretoria, South Africa.

Development Bank of Southern Africa. 1991. *Annual Report*. DBSA, Midrand, South Africa.

Du Toit, P.F. 1967. Bush encroachment with specific reference to *Acacia karroo* encroachment. *Proceedings of the Grassland Society of Southern Africa*, **2**: 119–126.

Ellery, W.N., Scholes, R.J. & Scholes, M.C. 1995. The distribution of sweetveld and sourveld in South Africa's grassland biome in relation to environmental factors. *African Journal of Range and Forage Science*, **12**: 38–45.

Ellis, J.E. & Swift, D.M. 1988. Stability of African pastoral ecosystems: alternate paradigms and implications for development. *Journal of Range Management*, **41**: 450–459.

FAO. 1973. Soil map of the world. Paris, France: UNESCO.

FAO. 2001. Data downloaded from FAOSTAT, the FAO online statistical database. FAO Rome, Italy. See: http://faostat.fao.org

Grossman, D., Holden, P.L. & Collinson, R.F.H. 1999. Veld management on the game ranch. *In:* N.M. Tainton (ed). *Veld Management in South Africa.* Pietermaritzburg, South Africa: University of Natal Press.

Hanson, J.D., Baker, B.B. & Bourdon, R.M. 1994. *SPUR2. Documentation and user guide.* GPSR [Great Plains System Research] Technical Report, No. 1. Fort Collins, Colorado, USA.

Henderson, L. 2001. Alien weeds and invasive plants. Plant Protection Research Institute Handbook, No. 12. Plant Protection Research Institute, Pretoria, South Africa.

Hoffman, M.T. 1997. *Human impacts on vegetation.* pp. 507–534, *in:* Cowling, Richardson & Pierce, 1997. q.v.

Hoffman, M.T. & O'Connor, T.G. 1999. Vegetation change over 40 years in the Weene/Muden area, KwaZulu-Natal: evidence from photo-panoramas. *African Journal of Range & Forage Science,* **16:** 71–88.

Hoffman, M.T. & Ashwell, A. 2001. *Nature divided. Land degradation in South Africa.* Cape Town, South Africa: University of Cape Town Press.

Le Houérou, H.N. 1984. Rain use efficiency: a unifying concept in land use ecology. *Journal of Arid Environments,* **7:** 213–247.

Le Houérou, H.N., Bingham, R.L. & Skerbek, W. 1988. Relationship between the variability of primary production and variability of annual precipitation in world arid lands. *Journal of Arid Environments,* **15:** 1–18.

Low, A.B. & Rebelo, A.G. 1996. *Vegetation of South Africa, Lesotho and Swaziland.* Pretoria, South Africa: Department of Environmental Affairs and Tourism.

Ludwig, J., Tongway, D., Freudenberger, D., Noble, J. & Hodgkinson, K. 1997. *Landscape Ecology. Function and Management. Principles from Australia's Rangelands.* CSIRO, Canberra, Australia. 158 p.

Lutge, B.U., Hardy, M.B. & Hatch, G.P. 1996. Plant and sward response to patch grazing in the Highland Sourveld. *African Journal of Range and Forage Science,* **13:** 94–99.

Maclean, G.L. 1993. *Roberts' Birds of southern Africa.* 6th ed. Cape Town, South Africa: John Voelcker Bird Book Fund.

National Botanical Institute. 2004. *Vegetation Map of South Africa, Lesotho and Swaziland.* Beta Version 4.0. National Botanical Institute, Cape Town, South Africa.

National Department of Agriculture. 1995. *White Paper on Agriculture.* Government Printer, Pretoria, South Africa.

National Department of Agriculture and Land Affairs. 1999. *Annual Report.*

National Department of Agriculture and Land Affairs. 2001. *Annual Report.*

O'Connor, T.G. & Bredenkamp, G.J. 1997. Grassland. *In:* Cowling, Richardson & Pierce, 1997, q.v.

Palmer, A.R. 1998. *Grazing Capacity Information System (GCIS). Instruction Manual.* ARC-Range & Forage Institute, Grahamstown, South Africa.

Palmer, A.R., Ainslie, A.M. & Hoffman, M.T. 1999. Sustainability of commercial and communal rangeland systems in southern Africa. pp. 1020–1022, *in: Proceedings of the 6th International Rangeland Congress*. 17–23 July 1999, Townsville, Australia.

Palmer, A.R., Novellie, P.A. & Lloyd, J.W. 1999. Community patterns and dynamics. pp. 208–223, *in:* Dean & Milton, 1999. q.v.

Palmer, A.R., Killer, F.J., Avis, A.M. & Tongway, D. 2001. Defining function in rangelands of the Peddie District, Eastern Cape, using Landscape Function Analysis. *African Journal of Range & Forage Science*, **18**: 53–58.

Partridge, T.C. 1997. Evolution of landscapes. pp. 5–20, *In:* Cowling, Richardson & Pierce, 1997, q.v.

Rethman, N.F.G. & Gouws, C.I. 1973. Foggage value of Kikuyu (*Pennisetum clandestinum* Hochst, ex Chiov.). *Proceedings of the Grassland Society of Southern Africa*, **8**: 101–105.

Rutherford, M.C. 1982. Above-ground biomass categories of the woody plants in the *Burkea africana-Ochna pulchra* savanna. *Bothalia*, **14**: 131–138.

Rutherford, M.C. & Westfall, R.H. 1986. The Biomes of Southern Africa – an objective categorization. *Memoirs of the Botanical Survey of South Africa*, **54**: 1–98.

Savory, A. 1988. *Holistic Resource Management*. Covelo, California, USA: Island Press.

Shackleton, C.M. 1991. Seasonal changes in above-ground standing crop in three coastal grassland communities in Transkei. *Journal of the Grassland Society of Southern Africa*, **8**: 22–28.

Schulze, R.E. 1997. *South African Atlas of Agrohydrology and -climatology*. Water Research Commission, Pretoria, South Africa. Report TT82/96.

Smithers, R.H.N. 1983. *The mammals of the southern African subregion*. Pretoria, South Africa: University of Pretoria.

Stats SA. 1996. *The People of South Africa. Population Census 1996*. National Census. South African Statistical Services.

Stuart-Hill, G.C. & Aucamp, A.J. 1993. Carrying capacity of the succulent valley bushveld of the eastern Cape. *African Journal of Range and Forage Science*, **10**: 1–10.

Tainton, N.M. (ed). 1999. *Veld management in South Africa*. University of Natal Press, Pietermaritzburg, South Africa. 472pp.

Tainton, N.M. (ed). 2000. *Pasture management in South Africa*. University of Natal Press, Pietermaritzburg, South Africa. 355pp.

Tainton, N.M., Aucamp A. J. & Danckwerts J. E. 1999. Principles of managing veld. Grazing programmes. pp. 169–180, *in:* Tainton, N.M. (ed). *Veld management in South Africa*. Pietermaritzburg, South Africa: University of Natal Press,.

Tanser, F.C. & Palmer, A.R. 1999. The application of a remotely-sensed diversity index to monitor degradation patterns in a semi-arid, heterogeneous, South African landscape. *Journal of Arid Environments*, **43**(4): 477–484.

Thackeray, A.I., Deacon, J., Hall, S., Humphreys, A.J.B., Morris, A.G., Malherbe, V.C. & Catchpole, R.M. 1990. *The early history of southern Africa to AD 1500*. Cape Town, South Africa: The South African Archaeological Society.

Trollope, W.S.W. 1980. Controlling bush encroachment with fire in the savanna areas of South Africa. *Proceedings of the Grassland Society of Southern Africa,* **15**: 173–177.

Wight, J.R. & Skiles, J.W. (eds). 1987. *SPUR: Simulation of production and utilization of rangelands.* Documentation and user guide. US Department of Agriculture, Agricultural Research Service, ARS 63. 372 p.

Van Rooyen, A.F. 2000. *Rangeland degradation in the southern Kalahari.* Unpublished PhD thesis. Department of Range and Forage Science, University of Natal, Pietermaritzburg, South Africa.

Volman, T.P. 1984. Early prehistory of southern Africa. pp. 169–220, *in:* R.G. Klein (ed). *Southern African Prehistory and Palaeoenvironments.* Rotterdam, The Netherlands: AA Balkema.

Vorster, M. 1999. Veld condition assessment. *In:* Tainton, 1999. q.v.

Zacharias, P.J.K., Clayton, J. & Tainton, N.M. 1991. *Leucaena leucocephala* as a quality supplement to *Pennisetum clandestinum* foggage: A preliminary study. *Journal of the Grassland Society of Southern Africa,* **8**: 59–62.

Chapter 4
Grasslands of Patagonia

Andrés F. Cibils and Pablo R. Borrelli

A.F. CIBILS

SUMMARY

Patagonia lies between 39° and 55°S, partly in Chile but mainly in Argentina; its extra-Andean portion is treeless semi-arid grass and shrub steppes that have been grazed by domestic livestock for a little over a century. The climate is arid to semi-arid, and cool to cold, with mean temperatures decreasing from 15.9°C in the north to 5.4°C in the south. Extra-Andean Patagonia is an area of semi-arid grass and shrub steppes; vegetation is characterized by xerophytes. Guanacos are the only large native ungulate herbivore and the region has evolved under light grazing pressure. Most vegetation has been seriously modified by sheep, particularly in the past 40–50 years, with palatable grasses being replaced by unpalatable woody plants. Private property is the main land tenure form. Human habitation probably began about 10 000 years BP, but European settlement began at the end of the nineteenth century, with commercial sheep farming. Aboriginal peoples were hunter-gatherers; private property limited their opportunity for migratory hunting. The success of early settlers encouraged more immigrants, who occupied progressively drier areas, until 1940. Sheep numbers peaked in 1952, at over 21 million head, and have since fallen to 8.5 million head. Cattle, kept at higher elevations near the Andes, are the next largest stock; herds have increased over the past 50 years. Horses and goats have decreased less dramatically than sheep. Sheep farming is almost a monoculture in the steppes. There are three kinds of farm: Large Commercial, with flocks of more than 6 000; Small and Medium farms in the drier areas, with 1 000 to 6 000 head; and Subsistence, with fewer than 1 000 sheep. Paddocks are grazed continuously, except for the high elevation (summer) ranges. Vast areas, with few paddocks, restrict the potential for controlling grazing. Guidelines for pasture management began in the 1980s, but much work has been done since on soil-plant-animal relations. Since areas are vast, Decision Support Systems (DSS) are a new frontier for range management. Development of agrotourism on sheep farms is incipient, mostly in the Andes.

INTRODUCTION

The vast area of southern Argentina and Chile between latitudes 39° and 55°S is referred to as Patagonia (Figure 4.1). Almost all of Patagonia's grazing lands are on the cool semi-arid steppes of the extra-Andean territory of southern Argentina (approximately 750 000 km²), extending into Chile around the Straits of Magellan (Paruelo, Jobbágy and Sala, 1998b; Villamil, 1997) – see Figure 4.2.

This chapter refers mainly to extra-Andean Argentinian Patagonia, an area of treeless semi-arid grass and shrub steppes that has been grazed by domestic ungulates for over a century.

Patagonia is mostly made up of sedimentary landscapes that blend with volcanic deposits from the Mesozoic and Tertiary eras, unfolding as a series of plateaus that lose elevation eastward from the Andes (Soriano, 1983). The Patagonian mesa landscape is interrupted by a series of rivers that flow from the Andes to the Atlantic, such as the Colorado, Negro, Chubut, Chico, Santa Cruz and Coyle. Irrigated floodplains in some valleys have allowed the development of agricultural oases (Table 4.1).

TABLE 4.1
Biozones of Patagonia grouped according to phytogeographical province.

Phytogeographical province	Biozone code[1]	Dominant physiognomic type	Area (km²)
Patagonia	Kg 11	Semi-deserts 1	95 400
	Kf 11	Semi-deserts 2	68 800
	Jg 11	Patagonian shrub steppes	134 800
	Jf 11	Shrub-grass steppes	99 900
	Jd 12	Grass-shrub steppes	43 600
	Id 12	Grass steppes	48 600
Monte	Hg 11	Scrub lands	48 300
	Jh 11	Monte shrub steppes 2	134 500
	Ig 4	Monte shrub steppes 1	54 400
Subantarctic	Ha 12	Ecotone forest-steppes and mesic grasslands	52 400
	Ea 2	Closed deciduous forests	69 100
Agro-ecosystems	Gd 12	Irrigated valleys	22 600

NOTES: (1) Biozone codes are those of Paruelo, Jobbágy and Sala, 1998.
SOURCE: Paruelo, Jobbágy and Sala, 1998. Reproduced by permission of authors and editors of *Ecología Austral*.

Figure 4.1
Extent of grasslands in Latin America.

Description of Patagonia's climate is hampered by the low density and very uneven distribution of weather stations (40 000 km²/station) (Paruelo *et al.*, 1998). Climate is influenced mostly by Pacific Ocean air masses forced inland by prevailing westerlies, across ocean currents that are warmer than the land masses and move towards the equator (MacArthur, 1972). The Andes

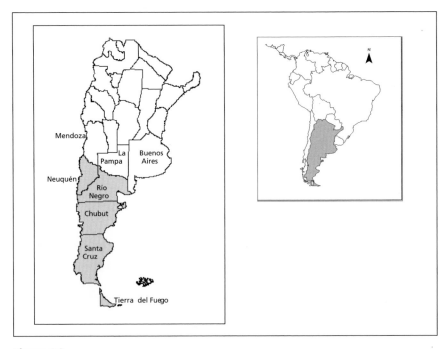

Figure 4.2
A map of the provinces of Argentinian Patagonia (shaded area) and neighbouring provinces (Digital Cartography by Ing. Ag. Liliana González).

stand between the moist air and the Patagonian steppes, creating an extensive rain-shadow that controls climatic patterns (Paruelo *et al.*, 1998). There is a very steep gradient of mean annual precipitation (MAP), decreasing towards the east, from 4 000 mm at the Andes eastern foothills (at about 42°S) down to 150 mm in the central plateau 180 km east of the mountains (Soriano, 1983). Inter-annual variation in precipitation increases exponentially with decreasing rainfall, reaching coefficients of variation greater than 45 percent at the drier end of the gradient (Jobággy, Paruelo and León, 1995). The east coast is influenced by moist air from the Atlantic, with somewhat higher annual precipitation (200 to 220 mm) evenly distributed, as opposed to the winter rainfall of most of Patagonia (Paruelo *et al.*, 1998; Soriano, 1983). The ratio of mean annual precipitation to potential evapotranspiration (MAP/PET ratio) of the steppes fluctuates between 0.45 and 0.11, with marked deficits in spring and summer (Paruelo *et al.*, 1998). Water is the most important factor regulating primary production. Some of the variation can be associated with El Niño-La Niña cycles (Paruelo *et al.*, 1998), but Cibils and Coughenour (2001) reported a longer-term cycle for MAP in southern Patagonia: a significant decrease in precipitation from 1930 to 1960 and a reversal of this trend (significant increase) over the subsequent thirty years in Río Gallegos.

Mean annual temperatures range from 15.9°C in the north (Cippoletti) to 5.4°C in the far south of Tierra del Fuego (Ushuaia) (Soriano, 1983). Mean temperatures of the coldest month (July) are above the frost mark, although absolute minimum temperatures can be below -20°C (Paruelo *et al.*, 1998). Cibils and Coughenour (2001) reported a significant increase in mean annual temperatures over the last 60 years of the twentieth century for Río Gallegos, a town with one of the longest weather records, on the steppes surrounding the Straits of Magellan. This trend is consistent with predictions of climate change from Global Circulation Models simulating enhanced atmospheric CO_2 concentration (Hulme and Sheard, 1999), but conclusions from weather station data analysis are still preliminary.

Strong, persistent westerly winds are an outstanding characteristic of Patagonia's climate. Because there is relatively little land in the Southern Hemisphere, westerlies between 40°S and 50°S gain impressive momentum, with annual intensities of between 15 and 22 km/h and frequent gusts of over 100 km/h, mostly in spring and summer (MacArthur, 1972; Paruelo *et al.*, 1998; Soriano, 1983). Strong winds increase evaporation and can have a considerable influence on sheep performance through chill (Borrelli, unpublished data; Soriano, 1983).

Over half of Patagonia's soils are Aridisols (desert soils), with Entisols (soils with little development) and Mollisols (dark coloured, base-rich steppe soils), respectively, as the second and third most important types (del Valle, 1998). Over 70 percent of topsoil is coarse-textured, ranging from sand to sandy-loam (del Valle, 1998). Soil textures can explain a large portion of the variation in dominant plant life form (grasses vs shrubs) across the region (Noy-Meir, 1973; Sala, Lauenroth and Golluscio, 1997). Small-scale spatial heterogeneity of soils tends to increase with aridity (Ares *et al.*, 1990); important differences in leaching and salinity occur over short distances, possibly causing soils within a taxonomic group to function differently (del Valle, 1998, and references therein). Over 90 percent of Patagonian soils are degraded to some degree, mostly because of improper land use; severe desertification affects 19 to 30 percent of the region (del Valle, 1998). Some of the most dramatic erosion processes occur in the form of sand macro-accumulations that, in the early 1970s, covered approximately 85 000 km² (Soriano, 1983). Both aerial photography and satellite imagery indicate that many of these accumulations are about 100 years old, suggesting that the rate of wind-driven erosion has been accelerated by the introduction of domestic livestock (Soriano, 1983).

Archaeological records from caves suggest that human occupation began around 11 000 BP (Borrero and McEwan, 1997). Native peoples were hunter-gatherers, although there are indications of limited agricultural activity in the north (Villamil, 1997). Bifacial stone weapons suggest that people of south Patagonia hunted guanaco (*Lama guanicoe*). The *Mapuche* tribe occupied the northern reaches, the *Tehuelches* the southern mainland, and the *Selknam*,

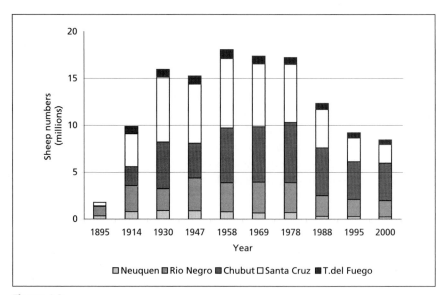

Figure 4.3
Sheep population by province in Argentinian Patagonia.
Source: SAGPyA, 2001.

Plate 4.1
Merino flock in Patagonia.

Haush and *Yámana* tribes occupied Tierra del Fuego and surrounding islands (McEwan, Borrero and Prieto, 1997, and references therein). European contact with natives began early in the sixteenth century; it is thought that conquerors named the natives after Patagón, a fantastical character of the Spanish chivalric tale *Primaleón* (Duviols, 1997: 129-130). European settlement only began at the end of the nineteenth century, mostly from Spain and the British Isles, or companies that established sheep farms (Barbería, 1995).

There are currently over 12 000 sheep farms (family or company owned) in Patagonia, with flocks ranging from less than 1 000 to over 90 000 head (Méndez Casariego, 2000). According to the latest on-farm population census (1988) there were 75 000 people on sheep farms and irrigated valley farms. From the 1970s to present, the rural population increased in Río Negro (+44%) and Tierra del Fuego (+132%), remained fairly stable in Neuquén, and decreased in Chubut (-33%) and Santa Cruz (-44%) (Méndez Casariego, 2000). Over the same period, the on-farm population increased in Neuquén (+51%) and Río Negro (+5%) and decreased in Chubut (-28%), Santa Cruz (-41%) and Tierra del Fuego (-26%) (Méndez Casariego, 2000).

Patagonia's grasslands have only been grazed by sheep for just over a century. Sheep numbers peaked in 1952, at over 21 million, and since then numbers have been slowly shrinking, to about 8.5 million in 1999 (Méndez Casariego, 2000) (Figure 4.3). Ranchers raise unherded Merino (Plate 4.1) or Corriedale flocks in continuously-grazed large pastures, usually for wool (Soriano, 1983). Wool production is fairly insensitive to forage scarcity associated with high stocking-rates or drought, so several authors have blamed present day land degradation on the wool-oriented operations (Borrelli *et al.,* 1997; Golluscio, Deregibus and Paruelo, 1998; Covacevich, Concha and Carter, 2000). Cattle have increased steadily over the last 50 years (Méndez Casariego, 2000) and although present numbers (836 000) are more than double those of 1952, this does not compensate for the decrease in sheep (Méndez Casariego, 2000). The numbers of horses and goats have decreased considerably, but not as dramatically as sheep. The most recent figures (1999) indicate that there are 180 000 horses and 827 000 goats – roughly half of the previous peak populations (Méndez Casariego, 2000). Goat farming is mainly in the north, such as Neuquén province, where numbers have remained fairly constant in spite of the general negative tendency (Méndez Casariego, 2000).

Guanacos are the only large native ungulate (Soriano, 1983) and although the region has generally been considered to have evolved under light grazing pressure (Milchunas, Sala and Lauenroth, 1988), pre-European numbers of guanacos may have been higher than previously thought (Lauenroth, 1998); recent counts show populations are fairly stable at approximately 500 000 (Amaya *et al.*, 2001). The native vertebrate fauna is poor (Soriano, 1983). The lesser rhea (*Pterocnemia pennata pennata*) and the upland goose (*Cloephaga picta*) are the most conspicuous birds. The Patagonian hare (*Dolichotis patagonum*) and the small armadillo (*Zaedyus pichyi*), together with the lesser rheas, are important zoogeographical indicators (Soriano, 1983). There are significant numbers of predators, such as red foxes (*Dusicyon culpaeus*), grey foxes (*Ducisyon griseus*), pumas (*Felis concolor*) and skunks (*Conepatus humboldtii*) (Soriano, 1983). Red foxes and pumas are responsible for most predation, and lamb losses due to red fox predation can be as high as 75 to 80 percent (Manero, 2001).

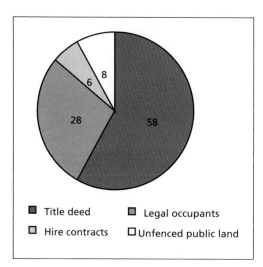

Figure 4.4
*Land tenure regimes in
Argentinian Patagonia*
(Source: Adapted from Peralta, 1999)

POLITICAL SYSTEM

Argentinian Patagonia has five provinces: Neuquén, Río Negro, Chubut, Santa Cruz and Tierra del Fuego (Figure 4.2). Parts of other provinces, such as Buenos Aires, La Pampa and Mendoza, are in the Patagonian environment. As a Federal Republic, each province of Argentina has an elected government. A Governor, the executive, is elected every four years. Each province has a Constitution, Legislative Power and an independent Judicial Power. Argentinian Patagonian provinces are relatively new because most of them were national territories until after the Second World War; national territories depended entirely on the central government in Buenos Aires. Irruption of dictatorships in Argentina between 1966 and 1983 prevented the exercise of democracy, so Patagonian provinces are young democratic states, in which political forces and institutions are beginning to organize and evolve.

LAND TENURE

Private property is the most important land tenure form, as shown in Figure 4.4 (Peralta, 1999). Permanent title deeds predominate, but legal occupation is also significant. Unfenced public lands comprise a small percentage of farms, and are locally important in Neuquén. Land tenure variation is related to the colonization process, which is summarized below.

Aboriginal distribution

There were many ethnic groups prior to colonization. Mapuches lived in the northwest, Tehuelches lived on most of the continental part of the steppe, and Onas lived on the steppes of Tierra del Fuego. All of these were "terrestrial cultures" (Borrero, 1997). Tehuelches and Onas were migratory hunters. There were also "canoe cultures" on the coasts of the Beagle Channel in Tierra del Fuego, which were reduced, absorbed or exterminated by Europeans (Martinic, 1997). Tehuelches were severely reduced and absorbed by European colonization. Fences and the concept of private property limited the opportunity for migratory hunting. As Martinic (1997) pointed out, "cultural exchange was unidirectional, from the colonists to the Indians, which affected the latter's hunting and fishing tools and customs, relationship with natural resources, social behaviour, health and very survival as people". Survivors mostly became farm employees and in a few generations had lost most of their language and culture. There are a few reservations suitable for raising sheep and horses where Tehuelche descendants subsist.

The Mapuches were better able to maintain their culture and survive under conditions imposed by colonizing groups, and their descendants live in Neuquén, western Río Negro and northwest Chubut. More than 3 000 family groups live on public pastures raising goats and sheep (Casas, 1999). Some families have fenced or demarcated individual grazing lands, which they run as legal occupants. Many others graze on common lands, where transhumance is still practiced, from low winter ranges (*invernadas*) to high summer ranges (*veranadas*) (Casas, 1999).

Welsh colonization

In 1866 a colony of Welsh immigrants established themselves in the lower valley of the Río Chubut, close to the Atlantic coast (Mainwaring, 1983); the settlers had enormous difficulty in surviving. They made little progress until 1885, when several horsemen rode west and settled as sheep farmers in the Andes foothills. The colony did not prosper until settlers managed to develop irrigation and learn basic farming skills (Mainwaring, 1983).

First settlers

The first sheep farmers arrived in 1885 (Barbería, 1995). The government in Buenos Aires granted land concessions to settlers. After a visit of Governor Moyano to the Falkland Islands, colonization started on the most suitable land for sheep, i.e. grass steppes close to the Andes foothills and in southern Santa Cruz and northern Tierra del Fuego (Lafuente, 1981). By 1908, families and large companies occupied the most productive land. Settlers were mainly Spanish, Scottish, English, German and French. By the end of land concessions, settlers had obtained private title to their lands (Lafuente, 1981; Barbería, 1995)

Last settlers

The success of the first settlers encouraged new waves of immigrants, who occupied prtogressively drier areas until 1940, by when Patagonia was fully colonized (Barbería, 1995). In 1908, national legislation prevented liberal distribution of remaining public range (Lafuente, 1981). In an attempt to restrict the amount of land purchased by an individual, Patagonia was divided into equal-sized blocks that were assigned to settlers without considering carrying capacity (Barbería, 1985), so most settlers received a limited amount of relatively unproductive land, which thereafter was subject to high grazing pressure. Most farms are now privately owned, under legal occupation or with permanent title (Casas, 1999).

Management authorities

The responsibility of provincial government to ensure sustainable management of natural resources is recognized in Provincial Constitutions, which were mostly amended in the 1990s and clearly define this role, but legislation is either weak or not enforced. By the end of the 1980s, "desertification" was well established as a subject of discussion, but sustainable use policies have still not been achieved. There is lack of institutional development for natural resources administration at provincial and national levels (Consorcio DHV, 1999). The federal Department of Sustainable Development and Environmental Policy, which is responsible for national policies on sustainable management, carries out planning, coordination and training. A National Plan for Desertification Control was formulated in 1998, but has not been implemented due to funding constraints.

MARKET SYSTEMS
Wool market systems

Patagonian wool is mainly exported; domestic consumption is less than 10 percent of greasy wool produced. Wool is mainly exported as tops and scoured wool. China, Italy, Germany and France have been the main customers (Argentine Wool Federation, 2001). Scouring and combing is done by multinational companies and some local industries in Trelew (Chubut), the main wool textile centre of Argentina. Sheep farms in northern and central Patagonia produce fine Merino wool, while farms in the south produce fine crossbred Corriedale-type wool (Argentine Wool Federation, 2001). Direct sales from farmers to wool processors and exporters predominate, but there are a few wool concentration and auction sale mechanisms (Peralta, 1999). In the 1980s, many wool cooperatives were created, but most collapsed due to financial problems and lack of managerial skills. Subsistence farmers with small quantities usually barter for basic goods with middlemen (Peralta, 1999).

In 1994, the government launched PROLANA, a joint wool quality programme with provincial governments, to improve shearing, handling, grading and packing, prevent contamination and improve wool appearance. By 2000, 37 percent of Patagonia's wool was processed under PROLANA procedures (SAGPyA, 2001). This Programme increased market transparency significantly by expanding farmer awareness regarding the characteristics and value of wool.

Meat marketing

Grassland-based systems produce about 10 500 tonne/year of high quality lamb and mutton (SAGPyA, 2001), which is natural, free from diseases and contaminants, with low fat content and a mild flavour, but the local markets are not sensitive to meat quality. Most lamb is exported to Europe (SAGPyA, 2001). Wool-oriented Merino farms have a low reproductive efficiency (less than 60 percent lambing) and produce few lambs. The meat production areas are southern Santa Cruz and northern Tierra del Fuego, where forage production is higher and Corriedale operations are oriented to lamb production (Borrelli *et al.,* 1997; Méndez Casariego, 2000).

Farmers sell to local abattoirs, which supply supermarkets and retail butchers. Overseas markets were historically the most important meat buyers (Lafuente, 1981). The progressive reduction in the number of animals for slaughter caused the collapse of large (mostly foreign) companies that had operated in the region from the beginning of the twentieth century. Most lamb was marketed locally during the 1990s (SAGPyA, 2001). Recently, a farmer-owned company began processing and exporting lamb from Santa Cruz. Many farmers in this project have organic certification that allows them to enter premium market niches.

DOMINANT NATURAL VEGETATION

Extra-Andean Patagonia is covered by treeless shrub and grass steppes that give way to dwarf-shrub semi-deserts in the drier areas of the central plateaus (Roig, 1998). Vegetation is characterized by the dominance of xerophytes, which have evolved remarkable adaptations to cope with severe water deficit (León *et al.,* 1998). Shrubs, for example, have either very small sclerophyllous leaves with abundant glandular hairs, or leaves with thick cuticles, and often dwarf cushion growth habits. Grasses commonly have leaves with a thick cuticle, convoluted laminae and bunch growth habits, with fairly large accumulations of dead biomass (León *et al.,* 1998). Blended in the steppe landscapes are small areas associated with rivers or permanent water sources, with more mesic plant communities comprising mostly grasses, sedges and rushes, referred to as riparian meadows (Golluscio, Deregibus and Paruelo, 1998; Roig, 1998), and, although they account for a very small proportion of the total area, they play a key role in livestock production and, in many instances, suffer most from the effects of bad land management (Golluscio, Deregibus and Paruelo, 1998).

Two phytogeographic provinces occupy all of arid and semi-arid Patagonia: the Patagonian phytogeographic province, and the Monte phytogeographic province (Cabrera, 1971). The latter occupies most of the arid west of Argentina; its southern tip enters Patagonia, occupying approximately the northern third of the region. The remaining two thirds of extra-Andean Patagonia correspond to the Patagonian phytogeographic province (Table 4.1) (Cabrera, 1971). Most classifications of natural vegetation types of have used either structural

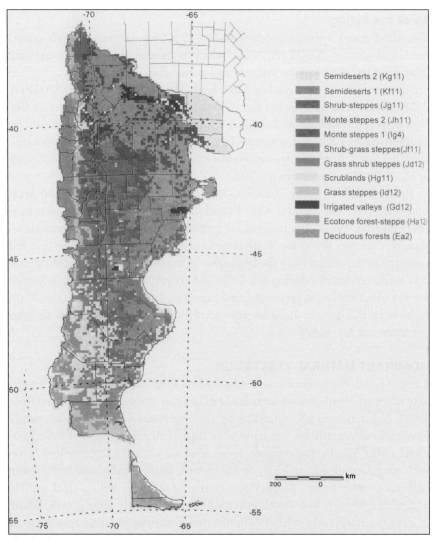

Figure 4.5
Biozones of Patagonia, from Paruelo, Jobággy and Sala (1998).
(Reproduced with permission of the authors and the editors of *Ecología Austral*)

(physiognomic) characteristics of dominant plant life-forms (Cabrera, 1971; Soriano, 1983; León *et al.,* 1998; Roig, 1998) or phytosociological approaches as the main grouping criteria (Collantes, Anchorena and Cingolani, 1999; Golluscio, León and Perelman, 1982; Boelcke, Moore and Roig, 1985). Recently, Paruelo, Jobbágy and Sala (1998b) classified the vegetation of the region on the basis of functional characteristics, using productivity-related indices derived from NOAA satellite imagery analysis (Figure 4.5 and Table 4.1). An advantage of this approach is that it provides a functional up-to-date classification of vegetation, reflecting the current state of rangelands,

V.A. DEREGIBUS & M.F. GARBULSKY

Plate 4.2
A typical Patagonian shrub steppe.

rather than the potential expected vegetation types typical of most structural classification maps. This section follows the grouping of biomes proposed by Paruelo *et al.* (1998), but endeavours to produce a synthesis of both structural and functional aspects of the vegetation of each biome.

Patagonian shrub steppes

This vegetation type (Unit Jg 11 in Figure 4.5) accounts for close to 20 percent of the semi-arid area (Paruelo, Jobbágy and Sala, 1998b) (Plate 4.2). Overall, the MAP of this area is below 200 mm; vegetation cover varies between 30 and 50 percent and annual above ground net primary productivity (ANPP) estimated from NDVI-I values (the annual integral of the Normalized Difference Vegetation Index) is 490 kg/ha/yr (León *et al.*, 1998; Paruelo, Jobbágy and Sala, 1998b). The physiognomy of this unit is that of a bi-layered shrubland: an upper layer of shrubs circa 100 cm high, and a lower layer made up of shrubs with crown heights that rarely exceed 15–20 cm (León *et al.*, 1998). The most conspicuous shrubs are *Chuquiraga avellanedae*, *Lycium ameghinoi*, *L. chilense*, *Verbena ligustrina*, *Prosopis denudans* and *Colliguaya integerrima* (León *et al.*, 1998; Roig, 1998). Grasses of the genera *Stipa*, *Festuca* and *Poa*, such as *Stipa neaei*, *S. speciosa*, *Festuca argentina* and *Poa ligularis*, occur as a sparse understorey (León *et al.*, 1998). Shrub steppes occur in transition areas between the grass steppes and the semi-deserts (Paruelo, Jobbágy and Sala, 1998b).

Semi-deserts and shrub steppes

Semi-deserts and shrub steppes (Units Kg 11 and Kf 11 in Figure 4.5) exhibit similar latitudinal extents; together, both variants of semi-desert cover 22 percent of the region, with plant communities of low diversity, including, on average, 19 plant species (Golluscio, León and Perelman, 1982). The MAP of much of the area is less than 150 mm. Patagonian semi-deserts are less productive than shrub steppes; ANPP calculated from NDVI-I values by Paruelo, Jobbágy and Sala (1998b) are 450 and 390 kg/ha/yr for units Kg 11 and Kf 11, respectively (Table 4.1). From a species composition standpoint, Kf 11 is the most typical and less degraded semi-desert type, in spite of being less productive (Soriano, 1983). Dwarf shrubs with cushion habits are typical of this vegetation type in the Kg 11 and Kf 11 units. *Nassauvia glomerulosa, N. ulicina* and *Chuquiraga aurea* are dominant, accompanied by others such as *Chuquiraga kingii, Brachyclados caespitosus* and *Perezia lanigera* (León *et al.*, 1998). Grasses such as *Stipa humilis, S. ibarii, S. ameghinoi* and shrubs such as *Chuquiraga avellanedae, Schinus polygamus* and *Lycium chilense* are secondary species in semi-desert plant communities. Some co-dominant species occur, but only in the Kg 11 semi-deserts: dwarf shrubs such as *Azorella caespitosa, Mullinum microphyllum* and *Frankenia* sp., grasses such as *Poa dusenii, P. ligularis* and, less frequently, *Stipa neaei,* and shrubs such as *Junellia tridens,* which occur in clumps on paleo-depressions and natural drainage networks (León *et al.*, 1998; Roig, 1998).

Shrub-grass and grass-shrub steppes

Shrub-grass and grass-shrub steppes span almost the entire latitudinal extent of Patagonia and cover approximately 20 percent of the arid area (Units Jf 11 and Jd 12 in Figure 4.5). According to Paruelo, Jobbágy and Sala (1998b), both types have similar ANPP levels (650 kg/ha/yr), although NDVI values peak somewhat later in the growing season in grass-shrub steppes. Vegetation cover of the shrub-grass steppes is 47 percent, with plant communities that contain about 26 vascular plant species (Golluscio, León and Perelman, 1982). *Adesmia campestris, Mullinum spinosum, Senecio filaginoides, Berberis heterophylla, Colleguaya integerrima, Trevoa patagonica* and *Schinus polygamus* are the most conspicuous shrubs (León *et al.*, 1998). The most important grasses are *Stipa speciosa, S. humilis, Poa ligularis, P. lanuginosa, Festuca argentina* and *F. pallescens,* and occur with sedges of the genus *Carex* (León *et al.*, 1998). Grass-shrub steppes are a transition between the shrub steppes and grass steppes on the one hand and the grass-steppes and the *Nothophagus* subantarctic forest ecotone on the other (Figure 4.5) (Roig, 1998). Paruelo, Jobbágy and Sala (1998b) combine the latter (*Chiliotrichum diffusum* grass-shrub steppes) and the steppe-forest ecotones in southern Santa Cruz and northern Tierra del Fuego into a single biozone (unit Ha 12). Physiognomically, these are different domains; they may exhibit similar functional attributes and should be significantly more productive than the grass-shrub steppes at the opposite end of the moisture gradient. Dominant species of the grass-shrub steppes are the same as those mentioned above, except for the shrubs *Junellia tridens, Nardophyllum obtusifolium, Berberis buxifolia* and *Chiliotrichum diffusum,* and the grasses *Stipa ibarii, Poa dusenii, Festuca pallescens, F. gracillima* and *F. pyrogea* (León *et al.,* 1998; Roig, 1998).

Grass steppes

Grass steppes (Unit Id 12 in Figure 4.5) also span the latitudinal extent of mainland Patagonia as a belt along the Andean foothills, that widens in the south, reaching the Atlantic Ocean, and giving way to the Magellanic steppes that occupy all of the area surrounding the Straits of Magellan, on the mainland and the northern tip of Tierra del Fuego (Figure 4.5) (Paruelo, Jobbágy and Sala, 1998; Cibils and Coughenour, 2001). This vegetation unit occurs in areas where MAP exceeds 250 mm. Average ANPP is about 900 kg/ha/yr according to NDVI-I-derived estimates reported by Paruelo, Jobbágy and Sala (1998). There are about 34 and 40 plant species in the sub-Andean and Magellanic steppes, respectively (Golluscio, León and Perelman, 1982; Boelcke, Moore and Roig, 1985). Vegetation cover is about 65 percent on sub-Andean grass steppes, where *Festuca pallescens* accounts for up to 70 percent of plant cover and occurs along with *F. magellanica, F. pyrogea, Deschampsia elegantula, D. flexuosa, Phleum commutatum, Elymus patagonicus* and *Rytidosperma virescens* (León *et al.,* 1998). Magellanic steppes exhibit two main variants: dry steppes on the eastern portion of the mainland, and mesic grasslands in the west and southeast of the mainland and the northern region of Tierra del Fuego, where MAP exceeds 350 mm. Vegetation cover ranges from 60 to over 80 percent; the dominant plant on both variants of the Magellanic steppe is *Festuca gracillima,* a 25-cm-tall tussock-forming bunchgrass that is the most conspicuous life form of this ecosystem (Boelcke, Moore and Roig., 1985; Collantes, Anchorena and Cingolani, 1999). Other grass and grass-like species are associated with the tussocks, such as *Poa dusenii, P. poecila, Rytidosperma virescens, Bromus setifolius, Deschampsia flexuosa, Agropyron magellanicum, Festuca magellanica, Agrostis tenuis, Carex andina, C. argentina,* among others (Boelcke, Moore and Roig, 1985). *Empetrum rubrum*-dominated communities occur as heathland blended in the grass steppes on south-facing slopes of moraine hills on moister Magellanic steppes (Collantes, Anchorena and Cingolani, 1999).

Monte shrublands and Monte ecotone

A third of semi-arid Patagonia is taken up by Monte vegetation units (Units Jh 11, Ig 4 and Hg 11 in Figure 4.5) (Plate 4.3), exhibiting ANPP levels ranging from 650 to 730 kg/ha/yr (Paruelo, Jobbágy and Sala, 1998b). Hg 11 scrubland is the most productive and is an ecotone between the Monte and Espinal phytogeographic provinces (Cabrera, 1971; Paruelo, Jobbágy and Sala,

V.A. DEREGIBUS & M.F. GARBULSKY

Plate 4.3
A shrub steppe in the Monte.

1998b). Rainfall rarely exceeds 200 mm and tends to be evenly distributed throughout the year (León *et al.,* 1998; Paruelo, Jobbágy and Sala, 1998b). The most conspicuous plant of these biomes is *Larrea divaricata,* which occurs with *L. cuneifolia* and *L. nitida* and other shrubs such as *Prosopis alpataco* and *P. flexuosa* and species of *Lycium, Chuquiraga, Ephedra* and *Atriplex.* Grasses such as *Stipa tenuis, S. speciosa, S. neaei, Poa ligularis* and *P. lanuginosa* make up the herbaceous stratum (León *et al.,* 1998). For a description of units corresponding to subantarctic forests and forest ecotones, see Veblen, Hill and Read (1996) and references therein.

PASTORAL AND AGRICULTURAL SYSTEMS

Sheep farming is almost a monoculture in the arid and semi-arid steppes (see Plates 4.4 and 4.5). Intensive agricultural activities such as fruit and horticultural crops are important in a few irrigated valleys, but are almost absent on sheep farms (Borrelli *et al.,* 1997). Cattle production has become important on mountain ranges near the Andes, where sheep farming is more difficult due to the presence of forests, steep landscapes and losses to predators. There has been an important substitution of sheep for cattle in the Monte region. Agrotourism activities on sheep farms are developing, mostly in the Andes, where there are scenic lakes, mountains and glaciers (Borrelli *et al.,* 1997; Méndez Casariego, 2000).

PABLO BORELLI

Plate 4.4
Sheep being driven up to summer range paddocks in the Magellan Steppe.

PABLO BORELLI

Plate 4.5
Gauchos herding a Corriedale flock on bunchgrass rangelands in southwestern Patagonia.

Sheep farming is extensive; each farm has, on average, three to four 5 000-ha fenced paddocks. No supplementary feeding is used. On-farm hay or silage production is insignificant and off-farm feeds are too expensive. Animals graze freely in large areas and are never housed, in spite of periodic severe winters. There is significant mortality during big snow falls (Sturzenbaum and Borrelli,

2001). Sheep are gathered three or four times each year. Drinking water comes from springs and lagoons, rivers, artificial ponds and windmill-pumped groundwater.

Patagonia is free of Bovine Spongiform Encephalopathy (BSE disease) and Foot-and-Mouth Disease (FMD) (Robles and Olaechea, 2001). Environmental conditions constrain the development of internal parasites and anthelmintics are often not necessary (Iglesias, Tapia and Alegre, 1992); no antibiotics or hormonal treatments are used. Patagonian farms supply wool and meat that can naturally reach the highest standards of quality in terms of food safety and lack of contaminants. Despite this, sheep stocks have declined continuously since the 1980s (Figure 4.4) and, under current conditions, sheep farming is unsustainable, whether in economic, ecological or social terms (Noy-Meir, 1995; Borrelli and Oliva, 1999; Pickup and Stafford-Smith, 1993). Factors contributing to this are low wool prices, small farm size, poor adoption of available technology, desertification, high winter losses, predator losses, high farmer indebtedness and lack of sustainable development policies (Borrelli *et al.*, 1997; Consorcio DHV, 1999).

Sheep farming systems

Conditions and attributes of sheep farming in Patagonia are quite heterogeneous, in spite of the general characteristics summarized above. The main sources of variation are:

- rain and temperature gradients, which form twelve biomes that differ in rangeland vegetation, primary and secondary productivity and potential for rangeland improvement (as discussed in the natural vegetation section, above); and
- farm size, as the sustainable number of sheep that can be kept on a farm depends on the area for grazing and its carrying capacity. Because sheep products are the only source of income, flock size determines farm income.

Three kinds of farms can be recognized (Table 4.2): (1) Large commercial farms, with more than 6 000 head and which are usually derived from the first

TABLE 4.2.
Farm distribution by size in Argentinian Patagonia.

Province	Criterion	Subsistence farms	Small to medium units	Big compani
Chubut	By no. of farms:	52%	43%	5%
	By no. of sheep:	8%	61%	31%
Neuquén	By no. of farms:	89%	9%	2%
	By no. of sheep:	20%	44%	36%
Río Negro	By no. of farms:	69%	30%	1%
	By no. of sheep	20%	64%	16%
Santa Cruz	By no. of farms:	16%	65%	6%
	By no. of sheep:	2%	49%	49%
Tierra del Fuego	By no. of farms:	–	37%	63%
	By no. of sheep:	–	10%	90%
Total Argentinian Patagonia	By no. of farms:	54%	40%	6%
	By no. of sheep:	8%	54%	38%

SOURCE: Data from Casas, 1999.

settlements and on the best pastures. (2) Small and medium commercial farms, in the drier areas, with flocks of 1 000 to 6 000; these have serious financial problems due to present wool prices. (3) Subsistence farms, with less than 1 000 sheep, mainly in northwestern Patagonia, which belong mostly to aboriginal families and graze on unfenced public lands.

More than half of sheep farmers in Patagonia are very poor and together own less than 10 percent of total sheep (Casas, 1999; Table 4.2). Most of the other half is limited by farm size, so at present net farm income does not satisfy their economic expectations. A few companies run sheep farms that can be considered economically viable. Company farms own approximately 40 percent of the sheep. There is a marked increasing north-south farm size gradient, beginning in the northwest (Neuquén), where subsistence farms are commonest, to Tierra del Fuego, where large company-owned farms are more frequent than in any other province (Table 4.2). The combination of biozone and farm size (which is related to the kind of farm operation) gives a wide range of pastoral systems, differing in terms of objectives, productivity and sustainability.

GRAZING MANAGEMENT

Farmers make grazing management decisions based on subjective criteria and previous experience (Golluscio *et al.*, 1999). Paddocks are grazed continuously (year-round), except on high altitude ranges grazed in summer (Borrelli and Oliva, 1999). Vast areas, with few paddocks, restrict the possibilities of controlling grazing, especially when paddocks include grazing sites with contrasting forage availability (e.g. meadows and arid steppes) (Golluscio *et al.*, 1999).

Determining stocking rates is the most important decision in developing a grazing plan (Heady and Child, 1994). The National Institute for Agricultural Technology (INTA), Argentina, with the aid of GTZ (Deutsche Gesellschaft für Technische Zusammenarbeit), developed range evaluation methods, based on satellite imagery and field measurements, which provide objective information for the formulation of sound grazing plans. Improved management is based on adaptive management that consists of a planning-execution-monitoring-evaluation cycle (Borrelli and Oliva, 1999).

Traditional management caused continuous overgrazing in most of the region, which in turn led to general degradation (Oliva, Rial and Borrelli, 1995; Consorcio DHV, 1999). Del Valle (1998) estimated that 65 percent of Patagonia was seriously degraded, 17 percent was moderately degraded and only 9 percent was lightly affected. In no area was grazing impact negligible. The DHV report estimated that 75 percent of Patagonian meadows were severely degraded (Consorcio DHV, 1999). A few small-scale farmers have adopted the recommended practices, with good results in terms of both animal production and rangeland conservation (Borrelli and Oliva, 1999).

SHEEP MANAGEMENT

Severe winters and the importance of spring forage growth relative to other seasons led to a farming pattern of autumn mating and spring lambing. Shearing was traditionally done between November and January, but with increasing pre-lambing shearing (due to gains in lamb and ewe survival and wool quality), dates have shifted to September-October. Tally Hi and Bowen shearing promoted by PROLANA (SAGPyA, 2001) are now widespread. Sheep are eye-shorn two or three times annually, and lamb tails are generally docked during marking. Male lambs are castrated and marked shortly before being shipped to the abattoir. Scabies (sarcoptic mange) is the commonest sheep disease (Robles and Olaechea, 2001) but its impact is limited to a few areas and so the use of veterinary products to treat it is almost unnecessary.

SHEEP BREEDS AND GENETIC IMPROVEMENT

There are two dominant sheep breeds: Merino and Corriedale. Each is used in production systems with different relative emphases on wool or lamb production.

Fine-wool production systems

Merino flocks predominate in the provinces of Neuquén, Río Negro, Chubut and northern Santa Cruz, comprising almost 75 percent of all sheep in Patagonia; their distribution closely matches the distribution of drier environments, where meat production is limited by nutritional constraints and farming is oriented to fine wool production (mean fibre diameter: 20.5 microns). On these farms, wool sales can represent up to 80 percent of total farm income (Méndez Casariego, 2000). Patagonian Merinos were selected from old Argentine Merino strains, improved by the introduction of Australian Merino, mainly in the past three decades. The Argentine Merino Breeder Association (AMBA) has implemented a genetic improvement programme, including progeny testing of rams, with INTA's technical support There are about 50 Merino studs with pedigree records and several open nucleus flocks, which are inspected by AMBA (Mueller, 2001).

Lamb and fine-crossbred-wool production systems

Grass steppe rangelands of southern Santa Cruz and northern Tierra del Fuego have higher forage production and are therefore more suitable for meat production. In this area, Corriedales introduced in the mid-twentieth century have been very successful. Local stud breeders provide superior rams to commercial farmers. A progeny testing service for top sire evaluation is being conducted under INTA-GTZ direction and funding. Many meat breeds (Texel, Southdown and Hampshire Down) are being introduced to improve lamb traits such as growth rate, low carcass fat and improved carcass conformation (Mueller, 2001).

TABLE 4.3.
Vegetation shifts under grazing in Patagonia.

Biozone	Vegetation transitions under grazing[1]		Reference
	From	To	
Semi-deserts	*Nassauvia glomerulosa* (forage dwarf shrub) + *Poa dusenii* (palatable grass)	*N. ulicina* (unpalatable dwarf shrub)	Bertiller, 1993a
Shrub-grass steppes	*Mullinum spinosum* (forage shrub) + *P. ligularis* (palatable grass)	*Senecio* sp. (unpalatable shrub) + *Stipa humilis* (unpalatable grass)	Bonvissuto *et al.*, 1993; Fernández and Paruelo, 1993
Grass-shrubs teppes	*Festuca pallescens* (palatable grass) + *M. spinosum* (forage shrub)	*Senecio filaginoides* (unpalatable shrub) + *M. spinosum* (forage shrub) + *Stipa* spp. (low palatability grasses)	Paruelo and Golluscio, 1993
Grass steppes	*F. pallescens* (palatable grass)	*F. pallescens* (palatable grass) + *M. spinosum* (forage shrub) + *Senecio* sp. (unpalatable shrub)	Bertiller and Defossé, 1993
	F. pallescens (palatable grass)	*Acaena* sp. (low palatability dwarf shrub)	Bertiller and Defossé, 1993
	F. gracillima (low palatability grass)	*Nassauvia* sp. (unpalatable dwarf shrub) + *Stipa* sp. (unpalatable grasses)	Oliva and Borrelli, 1993
Shrub steppes	*Schinus* sp. (palatable shrub) + *Prospidastrum* sp. (palatable shrub) + *Stipa tenuis* (palatable grass)	*Grindelia chiloensis* (unpalatable low shrub)	Nakamatsu *et al.*, 1993
	Chuquiraga avellanedae (low palatability shrub) + *Stipa tenuis* (palatable grass)	*Chuquiraga avellanedae* (low palatability shrub)	Rostagno, 1993

NOTES: (1) The order in which species appear is associated with their status in the plant community.
SOURCE: The table is a synthesis of state-and-transition catalogues developed for different biozones of Patagonia and compiled in Paruelo *et al.,* 1993.

EVOLUTION OF PATAGONIAN GRASSLANDS OVER THE LAST 40 YEARS

Patagonian vegetation is generally described as having few adaptations to cope with grazing by domestic ungulates, since the entire region is thought to have evolved under conditions of light grazing by native ungulates (Milchunas, Sala and Lauenroth, 1988). Although this notion has recently been challenged by Lauenroth (1998), there is general consensus that vegetation throughout most of Patagonia has been modified significantly by sheep over the last century, particularly in the last 40–50 years (Golluscio, Deregibus and Paruelo, 1998; Paruelo *et al.,* 1993).

Deterioration of grazed vegetation has usually been demonstrated by replacement of palatable grasses by unpalatable woody plants (Bertiller, 1993a). The severity of plant life-form replacements varies among biozones, depending on abiotic constraints within each ecosystem (Sala, Lauenroth and Golluscio, 1997; Perelman, León and Bussacca, 1997). The process of plant species replacement has been described for most of Patagonia's bio-zones following the conceptual model of "states-and-transitions" proposed by Westoby, Walker and Noy Meir (1989) for non-equilibrium rangeland ecosystems (Table 4.3). According to this model, plant communities shift between alternative steady states rather than progressing in a linear manner toward a predictable climax. Shifts in vegetation composition (transitions) are produced by particular combinations of biotic and abiotic stressors. In

Patagonia, transitions in the plant community are frequently close-to-irreversible and involve not only a reduction in forage biomass for livestock but also a decrease in water-use efficiency that leads to an overall decline in ANPP (Aguiar *et al.*, 1996). In some instances, degradation involves permanent physical changes in soils, resulting in shifts in the soil texture of superficial layers (Oliva, Bartolomei and Humano, 2000).

Although alternative steady states of vegetation in Patagonia have been described with a reasonable level of detail, the factors that trigger transitions from one state to another have not been tested under controlled experimental conditions (Bertiller, 1993b). Overestimation of carrying capacity, uneven distribution of sheep in large pastures and year-long continuous grazing have been suggested as possible factors responsible for vegetation degradation over the last 50 years (Golluscio, Deregibus and Paruelo, 1998).

An analysis of peak sheep numbers in the province of Santa Cruz shows that pioneering sheep farmers did overestimate the carrying capacity of the system. This is especially true of operations on the semi-deserts of the central plateau (Unit Kg 11 in Figure 4.5), where stocking rates were consistently 60 percent above the estimated carrying capacity (Oliva *et al.*, 1996) and the current sheep population has fallen well below the expected carrying capacity of the system (Cibils, 2001). Most of the variability in sheep numbers between 1931 and 1960 on the drier grass steppes north of the Straits of Magellan can be explained by the variation in MAP ($r^2 = 0.97$, $p = 0.02$; Cibils and Coughenour, 2001), a variable that has been shown to relate linearly to ANPP (Sala *et al.*, 1988; Paruelo and Sala, 1995). After 1970, this relation disappears, giving way to a second period in which sheep numbers decrease despite an apparent phase of overall increase in MAP (Cibils and Coughenour, 2001). Interestingly, 1960–1970 was the driest decade in the century; there could have been a breaking point in the system sometime around or after this decade as a consequence of excessive stocking combined with prolonged droughts that caused a significant shift in the relation between rainfall (or ANPP) and sheep numbers (Cibils and Coughenour, 2001).

The spatial distribution of sheep grazing in very large pastures is very uneven and primarily related to the distribution of watering points (Lange, 1985). Sheep densities at a given point within a pasture can vary from 8 to 0.02 times the mean density assigned to the whole pasture (Lange, 1985). Although there have been few efforts to measure grazing distribution in Patagonian-type pastures, there is circumstantial evidence that confirms the occurrence of the grazing patterns described by Lange (1985). Heterogeneous grazing distributions generate local areas of degradation that can trigger severe erosion, particularly when highly-affected areas are sensitive sites, such as riparian meadows (Borrelli and Oliva, 1999; Golluscio, Deregibus and Paruelo, 1998).

Because sheep are selective grazers, continuous year-long grazing tends to intensify the pattern of uneven utilization. Grazing systems have been tested at several sites in the grass-steppe biome as a possible means of attenuating the undesired effects of sheep selectivity. The results of these trials, in terms of both animal production and range condition trend, were mostly comparable to the continuous moderately grazed system (Borrelli, 1999; Anchorena *et al.*, 2000, but see also Paruelo, Golluscio and Deregibus, 1992). In most cases, the application of flexible moderate stocking rates (even in year-long grazing schemes) may be the most reasonable way to manage Patagonia's steppes for long-term sustainability.

ONGOING RESEARCH, MANAGEMENT, RESTORATION AND BIODIVERSITY MAINTENANCE ACTIVITIES
Research activities
A review of abstracts of both poster and oral presentations of current research in the arid and semi-arid ecosystems and published in the proceedings of recent meetings of the Argentine Ecological Association (April 2001 meeting) and the Argentine Association for Animal Science (October 2000 meeting) was undertaken to assess research trends. Approximately 30 percent of research in Patagonia is in the Monte region, close to 40 percent on the shrub and shrub-grass steppes and about 20 percent on the Patagonian grass steppe. The remaining 10 percent is regional-scale, greenhouse or riparian meadow (Plate 4.6) research. A common feature of the results reviewed is the relative

V.A. DEREGIBUS & M.F. GARBULSKY

Plate 4.6
Winter view of a riparian meadow or mallin.

scarcity of manipulation experiments; most results are derived primarily from observation-type studies. The most frequent issue is the influence of grazing by domestic herbivores on a number of vegetation and soil variables (over 30 percent of studies reviewed). Next come studies on the influence of water or nitrogen on ecosystems (13 and 10 percent of reviewed studies, respectively) and, thirdly, research on the impact of fire on ecosystems (10 percent of current studies). Research and surveys on wildlife account for 9 percent of abstracts, and studies of ecosystem processes such as primary productivity and decomposition are 9 and 5 percent of all studies, respectively. Satellite image analysis or simulation modelling are only used in about 4 percent of ongoing research activities.

Grazing (mostly by sheep) is currently being studied in relation to its effect on: vegetation structure in the shrub-dominated ecosystems of Patagonia at either patch or landscape scale (Ares, Bertiller and Bisigato, 2001b; Cecchi, Distel and Kröpfl, 2001; Ciccorossi and Sala, 2001; Ghersa *et al.*, 2001; Ripol *et al.*, 2001); overall community plant diversity or population genetic diversity of endangered plant species at local spatial scales (Aguiar, Premoli and Cipriotti, 2001; Cesa and Paruelo, 2001; Cibils *et al.*, 2000); riparian meadow productivity (Collantes, Stoffella and Pomar, 2001; Golluscio *et al.*, 2000; Utrilla *et al.*, 2000); the demography of native dominant tussock grasses (Weber *et al.*, 2000; Oliva, Collantes and Humano, 2001); interspecific relations between shrubs (Cipriotti and Aguiar, 2001); shrub crown shapes (Siffredi and Bustos, 2001); soil nitrogen mineralization rates in relation to changes in vegetation composition (Anchorena *et al.*, 2001); shrub recruitment in relation to soil compaction (Stofella and Anchorena, 2001); and microphytic crusts in the Monte shrub steppes (Silva *et al.*, 2001). Finally, grazing is also currently being researched in relation to herbivore diets and lambing rates at regional scales (Hall and Paruelo, 2001; Pelliza *et al.*, 2001). Water is the single most important factor regulating processes such as primary and secondary productivity in Patagonian ecosystems. Nitrogen dynamics is closely tied to moisture availability. Although there has been much research in the past decades addressing the use of water by different life forms (Sala, Lauenroth and Golluscio, 1997, and references therein), only recently have studies begun to address issues related to the joint effects of water and nitrogen. One of the few ongoing manipulative field experiments is being conducted in this area, studying the effects of drought on productivity and N mineralization, using rain shelters in the shrub steppe ecosystem (Sala, Yahdjian and Flombaum, 2001). Current studies on the influence of water (alone) include: effects of water deficit on the germination of an endangered grass species (Flombaum *et al.*, 2001); simulation of competition for water and light in *Festuca* tussocks growing in a grass-forest ecotone (Fernández, Gyengue and Schlichter, 2001); effects of stem flow on soil water content beneath shrubs (Kröpfl *et al.*, 2001); and *Poa ligularis* response to defoliation and water stress in a greenhouse experiment (Sáenz and Deregibus,

2001). Currently, nitrogen dynamics are being studied in relation to: the effect of litter nitrogen content of different plant life forms on soil N fractions in the grass-steppe ecosystems (Sain, Bertiller and Carrera, 2001) and the Monte shrub steppes (Carrera *et al.*, 2001); effects of levels of soil nitrogen fractions on the segregation of male and female *Poa ligularis* individuals (Bertiller, Sain and Carrera, 2001); soil nitrogen mineralization rates in relation to grazing (Anchorena *et al.*, 2001); decomposition rates of litter with different nitrogen content (Semmartin *et al.*, 2001); and nitrogen use efficiency (together with water use efficiency) of 26 species of plants from Patagonian ecosystems (Golluscio, Oesterheld and Soriano, 2001).

Current studies on the effects of fire on Patagonian ecosystems mostly include monitoring of vegetation following natural wildfire outbreaks. Such studies include: descriptions of post-burn secondary succession patterns (Ghermandi, Guthmann and Bran, 2001; González *et al.*, 2001; Rafaelle and Veblen, 2001); study of biotic and abiotic (including weather) conditions that promote wildfire outbreaks (Defossé *et al.*, 2001; De Torres Curth, Ghermandi and Pfister, 2001); and effects of wildfires on survival of adult tussocks or seeds in soil seed-banks (Gittins, Bran and Ghermandi, 2001; González, Ghermandi and Becker, 2001). Almost all fire-related studies have been conducted either in the shrub-steppe ecosystems or the steppe-forest ecotones.

Current studies on wildlife in Patagonia include: surveys of animal numbers such as guanaco population numbers in relation to sheep density and forage availability (Baldi, Albon and Elston, 2001); calculations of *Rhea* densities using improved field methods (Funes *et al.*, 2001); census of migratory bird species in southern Patagonia (Manero *et al.*, 2001); predator-prey relations studying fox and European hare populations and diets of a number of predators of the shrub steppe ecosystems (Donadío *et al.*, 2001; Novaro *et al.*, 2001); habitat use by *Rheas* (Bellis *et al.*, 2001); and deer reproductive ecology in relation to droughts (Flueck, 2001).

ANPP of Patagonian ecosystems is currently being studied in relation to range condition (Bonvissuto, González Carteau and Moraga, 2001), grazing system (Collantes, Stoffella and Pomar, 2001), competition among plant life-forms (Schlichter, Fernández and Gyenge, 2001), or forage production (Bustos and Marcolín, 2001). Satellite image analysis using NDVI at regional scales continues to be used as a tool to estimate ANPP (Fabricante *et al.*, 2001). Decomposition is being studied at regional scales either along rainfall gradients (Austin and Sala, 2001), or in relation to a species' successional status within the plant community and its litter N content (Semmartin *et al.*, 2001). At local scales, decomposition of forbs is being studied in relation to increased ultraviolet-B radiation, derived from the thinning in the ozone layer at high latitudes in the southern hemisphere (Pancotto *et al.*, 2001).

A number of ongoing research projects include the study of aspects of the biology of a few shrub species, namely: shrub secondary compounds

(Cavagnaro *et al.*, 2001; Wassner and Ravetta, 2001); within-genus shrub genetic diversity (Bottini *et al.*, 2001); the effects of pruning or cloning treatments (Arena, Peri and Vater, 2001; Peri, Arena and Vater, 2001); segregation of shrub species in relation to rainfall gradients (Marcolin and Bustos, 2001); allocation patterns or morphological attributes in sympatric shrub species (Stronatti *et al.*, 2001; Vilela, Agüero and Ravetta, 2001); and factors influencing insect herbivory in shrubs (D'Ambrogio and Fernández, 2001; Villacide and Farina, 2001).

A few researchers are studying seed biology or germination dynamics in relation to presence of microphytic crusts (Villasuso *et al.*, 2001), litter accumulation (Rotundo and Aguiar, 2001), plant life-form (Vargas and Bertiller, 2001), or grazing (Oliva, Collantes and Humano, 2001). Finally, there are a small number of studies addressing miscellaneous issues ranging from secondary succession patterns on cultivated rangelands to endophyte fungi in a series of grasses from Patagonia (Cibils, Peinetti and Oliva, 2001; Vila Aiub *et al.*, 2001).

Management activities

The need for management tools to regulate grazing and slow down rates of vegetation deterioration has led to the development of a number of vegetation-based pasture assessment routines over the past decade. Most of these (developed primarily by INTA) are being used in almost all provinces of Argentinian Patagonia, either by government agencies or private consultants (Borrelli and Oliva, 1999; Nakamatsu, Escobar and Elissalde, 2001; Bonvissuto, 2001; Siffredi *et al.*, 2002).

The rangeland assessment methods used in the provinces of Río Negro and Chubut (generally areas of shrub-steppe vegetation) basically involve: the measurement of vegetation cover (forage species cover, in particular); and estimation of ANPP using annual precipitation data (see appendix in Golluscio, Deregibus and Paruelo, 1998). The routine used in Santa Cruz (generally applied to grass-steppes and semi-deserts) involves: the measurement of forage biomass (short-grasses, sedges and forbs); and grass key species stubble heights (Borrelli and Oliva, 1999). The output of all methods is an estimate of sheep carrying capacity. Whereas the biomass-based method involves yearly monitoring, the vegetation-cover-based methods do not. In all cases, however, assessment routines are fairly labour-intensive and therefore, in some instances, their use becomes economically unviable. A number of efforts aim at reducing labour costs by using up-to-date technological tools to facilitate a more widespread adoption of range assessment routines.

Scientists at the Universidad de Buenos Aires (IFEVA-UBA) are using Landsat TM image analysis to derive primary productivity estimates from NDVI values to calculate carrying capacity at individual pasture scales (Paruelo *et al.*, 2001). Another approach that is currently being investigated by INTA scientists is the use of either empirical or mechanistic simulation models to predict year-to-year fluctuations in forage availability and adjust animal numbers accordingly. The empirical approach involves the use of seasonal rainfall data to make stocking rate adjustment decisions following within-year patterns of drought or moisture surpluses (Rimoldi and Buono, 2001). The mechanistic approach includes the parameterization of existing mechanistic spatially-explicit models that allow landscape-scale simulation of primary productivity and grazing at a number of different time scales of interest. This approach involves the use of satellite image analysis to calibrate productivity estimates (Ellis and Coughenour, 1996).

In recent years there has been increasing demand for long-term range monitoring tools at scales ranging from individual pastures to landscapes and ecosystems. Current range assessment routines cannot (in most cases) provide useful long-term monitoring information. Furthermore, land uses other than grazing, such as oil extraction or other mining, require the development of tools tailored to the type of environmental disturbance they produce. Landsat TM satellite image analysis has been used over the last decade to make an inventory of the state of Patagonian rangelands (degrees of desertification) in several key areas of the region (del Valle *et al.*, 1995). As the availability of satellite images increases, much of the installed capabilities in research institutes throughout the region will be used as a basis for multi-temporal monitoring of rangelands at regional scales. At smaller spatial scales, Ares *et al.* (2001a,b) are developing methods of monitoring changes in vegetation structure under grazing at landscape scales in the Monte shrub steppes using aerial photographs and spatially-explicit simulation modelling.

RESTORATION ACTIVITIES

Restoration activities have traditionally been restricted to the stabilization of sand accumulations in severely eroded areas, using special cultivation techniques and generally involving the seeding of rhizomatous grasses of the genus *Elymus* (Castro, Salomone and Reichart, 1983). Almost all of these activities have been conducted successfully, by both INTA and the Board of Agriculture (Consejo Argario Provincial) of the Province of Santa Cruz. Although this and other variants of grazing-related restoration activities continue (Magaldi *et al.*, 2001; Becker, Bustos and Marcolín, 2001; Rostagno, 2001), current efforts in this field have mostly shifted toward the reclamation of disturbances associated with the mining and oil industries (Baetti *et al.*, 2001; Ciano *et al.*, 2001).

Currently, restoration activities involve: the developing or adaptation of technologies to promote *in situ* biodegradation of oil (especially in situations where oil spills affect valuable riparian meadow habitats) (Luque *et al.*, 2000; Nakamatsu *et al.*, 2001b); conducting conservationist tillage in areas of topsoil decapitation (Ciano *et al.*, 2000); and selection of native ruderal species for revegetation of highly degraded environments (Ciano *et al.*, 1998). Shrubs of the genera *Atriplex*, *Grindelia* and *Tamarix* are being used in many current restoration projects, with establishment rates of almost 70 percent (Ciano *et al.*, 2001).

Most land reclamation activities are currently in a region with some of the oldest oil fields of southern Patagonia (northern Santa Cruz and southern Chubut), and lie mostly within the shrub-grass steppes and semi-desert bio-zones. Recently, there has been a rapid growth in the demand for further land reclamation technology by a number of large mining projects in the southern semi-desert biozone (Province of Santa Cruz), a need that is currently being met by local Universities. Mine reclamation will possibly be one of the fastest growing applications of restoration in certain areas of Patagonia during the decades to come.

BIODIVERSITY MAINTENANCE

There are 1 378 recorded vascular plant species in arid and semi-arid Patagonia (Correa, 1971), almost all of which are angiosperms and close to 30 percent of which are endemic species. Of all species recorded in the Flora of Patagonia, there are about 340 exotic plants that are restricted to areas surrounding houses, pens and roads, but they are, in all cases, unable to become part of the native steppe plant communities (Soriano, Nogués Loza and Burkart, 1995). Due to its relatively high level of endemism, Patagonia has been recently included as a "Centre of Plant Diversity" (CPD Site A46) in a worldwide diversity conservation project under the auspices of the Museum of Natural History of the Smithsonian Institution (USA), IUCN and WWF (Smithsonian Institution, 1997).

Sheep grazing has been shown to reduce vascular plant diversity in several Patagonian ecosystems, both by promoting local extinction of preferred forage plants and by altering the relative abundance of species in the grazed plant communities (Schlichter *et al.*, 1978; Perelman, León and Bussacca, 1997; Oliva *et al.*, 1998; Cibils *et al.*, 2000; Cesa and Paruelo, 2001). Soriano, Nogués Loza and Burkart (1995) assembled a list of 76 endangered species in Patagonia, of which a quarter are grasses, on the basis of the plant species replacement patterns under grazing described by several authors in Paruelo *et al.* (1993). Although the severity of extinction risk is not equal for all species listed by Soriano, Nogués Loza and Burkart (1995), this list would clearly be a good starting point to guide conservation efforts. Current efforts to prevent over-grazing may contribute to slowing down the rate of loss of endemic species, although these programmes do not address the biodiversity issue explicitly. Unfortunately there are few nature reserves in arid and semi-arid Patagonia, although many of the National Parks along the Patagonian Andes include areas of steppe-forest ecotone (Villamil, 1997). There are currently only two reserves well within arid and semi-arid Patagonia, which account for less than 0.1 percent of the region, namely Laguna Blanca National Park (about 110 km^2

in the province of Neuquen, created in 1940), and Bosques Petrificados Natural Monument (100 km² in the province of Santa Cruz) (Villamil, 1997).

Seed production

Although experimental sowing of native species has been successful in southern Patagonia, forage productivity of native plant species under cultivation was lower than that of introduced grasses and legumes (Mascó, 1995). Reseeding trials on degraded land were conducted in the sixties by an INTA-FAO Project (Molina Sanchez, 1968). Reseeding was biologically successful at many sites, but productivity under low moisture regimes was considered limiting for commercial application (Mascó and Montes, 1995), mostly because sheep production was the only activity considered in the economic analyses.

These results constrained local seed production to limited areas, namely: harvesting small stands of *Elymus sabulosus* and *E. arenarius* in western Santa Cruz and south-central Chubut to obtain seed for sand dune fixation; setting up two active gene banks in the region, which not only stored seed collections from natural stands, but also multiplied some material in experimental plots (Montes *et al.,* 1996); and developing oil spill reclamation technology by scientists at INTA's Research Station in Trelew (Chubut), which included the setting up of a nursery to multiply native shrub germplasm such as *Atriplex lampa* to provide plantations at disturbed sites. There is currently no public or private funding for seed production of native species nor for rehabilitation of desertified areas with native plant species.

RECOMMENDATIONS AND LESSONS LEARNED

Most of the grazing management and ecology research in Patagonia has been conducted by INTA and institutions such as CONICET and the University of Buenos Aires. Beginning in the 1980s, pasture condition guides were proposed for evaluating different vegetation types. Initially, grazing treatments were recommended based on range management literature. The lack of understanding of soil-plant-animal relations thwarted further progress. Soil and vegetation responses to different grazing treatments were unknown. The nutritional and behavioural aspects of the grazing process were ignored. Realizing this, two long-term grazing trials were designed and conducted by INTA, one in SW Chubut (Siffredi *et al.,* 1995) and one in southern Santa Cruz (Oliva *et al.,* 1998).

Many rangeland evaluation techniques and recommended grazing strategies were thereafter based on the findings of INTA grazing trials. Short-grass biomass and key species height were used to assess carrying capacity and grazing intensity, respectively, in grass-dominated rangelands of Southern Patagonia (Borrelli and Oliva, 1999; Cibils, 1993). Pastoral Value (Daget and Poisonnet, 1971), a method based on step-point cover data, was proposed for shrubland steppes in northern Patagonia (Elizalde, Escobar and Nakamatsu, 1991; Ayesa and Becker, 1991)

In 1989, INTA and GTZ launched a joint project to control and prevent desertification in Patagonia, which was implemented during the 1990s. This project increased societal awareness regarding desertification problems, and 3 percent of all sheep farmers in the region adopted the techniques recommended. Since the early 1990s, interaction between farmers and range scientists has increased and has resulted in the application of grazing plans at an individual farm scale. This was possibly the birth of range management as a practical discipline in Patagonia. After more than two decades of research activities and one decade of practical experience, we have both recommendations and many new questions.

Adaptive management – the Santa Cruz example

The designing of a grazing plan with little research background and a lot of variation coming from weather, soils, vegetation and previous grazing management is highly problematic. Stuart-Hill (1989), working in South Africa, stated that it is almost impossible to define "proper" management in a one-step plan. He proposed adaptive management as the only way to deal with urgent decisions and limited knowledge rangelands. Our experience confirms his hypothesis: proper management is a process rather than a single decision.

In Santa Cruz, for instance, many farms began to apply adaptive management in the 1990s (Borrelli and Oliva, 1999) (Figure 4.6). Range evaluation methods were used to support stocking rate adjustments and other grazing allocation decisions. Annual monitoring of weather, vegetation and animal production variables at the level of individual paddocks provided feedback information that allowed the implementation of opportunistic grazing plans and corrections for possible errors in the initial stocking proposal. Farmer objectives and perceptions were very important in the planning process. Opportunistic grazing plans in southern Santa Cruz proved to be effective in terms of optimizing sheep production. Variable stocking rates were used to take advantage of favourable years and also to reduce the impact of periodic droughts, although it is not clear whether variable stocking rates were more beneficial to vegetation than moderate fixed stocking rates. Unfortunately, the vegetation attributes used as criteria for stocking rate adjustments (short-grass biomass and key species height) were inadequate for long-term monitoring.

The information collected on many sheep farms in southern Patagonia was used by INTA Santa Cruz to create a regional database. This proved to be a useful and simple tool to analyse the internal variation of carrying capacity estimations within each natural environment and grazing site. Many inferences made from small paddock grazing studies were confirmed at the commercial scale. This information on animal and vegetation responses to grazing management was important to calibrate stocking rate recommendations across range types in Santa Cruz (Kofalt and Borrelli, unpublished data).

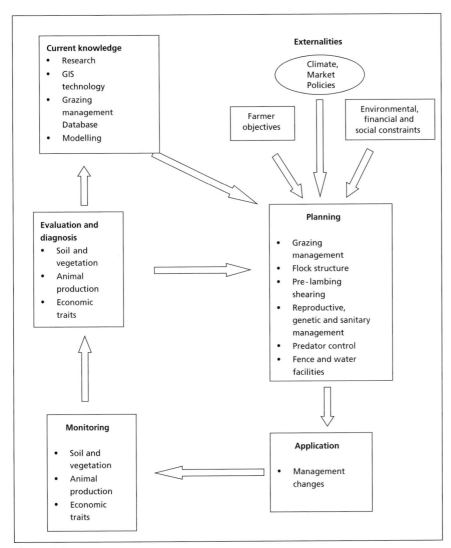

Figure 4.6
Adaptive management for sustainable sheep production.
(Based on Borrelli and Oliva, 1999)

The value of simple or flexible stocking strategies

Grazing management practices in Patagonia can be classified in terms of complexity (Table 4.4). The shift from a subjective, low-knowledge-level input, continuous stocking scheme (level 0), to an objectively-based, moderate and flexible continuous stocking strategy (level 1) promotes the greatest progress in grazing management (Borrelli and Oliva, 1999). Further increases in management complexity or sophistication can be expected to have less impact, at least in the drier and homogeneous environments of Patagonia. Level 1 recommended procedures have proved highly efficient in eliminating general-

TABLE 4.4

Complexity levels of grazing management in Patagonia.

Level	Description	Limitations	Application
0	**Traditional management** Continuous grazing with subjectively estimated, fixed stocking rates	Overgrazing in 50% of cases. Land degradation. Low lambing rates, with high mortality.	97% of the farms of Argentinian Patagonia
1	**Continuous flexible stocking** Range evaluation provides objective information for animal allocation. Range monitoring allows for yearly adjustments, to deal with climatic variation. Opportunistic rest of paddocks in rainy years Fencing of meadows and separate management	Moderate continuous grazing could promote undesirable transitions in some environments.	2 grazing studies and more than 200 farms with grazing plans
2	**Deferred rotation systems** Schematic rotation with low animal concentration (less than 50% of the farm is rested at any time)	Deferred rotation did not produce the results expected. Moderate managerial skills are required.	2 grazing studies 5 farms
3	**Specialized grazing systems** Schematic rotation with high animal concentration. (High intensity-low frequency, low intensity-low frequency and short duration grazing)	High requirement for fencing and managerial skills. Limited information about the benefits of the practice.	3 farms

SOURCE: Golluscio *et al.*, 1999, who adapted from a 1993 unpublished report.

ized continuous overgrazing (Borrelli and Oliva, 1999), identified as the most important cause of range degradation elsewhere (Heady and Child, 1994).

Simple Level-2 rotational grazing systems (Table 4.4) were tested in southern Patagonia, but the advantage of changing from Level 1 was not evident (Borrelli, 1999). Only opportunistic rest of some paddocks and fencing of meadows proved to be worthwhile "sophistication" in grazing management. Intensive grazing of fenced meadows showed impressive results in terms of sheep production in NW Patagonia (Giraudo *et al.*, 1996).

More specialized grazing systems (Level 3-type) are regarded as promising by researchers of the University of Buenos Aires on a large farm in NW Chubut, Argentina (Paruelo, Golluscio and Deregibus, 1992). The generalized adoption of these systems is limited by: scarce information regarding responses in other environments; the limited availability of paddocks for complex rotations; and the lack of managerial skills of most farmers. In the last decades there has been a debate in the range management literature about grazing systems (Kothmann, 1984) and the value of the optimal stocking rate concept (e.g. Ash and Stafford-Smith, 1996; Stafford-Smith, 1996). As an example, continuous moderate grazing has been shown as beneficial for combating undesirable shrub invasions (Westoby, Walker and Noy Meir, 1989). Many authors have considered that defoliation frequency was more important than defoliation intensity for proper grazing management, and proposed specialized grazing systems (Kothmann, 1984). Stafford-Smith (1996) pointed out that both temporal and spatial heterogeneity limit the possibility of controlling grazing intensity in continuous grazing treatments. However, for Patagonian conditions, these debates are stimulating but somewhat theoretical. Simple and flexible grazing strategies proved to be useful to optimize sheep production and to prevent rangeland deterioration for most situations. Severe restrictions limit the practical application of more complex grazing strategies.

Conflict between short- and long-term production

Many economic activities exhibit conflicts between short-term and long-term profitability when environmental impact is considered. Maximum short-term profits are attained by methods that may be harmful to natural resources, especially if hidden environmental costs are, as usual, not included in economic calculations. In this case, less profitable procedures in the short-term might be chosen for environmental protection, or environmental costs should be included in the economic analysis.

This seems not to be the case for Patagonian sheep farming systems. While overgrazed farms are likely to produce not only more but also finer wool, nutritional restrictions will decrease lambing rates and survival of adult sheep, promoting decreases in overall meat sales. If overgrazing occurs in the most arid biomes, reproduction and survival is depressed beyond the equilibrium point of the flock and sheep population numbers decline (Golluscio *et al.*, 1999). A properly managed sheep farm sells 24 to 44 percent of the herd annually (depending on the natural environment), whereas sales from overgrazed farms range from zero to 15 percent (Borrelli *et al.*, 1997). Consequently, sound management pays off in the short term, even using conventional economic analysis. This becomes more evident for mixed lamb and fine-crossbred-wool production systems, but is also valid for fine-wool production systems.

The role of Decision Support Systems

The availability of computers broadens the possibilities for environmental assessment and management by range technicians. The joint INTA-GTZ project, mentioned above, introduced satellite imagery processing facilities and skills in Patagonia. The use of Landsat TM images was adopted as a cost- and time-efficient service to help make accurate inventories for rangeland surveys. In some areas, carrying capacity could be estimated directly from Landsat TM Images (Oliva *et al.*, 1996). In others, image processing provided accurate range site maps and useful information to guide field sampling. Geographical Information System (GIS) technology was used in 1994 to combine satellite information with other data sources, such as soil maps, climatic data, property boundaries and other significant variables. For vast and isolated regions such as Patagonia, where farms cover big areas that are often hard to access with vehicles and where there are few trained people to conduct range evaluations, this technology multiplies human power and reduces operation costs.

Decision Support Systems (DSS) are clearly a new dimension for range management. Adaptive management information at the individual farm level could be loaded into a GIS database. Modelling would provide integration of different sources of information, to assist range managers and scientists to predict probable outcomes of specific problems at farm and regional scales, such as: flock allocation, mixed grazing, native flora and fauna conservation, spatial heterogeneity of grazing, long-term vegetation changes, economic evaluation of grazing strategies, and many other parameters (Bosch *et al.*, 1996). Feedback information from associated farmers would be used to improve the power of predictive models. The development of DSS should increase the accuracy and soundness of grazing management strategies and also allow for further reduction in the labour and time costs associated with range evaluation and management.

Priorities for development programmes and research

Development programme priorities for Argentinian Patagonia over the next five years, as set out by INTA (Carlos Paz, pers. comm.) involve developing or adapting technology for: sustainable sheep farming systems (including the development of eco-certification protocols); management and reclamation of degraded grazing land, in particular areas that have been severely disturbed by mining or oil extraction; regional GIS to develop DSS; genetic improvement of ultra-fine Merino sheep and Angora goats (including the use of biotechnology); and improvement of wildlife use (guanacos and rheas).

Sustainable sheep farming priorities include both the development of ultra-fine Merino wool production systems, especially in the provinces of Chubut, Río Negro and Neuquén, and the improvement of meat production systems on sheep farms of the grass-steppe biozone, either along the Andes foothills or on the Magellanic steppes in southern Santa Cruz and northern Tierra del Fuego. The latter include the development of quality protocols. Rangeland management and reclamation priorities include the development of routines for long-term monitoring of pasture vegetation, the improvement of technology to reclaim old mining and oil field areas, areas severely overgrazed by sheep (with particular emphasis on riparian meadow ecosystems), and the development of GIS to run DSS at both regional and single-farm scales (INTA-CRPS, 2001b; INTA-CRPN, 2001). Besides these main lines of development, agrotourism programmes will also continue to be developed, especially in areas with outstanding scenic values and adequate infrastructure support.

Research priorities are obviously related (but not limited) to development priorities for the region mentioned above. The main priorities as stated by the Secretaría para la Tecnología, la Ciencia y la Innovación Productiva (National Science and Technology Department) (one of the few local science and technology funding agencies) for the next five years are (SETCIP, 2000): impact of climate change at regional scales; study of ozone-layer dynamics and the consequences of increased ultraviolet radiation levels; catchment conservation and management for improved soil and water quality; evaluation and preservation of biodiversity; improvement of ecological risk assessment, including the development of monitoring systems; studies regarding appropriate use by tourism of natural reserve areas; improvement of sustainable sheep and goat production, including the development of quality protocols; production of organic foods; and study of rural and urban labour conditions.

REFERENCES

Aguiar, M.R., Paruelo, J.M., Sala, O.E. & Lauenroth, W.K. 1996. Ecosystem responses to changes in plant functional type composition: An example from the Patagonian steppe. *Journal of Vegetation Science,* 7: 381–390.

Aguiar, M.R., Premoli, A.C. & Cipriotti, P.A. 2001. Consecuencias genéticas del sobrepastoreo en dos gramíneas de la estepa patagónica: *Bromus pictus y Poa ligularis.* p. 40, *in: Resúmenes de la I Reunión Binacional de Ecología (XX Reunión Argentina de Ecología – X Reunión Sociedad de Ecología de Chile).* Bariloche, Argentina, 23–27 April 2001.

Amaya, J.N., von Thüngen, J. &Delamo, D.A. 2001. Relevamiento y distribución de guanacos en la Patagonia: Informe Final. Comunicación Técnica, No.111. Area Recursos Naturales-Fauna 111. INTA, Bariloche.

Anchorena, J., Cingolani, A., Livraghi, E., Collantes, M. & Stofella, S. 2000. Pastoreo ovino en Tierra del Fuego. Pautas ecológicas para aumentar la producción. Unpublished report. 27 p.

Anchorena, J., Mendoza, R., Cingolani, A. & Marbán, L. 2001. ¿El régimen de pastoreo promueve o deprime la fertilidad en suelos ácidos? p. 44, *in: Actas de la I Reunión Binacional de Ecología (XX Reunión Argentina de Ecología – X Reunión Sociedad de Ecología de Chile).* Bariloche, Argentina, 23–27 April 2001.

Arena, M.E., Peri, P. & Vater, G. 2001. Crecimiento de los brotes en plantas de *Berberis heterophylla* Juss. "Calafate". 2. Arqueado de ramas. p. 47, *in: Actas de la I Reunión Binacional de Ecología (XX Reunión Argentina de Ecología – X Reunión Sociedad de Ecología de Chile).* Bariloche, Argentina, 23–27 April 2001.

Ares, J.O., Bertiller M. & Bisigato, A. 2001a. Indicadores estructurales a escala de paisaje para evaluar el impacto relativo del pastoreo. pp. 38–39, *in: Resúmenes del taller de actualización sobre métodos de evaluación, monitoreo y recuperación de pastizales naturales patagónicos.* IV Reunión del Grupo Regional Patagónico de Ecosistemas de Pastoreo. INTA-INIA-FAO. Esquel, Argentina, 26–27 June 2001.

Ares, J.O., Bertiller, M. B. & Bisigato, A. 2001b. Análisis en dos escalas y modelos espacial-explícitos de la destrucción y regeneración del canopeo vegetal en el monte austral. p. 48, *in: Resúmenes de la I Reunión Binacional de Ecología (XX Reunión Argentina de Ecología – X Reunión Sociedad de Ecología de Chile).* Bariloche, Argentina, 23–27 April 2001.

Ares, J.O., Beeskow, A.M., Bertiller, M., Rostagno, M., Irisarri, M., Anchorena, J. & Deffossé, G. 1990. Structural and dynamic characteristics of overgrazed lands of northern Patagonia, Argentina. pp. 149–175, *in:* A. Breymeyer (ed). *Managed Grasslands.* Amsterdam, The Netherlands: Elsevier Science Publishers.

Argentine Wool Federation. 2001. *Argentine Wool Statistics*, Vol. 512. 22 p.

Ash A. & Stafford-Smith, M. 1996. Evaluating stocking rate impacts in rangelands: animals don't practice what we preach. *Rangeland Journal,* **18**: 216–243.

Austin, A.T. & Sala, O.E. 2001. Descomposición a lo largo de un gradiente de precipitación en la Patagonia: interacciones entre especies y precipitación. p. 251, *in: Actas de la I Reunión Binacional de Ecología (XX Reunión Argentina de Ecología – X Reunión Sociedad de Ecología de Chile).* Bariloche, Argentina, 23–27 April 2001.

Ayesa J. & Becker, G. 1991. Evaluación forrajera y ajuste de la carga animal. Proyecto de Prevención y Control de la desertificación en la Patagonia. PRECODEPA. *Comunicación Técnica Recursos naturales (Pastizales)*, No. 7. 17 p.

Baetti, C., Ferrantes, D., Cáceres, P. & Cibils, A. 2001. Respuesta de los estratos y atributos de la vegetación en relación al impacto que genera la construcción de un ducto. pp. 54–55, *in: Resúmenes del taller de actualización sobre métodos de evaluación, monitoreo y recuperación de pastizales naturales patagónicos.* IV Reunión del Grupo Regional Patagónico de Ecosistemas de Pastoreo. INTA-INIA-FAO. Esquel, Argentina, 26–27 June 2001.

Baldi, R., Albon, S.D. & Elston, D.A. 2001. Guanacos, ovinos y el fantasma de la competencia en la Patagonia árida. p. 252, *in: Actas de la I Reunión Binacional de Ecología (XX Reunión Argentina de Ecología – X Reunión Sociedad de Ecología de Chile).* Bariloche, Argentina, 23–27 April 2001.

Barbería, E. 1995. *Los dueños de la tierra de la Patagonia Austral:1880–1920.* Río Gallegos, Argentina: Universidad Federal de la Patagonia Austral.

Becker, G.F., Bustos, C. & Marcolín, A.A. 2001. Ensayos de revegetación de veranadas degradadas por sobrepastoreo de Lonco Puan (provincia del Neuquén). pp. 57–58, *in: Resúmenes del taller de actualización sobre métodos de evaluación, monitoreo y recuperación de pastizales naturales patagónicos.* IV Reunión del Grupo Regional Patagónico de Ecosistemas de Pastoreo. INTA-INIA-FAO. Esquel, Argentina, 26–27 June 2001.

Bellis, L.M., Martella, M.B., Vignolo, P.E. & Navarro, J.L. 2001. Requerimientos espaciales de choiques (*Pterocnemia pennata*) en la Patagonia Argentina. p. 57, *in: Actas de la I Reunión Binacional de Ecología (XX Reunión Argentina de Ecología – X Reunión Sociedad de Ecología de Chile).* Bariloche, Argentina, 23–27 April 2001.

Bertiller, M.B. 1993a. Catálogo de estados y transiciones: Estepas subarbustivo-herbáceas de *Nassauvia glomerulosa* y *Poa dusenii* del centro-sur del Chubut. pp. 52–56, *in:* Paruelo *et al.*, 1993, q.v.

Bertiller, M.B. 1993b. Conclusiones. p. 110, *in:* Paruelo *et al.*, 1993, q.v.

Bertiller, M.B. & Defossé, G.E. 1993. Catálogo de estados y transiciones: Estepas graminosas de *Festuca pallescens* en el SW del Chubut. pp. 14–22, *in:* Paruelo *et al.*, 1993, q.v.

Bertiller, M.B., Sain C.L. & Carrera. A.L. 2001. Respuesta de los sexos de *Poa ligularis* a la variación del nitrógeno del suelo en Patagonia. Implicancias para su conservación. p. 253, *in: Actas de la I Reunión Binacional de Ecología (XX Reunión Argentina de Ecología – X Reunión Sociedad de Ecología de Chile)*. Bariloche, Argentina, 23–27 April 2001.

Boelcke, O., Moore, D.M. & Roig, F.A. (eds). 1985. *Transecta Botánica de la Patagonia Austral*. Buenos Aires, Argentina: Conicet (Argentina); Royal Society (Great Britain); Instituto de la Patagonia (Chile).

Bonvissuto, G.L. 2001. Desarrollo y uso de guías de condición utilitaria de los pastizales naturales de Patagonia, para el ajuste de la carga animal. pp. 25–26, *in: Resúmenes del taller de actualización sobre métodos de evaluación, monitoreo y recuperación de pastizales naturales patagónicos*. IV Reunión del Grupo Regional Patagónico de Ecosistemas de Pastoreo. INTA-INIA-FAO. Esquel, Argentina, 26–27 June 2001.

Bonvissuto, G.L., González Carteau, A. & Moraga, S. H. 2001. La condición del pastizal en la estepa arbustiva de *Larrea divaricata* y *Atriplex lampa* del Monte Austral Neuquino. p. 61, *in: Actas de la I Reunión Binacional de Ecología (XX Reunión Argentina de Ecología – X Reunión Sociedad de Ecología de Chile)*. Bariloche, Argentina, 23–27 April 2001.

Bonvissuto, G.L., Siffredi, G., Ayesa, J., Bran, D., Somlo, R. & Becker, G. 1993. Catálogo de Estados y Transiciones: Estepas subarbustivo-graminosas de *Mullinum spinosum* y *Poa ligularis*, en el área ecológica de Sierras y Mesetas Occidentales en el noroeste de la Patagonia. pp. 23–30, *in: Paruelo et al.*, 1993, q.v.

Borrelli, G., Oliva, G., Williams, M., Gonzalez, L., Rial, P. & Montes, L. (eds). 1997. Sistema Regional de Soporte de Decisiones. Santa Cruz y Tierra del Fuego. Proderser (Proyecto de Prevención y Control de la Desertificación en Patagonia), Río Gallegos, Argentina.

Borrelli, P. 1999. Informe ampliado del efecto de la intensidad de pastoreo sobre variables del sistema suelo-planta-animal y limitantes del pastizal para la producción ovina (1991–1997). *In: El ensayo de pastoreo de Moy Aike Chico (1986-1999). Una experiencia compartida entre Estancia Moy Aike Chico y la Estación Experimental Agropecuaria Santa Cruz*. INTA Río Gallegos, Argentina.

Borrelli, P. & Oliva, G. 1999. Managing grazing: experiences from Patagonia. pp. 441–447 (Vol. 1), *in: Proceedings of the 6th International Rangeland Congress*. Townsville, Queensland, Australia, 19–23 July 1999.

Borrero, J.L. 1997. The origins of ethnographic subsistence patterns in Fuego-Patagonia. pp. 60–81, *in:* McEwan, Borrero and Priero, 1997, q.v.

Borrero, L.A. & McEwan, C. 1997. The Peopling of Patagonia. pp. 32–45, *in:* McEwan, Borrero and Priero, 1997, q.v.

Bosch, O., Williams, J., Allen, W. & Ensor, A. 1996. Integrating community-based monitoring into the adaptive management process: The New Zealand experience. pp. 105–106, *in: Proceedings of the 5th International Rangeland Congress*. Salt Lake City, Utah, USA, 23–28 July 1996.

Bottini, C.M., Premoli, A.C. & Poggio, L. 2001. ¿Conformarían una unica identidad *Berberis cabrerae, B.chillanensis* y *B. montana*? p. 62, *in: Actas de la I Reunión Binacional de Ecología (XX Reunión Argentina de Ecología – X Reunión Sociedad de Ecología de Chile).* Bariloche, Argentina, 23–27 April 2001.

Bustos, J.C. & Marcolín, A.A. 2001. Producción estacional de biomasa forrajeable de *Atriplex lampa*. p. 70, *in: Actas de la I Reunión Binacional de Ecología (XX Reunión Argentina de Ecología – X Reunión Sociedad de Ecología de Chile).* Bariloche, Argentina, 23–27 April 2001.

Cabrera, A.L. 1971. Fitogeografía de la República Argentina. *Boletín de la Sociedad Argentina de Botánica,* **XIV**: 1–42.

Carrera, A.L., Sain, C.L., Bertiller, M.B. & Mazzarino, M.J. 2001. Patrones de conservación del nitrógeno en la vegetación del Monte Patagónico y su relación con la fertilidad del suelo. p. 74, *in: Actas de la I Reunión Binacional de Ecología (XX Reunión Argentina de Ecología – X Reunión Sociedad de Ecología de Chile).* Bariloche, Argentina, 23–27 April 2001.

Casas, G. 1999. Recomendaciones y estrategias para compatibilizar el desarrollo productivo en la Patagonia con la prevención y el control de la desertificación. 29 pp. *In:* Consorcio DHV, 1999, q.v.

Castro, J.M., Salomone, J.M. & Reichart, R.N. 1983. Un nuevo método para la fijación de médanos en la Región Patagónica. *Séptima reunión nacional para el estudio de las regiones Aridas y Semiáridas. Revista IDIA,* **36**: 254–255.

Cavagnaro, F.P., Golluscio, R.A., Wassner, D.F. & Ravetta. D.A. 2001. Caracterización química de especies crecientes y decrecientes con la herbivoría bajo dos presiones de pastoreo constantes en la Estepa Patagónica. p. 77, *in: Actas de la I Reunión Binacional de Ecología (XX Reunión Argentina de Ecología – X Reunión Sociedad de Ecología de Chile).* Bariloche, Argentina, 23–27 April 2001.

Cecchi, G.A., Distel, R.A. & Kröpfl, A.I. 2001. Islas de vegetación en el monte austral; ¿Formaciones naturales o consecuencia del pastoreo? p. 259, *in: Resúmenes de la I Reunión Binacional de Ecología (XX Reunión Argentina de Ecología – X Reunión Sociedad de Ecología de Chile).* Bariloche, Argentina, 23–27 April 2001.

Cesa, A. & Paruelo, J.M. 2001. El pastoreo en el noroeste de la Patagonia reduce la diversidad vegetal y modifica diferencialmente la cobertura específica. p. 259, *in: Resúmenes de la I Reunión Binacional de Ecología (XX Reunión Argentina de Ecología – X Reunión Sociedad de Ecología de Chile).* Bariloche, Argentina, 23–27 April 2001.

Ciano, N., Salomone, J., Nakamatsu, V. & Luque, J. 2001. Nuevos escenarios para la remediación de áreas degradadas en la Patagonia. pp. 40–42, *in: Resúmenes del taller de actualización sobre métodos de evaluación, monitoreo y recuperación de pastizales naturales patagónicos.* IV Reunión del Grupo Regional Patagónico de Ecosistemas de Pastoreo. INTA-INIA-FAO. Esquel, Argentina, 26–27 June 2001.

Ciano, N., Nakamatsu, V., Luque, J., Amari, M., Owen, M. & Lisoni, C. 2000. Revegetación de áreas disturbadas por la actividad petrolera en la Patagonia extrandina (Argentina). *XI Conferencia de la International Soil Conservation Organization (ISCO 2000).* 22-27 October 2000. Resúmenes ISCO, Buenos Aires, Argentina.

Ciano, N., Nakamatsu, V., Luque, J., Amari, M., Mackeprang, O. & Lisoni, C. 1998. Establecimiento de especies vegetales en suelos disturbados por la actividad petrolera. *Terceras Jornadas de Preservación de Agua, Aire y Suelo en la Industrial del Petróleo y del Gas.* Comodoro Rivadavia, Chubut, Argentina.

Cibils, A.F. 2001. Evaluación de las estimaciones de receptividad ovina calculadas mediante la aplicación del Método Santa Cruz. pp. 15–16, *in: Resúmenes del taller de actualización sobre métodos de evaluación, monitoreo y recuperación de pastizales naturales patagónicos.* IV Reunión del Grupo Regional Patagónico de Ecosistemas de Pastoreo. INTA-INIA-FAO. Esquel, Argentina, 26–27 June 2001.

Cibils, A. 1993. Manejo de pastizales. *In:* Cambio Rural-INTA EEA Santa Cruz (eds). *Catálogo de Prácticas. Tecnología disponible.* INTA, Río Gallegos, Santa Cruz, Argentina.

Cibils, A.F. & Coughenour, M.B. 2001. Impact of grazing management on the productivity of cold temperate grasslands of Southern Patagonia – a critical assessment. pp. 807–812, *in: Proceedings of the XIX International Grassland Congress.* 11–21 February 2001, Sao Paulo, Brazil.

Cibils, A., Castillo, M., Humano, G., Rosales, V. & Baetti, C. 2000. Impacto del pastoreo mixto de bovinos y ovinos sobre un pastizal de la Estepa Magallánica – Estudio preliminar. pp. 241–242, *in: Actas del 23º Congreso Argentino de Producción Animal.* Corrientes, Argentina, 5–7 October 2000.

Cibils, A., Humano, G., Paredes, P., Baumann, O. & Baetti, C. 2001. Patrones de sucesión secundaria en parcelas cultivadas con forrajeras exóticas en la estepa magallánica (Santa Cruz). p. 81, *in: Actas de la I Reunión Binacional de Ecología (XX Reunión Argentina de Ecología – X Reunión Sociedad de Ecología de Chile).* Bariloche, Argentina, 23–27 April 2001.

Ciccorossi, M.E. & Sala, O.E. 2001. Cambios estructurales provocados por el pastoreo ovino en una estepa arbustiva semi-arida del sudoeste del Chubut. p. 81, *in: Resúmenes de la I Reunión Binacional de Ecología (XX Reunión Argentina de Ecología – X Reunión Sociedad de Ecología de Chile).* Bariloche, Argentina, 23–27 April 2001.

Cipriotti, P.A. & Aguiar, M.R. 2001. Interacciones entre especies de arbustos de la estepa patagónica. Efecto de la clausura al pastoreo. p. 260, *in: Actas de la I Reunión Binacional de Ecología (XX Reunión Argentina de Ecología – X Reunión Sociedad de Ecología de Chile).* Bariloche, Argentina, 23–27 April 2001.

Collantes, M.B., Anchorena, J. & Cingolani, A. 1999. The steppes of Tierra del Fuego: Floristic and growthform patterns controlled by soil fertility and moisture. *Plant Ecology,* **140**: 61–75.

Collantes, M.B., Stoffella, S.F. & Pomar, M.C. 2001. Efecto del pastoreo sobre la composición florística, la productividad y el contenido de nutrientes de vegas de Tierra del Fuego. p. 84, *in: Actas de la I Reunión Binacional de Ecología (XX*

Reunión Argentina de Ecología – X Reunión Sociedad de Ecología de Chile). Bariloche, Argentina, 23–27 April 2001.

Consorcio DHV. 1999. Desertificación en la Patagonia. Informe Principal. Consorcio DHV Consultants-Sweedforest.

Correa, M.N. (ed.) 1971. *Flora Patagónica.* Buenos Aires, Argentina: Colección científica del INTA.

Covacevich, N., Concha, R. & Carter, E. 2000. Una experiencia historica en efectos de carga y sistema de pastoreo sobre la produccion ovina en praderas mejoradas en Magallanes. pp. 119–120, *in: Actas de la XXV Reunion Anual de SOCHIPA.* Puerto Natales, Argentina, 18–20 October 2000.

Daget, P. & Poissonet, S. 1971. Une méthode d'analyze phytologique des prairies. *Annales Agronomiques,* **22**(1): 5–41.

D'Ambrogio, A. & Fernández, S. 2001. Estructura de agallas foliáceas en *Schinus* (Anacardiaceae). p. 89, *in: Actas de la I Reunión Binacional de Ecología (XX Reunión Argentina de Ecología – X Reunión Sociedad de Ecología de Chile).* Bariloche, Argentina, 23–27 April 2001.

Defossé, G.E., Rodriguez, N.F., Dentoni, M.C., Muñoz, M. & Colomb, H. 2001. Condiciones ambientales y bióticas asociadas al incendio "San Ramón" en Bariloche, Río Negro, Argentina en el verano de 1999. p. 91, *in: Actas de la I Reunión Binacional de Ecología (XX Reunión Argentina de Ecología – X Reunión Sociedad de Ecología de Chile).* Bariloche, Argentina, 23–27 April 2001.

del Valle, H.F. 1998. Patagonian soils: a regional synthesis. *Ecologia Austral,* **8**: 103–122.

del Valle, H.F., Eiden, G., Mensching, H. & Goergen, J. 1995. Evaluación del estado actual de la desertificación en áreas representativas de la Patagonia. Informe Final Fase I. Proyecto de Cooperación Técnica entre la República Argentina y la República Federal Alemana. Cooperación técnica argentino-alemana, proyecto INTA-GTZ, Lucha contra la Desertificación en la Patagonia a través de un sistema de Monitoreo Ecológico. 182 p.

De Torres Curth, M., Ghermandi, L. & Pfister, G. 2001. Relación entre precipitación y área quemada en incendios de bosque y estepa en el noroeste de la Patagonia. p. 93, *in: Actas de la I Reunión Binacional de Ecología (XX Reunión Argentina de Ecología – X Reunión Sociedad de Ecología de Chile).* Bariloche, Argentina, 23–27 April 2001.

Donadío, E., Bongiorno, M.B., Monteverde, M., Sanchez, G., Funes, M.C., Pailacura, O. & Novaro, A.J. 2001. Ecología trófica del puma (*Puma concolor*), culpeo (*Pseudalopex culpaeus*), águila (*Geranoaetus melanoleucus*) y lechuza (*Tyto alba*) en Neuquén, Patagonia Argentina. p. 96, *in: Actas de la I Reunión Binacional de Ecología (XX Reunión Argentina de Ecología – X Reunión Sociedad de Ecología de Chile).* Bariloche, Argentina, 23–27 April 2001.

Duviols, J.-P. 1997. The Patagonian "Giants". pp. 127–139, *in:* McEwan, Borrero and Priero, 1997, q.v.

Elizalde N., Escobar, J. & Nakamatsu, V. 1991. Metodología expeditiva para la evaluación de pastizales de la zona árida del Chubut. pp. 217–218, *in: Actas de la X Reunión Nacional para el Estudio de las Regiones Aridas y Semiáridas.* Bahía Blanca, Argentina, October 1991.

Ellis, J.E. & Coughenour, M.B. 1996. The SAVANNA integrated modelling system: an integrated remote sensing, GIS and spatial simulation modelling approach. pp. 97–106, *in:* V.R. Squires and A.E. Sidahmed (eds). *Drylands: Sustainable Use of Rangelands into the Twenty-First Century.* IFAD Technical Reports Series. 480 p

Fabricante, I., Oesterheld, M., Paruelo, J.M. & Cecchi, G. 2001. Variaciones espaciales y temporales de productividad primaria neta en el norte de la Patagonia. p. 100, *in: Actas de la I Reunión Binacional de Ecología (XX Reunión Argentina de Ecología – X Reunión Sociedad de Ecología de Chile).* Bariloche, Argentina, 23–27 April 2001.

Fernández, A. & Paruelo, J.M. 1993. Catálogo de estados y transiciones: Estepas arbustivo-graminosas de *Stipa* spp. del centro-oeste del Chubut. pp. 40–46, *in:* Paruelo *et al.*, 1993, q.v.

Fernández, M.E., Gyengue, J.E. & Schlichter, T.M. 2001. Viabilidad de *Festuca pallescens* en sistemas silvopastoriles. II Simulación de fotosíntesis y conductancia estomática bajo distintos niveles de cobertura arbórea. p. 103, *in: Actas de la I Reunión Binacional de Ecología (XX Reunión Argentina de Ecología – X Reunión Sociedad de Ecología de Chile).* Bariloche, Argentina, 23–27 April 2001.

Flombaum, P., Cipriotti, P., Aguiar, M.R. & Sala, O.E. 2001. Sequía y distribución heterogénea de la vegetación: Efectos sobre el establecimiento de una gramínea patagónica. p. 108, *in: Actas de la I Reunión Binacional de Ecología (XX Reunión Argentina de Ecología – X Reunión Sociedad de Ecología de Chile).* Bariloche, Argentina, 23–27 April 2001.

Flueck, W. 2001. La proporción de sexo de la progenie del ciervo colorado antes y después de una sequedad intensa en Patagonia. p. 109, *in: Actas de la I Reunión Binacional de Ecología (XX Reunión Argentina de Ecología – X Reunión Sociedad de Ecología de Chile).* Bariloche, Argentina, 23–27 April 2001.

Funes, M.C., Rosauer, M.M., Novaro, A.J., Sanchez Aldao, G. & Monsalvo, O.B. 2001. Relevamientos poblacionales del choique en la provincia del Neuquén. p. 268, *in: Actas de la I Reunión Binacional de Ecología (XX Reunión Argentina de Ecología – X Reunión Sociedad de Ecología de Chile).* Bariloche, Argentina, 23–27 April 2001.

Ghermandi, L., Guthmann, N. & Bran, D. 2001. Sucesión post-fuego en un pastizal de Stipa speciosa y Festuca pallescens. p. 118. , *in: Actas de la I Reunión Binacional de Ecología (XX Reunión Argentina de Ecología – X Reunión Sociedad de Ecología de Chile).* Bariloche, Argentina, 23–27 April 2001.

Ghersa, C.M., Golluscio, R.A., Paruelo, J.M., Ferraro, D. & Nogués Loza, M.I. 2001. Efecto del pastoreo sobre la heterogeneidad espacial de la vegetación de la Patagonia a distintas escalas. p. 119, in: *Resúmenes de la I Reunión Binacional de*

Ecología (XX Reunión Argentina de Ecología – X Reunión Sociedad de Ecología de Chile). Bariloche, Argentina, 23–27 April 2001.

Giraudo C., Somlo, R., Bonvisutto, G., Siffredi, G. & Becker, G. 1996. Unidad experimental de pastoreo. 1. Con ovinos en mallín central y periférico. Actas del XX Congreso Argentino de Producción Animal. *Revista Argentina de Producción Animal,* **16**(Suppl. 1): 50–51.

Gittins, C.G., Bran, D. & Ghermandi, L. 2001. Determinación de la tasa de super-vivencia post-fuego de dos especies de coirones norpatagónicos. p. 120, *in: Actas de la I Reunión Binacional de Ecología (XX Reunión Argentina de Ecología – X Reunión Sociedad de Ecología de Chile).* Bariloche, Argentina, 23–27 April 2001.

Golluscio, R., Giraudo, C., Borrelli, P., Montes, L., Siffredi, G., Cechi, G., Nakamatsu, V. & Escobar, J. 1999. Utilización de los Recursos Naturales en la Patagonia. Informe Técnico. 80 p. *In:* Consorcio DHV, 1999, q.v.

Golluscio, R.A., León, R.J.C. & Perelman, S.B. 1982. Caracterización fitosoci-ológica de la estepa del Oeste del Chubut. Su relación con el gradiente ambien-tal. *Boletín de la Sociedad Argentina de Botánica,* **21**: 299–324.

Golluscio, R.A., Deregibus, V.A. & Paruelo. J.M. 1998. Sustainability and range management in the Patagonian steppes. *Ecologia Austral,* **8**: 265–284.

Golluscio, R.A., Paruelo, J.M., Hall, S.A., Cesa, A., Giallorenzi, M.C. & Guerschman, J.P. 2000. Medio siglo de registro de la dinámica de la población ovina en una estancia del noroeste del Chubut: ¿Dónde está la desertificación? pp. 106–107, *in: Actas del 23° Congreso Argentino de Producción Animal.* Corrientes, Argentina, 5–7 October 2000.

Golluscio, R.A., Oesterheld, M. & Soriano, A. 2001. Eficiencia del uso del agua y el nitrógeno en 26 especies patagónicas que difieren en la limitación de ambos recursos. p. 122, *in: Actas de la I Reunión Binacional de Ecología (XX Reunión Argentina de Ecología – X Reunión Sociedad de Ecología de Chile).* Bariloche, Argentina, 23–27 April 2001.

González, C.C., Ciano, N.F., Buono, G.G., Nakamatsu, V. & Mavrek, V. 2001. Efecto del fuego sobre un pastizal del Monte austral del noreste del Chubut. p. 124, *in: Actas de la I Reunión Binacional de Ecología (XX Reunión Argentina de Ecología – X Reunión Sociedad de Ecología de Chile).* Bariloche, Argentina, 23–27 April 2001.

González, S.L., Ghermandi, L. & Becker, G. 2001. Banco de semillas post-fuego en un pastizal del noroeste de la Patagonia. p. 125, *in: Actas de la I Reunión Binacional de Ecología (XX Reunión Argentina de Ecología – X Reunión Sociedad de Ecología de Chile).* Bariloche, Argentina, 23–27 April 2001.

Hall, S.A. & Paruelo, J. M. 2001. Controles ambientales de la dinámica de la población ovina en Patagonia. p. 132, *in: Actas de la I Reunión Binacional de Ecología (XX Reunión Argentina de Ecología – X Reunión Sociedad de Ecología de Chile).* Bariloche, Argentina, 23–27 April 2001.

Heady, H. & Child, R.D. 1994. *Rangeland Ecology and Management.* Boulder, Colorado, USA: Westview Press.

Hulme, M. & Sheard, N. 1999. Escenarios de Cambio Climático para Argentina. Norwich, UK: Climatic Research Unit at University of East Anglia. Available from: http://www.cru.uea.ac.uk/%7Emikeh/research/argentina.pdf

Iglesias, R., Tapia, H. & Alegre, M. 1992. Parasitismo gastrointestinal en ovinos del Departamento Guer Aike. Provincia de Santa Cruz, Argentina. pp. 305–322, *in: III Congreso Mundial de Ovinos y Lanas.* Buenos Aires, Argentina, August 1992.

Jobággy, G.E., Paruelo, J.M. & León, R.J.C. 1995. Estimación de la precipitación y de su variablilidad interanual a partir de información geográfica en el NW de la Patagonia, Argentina. *Ecologia Austral,* **5**: 47–53.

Kothmann, M.M. 1984. Concepts and Principles underlying grazing systems. A discussion paper. pp. 903–916, *in:* NAS-NRC Committee on Developing Strategies for Rangeland Management. *Developing strategies for rangeland management.* Westview special studies in Agricultural Research. Boulder, Colorado, USA: Westview Press.

Kröpfl, A.I., Cecchi, G.A., Distel, R.A., Villasuso, N.M. & Silva, M.A. 2001. Diferenciación espacial en el uso del agua del suelo entre *Larrea divaricata* y *Stipa tenuis* en el Monte rionegrino. p. 141, *in: Actas de la I Reunión Binacional de Ecología (XX Reunión Argentina de Ecología – X Reunión Sociedad de Ecología de Chile).* Bariloche, Argentina, 23–27 April 2001.

Lafuente, H. 1981. La región de los Césares. Apuntes para una historia económica de Santa Cruz. Argentina: Editorial de Belgrano. 175 p.

Lange, R.T. 1985. Spatial distributions of stocking intensity produced by sheep flocks grazing Australian Chenopod shrublands. *Transactions of the Royal Society of South Australia,* **109**: 167–179.

Lauenroth, W. 1998. Guanacos, spiny shrubs and the evolutionary history of grazing in the Patagonian steppe. *Ecologia Austral,* **8**: 211–215.

León, R.J.C., Bran, D., Collantes, M., Paruelo, J.M. & Soriano, A. 1998. Grandes unidades de vegetación de Patagonia extra andina. *Ecologia Austral,* **8**: 125–144.

Luque, J., Ciano, N., Nakamatsu, V., Amari, M. & Lisoni, C. 2000. Saneamiento de derrames de hidrocarburos por la técnica de biodegración "in situ" en Patagonia, Argentina. *XI Conferencia de la International Soil Conservation Organization (ISCO 2000).* Buenos Aires, Argentina, 22–27 October 2000. Resúmenes ISCO.

MacArthur, R. 1972. Climates on a Rotating Earth. pp. 1–19, in: R. MacArthur (ed). *Geographical Ecology.* New York, NY, USA: Harper & Row.

Magaldi, J.J., Cibils, A., Humano, G., Nakamatsu, V. & Sanmartino, L. 2001. Ensayo de riego e intersiembra en estepas degradadas de la meseta central santacruceña: Resultados preliminares. pp. 62–63, *in: Actas del taller de actualización sobre métodos de evaluación, monitoreo y recuperación de pastizales naturales patagónicos.* IV Reunión del Grupo Regional Patagónico de Ecosistemas de Pastoreo. INTA-INIA-FAO. Esquel, Argentina, 26–27 June 2001.

Mainwaring, M.J. 1983. *From the Falklands to Patagonia.* London, UK: Allison & Busby. 287 p.

Manero, A. 2001. El zorro colorado en la producción ovina. pp. 243–252, *in:* P. Borrelli and G. Oliva (eds). *Ganadería ovina sustentable en la Patagonia Austral.* Rio Gallergos, Argentina: Prodesar/INTA-Centro Regional Patagonia Sur.

Manero, A., Ferrari, S., Albrieu, C. & Malacalza. V. 2001. Comunidades de aves en humedales del sur de Santa Cruz, Argentina. p. 156, *in: Actas de la I Reunión Binacional de Ecología (XX Reunión Argentina de Ecología – X Reunión Sociedad de Ecología de Chile).* Bariloche, Argentina, 23–27 April 2001.

Marcolin, A.A. & Bustos, J.C. 2001. Características ambientales y biológicas de poblaciones naturales del género Atriplex en la Linea Sur de Río Negro. p. 157, *in: Actas de la I Reunión Binacional de Ecología (XX Reunión Argentina de Ecología – X Reunión Sociedad de Ecología de Chile).* Bariloche, Argentina, 23–27 April 2001.

Martinic, B.M. 1997. The Meeting of Two Cultures. Indians and colonists in the Magellan Region. pp. 85–102, *in:* McEwan, Borrero and Priero, 1997, q.v.

Mascó, E.M. 1995. Intoducción de especies forrajeras nativas y exóticas en el sur de la Patagonia (Pcia. de Santa Cruz). *Revista Argentina de Producción Animal,* **15**: 286–290.

Mascó, E.M. & Montes, L. 1995. Evaluación preliminar de especies forrajeras. p. 222, *in:* L. Montes and G.E. Oliva (eds). *Patagonia.* Actas del Taller Internacional sobre Recursos Fitogenéticos, Desertificación y Uso Sustentable de los Recursos Naturales de la Patagonia. Río Gallegos, Argentina, November 1994. INTA Centro Regional Patagonia Sur.

McEwan, C., Borrero, L.A. & Prieto, A. (eds). 1997. *Patagonia: Natural history, prehistory and ethnography at the uttermost end of the earth.* New Jersey, USA: Princeton University Press.

Méndez Casariego, H. 2000. Sistema de soporte de decisiones para la producción ganadera sustentable en la Provincia de Río Negro (SSD-Río Negro). INTA-GTZ. Centro Regional Patagonia Norte. EEA Bariloche. EEA Valle Inferior. Proyecto Prodesar.1 CD-ROM.

Milchunas, D.G., Sala, O.E. & Lauenroth, W.K. 1988. A generalized model of the effects of grazing by large herbivores on grassland community structure. *The American Naturalist,* **132**: 87–106.

Molina Sanchez, D. 1968. Pasturas perennes artificiales en la Provincia de Santa Cruz. pp. 80–82, *in: Actas de la III reunión Nacional para el Estudio de las Regiones Aridas y Semiáridas.* Trelew, Argentina, October 1968.

Montes, L., Zappe, A., Becker, G. & Ciano, N. 1996. Catálogo de semillas. INTA Centro Regional Patagonia Norte - Centro Regional Patagonia Sur. Proyecto MAB-UNESCO, PRODESER (INTA-GTZ), 25 p.

Mueller, J. 2001. Mejoramiento genético de las majadas patagónicas. pp. 211–224, *in:* P. Borrelli and G. Oliva (eds). *Ganadería ovina sustentable en la Patagonia Austral.* Rio Gallergos, Argentina: Prodesar/ INTA-Centro Regional Patagonia Sur.

Nakamatsu, V.B., Elissalde, N., Pappalardo, J. & Escobar, J.M. 1993. Catálogo de estados y transiciones: Matorrales del monte austral del Chubut. pp. 57–64, *in:* Paruelo *et al.*, 1993, q.v.

Nakamatsu, V.B., Escobar, J.M. & Elissalde, J.M. 2001a. Evaluación forrajera de pastizales naturales de estepa en establecimientos ganaderos de la provincia de Chubut (Patagonia, Argentina), Resultados de 10 años de trabajo. pp. 19–20, *in: Resúmenes del taller de actualización sobre métodos de evaluación, monitoreo y recuperación de pastizales naturales patagónicos.* IV Reunión del Grupo Regional Patagónico de Ecosistemas de Pastoreo. INTA-INIA-FAO. Esquel, Argentina, 26–27 June 2001.

Nakamatsu, V., Luque, J., Ciano, N., Amari, M.E. & Lisoni, C. 2001b. Revegetación natural en un suelo empetrolado biodegradado in situ. Caleta Olivia, Santa Cruz. pp. 52–53, *in: Actas del taller de actualización sobre métodos de evaluación, monitoreo y recuperación de pastizales naturales patagónicos.* IV Reunión del Grupo Regional Patagónico de Ecosistemas de Pastoreo. INTA-INIA-FAO. Esquel, Argentina, 26–27 June 2001.

Novaro, A.J., Funes, M.C., Mosalvo, O.B., Sanchez, G., Pailacura, O. & Donadío, E. 2001. Rol de la predación por zorros culpeos en la regulación poblacional de la liebre europea en Patagonia. p. 282, *in: Actas de la I Reunión Binacional de Ecología (XX Reunión Argentina de Ecología – X Reunión Sociedad de Ecología de Chile).* Bariloche, Argentina, 23–27 April 2001.

Noy-Meir, I. 1973. Desert Ecosystems: Environment and producers. *Annual Review of Ecology and Systematics*, **4**: 25–51.

Noy-Meir, I. 1995. Working Group on Sustainability and Management of Natural Resources in Patagonia. Conclusions and Recomendations. pp. 204–205, *in:* L. Montes and G.E. Oliva (eds). *Patagonia.* Actas del Taller Internacional sobre Recursos Fitogenéticos, Desertificación y Uso Sustentable de los Recursos Naturales de la Patagonia. Río Gallegos, Argentina, November 1994. INTA Centro Regional Patagonia Sur.

Oliva, G. & Borrelli, P. 1993. Catálogo de estados y transiciones: Estepas del sudeste de Santa Cruz. pp. 73–83, *in:* Paruelo *et al.*, 1993, q.v.

Oliva, G.E., Bartolomei, C. & Humano, G. 2000. Recuperación de vegetación y suelos de la estepa magallánica (Patagonia) en exclusión del pastoreo. *In:* Resúmenes ISCO – Buenos Aires, 22–27 October 2000.

Oliva, G.E., Collantes, M.B. & Humano, G. 2001. Un modelo demográfico de la reproducción vegetativa del Coirón fueguino (Festuca gracillima) basada en diez años de observaciones de campo. p. 282, *in: Actas de la I Reunión Binacional de Ecología (XX Reunión Argentina de Ecología – X Reunión Sociedad de Ecología de Chile).* Bariloche, Argentina, 23–27 April 2001.

Oliva, G., Rial, P. & Borrelli, P. 1995. Desertificación y posibilidades de uso sustentable en la Provincia de Santa Cruz. pp. 48–55, *in:* L. Montes and G.E. Oliva (eds). *Patagonia.* Actas del Taller Internacional sobre Recursos Fitogenéticos, Desertificación y Uso Sustentable de los Recursos Naturales de la Patagonia. Río Gallegos, Argentina, November 1994. INTA Centro Regional Patagonia Sur.

Oliva, G., Cibils, A., Borrelli, P. & Humano, G. 1998. Stable states in relation to grazing in Patagonia: a 10-year experimental trial. *Journal of Arid Environments*, **40**: 113–131.

Oliva, G., Rial, P., González, L. Cibils, A. & Borrelli, P. 1996. Evaluation of carrying capacity using Landsat MSS images in South Patagonia. pp. 408–409, *in: Proceedings of the 5th International Rangeland Congress*. Salt Lake City, Utah, USA, 23–28 July 1995.

Pancotto, V.A., Sala, O.E., Ballare, C.L., Scopel, A.L. & Caldwell, M.M. 2001. Efectos de la radiación ultravioleta-B sobre la descomposición de *Gunnera magellanica* en Tierra del Fuego. p. 176, *in: Actas de la I Reunión Binacional de Ecología (XX Reunión Argentina de Ecología – X Reunión Sociedad de Ecología de Chile)*. Bariloche, Argentina, 23–27 April 2001.

Paruelo, J.M. & Golluscio, R.A. 1993. Catálogo de estados y transiciones: Estepas graminoso-arbustivas del NW del Chubut. pp. 5–13, *in:* Paruelo *et al.*, 1993, q.v.

Paruelo, J.M. & Sala, O.E. 1995. Water losses in the patagonian steppe: a modelling approach. *Ecology*, **76**: 510–520.

Paruelo, J., Golluscio, R. & Deregibus, V.A. 1992. Manejo del pastoreo sobre bases ecológicas en la Patagonia extra andina: una experiencia a escala de establecimiento. *Anales de la Sociedad Rural Argentina*, **126**: 68–80.

Paruelo, J.M., Jobbágy, E.G. & Sala, O.E. 1998. Biozones of Patagonia (Argentina). *Ecologia Austral*, **8**: 145–154.

Paruelo, J.M., Beltrán, A. Jobbágy, E.G., Sala, O.E. & Golluscio, R.A. 1998. The climate of Patagonia: general patterns and controls on biotic processes. *Ecologia Austral*, **8**: 85–102.

Paruelo, J.M., Cesa, A., Golluscio, R.A., Guerschman, J.P., Giallorenzi, M.C. & Hall, S.A. 2001. Relevamiento de la vegetación en la Ea. Leleque: Un ejemplo de aplicación de sistemas de información geográfica en la evaluación de recursos forrajeros. pp. 61–62, *in: Resúmenes del taller de actualización sobre métodos de evaluación, monitoreo y recuperación de pastizales naturales patagónicos*. IV Reunión del Grupo Regional Patagónico de Ecosistemas de Pastoreo. INTA-INIA-FAO. Esquel, Argentina, 26–27 June 2001.

Pelliza, A., Siffredi, G., Willems, P. & Vilagra, S. 2001. Tipos estructurales de dieta del ganado doméstico a nivel de un paisaje de Patagonia. p. 180, *in: Actas de la I Reunión Binacional de Ecología (XX Reunión Argentina de Ecología – X Reunión Sociedad de Ecología de Chile)*. Bariloche, Argentina, 23–27 April 2001.

Peralta, C. 1999. Algunas características sociales de la Patagonia. 16 p. *In:* Consorcio DHV, 1999, q.v.

Perelman, S.B., León, R.J.C. & Bussacca, J.P. 1997. Floristic changes related to grazing intensity in a Patagonian shrub steppe. *Ecography*, **20**: 400–406.

Peri, P., Arena, M.E. & Vater, G. 2001. Crecimiento de los brotes en plantas de *Berberis heterophylla* Juss. "Calafate". 1. Tipos de poda. p. 184, *in: Actas de la I Reunión Binacional de Ecología (XX Reunión Argentina de Ecología – X Reunión Sociedad de Ecología de Chile)*. Bariloche, Argentina, 23–27 April 2001.

Pickup, G. & Stafford-Smith, M. 1993. Problems, prospects and procedures for assessing the sustainability of pastoral land management in arid Australia. *Journal of Biogeography*, **20**: 471–487.

Rafaele, E. & Veblen, T. 2001. Evidencias de la interacción fuego-herbívoro sobre los matorrales: hipótesis y experimentos. p. 124, *in: Actas de la I Reunión Binacional de Ecología (XX Reunión Argentina de Ecología – X Reunión Sociedad de Ecología de Chile)*. Bariloche, Argentina, 23–27 April 2001.

Rimoldi, P. & Buono, G. 2001. Esquema flexible de ajuste de cargas por precipitación. pp. 13–14, *in: Resúmenes del taller de actualización sobre métodos de evaluación, monitoreo y recuperación de pastizales naturales patagónicos*. IV Reunión del Grupo Regional Patagónico de Ecosistemas de Pastoreo. INTA-INIA-FAO. Esquel, Argentina, 26–27 June 2001.

Ripol, M.P., Cingolani, A.M., Bran, D. & Anchorena, J. 2001. Diferenciación de la estructura de parches en campos de la estepa patagónica con distintas historias de pastoreo a partir de imágenes Landsat TM. p. 198, in: *Resúmenes de la I Reunión Binacional de Ecología (XX Reunión Argentina de Ecología – X Reunión Sociedad de Ecología de Chile)*. Bariloche, Argentina, 23–27 April 2001.

Robles, C. & Olaechea, F. 2001. Salud y enfermedades de las majadas. pp. 225–243, *in:* P. Borrelli and G. Oliva (eds). *Ganadería ovina sustentable en la Patagonia Austral.* Rio Gallergos, Argentina: Prodesar/INTA-Centro Regional Patagonia Sur.

Roig, F.A. 1998. La vegetación de la Patagonia. pp. 48–166, *in:* M.N. Correa (ed). *Flora Patagónica: Parte I.* Buenos Aires, Argentina: Colección científica del INTA.

Rostagno, C.M. 1993. Catálogo de estados y transiciones: Estepas arbustivo-herbáceas del área central de Península Valdés e Itsmo Ameghino. Pcia. del Chubut. pp. 47–51, *in:* Paruelo *et al.*, 1993, q.v.

Rostagno, C.M. 2001. La degradación de los suelos en el sitio ecológico Punta Ninfas: Procesos y posible práctica para su recuperación. pp. 44–45, *in: Resúmenes del taller de actualización sobre métodos de evaluación, monitoreo y recuperación de pastizales naturales patagónicos*. IV Reunión del Grupo Regional Patagónico de Ecosistemas de Pastoreo. INTA-INIA-FAO. Esquel, Argentina, 26–27 June 2001.

Rotundo, J.L. & Aguiar, M.R. 2001. Efecto de la broza sobre la regeneración de gramíneas en peligro de extinciónpor sobrepastoreo. p. 205, *in: Actas de la I Reunión Binacional de Ecología (XX Reunión Argentina de Ecología – X Reunión Sociedad de Ecología de Chile)*. Bariloche, Argentina, 23–27 April 2001.

Sáenz, A.M. & Deregibus, V.A. 2001. Morfogénesis vegetativa de dos subpoblaciones de *Poa ligularis* bajo condiciones de estrés hídrico periódico. p. 210, *in: Actas de la I Reunión Binacional de Ecología (XX Reunión Argentina de Ecología – X Reunión Sociedad de Ecología de Chile)*. Bariloche, Argentina, 23–27 April 2001.

SAGPyA. 2001. Boletín ovino. [Web page accessed 3 October 2001]. Located at www//http.sagyp.mecon.gov.ar

Sain, C.L., Bertiller, M.B. & Carrera, A.L. 2001. Relación entre la composición florística y la conservación de nitrógeno del suelo en el SW del Chubut. p. 211, *in: Actas de la I Reunión Binacional de Ecología (XX Reunión Argentina de Ecología – X Reunión Sociedad de Ecología de Chile).* Bariloche, Argentina, 23–27 April 2001.

Sala, O.E., Yahdjian, M.L. & Flombaum, P. 2001. Limitantes estructurales y biogeoquímicos de la productividad primaria: efecto de la sequía. p. 211, *in: Actas de la I Reunión Binacional de Ecología (XX Reunión Argentina de Ecología – X Reunión Sociedad de Ecología de Chile).* Bariloche, Argentina, 23–27 April 2001.

Sala, O.E., Lauenroth, W.K. & Golluscio, R. 1997. Plant functional types in temperate semi-arid regions. pp. 217–233, *in:* T.M. Smith, H.H. Shugart and F.I. Woodward (eds). *Plant Functional Types – their relevance to ecosystem properties and global change.* Cambridge, UK: Cambridge University Press.

Sala, O.E., Parton, W.J., Joyce, L.A. & Lauenroth, W.K. 1988. Primary production of the Central Grassland Region of the United States. *Ecology,* **69**: 40–45.

Schlichter, T.M., León, R.J.C. & Soriano, A. 1978. Utilización de índices de diversidad en la evaluación de pastizales naturales en el centro-oeste del Chubut. *Ecologia Austral,* **3**: 125–131.

Schlichter, T.M., Fernández, M.E. & Gyenge, J. E. 2001. Viabilidad de *Festuca pallescens* en sistemas silvopastoriles. I. Distribución de recursos agua y luz bajo distintos niveles de cobertura arbórea. p. 216, *in: Actas de la I Reunión Binacional de Ecología (XX Reunión Argentina de Ecología – X Reunión Sociedad de Ecología de Chile).* Bariloche, Argentina, 23–27 April 2001.

SETCIP [Secretaría para la Tecnología, la Ciencia y la Innovación Productiva]. 2000. Convocatoria PICT 2000/2001. Anexo I.2. Líneas de investigación prioritarias. [Web page accessed 22 October 2001] See: http://www.agencia.secyt.gov.ar/fct/pict2000/BasesIIC.htm#6

Semmartin, M., Aguiar, M.R., Distel, R.A., Moretto, A. & Ghersa, C.M. 2001. Efecto de los reemplazos florísticos inducidos por la herbivoría sobre la dinámica de carbono y nitrógeno en tres pastizales naturales. p. 293, *in: Actas de la I Reunión Binacional de Ecología (XX Reunión Argentina de Ecología – X Reunión Sociedad de Ecología de Chile).* Bariloche, Argentina, 23–27 April 2001.

Siffredi, G.L. & Bustos, J.C. 2001. El efecto del ramoneo sobre el crecimiento de arbustos en Patagonia. p. 220, *in: Actas de la I Reunión Binacional de Ecología (XX Reunión Argentina de Ecología – X Reunión Sociedad de Ecología de Chile).* Bariloche, Argentina, 23–27 April 2001.

Siffredi, G., Becker, G., Sarmiento, A., Ayesa, J., Bran, D. & López, C. 2002. Métodos de evaluación de los recursos naturales para la planificación integral y uso sustentable de las tierras. p. 35, *in: Resúmenes del taller de actualización sobre métodos de evaluación, monitoreo y recuperación de pastizales naturales patagónicos.* IV Reunión del Grupo Regional Patagónico de Ecosistemas de Pastoreo. INTA-INIA-FAO. Esquel, Argentina, 26–27 June 2001.

Siffredi, G., Ayeza, J., Becker, G.F., Mueller, J. & Bonvisutto, G. 1995. Efecto de la carga animal sobre la vegetación y la producción ovina en Río Mayo (Chubut) a diez años de pastoreo. pp. 91–92, *in:* R. Somlo and G.F. Becker (eds). *Seminario-Taller sobre Producción, Nutrición y Utilización de pastizales.* Trelew. FAO-UNESCO/MAB-INTA.

Silva, M.A., Kröpfl, A.I., Cecchi, G.A. & Distel, R.A. 2001. Reducción de la cobertura de costra microfítica en áreas pastoreadas del Monte rionegrino. p. 220, *in: Actas de la I Reunión Binacional de Ecología (XX Reunión Argentina de Ecología – X Reunión Sociedad de Ecología de Chile).* Bariloche, Argentina, 23–27 April 2001.

Smithsonian Institution. 1997. Centers for Plant Diversity. The Americas. [Web page accessed 19 October 2001]. See: http://www.nmnh.si.edu/botany/projects/cpd/index.htm.

Soriano, A., Nogués Loza, M. & Burkart, S. 1995. Plant biodiversity in the extra-andean Patagonia: Comparisons with neighboring and related vegetation units. pp. 36–45, *in:* L. Montes and G.E. Oliva (eds). *Patagonia.* Actas del Taller Internacional sobre Recursos Fitogenéticos, Desertificación y Uso Sustentable de los Recursos Naturales de la Patagonia. Río Gallegos, Argentina, November 1994. INTA Centro Regional Patagonia Sur.

Soriano, A. 1983. Deserts and semi-deserts of Patagonia. pp. 423–460, *in:* N.E. West (ed). *Ecosystems of the World - Temperate Deserts and Semi-Deserts.* Amsterdam, The Netherlands: Elsevier Scientific.

Stafford-Smith. M. 1996. Management of rangelands: paradigms at their limits. pp. 325–357, *in:* J. Hodgson and A. Illius (eds). *The Ecology and Management of Grazing Systems.* Wallingford, UK: CAB International.

Stofella, S.L. & Anchorena, J. 2001. Efecto de la compactación y la competencia sobre el desarrollo del arbusto *Chillotrichum diffusum* en la estepa magallánica. p. 225, *in: Actas de la I Reunión Binacional de Ecología (XX Reunión Argentina de Ecología – X Reunión Sociedad de Ecología de Chile).* Bariloche, Argentina, 23–27 April 2001.

Sturzenbaum, P. & Borrelli, P.R. 2001. Manejo de riesgos climáticos. pp. 255–270, *in:* P. Borrelli and G. Oliva (eds). *Ganadería ovina sustentable en la Patagonia Austral.* Rio Gallergos, Argentina: Prodesar/INTA-Centro Regional Patagonia Sur.

Stronati, M.S., Arce, M.E., Feijoo, M.S. & Barrientos, E. 2001. Evakuación de la diversidad morfológica en poblaciones de dos especies leñosas del género *Adesmia.* p. 226, *in: Actas de la I Reunión Binacional de Ecología (XX Reunión Argentina de Ecología – X Reunión Sociedad de Ecología de Chile).* Bariloche, Argentina, 23–27 April 2001.

Stuart-Hill, C. 1989. Adaptive Management: The only practicable method of veld management. pp. 4–7, *in:* J.E. Danckwerts and W.R. Teague (eds). *Veld management in the Eastern Cape.* Department of Agriculture, Republic of South Africa. 196 p.

Utrilla, V., Clifton, G., Larrosa, J. & Barría, D. 2000. Engorde de ovejas de refugo con dos tipos de uso y dos intensidades de pastoreo en un mallín de la Patagonia austral. pp. 243–244, *in: Actas del 23° Congreso Argentino de Producción Animal.* Corrientes, Argentina, 5–7 October 2000.

Vargas, D. & Bertiller, M.B. 2001. Patrones de germinación de distintos grupos de la vegetación en la Patagonia. p. 236, *in: Actas de la I Reunión Binacional de Ecología (XX Reunión Argentina de Ecología – X Reunión Sociedad de Ecología de Chile).* Bariloche, Argentina, 23–27 April 2001.

Veblen, T.T., Hill, R.S. & Read, J. (eds). 1996. *The ecology and biogeography of Nothofagus forests.* New Haven, USA: Yale University Press.

Vila Aiub, M.M., Demartín, E.B., Maseda, P., Gundel, P.E. & Ghersa, C.M. 2001. Exploración de la presencia de hongos endofíticos en pastos de la Estepa Patagónica. p. 239, *in: Actas de la I Reunión Binacional de Ecología (XX Reunión Argentina de Ecología – X Reunión Sociedad de Ecología de Chile).* Bariloche, Argentina, 23–27 April 2001.

Vilela, A., Agüero, R. & Ravetta, D.A. 2001. Comparación del esfuerzo reproductivo en *Prosopis alpataco* y *Prosopis denudans* (Mimosaceae) en el ecotono Monte-Patagonia. p. 240, *in: Actas de la I Reunión Binacional de Ecología (XX Reunión Argentina de Ecología – X Reunión Sociedad de Ecología de Chile).* Bariloche, Argentina, 23–27 April 2001.

Villacide, J.M. & Farina, J. 2001. Insectos formadores de agallas de *Schinus patagonicus*: efecto del ambiente sobre el sistema insecto-planta. p. 240, *in: Actas de la I Reunión Binacional de Ecología (XX Reunión Argentina de Ecología – X Reunión Sociedad de Ecología de Chile).* Bariloche, Argentina, 23–27 April 2001.

Villamil, C.B. 1997. Patagonia. Data Sheet - CDP South America - Site A46 - Diversity Conservation Project - NMNH Smithsonian Institution. Downloaded 19 October 2001 from: http//www.nmnh.si.edu/botany/projects/cpd/sa/sa46.htm

Villasuso, N.M., Kröpfl, A.I., Cecchi, G.A. & Distel, R.A. 2001. Efecto facilitador de las costras microfíticas sobre la instalación de semillas en el suelo en el Monte rionegrino. p. 241, *in: Actas de la I Reunión Binacional de Ecología (XX Reunión Argentina de Ecología – X Reunión Sociedad de Ecología de Chile).* Bariloche, Argentina, 23–27 April 2001.

Wassner, D.F. & Ravetta, V. 2001. Suelo encostrado bajo *Grindelia chiloensis*. Relación con la pérdida de resinas de las hojas y cambios en propiedades del suelo. p. 243, *in: Actas de la I Reunión Binacional de Ecología (XX Reunión Argentina de Ecología – X Reunión Sociedad de Ecología de Chile).* Bariloche, Argentina, 23–27 April 2001.

Weber, G.E., Paruelo, J.M., Jeltsch, J. & Bertiller, M.B. 2000. Simulación del impacto del pastoreo sobre la dinámica de las estepas de *Festuca pallescens*. pp. 108–109, *in: Actas del 23° Congreso Argentino de Producción Animal.* Corrientes, Argentina, 5–7 October 2000.

Westoby, M., Walker, B. & Noy Meir, I. 1989. Opportunistic management for rangelands not at equilibrium. *Journal of Range Management,* **42**: 266–273.

Chapter 5
The South American Campos ecosystem

Olegario Royo Pallarés (Argentina), Elbio J. Berretta (Uruguay) and Gerzy E. Maraschin (Brazil)

SUMMARY

The *Campos*, grassland with few trees or shrubs except near streams, lies between 24°S and 35°S; it includes parts of Brazil, Paraguay and Argentina, and all of Uruguay. Grassland-based livestock production is very important, based on the natural grassland that covers most of the area. Stock rearing is on large, delimited holdings and is commercial. Both tussock-grass and short-grass grasslands occur. There is a dominance of summer-growing C_4 grasses, with C_3 grasses associated with the winter cycle. Cattle and horses were introduced in the seventeenth century and sheep in the nineteenth. Production is based on spring–summer growing grassland, with little use of sown pastures. Beef cattle predominate; sheep are mainly for wool, but some lamb is produced. Limited winter production and poor herbage quality are major limiting factors in livestock production. Soil phosphorus is generally low and this deficiency affects stock. Campos pastures are highly responsive to fertilizers, which can modify the specific composition of natural grassland; application of phosphate increases legume cover and the phosphorus content of forage. Fattening off grass can take up to four years; intensive fattening of younger stock uses some sown pasture. Sheep may be grazed with breeding herds of cattle. Exotic temperate legumes can be grown and may be over-sown into native swards after land preparation; once established, legumes encourage the development of winter grasses. This paper shows that it is possible to improve forage consumption from natural grasslands, implying an annual increase of 784 000 tonne of liveweight, without cost, in Rio Grande do Sul alone, through a strategy of high forage offer to the grazing animal, which also optimizes forage accumulation rates in the pasture.

INTRODUCTION

The South American *Campos* is an ecological region lying between 24°S and 35°S, which includes parts of southern Brazil, southern Paraguay and northeastern Argentina, and the whole of Uruguay (see Figure 5.1), covering an area of approximately 500 000 km². The term Campos refers to grasslands or pastures with a vegetation cover comprising mainly grasses and herbs; scattered small shrubs and trees are occasionally found, generally by the banks of streams.

Figure 5.1
The Campos region of South America.

The grasslands of the Campos have enormous potential for cattle, sheep and horse production for meat, and for various wildlife products. This potential derives from the good environmental conditions, particularly the climate, which allows the growth of a great floristic diversity of edible plants that produce a huge bulk of forage throughout the year.

The climate is subtropical to temperate, with very marked seasonal fluctuations; it is subhumid, because potential evapotranspiration in summer is greater than precipitation, which leads to moisture deficiencies in the soil. Although rainfall is distributed throughout the year, it is characterized by great variations between years; this irregularity is the main source of problems in forage production. The highest precipitation is usually in summer and autumn.

Livestock production is one of the most important agricultural activities of the region, based on the natural grasslands that cover 95 percent of the area. Hence the great importance of this economic resource: its utilization in terms of maximum productivity while avoiding deterioration is an issue that concerns farmers, researchers and others with an interest in natural resource conservation.

GENERAL DESCRIPTION OF THE REGION
Climate
The Campos has a subtropical climate, very warm in summer but with frosts in winter. It is humid, often with moisture surplus in autumn and spring, but moderate deficits in summer (Escobar *et al.*, 1996) Average annual temperature in Corrientes Province varies from 19.5°C in the south of the province to 22.0°C in the north. The average of the coldest month varies from 13.5°C to 16.0°C. Meteorological frosts are registered in the whole region, with low frequency, from one to six frosts per year, mainly in June and July, with records of first and last frosts from May to September.

Average annual precipitation ranges between 1 200 and 1 600 mm, increasing from east to west. There is an unexplained increasing trend in mean annual precipitation; in the last 30 years autumn rainfall increased by more than 100 mm, while spring rainfall tended to decrease. Monthly rainfall distribution is variable: April, March and February have averages above 170 mm/month. A second rainfall peak occurs in October–November, with 130–140 mm/month, and lower values are recorded in winter. The moisture balance shows periods of excess (precipitation higher than evapotranspiration) in autumn and spring (March–April and September–October) and deficits in summer (December–January). Annual average relative humidity for all locations ranges between 70 and 75 percent, the lower values in summer and the higher in winter.

Livestock production
Cattle stock is about 4.2 million head in Corrientes Province (Argentina) and 10.1 million in Uruguay, with little variation in recent years. Sheep stocks have been declining consistently, and in 1996 there were 1.2 million head in Corrientes and 13 million in Uruguay. Low wool prices, reduction in domestic consumption of mutton and farmers discouraged by sheep rustling are the main causes.

Wildlife
The Campos Ecosystem, with abundant open tussock ranges and gallery forests along watercourses, provides a suitable environment for the development of a varied and abundant fauna. The great diversity of water bodies, flooded areas, small and big lagoons allowed the development of important populations of *carpinchos* or capybaras (*Hydrochoerus hidrochaeris*) in almost all the territory. Hunting of this animal for its valuable pelt is controlled by provincial authorities, and populations remain relatively stable. Deer are found in aquatic environments. Marsh deer (*Odocoileus blastocerus*) was an endangered species and now is controlled in protected areas in Brazil. In Uruguay, *Ozotocerus*

bezoarticus is the typical deer. Other abundant species are *yacares* (*Caiman* spp.) and river wolves (giant otters, *Pteronura brasiliensis*). On the grassland part of the Campos there are armadillos (*Dasypus* spp.), viscachas (*Lagostomus maximus*), hares, foxes, partridges, rheas and ducks, which are rarely harmed by humans.

Floristic composition

Within the Campos there are various econiches, defined more by inherent botanical composition than by effect of use. The dominant vegetation in Corrientes is herbaceous, with few or no trees and shrubs, except for the Ñandubay forest. Hence the name Campos or *Campos limpios*. Perennial summer grasses dominate, with sedges next in importance, and are found in every grassland of the region. There are numerous legumes, but at very low frequencies. More than 300 species from 39 botanical families have been listed in the herbaceous strata (J.G. Fernández, pers. comm.), which reflects the great floristic diversity and botanical richness of these grasslands. Perennial grasses contribute 70–80 percent of the total dry matter (DM) yield; Cyperaceae follow, with 7 percent on higher ground and up to 20 percent in the marshy, low-lying wetlands (*malezales*). Legume contribution is always low, ranging from 3 to 8 percent of total DM yield on higher ground, and is practically nil in the lowlands of the *malezales*.

In the Rocky Outcrops (*afloramiantos rocosos*) zone, natural grasslands have been regularly studied since the mid-1980s. In a grazing trial on 70 ha, 178 species were noted. The three most important grasses were *Andropogon lateralis*, *Paspalum notatum* and *Sporobolus indicus*. Other important grasses were *Paspalum almum*, *P. plicatulum*, *Coelorachis selloana* and *Schizachyrium paniculatum*. Other species seldom contributed more than 10 percent of total biomass. *Desmodium incanum* was the only legume that regularly contributed to summer forage. The most abundant Cyperaceae was *Rhynchospora praecincta*.

A greater range of species contributes to the total biomass of short-grass grasslands, although three grasses – *Paspalum notatum*, *Sporobolus indicus* and *Axonopus argentinus* – are the most frequent. An important feature of this grassland is that winter grasses can contribute from 3 to 20 percent of winter forage, depending on grazing management. The commonest winter species are *Stipa setigera*, *Piptochaetium stipoides*, *P. montevidense* and *Trifolium polymorphum*.

Climax vegetation

Cattle and horses were the first domestic herbivores, introduced by Spanish settlers at the beginning of the seventeenth century; sheep arrived in the mid-nineteenth century. The introduction of domestic livestock to the natural grassland ecosystem has changed the vegetation type, as grazing is the main factor that keeps the grasslands in a herbaceous pseudoclimax phase (Vieira da Silva, 1979). Exotic plants, mainly from Europe, were introduced along with livestock, increasing the disturbance. There is little information about the characteristics of the grasslands previous to the introduction of domestic herbivores. According to Gallinal *et al.* (1938) "We do not know descriptions or precise indicators of existing vegetation prior to livestock introduction nor from the native immigration over areas that now are Campos". Some imprecise references to vegetation were made at the beginning of nineteenth century by travellers such as the foreigners Azara, Darwin and Saint Hilaire, and by criollos such as Father Dámaso Antonio Larrañaga. From their descriptions it can be deduced that there were no forest zones, except for the banks of rivers, and that the landscape was characteristically a prairie with some small trees, shrubs and sub-shrubs.

In an exclosure made in 1984 at the INIA Experimental Unit of Glencoe, Uruguay, (32°01′32″S and 57°00′39″W), where grazing was excluded on land that had been grazed for centuries, tall bunchgrass-like plants began to increase and short-grasses showed reduced cover. There was also an increase of sub-shrubs and shrubs such as *Eupatorium buniifolium*, *Baccharis articulata*, *B. spicata* and *B. trimera*, while *B. coridifolia* decreased, as it is a species that thrives when grasses are weakened by grazing. *B. dracunculifolia*, a shrub of three metres, which has branches that are easily broken by domestic herbivores, was found after six years of exclosure. The population of *B. articulata* remained stable for five years; thereafter all the plants died almost simultaneously, but after a similar period, the population re-established and died again, and now there are new plants developing. Original plants of *Eupatorium buniifolium* remain, and there are other, younger plants. The size of the grass bunches increased and the number of individual plant decreased, as shown by *Stipa neesiana*, *Paspalum dilatatum*, *Coelorachis selloana* and *Schizachyrium microstachyum*. There is a great development of grasses that were of very low frequency and rarely flowered under grazing, such as *Paspalum indecorum*, *Schizachyrium imberbe* and *Digitaria saltensis*. Native legumes, although of low frequency, also increased in vigour. The continued exclusion of grazing leads to increased litter accumulation, which changes the moisture retention capacity of the soil markedly. This effect, coupled with taller grasses, modifies the microclimate. The interruption of a factor that has driven vegetation to a new equilibrium point returns it to an earlier stage, but not exactly to the same starting point (Laycock, 1991). The situation after two decades of exclosure might be similar to that prior to domestic livestock introduction.

GRASSLAND TYPES AND PRODUCTION SYSTEMS IN ARGENTINA

The structure of the main grassland types of the Mesopotamia Region of Argentina was described by Van der Sluijs (1971). A paper on *Grassland types in the Centre-South of Corrientes* was published by INTA Mercedes (INTA-EEA, 1977). Two different canopy structures are found, determined by the growth form and habit of the dominant species.

On the one hand there are the tussock prairies, called generically *pajonales* (straw), with *Andropogon lateralis* being the commonest species, and there are grasslands dominated by *Sorghastrum agrostoides,* others by *Paspalum quadrifarium* and others by *P. intermedium.* These are typical of the ecological regions of Albardón del Paraná Sandy Hills (*lomadas arenosas*); with lateritic hills and malezales on higher sites.

On the other hand there are short-grass grasslands, where dominant species rarely exceed 30–40 cm in height. Here the commonest grasses are *Paspalum notatum, Axonopus argentinus* and *Sporobolus indicus.* Long-term overgrazing causes grassland deterioration, which leads to a lower canopy, reduced floristic diversity and reduced vegetative growth. In this situation, flechilla becomes the dominant grass (*Aristida venustula*), so these grasslands are named *flechillares.* Deteriorated short-grass grasslands dominate the centre-south of the province, in the Rocky Outcrops regions and Ñandubay forest. Intermediate situations are found between the two grassland types, where pajonales and short-grass are mixed. These are mosaic grasslands, characteristic of the *floramientos* region.

Growth and forage production

Annual production from various grassland types and daily growth rates per hectare were evaluated for a 19-year period on Mercedes Experimental Station. A regrowth cutting methodology was employed, with mobile temporary enclosures (Brown, 1954; Frame, 1981). The main results were:

- **Pajonales** Mean annual production was 5 077 kg DM/ha. Average monthly growth (Figure 5.2) showed regrowth in every month, including winter, when growth was 5 kg DM/ha/day. The average monthly growth rate was at a maximum in February, March and December. Growth rate distribution

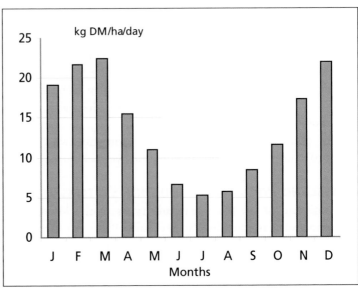

Figure 5.2
Average daily growth rates of a Pajonal grassland (19-year average).

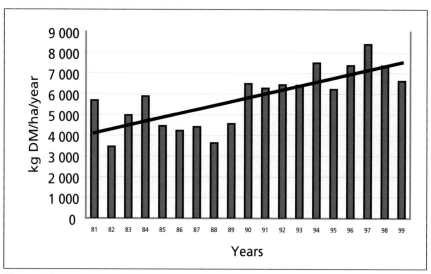

Figure 5.3
Yearly growth rate of a short-grass grassland over a 19-year period.

through the year correlated positively with monthly variations in temperature, showing an autumn peak higher than the spring one. Variability between years is high, particularly in summer, which is related to rainfall variation and high temperatures. Grassland production of the main grassland types of the northwest of the province was studied by Gándara and co-workers (1989, 1990a, b). These authors evaluated three pajonal-dominated sites: malezales, Corrientes and Chavarria, and mean aboveground production for four clipping frequencies was 5 260, 4 850 and 4 120 kg DM/ha/year for the three sites, respectively.

- *Short-grass* Average production of a short-grass grassland was 5 803 kg DM/ha/year, with great variation between years and an increasing trend over time (Figure 5.3). Maximum growth rate was attained at the end of the summer or early autumn (February–March), when growth rates were estimated at 25 kg DM/ha/day. July was the month with least growth; it was estimated at 5.5 kg DM/ha/day. Yearly forage production showed an increasing trend over time, but this could be related to an increasing trend in annual precipitation over the same period. Such an increase could lead to a progressive increase in carrying capacity. Nevertheless, the most remarkable conclusion from the data is the great inter-annual variability.

- *Flechillares* Average production of the flechillares was 2 774 kg DM/ha/year. The highest growth rate was in February and March, followed by December; the lowest in June–July. This grassland has a seasonal distribution similar to the original short-grasses but has a proportionally better growth distribution between winter and spring. The carrying capacity of such grassland is low, and it becomes critical in years when rainfall is below average.

Production systems

Livestock production is based on the use of spring–summer growing grassland, with little use of sown pastures or other supplementary sources of feed. The main production system is a mix of breeding and fattening, with increasing preference for breeding. Specialized fattening systems are irrelevant. Predominant breeds are Zebu-based, followed by European breeds, Indian breeds and criollas. The main systems are characterized by low production efficiency. The average extraction rate for sale is only 18.9 percent, while the national average in Argentina reaches 23 percent.

Sheep rearing is mainly for wool, and to a lesser extent for lamb. A cattle-sheep production system is applied by 3 400 farmers in the centre-south of the province. Predominant breeds are Corriedale, Romney Marsh and Ideal. Lambing rates in Corrientes average 60 to 65 percent, with a mean greasy fleece weight of 3.18 kg/head. Provincial sheep stocks have declined in recent decades, following the same trend as the national stock. The sheep stock in 1993 was 1.39 million head, with a greasy wool production of 4 427 000 kg.

Productivity levels are low when compared with potential productivity in this environment. The reasons for this have been analysed by Royo Pallarés (1985), who indicated a series of environmental, social, economic and technical factors as the causes of low productivity in an economic inflation scenario. Gándara and Arias (1999) noted recently that resource mismanagement, limited adoption of improved technology, lack of service structures, poor cattle markets and small farm size were factors determining low productivity.

Productivity of the best farms

Many authors have reported productivity increases when some basic management technologies have been applied (Arias, 1997; Benitez Meabe, 1997; Royo Pallarés, 1985, 1999). In the north of Corrientes, average productivity at subregional level is 30 kg/ha/year, while at the Experimental Unit, where basic management practices were applied, 67.7 kg/ha/year were obtained (Table 5.1).

GRASSLAND TYPES AND PRODUCTION SYSTEMS IN URUGUAY

Grassland is defined as a vegetation cover formed by grasses, with associated herbs and dwarf shrubs, where trees are rare (Berretta and Nascimento, 1991). The most numerous botanical family is the Gramineae, both summer (C_4) and temperate (C_3) types; this association is an unusual characteristic of these grasslands. The most important Tribes are: Paniceae, including the genera with most species, *Paspalum, Panicum, Axonopus, Setaria, Digitaria*, etc.; Andropogoneae, with *Andropogon, Bothriochloa, Schizachyrium*, etc.; Eragrostea, with the genera *Eragrostis, Distichlis*, etc.; and Chlorideae, with *Chloris, Eleusine, Bouteloua*, etc. Winter-grass tribes, where most of the cultivated forages belong, are: Poeae, with the genera *Bromus, Poa, Melica, Briza*,

TABLE 5.1
Average productivity in northwest Corrientes in comparison with an experimental unit.

Production indexes		NW Corrientes	Experimental Breeding Unit
Marketing rate	(%)	45	69.2
Weaning weight	(kg)	150	197
Weaning weight per cow	(kg)	67	136
Cows/total stock		0.43	0.65
Liveweight production	(kg/ha/year)	30	67.7
Carrying capacity	(Animal Units/ha)	—	0.56 – 0.73[1]

NOTES: (1) September–March.
SOURCE: After Arias, 1997.

TABLE 5.2
Daily Growth Rates (DGR) and their standard deviation (kg DM/ha/day), and Seasonal Distribution (SD) (%) of yearly forage production from grasslands on the main soil types.

Soil type				Season			
				Summer	Autumn	Winter	Spring
Basalt	SBR		DGR	10.1 ± 4.9	6.8 ± 2.9	4.9 ± 2.5	9.9 ± 3.9
			SD	31.4	21.2	15.7	31.7
	SB		DGR	13.6 ± 5.9	8.8 ± 3.9	6.1 ± 2.4	13.0 ± 4.3
			SD	32.1	21.0	14.9	32.0
	D		DGR	17.2 ± 7.8	10.9 ± 4.2	7.3 ±3.1	14.8 ±4.4
			SD	33.3	21.5	15.1	30.1
Eastern Sierras			DGR	15.3	9.2	3.8	11.5
			SD	38.0	23.4	9.7	28.9
Crystalline Soils (granitic) D			DGR	13.1 ± 7.3	8.6 ± 3.3	6.5 ± 3.2	17.0 ± 6.8
			SD	28.6	19.3	14.5	37.6
Sandy Soils	Upper hill		DGR	27.7 ± 5.6	7.3 ± 4.2	4.1 ± 2.3	17.6 ± 3.3
			SD	48.5	13.1	7.3	31.1
	Low hill		DGR	27.3 ± 8.4	7.5 ± 4.4	3.7 ± 1.5	22.2 ± 4.1
			SD	44.5	13.6	6.1	36.8
North East Soils			DGR	5.1	6.9	4.7	11.0
			SD	18.3	25.0	17.1	39.6

NOTES: SBR = Shallow Brown-Reddish. SB = Shallow Black. D = Deep.

Lolium, Dactylis, Festuca, etc.; Stipeae, with *Stipa* and *Piptochaetium* – the bulk of the native species; and Agrostideae, with the genera *Calamagrostis, Agrostis*, etc., with only a few species (Rosengurtt, Arrillaga de Maffei and Izaguirre de Artucio, 1970). In general terms, the presence of winter species is associated with soil type, topography, altitude, fertility and grazing management. Plants from other families grow with the grasses, such as Compositae, Leguminoseae, Cyperaceae, Umbelliferae, Rubiaceae, Plantaginaceae and Oxalidaceae. Native herbaceous legumes are represented by many genera – *Trifolium, Adesmia, Desmodium, Desmanthus, Galactia, Zornia, Mimosa, Tephrosia, Stylosanthes* – but their net frequency is low, always below 3 percent in all types of grassland, except in very special habitats (Berretta, 2001). The natural grasslands are used for extensive livestock production, with little improvement, and correspond with the main soil types (see Table 5.2). Vegetation characteristics of each grassland type are defined firstly by the soil type, its physical and chemical properties, and to a lesser extent by topography and aspect.

Some species are present in all grassland types, although with variable frequencies; others are present in some grasslands; others are characteristic and indicators of certain habitats. Within each grassland type there are vegetation gradients associated with topography (upper slope, middle and valley) that with soil depth differences and moisture conditions produce a range of associations. In swampy, flooded places there are *Cyperus* spp., *Heleocharis* spp., *Canna glauca*, *Leersia hexandra*, *Luziola peruviana*, *Paspalum hydrophylum*, *Pontederia cordata*, *Sagittaria montevidensis* and *Thalia* spp.

Perennials from the various families predominate in all grasslands. Annuals are infrequent, but may become more prominent at some seasons of the year or due to management practices, such as grazing methods, fertilization, or the introduction of exotics or legumes.

In grassland communities, a relationship can be established between the percentage contribution of each species to total biomass and its degree of contribution to soil cover. Theoretical studies (Poissonet and Poissonet, 1969; Daget and Poissonet, 1971) indicate that this relationship is commonly close to 20:80 – a Gini-Lorenz relationship. Vegetation surveys carried out in different grasslands and through several seasons showed relationships varying between 30:70 and 20:80 (Coronel and Martínez, 1983; Olmos and Godron, 1990). Despite the number of species found, which is generally high, only about ten species make a major contribution to forage production. Identification of these species is of particular interest when monitoring community evolution and planning cattle management.

Identification of growth habit types (Rosengurtt, 1979) can help in making grazing management decisions. Most summer and winter grasses are of a caespitose vegetative type. Stoloniferous grasses are all summer cycle, except for one. Rhizomatous species belong to various families (Gramineae, Cyperaceae, Compositae, Leguminosae, Umbelliferae, etc.) and there are both winter- and summer-cycle rosette plants, primarily Compositae and Umbelliferae. Growth habit types are used as a substitute where there is a lack of precise data on the nutritive value of forages and enabling the ranking of hundreds of species in a useful way for consideration in present and future vegetation management (Rosengurtt, 1946, 1979; Rosengurtt, Arrillaga de Maffei and Izaguirre de Artucio, 1970).

Table 5.2 shows detailed Daily Growth Rates and their standard deviation, and seasonal distribution of grass production in different types of grasslands. On some soils, forage growth reflects soil depth or topographic position, leading to different botanical compositions.

On basalt soils, three vegetation types can be distinguished, directly related to soil depth. On shallow brown-reddish soils, vegetation cover is about 70 percent, while rocks and stones cover 10 percent and the rest is bare soil and litter. These values have some seasonal variations and show marked changes during droughts. Daily Growth Rates, expressed as kg DM/ha/day, is variable according to season and between years. Most annual forage grows in summer, but this season is the most variable due to high risk of drought on this soil. The commonest species are *Schizachyrium spicatum, Chloris grandiflora, Eragrostis neesii, Eustachys bahiensis, Microchloa indica, Bouteloua megapotamica, Aristida venustula, Dichondra microcalyx, Oxalis* spp. (*macachines*) and *Selaginella* sp. On the same soil type, but where the upper horizon reaches 15–20 cm in depth, other species are found, such as the summer grasses *Paspalum notatum* and *Bothriochloa laguroides,* and winter cycle grasses *Stipa setigera* (= *S. neesiana*) and *Piptochaetium stipoides.* The presence of more productive species changes the seasonal distribution of growth, so highest productivity is in spring and autumn, although total annual production is similar.

Vegetation cover is 80 percent on shallow black soils – the rest is litter and bare soil – and varies between seasons and years. The most frequent species are *Schizachyrium spicatum, Chloris grandiflora, Eustachys bahiensis, Bouteloua megapotamica, Aristida murina, A. uruguayensis, Dichondra microcalyx, Oxalis* spp., *Nostoc* sp. and *Selaginella* sp. Less frequent are *Stipa setigera, Piptochaetium stipoides, Bothriochloa laguroides, Paspalum notatum, P. plicatulum, Coelorhachis selloana* and *Adesmia bicolor.* When the upper horizon is deeper, the usually less frequent species become more frequent. Total annual forage production on deeper soils is slightly greater, but seasonal distribution is different, with 70 percent of total forage being produced in spring and autumn.

Deep fertile soils have a vegetation cover close to 90 percent, and the rest is litter. The main species on these soils are *Paspalum notatum, P. plicatulum, P. dilatatum, Coelorachis selloana, Andropogon ternatus, Bothriochloa laguroides, Axonopus affinis, Aristida uruguayensis, Schizachyrium spicatum, S. setigera,* Cyperaceae, *Piptochaetium stipoides, Poa lanigera, Trifolium polymorphum* and *Adesmia bicolor* (Berretta, 1998).

On all three soil types, the deeper the upper horizon, the greater the spring growth, by up to 40 percent. This may be related to higher frequency of winter species which flower in spring and again in autumn when they regrow, and when growth can be as high as 28 percent of the total.

On sandy soils, botanical composition changes are mainly associated with topographic position. Table 5.2 shows daily growth rate and seasonal distribution of forage production from upper and lower parts of a hillside, in the same topographic sequence. Annual forage yields from upper and lower areas averaged 5 144 kg DM/ha and 5 503 kg DM/ha, respectively, over eight years (Bemhaja, 2001). In such grassland, growth peaks in spring and summer, with 80 percent of total production. This is related in part to edaphic factors (depth, texture, moisture retention capacity), but more to the dominance of summer species, such as *Paspalum notatum, Axonopus compressus, A. argentinus, Sporobolus indicus, Coelorachis selloana, Panicum milioides, P. sabulorum, P. nicorae* (which is a characteristic species of such soils) and *Eragrostis*

ELBIO BERRETTA

Plate 5.1
Landscape in the Sierras zone.

purpurascens. The commonest winter grass is *Piptochaetium montevidense*. Dwarf herbs, such as *Soliva pterosperma*, *Eryngium nudicaule*, *Chevreulia sarmentosa*, and *Dichondra microcalyx*, are relatively frequent. Native legumes are infrequent, with *Desmodium incanum* the most representative. *Baccharis coridifolia* and *Vernonia nudiflora* are the main weeds in invaded fields (*campo sucio*).

Managed burning is common on these soils, as a tool to reduce dead material and to promote green spring regrowth and hence improve forage quality. Summer grasses are rough, clearly overshadow the sward and are little or not liked by livestock, except in very special circumstances; dead leaves and stems accumulate in winter, becoming even less palatable. The main such grasses are *Erianthus angustifolius*, *Paspalum quadrifarium*, *Andropogon lateralis* and *Schizachyrium microstachyum*, associated with some dwarf shrub and shrub weeds that thrive in this conditions and give place to *campos sucios* and *pajonales* (straw fields).

Natural grasslands on Brunosols are species rich. It is possible to find 50 to 60 species in a 12 m² plot. Some 30 percent of the species present represent 70 percent of total vegetation cover. Grasses are the most abundant, and 70 percent of them are summer growing. Depending on local management practices, natural grasslands may be covered by small shrubs or native trees. Legume presence under grazing conditions is sparse.

Forage production averages 3 626 kg DM/ha/year in the lomadas zone and about 1 500 kg DM/ha/year in the Sierras zone (Plate 5.1). Most of the plants (80–85 percent) are summer-cycle perennials. In spite of rich biodiversity, the

Plate 5.2a
Typical grassland scenes on the Campos of Uruguay – Campos on shallow basaltic soil.

Plate 5.2b
Typical Grassland Scenes on the Campos of Uruguay – Campos on granitic soils.

number of species that contribute to forage production is low; the *Paspalum notatum–Axonopus compressuss* association is notably the main contributor. Forage digestibility is usually low (48–62 percent) (Ayala *et al.*, 2001). Typical grassland scenes on the Campos of Uruguay are shown in Plates 5.2a–f.

Plate 5.2c
Typical grassland scenes on the Campos of Uruguay – Campos on eastern hillocks.

Plate 5.2d
Typical grassland scenes on the Campos of Uruguay – Campos on sandy soils.

VEGETATION LIMITATIONS FOR ANIMAL PRODUCTION

The main limitation of the humid subtropical grasslands is their poor herbage quality. Although this is well known, and has been the subject of many papers (Royo Pallarés, 1985; Deregibus, 1988), little progress has been made in overcoming it. C_4-dominated grasslands, with high temperatures and good rainfall produce high growth rates, which leads to a dilution of nutrients and

ELBIO BERRETTA

Plate 5.2e
Typical grassland scenes on the Campos of Uruguay – Winter sunset over the Campos on granitic soils in southern Uruguay.

ELBIO BERRETTA

Plate 5.2f
Typical Grassland Scenes on the Campos of Uruguay – Campos in Central Uruguay with cows grazing on basaltic soils.

a marked decrease in digestibility, which rarely exceeds 60 percent; forage crude protein levels barely reach basic cattle requirements. This situation is aggravated in winter by frost. Most of the year there is a "green desert" – a great bulk of low quality forage, in a difficult-to-graze pasture structure. The animals graze in a "sea of forage", but have low intake. Fire is used in most cases to stimulate regrowth and improve grassland quality

Salt deficiency was noted as a problem at the end of the nineteenth century in the Campos. Phosphorus deficiency was identified (Kraemer and Mufarrege, 1965), and since then it has become increasingly obvious that phosphorus deficiency is one of the main constraints on livestock production in Corrientes. The soils have less than 5 ppm of available phosphorus, so forage has a phosphorus content below 0.10 percent. This strongly limits both forage production and quality, which in turn limits the animal output that can be obtained. Research on many aspects of phosphorus nutrition of cattle and pastures have been conducted in Corrientes (Arias and Manunta, 1981; Arias *et al*, 1985; Mufarrege, Somma de Fere and Homse, 1985; Wilken, 1985; Royo Pallarés and Mufarrege, 1969; Royo Pallarés, 1985). Mineral supplementation to correct phosphorus deficiencies is the technology most accepted and adopted by farmers; but there are still doubts, misconceptions and practical problems in its implementation.

Production systems
The main production systems are:
- calf production (*Cría*) only, with sales of weaned male calves and rejected cows, keeping replacement females;
- breeding and growth (*Recría*), where male calves are kept after weaning, to be sold to other farmers at 18 to 30 months, before winter;
- complete cycle, which is the breeding and fattening of all calves to slaughter, which can occur at different ages and weights; and
- fattening, which can be on natural grasslands. In that case steers are finished for slaughter at over four years old, starting with one-year-old or older steers. Intensive fattening starts from weaned calves or young steers, using variable proportions of improved grassland or cultivated pastures.

In any of these cases, cattle rearing may be accompanied by sheep (Plate 5.3). This is commoner in breeding than in fattening systems. Sheep breeding systems are similar. Castrated weaned lambs and rejected ewes are the main income source, but the current trend is to sell heavier lambs of more than 40 kg liveweight.

According to grassland characteristics, mixed set stocking in cattle production has many limitations, mainly nutritional. Some of the major constraints are advanced age of heifers at first mating (a mean of three years old); low calving rate (65 percent); low liveweight gain of calves, with consequently low weaning weight (130–140 kg); advanced slaughter age (4 years); and low extraction rate (18–20 percent). Under such conditions, beef production on natural grasslands is about 65 kg/ha/year.

Table 5.3 compares two management systems, with and without sheep, on basalt grasslands. Both systems were evaluated under grazing conditions with a continuous fixed stocking rate of 1 cow-equivalent per hectare, for four years.

Despite the high stocking rate and simple management, the results show higher productivity levels than those of extensive production systems. Yearly variations in birth and weaning rates are the main factors determining animal

ELBIO BERRETTA

Plate 5.3
Mixed grazing.

TABLE 5.3
Reproductive performance and productivity of two management systems.

Year	Birth rate (%)	Weaning rate (%)	Weaning weight (kg)	Productivity (kg/ha)	
				Liveweight	Wool
Cattle system					
1	80.0	77.5	141	109	–
2	60.0	55.5	141	78	–
3	87.5	75.0	137	103	–
4	75.0	70.0	143	100	–
Average	75.6	69.5	141	988	-
Mixed system					
1	75.0	70.0	153	107	10.1
2	55.0	50.5	143	72	9.0
3	78.0	75.0	166	125	10.3
4	65.0	60.0	160	96	9.8
Average	68.0	64.0	156	100	9.8

Source: Adapted from Pigurina, Soares de Lima and Berretta, 1998.

production. Weaning rates are higher in the cattle-only system, but weaning weight and total productivity were higher in the mixed system.

Fattening steers on natural grasslands takes a long time because liveweight gains are variable between seasons, related to availability and quality of forage, stocking rate and presence or absence of sheep (Table 5.4).

Different feeding, management and sanitary control strategies affect sheep production. Research programmes focus on increasing wool and lamb production efficiency, and the quality of both products.

Technical options for extensive conditions are presented in Table 5.5. In traditional systems, nutritional levels are insufficient for breeding ewes in the last third of pregnancy, with consequent low weight and low fat score at lambing.

TABLE 5.4

Steer liveweight variation (kg/head/day) and productivity (kg/ha/year) in relation to stocking rate and sheep:cattle ratio (S:C) in continuous set stocking on natural grasslands.

Stocking rate (AU/ha)	0.6[1]	0.8[1]	0.8[1]	0.9[2]	1.06[1]	1.06[1]
S:C ratio	2:1	2:1	5:1	0:1	2:1	5:1
Season	Liveweight variation, kg/day					
Autumn	0.196 bc	0.194 c	0.139 bc	-0.248 c	-0.076 c	-0.130 c
Winter	0.089 c	-0.176 d	-0.086 c	0.075 b	-0.312 d	-0.397 d
Spring	0.915 a	0.858 a	0.828 a	0.758 a	0.667 a	0.720 a
Summer	0.351 b	0.413 b	0.297 b	0.604 a	0.431 b	0.436 b
Yearly average	0.388 A	0.322 A	0.295 AB	0.297 AB	0.178 B	0.157 B
Total steer production						
kg/head/year)	141 A	118 A	108 B	108 B	65 B	57 B
kg/ha[3]	75	84	54	125	62	38

NOTES: a, b, c – Averages in the same column with distinct letters differ significantly (P<0.05). A, B – Averages in the same row with distinct letters differ significantly (P<0.05). (1) Based on UE Glencoe data (1984–92). (2) Adapted from Risso *et al.*, 1998. (3) Adjusted by effective area. Lamb and wool production is not included.

SOURCE: Pigurina *et al.*, 1998.

TABLE 5.5

Summary of the experiments carried out by Montossi *et al.* (1998a) using fat condition score and autumn deferment in natural and improved grasslands.

Pasture and animal characteristics	Traditional	Deferred	
		Natural	Improved
Available forage at lambing (kg DM/ha)	400–700	1 300–1 500	1 100[1]–1 900
Sward height at lambing (cm)	2–3	5–8	4 – 7
Stocking rate (ewes/ha)	4 (0.8 AU/ha)	5 (1 AU/ha)	10 (2 AU/ha)
Ewe liveweight at lambing (kg)	35–40	42–45	45–48
Fat score at lambing (grades)	2–2.5	3–3.5	3.3–3.7
Birth liveweight (kg)	2.5 – 3.0	3.6 – 3.8	3.8 – 4.6
Lamb mortality rate (%)	20 – 30	10 –13	9 –10

NOTES: (1) Required forage availability according to amount of legumes in improved grassland.

The effects of poor nutrition on lamb survival (20–30 percent mortality) is the major cause of the low reproductive performance of the national flock. To improve reproductive performance of single-lamb pregnant ewes and to reduce lamb mortality to 10 percent, it is necessary to apply deferred grazing (Plate 5.4), accumulating 1 300 to 1 500 kg DM/ha (5 to 8 cm height) at the beginning of the last third of gestation. The fat score of Corriedale ewes at lambing should be between grades 3 and 3.5 (Montossi *et al.*, 1998b).

In improved grasslands, with a stocking rate of twice that on natural grasslands (10 sheep/ha) with the same fat score at lambing it is possible to reduce lamb mortality to 10 percent. The recommended amount of deferred forage is from 1 100 to 1 900 kg DM/ha, equivalent to heights of about 4 to 7 cm, respectively. The amount of forage available will depend on the proportion of legumes in the improved grassland.

Considering the average autumn growth rate of natural and improved grasslands on basalt soils (Berretta and Bemhaja, 1998) and a normal breeding season, it is necessary to start deferring natural grassland 70 to 50 days before

ELBIO BERRETTA

Plate 5.4
Grazing management: forage deferred for winter grazing.

lambing and improved grasslands 40 to 30 days before lambing. These values are modified by weather conditions, which affect the growth rate, and also by the amount of forage present at the start of the accumulation period.

Most ewe hoggets are mated at 2.5 years (four teeth) since many of them (40–60 percent) do not reach the minimum liveweight for mating at 1.5 years). This has adverse productive and economic consequences for the industry, as it reduces the number of lambs produced by each ewe in her lifetime, reduces genetic progress of the flock and constrains the overall efficiency of the system. To increase lamb production it is very important to increase the reproduction rate of hoggets.

Several management strategies have been defined to improve the liveweight gain of hoggets on natural grassland on basalt soils (San Julián *et al.*, 1998). The use of improved grassland and sown pastures allows winter liveweight gains of 60 to 90 g/head/day. Such rates of gain allow a high proportion of hoggets (80–90 percent) to attain mating weight at two-tooth, implying weights exceeding 32 and 35 kg for Merino and Corriedale hoggets, respectively. To attain these gains in winter it is necessary to provide 1 500 kg DM/ha of deferred forage, with a height of 5 to 6 cm, on natural grasslands or 1 000 kg DM/ha, with a height of 4 to 5 cm, on improved grasslands (San Julián *et al.*, 1998).

In a study in the basalt zone (Ferreira, 1997), three groups of farmers could be distinguished according to production systems and technical demands. The first group, 56 percent of farmers studied, had low-potential natural resources and used a defensive strategy in their decision-making, which resulted in very low levels of technology adoption, and the technology available for shallow soils did not show sufficiently attractive response levels and stability to cross the risk aversion thresholds of these farmers. The second group, 18 percent of the sample, responded better to technology adoption and behaved proactively to technical change: they were not only receptive to new technologies, but also experimented and constantly analysed the effects of the introduction of technical changes. The third group (26 percent) were the bigger farmers, with a reactive and imitative attitude that incorporated technologies that have been successfully applied by others. The author concludes that the technology offered must be matched to each group, and – even more important – the technology identification process should be different for each group.

GRASSLAND PRODUCTION SYSTEMS IN SOUTHERN BRAZIL

The natural grasslands of Southern Brazil include native forests and herbaceous vegetation, both as open grasslands and dwarf shrub associations, forming a mosaic with savannah characteristics. Herbaceous vegetation, of diverse forms and botanical composition, is strongly influenced by temperature, showing seasonal productivity variations. Grasses predominate, accompanied by some legumes. Herbage develops under the influence of latitude, altitude and soil fertility, with a dominance of the C_4 species that grow in the warm season, associated with C_3 species in the winter cycle. Relative dominance of species on grasslands determines its growth capacity in each season and the balance of forage production. More than 800 grass species have been recorded, with 200 legume species. These grow in associations with herbs such as Compositae and Cyperaceae, besides shrubs, resulting in a very rich floral biodiversity. Edaphic factors lead to marked variations in botanical composition and substantial productivity differences as a function of the dominance of particular species. Extensive and extractive livestock production has developed in this ecosystem since the colonization of the region.

An ecological understanding of natural processes is the basis for management. Factors include productivity, vegetation cover preservation, pastoral value, environmental limitations and recognition of the natural succession process. Grassland ecology is closely associated with human activity and management of domestic herbivores. Grazing animals are major determinants of vegetation structure, as consumption may reach 50 percent of above ground net primary production (ANPP) and up to 25 percent of subterranean productivity (Sala, 1988). Plants differ in their responses to defoliation, with differential seasonal growing rates, and herbivores select and consume species and parts of plants disproportionately to their abundance in the pasture (Boldrini, 1993). This natural resource is useful for herbivores; grazing influences species, life forms and growth of the vegetation and it can be managed to satisfy economic needs. Different animal species use a wider range of forage and may direct succession to vegetation states that are ecologically and economically attractive (Araujo Filho, Sousa and Carvalho, 1995).

Plate 5.5
Grasslands of southern Brazil. (a) Grasslands with Araucaria trees.

(b) Representative grassland on the mid-level plateau, with "barba-de-bode"
(Aristida jubata).

The 12–15 million hectares of natural grasslands in Southern Brazil show great structural diversity (see Plate 5.5), with grass dominance and few legumes. Ignorance of their nature and potential led to the belief that they were unproductive and should be replaced by sown forages. This was associated with the concept of selective grazing and ignorance about its advantages to promote

(c) Grassland with Melica macra.

(d) Upland grassland in winter.

faster regrowth after grazing. Animal type, their genetics and aptitudes condition the development of natural grasslands. Society is now promoting conservation of natural ecosystems in managed recreation areas, where herbivores are always landscape modellers. A number of technical reports on this situation are available.

Forage from natural grasslands can only be marketed in the form of animal products. Nationally, there is still an instinctive resistance, if not dislike, to exploitation and use of natural grasslands through pastoralism (Tothill, Dzowela and Diallo, 1989). The measure of communal grazing is yield per unit of area, as the number of animals represents the economic value of the activity. In the philosophy of managed ecosystems (ranching), yield per animal and commercial value of the product represent the economic value. This philosophy of forage use is based on management of pastures and stock in delimited areas, with the possibility of external inputs. There are still many natural grassland properties operating with the philosophy and yield of pastoralism, which could attain the yield of managed ecosystems.

Until recently, stock rearers did not understand basic grassland management technology: to maintain vegetation and make long-term decisions on sustainability. The need is now appreciated of understanding natural grasslands and recognizing the availability level that does not restrict animal intake, in order to attain high individual performance and high per-hectare production.

Dry matter accumulation in natural grasslands

The climatic transition strip in the south of Brazil favours summer grasses, which explains the seasonal differences in forage production (Apezteguia, 1994; Correa and Maraschin, 1994; Maraschin *et al.*, 1997). In the cool season, which covers from a third to half of the year, there is slower growth due to low temperature, frost and irregular rainfall. Rejected forage increases errors in pasture evaluation (Moojen, 1991). Native winter species contributed 17 percent of yearly DM production in Uruguay (Berretta and Bemhaja, 1991) and 18 percent in Rio Grande do Sul (Gomes, 1996). But the warm season covers two-thirds to half the year (Maraschin *et al.*, 1997). Daily growth is termed the DM Accumulation Rate (AR) and represents what can be grazed. Table 5.6 shows ARs (in kg DM/ha/day) in a Rio Grande do Sul natural grassland, influenced by forage offer (FO) levels per head and per day, with corresponding residual DM (Moojen, 1991; Correa and Maraschin, 1994). ARs increase with increasing levels of FO until more than 12 percent of liveweight, and tends to decrease after FO exceeds 16 percent of liveweight. Maximum recorded AR was 16.3 kg DM/ha/day, with an FO of 13.5 percent of liveweight, which corresponded to forage availability of 1 400–1 500 kg DM/ha at any time.

Unfertilized natural grasslands produced 2 075 to 3 393 kg DM/ha considered as available forage, defining the number of animals that could be grazed on

TABLE 5.6
Pasture parameters and radiant energy conversion efficiency on a natural grassland in the Central Depression of Rio Grande do Sul, with dominance of *P. notatum* and different forage offer (FO) levels (5-year average; 21.6 TJ/ha of incident PAR).

Parameters		Dry matter on offer – percent liveweight			
		4.0	8.0	12.0	16.0
Accumulation Rate (AR)	kg DM/ha/day	11.88	15.52	16.28	15.44
DM Production	kg/ha	2 075	3 488	3 723	3 393
Primary Aerial Productivity (PAP)	MJ/ha	40.877	68.714	73.343	66.842
PAR/PAP Efficiency	%	0.20	0.34	0.36	0.33
Daily liveweight gain (DLWG)	kg/head	0.150	0.350	0.450	0.480
Animal-day/ha	no.	572	351	286	276
Stocking rate	kg LW/day/ha	710	468	381	368
Residual DM	kg/ha	568	1 006	1 444	1 882
Liveweight gain (LWG)	kg/ha	80	120	140	135
Secondary production (SP)	MJ/ha	1 880	2 820	3 290	3 173
PAR/SP Efficiency	%	0.009	0.0015	0.017	0.013
PAP/SP	%	4.48	4.53	4.66	4.10

Source: Adapted from Maraschin *et al.*, 1997; Nabinger, 1998.

them. With plant development and dead matter accumulation at the base of the plants, there seems to be a reduction in AR and also a liveweight gain inhibition, as the treatment with an FO of 16 percent of liveweight suggested. The parallelism of both development curves suggests liveweight gain variations are closely related to AR (kg DM/ha/day), as both showed optimal response at an FO of 13 percent liveweight.

Grazing intensity effects can be evaluated on the energy flow of the system, as a function of FO levels. Forage availability (kg DM/ha) and liveweight gain (kg LW/ha) are multiplied by 19.7 and 23.5 MJ/kg, respectively (Briske and Heitschmidt, 1991). Based on normal global radiation and photosynthetically active radiation (PAR), Nabinger (1998) determined conversion efficiency indexes, which represent the quotient between the energy values considered, multiplied by 100 (Table 5.6). With an FO of 4.0 percent LW, conversion efficiency of PAR to DM is estimated at close to 0.20 percent. Conversion increased to 0.34 percent with an FO of 8 percent LW, peaked at 0.36 percent with an FO of 12.0 percent LW and declined to 0.33 percent with an FO of 16.0 percent LW, as a consequence of age and senescence of natural grasslands, influenced by FO levels. Primary production of natural grassland increased markedly (+80 percent) when FO was 12 percent.

The grazing animal prefers green grass to dry, leaf to stem, and the upper half of young leaves; this shows clearly what forage is desirable and what should therefore be encouraged in the sward. It is necessary to distinguish between the total aerial biomass of plants and the available DM for the grazing animal; the former is the forage technically within reach of the animal, while the latter is the forage selected. It has to be clear what should be the optimum height of the pasture after grazing to maintain regrowth capacity (Maraschin, 1993). Understanding this provides understanding of how animals behave on different swards and pasture conditions.

Data in Table 5.6 show that the highest liveweight gain (LWG) per head is when the number of animal-days per ha is low and LWG/ha reaches its maximum close to the maximum pasture AR, with an FO of 12 percent LW. Similarly, observing the efficiency of secondary production as a function of the energy fixed by primary production, the energy flow of the system shows that the efficiency of secondary production (kg LW/ha) in relation to PAR was 0.009 percent with an FO of 4.0 percent LW, increased to 0.015 percent at an FO of 8.0 percent LW, peaked at 0.017 percent at an FO of 12.0 percent LW, and then decreased in the FO of 16.0 percent LW treatment. Increasing FO increases the amount of dead material in the sward profile, which is wrongly considered as a forage component of pasture biomass (Maraschin, 1996). This is an important issue in animal-plant relationships, which has to be better understood, as it relates to quality expression and global yield of grasslands. This dry matter plays an important role in nutrient recycling in ecologically managed natural ecosystems, promotes moisture retention capacity of soils and conservation of soil, flora and fauna.

Optimizing animal production from natural grassland ecosystems

The amount and botanical composition of available forage determines the sustainable animal production level (Moraes, Maraschin and Nabinger, 1995), which depends on forage on offer for a specific animal class (Maraschin, 1996). Firstly, it is necessary to know how much forage is available to feed the stock properly in relation to their biological functions. Knowledge developed by the Forage Plants and Agrometeorology Department of the Federal University of Rio Grande del Sul (UFRGS) on forage transformation into animal products allowed the natural grassland heritage to be rescued and production raised to a level not seen before, due to better understanding of soil-plant-animal relationships. Seasonality of forage production reflects the favourable environment, with rainfall well distributed throughout the year. Grassland growth is different in the cool season (40–30 percent of the year) and warm season (Moojen, 1991). Fixed stocking may contribute to animal yield losses because of seasonal fluctuations, and may damage the grassland ecosystem and increase farmers' vulnerability. Since true forage production is in the warm season, it is mainly in spring that animals gain weight, thus defining overall performance for the year (Correa and Maraschin, 1994), because it is dependent on grassland daily growth rate (Table 5.6) and forage availability (Setelich, 1994; Maraschin *et al.*, 1997). If farmers do not make use of spring forage correctly, capitalizing it as animal products, they will not be able to catch up in summer.

FO levels determine sward profiles. With low FO (4.0 percent LW = high grazing pressure), pasture seems uniform, like a low sward, and forage from new leaves has 8 percent of crude protein. Prostrate summer species pre-

Figure 5.3

Forage offer (FO) and daily liveweight gains per animal (DLWG) and per hectare (LW) and its effect on solar radiation conversion efficiency, on a natural grassland of Rio Grande do Sul, Brazil.

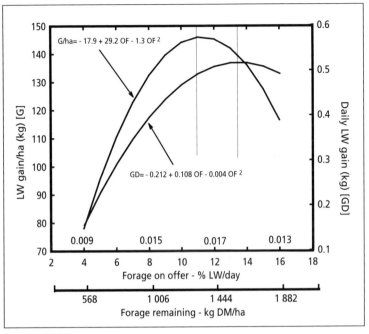

dominate, with near disappearance of winter species and little contribution of legumes, decrease in *Andropogon lateralis, Aristida jubata* and *Eryngium horridum,* and increased bare soil. Regrowth does not reflect its forage production and daily LWG is low. With an increase of FO to 8.0 percent LW, animals show better body condition but the grassland is vulnerable, lacking protection for grazing-sensitive species.

At medium and low grazing pressures (12.0 and 16.0 percent LW) and higher FO, the grassland showed greater height, with more bunchgrasses of varying diameter. Winter species were more frequent and increased grassland quality, such as *Stipa neesiana, Piptochaetium montevidense* and *Coelorachis selloana,* besides native legumes, with an important presence of *Desmodium incanum.* Forage production and seed production of native legumes was only seen after 8–10 years of this grazing treatment. Under lighter stocking rates, animals graze more selectively and choose higher quality fractions of available forage, leaving higher, less grazed plants. This contributes to maintaining higher leaf area and promotes faster regrowth after each defoliation under continuous grazing. With selective grazing, on lightly stocked swards, forage production is higher, as is the voluntary intake of the animals, which produced daily liveweight gain (DLWG) of 0.500 kg per head (Figure 5.3). This DLWG would not be possible if one considers the average crude protein contents of the forage. The increased FO allows the animals to select a more nutritious diet than average; the animal is harvesting more because it is harvesting better.

With increasing levels of FO, ground cover increases; as leaves increase in relation to stems, forage and animal production also increase. The PAR/SP [Secondary Production] relationship nearly doubles when FO changes from 4.0 to 12.0 percent LW. Maximum LW is attained at lower stocking rates, which are exactly those that promote high DLWG, related to high AR and light grazing. The Primary Aerial Productivity (PAP):SP relationship had an efficiency of 4.48 percent with an FO of 4.0 percent, reaching 4.66 percent with an FO of 12.0 percent, as a consequence of increased DLWG. Lighter grazing pressures allow tall species to make important contributions to increase animal diet quality, and also protects native fauna.

Optimal utilization ranges for natural grasslands can be derived from a curvilinear response model, promoting productivity and ensuring sustainability, which is attained by higher utilization efficiency of incident PAR (Table 5.6 and Figure 5.3). Optimal utilization ranges are estimated from FOs of 13.5 percent of LW (maximum DLWG per head) to 11.5 percent of LW (maximum LW), where there is compromise between individual and per-hectare production. As there is considerable variation between the nutritional requirements of species and classes of animal (cow+calf, ewe+lamb, heifers, steers, bulls, horses, etc.) each pasture has to be managed according to the specific animal class requirements. Stocking rate and carrying capacity can only be defined as a function of the animal product involved and cannot be fixed, because they depend on environmental variations.

Table 5.7 can be prepared as a function derived from the grassland optimization model, which reflects natural grassland grazing optimization and the stocking rate that this pasture could feed at optimal carrying capacity. In the warm season – a nearly 200-day grazing period for natural grassland – these results adjust to the animal product yield equation in the following way:

$$
\begin{aligned}
\text{Yield} &= \text{Quality} \times \text{Quantity} \\
\text{Liveweight/ha (LW)} &= \text{DLWG} \times \text{Animal-day/ha} \\
146 \text{ kg} &= 0.517 \text{ kg} \times 282
\end{aligned}
$$

Forage harvest from natural grasslands could be improved, representing an annual increase of 784 000 t live weight, without cost, in Rio Grande do Sul alone through the recommended strategy of high FO to the grazing animal,

TABLE 5.7
Natural grassland and animal performance in the optimal utilization range.

Parameters		Responses	
DM/ha/day	(kg)	16.30	(evaluated)
Animal-day/ha		282	(counted)
Daily LWG	(kg)	0.517	(evaluated)
Liveweight gain/ha	(kg)	146	(calculated)
Carrying capacity		1.17 two-year-old steers	(calculated)
Stocking rate	(kg/ha)	370	(observed)

which also optimizes forage accumulation rates in the pasture. This approach is expanding opportunities in southern Brazil.

Natural grassland dynamics

The natural grasslands of southern Brazil evolved without the presence of large herbivores, and were altered by the introduction of livestock at the beginning of colonization, changing from a climax condition to a productive disclimax with a range of growth habits and life forms. Knowledge of grassland ecology became important when the value of natural grassland was acknowledged in parallel with the need for controlling grazing-induced land degradation. Boldrini (1993) studied vegetation cover variations as part of the long-term grazing experiment described earlier, and then verified that soil type has a greater influence on botanical composition than FO levels. Erect plants were more sensitive to defoliation than prostrate ones, because leaf tissues and growing buds are more exposed to grazing. With lighter grazing, they stood above the sward canopy and dominated prostrate species.

Some important natural grassland species were selected to evaluate vegetation dynamics: *Paspalum notatum* is the one with greatest presence and contribution. Like *P. paucifolium*, it is a rhizomatous species, and they are both pioneers in more eroded and leached areas, with higher cover in FOs of 4.0 and 12.0 percent of LW. *Andropogon lateralis* benefits from high soil moisture levels, but is very sensitive to increases in grazing pressure. Its frequency decreases drastically with low FO (from 2.4 to 4.5 percent of LW) but it remains stable under optimal stocking and offers protection to other highly palatable grasses, allowing them to reseed. *Axonopus affinis*, with long stolons, thrives in damp areas of low fertility and benefits from high intensity grazing under low-FO treatments. *Aristida filifolia* is adapted to drier soils and is favoured by low grazing pressures, where it remains stable. *Paspalum plicatulum* shows lignification at the base of the leaf blades, but still it is well accepted and consumed by animals and damaged by heavy grazing under low FO. It seems to benefit from light grazing and showed marked increases in density and cover after two or three years of light grazing. It benefits from the shelter of more vigorous vegetation and so produces seeds and increases in the grassland. *Piptochaetium montevidense,* which is important because it grows more in winter–spring, shows higher cover on hillsides and seems to suffer from competition in more humid niches, but tends to persist in less dense swards. Another important plant is the legume *Desmodium incanum*, which presents higher cover values under light spring grazing pressure and with the aid of protective species. It shows ecological versatility in the face of competition, and flowers and produce seeds, generating viable plants to increase the population.

In a study where FO levels were associated with soil fertility and deferred grazing (Gomes, 1996), the prostrate species *Paspalum notatum* was more frequent on heavily grazed treatments, whereas the caespitose species *Andropogon selloanus* and *Elionurus candidus* were commoner on lightly and very lightly grazed paddocks. Plant groups that are independent of growth habit, such as *Paspalum paucifolium*, *Eragrostis neesii* and *Eryngium ciliatum*, occurred on drier sites, while *Andropogon lateralis*, *Eryngium horridum*, *E. elegans*, *Schizachyrium microstachyum* and *Baccharis trimera* occurred on sites with higher soil moisture levels, and were also sensitive to heavy grazing.

An interesting issue was the tolerance of heavy grazing shown by *Coelorachis selloana* and *Piptochaetium montevidense*, both low growing with buds close to the soil. However, when FO is higher they grow along with the height of the sward profile and remain as contributors to DM production. The ability to adapt growth habit is also seen in the native legume *Desmodium incanum*: it remains prostrate under heavy grazing, but its branches rise to sward height when grazing is reduced. The legumes *Aeschynomene falcata*, *Chamaecrista repens*, *Stylosanthes leiocarpa*, *Trifolium polymorphum* and *Zornia reticulata* are associated with higher utilization intensities, but need resting periods. Non-limiting FO management practices on natural grasslands seem to be an ecologically efficient procedure to restore and maintain grassland productivity in a sustainable manner.

FERTILIZING CAMPOS GRASSLAND
Fertilization in Argentina
In the past 30 years the Mercedes Research Station has evaluated the effects of fertilizing natural grasslands on animal production in the Rocky Outcrops region. Large increases in stocking rate, liveweight gain per animal and annual beef production per unit area have been registered in all trials. The first study showed that, with NPK fertilization, animal production increases yearly, reaching 210 kg LW/ha/year by the third year, which represented a 138 percent increase over the control (Royo Pallarés and Mufarrege, 1970). Subsequently, different N levels were applied to natural grassland, which raised animal production in the third year to 254 kg LW/ha/year at 120 kg N/ha/year (Mufarrege, Royo Pallares and Ocampo, 1981).

Phosphorus fertilization was evaluated for 11 years at the Estancia Rincón de Yeguas. Average animal production on fertilized paddocks was 40 percent higher, for the three stocking rates evaluated, with production levels that rose to 188 kg LW/ha/year (Benitez, unpublished). In another eight-year fertilization and stocking rate trial by Mercedes Research Station, production reached 176 kg LW/ha/year at the higher stocking rate. The increase in total animal production at the same individual performance level was 76 percent (Royo Pallarés *et al.*, 1998). Observed effects of phosphorus fertilization on grasslands are increased forage production, a large increase in the phosphorus content of the forage and increased legume cover.

Fertilization of Campos Grasslands in Uruguay

The reduced winter growth of natural grasslands due to P and N deficiencies in most of the soils of the region led to the use of inorganic nitrogen and to legume introduction with phosphatic fertilization to foster establishment and production. Phosphatic fertilization alone has little impact on botanical composition and production increases are low (less than 15 percent) because of the low frequency of native legumes.

The use of relatively low doses of N and P_2O_5 (90 kg N/ha/year; 44 kg P_2O_5 ha/year) favours an increase in the fertility level of the soil, especially if the fertilizer is split: the first dose at the beginning of the autumn and the other at the end of the winter. This can only be done when relative frequency of winter forages in the total vegetation is above 20 percent. Autumn application promotes regrowth of winter grasses and extends the growth of summer grasses into late autumn. Winter application favours longer growth of winter species and earlier regrowth of summer ones (Bemhaja, Berretta and Brito, 1998).

As the fertility level of the system increases, forage growth starts to stabilize at a level that is 60 percent higher than an unfertilized grassland. The seasons in which fertilization can make significant improvements to livestock production are autumn and winter. Autumn daily forage growth is higher on fertilized grasslands. To defer forage for winter feeding, autumn growth should be sufficient to accumulate more than 1 000 kg DM/ha, plus the available forage prior to deferment or stocking rate reduction. Fertilized grasslands show 100 percent increments in daily forage growth rates during winter, compared with unfertilized grasslands (Figure 5.4).

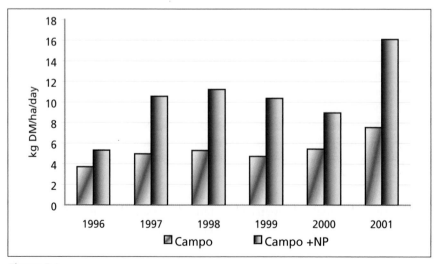

Figure 5.4
Winter daily forage growth rate (kg DM/ha/day) of unfertilized and N+P fertilized natural grasslands.

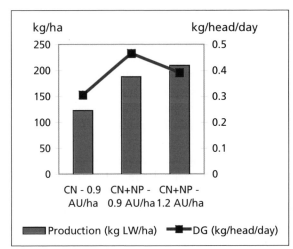

Figure 5.5
Daily liveweight gain (kg/head/day) and beef production (kg liveweight/ ha) on natural grasslands with rotational grazing stocked at 0.9 AU/ ha, and on fertilized natural grassland with rotational grazing and stocking rates of 0.9 and 1.2 AU/ha.

Spring forage growth for these grasslands exceeds 1 600 kg DM/ha, while unfertilized grasslands produce about 1 000 kg DM/ha. Maximum registered daily forage growth rate without fertilization was 19 kg DM/ha/day, while fertilized grasslands shown a maximum of 35 kg DM/ha/day. Summer growth is tightly tied to precipitation and therefore highly variable. Annual addition of 92 and 44 kg/ha of N and P, respectively, increased forage production, adding 7.5 kg DM/kg nutrient in the first year and about 24.0 kg DM/kg nutrient in subsequent years.

Nitrogen and phosphorus content in the forage is always higher in fertilized grasslands. In natural grasslands, the highest N and P values occur in winter and spring, and the lowest are in summer, when forage is mature and, as usual, there is a moisture deficit (Berretta, 1998). In winter, N content of forage reaches 2.3 percent, while unfertilized grasslands reach 1.7 percent; in spring the values are 2.8 and 1.9 percent, respectively. In summer, N contents decreases to 1.4 and 1.1 percent, respectively. Taking winter as an example, natural grasslands produce about 38 kg/ha of crude protein (CP), while fertilized grasslands produce about 95 kg CP/ha. Forage P content during winter and spring is about 2.3 mg P/g DM with fertilizer and 1.8 mg P/g DM without fertilizer (Berretta *et al.*, 1998). The values are 1.9 and 1.5 mg P/g DM, in summer and 1.5 and 2.2 mg P/g DM in autumn, respectively.

Throughout the year, the relative frequency of winter grasses is higher in fertilized grassland. The increase in the C_3 grasses is related to nutrient input, which raises the fertility level of the soil. Fertilization is a way of changing the botanical composition of grasslands and consequently to increase winter forage production.

Winter-productive species such as *Stipa neesiana*, *Piptochaetium stipoides*, *Poa lanigera* and *Adesmia bicolor* tend to increase their cover with fertilization. Summer grasses such as *Paspalum notatum* and *P. dilatatum* also increase their cover. Ordinary grasses, such as *Bothriochloa laguroides* and *Andropogon ternatus,* decrease and *Schizachyrium spicatum* becomes less frequent than the others following fertilization, as it is most competitive in a poor environment. *Paspalum plicatulum* also decreases with fertilization, although this may be linked to a palatability increase, as its leaves keep green for longer than unfertilized grassland. Native legumes increase in frequency, reaching values close to 5 percent. Weeds, typically *Baccharis coridifolia, B. trimera* and *Heimia* sp., are scarce and do not increase with fertilization.

Fertilized grasslands managed under rotational grazing provided the highest beef production per unit area when stocked with 1.2 AU/ha, and the highest liveweight gains per animal at the lower stocking rate of 0.9 AU/ha (Figure 5.5). At lower stocking rates on fertilized grasslands, steers grew to 440 kg liveweight at 2.5 years, while at the higher stocking rate they did not exceed 400 kg.

Results can be quite different if the grassland has a high proportion of summer species and the winter species are mainly annuals, like the soils of the Crystalline and Eastern Hills. Fertilization at the start of the winter favours the presence of winter annual grasses such as *Vulpia australis* and *Gaudinia fragilis,* which have limited productive potential at the end of the season. The disappearance of these species as they finish their growth cycle leaves spaces that can be occupied by undesirable plants. Spring fertilization increases forage growth at the end of the summer, when summer grasses flower and produce seeds. Organic matter digestibility of fertilized forage was greater than unfertilized grassland (Formoso, pers. comm.). N fertilization increases spring and summer production markedly, but has little effect on winter growth. This nutrient increases the frequency of annuals and decreases perennials (Ayala *et al.,* 1999). N+P fertilization produces a threefold increase in beef production in comparison with untreated natural grassland.

Fertilization of natural grasslands in southeast Brazil

The quality and production potential of natural grasslands were always considered to be limited. There was uncertainty about their responses until Scholl, Lobato and Barreto (1976) showed forage production increases on natural grassland with N applications in summer, and Barcellos *et al.* (1980) obtained significant responses of natural grassland to high P fertilizer rates. After the results of Rosito and Maraschin (1985) on secondary succession on fertilized grasslands, a new scenario was clear for southern Brazil, with animal production results in the Central Depression (Perin and Maraschin, 1995) similar to those obtained in Campaña fields (Barcellos *et al.,* 1980). On poor soils of the Central Depression of Rio Grande del Sul (30°S), blanket application of lime and fertilizers (Moojen, 1991) evaluated five years later (Gomes, 1996) showed a rise of pH and reduction in Al^{+++}, while calcium, magnesium and phosphorus contents of the upper 7.5 cm of the soil increased. Organic matter content of this horizon also increased with fertilizer increase, in the same way as deferment accumulation, which increased the litter content in the pastures. From the beginning of this study, *Desmodium incamun* responded rapidly to increasing fertilizer levels, rising to 12.5 percent (Moojen, 1991) and reaching close to 24.4 percent of contribution to total DM of the natural grassland five years later (Gomes, 1996).

Residual effects of fertilizers reduced the number of species, from 137 species noted by Moojen, (1991) to 122 recorded by Gomes (1996); this was attributed to better conditions offered to species that were formerly limited by low soil fertility. These species become dominant, modifying the flora. The presence and contribution of *Paspalum dilatatum, P. maculosum, P. pauciciliatum* and *P. urvillei* was noted, yet these desirable grasses were not mentioned in the report of Moojen (1991). There was also development of the legume *Trifolium polymorphum*. Another important observation reported by Gomes (1996) was the increased frequency of *Desmodium incanum, Agrostis montevidense, Coelorachis selloana, Paspalum notatum, Sporobolus indicus* and *Stipa* spp. when more than 250 kg/ha of P_2O_5, were applied; the species also increased their contribution to DM production of grasslands. *Elionurus candidus, Aristida* spp. and dead material were less. When fertilization rates were below 250 kg P_2O_5/ha, *Paspalum plicatulum, Piptochaetium montevidense* and *Axonopus affinis* increased their presence and made some contribution to DM production, while *Andropogon lateralis, Elionurus candidus* and *Piptochaetium montevidense* were intermediate contributors.

With blanket N+P fertilization of natural grassland, Moojen (1991) and Gomes (1996) raised forage production to 7.0 t DM/ha. Subsequently, through increasing N and avoiding moisture stress, Costa (1997) reported 12.0 t DM/ha and derived the following DM production model for unit area (m²) per day of *Paspalum notatum*:

$$DM = 0.44. \text{ Rs } (1 \exp(-0.0031. \text{ ST})) + R$$

where Rs is global solar radiation, ST is thermal addition and R is green residual DM. Following this model, Boggiano (2000) obtained 18.0 t/ha of total DM, including stolons and roots to 8 cm deep, on a natural grassland dominated by *P. notatum*. Liveweight gain per hectare was 700 kg in 200 grazing days, under continuous stocking. This response removed suspicions about limited growth potential of natural grasslands, creating expectations for this natural resource.

Structural changes on fertilized natural grasslands in SE Brazil

As research programmes evolved, fertilizer studies on natural grassland were extended to consider different fodder offers and N fertilization levels applied in a Composite Central Rotation with Uniform Precision experimental design, using three-day spells of grazing on a grazing cycle of 38 days. This study exposed a lack of knowledge about N fertilization responses of natural grasslands. Nitrogen action was reliable on some important species, such as

Paspalum notatum. Following Lemaire (1997), DM production of vegetative grasslands depends mainly on three morphogenic variables: Leaf Appearance Rate (LAR), Leaf Expansion Rate (LER) and Leaf Life Span (LLS). These variables are genetically defined, but modified by environmental factors. The combination of these variables determines the structural characteristics of the grassland, such as tiller density, leaf size and number of leaves per tiller, and the integral outcome gives the Leaf Area Index (LAI). Boggiano (2000) verified that LER and the number and size of leaves and tillers were very sensitive to N effects and defoliation management, leading to different recovery rates of *Paspalum notatum* after grazing. LAR was 5.5–7.0 days, influenced by N and FO, suggesting that lighter grazing increases sheath length, the expansion period and the size of new leaves. With low N applications, there is an increase in the number of small leaves and a longer LLS. Average LLS varied from 21 to 31 days, increasing with FO and with reducing N. It was evident that LAR and tiller density increase with higher defoliation intensities.

Tiller density depends on LAR and increases with lower FO, which provoke higher grazing frequency (more defoliations). At the same time, N increases LAR and stimulates higher tiller densities under lower FO, while contributing to low tiller number in high FO conditions, where defoliations are less frequent. N × FO interaction alters compensatory relationships, with a trend towards higher tiller density on high N–low FO swards. N reduction decreases tiller density and increasing N raises the weight per tiller. This gives us the parameters for an area covered by *Paspalum notatum*, modelling a compact sward with low production. It differs from a productive grazing pasture, with fewer, bigger tillers, in a higher sward profile that ensures high DM accumulation rates and it is more favourable for animal production.

Average final length of the laminae is more dependent on previous defoliation intensity (residual LAI) than on nitrogen supply. Bigger tillers have greater LER (Table 5.8). It seems to be desirable to promote management practices that promote larger tillers. LAI is the main factor determining interception of incident solar radiation, which has direct effect on the DM accumulation rates

TABLE 5.8
Estimated LAI values for *Paspalum notatum* as a function of surface response models for residual LAI and after 33 days of regrowth (Boggiano, 2000).

FO (percent of LW)	N (kg/ha)	LAI after grazing	LAI after 33 days regrowth
4.0	0	1.992	3.956
4.0	100	1.555	4.093
4.0	200	0.644	4.144
9.0	0	0.962	2.536
9.0	100	1.462	3.675
9.0	200	1.614	5.924
14.0	0	1.480	2.816
14.0	100	3.045	6.153
14.0	200	4.130	9.404

Source: Adapted from Boggiano, 2000.

of grasslands (Brougham, 1959; Parsons, Carrère and Schwinning, 2000). For *Paspalum notatum*, responses to N and FO were observed reaching LAI values of 9.4, which is high for this kind of plant.

With low N, the pasture is more prostrate and less exposed to animal defoliation. With increased FO, grazing is more selective, leaving more residues that contribute to regrowth. With frequent grazing and low N there are smaller leaves with low LAI values, less light interception and lower DM production. Increasing N promotes faster LAI recovery, which in the higher FO promotes a faster regrowth start, with higher LAI at the end of the regrowth period. Therefore there is higher radiation interception, higher carbon sequestration, higher forage production and higher efficiency of applied N.

Green DM of the grassland is produced from the grazing stubble, which increases according to the net AR of the regrowth period, which is increased by the action of N. The effect of management has been well documented, because Boggiano (2000) observed available DM increases of 1 000 kg/ha for each 35 days of regrowth, as this is the response to lighter grazing on fertilized grasslands. The low LLS makes difficult to maintain high LAI values, while low FO, with low LAI, consistently show less leaf length and less final length. Higher grazing intensity leads to reduced forage production, lower forage accessibility for grazing animals and consequently lower intake.

In terms of plants and pastures, with low FO and poor N status, the priority is to accumulate dry matter in stolons and roots, preserving meristems and increasing the proportion of stolons in total aerial biomass, so as to supply the demands of the next growth period. At intermediate FO, stolon biomass is maximal and root biomass minimal. This topic requires more study. Stolons cannot be grazed, so *Paspalum notatum* and its biological forms show greater cover on grazed grassland. Defoliation and shading alter the carbon supply to plants and increase the proportion used for leaf production, while factors that reduce meristem activity (N, moisture) promote higher carbon accumulation in the roots (Lemaire, 1997). Careful use of N increases the capacity of natural grasslands to sequestrate carbon from the atmosphere, storing it in permanent plant structures for growth, organ and tissue development, DM production, and consequently livestock feeding. Better performance tends to reduce methane emissions and the litter that, with animal dejections, constitute the main source for renovation and increment of soil organic matter. This enrichment of the environment promotes favourable conditions for microfauna, which form part of the fertility chain of predator fauna, hence contributing to environmental health, nutrient recycling and strengthening of life expression in natural grassland.

IMPROVEMENT TECHNIQUES
Over-seeding
This technique for introducing valuable forages to the sward has been evaluated for a long time. Many forages, mainly winter legumes, have been

TABLE 5.9
Winter performance and yearly liveweight gain for two treatments on natural grassland.

Treatment	LWG winter period kg/day/head	Year		
		1997	1998 liveweight/ha/year	1999
P fertilization	0.615	151	219	267
P fertilization + over-seeding	0.695	173	245	302

tested and also seeding methods, previous grassland management, fertilization levels, over-seeding, grazing management, etc. Rarely do the introduced species persist for more than three years due to strong competition from native species. Despite this, when some winter species become established, animal production increases are large. Higher productivity has been obtained recently in a three-year grassland improvement trial. Preliminary results of two treatments are shown in Table 5.9 (Pizzio, unpublished).

The most interesting results from this trial are the excellent animal performance in winter, which exceeded 0.6 kg/day when normally there is no gain at this season, and the year-on-year productivity increases.

This experiment considered some factors not previously evaluated: (1) a higher level of phosphorus fertilization in comparison with previous research, which brought the phosphorus content in grass above 0.22 percent, which had not previously been recorded; (2) a sward structure that offered a good quantity of green, easy-to-graze grass; and (3) a diverse and desirable botanical composition, that offered good quality green feed in winter, with species such as red clover, *Lotus* cv. Rincón, ryegrass and oats. These factors, with others, allowed the animals to harvest a large quantity of high quality of forage in the available grazing time, to attain performance similar to those from sown pastures.

Legume introduction

The need to improve the primary production and quality of Uruguayan grasslands led to legume introduction using minimum- or no-tillage techniques, as a way to increase secondary production. Correcting soil P deficiencies is a crucial element in this process (Bemhaja and Levratto, 1988; Berretta and Formoso, 1993; Berretta and Risso, 1995; Risso and Berretta, 1997; Bemhaja, 1998). The study of anthropogenic factors provides an understanding of various aspects of induced vegetation succession, which contributes to success in the application of the technology. To make a proper improvement in natural grasslands, the following must be considered:

- *Vegetation sward* as botanical composition defines the quality of the grassland, related to productive types, vegetative types and growing cycle.
- *Soil* type, topography, stoniness, drought and erosion risks, drainage, etc.
- *Grazing objective* for the improved paddock: cattle, sheep, fattening, weaning, etc.

These factors influence the selection of forages to be introduced and the way the seed will be in contact with the soil, for efficient moisture and nutrient supply to the seedling. The establishment, productivity and persistence of introduced forages depends mainly on the way that competition from natural herbage is reduced, the quality of the seedbed and the adaptation of introduced species to the environment. Forage yield of improved pastures depends on soil type and botanical composition, and can be 50 to 100 percent higher than unimproved grasslands, with winter yield up to three times higher (Berretta *et al.*, 2000).

Sward preparation for seeding

Generally it is necessary to graze with cattle beforehand to reduce tall-grasses and accumulated dead material. Stocking rates will depend on forage availability at the end of the spring and summer, but should be high. If the summer is wet, grass growth will be high and dry matter and seed stalks will remain at the end of the season, so stocking must be increased to eliminate this material. Sheep are used in the final stages, to reduce sward height to 2 cm. This grazing could be continuous, but rotational grazing is better to allow regrowth and regrazing; this reduces wild plant reserves, thus favouring the germination, emergence and establishment of the introduced forages. Depending on grass growth, grazing must be done every 30–45 days. If grazing is alternated with resting, stocking rates must be much higher than with continuous grazing. Sward preparation aims to provide safe sites for good seed-soil contact. Generally it is very difficult to reduce vegetation cover below 50 percent, although sward height may be low. Some herbage at sowing time is, however, important to protect seeds from bad weather.

Chemicals must be used carefully. Non-selective contact herbicides are preferred, to avoid reducing the growth capacity of native plants. When systemic herbicides are used, the dose must be low enough to preserve valuable native species (Berretta and Formoso, 1993).

Legumes for improvement

Many evaluations of different genera and species of legumes have been carried out. Recent studies include several species of *Trifolium, Lotus, Medicago, Ornithopus, Desmanthus, Vicia*, etc. (Bemhaja, 1998). On medium and deep soils, the best forages tested have been white clover cvs Zapicán and Bayucuá, and *Lotus corniculatus*. Less reliable have been *L. pedunculatus* cv Maku, *L. hispidus* cv. El Rincón and red clover (*Trifolium pratense*).

Recommended seed rates are 4–5 kg/ha for white clover, 10–12 kg/ha for *L. corniculatus*, 2.5–3.5 kg/ha for *L. pedunculatus* cv Maku, 4–5 kg/ha for *Lotus* cv. El Rincón, 6–8 kg/ha for red clover, and for a mix of white clover and *L. corniculatus*, 2–3 kg/ha of the former and 8–10 kg/ha of the latter are recommended (Risso, 1991; 1995; Risso and Morón, 1990).

TABLE 5.10
Production of steers in rotational grazing on improved native grasslands in different regions of Uruguay.

Soils	Stocking rate (AU/ha)	Liveweight gain (kg/ha)	Individual performance (kg LW/head)
Crystalline	1.55	533	406
Medium and deep Basalt	1.85	680	485
Hills	1.53[1]	700	473

NOTES: (1) Includes mixed grazing with wethers in a ratio of two wethers per steer.
SOURCE: Adapted from Ayala and Carámbula, 1996; Bemhaja, Berretta and Brito, 1998; Risso and Berretta, 1997.

This improvement technique is low-input and environmentally friendly, promotes sustainable development of native vegetation and improves productivity, accelerating fattening by means of better individual performance and higher stocking capacity (Table 5.10). These results were obtained in rotational grazing conditions, 5–8 paddocks, 7–12 grazing days and 30–40 rest days, in grazing seasons of about 300 days (Berretta *et al.*, 2000).

Effect of legume introduction on composition of native grasslands

Once legumes have been established for some years, an important change is an increase of winter grasses (C_3) (Berretta and Levratto, 1990; Bemhaja and Berretta, 1991). On similar unimproved grasslands of the basalt region, summer species are always more frequent than winter ones (Formoso, 1990; Berretta, 1990). On improved grasslands, the relative frequency of winter forage species is around 75 percent, with similar values for native grasses and introduced *Trifolium repens*. The increased frequency of better quality species raises the N content of the forage to 3.2 percent.

Flowering and seed production are necessary to maintain introduced species in the pasture. This ensures regeneration the next autumn, since they pass the summer partly as plants and partly as seeds (Berretta and Risso, 1995). Reduction or total exclusion of grazing also favours seed production of native winter grasses, including *Poa lanigera*, *Stipa setigera*, *Piptochaetium stipoides* and *Adesmia bicolor*. Therefore conservation of these species in native grasslands is related both to rest periods to allow flowering and seed production, and to increased soil fertility. In many improved grasslands, there is a remarkable increase in the frequency of *Lolium multiflorum*, which has adapted, and in many cases is introduced and thrives with increased fertility.

Legume introduction can have positive effects in more degraded grasslands, dominated by unproductive or unpalatable grasses and short herbs. Relative legume frequency (*Trifolium repens*, *Lotus corniculatus*) is about 60 percent. Native, productive winter grasses – *Stipa neesiana* and *Piptochaetium stipoides* – and naturalized species, such as *Lolium multiflorum*, increase in frequency, while unproductive grasses and herbs decrease (Berretta and Risso, 1995; Risso and Berretta, 1997). Oversowing of perennial and annual legumes in C_3-dominated grasslands that had a yearly forage production of

3 400 kg DM/ha, increased forage production to 8 600 kg DM/ha (Ayala *et al.*, 1999).

Stock management

Managing livestock is one of the most important options for farmers in improving the utilization efficiency of available forage and to increase its productivity. This low-cost technique is based on adapting the nutritional requirements of stock classes to the grassland growth curve. Stock management involves short seasonal mating, early weaning, pregnancy diagnosis, stock classification according to nutritional requirements, and sales organization. An example of the impact of this technology is found in Curuzu Cuatiá Department. While the average liveweight gain for the Department is 56 kg/ha/year, twelve farms that adopted these practices averaged 88 kg/ha/year over five years.

Mineral supplementation

Phosphorus deficiency in diets is one of the limiting factors for animal production in the region. Unsupplemented steers have a liveweight gain of 66 kg/year, while supplemented steers can gain 106 kg/year.

Other management practices

Other management practices that increase productivity include mowing of tussock grasslands, burning, autumn deferments for winter grazing, strategic rests for paddocks, energy-protein supplementation, and "protein banks".

RESEARCH AND DEVELOPMENT PRIORITIES

Advances in knowledge over the last 35 years concerning the structure, function and management of natural grasslands show that there is great potential, at least in the Rocky Outcrops region. The next task should be to evaluate these technologies in other ecological regions where this could be applicable. In regions such as the *malezales*, factors such as drainage and use of fire have to be studied before thinking of any further improvement. The relationship between soil series, grass production and carrying capacity is an issue that has received little attention. Soil has a great effect on grassland production and stability, but research has paid little attention to this topic.

A task that has to be completed, validated and then extended is paddock ranking. Managing natural grasslands means to manage soil, vegetation and stock within the constraints of climate to get the best results from the combination of factors. Each stock class has specific nutritional requirements; each paddock has different FO and potential. Today, the pastoral value of a paddock is subjectively evaluated. Methodology development is required to enable simple objective paddock ranking, and to match paddock FO with animal requirements.

Research has focused on technology for increased production. Monitoring the effects of recommended technology with respect to biological and economic sustainability has received little attention. The search for alternative production from grasslands, such as agrotourism and game harvesting, would allow diversification of use of these ecosystems. There is a need to find reliable sustainability indicators to allow us to ensure that recommended technologies are sustainable, so coming generations receive a better resource than we inherited.

Ecological grassland management for maintaining productivity

Natural grasslands are the main basis for meat and fibre production in the region, and are also a huge reservoir of valuable grass and legume species, which it is necessary to select and screen under cultivation. Only with deep knowledge of the behaviour of native species will it be possible to conserve and improve the natural grasslands and protect the soil from erosion and degradation. Research in the region suggests that the potential of natural grasslands is very high, close to cultivated pastures, with better persistence.

Studies on natural grassland dynamics with several management-controlled factors reflect ongoing changes that occur slowly, with seasonal variations more important than grazing effects. Over longer periods, high continuous grazing and a high sheep:cattle ratio encourages pasture degradation and lower primary production. Quite often, high stocking rates are maintained for economic and social reasons, but ultimately lead to poorer animal production. Higher stocking rates may increase short-term economic returns, but they increase operational risks. Continuous and deeper studies of native grasslands and native forage species will increase understanding of the factors that promote high secondary productivity – meat and wool in this case – through primary production increases related to better use and conservation of forage.

When stocking rates are adjusted to grassland potential and grazing methods include rest periods, grasslands can be maintained, with variations due to seasonal changes. These prairie ecosystems are highly stable and are capable of recovering after severe impacts, such as droughts.

Spatial heterogeneity is high on most of the grasslands, mainly due to soil type, combined with weather fluctuations and grazing management. Vegetation types must have management practices adjusted to the morphological and physiological characteristics of the dominant species, so they are better managed as independent units. When planning grazing systems, it is necessary to know precisely which species are present in the vegetation, concentrating on productive types, particularly when coarse ordinary grasses are dominant, because prolonged rests and low stocking rates may be beneficial. Determining a proper stocking rate that achieve animal performance objectives without ecosystem deterioration is the most important management decision. Each grassland has a production potential that determines its carrying capacity. The main problem in developing an optimum stocking rate criterion is the need to preserve forage to be used when grass growth is limited by moisture stress or low temperatures.

Liveweight gains are highly variable, being a function of weather and forage availability. When pastures have winter species, autumn deferment is recommended to supply forage for winter. When winter grasses are scarce, forage accumulation must be achieved in other periods because of fast declining forage quality in autumn; under conditions of low autumn growth and quality loss as the resting period extends, the accumulated forage is inadequate to supply animal requirements and provide the desired liveweight gains (Ayala *et al.*, 1999).

Inadequate grazing management – such as overgrazing, inadequate subdivision and continuous grazing – prevent flowering and seed production of winter grasses, leaving reliance on vegetative mechanisms alone for persistence. This may be the main reason for decreased cover of winter grasses in natural grasslands of the Campos.

Raising the fertility level of the soil by means of N and P fertilization increases the production and quality of natural grassland. The process is relatively slow, with increased responses as more nutrients are applied. Fertilization "disturbance" leads vegetation to a new equilibrium point, with botanical changes consisting of an increase in productive species frequency, and therefore increased secondary production. This technology complements grassland improvement with legume introduction, as well as cultivation of perennial and annual forages. Natural grassland fertilization allows increased production and quality of vegetation on soils too shallow for more productive forages. At the same time, the residual benefits of N and P fertilization must also be considered.

N and P additions, particularly the latter, should help to return to natural grassland something that has been extracted during centuries of grazing, from livestock introduction at the beginning of the seventeenth century, besides its contribution to plant and animal biodiversity maintenance on natural grasslands. It is important to conserve this natural resource without degrading it, maintaining an awareness of the economic, ecological and social aspects implicit in sustainable development.

The introduction of legumes, coupled with fertilizing at sowing, yearly maintenance phosphorous dressings and grazing management, move vegetation, in a slow biotic process, to a new equilibrium point where yield and quality are higher than the original. Grazing management and fertilization have to be closely controlled to maintain the pasture at this higher equilibrium point. The result should be a sward dominated by winter species, where high quality native perennial species are outstanding. This is an alternative route to increasing annual primary production without using herbicides while conserving productive species of the natural grassland.

It is necessary to improve the extension of available technologies and to promote the training of scientists specialized in management and conservation of natural grasslands. This discipline does not exist in Uruguay, despite its main agricultural exports being based on natural grassland outputs.

Scientific knowledge has contributed to better natural grasslands management practice, which has resulted in biological and economic benefits for farmer communities and society in the long term, with special care for animal and vegetation biodiversity and water conservation for the use of all living creatures. Plants and domestic animals will continue to provide the main food and fibre source of the world, conditioning our actions and behaviour to preserve natural resources for future generations.

In 1943, Professor Bernardo Rosengurtt wrote:

"Let us conserve with infinite care the prairie heritage, simultaneously national and private, to transfer it whole to the coming generations."

REFERENCES

Apezteguia, E.S. 1994. Potencial produtivo de uma pastagem natival do Rio Grande do Sul submetida a distintas ofertas de forragem [Productive potential of a natural grassland of Rio Grande do Sul under different forage offer]. Magisterial thesis. UFRGS, Porto Alegre, Brazil. 123 p.

Araujo Filho, J.A., Sousa, F.B. de & Carvalho, F.C. de. 1995. Pastagens no semi-árido: pesquisa para o desenvolvimento sustentável [Semi-arid grasslands: a study for sustainable development]. pp. 63–75, *in:* R.P. Andrade, A.O. Barcellos and C.M.C. Rocha (eds). *Simpósio sobre pastagens nos ecossistemas brasileiros, Anais XXXII Reun. Anual da SBZ.* Brasilia, DF, Brazil, 1995.

Arias, A. 1997. Intensificación y diversificación de la ganadería bovina de carne en la región NEA.

Arias, A.A. & Manunta, O.A. 1981. Suplementación con harina de hueso y sal en un área deficiente en fósforo. Su efecto sobre el crecimiento de novillos. *Producción Animal (Buenos Aires),* **7**: 64–76.

Arias, A.A., Peruchena, C.O., Manunta, O.A. & Slobodzian, A. 1985. Experiencias de suplementación mineral realizadas en la Estación Experimental Agropecuaria Corrientes. *Revista Argentina de Produccion Animal,* **4**(Suppl. 3): 57–70.

Ayala, W., Bermúdez, R., Carámbula, M., Risso, D. & Terra, J. 1999. Diagnóstico, propuestas y perspectivas de pasturas en la región. pp. 1–41, *in: Producción animal. Unidad Experimental Palo a Pique.* INIA Treinta y Tres, Uruguay. (*INIA Serie Actividades de Difusión,* No. 195).

Ayala, G., Bermúdez, R., Carámbula, M., Risso, D. & Terra, J. 2001. Tecnologías para la producción de forraje en suelos de Lomadas del Este. pp. 69–108, *in: Tecnologías forrajeras para sistemas ganaderos de Uruguay.* INIA Tacuarembó, Uruguay. Montevideo, Uruguay: Hemisferio Sur. (*INIA Boletín de Divulgación,* No. 76)

Ayala, W. & Carámbula, M. 1996. Mejoramientos extensivos en la región Este: manejo y utilización. [Extensive improvement in the Eastern Region: management and utilization]. pp. 177–182, *in:* D.F. Risso, E.J. Berretta and A. Morón (eds). *Producción y manejo de pasturas.* INIA Tacuarembó, Uruguay. Montevideo, Uruguay: Hemisferio Sur. (*INIA Serie Técnica*, No. 80).

Barcellos, J.M., Severo, H.C., Acevedo, A.S. & Macedo, W. 1980. Influência da adubação e sistemas de pastejo na produção da pastagem natural. p. 123, *in: Pastagens e Adubação e Fertilidade do Solo.* Bagé, Rio Grande do Sul, Brazil. *UEPAE/ Embrapa, Miscelânea*, No. 2, 1980.

Bemhaja, M. 1998. Mejoramiento de campo: manejo de leguminosas. [Grassland improvement: legume management]. pp. 53–61, *in:* E.J. Berretta (ed). *Seminario de Actualización en Tecnologías para Basalto.* INIA Tacuarembó, Uruguay. Montevideo, Uruguay: Hemisferio Sur. (*INIA Serie Técnica,* No. 102).

Bemhaja, M. 2001. Tecnologías para la mejora de la producción de forraje en suelos arenosos. pp. 123–148, *in: Tecnologías forrajeras para sistemas ganaderos de Uruguay.* INIA Tacuarembó,Uruguay. Montevideo, Uruguay: Hemisferio Sur. (*INIA Boletín de Divulgación*, No. 76)

Bemhaja, M. & Berretta, E.J. 1991. Respuesta a la siembra de leguminosas en Basalto profundo. [Response to legume seeding on deep Basalt]. pp. 103–114, *in: Pasturas y producción animal en áreas de ganadería extensiva.* Montevideo, Uruguay: INIA. (*INIA Serie Técnica*, No. 13).

Bemhaja, M., Berretta, E.J. & Brito, G. 1998. Respuesta a la fertilización nitrogenada de campo natural en Basalto profundo. pp. 119–122, *in:* E.J. Berretta (ed). *14th Reunión del Grupo Técnico Regional del Cono Sur en Mejoramiento y Utilización de los Recursos Forrajeros del Area Tropical y Subtropical.* Grupo Campos, 1994, Uruguay. Anales. INIA Tacuarembó, Uruguay. Montevideo, Uruguay: Hemisferio Sur. (*INIA Serie Técnica*, No. 94).

Bemhaja, M. & Levratto, J. 1988. Alternativas para incrementar la producción de pasturas con niveles controlados de insumos en suelos de Areniscas y Basalto. pp. 105–106, *in: 9th Reunión del Grupo Técnico Regional del Cono Sur en Mejoramiento y Utilización de los Recursos Forrajeros del Area Tropical y Subtropical.* Grupos Campos y Chaco. Tacuarembó, Uruguay.

Benitez Meabe, O. 1997. Modelos de cría en Corrientes. pp. 19–24, *in: IV Jorn. de Ganadería Subtropical.*

Berretta, E.J. 1990. Técnicas para evaluar la dinámica de pasturas naturales en pastoreo. pp. 129–147, *in:* N.J. Nuernberg (ed). *11th Reuniao do Grupo Técnico Regional do Cone Sul em Melhoramento e Utilizaçaô dos Recursos Forrageiros das Areas Tropical e Subtropical.* Grupo Campos, 1989, Brasil. Relatório. Lages, SC, Brazil.

Berretta, E.J. 1998. Principales características de las vegetaciones de los suelos de Basalto. [Main characteristics of Basalt soil natural grasslands]. pp. 11–19, *in:* E.J. Berretta (ed). *14th Reunión del Grupo Técnico Regional del Cono Sur en Mejoramiento y Utilización de los Recursos Forrajeros del Area Tropical y*

Subtropical. Grupo Campos, 1994, Uruguay. INIA Tacuarembó, , Uruguay. Montevideo, Uruguay: Hemisferio Sur. (*INIA Serie Técnica*, No. 94).

Berretta, E.J. 2001. Ecophysiology and management response of the subtropical grasslands of Southern America. pp. 939–946, *in: Proceedings of the 19th International Grassland Congress.* Sao Pedro, Sao Paulo, Brazil, 11–21 February 2001.

Berretta, E.L. & Bemhaja, M. 1991. Produccion de pasturas naturales en el Basalto. B. Produccion estacional de forraje de tres comunidades nativas sobre suelo de basalto. pp. 19–21, *in: Pasturas y producción animal en áreas de ganadería extensiva.* Montevideo, Uruguay: INIA. (*INIA Serie Técnica*, No. 13).

Berretta, E.J. & Bemhaja, M. 1998. Producción estacional de comunidades de campo natural sobre suelos de Basalto de la Unidad Queguay Chico. pp. 11–20, *in:* E.J. Berretta (ed). *Seminario de Actualización en Tecnologías para Basalto.* INIA Tacuarembó, Uruguay. Montevideo, Uruguay: Hemisferio Sur. (*INIA Serie Técnica*, No. 102).

Berretta, E.J. & Formoso, D. 1993. Manejo y mejoramiento del campo natural. Campos de Basalto. Campos de Cristalino. pp. I-10–I-11, *in: 6th Congreso Nacional de Ingeniería Agronómica,* Montevideo, Uruguay. Asociación de Ingenieros Agrónomos del Uruguay.

Berretta, E.J. & Levratto, J.C. 1990. Estudio de la dinámica de una vegetación mejorada con fertilización e introducción de especies. pp. 197–203, *in: 2nd Seminario Nacional de Campo Natural.* Tacuarembó, Uruguay, 15–16 November 1990. Montevideo, Uruguay: Hemisferio Sur.

Berretta, E.J. & Nascimento D. 1991. Glosario estructurado de términos sobre pasturas y producción animal. Montevideo: IICA - PROCISUR. (*Diálogo IICA - PROCISUR,* No. 32)

Berretta, E.J. & Risso, D.F. 1995. Native grassland improvement on Basaltic and Granitic soils in Uruguay. pp. 52–53 (vol. 1), *in:* N.E. West (ed). *Proceedings of the 5th International Rangeland Congress.* Salt Lake City, USA, 23-28 July 1995. Denver, Colorado, USA: Society for Range Management.

Berretta, E.J., Risso, D.F., Levratto, J.C. & Zamit, W.S. 1998. Mejoramiento de campo natural de Basalto fertilizado con nitrógeno y fósforo. pp. 63–73. *in:* E.J. Berretta (ed). *Seminario de Actualización en Tecnologías para Basalto.* INIA Tacuarembó, Uruguay. Montevideo, Uruguay: Hemisferio Sur. (*INIA Serie Técnica*, No. 102).

Berretta, E.J., Risso, D.F., Montossi, F. & Pigurina, G. 2000. Campos in Uruguay. pp. 377–394, *in:* G. Lemaire, J. Hodgson, A. Moraes, C. Nabinger and P.C.F. Carvalho (eds). *Grassland Ecophysiology and Grazing Ecology.* Wallingford, Oxon., UK: CAB International.

Boggiano, P.R.O. 2000. Dinâmica da produção primária da pastagem nativa sob efeito da adubação nitrogenada e de ofertas de forragem. Doctor of Zootechnology thesis. UFRGS, Porto Alegre, Brazil. 166 p.

Boldrini, I.I. 1993. Dinâmica de Vegetação de uma Pastagem Natural sob Diferentes Níveis de Oferta de Forragem e Tipos de Solos, Depressão Central, Rio Grande do Sul. Doctoral thesis. Faculty of Agronomy, UFRGS, Porto Alegre, Brazil. 266 p.

Briske. D.D. & Heitschmidt, R.K. 1991. An ecological perspective. pp. 11-26, *in:* R.K. Heitschmidt and J.W. Stuth (ed). *Grazing Management – An Ecological Perspective.* Portland, Oregon, USA: Timber Press.

Brougham, R.W. 1959. The effects of frequency and intensity of grazing on the productivity of pasture of short-rotation ryegrass, red and white clover. *New Zealand Journal of Agricultural Research,* 2(6): 1232–1248.

Brown, D. 1954. Methods of surveying and measuring vegetation. *Commonwealth Agricultural Bureaux Bulletin,* No. 42. 223 p.

Coronel, F. & Martínez, P. 1983. Evolución del tapiz natural bajo pastoreo continuo de bovinos y ovinos en diferentes relaciones. Ing. Agr. thesis. Faculty of Agronomy, Universidad de la República, Uruguay. 295 p.

Correa, F.L. & Maraschin, G.E. 1994. Crescimento e desaparecimento de uma pastagem nativa sob diferentes níveis de oferta de forragem. *Pesquisa Agropecuaria Brasileira,* 29(10): 1617–1623.

Costa, J.A.A. 1997. Caracterização ecológica de ecotipos de *Paspalum notatum* Flügge var. *notatum* naturais do Rio Grande do Sul e ajuste de um modelo de estimação do rendimento potencial. Master of Agronomy-Zootechnology thesis. PPGAg, UFRGS, Porto Alegre, Brazil. 98 p.

Daget, PH. & Poissonet, J. 1971. Une méthode d'analyse phytologique des prairies. Critères d'application. *Annales Agronomiques,* 22: 5–41.

Deregibus, V.A. 1988. Importancia de los pastizales naturales en la República Argentina. Situación presente y futura. *Revista Argentina de Produccion Animal,* 8(1): 67–78.

Escobar, E.H., Ligier, D.H., Melgar, R., Maheio, H. & Vallejos, O. 1996. *Mapa de suelos de la Provincia de Corrientes* 1:500 000. INTA EEA Corrientes.

Ferreira, G. 1997. An evolutionary approach to farming decision in extensive rangelands. PhD thesis. Faculty of Science and Engineering, University of Edinburgh, Scotland, UK.

Formoso, D. 1990. Pasturas naturales. Componentes de la vegetación, producción y manejo de diferentes tipos de campo. pp. 225–237, *in: 3rd Seminario Técnico de Producción Ovina.* Paysandú, Uruguay, August 1990. Uruguay: SUL.

Frame, J. 1981. Herbage mass. pp. 39–69, *in:* J. Hodgson, R. Barker, A. Davies, A.S. Laidlaw and J. Leaver (eds). *Sward measurement handbook.* UK: British Grassland Society.

Gallinal, J.P., Bergalli, L.U., Campal, E.F., Aragone, L. & Rosengurtt, B. 1938. *Estudio sobre praderas naturales del Uruguay. 1ª Contribución.* Montevideo: Germano Uruguaya.

Gandara, F. and Arias, A.A. 1999. Situación actual de la ganadería. pp. 31–39, *in:* Técnica Jornada Ganadera del NEA, INTA Publicación, Corrientes, Argentina.

Gándara, F.R., Casco, J.F. Goldfarb, M.C., Correa, M. & Aranda, M. 1989. Evaluación agronómica de pastizales en la Región Occidental de Corrientes

(Argentina). I. Sitio malezales. Epoca agosto. [Agronomic evaluation of grasslands in the Western Region of Corrientes (Argentina). I. Malezales Site. August Season]. *Revista Argentina de Produccion Animal,* 9(Suppl. 1): 31–32.

Gándara, F.R., Casco, J.F., Goldfarb, M.C. & Correa, M. 1990a. Evaluación agronómica de pastizales en la Región Occidental Corrientes (Argentina). II Sitio Chavarria. Epoca agosto. [Agronomic evaluation of grasslands in the Western Region of Corrientes (Argentina). II. Chavarría Site. August Season]. *Revista Argentina de Produccion Animal,* 10: 21–22.

Gándara, F.R., Casco, J.F., Goldfarb, M.C. & Correa, M. 1990b. Evaluación agronómica de pastizales en la Región Occidental de Corrientes (Argentina) III. Sitio Corrientes. Epoca agosto. [Agronomic evaluation of grasslands in the Western Region of Corrientes (Argentina). III. Corrientes Site. August Season]. *Revista Argentina de Produccion Animal,* 10(Suppl. 1): 22–23.

Gomes, K.E. 1996. Dinâmica e produtividade de uma pastagem natural do Rio Grande do Sul após seis anos de aplicação de adubos, diferimentos e níveis de oferta de forragem. [Dynamics and productivity of a natural grassland of Rio Grande do Sul after six years of fertilization, deferments and forage offer levels]. Doctoral thesis. Faculty of Agronomy, UFRGS, Porto Alegre, Brazil. 225 p.

INTA EEA. 1977. Tipos de pasturas naturales en el Centro-Sur de Corrientes. INTA EEA Mercedes (Corrientes, Argentina). *Noticias y Comentarios,* No. 113. 5 p.

Kraemer, M.L. & Mufarrege, D.J. 1965. Niveles de fósforo inorgánico en sangre de bovinos y fósforo total en pasto de la pradera natural. INTA EEA Mercedes (Ctes), Argentina. *Serie Técnica,* No. 2. 13 p.

Laycock, W.A. 1991. Stable states and thresholds of range condition on North American rangelands: a viewpoint. *Journal of Range Management,* 44: 427–433.

Lemaire, G. 1997. The physiology of grass growth under grazing. Tissue turnover. pp. 117–144, *in:* J.A Gomide (ed). *Simpósio Internacional sobre Produção Animal em Pastejo.* November 1997. Viçosa, MG, Brazil.

Maraschin, G.E. 1993. Perdas de forragem sob pastejo. pp. 166–190, *in:* V. Favoretto, L.R. de A. Rodrigues and R.A. Reis (eds). *Anais do 2° Simpósio sobre ecossistema de pastagens.* FAPESP, FCAV- Jaboticabal.

Maraschin, G.E. 1996. Produção de carne a pasto. pp. 243–274, *in:* AM.M. Peixoto, J.C. Moura and V.P. de Faria (eds). *Anais do 13° Simpósio sobre Manejo da Pastagem. Produção de Bovinos a Pasto.* FEALQ. Piracicaba, SP.

Maraschin, G.E., Moojen, E.L., Escosteguy, C.M.D., Correa, F.L., Apezteguia, E.S., Boldrini, I.J. & Riboldi, J. 1997. Native pasture, forage on offer and animal response. Paper 288 (vol. 2), *in: Proceedings of the 18th International Grassland Congress.* Saskatoon, Sascatchewan and Winnipeg, Manitoba, Canada, 8–19 June 1997.

Montossi, F., Berretta, E.J., Pigurina, G., Santamarina, I., Bemhaja, M., San Julián, R., Risso, D.F. & Mieres, J. 1998b. Estudios de selectividad de ovinos y vacunos en diferentes comunidades vegetales de la región de basalto. pp. 275–285, *in:* E.J. Berretta (ed). *Seminario de Actualización en Tecnologías para Basalto.* INIA Tacuarembó, Uruguay. Montevideo, Uruguay: Hemisferio Sur. (*INIA Serie Técnica*, No. 102).

Montossi, F., San Julián, R., de Mattos, D., Berretta, E.J., Ríos, M., Zamit, W. & Levratto, J. 1998a. Alimentación y manejo de la oveja de cría durante el último tercio de la gestación en la región de Basalto. pp. 195–208, *in:* E.J. Berretta (ed). *Seminario de Actualización en Tecnologías para Basalto.* INIA Tacuarembó, Uruguay. Montevideo, Uruguay: Hemisferio Sur. (*INIA Serie Técnica*, No. 102).

Moojen, E.L. 1991. Dinâmica e Potencial Produtivo de uma Pastagem Nativa do Rio Grande do Sul submetida a pressões de pastejo. Épocas de Diferimento e Níveis de Adubação. Doctoral thesis. UFRGS, Porto Alegre, Brazil. 172 p.

Moraes, A. de, Maraschin, G.E. & Nabinger, C. 1995. Pastagens nos ecossistemas de clima subtropical – pesquisas para o desenvolvimento sustentável. pp. 147–200, *in: Anais do simpósio sobre pastagens nos ecossistemas brasileiros. XXXII Reun. Anual da SBZ.* Brasilia, DF, Brazil. 1995.

Mufarrege, D.J., Royo Pallares, O. & Ocampo, E.P. 1981. Recría de vaquillas en campo natural fertilizado con nitrógeno en el departamento Mercedes (Provincia de Corrientes). *TAAPA Producción Animal (Buenos Aires, Argentina),* **8**: 270–283.

Mufarrege, D.J., Somma de Fere, G.R. & Homse, A.C. 1985. Nutrición mineral del ganado en la jurisdicción de la EEA Mercedes. *Revista Argentina de Produccion Animal,* 4(Suppl. 3): 5–7.

Nabinger, C. 1998. Princípios de manejo e produtividade de pastagens. manejo e utilização sustentável de pastagens. pp. 54–107, *in: Anais III Ciclo de Palestras em Produção e Manejo de Bovinos de Corte.* Universidade Luterano do Brasil (ULBRA), May 1998.

Olmos, F. & Godron, M. 1990. Relevamiento fitoecológico en el noreste uruguayo. pp. 35–48, *in: 2nd Seminario Nacional sobre Campo Natural.* Tacuarembó, Uruguay, 15–16 November 1990. Montevideo, Uruguay: Hemisferio Sur.

Parsons, A.J., Carrëre, P. & Schwinning, S. 2000. Dynamics of heterogeneity in a grazed sward. *In:* G. Lemaire, J. Hodgson, A. de Moraes, C. Nabinger and P.C.F. Carvalho (eds). *Grassland Ecophysiology and Grazing Ecology. A Symposium.* Wallingford, Oxon, UK: CABI Publishing.

Perin, R. & Maraschin, G.E. 1995. Desempenho animal em pastagem nativa melhorada sob pastejo contínuo e rotativo. pp. 67–69, *in: Na. XXXII Reun. Anual Soc. Bras. Zoot.* Brasilia, DF, Brazil, 17–21 July 1995.

Pigurina, G., Soares de Lima, J.M. & Berretta, E.J. 1998. Tecnologías para la cría vacuna en el Basalto [Cattle breeding technologies for Basalt soils]. pp. 125–136, *in:* E.J. Berretta (ed). *Seminario de Actualización en Tecnologías para Basalto.* INIA Tacuarembó, Uruguay. Montevideo, Uruguay: Hemisferio Sur. (*INIA Serie Técnica*, No. 102).

Pigurina, G., Soares de Lima, J.M., Berretta, E.J., Montossi, F., Pittaluga, O., Ferreira, G. & Silva, J.A. 1998. Características del engorde a campo natural. pp. 137–145, *in:* E.J. Berretta (ed). *Seminario de Actualización en Tecnologías* *para Basalto.* INIA Tacuarembó, Uruguay. Montevideo, Uruguay: Hemisferio Sur. (*INIA Serie Técnica,* No. 102).

Poissonet, P. & Poissonet, J. 1969. Étude comparé de diverses méthodes d'analyse de la végétation des formations herbacées denses et permanentes. CNRS-CEPE, Montpellier, France. 120 p. Document No. 50.

Risso, D.F. & Morón, A.D. 1990. Evaluación de mejoramientos extensivos de pasturas naturales en suelos sobre Cristalino. pp. 205–218, *in: 2nd Seminario Nacional de Campo Natural.* Tacuarembó, Uruguay, 15–16 November 1990. Montevideo, Uruguay: Hemisferio Sur.

Risso, D.F. 1991. Siembras en el tapiz: consideraciones generales y estado actual de la información en la zona de suelos sobre Cristalino. pp. 71–82, *in: Pasturas y producción animal en áreas de ganadería extensiva.* Montevideo, Uruguay: INIA. (*INIA Serie Técnica,* No. 13).

Risso, D.F. 1995. Alternativas en el mejoramiento de campos en el Cristalino. pp. 9–11, *in: Mejoramientos extensivos en el área de Cristalino.* IPO; CIE Dr. Alejandro Gallinal; SUL. Montevideo, Uruguay: Multigraf.

Risso, D.F. & Berretta, E.J. 1997. Animal productivity and dynamics of native pastures improved with oversown legumes in Uruguay. p. 22-29–22-30, *in: Proceedings of the 8th International Grassland Congress.* Saskatoon, Saskatchewan and Winnipeg, Manitoba, Canada, 8–19 June 1997.

Risso, D.F., Pittaluga, O., Berretta, E.J., Zamit, W., Levratto, J., Carracelas, G. & Pigurina, G. 1998. Intensificación del engorde en la región Basáltica: I. Integración de campo natural y mejorado para la producción de novillos jóvenes. pp. 153–163, *in:* E.J. Berretta (ed). *Seminario de Actualización en Tecnologías para Basalto.* INIA Tacuarembó, Uruguay. Montevideo, Uruguay: Hemisferio Sur. (*INIA Serie Técnica,* No. 102).

Rosengurtt, B. 1946. *Estudio sobre praderas naturales del Uruguay. 5ª. Contribución.* Montevideo, Uruguay: Rosgal.

Rosengurtt, B. 1979. Tabla de comportamiento de las especies de plantas de campos naturales en el Uruguay. Departamento de Publicaciones y Ediciones, Universidad de la República, Montevideo, Uruguay. 86 p.

Rosengurtt, B., Arrillaga de Maffei, B. & Izaguirre de Artucio, P. 1970. *Gramíneas uruguayas.* Montevideo, Uruguay: Departamento de Publicaciones, Universidad de la República.

Rosito J. & Maraschin, G.E. 1985. Efeito de sistemas de manejo sobre a flora de uma pastagem. *Pesquisa Agropecuaria Brasileira,* **19**(3): 311–316.

Royo Pallarés, O. 1985. Posibilidades de intensificación de la ganadería del NEA. *Revista Argentina de Produccion Animal* **4**(Suppl. 2): 73–101.

Royo Pallarés, O. 1999. Panorama ganadero de los próximos años. pp. 23–29, *in: INTA Jornada Ganadera del NEA.* Publicación Técnica Corrientes, Argentina.

Royo Pallarés, O. & Mufarrege, D.J. 1969. Respuesta de la pradera natural a la incorporación de nitrógeno, fósforo y potasio. INTA EEA Mercedes (Ctes), Argentina. *Serie Técnica* No. 5. 14 p.

Royo Pallarés, O. & Mufarrege, D.J. 1970. Producción animal de pasturas sub-tropicales fertilizadas. INTA EEA Mercedes (Ctes), Argentina. *Serie Técnica*, No. 6. 23 p.

Royo Pallarés, O., Pizzio, R.M., Ocampo, E.P., Benitez, C.A. & Fernandez, J.G. 1998. Carga y fertilización fosfórica en la ganancia de peso de novillos en pastizales de Corrientes. *Revista Argentina de Produccion Animal*, 18(Suppl. 1): 101–102.

Sala, O.E. 1988. Efecto del pastoreo sobre la estructura de la vegetación a distintas escalas de tiempo y espacio. *Revista Argentina de Produccion Animal* 8(Suppl. 1): 6–7.

San Julián, R., Montossi, F., Berretta, E.J., Levratto, J., Zamit, W. & Ríos, M. 1998. Alternativas de manejo y alimentación invernal de la recría ovina en la región de Basalto. pp. 209–228, *in:* E.J. Berretta (ed). *Seminario de Actualización en Tecnologías para Basalto.* INIA Tacuarembó, Uruguay. Montevideo, Uruguay: Hemisferio Sur. (*INIA Serie Técnica*, No. 102).

Setelich, E.A. 1994. Potencial produtivo de uma pastagem nativa do Rio Grande do Sul submetida a distintas ofertas de forragem. Magisterial thesis. Faculty of Agronomy, UFRGS, Porto Alegre, Rio Grande do Sul, Brazil. 123 p.

Scholl, J.M., Lobato, J.F.P. & Barreto, I.L. 1976. Improvement of pasture by direct seeding into native grass in Southern Brazil with oats, and with nitrogen supplied by fertilizer or arrowleaf clover. *Turrialba*, 26(2): 144–149.

Tothill, J.C., Dzowela, B.D. & Diallo, A. K. 1989. Present and future role of grasslands in inter-tropical countries, with special references to ecological and sociological constraints. pp. 1719–1724, *in: Proceedings of the 16th International Grasslands Congress.* Nice, France.

van der Sluijs, D.H. 1971. Native grasslands of the Mesopotamia region of Argentina. *Netherlands Journal of Agricultural Science, 19:* 3–22.

Vieira da Silva, J. 1979. *Introduction à la théorie écologique.* Paris, France: Masson.

Wilken, F. 1985. Aspectos económicos de la suplementación mineral. Resultados en campos de cría del sur de Corrientes. *Revista Argentina de Produccion Animal,* 4(Suppl. 3): 71–74.

Chapter 6
Grasslands of central North America

Rex D. Pieper

SUMMARY

At the time of colonial settlement there was extensive grassland from the prairies of Canada to the Gulf of Mexico on mainly level topography. Great Plains grassland is in three strips running north-south: tall-grass, mixed-grass and short-grass, with the tall-grass in the better watered west. Precipitation increase from west to east (320 to 900 mm) is the main factor governing primary productivity; periodic droughts occur. Bison, the dominant large herbivore until the mid-nineteenth century, have largely been replaced by cattle. About half of the beef cattle in the United States of America are in the Great Plains. Woody vegetation types are embedded, with the trees varying according to latitude. C_4 species comprise more than 80 percent from 30° to 42°N, while C_3 species increase dramatically north of 42°N. Only 1 percent of the tall-grass remains; half of the short-grass is uncultivated; unproductive cropland is being put back to grass. Cattle predominate; sheep are far fewer and declining. Most land is privately owned, much in small farms. There is extensive ranching in dry areas. Grazing is seasonal, especially in the north with supplemental feed in winter. In favourable areas, sown pasture are used sometimes alongside range grazing. Rotational grazing is common, although research results on its advantage are mixed. Fire is used to suppress undesirable plants and increase fodder production. Grassland monitoring includes long-term ecological research sites. Introduced plants can cause problems: *Euphorbia esula* is an aggressive weed and *Bromus japonicus* often competes with native grasses. Many small operations are no longer economically viable, so many are being abandoned. Livestock enterprises should remain viable, although they have to compete with systems based on forage grown under irrigation.

INTRODUCTION

When European settlers first moved into the central portion of what is now the United States of America (USA), they encountered an extensive, unbroken grassland extending from the prairies of Canada to the Gulf of Mexico and Mexico. While this grassland was generally free from woody plants, apparently there was a dynamic ecotone between the mountains and deserts to the west and the eastern deciduous forests in central and northern portions of the grassland (Bazzaz and Parrish, 1982; Gleason, 1913; Transeau, 1935). The general impression held by many observers was that conditions in this vast

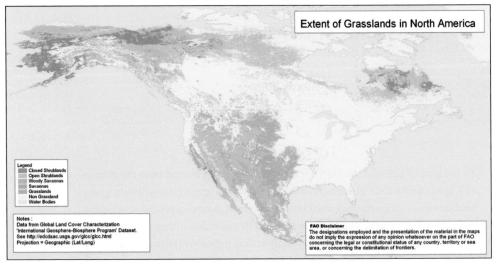

Figure 6.1
The extent of grasslands in North America.

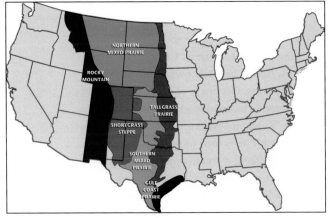

Figure 6.2
Map showing grassland types in central USA.
Source: Lauenroth *et al.*,1994.

grassland prior to European settlement were pristine and little modified by man (Deneven, 1996; Leopold *et al.*, 1963). However, Flores (1999) presents persuasive arguments that native American populations were relatively high in the Great Plains and probably exerted considerable influence on other components of these grassland ecosystems.

LOCATION AND GENERAL DESCRIPTION OF THE REGION

The extent of grasslands in North America is shown in general terms in Figure 6.1. At coarse scales the Great Plains grassland is commonly divided into tall-grass (true prairie), mixed- (or mid-)grass, and short-grass (Bazzaz and Parrish, 1982; Gleason and Cronquist, 1964; Lauenroth, *et al.*, 1994; Laycock, 1979; Sieg, Flather and McCanny, 1999; Sims, 1988) (Figure 6.2). Plates 6.1a–c show examples of the

Plate 6.1a
Examples of the three major grassland types, from North Dakota in the north to New Mexico in the south – (a) Short-grass prairie (central New Mexico).

Plate 6.1b
Examples of the three major grassland types, from North Dakota in the north to New Mexico in the south – (b) Northern mixed-grass prairie (central North Dakota).

three major grassland types from North Dakota to New Mexico. The map in Lauenroth *et al.* (1994) (Figure 6.2) shows that the tall-grass prairie formed a narrow band from Canada south to the Gulf Coast Prairie in Texas. The diagram in Barbour, Burk and Pitts (1987) shows a transect (Figure 6.3) from the Pacific Ocean to the Atlantic at latitude 37°N (the northern boundary of Arizona and

REX PIEPER

Plate 6.1c
Examples of the three major grassland types, from North Dakota in the north to New Mexico in the south – (c) Tall-grass prairie (eastern Kansas).

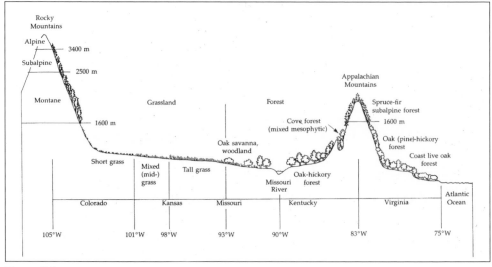

Figure 6.3
Transect showing topographical changes across central USA.
Source: Barbour, Burk and Pitts, 1987.

New Mexico). This diagram shows short-grass vegetation occupying the area between 105° and 101°W, the mixed prairie to 98°W and the tall-grass prairie to 93°W. The map in Lauenroth *et al.* (1994) shows that the northern mixed prairie forms a broad band in Canada, eastern Montana, the Dakotas and eastern Wyoming (Figure 6.2). The southern mixed-grass prairie is constricted between the tall-grass prairie to the east and the short-grass prairie to the west, and found in southern Nebraska, central Kansas and Oklahoma, and Texas (Lauenroth *et al.*, 1994; Lauenroth, Burke and Gutmann, 1999).

CLIMATE

Figure 6.4 shows the precipitation gradient east of the Rocky Mountains in the central part of the Great Plains resulting from the rain-shadow effect of the Rocky Mountains. Annual precipitation increases from about 320 mm at Greeley, Colorado, to nearly 900 mm at Kansas City, Missouri. Seasonal precipitation patterns also vary from south to north in the central plains (Trewartha, 1961). In southern portions of the short-grass prairie, summer maxima are the rule, while further east there is one peak in the late spring-early summer and another in late summer-early autumn (type 3b in Trewartha, 1961). In the northern Great Plains, spring peaks are common (type 3c in Trewartha, 1961) while in the upper Mississippi Valley-Great Lakes region, summer and autumn peaks occur (Trewartha, 1961).

The major temperature gradient is from warm temperatures in southern grassland to cooler temperatures in the north (Figure 6.5). The gradient is steeper for January temperatures than for July temperatures. Colder winter temperatures in the north have many implications for both plants and animals. However, snow cover in the north may ameliorate extremely cold air temperatures at the soil surface. Winter temperatures in southern locations allow cool-season plant growth almost any time that there is adequate soil moisture (Smeins, 1994; Holechek, Pieper and Herbel, 2001).

Before European settlement, the three grassland types in the central portion of the continent were fairly comparable in area: short-grass was 615 000 km², mixed prairie was 565 000 km² and tall-grass prairie was 570 000 km² (Van Dyne and Dyer, 1973). Today, the tall-grass prairie is much constricted because of conversion to intensive agriculture; originally, it extended eastward into southern Minnesota, most of Iowa, northern Missouri and northern Illinois and western Indiana (Lauenroth, Burke and Gutmann, 1999). Currently, the

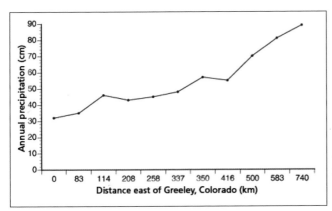

Figure 6.4
Mean annual precipitation gradient for various sites on the Great Plains east of the Rocky Mountains.

Figure 6.5
Average January and July temperatures for various sites on a south-north transect in the Great Plains.

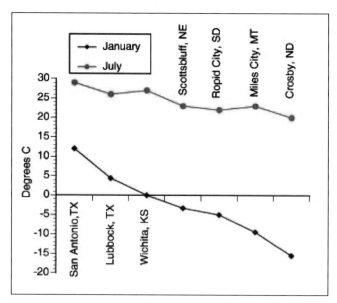

tall-grass prairie occurs mostly as isolated tracts, such as the Osage Hills in Oklahoma and the Flint Hills in Kansas.

TOPOGRAPHY AND SOILS

Topographically, the Great Plains are relatively level, but minor topographic variations are important in influencing plant species distributions and other inclusions within the grassland. Often, poorly drained sites in depressions, either with or without standing water, offer habitats for plants and animals not found in adjacent grassland.

Grassland soils have developed from a variety of parent materials: limestone, sandstone, shale, metamorphic and igneous outwash, and loess (Buol, Hole and McCracken, 1980; Dodd and Lauenroth, 1979; Miller and Donohue, 1990; Sims, Singh and Lauenroth, 1978). The major soils are mollisols, deep soils with dark A horizons and high (>50 percent) base saturation (especially calcium) (Miller and Donohue, 1990). Surprisingly, the A horizon has a clay content nearly equal to that of the B horizon (Baxter and Hole, 1967). Several soil organisms including a common prairie ant (*Formica cinerea*) are apparently involved in translocation of clays from the B horizon to the A (Buol, Hole and McCracken, 1980). Buol, Hole and McCracken (1980) describe the soil forming process for mollisols as "melanization". This process consists of five specific processes (Hole and Nielsen, 1968):

1. Growth of plant roots into the soil profile.
2. Partial decay of organic material in the soil.
3. Mixing of the soil by soil micro-organisms.
4. Eluviation and illuviation of organic colloids and some inorganic colloids.

5. Formation of resistant "ligno-protein" residues producing the dark colour in the soil.

Soils developed in semi-arid portions of the grassland, classified as aridisols formed by calcification, often develop calcium carbonate (caliche) layers at varying depths below the surface (Breymeyer and Van Dyne, 1979). Other soils found in the grassland include alfisols, found extensively in Kansas, Oklahoma and Texas (Sims, 1988).

FAUNA

At the time of early exploration of the American grassland, bison (*Bison bison*) were the dominant large herbivore in the Great Plains (Plate 6.2), although pronghorn antelope (Plate 6.3) were also abundant (Shaw, 1996; Yoakum, O'Gara and Howard, 1996). Seton (1927), Garretson (1938) and Danz (1997) estimated that as many as 40–60 million head of bison were present in the North American grassland before settlement. Numbers of pronghorn were probably comparable to those for bison (Nelson, 1925; Yoakum, O'Gara and Howard, 1996).

Grasslands also provided habitat for a wide variety of small mammals, including prairie dogs (*Cynomys* spp.), jackrabbits (*Lepus* spp.), ground squirrels (*Spermophilus* spp.), gophers (*Geomys* spp. and *Thomomys* spp.) and voles (*Microtus* spp.). Originally, several species of prairie dogs occupied over 800 000 ha of grasslands in central USA (Kreitzer and Cully, 2001; Summer and Linder, 1978), but by the early 1990s their distribution had been reduced by 98 percent (Vanderhoff, Robel and Kemp, 1994).

A wide number of invertebrates such as grasshoppers, beetles, ants, sap feeders and members of other orders are important components of grassland

S.G. REYNOLDS

Plate 6.2
Remnant herd of bison (Bison bison).

Plate 6.3
Pronghorn antelope on mixed grass prairie – North Dakota.

ecosystems (Blocker, 1970; McDaniel, 1971; Risser *et al.*, 1981). Some, such as grasshoppers, have been studied because of their economic importance (Hewitt, 1977; Hewitt and Onsager, 1983) while others, such as nematodes, have only recently been properly assessed as to abundance and importance (Freckman, Duncan and Larson, 1979; Smolik, 1974).

Central plains grasslands also support diverse populations of birds (Bolen and Crawford, 1996; Guthery, 1996; Knopf, 1996; Wiens, 1973). However, within the grassland geographical region, habitats other than grasslands have higher numbers of avian species. Only 11 percent of the bird species within the grassland geographic area were actually inhabitants of grassland *per se*: 51 percent were associated with woodland and forest habitats and 22 percent with wetland habitats (Bolen and Crawford, 1996). Nevertheless, birds are abundant in grasslands. Glover (1969) listed over 150 species found on the Central Plains Experimental Range in short-grass habitat in north-central Colorado. These included both primary consumers and secondary consumers. Common grassland birds include western meadowlark (*Sturnella neglecta*), grasshopper sparrow (*Ammodramus savannarum*), horned lark (*Eremophila aplestris*) and chestnut-collared longspur (*Calcarius ornatus*) (Wiens, 1973, 1974).

Cattle (Plates 6.4 and 6.5) have largely replaced bison as the dominant large herbivore on the Great Plains. The importance of Great Plains cattle to the beef industry in the USA is reflected in data quoted by Holechek, Pieper and Herbel (2001) indicating that 50 percent of all USA beef cattle are found in the northern and southern Great Plains. Although Lauenroth *et al.* (1994) concluded that vegetation changes resulting from the shift from bison to cattle have been minimal, there are differences in grazing patterns and behaviour: bison select a

MAE ELSINGER

Plate 6.4
Herding cattle in a mixed-grass zone, Saskatchewan, Canada.

DUANE McCARTNEY

Plate 6.5
Cattle grazing on Deseret Ranch near Salt Lake City, Utah, USA.

diet higher in grasses than cattle; bison select a diet higher in digestibility than cattle; bison spend less time grazing than cattle; and cattle are restricted in grazing by fences while bison were free to move over the landscape (Danz, 1997; Donohue, 1999; Stueter and Hidinger, 1999; Pieper, 1994).

VEGETATION PATTERNS

While the Central Plains grassland of North America is often divided into three subdivisions, as noted earlier, the patterns are more complex at finer scales. For example, Sieg, Flather and McCanny (1999) show 24 major vegetation types extending from Canada to the coastal prairies in Texas. Similar rangeland also occurs in northern Mexico. Woody vegetation types embedded in the grassland includes aspen parkland in the north, mesquite-acacia savannah, shinnery oak savannah, cross timbers, mesquite-buffalo grass, juniper-oak savannah, oak-hickory forest and oak-hickory-pine forest in the south (Sieg, Flather and McCanny, 1999). These woodland types have been described in more detail by Dahl (1994), McClendon (1994), Pettit (1994), Engle (1994) and Smeins (1994). Several species of juniper have expanded into grasslands in recent times. In Oklahoma some estimates of expansion of eastern red cedar (*Juniperus virginiana*) are as high as 113 000 ha annually (Engle, 2000; Gehring and Bragg, 1992). In Texas, ash (*Juniperus ashei*) and redberry (*Juniperus pinchoti*) junipers have also expanded into grasslands (Smeins, 2000). Reduced fire intensity and frequency is considered one of the primary factors in this expansion (McPherson, 1997).

Major grass dominants in the tall-grass prairie (Plate 6.6) are big bluestem (*Andropogon gerardii*) little bluestem (*Schizachyrium scoparium*), Indian grass (*Sorghastrum nutans*) and switchgrass (*Panicum virgatum*). In the mixed-grass prairie (see Plates 6.7, 6.8 and 6.9), needle-and-thread grass (*Stipa comata*) and western wheatgrass (*Pascopyrum smithii*) are common grasses, but many other species are abundant on specific sites. Sims (1988) states that the vegetational

JEFF PRINTZ, USDA-NRCS

Plate 6.6
Tall-grass prairie – Sheyenne National Grassland area, North Dakota, USA.

JEFF PRINTZ, USDA-NRCS

Plate 6.7
*Mixed-grass prairie – west side of the Missouri river, just south of Mandan,
North Dakota.*

JEFF PRINTZ, USDA-NRCS

Plate 6.8
Mixed-grass prairie – north-central North Dakota, USA.

diversity of the mixed prairie is highest of all grassland types in the USA (not
unusual for vegetation often considered an ecotone). Two major grass dominants of short-grass (Plate 6.10) vegetation are blue grama (*Bouteloua gracilis*)
(Plate 6.11) and buffalo grass (*Buchloe dactyloides*). Many forb species are also
common in the grassland. Thus, the term "grassland" may be somewhat mis-

MAE ELSINGER

Plate 6.9
Mixed-grass prairie on the Monet Prairie Farm Rehabilitation Community Pasture,
Saskatchewan, Canada.

JEFF PRINTZ, USDA-NRCS

Plate 6.10
Short-grass prairie – from a badlands area.

leading if it implies only grasses are present in high abundance. Typical grassland scenes near Mandam in North Dakota and near Salt Lake City, Utah, are
shown in Plates 6.12 and 6.13, respectively.

Within the central North American grassland, there are also minor
variations in species composition related to micro-relief patterns. Ayyad and
Dix (1964) reported that three species (*Festuca scabrella, Carex obtusata* and

S.G. REYNOLDS

Plate 6.11
Bouteloua gracilis – *Blue grama.*

DUANE McCARTNEY

Plate 6.12
Mixed grass prairie near Mandan, North Dakota.

Galium boreale) were most abundant on moist and cool north-facing slopes, while other species (*Phlox hoodii, Carex filifolia, Stipa comata, Artemisia frigida*) reached highest abundance on relatively warm and dry south-facing slopes. Species occupying intermediate habitats were *Koeleria cristata, Carex eleocharis, Stipa spartea* and *Agropyron dasystachum*. Redmann (1975) and Sims (1988) reported on micro-topographical and soils variations in mixed

DUANE McCARTNEY

Plate 6.13
Grassland with sagebrush near Salt Lake City, Utah.

prairie vegetation in North Dakota. *Agropyron smithii, Carex pennsylvanica* and *Stipa comata* were dominant species on rolling upland with fine-textures soils, while sites at lower elevations with medium-textured soils supported stands of *Sporobolus heterolepis*. In short-grass vegetation in New Mexico, blue grama was present in all topographic positions, while *Lycurus phleoides, Aristida wrightii, Stipa neomexicana* and *Bouteloua curtipendula* occurred on upper slopes. *Sporobolus cryptandrus* and *Muhlenbergia torreyi* along with blue grama were dominant on lower slopes, with blue grama and buffalo grass, *Muhlenbergia repens* and *Hilaria jamesii* in moister depressions (Beavis *et al.*, 1981).

There is also a north-south gradient in the relative proportion of C_3 and C_4 species (Sims, Singh and Lauenroth, 1978). C_4 species comprise more than 80 percent of the flora from 30° to 42°N, while C_3 species increase dramatically north of 42°N (Sims, 1988).

PRIMARY PRODUCTION
Several environmental variables act to control primary production in the Central Plains grasslands in North America. Precipitation, as it is translated into soil water content through infiltration, is often considered the main control for primary production (Laurenroth, 1979; Sims, Singh and Lauenroth, 1978; Sims and Singh, 1978a, b). Several studies have provided regression analyses showing the relationship between precipitation and above ground net primary productivity (ANPP). Lauenroth (1979) showed a linear relationship between ANPP and mean annual precipitation for 52 grassland sites around the world, with r^2 of 0.51 under mean annual precipitation ranging from about 100 mm to about 1500 mm. Later, Lauenroth, Burke and

Gutmann (1999) presented similar analyses for a much larger data set from central USA grasslands for normal rainfall, favourable and unfavourable rainfall patterns. The r^2 values were 0.56 for normal years, 0.66 for favourable years and 0.43 for unfavourable years (favourable years represent the wettest 10 percent of the years; unfavourable are the driest 10 percent of the years; and normal the middle 80 percent (Soil Conservation Service, 1973)). Of course, the ANPP–precipitation relationship is not linear over the complete range of precipitation values, and often annual precipitation is a relatively poor predictor of ANPP or end-of-season standing crop (Pieper, 1988). For example, Smoliak (1956) found that May-June precipitation was highly related to end-of-season standing crop in northern Great Plains short-grass prairie (r^2= 0.86), while Hart and Samuel (1985) found a high correlation between spring-summer precipitation and herbage yield in short-grass vegetation in eastern Wyoming (r^2 = 0.95). Since primary production is so closely related to precipitation, the general pattern of primary production (Plate 6.14) follows those gradients of precipitation, increasing from west to east. Lauenroth (1979) reported that general average annual production was about 200 g/m² for short-grass, 300 g/m² for mixed-grass prairie and 500 g/m² for USA International Biological Programme locations. These general averages mask the tremendous variation across these grasslands. For example, Risser *et al.* (1981) reported that above ground peak live standing crop for 23 tall-grass locations varied from 180 g/m² at Junction, Kansas, to nearly 600 g/m² in Oklahoma County, Oklahoma.

Plate 6.14
Estimating annual biomass productivity on the Monet Prairie Farm Rehabilitation Area, Saskatchewan, Canada.

PASTORAL AND AGRICULTURAL SYSTEMS

Considerable portions of the central grasslands of the USA have been converted to intensive agriculture (Gunderson, 1981). Thomas, Herbel and Miller (1990) estimated that only about 1 percent of the original tall-grass prairie is still in native vegetation, while Lauenroth, Burke and Gutmann (1999) estimated that approximately 50 percent of the short-grass prairie is still uncultivated.

Crop production

Wheat is the major crop grown on the western edge of the Great Plains, although larger percentages of the land in wheat occurred in central and eastern Kansas and Oklahoma and northeastern North Dakota (Lauenroth, Burke and Gutmann, 1999). The pattern of acreage of wheat grown in the Great Plains was one of breaking native sod during times of plentiful precipitation and high wheat prices, and abandonment of these lands during drought and periods of low wheat prices (Holechek, Pieper and Herbel, 2001; Sims, 1988; Stoddart, Smith and Box, 1975). The dust bowl of the 1930s occurred in southeastern Colorado, southeastern Kansas and the Texas and Oklahoma panhandles, largely on land unsuited for cultivation without irrigation (Costello, 1944; Holechek, Pieper and Herbel, 2001; Jordan, 1995; Sims, 1988). Considerable effort has been expended in developing seeding techniques to "recover" these abandoned fields (Bement *et al.*, 1965).

In 1985, the Food Security Act provided the opportunity for land owners to retire cropland, and provided cost-share funding to establish grass cover, wild-life habitat or trees (Joyce, 1989). Under the Conservation Reserve Programme (CRP) of this USA Act, many land owners converted cropland to grassland (Mitchell, 2000). The CRP is a voluntary cropland retirement programme under which the Federal Government pays an annual rental fee and a cost share for conversion from cropland to a permanent cover of grass, wildlife or trees. The basic goals for creation of the CPR were to: (1) take highly erosive cropland out of production and to establish a permanent perennial vegeta-tion cover; (2) to decrease farm commodity surpluses; (3) to generate stable incomes for participants; and (4) to enhance natural resource values, including soil, water, air quality and wildlife (Goetz, 1989; Heimlich and Kula, 1989). The map presented by Mitchell (2000) shows that CRP lands are concentrated in the plains states, with high densities in the northern Great Plains (Montana and North Dakota), the corn belt (southern Iowa and northern Missouri) and the southern Great Plains (eastern Colorado, western Kansas and the panhan-dles of Oklahoma and Texas). Originally, the CRP programme was designed for a 10–15-year period, but in separate Acts in 1990 and 1996, the CRP was extended and broadened (Mitchell, 2000).

Most land in the Great Plains is under private ownership (Holechek, Pieper and Herbel, 2001). For example, Neubauer (1963) reported that there was nearly 34 million hectares of private range and pasture land in the Dakotas,

Nebraska and Kansas, but only 1 million hectares of state and Indian land and 1.4 million hectares of federal land. There are National Forest lands in the Dakotas, Nebraska, Arkansas and Missouri, but most of these are forest or woodlands (Mitchell, 2000). Some Forest Service Land is in National Grasslands, but these are relatively small compared with non-federal land. Licht (1997) lists 15 separate National Grasslands in the Plains states. These vary in size from less than 600 ha for McClelland Creek National Grassland, to over 400 000 ha in the Little Missouri National Grassland in North Dakota. The Bureau of Land Management (BLM) has mineral rights to considerable areas outside the West, but little surface rights in the Great Plains (Holechek, Pieper and Herbel, 2001). Most of the BLM holdings in the Plains grassland is in Montana and Wyoming, but there are also a few allotments in South Dakota (Licht, 1997; Wester and Bakken, 1992).

Major crops in tall-grass regions are maize and soybeans (Lauenroth, Burke and Gutmann, 1999), with maize more important in the north and soybean in the central and southern portions of the grasslands. Wheat is the other major cereal crop, with higher yields in eastern portions, but greater areas in the west and north in locations with less than 500 mm/yr precipitation (Lauenroth, Burke and Gutmann, 1999). Cotton is important in eastern New Mexico, western Oklahoma and northern Texas.

Grazing management
Livestock production
Several types of enterprises constitute the livestock production systems of Central North America. In the drier portions of the region (short-grass and mixed-grass), extensive range grazing operations are the norm. These operations are typically cow-calf operations with the young animal sold for finishing in feedlots (Neumann and Lusby, 1986). In other cases, stocker programmes – whereby weaned animals are retained and maintained by feeding roughages to ensure growth but not improvement in condition – are practised (Neumann and Lusby, 1986; Wagnon, Albaugh and Hart, 1960). Stocking rates on native short-grass prairie vary considerably depending on precipitation, range condition and other environmental factors. Klipple and Costello (1960) reported that moderate stocking in eastern Colorado was about 21 ha per animal unit year (AUY), while Bement (1969) recommended 19.4 ha to support 1 AUY. In the panhandle of Nebraska, Burzlaff and Harris (1969) reported that moderate stocking was 14 ha per AUY. These stocking rates were based on summer grazing from May through October. In mixed-grass regions, stocking rates are normally higher, e.g. 9.3 ha AUY in North Dakota (Rogler, 1951). In tall-grass prairie, stocking rates are much higher: 4 ha AUY in Oklahoma (Harlan, 1960). In the Prairie Provinces of Canada (see Plates 6.15, 6.16 and 6.17), Smoliak *et al.* (1976) reported that carrying capacities ranged from 21.6 to 10.9 ha AUY depending on range type and

MAE ELSINGER

Plate 6.15
Mixed-grass zone: roped steer on the Tecumseh Prairie Farm Rehabilitation Area,
Saskatchewan, Canada.

MAE ELSINGER

Plate 6.16
Mixed-grass zone: cattle on the Caledonia Prairie Farm Rehabilitation Area,
Saskatchewan, Canada.

condition. Holechek, Pieper and Herbel (2001) reviewed several grazing studies
in the Great Plains, and recommended 35–40 percent removal (utilization) of
current annual production to maintain vigorous plants and grassland ranges
in a highly productive condition. Bement (1969) recommended leaving 300–

MAE ELSINGER

Plate 6.17
Winter grazing on the Canadian prairie.

350 kg/ha at the end of the summer grazing period to support both livestock performance and desirable vegetation condition for short-grass rangeland in eastern Colorado.

Most livestock operations in the Great Plains are relatively small. Over 85 percent of the farms and ranches in the Great Plains (including North and South Dakota, Nebraska, Montana, Wyoming, Kansas and Oklahoma) had less than 100 head of cattle, and only 5 percent had more than 500 head (Mitchell, 2000). Over 46 percent had less than 50 head. These were probably small operations where cattle were produced in conjunction with cropping operations. There were over 180 000 individual units in these seven states in 1993. Numerically, cattle are much more important than sheep in the Central Plains grasslands (Mitchell, 2000). Total cattle numbers for most of the states making up the Great Plains was about 25 million head, compared with about 5 million sheep (Ensminger and Parker, 1986; Mitchell, 2000). Sheep numbers have declined during the last 50 years because of predator problems, economic conditions, lack of herders in some western states, lack of demand for mutton and lamb, and other factors. These data on livestock numbers do not distinguish among different types of operations.

The northern and southern Great Plains (including Texas) support about half of the total beef cattle in the USA (Holechek, Pieper and Herbel, 2001), while the rest of the West supports less that 10 percent of the total. There was no distinction between those in feedlots and those on farms and ranches, but these numbers illustrate the importance of the Great Plains as a livestock-producing area.

Balancing seasonal variations of forage supply

In more mesic situations, mixed operations are common, whereby animals are raised under pasture or confined conditions in combination with cultivated agriculture practices (Neumann and Lusby, 1986). In many cases, the number of animals in these situations is relatively small.

Although grasslands have the potential to be grazed year long, they are grazed mostly seasonally by livestock. In northern areas, inclement weather largely precludes grazing during the winter (Holechek, Pieper and Herbel, 2001; Neumann and Lusby, 1986; Stoddart and Smith, 1955). Native grass hay and alfalfa have been used extensively as winter feed in northern areas and as supplemental feed in southern areas (Neumann and Lusby, 1986; Newell, 1948; Rogler and Hurtt, 1948). Keller (1960) showed that wild hay (native grasses) occupied over 3.6 million hectares in the six plains states, followed by alfalfa on about 2.8 million hectares and cereal hay on about 0.4 million hectares.

Another factor involved in decisions for seasonal grazing is that of declining nutritive quality of forage as the growing season progresses (Adams *et al.*, 1996; Rao, Harbers and Smith, 1973; Scales, Streeter and Denham, 1971). Protein content of Great Plains forage generally reaches a peak during the early summer period and declines sharply as the forage matures into winter (Adams *et al.*, 1996). During the late summer, forage quality was rated as moderate, while in the winter it was rated as low quality. Other nutritional variables often change in a similar pattern, such as phosphorus content, digestibility and intake. Changes in nutritive quality of forage depend to some degree on species composition: cool-season grasses (C_3) have higher nutritive quality early in the season than warm-season species (C_4) that grow later, during the heat of the summer. Presence of forbs may also increase mineral content of herbivore diets (Pieper and Beck, 1980; Holechek, 1984). In New Mexico, protein and phosphorus content of side-oats grama (*Bouteloua curtipendula*) was significantly lower than that of five other grass species (Pieper *et al.*, 1978). Tall-grass prairie plants often become coarse and relatively unpalatable late in the growing season.

One approach to mitigation of the problems of low nutritive quality and palatability of forage late in the growing season is intensive early stocking (Bernardo and McCollum, 1987; Lacey, Studiner and Hacker, 1994; Smith and Owensby, 1978; McCollum *et al.*, 1990; Olson, Brethour and Launchbaugh, 1993). In Montana, early spring grazing was beneficial for most vegetational characteristics compared with summer grazing, but livestock performance was not reported (Lacey, Studiner and Hacker, 1994). In tall-grass prairie in Kansas, intensive early grazing improved steer gains per unit area compared with season-long grazing, resulted in more even utilization of the pastures and increased desirable perennial grass production, but reduced gain per steer (Smith and Owensby, 1978). Other studies in Kansas indicated that stocking density could be increased 2 to 3 times by early-season grazing compared with summer-season grazing (Launchbaugh and Owensby, 1978). However, Olson, Brethour and Launchbaugh (1993) cautioned against using early-season grazing at high stocking rates when vigour of cool-season plant species is a concern. McCollum *et al.* (1990) reported that total beef production was increased 19 percent under increased early-season stocking compared with traditional season-long stocking.

Grazing systems

Other stocking plans for the Great Plains include several types of rotational grazing systems (Holechek, Pieper and Herbel, 2001). The objective of many of these plans is to increase individual plant vigour and overall plant productivity. The basic design for rotation systems is to defer grazing on different pastures or portions of the entire area at different seasons in different years (Vallentine, 1990). This objective is met by adjusting the number of pastures and herds to ensure that the same area is not grazed at the same period each year. Research results comparing specialized grazing systems to continuous grazing have been mixed (Herbel, 1974; Herbel and Pieper, 1991; Hickey, 1969; Van Poolen and Lacey, 1979). In some cases there has been little difference in either cattle production or vegetation status between continuous grazing and some form of rotation grazing in the central Great Plains (Hart *et al.*, 1988; Lodge, 1970; Rogler, 1951; McIlvain and Shoop, 1969; McIlvain and Savage, 1951; McIlvain *et al.*, 1955). Generally, rotational grazing systems, whereby livestock are concentrated in one pasture for short periods, decreased livestock performance (gain per head), presumably because of lower selection, lower nutritive quality of forage selected and lower digestibility (Malechek, 1984; Pieper, 1980). Field studies in some cases confirmed this (Fisher and Marion, 1951; Heitschmidt, Kothmann and Rawlins, 1982; Pieper *et al.*, 1991; Smith *et al.*, 1967). Other studies indicated that there was some vegetation improvement, including higher production, increases in abundance of plant species desirable for grazing, or increases in plant cover (Herbel and Anderson, 1959; Smith and Owensby, 1978; Pieper *et al.*, 1991) under specialized grazing systems. Van Poollen and Lacey (1979) reported that six studies in the northern Great Pains showed virtually no difference in herbage yields under continuous grazing and rotation systems, while in tall-grass prairie (Flint Hills in Kansas) herbage yields were 17 percent higher under specialized grazing systems than under continuous grazing. In some cases, improved management and more uniform grazing distribution under specialized grazing systems are confounded with the grazing system.

During the 1970s and 1980s, interest in short-duration or time-controlled grazing, as advocated by Savory (1999), peaked. This grazing approach is based on having a large number of paddocks and moving livestock rapidly through the paddocks, especially during periods of rapid plant growth (Savory, 1983, 1999; Savory and Parsons, 1980). The grazing period is often only a matter of a few days or even, in extreme cases, hours, since all the livestock normally allocated to the entire area are concentrated into one paddock at a time. Savory has stated that stocking could be doubled over that recommended by standard Soil Conservation Service procedures (Bryant *et al.*, 1989). Results of experiments involving short-duration grazing in the Great Plains have been mixed. Holechek, Pieper and Herbel (2001) evaluated nine studies conducted on USA and Canadian grasslands. Many of these studies showed little difference in herbage yield between short-duration grazing and continuous grazing (Manley *et al.*, 1997; Pitts and Bryant, 1987; Thurow, Blackburn and Taylor, 1988; White *et al.*, 1991). In some cases there was some advantage for short-duration grazing, depending on stocking rate (Heitschmidt, Downhower and Walker, 1987). In New Mexico, on blue grama rangeland, short-duration grazing apparently benefited blue grama compared with continuous grazing (White *et al.*, 1991). Stocking rate was more influential than grazing system in most of these studies (Bryant *et al.*, 1989; Holechek, Pieper and Herbel, 2001; Pieper and Heitschmidt, 1988).

Short-duration grazing apparently reduced infiltration and increased runoff compared with non-grazed or continuous grazing conditions in grasslands (McCalla, Blackburn and Merrill, 1984; Pluhar, Knight and Heitschmidt, 1987; Weltz and Wood, 1986). Concentrating livestock, even for short periods, tends to compact the soil and negates any possible benefit from hoof action. However, in New Mexico, infiltration and runoff had returned nearly to normal in short-duration pastures following the rest period (Weltz and Wood, 1986).

Intensification?

Since grasslands are generally grazed seasonally, provision for feed for the rest of the year is necessary. The use of complementary pastures along with native range is one approach for meeting the nutritional needs of livestock during periods when grazing of native rangeland is not practical (Gillen and Berg, 2001; Hart *et al.*, 1988; Hoveland, McCann and Hill, 1997; Keller, 1960; Lodge, 1970; Nichols, Sanson and Myran, 1993; Smoliak, 1968). Such complementary pastures may involve old world bluestems (Gillen and Berg, 2001), introduced grasses such as crested (Plate 6.18) and other wheatgrasses (Holechek, 1981; Rogler, 1960), other cool-season grasses (Nichols, Sanson and Myran, 1993) and legumes.

Fertilization is another practice used to enhance livestock performance in the Great Plains (Nyren, 1979; Wight, 1976). Nitrogen is most often the limiting nutrient, but in some cases phosphorus and potassium may also be limiting (Nyren, 1979; Vallentine, 1989; Wight, 1976). An extensive literature on range fertilization has developed that shows, in general, greater vegetational response in northern mixed prairie rangelands than in southern areas (Vallentine, 1989). Nitrogen fertilization may change species composition by favouring cool-season species if applications are made early in the grow-

S.G. REYNOLDS

Plate 6.18
*Crested wheatgrass (*Agropyron cristatum*).*

ing season (Nyren, 1979; Vallentine, 1989). In northern mixed prairie, early application of nitrogen may stimulate the aggressive cool-season species western wheatgrass (originally *Agropyron smithii*, now *Pascopyrum smithii*) at the expense of warm-season species (Nyren, 1979). High nitrogen fertilizer rates late in the growing season to benefit warm-season species such as blue grama may stimulate cool-season species the next spring (Wight, 1976). In southern areas, cool-season introduced species such as Kentucky bluegrass (*Poa pratensis*) may be stimulated (Owensby, 1970; Rehm, Sorensen and Moline, 1976; Vallentine, 1989).

Power (1972) argued that on many northern Great Plains rangelands, inorganic nitrogen is immobilized when nitrogen is added as fertilizer and sufficient nitrogen must be added to overcome that immobilized. He stated that the system could be maintained if annual fertilizer additions plus mineralization equals immobilization plus irreversible losses.

Even though substantial responses in herbage yield can be accomplished with range fertilization in grasslands, the practice may be only marginally feasible economically. In blue grama rangeland in south-central New Mexico, despite doubling of herbage and cattle production from annual additions of 40 kg/ha, economic returns were marginal (Chili *et al.*, 1998). The economics of range fertilization depend mostly on cost of fertilizer and livestock prices.

MAE ELSINGER

Plate 6.19
*Prescribed burn to control aspen growth on the mixed-grass of the Wolverine
Prairie Farm Rehabilitation Area, Saskatchewan, Canada.*

Rangeland burning

Fire is another useful tool in managing Great Plains grassland (Wright, 1974,
1978; Wright and Bailey, 1982). Vallentine (1989) lists 18 separate objectives in
rangeland burning but suggests that there are three main reasons to burn: 1. To
kill or suppress undesirable brush plants (Plate 6.19). 2. To prevent invasion of
inferior species in the understorey. 3. To increase forage production and thus
grazing capacity.

Especially in tall-grass prairie, prescribed burning is often used to reduce
old growth and stimulate new, more palatable growth (Anderson, Smith and
Owensby, 1970; McMurphy and Anderson, 1965; Smith and Owensby, 1972).
Wright (1978) suggested that burning in tall-grass vegetation increased palatability, suppressed encroachment of trees and shrubs and reduced competition
from cool-season plants. However, timing of the burning is very important.
Cool-season grasses are detrimentally affected by spring burning (Hensel, 1923;
Wright, 1978). Spring burning tends to increase summer gains of cattle, but
gains may not hold up into the autumn (Anderson, Smith and Owensby, 1970;
Vallentine, 1989). Late winter burning may initiate spring growth two to three
weeks earlier than in the absence of burning (Ehrenreich and Aikman, 1963).

Development of grasslands

Grasslands are very dynamic, both spatially and temporally (Dix, 1964; Sims,
1988). Consequently, different authors have considered different factors as

influential in the development of grassland vegetation and animal communities. Since grasslands operate as ecosystems, it may be futile to try to isolate causal factors, since some internal components may interact with others to change the nature of the system. For example, Larson (1940) considered that heavy bison grazing prior to settlement helped maintain the short-grass prairie. However, bison evolved under grassland conditions – vegetation, climate, other herbivores and predators – and attaching causality to one component may involve circular reasoning.

Sauer (1950), in contrast, argued that grasslands were maintained by periodic fires. Without fires, grasslands would progress to woodlands or forest. Indeed, grasslands of central North America have developed under frequent fire regimes, caused both naturally and by man (Flores, 1999; Sauer, 1950). Flores (1999) suggested that natural lightning fires had results that differed from those set by native Americans. He argued that maintenance of southern Great Plains grasslands populated by large grazing animals depended on fire management by native Americans.

One prominent feature of grasslands is a variable climate, with periodic droughts a common feature (Dix, 1964). The drought of the 1930s that resulted in the dust bowl in the Great Plains has been well documented (Albertson and Weaver, 1942; Robertson, 1939; Savage, 1937; Weaver and Albertson, 1936, 1939, 1940; Whitman, Hanson and Peterson, 1943). During the drought of the 1930s, blue grama abundance was reduced dramatically (by as much as 70 to 80 percent) in Kansas (Weaver and Albertson, 1956). In North Dakota mixed prairie, blue grama was reduced to about 40 percent of pre-drought (1933) levels in 1936–37 (Whitman, Hanson and Peterson, 1943). Other species negatively affected by the drought were western wheatgrass, needle-and-thread and prairie junegrass *(Koeleria macrantha)*. The one species not affected by the drought was threadleaf sedge *(Carex filifolia)* (Whitman, Hanson and Peterson, 1943).

In western Nebraska, tree ring analyses indicated that over the last 400 years nearly 160 were "drought" years and 237 "wet" years (Weakly, 1943). Borchert (1950) reported that drought years tended to be clumped, with an average duration of nearly 13 years, compounding the effects of the drought.

Geologically, the Great Plains consists of a valley between the relatively young Rocky Mountains to the west and the older Appalachian chain to the east. The valley is drained by the Missouri and Mississippi River systems, which have carried sediment from both the Rocky and Appalachian Mountains and sorted and deposited these sediments (Dix, 1964).

In geological time, the central North American grasslands have undergone many transformations since the late Cretaceous period (Axelrod, 1958; Dix, 1964; Donart, 1984). At this time the deciduous Pan Tropical Forest covered most of the present USA (Axelrod, 1979). From these forests, two distinct forests developed during Eocene times: the Arcto-tertiary and Neotropical-tertiary forests (Dix,

1964; Axelrod, 1958). Both of these forests contributed to the central grasslands that probably developed in more recent times (Pliocene and Pleistocene series) as the forests retreated (Dix, 1964). These vegetational shifts were also accompanied by climatic shifts, geologic events and changing patterns of herbivore utilization of these grasslands. Glaciation during the Pleistocene had dramatic influences on landscapes and vegetation, but the influence on the grasslands is not completely understood (Dix, 1964; Flint, 1957; Love, 1959).

Current status of grassland research and management

Traditionally, research on grasslands of the Great Plains has been conducted by the Land Grant Universities. These were established by the Morrill Act of 1862, whereby one university in each state was designated the Land Grant University (Holechek, Pieper and Herbel, 2001). The Hatch Act of 1887 and the Smith-Lever Act of 1914 completed the tripartite focus of the Land Grant Universities in teaching, research and service (National Research Council, 1996). Each of these universities in the grassland states has been conducting research into agricultural practices and they have received research support from federal, state and other grant sources. Departments involved in these efforts have been those of Agronomy, Horticulture, Agricultural Economics, Animal Science and allied disciplines. The Cooperative Extension Service has served as the link between the research and application by farmers and ranchers (see Plates 6.20 and 6.21 with examples from Canada). Range research in the Land Grant Universities has been conducted by researchers attached to other departments in the main grassland states: with Animal Science in Montana,

Plate 6.20
Plant identification by range management officers on native prairie in the mixed-grass zone at Big Muddy, Saskatchewan, Canada.

Plate 6.21
Pasture sampling in the mixed-grass zone, Saskatchewan, Canada.

New Mexico, North and South Dakota; and with Agronomy in Nebraska, Kansas and Oklahoma. The School of Forestry at the University of Montana also has a range faculty offering degrees in Range Science (Bedell, 1999). Colorado State University has a separate Range Science Department, as does Texas Tech (with Wildlife Science) and Texas A & M University.

Research in grassland agriculture has also been conducted by the Agriculture Research Service. Experimental stations have concentrated on range and livestock problems in the Northern Great Plains in North Dakota; Sydney, Montana (now closed); Central Plains in Colorado; and the Southern Great Plains in Oklahoma. Research conducted at the universities and Agricultural Research Service (ARS) experimental stations has been broad based, featuring both basic and applied research.

Grassland research has also been conducted by ecologists in Biology or Botany Departments in Great Plains states. The University of Nebraska was in the forefront of ecological research under the direction of Dr John E. Weaver during the 1930s and 1940s, although earlier scientists, including Dr Frederic E. Clements, were instrumental in establishing ecology at the University of Nebraska (Tobey, 1981). Drs Clair Kucera at the University of Missouri, Warren Whitman at North Dakota State University, Lloyd C. Hulbert at Kansas State University, William Penfound, Elroy Rice and Paul G. Risser at Oklahoma State University and John Aikman at Iowa State University also had strong grassland research programmes (Kucera, 1973; Tobey, 1981).

In the late 1960s and early 1970s, another major research effort in grassland ecology was launched with the International Biological Programme (IBP) (Golley, 1993). The Grassland Biome was established with its focus at Colorado State University, with Dr George M. Van Dyne as Director. Satellite research areas were established at the Cottonwood site in mixed prairie vegetation in South Dakota (operated by South Dakota State University); tall-grass vegetation in Oklahoma at the Osage site (operated by Oklahoma State University); and short-grass vegetation at the Pantex Site in Texas (operated by Texas Tech University) and the Pawnee Site in Colorado (operated by Colorado State University) (Van Dyne, Jameson and French, 1970). Other grassland sites, such as desert grassland, mountain grassland and California annual grassland, were also included in the project. Although the project generated much ecological information and extensive literature on aspects of grassland ecology, the goal of publishing a synthesis volume for each of the grassland types was not realized (Golley, 1993). Only the tall-grass volume was actually published (Risser *et al.*, 1981).

The other major outcome of the IBP programme was establishment of Long-Term Ecological Research (LTER) sites. The argument was made that ecological problems could only be approached by looking at dynamics of ecosystems in a long time frame – 10 years or more. The Conyza Prairie in Kansas (Knapp *et al.*, 1998) and the Central Plains Experimental Range (the old Pawnee Site of the IBP) are currently LTER sites.

Great Plains agriculture is now facing many challenges from various sources. This analysis will focus on only a few of these. In the Great Plains, as well as most of the West, many small towns and communities are facing extreme economic conditions and many are being abandoned (Flores, 1999; Licht, 1997). Licht (1997) reported that 81 percent of the Great Plains counties lost population between 1980 and 1990. There are probably multiple reasons for this decline in rural communities such as reliance on railroads; influence of technology and government; better transportation to larger urban areas; location of agricultural agents in county seats; and governmental policies (Burns, 1982). However, Licht (1997) argues that:

> "...the main reason for the collapse of rural communities in the Great Plains is indisputable; the region's inhospitable climate, lack of economically valuable natural resources, high transportation costs and other factors meant that it was never capable of supporting numerous vibrant economies with high human densities."

Along with the constriction of rural communities, many agricultural enterprises have been caught in an economic squeeze, with, on the one hand, high production costs and, on the other, low prices for their products. This is true in both intensive agriculture and the livestock sector. Consequently, many small-scale operators (such as family farms) are no longer able to operate economically (Licht, 1997).

Other biological problems relate to environmental concerns. Even though Lauenroth *et al.* (1994) considered that grazing lands in the Great Plains had changed little since European settlement, farming and other disturbances have had a great effect. For example, Klopatek *et al.* (1979) showed that most counties in the Great Plains had lost some of the potential natural vegetation, with the greatest impact in the mesic eastern edge and the least disturbed being the more xeric western short-grass plains. From 85 to 95 percent of the bluestem prairie vegetation types had been converted to cropland (Sieg, Flather and McCanny, 1999). These types of disturbance and vegetation shifts represent habitat fragmentation for many wildlife species that developed in unbroken tracts of grassland. Conversion to cropland created habitats for other species, but loss of both plant and animal diversity in the grassland is a concern (Sieg, Flather and McCanny, 1999; Leach and Givnish, 1996; Licht, 1997). For example Sieg, Flather and McCanny (1999) reported that in the Canadian province of Saskatchewan and six Great Plains states in the USA, 19 percent of the breeding bird species declined in numbers from 1966 to 1996. However, the number of listed, threatened and endangered (LT&E) plant and animal species is relatively low compared with other regions of the country (Ostlie *et al.*, 1997; Sieg, 1999). No pattern of LT&E species could be discerned for the Great Plains. Large blocks of counties showed no known LT&E species, up to a maximum of 9–12 species. These counties were scattered throughout the Great Plains (Sieg, 1999). Examples of LT&E species are the black-tailed prairie dog (*Cynomys ludovicianus*), the black-footed ferret (*Mustela nigrepes*) and the western prairie fringed orchid (*Platanthera praeclara*) (Sieg, Flather and McCanny, 1999).

Other environmental concerns regard use of pesticides and herbicides, commercial fertilizers, grazing by introduced domestic livestock, status of riparian areas and introduction of invasive plants and animals. Crested wheatgrass was introduced into the Great Plains in the early 1900s (Holechek, 1981; Rogler, 1960). The species played a major role in restoration of abandoned wheat fields in the northern Great Plains in the 1930s (Rogler, 1960), but some workers regard crested wheatgrass as an invader species leading to near monocultures.

One of the most troublesome introduced plant species is leafy spurge (*Euphorbia esula*) (Plate 6.22), a perennial forb accidentally introduced into the USA from eastern Europe or western Asia (Biesboer and Koukkari, 1992). It is an aggressive weed that currently infests over one million hectares in the USA (DiTomaso, 2000) and over 650 000 ha in the northern Great Plains (Leistritz, Leitch and Bangsund, 1995). Estimates of loss of livestock grazing because of leafy spurge encroachment onto northern Great Plains rangelands were 736 000 Animal Unit Months (AUMs), or US$ 37 million annually (Leistritz, Leitch and Bangsund, 1995).

Introduction of annual grasses such as Japanese brome (*Bromus japonicus*) has also altered grassland vegetation (Haferkamp *et al.*, 1993; Haferkamp, Heitschmidt and Karl, 1997). Japanese brome occurs throughout the Great Plains (Hitchcock, 1950) and often competes with native perennial grasses.

MAE ELSINGER

Plate 6.22
*Leafy spurge (*Euphorbia esula*) infestation on sandy soils in the mixed-grass zone,
Saskatchewan, Canada.*

Haferkamp, Heitschmidt and Karl (1997) reported that presence of Japanese
brome reduced yield of western wheatgrass in eastern Montana, but removal
of Japanese brome reduced total standing crop since other species did not completely replace the brome. In addition to economic consequences, Huenneke
(1995) and Hobbs and Huenneke (1992) listed the following ecological impacts
of plant invasions (for lack of a more appropriate word): spread of toxic sub-
stances, replacement of native species, alteration of hydrological characteristics,
alteration of soil properties, and changed nutrient cycling.

Other suggestions for managing the Great Plains include increasing the
number of national grasslands and developing a "buffalo commons" for certain
portions of the Great Plains (Licht, 1997; Popper and Popper, 1994). Although
such proposals have appeal to some environmental groups, Licht (1997) discusses several limitations of such proposals.

Riparian areas in the Great Plains are also of concern, as they are in many
other areas of the country (Johnson, 1999). These systems occupy less than one
percent of the land surface, yet are vitally important for catchment processes;
plant and animal diversity; and uses by man, including both industrial and agricultural purposes (Johnson and McCormick, 1979; Swanson, 1988). Riparian
systems in the Great Plains have been modified by human activities such as
clearing for agriculture, grazing, canalization, damming and water diversion
(Johnson, 1999). Johnson (1999) presents case studies on how these activities
have altered the Missouri River in North Dakota, the Platte River in Nebraska
and Foster Creek in South Dakota.

FUTURE OF THE GREAT PLAINS

It is likely that agriculture will continue to dominate the Great Plains into the foreseeable future. While technology will continue to develop new approaches, such as no-till cultivation, more efficient use of water and fertilizer, and methods to survey and monitor landscapes, some of these technologies will be difficult to apply because of economic, sociological and biological constraints.

For example, we now have the technology to consider management at relatively large scales (Ludwig *et al.*, 1997). Modern tools. including remote sensing (Tueller, 1989), geographical information systems (GIS) and global positioning systems (GPS), provide the opportunity to consider land management and ecological situations across landscapes and habitats. However, these approaches need to be applied with consideration of some of the limitations, such as lack of adequate ground truth data for remote sensing and GIS applications. Development of landscape-scale planning for the Great Plains might entail consideration of crop agriculture areas, riparian habitats and "natural" vegetation types. The extent and arrangement of agricultural areas and grassland vegetation types would be challenging, even if all those concerned could agree on percentages of land areas devoted to each and the spatial distribution of land devoted to different or several uses because of differences in land ownership patterns and extent of agricultural development. Developments such as the buffalo commons would be difficult to effect because of the large extent of private land in the region. Eventually, lack of water resources will have heavy impacts on both agricultural and industrial development.

Major cities in the Great Plains may not expand into adjacent farmland and wild land to the same extent as those in other western cities, but there will probably be some expansion. Cities along the western edge of the Great Plains – Fort Collins, Denver, Colorado Springs, Pueblo, etc. – will continue to grow because of favourable perceptions of location near the mountains.

Livestock enterprises, although stressed economically, will probably remain relatively stable. Walker (1995) stated that grazing systems have largely not changed the selective nature of livestock grazing. Stocking rate is the primary factor determining livestock and vegetational responses (Holechek, 1988; Walker, 1995). Competition with forages produced under irrigation will probably continue to erode livestock production from rangelands in the Great Plains (Glimp, 1991).

Genetic modification of both plants and animals has the potential to change plant and animal agriculture in the Great Plains (Walker, 1997). However, public acceptance of genetically modified plants and animals will influence how fast these technologies are used.

REFERENCES

Adams, D.C., Clark, R.T., Klopfenstein, T.J. & Volesky, J.D. 1996. Matching the cow with the forage resources. *Rangelands*, **18**: 57–62.

Albertson, F.W. & Weaver, J.E. 1942. History of the native vegetation of western Kansas during seven years of continuous drought. *Ecological Monographs,* **12**: 23–51.

Anderson, K.L, Smith, E.F. & Owensby, C. 1970. Burning bluestem range. *Journal of Range Management,* **23**: 81–92.

Axelrod, D.E. 1958. Evolution of the Madro-tertiary Geoflora. *Botanical Review,* **24**: 434–509.

Axelrod, D.E. 1979. Desert vegetation, its age and origin. pp. 75–82, *in:* J.R. Goodin and D.K. Northington (eds). *Aridland plant resources.* Lubbock, Texas, USA: ICASALS, Texas Tech University Press.

Ayyad, M.A.G. & Dix, R.L. 1964. An analysis of a vegetation-microenvironemtal complex on prairie slopes in Saskatchewan. *Ecological Monographs,* **34**: 421–442.

Barbour, M.G., Burk, J.H. & Pitts, W.D. 1987. *Terrestrial plant ecology.* 2nd ed. Menlo Park, California, USA: The Benjamin Cummings Pub. Co.

Baxter, F.P. & Hole, F.D. 1967. Ant (*Formica cinerea*) pedoturbation in a Prairie soil. *Soil Science Society of America Proceedings,* **31**: 425–428.

Bazzaz, F.A. & Parrish, J.A.D. 1982. Organization of grassland communities. pp. 233–254, *in:* J.R. Estes, R.J. Tyrl and J.N. Brunken (eds). *Grasses and Grasslands. Systematics and ecology.* Norman, Oklahoma, USA: University of Oklahoma Press.

Beavis, W.D., Owens, J.C., Ortiz, M., Bellows, T.S. Jr., Ludwig, J.A. & Huddleston, E.W. 1981. Density and developmental stage of range caterpillar *Hemilueca oliviae* Cockerill, as affected by topographic position. *Journal of Range Management,* **34**: 389–392.

Bedell, T.E. 1999. *The educational history of range management in North America.* Denver, Colorado, USA: Society for Range Management.

Bement, R.E. 1969. A stocking-rate guide for beef production on blue-grama range. *Journal of Range Management,* **22**: 83–86.

Bement, R.E., Barmington, R.D., Everson, A.C., Hylton, L.O. Jr. & Remmenga, E.E. 1965. Seeding of abandoned cropland in the Central Great Plains. *Journal of Range Management,* **18**: 53–65.

Bernardo, D.B. & McCullom, F.T. 1987. An economic analysis of intensive-early stocking. *Oklahoma State University Agricultural Experiment Station Research Report,* No. 887.

Biesboer, D.D. & Koukkari, W.L. 1992. The taxonomy and biology of leafy spurge. pp. 51–57, *in:* R.A. Masters, S.J. Nissen and G. Friisoe (eds). *Leafy spurge symposium.* Lincoln, Nebraska, USA, 1992. Lincoln, Nebraska, USA: Dow Elanco and Nebraska Leafy Spurge Working Task Force.

Blocker, H.D. 1970. The impact of insects in grassland ecosystems. pp. 290–299, *in:* R.L. Dix and R.G. Beidleman (eds). *The grassland ecosystem.* Range Science Department Series, No. 2. Colorado State University, Fort Collins, Colorado, USA.

Bolen, E.C. & Crawford, J.A. 1996. The birds of rangelands. pp. 15–27, *in:* P.R. Krausman (ed). *Rangeland wildlife.* Denver, Colorado, USA: Society for Range Management.

Borchert, L.R. 1950. The climate of the central North American grassland. *Annals of the Association of American Geographers*, **40**: 1–39.

Breymeyer, A.I. & Van Dyne, G.M. (eds). 1979. *Grasslands, systems analysis and management*. New York, New York, USA: Cambridge University Press.

Bryant, F.C., Dahl, B.E., Pettit, R.D. & Britton, C.M. 1989. Does short-duration grazing work in arid and semiarid regions? *Journal of Soil and Water Conservation*, **44**: 290–296.

Burns, N. 1982. The collapse of small towns on the Great Plains: a bibliography. Emporia State Research Studies, Emporia, Kansas, USA.

Buol, S.W., Hole, F.D. & McCracken, R.J. 1980. *Soil genesis and classification*. 2nd ed. Ames, IA, USA: Iowa State University Press.

Burzlaff, D.F. & Harris, L. 1969. Yearling steer gains and vegetation changes of western Nebraska rangeland under three rates of stocking. *University of Nebraska Agricultural Experiment Station Bulletin*, No. SB.505.

Chili, P., Donart, G.B., Pieper, R.D., Parker, E.E., Murray, L.W. & Torell, L.A. 1998. Vegetational and livestock response to nitrogen fertilization in south-central New Mexico. *New Mexico State University Agricultural Experiment Station Bulletin*, No. 778.

Costello, D.F. 1944. Natural revegetation of abandoned plowed land in the mixed prairie association of northeastern Colorado. *Ecology*, **25**: 312–326.

Deneven, W. 1996. Carl Sauer and native American population size. *The Geographical Review*, **86**: 385–397.

Dahl, B. 1994. Mesquite-buffalograss. pp. 27–28, *in:* T.N. Shiflet (ed). *Rangeland cover types of the United States*. Denver, Colorado, USA: Society for Range Management.

Danz, D.P. 1997. *Of bison and man: from the annals of a bison yesterday to a refreshing outcome from human involvement with America's most valiant of beasts*. Boulder, Colorado, USA: University of Colorado Press.

DiTomaso, J.M. 2000. Invasive weeds in rangelands: species, impacts and management. *Weed Science*, **48**: 255–265.

Dix, R.L. 1964. A history of biotic and climatic changes within the North American Grassland. pp. 71–89, *in:* D.J. Crisp (ed). *Grazing in terrestrial and marine environments*. Oxford, UK: Blackwell Scientific.

Dodd, J.L. & Lauenroth, W.K. 1979. Analysis of the response of a grassland ecosystem to stress. pp. 43–58, *in:* N.R. French (ed). *Perspectives in grassland ecology*. New York, New York, USA: Springer-Verlag.

Donart, G.B. 1984. The history and evolution of western rangelands in relation to woody plant communities. pp. 1235–1258, *in: Developing strategies for rangeland management*. Boulder, Colorado, USA: Westview Press.

Donohue, D.L. 1999. *The western range revisited. Removing livestock from public lands to conserve native biodiversity*. Norman, Oklahoma, USA: University of Oklahoma Press.

Engle, D. 1994. Cross timbers – Oklahoma. p. 37, *in:* T.N. Shiflet (ed). *Rangeland cover types of the United States.* Denver, Colorado, USA: Society for Range Management.

Ehrenreich, J.H. & Aikman, J.M. 1963. An ecological study of certain management practices on native plants in Iowa. *Ecological Monographs*, **33**: 113–130.

Engle, D.M. 2000. Eastern redcedar (*Juniperus virginiana*). Expanded abstract. 53rd Annual Meeting of the Society for Range Management, Boise, Idaho, USA. Society for Range Management, Denver, Colorado, USA.

Ensminger, M.E. & Parker, R.O. 1986. *Sheep and goat science.* 5th ed. Danville, Illinois, USA: Interstate Printers and Pub.

Fisher, C.E. & Marion, P.T. 1951. Continuous and rotation grazing on buffalo and tobosa grassland. *Journal of Range Management*, **4**: 48–51.

Flint, R.F. 1957. *Glacial and Pleistocene geology.* New York, New York, USA: John Wiley and Sons.

Flores, D. 1999. Essay: the Great Plains "wilderness" as a human-shaped environment. *Great Plains Research*, **9**: 343–355.

Freckman, D.W., Duncan, D.A. & Larson, J.R. 1979. Nematode density and biomass in an annual grassland ecosystem. *Journal of Range Management*, **32**: 418–422.

Garretson, M.S. 1938. *The American bison.* New York, New York, USA: New York Zoological Society.

Gehring, J.L. & Bragg, T.B. 1992. Changes in prairie vegetation under eastern red cedar (*Juniperus virginiana* L.) in an eastern Nebraska bluestem prairie. *American Midland Nauralist*, **128**: 209–217.

Gillen, R.L. & Berg, W.A. 2001. Complementary grazing of native pasture and old world bluestem. *Journal of Range Management*, **54**: 348–355.

Gleason, H.A. 1913. The relation of forest distribution and prairie fires in the Middle West. *Torreya*, **13**: 173–181.

Gleason, H.A. & Cronquist, A. 1964. *The natural geography of plants.* New York, New York, USA: Columbia University Press.

Glimp, H.A. 1991. Can we produce lambs for $0.40/lb? *Symposium Proceedings – Sheep Forage Production Systems.* Denver, Colorado, USA, 1991. Denver, Colorado, USA: American Sheep Industry.

Glover, F.A. 1969. *Birds in grassland ecosystems.* pp. 279–289, *in:* R.L. Dix and R.G. Beidleman (eds). *The grassland ecosystem. A preliminary synthesis.* Range Science Department Scientific Series, No. 21. Colorado State University, Fort Collins, Colorado, USA.

Goetz, H. 1989. The conservation reserve program – where are we heading? *Rangelands*, **11**: 251–252.

Golley, F.B. 1993. *A history of the ecosystem concept in ecology: more than the sum of the parts.* New Haven, Conneticut, USA: Yale University Press.

Guthery, F.S. 1996. Upland gamebirds. pp. 59–69, *in:* P.R. Krausman (ed). *Rangeland wildlife.* Denver, Colorado, USA: Society for Range Management.

Gunderson, J. 1981. True prairie – past and present. *Rangelands,* 3: 162.

Haferkamp, M.R., Karl, M.G., MacNeil, M.D., Heitschmidt, R.K. & Young, J.A. 1993. Japanese brome in the northern Great Plains. pp. 112–118, *in: Research & Rangeland Agriculture: past, present & future.* USDA Ft. Keogh Livestock and Range Research Laboratory, Miles City, Montana, USA.

Haferkamp, M.R., Heitschmidt, R.K. & Karl, M.G. 1997. Influence of Japanese brome on western wheatgrass yield. *Journal of Range Management,* 50: 45–50.

Harlan, J.R. 1960. Production characteristics of Oklahoma forages, native range. *Oklahoma State University Agricultural Experiment Station Bulletin,* No. B-547.

Hart, R.H. & Samuel, M.J. 1985. Precipitation, soils and herbage production on southeast Wyoming range sites. *Journal of Range Management,* 38: 522–525.

Hart, R.H., Samuel, M.J., Test, P.S. &Smith, M.A. 1988. Cattle, vegetation and economic responses to grazing systems and grazing pressure. *Journal of Range Management,* 41: 282–286.

Hart, R.H., Waggoner, J.W. Jr., Dunn, T.G., Kaltenbach, C.C. & Adams, L.D. 1988. Optional stocking rate for cow-calf enterprises on native range and complementary improved pastures. *Journal of Range Management,* 41: 435–440.

Heimlich, R.E. & Kula, O.E. 1989. Grazing lands: how much CRP land will remain in grass? *Rangelands,* 11: 253–257.

Heitschmidt, R.K., Downhower, S.L. & Walker, J.W. 1987. Some effects of a rotational grazing treatment on quantity and quality of available forage and amount of ground litter. *Journal of Range Management,* 40: 318–321.

Heitschmidt, R.K., Kothmann, M.M. & Rawlins, W.J. 1982. Cow-calf response to stocking rates, grazing systems, and winter supplementation at the Texas Experimental Ranch. *Journal of Range Management,* 35: 204–210.

Hensel, R.L. 1923. Recent studies on the effect of burning on grassland vegetation. *Ecology,* 4: 183–188.

Herbel, C.H. 1974. A review of research related to development of grazing systems on native ranges of the western United States. pp. 138–149, *in:* K.W. Kreitlow and R.H. Hart (Coordinators). *Plant morphogenesis as the basis for scientific management of range resources. USDA Miscellaneous Publication,* No. 1271.

Herbel. C.H. & Anderson, K.L. 1959. Response of true prairie vegetation on major Flint Hills range sites to grazing treatment. *Ecological Monographs,* 29: 171–186.

Herbel, C.H. & Pieper, R.D. 1991. Grazing management. pp. 361–385, *in:* J. Skujins (ed). *Semiarid lands and deserts. Soil resource and reclamation.* New York, New York, USA: Marcel Dekker.

Hewitt, G.B. 1977. Review of forage losses caused by rangeland grasshoppers. *USDA Miscellaneous Publication,* No. 1348. Washington, D.C., USA

Hewitt, G.B. & Onsager, J.A. 1983. Control of grasshoppers on rangeland of the United States – a perspective. *Journal of Range Management,* 36: 202–297.

Hickey, W.C. Jr. 1969. A discussion of grazing management systems and some pertinent literature (abstracts and excerpts) 1895-1966. USDA Forest Service Regional Office, Denver, Colorado, USA.

Hitchcock, A.S. 1950. *Manual of the grasses of the United States. USDA Miscellaneous Publication*, No. 200. U.S. Printing Office, Washington, D.C., USA

Hobbs, R.J. & Huenneke, L.F. 1992. Disturbance, diversity and invasion: implications for conservation. *Conservation Biology*, **6**: 324–337.

Hole, F.D. & Nielsen, G.A. 1968. Some processes of soil genesis under prairie. *Proceedings of a Symposium on Prairie and Prairie Restoration*. Galesburg, Illinois, USA, 1968. Galesburg, Illinois, USA: Knox College.

Holechek, J.L. 1981. Crested wheatgrass. *Rangelands*, **3**: 151–153.

Holechek, J.L. 1984. Comparative contribution of grasses, forbs and shrubs to the nutrition of range ungulates. *Rangelands*, **6**: 245–248.

Holechek, J.L. 1988. An approach for setting the stocking rate. *Rangelands*, **10**: 10–14.

Holechek, J.L., Pieper, R.D. & Herbel, C.H. 2001. *Range management principles and practices*. Upper Saddle River, New Jersey, USA: Prentice Hall.

Hoveland, C.S., McCann, M.A. & Hill, N.S. 1997. Rotational vs. continuous stocking of beef cows and calves on mixed endophyte-free tall fescue-bermudagrass pasture. *Journal of Production Agriculture*, **10**: 193–194.

Huenneke, L.F. 1995. Ecological impacts of plant invasions in rangeland ecosystems. *Abstracts of the Annual Meeting of the Society for Range Management*. Phoenix, Arizona, USA, 1992. Society for Range Management, Denver, Colorado, USA.

Johnson, R.R. & McCormick, J.F. 1979. Strategies for protection and management of floodplain wetlands and other riparian ecosystems. *USDA Forest Service General Technical Report*, No. WO-12.

Johnson, W.C. 1999. Response of riparian vegetation to streamflow regulation and land use in the Great Plains. *Great Plains Research*, **9**: 357–369.

Jordan, C.F. 1995. *Conservation. Replacing quantity with quality as a goal for global management*. New York, New York, USA: John Wiley & Sons.

Joyce, L.A. 1989. An analysis of the range forage situation in the United States, 1989–2040. *USDA Forest Service General Technical Report*, No. RM-180.

Keller, W. 1960. Importance of irrigated grasslands in animal production. *Journal of Range Management*, **13**: 22–28.

Klipple, G.E. & Costello, D.F. 1960. Vegetation and cattle response to different intensities of grazing on short-grass ranges of the central Great Plains. *USDA Agricultural Technology Bulletin*, No. 1216.

Klopatek, J.M., Olson, R.J., Emerson, C.J. & Jones, J.L. 1979. Land-use conflicts with natural vegetation in the United States. *Environmental Sciences Division, Oak Ridge National Laboratory Publication*, No. 1333. Oak ridge, Tennessee, USA.

Knapp, A.K, Briggs, J.M., Harnett, D.C. & Collins, S.L. 1998. *Grassland dynamics: long-term ecological research in tallgrass prairie*. New York, New York, USA: Oxford University Press.

Knopf, F.L. 1996. Perspectives on grazing nongame bird habitats. pp. 51–58, *in:* P.R. Krausmann (ed). *Rangeland wildlife.* Denver, Colorado, USA: Society for Range Management.

Kretzer, J.E. & Cully, J.F. Jr. 2001. Effects of black-tailed prairie dogs on reptiles and amphibians in Kansas shortgrass prairie. *Southwestern Naturalist,* **46**: 171–177.

Kucera, C.L. 1973. *The challenge of ecology.* Saint Louis, Missouri, USA: C.V. Mosby.

Lacey, J., Studiner, S. & Hacker, R. 1994. Early spring grazing on native range. *Rangelands,* **16**: 231–233.

Larson, F. 1940. The role of the bison in maintaining the short grass plains. *Ecology,* **21**: 113–121.

Lauenroth, W.K. 1979. Grassland primary production: North American grasslands in perspective. pp. 3–24, *in:* N.R. French (ed). *Perspectives in grassland ecology.* New York, New York, USA: Springer-Verlag.

Lauenroth, W.K., Milchunas, D.G., Dodd, J.L., Hart, R.H., Heitschmidt, R.K. & Rittenhouse, L.R. 1994. Effects of grazing on ecosystems of the Great Plains. pp. 69–100, *in:* M. Vavra, W.A. Laycock and R.D. Pieper (eds). *Ecological implications of livestock herbivory in the West.* Denver, Colorado, USA: Society for Range Management.

Lauenroth, W.K., Burke, I.C. & Gutmann, M.P. 1999. The structure and function of ecosystems in the Central North American Grassland Region. *Great Plains Research,* **9**: 223–259.

Launchbaugh, J.L. & Owensby, C.E. 1978. Kansas rangelands: their management based upon a half century of research. *Kansas State University Agricultural Experiment Station Bulletin,* No. 622.

Laycock, W.A. 1979. Introduction. pp. 1–2, *in:* N.R. French (ed). *Perspectives in grassland ecology.* New York, New York, USA: Springer-Verlag.

Leach, M.K. & Givnish, T.J. 1996. Ecological determinants of species loss in remnant prairies. *Science,* **273**: 1555–1558.

Leistritz, F.L, Leitch, J.A. & Bangsund, D.A. 1995. Economic impact of leafy spurge on grazingland and wildland in the northern Great Plains. *Abstracts of the Annual Meeting of the Society for Range Management.* Phoenix, Arizona, USA, 1995. Society for Range Management, Denver, Colorado, USA.

Leopold, A.S., Cain, S.A., Cottan, C.M., Gabrielson, I.N. & Kinball, T.L. 1963. *Wildlife management in the National Parks: the Leopold Report.* Advisory Board on Wildlife Management, Washington, D.C., USA.

Licht, D.S. 1997. *Ecology and economics of the Great Plains.* Lincoln, Nebraska, USA: University of Nebraska Press.

Lodge, R.W. 1970. Complementary grazing systems for the northern Great Plains. *Journal of Range Management,* **23**: 268–271.

Love, D. 1959. The post-glacial development of the flora of Manitoba: a discussion. *Canadian Journal of Botany,* **37**: 547–585.

Ludwig, J., Tongway, D., Fruedenberger, D., Noble, J. & Hodgkinson, K. 1997. *Landscape ecology, function and management: principles from Australia's rangelands*. Collingwood, Australia: CSIRO Publications.

Malechek, J.C. 1984. Impacts of grazing intensity and specialized grazing systems on livestock responses. pp. 1129–1165, *in: Developing strategies for rangeland management*. Boulder, Colorado, USA: Westview Press.

Manley, W.A., Hart, R.H., Samuel, M.J., Smith, M.A., Waggoner, J.W. & Manley, J.T. 1997. Vegetation, cattle and economic responses to grazing strategies and pressures. *Journal of Range Management*, 50: 638–646.

McClendon, T. 1994. Mesquite. pp. 46–47, *in:* T.N. Shiflet (ed). *Rangeland cover types of the United States*. Denver, Colorado, USA: Society for Range Management.

McCalla, G.R. II, Blackburn, W.H. & Merrill, L.B. 1984. Effects of livestock grazing on infiltration rates, Edwards Plateau of Texas. *Journal of Range Management*, 37: 265–269.

McCollum, F.T., Gillen, R.L., Engle, D.M. & Horn, G.W. 1990. Stocker cattle performance and vegetation response to intensive-early stocking of Cross Timbers rangeland. *Journal of Range Management*, 43: 99–103.

McDaniel, B. 1971. The role of invertebrates in the grassland biome. *In: Preliminary analysis of structure and function in grasslands*. Range Science Department Scientific Series, No. 10. Colorado State University, Fort Collins, Colorado, USA.

McIlvain, E.H. & Shoop, M.C. 1969. Grazing systems in the southern Great Plains. *Abstracts of the Annual Meeting of the American Society for Range Management*, 22: 21–22.

McIlvain, E.H. & Savage, D.A. 1951. Eight-year comparisons of continuous and rotational grazing on the Southern Great Plains Experimental Range. *Journal of Range Management*, 4: 42–47.

McIlvain, E.H., Baker, A.L. Kneebone, W.R. & Gates, D.H. 1955. Nineteen-year summary of range improvement studies at the U.S. Southern Great Plains Field Station, Woodward, Oklahoma. *USDA Agricultural Research Service Progress Reports*, No. 5506.

McMurphy, W.E.L. & Anderson, K.L. 1965. Burning Flint Hills range. *Journal of Range Management*, 18: 265–269.

McPherson, G.R. 1997. *Ecology and management of North American savannas*. Tucson, AZ, USA: University of Arizona Press.

Miller, R.W. & Donohue, R.L. 1990. *Soils – an introduction to soils and plant growth*. 6th ed. Englewood Cliffs, New Jersey, USA: Prentice Hall.

Mitchell, J.E. 2000. Rangeland resource trends in the United States: A technical document supporting the 2000 USDA Forest Service RPA assessment. *USDA Forest Service General Techical Report*, No. RMRS-GTR-68.

National Research Council. 1996. Colleges of Agriculture at the Land Grant Universities. Public service and public policy. Board on Agriculture, National Research Council. Washington, D.C., USA: National Academy Press.

Nelson, E.W. 1925. Status of pronghorn antelope, 1922-24. *USDA Bulletin*, No. 1346. Washington, DC., USA.

Neubauer, T.A. 1963. The grasslands of the West. *Journal of Range Management*, **16**: 327–332.

Neumann, A.L. & Lusby, K.S. 1986. *Beef cattle*. 7th ed. New York, New York, USA: John Wiley and Sons.

Newell, L.C. 1948. Hay, fodder and silage crops. pp. 281–287, *in: Grass, the [USDA] Yearbook of Agriculture*. Washington, DC., USA: U.S. Govt. Printing Office.

Nichols, J.T., Sanson, D.W. & Myran, D.D. 1993. Effect of grazing strategies and pasture species on irrigated pasture beef production. *Journal of Range Management*, **46**: 65–69.

Nyren, P.E. 1979. Fertilization of northern Great Plains rangelands: a review. *Rangelands*, **1**: 154–156.

Olson, K.E., Brethour, J.R. & Launchbaugh, J.L. 1993. Shortgrass range vegetation and steer growth response to intensive-early stocking. *Journal of Range Management*, **46**: 127–132.

Ostlie, W.R., Schneider, R.E., Aldrich, J.M., Faust, T.M., McKim, R.L.B. & Chaplin, S.J. 1997. *The status of biodiversity in the Great Plains*. Arlington, Virginia, USA: The Nature Conservancy.

Owensby, C.E. 1970. Effects of clipping and supplemental nitrogen and water on loamy upland bluestem range. *Journal of Range Management*, **23**: 341–346.

Pettit, R. 1994. Sand shinnery oak. pp. 42–43, *in:* T.N. Shiflet (ed). *Rangeland cover types of the United States*. Denver, Colorado, USA: Society for Range Management.

Pieper, R.D. 1980. Impacts of grazing systems on livestock. pp. 131–151, *in:* K.C. McDaniel and C.D. Allison (eds). *Proceedings grazing management systems for southwest rangelands symposium.*. Albuquerque, New Mexico, USA, 1980. Range Improvement Task Force, New Mexico State University, Las Cruces, New Mexico, USA.

Pieper, R.D. 1988. Rangeland vegetation productivity and biomass. pp. 449–467, *in:* P.T. Tueller (ed). *Vegetation science applications for rangeland analysis and management*. Dordrecht, The Netherlands: Kluwer Academic Publishers.

Pieper, R.D. 1994. Ecological implications of livestock grazing. pp. 177–211, *in:* M. Vavra, W.A. Laycock and R.D. Pieper (eds). *Ecological implications of livestock herbivory in the West*. Denver, Colorado, USA: Society for Range Management.

Pieper, R.D. & Beck, R.F. 1980. Importance of forbs on southwestern rangelands. *Rangelands*, **2**: 35–36.

Pieper, R.D. & Heitschmidt, R.K. 1988. Is short-duration grazing the answer? *Journal of Soil and Water Conservation*, **43**: 133–137.

Pieper, R.D., Nelson, A.B., Smith, G.S., Parker, E.E., Boggino, E.J.A. & Hatch, C.F. 1978. Chemical composition and digestibility of important range grass species in south-central New Mexico. *New Mexico State University Agricultural Experiment Station Bulletin*, No. 662.

Pieper, R.D., Parker, E.E., Donart, G.B., Wallace, J.D. & Wright, J.D. 1991. *Cattle and vegetation response of four-pasture rotation and continuous grazing systems. New Mexico State University Agricultural Experiment Station Bulletin*, No. 756.

Pitts, J.C. & Bryant, F.C. 1987. Steer and vegetation response to short duration and continuous grazing. *Journal of Range Management*, **40**: 386–390.

Pluhar, J.J., Knight, R.W. & Heitschmidt, R.K. 1987. Infiltration rates and sediment production as influenced by grazing systems in the Texas rolling plains. *Journal of Range Management*, **40**: 240–244.

Popper, D.E. & Popper, F.J. 1994. The buffalo commons: a bioregional vision of the Great Plains. *Landscape Architecture*, **84**: 144–174.

Power, J.F. 1972. Fate of fertilizer nitrogen applied to a northern Great Plains rangeland ecosystem. *Journal of Range Management*, **25**: 367–371.

Rao, M.R., Harbers, L.H. & Smith, E.F. 1973. Seasonal change in nutritive value of bluestem pastures. *Journal of Range Management*, **26**: 419–422.

Redmann, R.E. 1975. Production ecology of grassland plant communities in western North Dakota. *Ecological Monographs*, **45**: 83–106.

Rehm, G.W., Sorensen, R.C. & Moline, W.J. 1976. Time and rate of fertilizer application for seeded warm-season and bluegrass pastures. I. Yield and botanical composition. *Agronomy Journal*, **68**: 759–764.

Risser, P.G., Birney, E.C., Blocker, H.D., May, S.W., Parton, W.J. & Wiens, J.A. 1981. *The true prairie ecosystem.* Stroudsburg, PA, USA: Hutchinson Ross.

Robertson, J.H. 1939. A quantitative study of true-prairie vegetation after three years of extreme drought. *Ecological Monographs*, **9**: 431–492.

Rogler, G.A. 1951. A twenty-five year comparison of continuous and rotation grazing in the Northern Plains. *Journal of Range Management*, **4**: 35–41.

Rogler, G.A. 1960. Growing crested wheatgrass in the western states. *USDA Leaflet*, No. 469.

Rogler, G.A. & Hurtt, L.C. 1948. Where elbowroom is ample. pp. 447–482, *in: Grass, the [USDA] Yearbook of Agriculture.* U.S. Printing Office, Washington, DC, USA.

Sauer, C.O. 1950. Grassland, fire and man. *Journal of Range Management*, **3**: 16–21.

Savage, D.A. 1937. Drought, survival of native grass species in the central and southern Great Plains. *USDA Technical Bulletin*, No. 549.

Savory, A. 1983. The Savory grazing method or holistic resource management. *Rangelands*, **5**: 555–557.

Savory, A. 1999. *Holistic management, a new framework for decision making.* Washington, D.C., USA: Island Press.

Savory, A. & Parsons, S.D. 1980. The Savory grazing method. *Rangelands*, **2**: 234–237.

Scales, G.H., Streeter, C.L. & Denham, A.H. 1971. Nutritive value and consumption of range forage. *Journal of Animal Science*, **33**: 310–312.

Seton, E.T. 1927. *Lives of game animals.* Vol 3. New York, New York, USA: Literary Guild of America.

Shaw, J.H. 1996. Bison. pp. 227–236, *in:* P.R. Krausmann (ed). *Rangeland wildlife.* Denver, Colorado, USA: Society for Range Management.

Sieg, C.H., Flather, C.H. & McCanny, S. 1999. Recent biodiversity patterns in the Great Plains: implications for restoration and management. *Great Plains Research,* **9**: 277–313.

Sims, P.L. 1988. Grasslands. pp. 324–356, *in:* M.G. Barbour and W.D. Billings (eds). *North American terrestrial vegetation.* New York, New York, USA: Cambridge University Press.

Sims, P.L. & Singh, J.S. 1978a. The structure and function of ten western North American grasslands. II. Intra-seasonal dynamics in primary producer compartments. *Journal of Ecology,* **66**: 547–572.

Sims, P.L. & Singh, J.S. 1978b. Intra-seasonal dynamics in primary producer compartments in ten western North American grasslands, III. Net primary production, turnover and efficiency of energy capture and water use. *Journal of Ecology,* **66**: 573–597.

Sims, P.L., Singh, J.S. & Lauenroth, W.K. 1978. The structure and function of ten western North American grasslands. I. Abiotic and vegetational characteristics. *Journal of Ecology,* **66**: 251–285.

Smeins, F. 1994. Little bluestem-Indiangrass-Texas winter grass – SRM 717. pp. 65–66, *in:* T.N. Shiflet (ed). *Rangeland cover types of the United States.* Denver, Colorado, USA: Society for Range Management.

Smeins, F.E. 2000. Ecology and management of Ashe juniper and redberry juniper. *Abstracts of the Annual Meeting of the Society for Range Management.* Boise, Idaho, USA, 2000. Denver, Colorado, USA: Society for Range Management.

Smith. E.F., Anderson, K.L., Owensby, C.E. & Hall, M.C. 1967. Different methods of managing bluestem pasture. *Kansas State University Agricultural Experiment Station Bulletin,* No. 507.

Smith, E.F. & Owensby, C.E. 1972. Effects of fire on true prairie grasslands. *Proceedings of the Tall Timbers Ecology Conference,* **12**: 9–22.

Smith, E.F. & Owensby, C.E. 1978. Intensive-early stocking and season-long stocking of Kansas Flint Hills range. *Journal of Range Management,* **31**: 14–17.

Smoliak, S. 1956. Influence of climatic conditions on forage production of short-grass rangeland. *Journal of Range Management,* **9**: 89–91.

Smoliak, S. 1968. Grazing studies on native range, crested wheatgrass and Russian wildrye pastures. *Journal of Range Management,* **21**: 47–50.

Smoliak, S., Johnston, A., Kilcher, M.R. & Lodge, R.W. 1976. Management of prairie rangeland. Canada Department of Agriculture, Ottawa, Canada.

Smolik, J.D. 1974. Nematode studies at the Cottonwood Site. *US/IBP Grassland Biome Technical Report,* No. 251. Colorado State University, Fort Collins, Colorado, USA.

Soil Conservation Service. 1973. *National soils handbook.* Washington, D.C., USA: USDA.

Steuter, A.A. & Hidinger, L. 1999. Comparative ecology of bison and cattle on mixed-grass prairie. *Great Plains Research,* 9: 329–342.

Stoddart, L.A. & Smith, A.D. 1955. *Range management.* 2nd ed. New York, New York, USA: McGraw-Hill Book Co.

Stoddart, L.A., Smith, A.D. & Box, T.W. 1975. *Range Management.* 3rd ed. New York, New York, USA: McGraw-Hill Book Co.

Summer, C.A. & Linder, R.L. 1978. Food habits of the black-tailed prairie dog. *Journal of Range Management,* 31: 134–136.

Swanson, S. 1988. Riparian values as a focus for range management and vegetation science. pp. 425–445, *in:* P.T. Tueller (ed). *Vegetation science applications for rangeland anslysis and management.* Dordrecht, The Netherlands: Kluwer Academic.

Thomas, G.W., Herbel, C.H. & Miller, G.T. Jr. 1990. Rangeland resources. pp. 284–290, *in:* G.T. Miller Jr. (ed). *Resource conservation and management.* Belmont, California, USA: Wadsworth Pub. Co.

Thurow, T.L., Blackburn, W.H. & Taylor, C.A. 1988. Infiltration and interrill erosion responses to selected livestock grazing strategies, Edwards Plateau, Texas. *Journal of Range Management,* 41: 296–302.

Tobey, R.C. 1981. *Saving the prairies. The life cycle of the founding school of American Plant Ecology, 1895-1955.* Berkeley, California, USA: University of California Press.

Transeau, E.N. 1935. The prairie peninsula. *Ecology,* 16: 423–437.

Trewartha, G. 1961. *The earth's problem climates.* Madison, Wisconsin, USA: University of Wisconsin Press.

Tueller, P.T. 1989. Remote sensing technology for rangeland management applications. *Journal of Range Management,* 42(6): 442–453.

Vallentine, F.F. 1989. *Range development and improvements.* 3rd ed. San Diego, California, USA: Academic Press.

Vallentine, F.F. 1990. *Grazing management.* San Diego, California, USA: Academic Press.

Vanderhoff, J.L, Robel, R.J. & Kemp, K.E. 1994. Numbers and extent of black-tailed prairie dogs in Kansas. *Transactions of the Kansas Academy of Science,* 97: 36–43.

Van Dyne, G.M. & Dyer, M.I. 1973. A general view of grasslands – a human and ecological perspective. pp. 38–57, *in: Analysis of structure, function and utilization of grassland ecosystems.* Proposal submitted to the National Science Foundation. Colorado State University, Fort Collins, Colorado, USA.

Van Dyne, G.M., Jameson, D.A. & French, N.R. 1970. *Analysis of structure and function of grassland ecosystems.* A progress report and a continuation proposal. Colorado State University, Fort Collins, Colorado, USA.

Van Poollen, H.W. & Lacey, J.R. 1979. Herbage response to grazing systems and stocking intensities. *Journal of Range Management,* 32: 250–253.

Wagnon, K.A., Albaugh, R. & Hart, G.H. 1960. *Beef cattle production.* New York, New York, USA: MacMillan.

Walker, J.W. 1995. Viewpoint: grazing management and research now and in the next millennium. *Journal of Range Management,* **48**: 350–357.

Weakly. H.E. 1943. A tree ring record of precipitation in western Nebraska. *Journal of Forestry,* **41**: 816–819.

Weaver, J.E. & Albertson, F.W. 1956. *Grasslands of the Great Plains: their nature and use.* Lincoln, Nebraska, USA: Johnson Publishing.

Weaver, J.E. & Albertson, F.W. 1940. Deterioration of grassland from stability to denudation with decrease in soil moisture. *Botanical Gazette,* **101**: 598–624.

Weaver, J.E. & Albertson, F.W. 1939. Major changes in grassland as a result of continued drought. *Botanical Gazette,* **100**: 576–591.

Weaver, J.E. & Albertson, F.W. 1936. Effects of the great drought on the prairies of Iowa, Nebraska and Kansas. *Ecology,* **17**: 567–639.

Weltz, M. & Wood, M.K. 1986. Short-duration grazing in central New Mexico: effects on infiltration rates. *Journal of Range Management,* **39**: 365–368.

Wester, D. & Bakken, T. 1992. Early allotments in South Dakota revisited. *Rangelands,* **14**: 236–238.

White, M.R., Pieper, R.D., Donart, G.B. & White-Trifaro, L. 1991. Vegetation response to short-duration and continuous grazing in southcentral New Mexico. *Journal of Range Management,* **44**: 399–404.

Whitman, W., Hanson, H.C. & Peterson, R. 1943. Relation of drought and grazing to North Dakota range lands. *North Dakota Agricultural College Agricultural Experiment Station Bulletin,* No. 320.

Wiens, J.A. 1973. Pattern and process in grassland bird communities. *Ecological Monographs,* **43**: 237–270.

Wiens, J.A. 1974. Climatic instability and the "ecological saturation" of bird communities in North American grasslands. *The Condor,* **76**: 385–400.

Wight, J.R. 1976. Range fertilization in the northern Great Plains. *Journal of Range Management,* **29**: 180–185.

Wright. H.A. 1974. Range burning. *Journal of Range Management,* **27**: 5–11.

Wright, H.A. 1978. Use of fire to manage grasslands of the Great Plains: Central and Southern Great Plains. pp. 694–696, *in:* D.N. Hyder (ed). *Proceedings of the First International Rangeland Congress.* Denver, Colorado, USA, 1978. Society for Range Management, Denver, Colorado, USA.

Wright, H.A. & Bailey, A.W. 1982. *Fire ecology: United States and southern Canada.* New York, New York, USA: John Wiley and Sons.

Yoakum, J.D., O'Gara, B.W. & Howard, V.W. Jr. 1996. Pronghorn on western rangelands. pp. 211–226, *in:* P.R. Krausmann (ed). *Rangeland wildlife.* Denver, Colorado, USA: Society for Range Management.

Chapter 7
Grazing management in Mongolia

J.M. Suttie

SUMMARY

Eighty percent of Mongolia is extensive grazing and a further ten percent is forest or forest scrub that is also grazed. Its climate is arid to semi-arid and the frost-free period of most of the steppe is one hundred days; transhumant herding on natural pasture is the only sustainable way of using such land. Cattle, with yak in the higher areas, horses, camels, sheep and goats are raised; local breeds are used. During the past century management has changed from traditional transhumance, to collectives that retained herd mobility from the fifties, to private herding from 1992. While livestock are now privately owned, grazing rights have not yet been allocated; this causes problems for maintenance of pastoral infrastructure and respect of good grazing practice. Stock numbers have risen since privatization and are now above the previous high of 1950; weakness of the traditional export market and increase in the number of herding families are contributing factors. Pasture condition is generally sound, although, recently, localized overgrazing has occurred close to urban centres and main routes. Considerable tracts are undergrazed because of breakdown of water supplies or remoteness from services. Major improvement of grazing management and pastoral production requires enactment of legislation appropriate to the new management system and organization of the herding population. Increased family hay production from natural herbage would improve overwintering survival. Transhumant herding of hardy, local stock, has proved sustainable over centuries and is still thriving.

INTRODUCTION

Mongolia is one of the few countries that is truly pastoral and its economy depends largely on livestock, with little crop production, forestry or industry. The cold, arid climate is only suitable for extensive grazing and transhumance with local, hardy breeds, which are still used, with few inputs other than the hard work and skill of the herders (Plate 7.1). This ancient grazing system has proved productive and sustainable through the political changes of the past century. The grazing lands are in good condition and the local breeds intact and thriving; this contrasts with the situation in some neighbouring countries that are now facing the consequences of excessive use of exotic breeds and reliance on bought, imported winter feed.

Mongolia lies between 42° and 52°N and 88° and almost 120°E. About half the land is above 1 400 m. It is completely landlocked, bordering the Russian

Plate 7.1
Ger and sheep fold on summer pastures – Arkhangai.

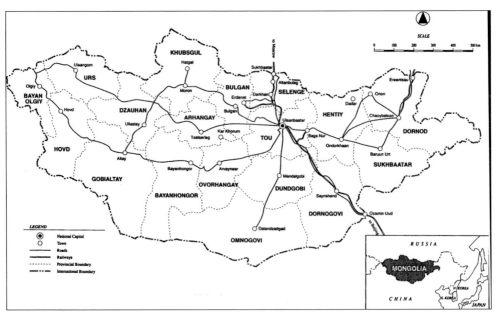

Figure 7.1
Map of Mongolia.

Federation and China (Figure 7.1) and with well-defined natural boundaries delimiting the Mongolian steppe: the Altai and Gobi Altai mountains to the west and southwest, the Khangai mountains in the central north, the Gobi

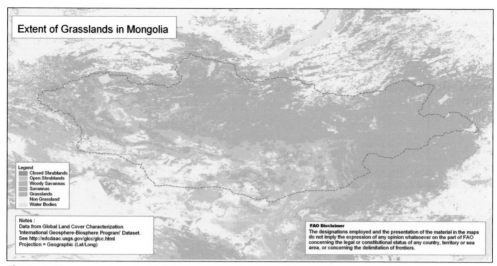

Figure 7.2
Extent of grasslands in Mongolia.

desert to the south and the taiga to the north; these facilitate neither trade nor transport. Access to the sea is through the Chinese port of Tianjin, 1 000 km from the frontier. There are very few hard-surfaced roads; the main Russia-China railway traverses the country, but there are few internal lines. Livestock move to market by droving; other commodities have to be transported over poor, unsurfaced roads and tracks. The pastoral and climatic situation has close parallels in neighbouring parts of Inner Asia: Buryatia, Tuva and some Chinese regions (Inner Mongolia Autonomous Region and the northern part of Xinjiang Autonomous Region), although the Mongolian economy and lifestyle are much more pastoral and its crop sector vestigial. Under slightly different climatic conditions, experience in the transition from collective to private herding is also relevant to parts of Central Asia – Kazakhstan, Kyrgyzstan and Tajikistan. Mongolia's pastoral industry was less drastically modified by collectivization than that of the CIS countries in that herder mobility was maintained as the key to assuring year-round feeding and risk avoidance, and hardy, local breeds remained the basis of the industry. Technologies and strategies developed in Mongolia may have relevance throughout the region.

Grasslands and arid grazing cover 1 210 000 km² (80 percent of the land area – see Figure 7.2) and forest and forest scrub 150 000 km² (10 percent). Some 90 000 km² are said to be used in settlement and infrastructure and 52 000 km² in national parks. The arable area is under 10 000 km², all mechanized, large-scale farms, although much fell out of cultivation following the demise of the state farms (about 7 000 km² are estimated to be recoverable). About 80 percent of the country, therefore, is extensive grazing exploited by traditional, pastoral methods (Plate 7.2). The five main biogeographical zones are:

- high mountains (70 000 km²);

TABLE 7.1
Land resources of Mongolia.

Land use	Proportion (%)	Area (km²)
Grasslands and arid grazing	80.7	1 210 000
Forest	6.9	104 000
Saxaul forest in Gobi	3.1	46 000
Arable[1]	0.5	7 000
National parks	3.5	52 000
Hay land[1]	1.3	20 000
Roads, buildings and miscellaneous	4.0	61 000
Total land area	100	1 500 000

NOTES: (1) Figures from the early 1990s. Much of that is now fallow.
SOURCE: Ministry of Agriculture and Food.

Plate 7.2
Mountain pastures above larch forest with yak – Zaghvan.

- mountain taiga (60 000 km²);
- forest-mountain and steppe – mixed forest and grazing (370 000 km²);
- dry steppe grassland (410 000 km²); and
- Gobi – desert steppe and desert (580 000 km²).

Extensive livestock production is, by far, the country's major land use and industry, as can be seen from Table 7.1.

The level-to-undulating topography of the Mongolian plateau is frequently interrupted by low mountain ranges and is surrounded by rough topography. Luvic xerosols associated with Orthic Solonchaks occupy the greatest part of the land: the steppes and the Gobi desert. Associations of Haplic Yermosols and Orthic Solonchaks also occur. Luvic Kastanozems associated with Orthic Solonchaks occupy a large area in the north and east, the best of Mongolia's pasture lands. Mountain ranges are covered by Lithosols associated with Luvic Xerosols or Haplic Yermosols (FAO/UNESCO, 1978).

The climate is cold, semi-arid and markedly continental. High mountain ranges isolate the country from the influence of the Atlantic and Pacific climates. The Siberian anticyclone determines the low temperature in winter and the low precipitation. The frost-free period at the capital is around 100 days. There are four distinct seasons: a windy spring with variable weather – spring rain is especially valuable to get the pasture growth started before the main summer rains; a hot summer, with the main rains falling in the earlier part; a cool autumn; and a long cold winter, with temperatures as low as -30°C. The growing season is, therefore, generally limited to about three months.

Precipitation is low, much falling between June and September. The largest grazing areas, the steppe and the mountain steppe and forest, get between 200 mm and 300 mm annually; the desert steppe receives between 100 and 200 mm; the desert gets below 100 mm; only the northern zone has over 300 mm. Most of the precipitation returns to the atmosphere through evapotranspiration; about four percent infiltrates to the aquifer and six percent contributes to surface flow. Strong winds (with velocities in excess of 20 m/s) are common in spring and early summer, and then dust storms can bring disaster to people and livestock. Such storms are commonest in the drier tracts.

The vast majority of the nation, about 80 percent, is Mongol; the extreme west is inhabited by Kazakhs and there are some reindeer people in the extreme north. Buryats, Tuvans and other Mongol-related peoples make up the rest. The total population has risen sharply, more rapidly than livestock numbers, tripling since 1950 (see Table 7.2). The degree of urbanization rose very steeply on collectivization. Originally urban dwellers were only 15 percent, but ten years on this had risen to 40 percent and by 1989, the end of the collective period, the urban population was 57 percent, including those in the *sum* centres. The 1997 figures show a slight decrease in the proportion (but not number) of town dwellers, perhaps reflecting some families returning to herding.

The population rise since 1950 has been large and rapid: the projections for the next twenty years (Table 7.3) show no slowing down, but rather a near doubling!

Education from 6 to 16 has been compulsory for many years and the level of literacy in the population is very high. There are strong training institutions to

TABLE 7.2
Population change, rural-urban distribution and total ('000s).

Year	1950	1956	1960	1963	1969	1970	1979	1980	1989	1997	1998
Urban	n.a.	183.0	n.a.	408.8	527.4	n.a.	817.0	n.a.	1 161.1	1 226.3	n.a.
Rural	n.a.	662.5	n.a.	608.3	670.2	n.a.	778.0	n.a.	877.9	1 127.0	n.a.
Total	772.4	845.5	968.1	1 017.1	1 197.6	1 265.4	1 595.0	1 682.0	2 044.0	2 353.3	2 422.8
Urban %		15.3		40.1	44.0		51.2		57.0	52.1	

NOTE: n.a. = information not available.
SOURCE: State Statistics Office.

TABLE 7.3
Projected total population to 2020.

2000	2005	2010	2015	2020
2 781 700	3 195 000	3 612 300	3 945 500	4 284 800

Source: Development scenario for 21st century. UNDP pilot project report. Ulaanbaatar, 1998. MAP-21, MON/95-G81.

J.M. SUTTIE

Plate 7.3
Migrating flock crossing the Ulan Dava pass on the way to summer pasture – Uvs.

university level – many post-graduates have trained abroad. There are technical schools in each *aimag* (≈ province). More girls than boys follow secondary and university studies – their families do not require them for herding and there are adequate women to attend to dairy duties.

The herders all practice transhumance; this means that they must move seasonally (see Plate 7.3) with their livestock on the pastures. They live in *gers* (yurt in Russian), cylindrical, domed structures (Plate 7.4) with a wooden framework covered with felt; They are free-standing, not held in place by guy-ropes like a tent. While the *ger* is easy to take down and erect and domestic equipment is designed for ease of transport, the moving of the family's *gers* and baggage requires frequent hard work and transport. Fuel for cooking and heating is generally dried dung, except in the forest zone, where firewood is also used.

Mongolia is rich in wildlife and its herds share the grazing with antelope, gazelle, elk and deer. Rodents are widespread and can cause much local damage to grassland through feeding and burrowing; control was once done through poisoning but this has now stopped. There are abundant predators, hawks, buzzards, eagles and foxes that feed on them. Wolves prey on sheep flocks and in the Gobi Altai the protected snow-leopard may cause damage.

ALICE CARLONI

Plate 7.4
Gers and autumn grass.

Crops and industry are very minor components in the present national economy; mineral resources have yet to be tapped on any scale, the forest area is relatively small and slow-growing. Agro-industrial processing, almost entirely livestock-based, has contracted since economic liberalization. Traditionally, herders did not till the land; their economy and life-style was entirely pastoral and the climate gave little incentive to do so with the technology available to them. A little irrigated cropping, mainly wheat and barley, was done in the region of the Great Lakes and the grain parched and ground to a pre-cooked flour (similar to the *tsampa* of Tibet).

With the availability of suitable agricultural machinery during the second half of the twentieth century, however, it became possible to undertake large-scale cereal production (Plate 7.5): in some of the less unfavourable areas of Central Mongolia over one million hectares were cultivated. The land used was, of course, among the best pasture. Some fodders (discussed in detail below) and potatoes were also grown, but the area was small compared to that of grain. The technology used, based on a rotation of alternating strips of crop and fallow, was adapted from Canadian practice.

State farms and *negdel* (see Plate 7.6) in suitable sites produced enough grain to satisfy the population's needs – more cereals were eaten during the collective period than previously or nowadays. FAO (1996) quotes a 40 percent reduction in the consumption of flour. In a semi-arid area with a very short thermal growing season, all agricultural operations must be carried out very rapidly, especially seed-bed preparation and sowing; yield potential is low, so production methods have, therefore, to be extensive. Considerable seasonal risk is

S.G. REYNOLDS

Plate 7.5
Wheat was once grown over much larger areas in Mongolia.

J.M. SUTTIE

Plate 7.6
Mountain and steppe with negdel *complex in background – Tuv.*

involved and harvest can be difficult if a dull summer delays ripening or there is early frost or snow. Cropping is not attractive to smallholders. Production was highly mechanized, and field sizes large – over a square kilometre. Harvesting was by combine harvester, often with assisted drying. Straw was recovered as feed and handled mechanically – some straw was ground up as a component of "concentrate" feed. The fallow strips had to be cultivated in summer to control weeds and prepared for the coming year's crop.

With the collapse of the former producing organizations, the crop area is greatly reduced, although some companies are still active. There are many financial as well as technical problems, including seed supply and competition from imported flour. The country is now very much dependent on its neighbours for grain supplies, a problem for national food security. Much of the former crop land is in tumble-down fallow, the area is not known but it is estimated that 700 000 hectares could be recovered for cropping; this provides some grazing but would require continual weed-control work were it to be cropped. Straw is not, therefore, an important source of fodder.

Changes in administrative systems in the twentieth century

The cold, arid climate is well suited to extensive grazing and transhumance, which makes best use of pastures, where forage availability in any one place can vary greatly from season to season and from year to year. The ancient, original systems were transhumance with a wide range of possible travel. According to Humphrey and Sneath (1996a)

"Banners were the main administrative units of the Manchu government in Inner Mongolia and Mongolia. They approximated in area to the present counties (banners) in Inner Mongolia. In Mongolia, territories of banner size no longer exist; they were amalgamated into aimags, which are divided into sum (more numerous and mostly smaller units than the previous banners).

The 'traditional' practice in the pre-revolutionary period in the open steppes of Inner Asia was based on general access to the bounded pasture territories coordinated by leaders and officials. In Mongol inhabited areas, along with small herder groups of a few families, there were large institutions, notably Buddhist monasteries and the economies of banners [administrative units] managed by the ruling princes. These institutions held their own property or funds (jas) consisting of livestock, land and money. In Mongolia and Inner Mongolia the animals were herded by monastery serfs (shabinar) or banner princes' serfs (hamjilaga), while a further class of State subjects (albat) paid taxes and performed labour services. The large monastic foundations, with their own territories and people, functioned as districts equivalent to banners, but there were also numerous smaller monasteries located inside the princely banners."

Feudal land ownership was done away with on the founding of the Mongolian Communist State in 1921; transhumance continued with government, instead of feudal, supervision.

In the late thirteenth century, Marco Polo described the Mongol transhumance and their *gers* (Latham, 1958: 67).

"They spend the winter in steppes and warm regions where there is good grazing and pasturage for their beasts. In summer they live in cool regions, among mountains and valleys, where they find water and pasturage. A further advantage is that in the cooler regions there are no horse flies and gad flies or similar pests to annoy them and their beasts. They spend two or three months climbing steadily and grazing as they go, because if they confined their grazing to one spot there would not be grass enough for the multitude of their flocks. They have circular houses

made of wood that they carry about with them on four-wheeled wagons wherever they go. The framework of rods is so neatly and lightly constructed that it is light to carry. And every time they unfold the house and set it up the door is always facing south. They also have excellent two-wheeled carts – these are drawn by oxen and camels. And in these carts they carry their wives and children and all they need in the way of utensils." Polo continues with more that is still apposite: "And I assure you that the womenfolk buy and sell and do all that is needful for their husbands and households. For the men do not bother themselves about anything but hunting and warfare and falconry."

The country's pastures have probably always been heavily stocked – hard grazing is a historical phenomenon, not something of recent development. Kharin, Takahashi and Harahshesh (1999) quote Przevalsky (1883) who "said that all suitable agricultural lands were reclaimed and all grazing lands were overloaded by livestock."

A fundamental change took place in 1950 with the collectivization of the livestock industry; while this facilitated the provision of government services and marketing (and probably control of a nomadic population), it decreased the range over which herds could travel and thus reduced opportunities for risk-avoidance in times of feed scarcity. The unit of management during the collective period was the *negdel* covering the same area as a single district (*sum*); it was primarily an economic unit responsible for marketing livestock products, supplying inputs and consumer goods as well as fodder and transport services to members; it provided health, education and veterinary services. Although livestock was collectivized, each family was allowed to keep two livestock units (*bod*[1]) per person so about a quarter of the herd was under private control. Collectivization, as noted above, led to a very large rise in the proportion of urban population.

During the collective period, the government was heavily involved in livestock production through the provision of breeding stock, fodder, marketing, transport and services. It was a heavily subsidized production system that did not allocate resources efficiently. The loss of mobility through collectivization was compensated by the production of supplementary forage and a State Emergency Fodder Fund was established as a mechanism to provide feed during weather conditions that would threaten survival, but, with heavily subsidized transport and undervalued prices, herders soon became dependent on it as a regular source of feed. By 1991, the State Emergency Fodder Fund was handling 157 600 t/yr and had become a major component of the state budget. A network of stock-routes was maintained that allowed slaughter stock to be trekked to market, fattening *en route*. There were marketing and primary processing facilities for hides, skins, wool and cashmere.

Eighteen *aimags* were subdivided into 225 districts – *sum* – that in turn were divided into brigades. *Negdel* headquarters had administration, schools

---

[1] A large-animal unit: a camel = 1.5 bod; cattle and horses = 1; 7 sheep or 10 goats = 1 bod.

ALICE CARLONI

Plate 7.7
Hay reserves for feed provision under the State Emergency Fodder Fund

ALICE CARLONI

Plate 7.8
Trucks distributing winter feed

(boarding), medical facilities, a veterinary unit, communications, recreational facilities and shops. *Negdels* were set production quotas and paid accordingly with bonuses – the system was production driven. A vast number of salaried administrators and specialist staff was built up at all levels, especially in the capital.

Negdels were divided into production herding brigades or teams, which were further sub-divider into *suuri* – individual units made up of one to four households (*sur*). There were other, salaried, brigades for haymaking, mechanization, etc. Brigades had production targets for each *sur*, determining the quantity of meat, wool and other products to be delivered according to the annual state procurement order. A *sur* was generally involved in the production of single-species herds for which a monthly salary was paid (each household, however, had some private livestock for subsistence). Pasture management was organized along rational lines and the seasonal movement of herds (and resting of grazing land) planned and the plans followed by the *sur*. Emphasis was on animal output rather than pasture improvement but the system did assure better pasture management than today's anarchy. Hay lands were reserved and managed separately from grazing.

The *negdels* were privatized in 1991; this was meant to take place in two stages. Thirty percent of *negdels'* assets were distributed between members; a further 10 percent of the livestock was distributed to *sum* inhabitants (administrative and health workers, etc.). The remaining 60 percent of assets was formed into a limited liability company; these companies were generally unsuccessful and the livestock industry reverted towards its earlier family-based transhumance. In some cases the livestock were distributed without the formation of a company.

Grazing lands, pasture and fodder

The natural grazing has a very short growing season, limited by low temperatures. Pasture growth begins in mid-May and usually ceases after mid-August because of drought. Frosts can occur at the end of August; the thermal growing season is shorter in the mountains and longer in the Gobi. The grazing lands were surveyed in detail and pasture maps covering the country produced about twenty years ago. Under *negdel* management, pastures were monitored and seasonal movements of livestock respected. The monitoring of pasture condition needs updating so that the present situation can be defined and policies formulated on a basis of fact rather than opinion. The dichotomy of interests between the grazers and the grazed is recognized at government level: livestock are under the Ministry of Agriculture and Food while the grazing lands and the monitoring of their vegetation are the responsibility of the Ministry of the Environment and Natural Resources; close inter-ministerial collaboration is essential in any work on pasture management at national level.

Opinions on the present state of Mongolia's pastures vary widely, especially those of external missions. There is general agreement that overstocking now occurs close to agglomerations, especially the capital and along roads. Damage through random track-making by vehicles, particularly in valley-bottoms, is also widespread. Thereafter opinions have varied from declaring that the nation's pastures are seriously degraded, risking an ecological disaster, to the view that overstocking is a localized phenomenon and labour availability, not pasture production is the main constraint to herding. While stock numbers are at an all-time high since recording began in 1918, the 1996 levels are only mar-ginally higher than those of 1950. The consensus is that problems vary from place to place and that outlying (summer and autumn) pastures are underu-tilized, while winter-spring pastures are often being abused. Natural control of stock numbers is the traditional way to correct overstocking. Periodic *zud* [winter natural disaster – discussed later] or prolonged drought kills large num-bers, and puts the grazing stock back in equilibrium with the forage supply, but however effective natural disasters are in protecting the grazing vegetation, they inevitably lead to poverty and suffering among the herders.

The vast grasslands of Mongolia are part of the steppe, a prominent transi-tion belt in Inner Asia and Central Asia between their forest and desert belts. Steppe vegetation is characterized by a predominance of grasses, especially species of *Stipa* and *Festuca*. Legumes are scarce; the commonest are *Medicago sativa* subsp. *falcata* and *Astragalus* spp. *Artemisia frigida* is frequent and is the main steppe-forming plant of the desert steppe. The montane forest steppe has *Festuca* spp. and *Artemisia* spp. as dominants.

There are typical plants associated with the main pasture zones. High mountain pasture is dominated by *Kobresia bellardii, Ptilagrostis mongolica, Arenaria, Formosa* and *Potentilla nivea*; Forest steppe is dominated by *Festuca lenensis, Carex pediformis, Aster alpinus* and *Androsace villosa*; the steppe zone is dominated by *Stipa capillata, Elymus chinensis, Cleistogenes squar-rosa, Koeleria macrantha, Agropyron cristatum, Carex duriuscula, Artemisia frigida* and *Potentilla acaulis*; the desert steppe is dominated by *Stipa gobica, S. glareosa, Allium polyrhizum, Artemisia xerophytica, A. caespitosa, Anabasis brevifolia* and *Eurotia ceratoides*; and the desert zone is dominated by shrubs and semi-shrubs like *Anabasis brevifolia, Salsola passerina, Sympegma regelii* and *Nanophyton erinaceum*.

The steppe has five major zones with different livestock production capaci-ties. The Khangai-Khosvol region in the northwest is mountainous with scat-tered larch forest. It includes Arkhangai, Khovsgol and part of Bulgan and Zhagvan *aimags*; this is mixed grazing, with yaks replacing cattle at the higher altitudes. Selenge-Onon in the north central area (Tuv, Selenge and parts of Bulgan) is the main area of agricultural production. These two regions drain to Lake Baikal. Altai (covering Uvs, Bayangol, Khovd and parts of Zhavakan and Gobi-Altai *aimags*) is a high, mountainous, area with internal drainage and contains large lakes. In the northern part of the region this again is grazed by the main types of livestock with yaks; there is some localized fodder and horticultural production under irrigation in the lower parts. The Central and Eastern steppes (comprising Dornod, Hentii – see Plate 7.9, Sukhbaatar and parts of Dorongobi and Dungovi) are characterized by broad, treeless plains; the Herlen river traverses part of the region; the primary activity is herding of horses, cattle, sheep, goats and camels. Gobi (mainly Bayankhongor, Omnogobi, much of Ovorkhangai and parts of Dungobi and Gobi-Altai) is desert steppe

J.M. SUTTIE

Plate 7.9
Saddle horses on hitching line in the eastern steppe – Hentii.

and desert, used for grazing camels, horses, cattle and goats, with very limited hay harvesting; drainage is internal; oases produce vegetables and fruit.

Sown fodder

Some fodder was grown during the collective period, for hay, by *negdels* and State Farms in the higher rainfall areas. Some silage was made by "mechanized dairies". The area dropped dramatically with the change of system, from 147 000 ha in 1989 (Table 7.4) to 25 000 ha in 1993 and is probably much lower now. Oat (*Avena sativa*) was the main hay crop; its cultivation suited the wheat-growing equipment already available, a crop could be grown to the hay stage in the short season available, and harvesting and curing was easy. All operations were, of course, mechanized. Locally-saved seed was mainly used. Sunflower (*Helianthus annuus*) was a common silage crop; in the main crop producing areas it can develop to the full heading stage with seed set, suitable for ensiling, before low temperatures affect growth; it is very drought tolerant. Sunflower seed cannot, however, be successfully ripened in the main silage-making zone; some farms arranged for seed production at lower, warmer sites in Eastern Mongolia, but much of the seed was imported from Central Asia.

Alfalfa (*Medicago* spp.) has been cultivated on a small scale, under irrigation, in the area of the Great Lakes in the northwest for a very long time. This was expanded greatly during the collective period but is now on a lesser scale. Local landraces are grown, probably *M. media* types, their seed set and production is good in that area; the conditions of western Mongolia are excellent for hay-making. Yellow-flowered alfalfa (*M. sativa* subsp. *falcata*), has been grown

TABLE 7.4
Fodder and straw production 1989-1993.

Fodder type		1989	1990	1991	1992	1993
Area of fodder	ha	147 700	117 800	79 900	52 900	25 600
Hay harvest	tonne	1 166 400	866 400	885 500	668 800	698 400
Straw used	tonne	99 500	58 300	54 600	31 900	26 500

SOURCE: State Statistical Office, 1994, quoted by FAO, 1996.

under irrigation on some State Farms, including Khar Horin. It was also grown on several small irrigated areas in the Gobi. Gobi sites have generally been converted to the more popular and profitable melons and vegetables.

Sown fodder does not have a high priority under the present economic and social conditions but could play a role in supplementing low quality winter and spring feed in favoured sites. Oat hay could be developed as a cash crop on cereal farms once the crop industry is re-established. Screening and selection of cultivars will, however, be necessary, as will development of a seed supply chain.

Because of the 1944 *zud* the government decided to encourage the creation of reserves of fodder by private herders, but this really developed during the collective period. The State Emergency Fodder Fund was set up in 1971, operating twelve centres and forty-one distribution points, but its origins date from the 1930s, when haymaking stations were started with horse-drawn technology brought in from Russia. By 1991, the State Emergency Fodder Fund operated 22 centres; because of financial problems, most were transferred to *aimag* administrations. The State Emergency Fodder Fund played an important part in reducing the impact of weather emergencies but, as economic liberalization progressed, its ability to continue its role became doubtful since central government could not provide the previous level of subsidy.

In 1997 total fodder production was estimated at 340 000 fodder units; the national average was 4.9 forage units per sheep, less than a tenth of the average of 1980. Hay production data for the 1960–1985 period are shown in Table 7.5. In 2000, hay production was estimated at 689 000 tonne. Problems of land use rights are a serious hindrance to herder haymaking; a further problem in some systems is the location of the hay lands: sometimes they are far from the summer pastures (Plate 7.10) and the herders are absent at the haymaking season; sometimes they are far from the spring and winter pastures where the hay is needed.

The biggest bottleneck in haymaking by herders is the amount of labour involved and the lack of machinery. Herbage reaches its maximum yield and feeding quality in the second half of August in most ecological zones; this is a season of relatively heavy rainfall and it is laborious to mow and turn low-yielding crops of hay to give a quality product.

HAY FROM NATURAL PASTURE IN ARKHANGAI

FAO has provided some support for work on haymaking in Arkhangai by the High Mountain Research Station, based in Ihk Tamir *sum*, which concentrates

TABLE 7.5
Haymaking by producer and year ('000 tonne).

Year	State farms	Cooperatives	Other statal	Private
1960	49.8	728.8	12.5	–
1970	116.2	328.9	34.4	42.7
1980	246.6	563.2	161.8	98.6
1985	323.8	615.3	228.3	108.2

Source: Ministry of Agriculture and Food.

S.G. REYNOLDS

Plate 7.10
Haylands – Arkhangai.

on montane pasture and livestock management questions, especially yaks. Arkhangai *aimag* is in the central area of the Khangai mountains, its head-quarters, Tsetserleg, is about 500 km west of Ulan Bator; its latitude is roughly 47° 30' N at 103° 15' E. It covers a range of ecological zones, including high mountain, mountain steppe and steppe zones.

The average elevation is 1 700–1 850 m; mean annual precipitation 363 mm, of which 80 percent falls in the period May to August; mean maximum temperature in August is around 16.0°C, falling to -16.0°C in the December to February period, with absolute maximum and minimum temperatures of 34.5 and -36.5°C. The *aimag* covers 55 300 km², of which 41 000 km² is pasture, 540 km² hay and 8 645 km² forest. The steppe zone, in the east of the province, has the mildest climate: mean January temperature is -16°C (absolute minimum -38°C) and July mean is 17.5°C (absolute maximum 35°C), with 98 to 125 frost-free days. The main ecological zones in Arkhangai are shown in Table 7.6.

The high mountains are summer yak pasture that is not really accessible to other species, although it can be used for horses. Because of the higher humidity in the high zone, small ruminants suffer there from foot-rot. The

TABLE 7.6
Ecological zones in Arkhangai.

Ecological zone	Altitude range (masl)	Rainfall (mm)	Frost-free days
Steppe & Mountain steppe	1 300 – 1 700	315 – 360	130 – 165
Mountain steppe	1 700 – 1 900	370 – 480	90 – 150
Mid-mountain	1 900 – 2 350	440 – 470	70 – 140
High mountain	2 350 – 2 500	450 – 550	50 – 120

area is well-watered by mountain streams and rivers; water for livestock is not generally a problem in the warmer months, although it may be locally. In winter, stock must be watered by cutting through ice to water, or by eating snow, with a consequent extra energy requirement. Forests are common in the mountain and mountain-and-steppe zones: *Larix, Betula* and aspen in mountain forests; poplar (*Populus*) and willow (*Salix*) in riparian forests. Timber and firewood are readily available in much of the *aimag*. Generally the sward is dominated by grasses, but broad-leaved species, including legumes, are common in areas of favoured moisture status. In the higher grazing areas, Cyperaceae are frequent – the dominant pasture in the high mountains is a *Carex-Kobresia* community.

At present, hay lands are not allocated to herders, so cutting is unregulated and competitive; maintenance or improvement of hay land is therefore impossible. The area of hay land is inadequate for the *aimag's* needs and yields are very low. The growing season is short throughout the project area and scarcity of winter and spring feed is a major constraint to intensification of livestock rearing. Herders are loath to give supplementary feed, except to special classes of stock (milking and pregnant animals; riding horses), because fed animals tend to graze less and come home early to wait for feed.

Now almost all hay is hand-mown from natural stands. Yields are very low, 600–700 kg/ha at 18 percent moisture, and haymaking is slow and laborious, and although yields are very strongly affected by rainfall it is likely that most hay fields are declining in yield and quality since they have been mown yearly over a long period without rest, manure or other fertilizer. The High Mountain Research Station has been working on improvement of hay yields from natural stands for some time (variation in cutting dates, dung and fertilizer application, irrigation, etc.). Traditional water-spreading methods practised in the mountain-and-steppe involve sporadic diversion of spring water in winter to develop ice-sheets over hay land, ice which will subsequently melt at the onset of the growing season.

Grazing on exposed and sheltered hills is reserved for the winter; autumn and spring grazing takes place on the slopes leading to the higher areas and tree covered areas that will be inaccessible in winter because of deeper snow. Haymaking "fields" (and potential sites), often meadows, lie in these areas in sheltered spots along streams and where natural drainage lines favour a concentration of moisture, one of the keys to good grass growth. These areas would

J.M. SUTTIE

Plate 7.11
Meadow grazing – Arkhangai.

be grazed early in spring (Plate 7.11) and then left for haymaking (and later autumn and winter feed), as the livestock (horses, goats, sheep, cattle and yak´ are moved down to lower elevations.

Haymaking has been carried out for a very long time. Historically, each herder is entitled to use certain land where hay has been cut for many years. After privatization, however, every hayfield has become a focus of disputes between individual herders and members within social groups, as well as with people from neighbouring communities. Also, the repeated cutting of the past few decades has led to a serious decline in the natural productivity of hay fields and there is no sign, at present, that herders will invest in their improvement. Natural hay fields have usually been mown for a long time, so stones and obstructions have largely been eliminated. Further study is required on sources of animal-drawn equipment such as mowers and trip-rakes (carts are available), as well as on how to finance their acquisition and organize their management. Ways of raising yields will also have to be investigated if haymaking is to be improved – haymaking costs, other than cartage and stacking, are proportional to the area dealt with rather than the quantity of hay made.

The botanical composition of the hayfields varies, of course, according to site. In the mountain steppe, the main grasses would be *Leymus chinensis, Stipa krylovi, Festuca lenensis* and *Koeleria cristata,* with *Carex duriscula, Artemisia lacenata, A. glauca, A. commutata* and *Plantago adpressi* as the main herbs. In a riparian meadow, the grasses would be *Leymus chinensis, Koeleria cristata* and *Agropyron cristatum,* with *Carex pediformis, Artemisia lacenata, Potentilla tanacetifolium, P. anserina, Galium verum* and *Plantago adpressa.* In a rainfed mountain meadow, the grasses and grass-like species would be *Agropyron cristatum, Poa subfastigata, Festuca* spp. and *Carex pediformis,* and the herbs would be typically *Artemisia lacenata, A. dracunculus, A. glauca, Thalictrum simplex* and *Galium verum.* A mountain meadow on a north-facing slope would have *Bromus inermis, Calamagrostis epidois, Elymus turczanovii, Stipa baicalensis* and *Carex pediformis* as the grasses and grass-like species, with *Artemisia lacenata, Geranium pratense* and *Galium boreale* as the main herbs. The overall proportion of plant types in hay is *Carex* 11–22 percent; grasses 20–37 percent; legumes 6–18 percent; and other herbs (considered to be of poor feeding value) 39–58 percent.

Haymaking trials and demonstrations were established in Ikh Tamir district in 1996. Initial trials focused on different rates of dung and their effects, with 50 t/ha being selected as the rate to be used in trials with ice irrigation and mineral fertilizer. Ice irrigation, dung and mineral fertilizer all increased the number of plants per square metre, the length of vegetative shoots and dry matter yield, but it is unlikely that mineral fertilizer will be an economic proposition under present conditions. Differences were particularly significant in 1996, but less so in the dry year 1997. In 1997, increases ranged from 253 percent with ice irrigation to 407 percent with ice irrigation plus dung, and 707 percent with ice irrigation and fertilizer. The percentage of grass on the treated plots rose while that of sedges fell. Land ownership (all land is currently state owned) and continued access to land are key questions. Although families have traditional grazing rights (but not ownership), any move to invest time and resources to increase soil fertility and haymaking brings with it the need for some security of access to an area of land for a reasonable period of time.

Herders in Arkhangai made 1 340 kg of hay per 100 head in 1995, less than a twelfth of the official norm. Part of this may be due to herders overestimating the weight of their harvest by a factor of three or four. Two families have recently taken up contract haymaking, with animal-drawn equipment, accepting payment in kind or a share of the crop.

Grazing livestock production

Mongolia's livestock are raised at pasture in traditional, extensive grazing; this is the best – and in most cases the only – type of exploitation suited to the grazing lands. Livestock are herded on the open pasture, by mounted stockmen, and return to the camp each night, to be penned or tethered, although camels may be left at pasture. The intensive sector, which was government-run on state farms, has largely broken down since it could not be based on natural pasture and depended on large external inputs of feed. Local cattle are poor milkers and exotic dairy cattle require good, warm housing to survive the long winter; provision of feed for housed dairy stock is expensive and forage for the eight-month winter has to be saved during a three-month growing season. Some small semi-intensive dairying is developing in peri-urban areas and where cropping and grazing land intermingle. Swine and poultry numbers have fallen drastically since decollectivization. Dogs were, previously, licensed but are now breeding rapidly and their numbers are uncontrolled. Gid, "circling disease" as translated locally, of sheep is common, according to herders interviewed in all areas, and is related to the dogs that are intermediate hosts of a tapeworm, probably *Taenia multiceps*, the intermediate stage of which is known as *Coenurus cerebralis*.

The major infectious diseases have been under control for many years through regular vaccination. Recently, veterinary services in the field have been privatized; the state still supplies vaccines, free of cost, for the major diseases, but herders now have to pay their veterinarian to deliver and carrying out the vaccination.

Nowadays livestock are privately owned: over 95 percent were in private hands in December 1998; there were 83 600 herding households with 409 600 herders. The average household herd was 170 head; 71 percent of the total herding families had herds between 51 and 500 head.

Livestock in herding systems

Six species are commonly raised – camels (Bactrian), horses, cattle, yaks, sheep and goats – with their distribution and frequency depending on ecological conditions and pasture type. Although small ruminants are by far the most numerous (Plate 7.12), large stock predominate in terms of livestock units – camels, horses and cattle account for about 69 percent of the total. Some data on liveweight are given in Table 7.9. Currently, the overall livestock population is estimated at over 31 million head; nation-wide statistics from 1918 to 1996 are given in Table 7.10 (yak are not differentiated from cattle and their hybrids, but see Table 7.7). In general, there has been a steady increase in numbers, except for camels, which have declined from a peak of 859 000 in 1960 to 358 000 in 1995. The drop in camel numbers coincided with collectivization, when motor transport became available for moving camp (and probably mechanization of the military) – their lack may be felt by the, now unmotorized, private herders.

The traditional livestock are all, of necessity, well adapted to the harsh climate; they can regain condition and build up fat reserves rapidly during the short growing season. The hump of the camel and the fat rump of the local sheep breeds provide energy reserves to help tide them over winter and spring. Yaks, camels and cashmere goats develop winter down among their coats, which helps reduce heat loss. All can survive outdoors throughout the long, cold winter with little or no shelter nor supplementary feed. The young are generally born in spring and their dams benefit from the fresh grass; generalized breeding seasons are given in Table 7.8. The livestock are generally small. Table 7.9 gives the average liveweight of animals sold to the national abattoir, which is probably a fair indication of the general run of stock; some

Plate 7.12
Sheep and goats being rounded up for milking.

TABLE 7.7
Cattle, yaks and their hybrids ('000s).

	1940	1950	1960	1970	1980	1990	1994
Total cattle and yak	2 634.9	1 950.3	1 905.5	2 107.8	2 397.1	2 848.7	3 005.2
Yak	725.8	561.0	495.6	452.2	554.5	566.9	570.8
Khainag (F_1)	73.6	52.4	69.2	69.1	50.7	70.0	56.3
Yak and khainag as % of total	30.3	31.5	29.7	24.7	25.2	22.4	20.9

NOTE: khainag are yak×cattle crosses.
SOURCE: after Cai Li and Weiner, 1995.

TABLE 7.8
Livestock husbandry patterns.

Species	Mating	Birth	Slaughter
Camels	early Dec. – late Feb.	late Feb. – mid-May	December
Mares	mid-May – late Aug.	mid-Apr. – late July	December
Cows	mid-May – late Sep.	mid-Mar. – late July	December
Yaks	early June – late Sep.	early Apr. – late May	December
Ewes	late Sep. – late Dec.	late Feb. – mid-May	Nov. – Dec.
Does	mid-Sep. – mid-Nov.	mid-Feb. – mid-Mar.	Nov. – Dec.

SOURCE: Telenged, 1996.

TABLE 7.9
Average liveweight (kg) of livestock sold to State Abattoirs.

Species	1950	1960	1970	1980	1985
Cattle	242	248	243	217	259
Sheep	37	36	36	33	41
Goats	28	28	28	26	32

ALICE CARLONI

TABLE 7.10
Evolution of stock numbers, 1918–2003 ('000 head).

Year	Camels	Horses	Cattle[(1)]	Sheep	Goats
1918	228.7	1 150.5	1 078.7	5 700.0	1 487.9
1924	275.0	1 389.8	1 512.1	8 444.8	2 204.4
1930	480.9	1 566.9	1 887.3	15 660.3	4 080.8
1940	643.4	2 538.1	2 722.8	15 384.2	5 096.3
1950	844.2	2 317.0	1 987.8	12 574.6	4 978.6
1961	751.7	2 289.3	1 637.4	10 981.9	4 732.6
1970	633.5	2 317.9	2 107.8	13 311.7	4 204.0
1980	591.5	1 985.4	2 397.1	14 230.7	4 566.7
1985	559.0	1 971.0	2 408.1	13 248.8	4 298.6
1992	415.2	2 200.2	2 840.0	14 657.0	5 602.5
1996	357.9	2 270.5	3 476.3	13 560.6	9 134.8
2000	322.9	2 660.7	3 976.0	13 876.4	10 269.8
2003	275.0	2 200.0	2 053.7	11 797.0	8 858.0

NOTE: (1) cattle includes yaks and their hybrids.
SOURCE: Ministry of Agriculture and Food; Data for 2003 from FAOSTAT.

ALICE CARLONI

Plate 7.13
Camels being watered in the Gobi.

authors claim heavier weights, which are, no doubt, possible with selected or better managed flocks.

Bactrian camels are important in the Gobi and other dry regions and are used in many other areas to pull carts or carry baggage; they are the only class of pastoral livestock whose numbers are falling – the decline has been steady from 860 000 at collectivization in 1960 (when motor transport for camp moves became available) to 360 000 today; there is anecdotal evidence to suggest that the fall has ceased and numbers may be beginning to rise. Camels are used for milk and meat as well as transport; camel-hair is a minor but high-priced product. Three breeds are recognized, all from the Gobi, but for moving herders' camps, camels are important in most of the country. Camel as subsistence herds and camel breeding is mainly found in the desert and semi-desert zones. (Plate 7.13).

Horses of the local breed are small but hardy; they are extremely important as part of the herders' essential equipment, as well as for sport, meat and milk – fermented mares' milk (*airag*) is a favourite, and highly saleable, beverage, although not all areas milk mares – in parts of Western Mongolia, such as Uvs, they are not milked. Only rough estimates of milk yields are available but it is an important revenue source in steppe and mountain steppe zones in places where there are market opportunities; herds of dairy mares are often brought to roadsides in the season. Mares are milked from mid-July through September, sometimes into October, every two to two-and-a-half hours during daylight – about six times daily. Yields are two to two-and-a-half litres – about 150 litres per lactation. In 2001, fermented mares' milk was selling at 400 tugriks[2] per litre at the roadside, about 40 US cents. Horse-racing is popular and herders' selection is for speed.

The small local breed of cattle is the basis of the pastoral beef industry; in many areas signs of admixture with exotic blood (Alatau, Simmental and, most obviously, White-faced Kazakh) are obvious, but pure Mongolian prevails in harder areas. They are very hardy, but poor milkers, and most dairy products are reserved for home consumption. Cows are dried off as the feed supply diminishes in late autumn and those that do not get in calf may be disposed of. At the colder limit of the range, cattle×yak hybrids (*khainag*) are also used.

Yaks and their hybrid with cattle, the *khainag,* are kept in the higher areas (Plate 7.14). There are no named breeds, and polled animals are common and are preferred by herdsmen. The proportion of yak and *khainag* in the national cattle herd fell (see Table 7.7) from one-third to one-fifth between 1950 and 1994. There is some anecdotal evidence that the proportion of yak is increasing again in their main areas.

Sheep unlike the other species, have several local breeds, adapted to different ecological zones. These have been described in detail in an article in *World Animal Review* (Batsukh and Zagdsuren, 1990). Sheep numbers have been declining slowly since 1990. In 1996 there were reportedly 13 560 600 sheep, which was 90 percent of the 1990 figure. Mongolian sheep produce mainly carpet wool and average annual production from adult sheep is 2.0 to 2.4 kg of greasy wool.

Mongolian goats are renowned for the quality of their cashmere; their number has increased rapidly in recent years, more than doubling since 1988. This is partly due to the ease of commercialization of a product with a high price-to-weight ratio since the old meat marketing organization broke down; traders now purchase cashmere direct from herders. Goats were traditionally kept in drier areas with plentiful browse – now they are increasing in many

J.M. SUTTIE

Plate 7.14
Polled yak in autumn – Arkhangai.

areas where previously they were a minor herd component. Production of raw combed product varies from 250 g (female) to 340 g (male castrates) per head. Twinning is commoner in goats than in local sheep, and weaning rates of 100 percent or more are claimed.

Most of the dairy products of the herding sector are consumed at home. Cows and mares are the main milk sources, but ewes are milked for a few weeks after weaning in some areas. Lactations are short and all cattle are usually dried off by December, when feed has become scarce, to avoid strain on the developing calf. Much of the milk in the short season is processed domestically to conserve it for later use. A wide range of traditional dairy products are made, but clotted cream and dried curd are the main ones. Fermented mares' milk, *airag*, is a favourite and saleable beverage; it is also distilled to produce an alcoholic drink, *rakhi*, and the residues of the distillation may be added to curd.

Evolution of stock numbers
The numbers of the five species between 1918 and 1996 were shown in Table 7.10. Since grazing pressure depends on species as well as overall numbers, these figures have been transformed into stock units (on the basis of the traditional *bod*) in Plate 7.3. The transformation is crude and does not take account of the different stages of maturity of animals within the herd, but serves for rough comparisons. Present stock numbers are high, but those of 1996, in terms of livestock units, are little higher, by about 6 percent, than those of 1950 immediately prior to the development of collective management. Historically, there was a very rapid rise between 1918, a time of troubles, and 1930, when the national herd reached levels approaching those of modern times.

TABLE 7.11
Evolution of the national herd in terms of composition by species and overall size in terms of stock units ('000s).

Year	Camels %	Horses %	Cattle %	Sheep %	Goats %	Total SU[1]
1918	9.7	32.5	30.5	23.0	4.2	3 535.3
1924	8.7	29.3	31.9	25.5	4.7	4 741.2
1930	10.6	23.0	27.7	32.8	6.0	6 820.8
1940	9.6	25.3	27.2	30.7	7.2	10 029.0
1950	10.8	28.4	30.5	24.6	5.7	8 933.4
1961	16.1	29.5	25.3	22.8	6.3	7 865.3
1970	15.9	32.2	23.1	22.1	6.7	7 096.4
1980	12.3	30.1	27.4	24.7	5.5	7 698.0
1985	11.1	26.1	31.9	25.1	5.7	7 540.2
1992	7.5	26.5	34.1	25.2	6.7	8 317.1
1996	5.9	24.9	38.6	21.2	10.0	9 134.4
2000	4.8	26.3	39.2	19.6	10.1	10 130.3
2003	5.7	30.4	28.4	23.3	12.2	7 372.7

NOTE: (1) Stock units converted as *"bod"* values, derived from Table 7.10.

From 1961 until the early 1990s, the overall number of livestock units remained relatively stable, reflecting the organized management and marketing arrangements of the period. Since economic liberalization there has been increase in both stock numbers and livestock units, although numbers are rising most rapidly because of the great increase in the goat flock. The greatest increase is in cattle, by about a million, or 12 percent of all livestock units. Small ruminants account for about 30 percent of the total. Between 1950 and 1996, in terms of livestock units, the sheep and goat population was in a very narrow range of between 28.8 and 31.9 million head; large ruminants and horses, therefore, account for by far the greater part of the grazing pressure.

Mongolia's pastures have, therefore, already carried livestock populations equivalent to modern ones (Table 7.11); how they were distributed in space in the early years is not known. The number of livestock per head of population, however, has been declining steadily since records began, from 34 head (11.6 units) in 1950 to 23.6 (8.1) in 1961, to 16.1 (5.6) in 1970, to 13.4 (4.5) in 1980 and to 12 (3.8) in 1996; the human population, in a largely livestock-based economy, now has only one third of the livestock per capita that it had in 1950.

The changes in overall stocking over time is shown graphically in Figure 7.3.

Herd composition, of course, reflects ecological conditions and the type of terrain. In Table 7.12 two aimags are compared. One, Tuv, is typical steppe; the other, Uvs, is semi-desert and mountainous. The aimags differ considerably in herd composition. Uvs, being arid, has far more camels than Tuv. The difference in horse numbers is striking, Tuv having double the Uvs percentage; Tarialan, at 10 percent, has a very low horse component. The arid sums have far higher proportions of small ruminants.

Figure 7.3
Evolution of stock units over time.

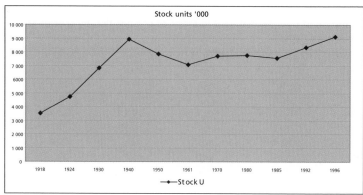

TABLE 7.12
Proportion of species in two aimags.

	Camels %	Horses %	Cattle %	Sheep %	Goats %
Uvs aimag	6.4	17.4	24.6	33.3	18.2
Turgen sum	5.7	14.7	25.6	35.4	18.6
Tarialan sum	6.1	10.4	25.0	37.2	21.2
Tuv aimag	0.8	35.9	26.5	26.4	10.4
Zaamar sum	0.0	31.1	34.0	22.2	12.7
Lun sum	0.6	31.6	29.4	27.3	11.0

SOURCE: Final report (September 2002) of the consultant on haymaking, pasture planning and fodder reserves, prepared for FAO TCP project TCP/MON/0066 – Pastoral risk management strategy.

Plate 7.15
Winter shelter.

Intensive livestock production

Localized intensive livestock production grew up with the collective movement; both state farms and some *negdels* were involved. The main enterprises were dairying, using exotic stock in "mechanized dairies", and pig and poultry rearing. All were aimed at supplying the urban market. An Artificial Insemination Service supported the dairy industry. Keeping exotic dairy stock in such a climate was always difficult and expensive, since they have to be warmly housed in winter, and producing or procuring high-quality feed to suffice for the eight- to nine-month period when there is no fresh grass was expensive in cultivated fodder and concentrates, which often had to be imported. Likewise pig and poultry farms were largely dependent on imported stock and feed. Since Economic Liberalization, most of the "mechanized dairies" and piggeries have collapsed, and there is a serious scarcity of dairy products in urban areas. Some small-scale, semi-intensive dairying is developing in peri-urban areas and where cropping and grazing land intermingle, but its progress is slow and economic viability still unclear.

Grazing management

Although the first land law was enacted in 1933, the introduction of collective production in the 1950s was the first major change from customary practice. A new law in 1971 introduced a classification of land according to its use, and the responsibilities, the obligations and rights of economic organizations and the administration were defined, and land tenure arrangements introduced. The pasture law of 2002 takes account of the changed political situation and deals with factors such as: individual ownership (by herders, economic entities and organizations) and group owners (*bag*) of natural pasture and areas for winter and spring camps; rules for use of grazing in emergencies; stock-raising in settled areas; rules for contracting grazing to rights-holders; setting up of inter-*aimag* and inter-*sum otor* [using distant pasture for fattening] areas; and granting of haymaking rights to individuals and groups of herders. There are three major periods of otor: (i) spring otor for grazing young grass; (ii) summer otor for developing enough muscle and internal fat; and (iii) autumn otor for consolidating fatness. There can also be emergency movement of large stock to grazing reserves in a hard winter. Customary grazing rights, however, remain powerful, and are a major factor when considering land issues.

Transhumance

The regular movement of herds between summer and winter pastures is a widespread practice in pastoral areas of Europe and Asia. The classic cycle is from low ground in winter to mountain pastures in summer, often associated with alpine herbage that is snow-covered in winter. Transhumant grazing systems in Temperate Asia are dealt with in detail by Suttie and Reynolds (2003). The pattern of transhumance in the Mongolian steppe is not usually of this classic kind; most of the precipitation is in the warmer months, wind-chill is a very serious winter hazard, and livestock are not housed in winter. Winter and spring camps, which are the key to transhumance, are chosen for availability of some shelter and access to forage and water. In the steppe, winter camps may be sited in valleys of suitable hills and in some areas riparian forests provide shelter. There are suggestions that in feudal times much of the transhumance in the non-desert parts of Mongolia was longer, and of the plains to mountains and down again type; these movements would generally have been north-south; the present aimags tend to run east-west and their alignment may have been partially intended to change the traditional migration pattern.

Movements may be more vertical in mountain areas, with winter camps generally at the hill-foot; mountain transhumance is usually over shorter hori-zontal distances than that of the steppe. Access to summer and autumn pasture is less contested than for winter camps and, within a *sum* or similar sub-unit, may be almost communally used. Grazing circuits cannot be firmly fixed under conditions of great variation in feed availability, which have many weather-related causes; transhumance must be flexible and highly mobile so that herds can be taken to where feed is available, which may be much further in some years than others – this presupposes a degree of cooperation between grazi-ers' groups insofar as one group will allow another group emergency grazing should weather events make it necessary.

Feed and shelter are not the only considerations governing movement; in some of the mountainous, western aimags, including Uvs, severe plagues of biting insects force the population and their stock to seek high altitudes for the hotter part of summer. Topography may determine migration routes; in high hills, stock movements may be obliged to use passes and this can influence itineraries and grazing systems; passes may only be open for limited seasons and this again affects timing of movements. Detailed studies on systems in Uvs and Khuvsgul are reported by Erdenebaatar (2003).

Risk in herding

Herding in Mongolia is a risky undertaking and much of the herders' work and planning involves avoiding or minimizing risks. The term *zud* describes serious weather events associated with snow and cold; the major risks can be classified as *zud*, drought, disease and others. Serious weather events, as defined for forecasting purposes, include: snowstorm: wind speed ≥12 m/s and visibility <2 000 m, with duration >3 hours; hail: ≥10 mm diameter, with no duration limit; ice cover on pastures: transformation of snow to ice by warming followed by sudden cold, lasting a week or longer. Risk in herding is discussed in detail by Baas, Erdenbaatar and Swift (2001). *Zud* and drought are traditional and effective controllers of stock numbers. From the point of view of pasture condition, a white *zud* has a double effect – it provides moisture for spring regrowth while reducing stock numbers. *Zud* takes several forms:

J.M. SUTTIE

Plate 7.16
Small stock grazing through snow – Tuv.

- Black *zud* occurs when, in winter, there is a prolonged lack of snow and continued want of water because of freezing of surface sources, so both stock and herders suffer from lack of water to drink. This type of *zud* does not occur every year, nor does it usually affect large areas. Wells provide water in black *zud* conditions, but often a long trek would be necessary and, at the wells, shelter and bedding would not be available in the camping area.
- White *zud* is caused by deep and prolonged snow cover (Plate 7.16). It is a frequent and serious disaster that has caused a great number of deaths. Opinion on how deep snow has to be to constitute *zud* varies: over 7 cm causes difficulties in Khangai yak pastures, while up to 10 cm leaves fodder accessible to small stock in the forest-steppe and steppe; in the steppe of less mountainous provinces, 6 cm is considered a *zud*. White *zud* is, of course, more serious if it follows a dry summer and herbage is short.
- Storm *zud* is caused by continuous snowfall and drifting over large areas. If it occurs at the coldest time of year it is very dangerous; animals may run many kilometres before the wind and most mortality is through exhaustion or falling into rivers.
- *Khuiten zud* is caused by extreme cold or freezing winds; when winter temperatures are 10°C below seasonal averages, stock can no longer graze freely, and expend much energy in maintaining body heat. It usually occurs when night temperatures drop sharply for two or more consecutive nights. Serious losses occur when *khuiten zud* follows white or storm *zud*.

Drought, from the herders' viewpoint, is a lack of rain during the warmer part of the year. Drought in late spring and early summer is the most serious since, at that season, the pasture recommences growth and the animals are in

TABLE 7.13
Stock ownership during the collective period (percentage distrbution on a per head basis).

Species	State farm %	Cooperatives %	Private %
Camels	1.7	84.5	13.8
Horses	2.4	54.8	40.8
Cattle[1]	2.2	46.0	43.6
Sheep	2.0	80.2	17.8
Goats	0.8	74.9	24.3

NOTES: (1) Cattle includes yaks and their hybrids.
SOURCE: Ministry of Agriculture and Food.

greatest need of good forage to rebuild body condition and provide milk for their young. Drought over a wide area leads to concentration of livestock around water-points and areas of better grazing and thus causes damage to the vegetation. In higher, cooler, sites, late summer rain has little effect on pasture growth since temperatures have already fallen too low.

Uncontrolled fire can be serious; it rarely originates from, or near, *gers* or winter shelters since great care is taken in such flammable surroundings. In the mountain regions, unprotected fires of hunters and gatherers of wild fruit are a common cause. While accidental fire destroys standing forage and causes scarcity and wastes much labour in control (to protect *gers* and property as well as grazing), controlled burning may be used to remove unpalatable old material and encourage a young flush. Predation, mainly from wolves, is an increasing risk now that the premium for wolf-killing has been removed. Protection of snow leopards in the Gobi Altai raises the problem of how to recompense herders for stock taken by these rare and protected beasts. Stock theft is a very rare risk, although there have been reports recently of trans-border rustling in northern frontier regions.

Grazing management on negdels

The grazing management of the collective period was based on limited mobility within the bounds of the *negdel,* and while brigades usually handled monospecific herds, they might overlap in space to provide multispecies grazing of the same pasture for greater efficiency; further mixed grazing pressure was provided by the private stock of the families. The areas and seasons of grazing were specified by management, giving a broader coverage than at present and avoiding undue concentration of stock. Organized marketing avoided both the build up of excess stock and the congregation of camps close to roads and centres. Details of stock ownership in the collective period are given in Table 7.13.

THE PRESENT GRAZING SITUATION

Change to private ownership shifted the responsibility for risk avoidance and economic management abruptly from state to household. Herders very rapidly reverted to traditional mobile transhumance in small family groups. Ex-salaried staff took to herding with stock allocated to them from *negdel* break-up, but not all succeeded: 100-150 head is considered to be the threshold herd size for a reasonable living; 50 is the poverty line. In 1995, over 40 percent of households had under 50 head, 45 percent had over 100, and only 15 percent owned over 200 animals. Controlled grazing has gone – in some areas pasture use is anarchic, with immigrant herders trespassing on the traditional lands of others. At neighbourhood and community levels, other customary institutions have re-emerged. Groups provide an approach to regulating access to grazing. They are often kinship-based and related to a natural grazing management unit, such as a valley, or, in dry areas, a water source. Hay and fodder are now negligible – overwintering survival depends on autumn condition and herding skills.

Extensive herding, of course, continues, but the controlled grazing of the collective period has gone. The transition has, however, given women a far greater role in decision-making since under the collective all the governmental bodies were overwhelmingly male although many veterinarians are women; women now take an active role in management and especially marketing.

Water is a determining factor in pasture use, especially in the steppe and Gobi regions (the mountain-steppe often has plentiful surface water); some areas can only be grazed in winter when snow is available as a water source; elsewhere wells supply, or used to provide, water; in the Gobi, herders' movements are governed by watering places. Breakdown of most of the deep "mechanical" water points has rendered many areas inaccessible, especially in the eastern steppe, where gazelle numbers are increasing as they colonize the deserted grazing.

Much pasture is not used or is under-used. According to studies by FAO project TCP/MON/0066, as much as one-third of the total may be under-used. These pastures include areas along the borders, where there are problems of stock theft; in the eastern part, infrastructure is poorly developed and social problems of herders have not been solved; and in parts of western Mongolia there is not enough water and other living materials. In 1990–1997, about 600 new wells were sunk, but 12 800 remained out of operation; 10 700 000 ha of pasture can not be used because of lack of water. Most unused land is far from administrative centres and many herders are increasingly loath to travel so far, especially when infrastructure is deficient. In western Mongolia, where there is shortage of pasture, there are large areas that could be used as joint pasture between aimags, yet they are not fully used.

All herding families now keep multispecies herds, i.e. have at least three kinds of livestock that each comprise over 15 percent of the herd; subsidiary species are those forming under 10 percent, such as camels in many areas and yak in the foothills of the mountain-and-steppe zone. Multispecies herds have many advantages, but increase the labour needed for herding. The different species vary in their grazing habits and preferences, so therefore a mixture makes better use of the overall forage available. Yak and horses, for example, can go further into the mountains than other stock; goats and camels make better use of browse. There is a complementarity of species in winter grazing: large stock, especially horses, are used to open trails in heavy snow cover to facilitate grazing by sheep and cattle. A mixed herd spreads risk much more than a monospecific one. Part of the necessity of mixed herds is, of course, the herders' needs for a range of products, including transport and traction.

At pasture, the species (and at some seasons the sexes may be kept apart) are, of course, grazed in separate flocks. Breeding males may be herded out of season in a communal flock. The degree of attention varies with species. Small ruminants are usually closely supervised and brought back to the camp overnight as they are more prone to attacks by predators. Cattle may be left to graze, except those being milked. Horses often graze unsupervised. Camels are usually left to their own devices except when used for transport.

The herders' year is divided according to the seasons. The winter and spring camps and grazing are the key to their overall system; each must provide shelter as well as accessible forage through that difficult season. Rights to winter grazing are jealously guarded and are frequently subject to dispute; finding winter grazing is a major problem for many "new" herding families. In contrast to many transhumance systems elsewhere, herders often go to the hills in winter to find shelter from the cold winds that sweep the steppe; the hills frequently have less snow and more accessible forage than the plains. Some areas are used in winter because water scarcity precludes their use when there is no snow. Spring grazing is also critical, since it is there that most of the young are born, at a season when feed is very scarce. Summer and autumn pasture is usually grazed in common, with few problems of access or dispute.

Taking livestock to more distant fattening pastures – *otor* – is an important part of well organized herding and, if done with skill, can greatly improve the condition of stock before the long winter. Going on *otor*, of course, requires effort and labour, and camping away from the main group, and may reduce surveillance of winter camp sites, but it is a key to better herd survival. Many herders now undertake much shorter transhumance circuits than previously. They also produce far less hay. Herders' objectives in supplementary feeding are: to minimize loss of condition, ensuring better yield in the coming year and enable early mating, mainly for cows and camels; to improve disease resistance and lessen the incidence of abortion in small stock and mares; to support suckling females and their young; and to maintain working stock. The herders contend that supplements to weak stock, once begun, must not be withdrawn before both weather and pasture conditions are suitable for the stock to forage for themselves.

Winter and spring shelters were a very useful innovation of the *negdel*; they are generally simple wooden structures sited in a sheltered spot and often south-facing; they provide valuable protection to stock. With privatization, no rights to shelters have been assigned to herders, so they are often now dilapidated, although little other than labour input is required to make them useable. Mobility is an essential part of the system; previously *ger*-moving was facilitated by the provision of motor transport; now herders often have no access to or funds for lorries, and their movements are restricted. Carts and camels are returning as a means of moving, but their number is insufficient; wheels and axles are scarce outside the forest zone and using them to move requires much more labour and time than did a motorized move.

With state subsidies for inputs removed and services reduced or absent, herders have reverted to traditional risk-management (in what has always been a risky environment), including keeping multispecies herds and cooperating with other households in herding tasks to help cope with the greater labour needs of diversified herds. The basis of this collaboration is the *khot ail*, a traditional level of household collaboration, camping and working in a group, which existed before collectivization, especially for summer and autumn grazing. The *sur* of the *negdels* partly copied this, but avoided the kinship basis that is common in the *khot ail*. These units are often, but not necessarily, based on family ties, but associations between households with common interests are as important. The size of the *khot ail* varies with season and ecological zone: in the Gobi the *khot ail* often consists of a single household; in better watered areas up to five households may group together.

At neighbourhood and community levels, other customary institutions have re-emerged. At neighbourhood level, groups provide an approach to regulating access to grazing. They are often kinship-based and related to a natural grazing management unit, such as a valley, or, in dry areas, a water source. They exist within the limits of a wider traditional unit, the *bag*, a customary institution that was responsible for pasture allocation and dispute settlement in the pre-collective era. Present *bag* boundaries are generally based on those of the brigades. A further type of cooperation is appearing, in that many herders now store their winter gear that is not required on migration; since winter camps are not secure, the storage is often with people settled at the sum centre; payment may be in kind or by other services.

The socio-economic changes have had a marked effect on access to basic foodstuffs and the dietary pattern of the herders. FAO (1996) stated:

> *"Herders are self-sufficient in meat and milk products and consumption of those products increased by 30 percent and 50 percent, respectively, between 1990 and 1992. In the same period the consumption of other food decreased, e.g. by 40 percent for flour and by more than 80 percent for various food grains. This was a result of the worsening of rural trading services, as herders could only get commodity goods in sum centres, instead of from brigade centres and travelling agents as previously."*

Reforms have changed a highly organized grazing system into one where privately-owned livestock graze public land; this is often a certain recipe for pasture abuse. Although ownership of land is often a prerequisite for its good management, this is not the case for extensive grazing land in Mongolia (for arable, intensive livestock, residential and mining land the situation is different); some form of group registration of grazing rights is considered adequate and more desirable. The reasons quoted by Mearns and Swift (1996) and the Policy Alternatives for Livestock Development (PALD) team (Mearns, 1993), are:

"There are strong arguments in favour of increasing security of tenure over pasture land in Mongolia's extensive livestock sector in order to promote sustainable land management and reduce conflicts over pasture. It is more likely that individualized, private ownership of pasture land, under Mongolian conditions, would actually increase conflict and jeopardise environmental stability, particularly given the lack of administrative capacity to enforce such rights.

"While ownership often increases investment and creates a demand for and a supply of credit, since the land would be managed as a capital good in which investments must be made to promote sustainability and prevent land degradation. This assumption does not hold for most pasture land in Mongolia's extensive livestock sector in which few if any external inputs are required to maintain productivity. Sustainable pasture management in such an environment depends primarily on mobility and flexibility rather on capital investment. There are certain exceptions: investment may be made in winter/spring camps and shelters and in wells and other water resources and there may be a demand for credit to overcome transport constraints in seeking to maintain mobility. But it is not clear in the Mongolian case that lack of secure title is the principle obstacle to supply of such credit, nor that it could not be satisfied by means of certified possession rights at the level of a group such as the khot ail, which is the appropriate level at which most such investments are likely to be made.

"In addition there are strong ecological reasons why the development of a market in pasture land would be undesirable. Sustainable land use under an extensive grazing system requires mobility of livestock between pastures suitable for use in each season. Such seasonal pastures must be shared between neighbouring households since their patterns of movement overlap and vary between years according to forage availability. The spatial arrangement of Mongolian landscapes vary considerably between ecological zones; larger areas are required to encompass land suitable for all seasons in desert-steppe zones, while smaller areas are required in the steppe and mountain-forest-steppe zones. In most cases the risk of drought and/or zud, among other natural hazards, requires that herders have access to traditional areas of pasture for emergency use. Taken together these factors account for the indivisibility of pasture land in Mongolia below a certain spatial scale varying by ecological zone. On no account should transfers of land be permitted that would fragment in any way these minimum sustainable pasture resource areas."

Herders can obtain title to their winter camp-sites, but not to the winter grazing land. Winter migration from drier areas (Plate 7.17) to better watered sums is a serious problem. The incomers can graze all winter, by right, putting great pressure on already heavily used winter pasture. They then graze the early spring growth before returning to their home areas (Plate 7.18).

Improving pasture management and production
The constraints to sustainable grazing management in Mongolia have been discussed above. The harsh climatic conditions are not a constraint; they are the reason for the extensive, mobile, animal production, based exclusively

Plate 7.17
Desert steppe near Khyargas Lake – Uvs.

Plate 7.18
Baggage camel beside marshland pasture by Uvs Lake.

on natural pasture, that has proved sustainable over many centuries. Many constraints are organizational rather than technical, and have their roots either in the present economic situation of the region or changes in governmental policy during the twentieth century. The main organizational constraint is the lack of recognition, or title to, grazing rights, especially for winter camps and hayfields; legislation to deal with this is under consideration. Lack of regulation of grazing is becoming serious locally, with the abandonment of some areas and overuse of others; a revitalized monitoring system is needed to provide a factual basis for advice and control on the use and maintenance of grazing land. Herders are not organized above the family group, *khot ail*, level, which is too small for decision-making over the very large areas of land needed for management under extensive herding.

Guidelines on grazing management are a necessary adjunct to any advice and control of use; these must be developed with herder participation, after organization of the herding community. National guidelines may be necessary as a framework, but it will be necessary to develop a series of others that take into account the ecological conditions, situation, topography and production systems of individual areas: it is at that level that very close consultation with the users will be necessary. While rising stock numbers are a cause for concern, they were up to near present-day levels during the 1950s; the rapid rise in the human population and the increase in the number of herding families, however, is likely to make control of grazing pressure even more difficult.

Herders have been affected by a reduction in the levels of services available and have not yet come to terms with having to help themselves, where previously decisions were taken and services provided centrally. Lack of availability of selected breeding stock is noticeable, although that may change if markets and profitability improve. Lack of marketing infrastructure affects access to outside purchasers as well as both offtake and the quality of products on sale. Similarly, lack of access to consumer goods and supplies reduces the incentive to sell, and may lead to accumulation of non-breeding stock. The closure of the State Emergency Fodder Fund has thrown herders back on their own resources for supplementary fodder supply. Research, training and technical support services now operate on very reduced budgets.

Opportunities for improving grazing management and herbage condition while maintaining and increasing output are many. Mongolia's grazing lands are well suited to extensive livestock raising and are generally in good condition. Herding has always been the main national occupation, and the people are highly skilled and motivated. They also have the support of a solid body of technical expertise and knowledge. Once legal problems associated with grazing rights have been resolved, coupled with the organization of the herding population, the industry should be able to manage its resources properly while improving the livelihood of the rural population.

Many of the actions to remove or palliate these constraints require administrative decisions or actions: definition and granting of grazing rights, probably emphasizing winter camps and hay lands in the first instance; a structure for the organization of the herding population so that they can participate in the regulation of local land use as well as pasture management, development and maintenance, all of which must have functional user participation; monitoring of pasture condition and regulation of its use, which will also require the participation of herders' associations, as will the establishment of guidelines (down to local level) on the use of grazing land. Research and training must be maintained and, at herder level, expanded. Rehabilitation of water supplies and revitalization of haymaking are two very obvious activities for better pasture use and stock survival; these can now only be tackled by the herding communities, once organized. Haymaking by individual households needs access to simple implements, security and training. Water development must await both granting of grazing rights and organization of the users before it has a realistic chance of success.

Some large tracts of unused pasture were previously reserve *otor* areas for emergencies and could have been useful in recent *zuds*; however, to be useful, they require rehabilitation of the water supply and other basic infrastructure, and, when in use, the herders would need access to some sources of supplies and facilities.

THE RECENT DROUGHTS AND *ZUDS*

Stock numbers have risen sharply since decollectivization. A series of consecutive dry summers and the disastrously severe winters of 1999–2000 and 2000–2001 have shown up this lack of preparedness of herders for severe weather. Over 2 million head of stock were lost in each year (see Table 7.14) and much human poverty and misery has ensued.

Two consecutive years, 1999–2000 and 2000–2001 have had the harsh combination of drought followed by *zud*: stock suffering on thin pastures in the growing season and being unable to feed because of hardened snow in winter. This is, of course, a regular risk in herding under such climatic conditions. The greatest disaster was 1944–1945, when 8 million adult stock were lost. Eight *zud* winters have been recorded since then, the worst pre-2000 being in 1967. These *zuds* are defined by stock losses, not meteorological data; for much of the time when *zud* has been recorded there was a well organized system of grazing management, shelters were maintained and winter feed conserved – emergency

TABLE 7.14
Livestock losses through drought and *zud* (head).

Year	Type of disaster	Losses of adult stock	Losses of young stock
1944–45	Drought + *zud*	8 100 000	1 100 000
1954–55	*Zud*	1 900 000	300 000
1956–57	*Zud*	1 500 000	900 000
1967–68	Drought + *zud*	2 700 000	1 700 000
1976–77	*Zud*	2 000 000	1 600 000
1986–87	*Zud*	800 000	900 000
1993–94	*Zud*	1 600 000	1 200 000
1996–97	*Zud*	600 000	500 000
1999–00	Drought + *zud*	3 000 000	1 200 000
2000–01	Drought + *zud*	3 400 000	n. a.

NOTE: n.a. = data not available.

systems were probably better equipped as well. It is not clear, therefore, to what extent the recent losses are a reflection of severe weather events and how much is due to lack of preparedness by herders and authorities. Stock numbers have risen very steeply since 1990, and this may have been a contributing factor to the severe losses.

Relief, once *zud* has struck and local reserves are inadequate, is not only costly, it is often ineffective, since the time taken to procure, mobilize and deliver feed is such that the relief fodder arrives once many stock have died and often spring has come and the grass is greening up. This was strikingly demonstrated in 2001. The quality of fodder used in relief work is another problem: local hay is of low feeding value and the economics of transporting such a poor feed over long distances is dubious. Unfortunately, since Mongolia produces little in the way of crops, cereals, which would be a far better emergency fodder and cheaper to transport, are not available.

Following the 1993 *zud*, "restocking" of herders was undertaken on a fairly large scale in the hope that it would be an effective means of poverty alleviation, notably with IFAD financing in Arkhangai. Restocking is the redistribution of stock to herding families that have herds below the economic minimum. The recent *zuds*, however, have indicated that such restocking on its own is not really sustainable – restocked herders are just as prone to losses during *zud* as they were before. Unless the other faults are dealt with – preparedness of herders, maintenance of shelters, reconstitution of emergency services and resolution of the grazing rights problem – restocking is likely to be expensive and of transient benefit.

SUSTAINABILITY

Herding has been almost the sole land use of Mongolia for millennia and its pastures, although hard grazed, are still in reasonably good order. Extensive, mobile grazing systems are therefore sustainable and will continue to be the main economic activity of the country. During the collective period, Mongolia maintained a modified system of mobile grazing, using hardy local breeds of livestock and without external sources of feed; its pastures have remained in good order in contrast to most of the neighbouring countries that collectivized their livestock industry.

Most of the neighbouring countries (Kyrgyzstan, Buryatya, parts of Northern China) that collectivized livestock modified their grazing systems, often restricting movement or sedentarizing the herders. In some cases, exotic stock was introduced and imported feed brought in, permitting better overwintering but also leading to severe overstocking. Pasture condition in these countries is much worse than in Mongolia; for example, the degradation of pasture in the Ningxia Autonomous Region of China is described by Ho (1996). In the case of Kyrgyzstan, the sheep industry, based on exotic fine-wool breeds and imported feed, collapsed after decollectivization, with stock numbers falling from 9 500 000 in 1990 to 3 200 000 in 1999 (van Veen, 1995; Fitzherbert, 2000), as the exotic sheep could not survive without large, uneconomic inputs.

REFERENCES

Baas, S., Erdenbaatar, B. & Swift, J.J. 2001. Pastoral risk management for disaster prevention and preparedness in Central Asia – with special reference to Mongolia. *In: Report of the Asia-Pacific conference on early warning, prevention, preparedness and management of disasters in food and agriculture.* Chiangmai, Thailand, 12–15 June 2001. FAO RAP Publication No. 2001:4. Doc. no. APDC/01/REP.

Batsukh, B. & Zagdsuren, E. 1990. Sheep Breeds of Mongolia. *FAO World Animal Review.*

Cai Li & Weiner, J. 1995. *The Yak.* FAO RAP, Bangkok, Thailand.

Erdenebaatar, B. 1996. Socio-economic aspects of the pastoral movement pattern of Mongolian herders. pp. 59–110, *in:* Humphrey and Sneath, 1996b, q.v.

Erdenebaatar, B. 2003. Studies on long distance transhumant grazing systems in Uvs and Khuvsgul aimags of Mongolia, 1999–2000. pp. 31–68, *in:* Suttie and Reynolds, 2003, q.v.

FAO. 1996. *Trends in pastoral development in Central Asia.* Rome, Italy.

FAO/UNESCO. 1978. *Soil Map of the World.* Vol. III: *North and Central Asia.* Paris, France: UNESCO.

Fitzherbert, A.R. 2000. Pastoral resource profile for Kyrgyzstan. *Available at:* http://www.fao.org /waicent/faoinfo/agricult/AGP/AGPC/doc/Counprof/kyrgi. htm

Ho, P. 1996. Ownership and control in Chinese rangeland management: the case of free riding in Ningxia. *ODI Pastoral Network Paper,* No. 39c.

Humphrey, C. & Sneath, D. 1996a. Pastoralism and institutional change in Inner Asia: comparative perspectives from the MECCIA research project. *ODI Pastoral Network Paper,* No. 39b.

Humphrey C. & Sneath, D. (eds). 1996b. *Culture and environment in inner Asia: I. Pastoral economy and the environment.* Cambridge, UK: White Horse Press.

Kharin, N., Takahashi, R. & Harahshesh, H. 1999. Degradation of the drylands of Central Asia. Center for Remote Sensing (CEReS), Chiba University, Japan.

Latham, R.E. (translator). 1958. *The Travels of Marco Polo.* Harmondsworth, UK: Penguin.

Mearns, R. 1993. Pastoral Institutions, Land Tenure and Land Policy Reform in Post-Socialist Mongolia. PALD Research Report, No. 3. University of Sussex, UK.

Mearns, R. & Swift, J. 1996. Pasture and land management in the retreat from a centrally planned economy in Mongolia. pp. 96–98, *in:* N. West (ed) *Rangelands for a Sustainable Biosphere. Proceedings of the 5th International Rangeland Conference,* 1995. Denver, Colorado, USA: Society for Range Management.

Przevalsky, N.M. 1883. *The third expedition in Central Asia.* Sankt-Petersburg. Quoted by Kharin, Takahashi and Harahesh, 1999: 56.

Suttie, J.M. & Reynolds, S.G. (eds). 2003. *Transhumant grazing systems in Temperate Asia. FAO Plant Production and Protection Series,* No. 31.

Telenged, B. 1996. Livestock breeding in Mongolia. pp. 161–188, *in:* Humphrey and Sneath, 1996b, q.v.

van Veen, T.W.S. 1995. Kyrgyz sheep herders at crossroads. *ODI Pastoral Network Paper,* No. 38d.

Chapter 8
The Tibetan Steppe

Daniel J. Miller

SUMMARY

The Tibet Plateau is a vast area to the north of the Himalaya between roughly 26°50′ and 39°11′N. The climate is severe continental, and most of the plateau is arid to semi-arid. Snow events in winter increase risk. Its high, cold grazing lands vary from cold deserts and semi-arid steppe and shrublands, to alpine steppe and moist alpine meadows. Much is above 4 000 m; some camps are as high as 5 100 m. It is traditionally an area of transhumant herding, but has undergone vast changes in the past half century – from feudalism, through a collective period, to privatized livestock and individual grazing rights that are circumscribing the mobility necessary for herding risk avoidance in such a climate. Yak, sheep and goats are kept, with yak more important in the wetter east and sheep in the west. The steppe contains the headwaters of many of the major rivers of Asia and has a very rich flora and fauna, with many endemic species, so grazing management is not only important for herders' livelihoods but also for catchment maintenance and *in situ* preservation of genetic resources and biodiversity.

INTRODUCTION

The Tibetan Steppe is one of the earth's important grazing ecosystems, encompassing about 1.65 million km² (Figure 8.1). The Tibetan Steppe ecosystem actually extends into northwestern Bhutan, northern Nepal and northwestern India, but this paper deals only with the land within the Tibet Autonomous Region of the People's Republic of China. Grazing lands vary from cold deserts to semi-arid steppe and shrublands, to alpine steppe and moist alpine meadows. It contains the highest grasslands in the world, much is above 4 000 m; some herders maintain permanent camps at elevations as high as 5 100 m, among the highest inhabited places in the world. With a severe continental climate, it is one of the world's harshest grazing environments, yet these pastures supply forage for an estimated 12 million yak and 30 million sheep and goats (Plate 8.1), and provide livelihoods for about 5 million pastoralists and agropastoralists.

The remote, northwestern Steppe, one of the last notable examples of a grazing ecosystem relatively undisturbed by man, is home to a unique assemblage of wildlife. Wild yaks are still found in large herds, great concentrations of Tibetan antelope continue to migrate between their winter pastures and sum-

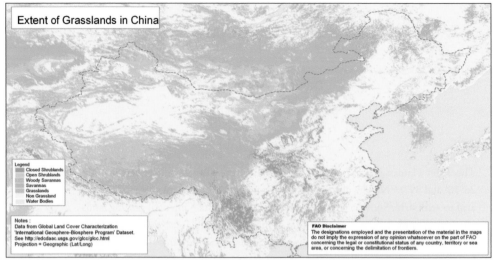

Figure 8.1
Location of the Tibetan Steppe and the extent of grasslands in the People's Republic of China.

Plate 8.1
Sheep flock.

mer fawning grounds, and troops of wild ass (Plate 8.2) run across the steppes. Because of its highly distinctive species, ecological processes and evolutionary phenomena, the Tibetan Steppe is included in the World Wildlife Fund's list of Global 200 ecoregions that are priority biodiversity conservation areas (Olson and Dinerstein, 1997).

DANIEL MILLER

Plate 8.2
*Wild ass (*Equus kiang*).*

Many major rivers originate in the Tibetan Steppe, including the Yellow, Yangtze, Mekong, Salween, Indus, Sutlej, Ganges and Brahmaputra. The preservation and management of these sources have global implications, as their waters will be of increasing importance in the future. The challenges facing the sustainable development of the steppe are considerable, but its pastures offer numerous opportunities for achieving the twin objectives of conservation and development of grassland resources. Properly managed, grazing lands can continue to be sources of water, provide wildlife habitat, feed for livestock and contribute to overall economic development of the region.

GENERAL DESCRIPTION

The Tibetan Steppe is on the Tibet-Qinghai plateau in the People's Republic of China and adjoining regions of Bhutan, Nepal and India. The Himalaya marks its southern boundary; the Kunlun, Arjin and Qilian Mountains delineate the northern boundary. The western limit is where the Himalaya, Karakoram, Kunlun and Pamir Mountains meet. In the east, the boundary extends along highlands in Qinghai, western Gansu and Sichuan and into northwestern Yunnan. Encompassing about a quarter of China's land, the plateau stretches for almost 1 500 km north to south and for about 3 000 km from east to west – the largest plateau on earth. Over 80 percent is above 3 000 m and about half over 4 500 m (Schaller, 1998). The vegetation is mainly grazing land, which is floristically distinctive, one of the largest of such ecosystems in the world (Schaller, 1998); at about 165 million hectares, it is 42 percent of China's grazing area (Miller, 1999a). This vast grassland is here termed the Tibetan Steppe; it

S.G. REYNOLDS

Plate 8.3
Harvested wheat in the Yarlung Tsangpo river valley.

includes all grassland in the Tibet Autonomous Region and Qinghai Province (118.4 million hectares), on the northern flanks of the Kunlun Mountains in southern Xinjiang (15 million hectares) and in western Sichuan (14 million hectares), northwestern Yunnan (5 million hectares) and western Gansu (12 million hectares). Less than one percent of the steppe is cultivated, although crops have expanded in recent decades, especially in the Qaidam Basin. In the east of the plateau, crop land is in the lower valleys; in western Tibet, along the valley and tributaries of the Yarlung Tsangpo (Brahmaputra River). The upper limit of cultivation, which is as low as 3 300 m in some eastern parts, can reach 4 400 m in the west. The major crops are barley, wheat (Plate 8.3), peas, rape and potatoes.

The Tibetan Steppe has several distinct topographic regions determined by drainage and the parallel mountain ranges that divide it (Schaller, 1998). Only the east and south have outlets to the ocean; rivers originating in the Kunlun Mountains flow north to the Taklimakan and Qaidam Deserts. Much of the Steppe consists of large lake basins with no outlets, ringed by mountains. Forests are limited to the eastern edge in western Sichuan, northwestern Yunnan, southeastern Qinghai and eastern Tibet, and in some valleys on the northern slopes of the Himalaya.

CLIMATE

The Tibetan Steppe has a severe continental climate and is affected by the southeastern monsoon in summer and western air circulation patterns and high Mongol-Siberian air pressures in winter (Huang, 1987). The Steppe slopes to the southeast, so moisture from the southwest monsoon comes up gorges from the east and south and precipitation in summer decreases in a gradient from east to west and from south to north. The east of the Steppe is humid, the south is semi-arid, and far western Tibet is arid. The central Steppe, in a broad band from Gansu and Qinghai west through Tibet, is sub-frigid, humid in the east and semi-arid in the west. The northern part Steppe is frigid and arid (Schaller, 1998).

In Lhasa, at 3 658 m, the average January temperature is -2°C, and in July it is 15°C; the absolute minimum is -16°C. Lhasa has about 130 frost-free days. In Naqu, at 4 507 m in northern Tibet, the average temperature in January is -14°C, and 9°C in July; there are only 20 frost-free days. Absolute minimum temperature in Naqu is -41°C. Temperature rises quickly during the day, but drops rapidly after sunset. The diurnal temperature range is 14 to 17°C (Huang, 1987), with an annual average of 2 500 to 3 000 sunshine hours.

Annual precipitation varies from about 600 mm in the east to under 60 mm in the west, most falls from June to September, often as wet snow and hail. Most of the pastoral area receives less than 400 mm per annum. Winters are generally dry, but periodical heavy snowfalls bury forage; low temperatures accompanying snowstorms put additional stress on livestock. Much of the steppe, especially in the west, has strong winds, with 100-150 days in a year with wind speeds over 17 m/s.

The eastern steppe receives enough precipitation (>400 mm) for the growth of forage, and the vegetation there probably exhibits characteristics of an equilibrium system (Schaller, 1998). Dry spells in late spring and early summer may delay growth, but rainfall is fairly reliable and many pastures have luxuriant vegetation. In the central and western Steppe, forage production is more variable from year to year due to fluctuating rainfall. There are even remarkable differences in grass growth within a small area due to local rainfall events. Here, non-equilibrium ecosystem dynamics may exert more influence on the landscape (Ellis and Swift, 1988; Laycock, 1991; Westoby, Walker and Noy-Meir, 1989a). Classical equilibrium theory may not be able to capture the uncertainty and variability in these environments, making such concepts as carrying capacity and stocking rate less effective in predicting ecosystem productivity and dynamics.

GRASSLAND BIODIVERSITY
Central Asia is normally divided into the Mongolian and Tibetan floristic provinces; the latter includes the entire Tibetan plateau with the exception of the Qaidam Basin, the Pamirs and southwestern Xinjiang. The Qaidam Basin is geographically part of Tibet, but its vegetation has more affinity with the Mongolian province (Walter and Box, 1983). The Tibetan floristic province is divided into four regions: (1) the Nan Shan and Chamdo in the northeast; (2) the deep river valleys in the southeast; (3) the deep longitudinal valley of the Yarlung Tsangpo in the south; and (4) the vast High Tibetan or Chang

Tang. The steppe is a meeting ground of several floras, including Central Asian desert species, East Asian temperate, and Himalayan. In Tibet, over 2 000 plant species have been identified (Gu, 2000), mainly in the families Compositae (330 species), Gramineae (277), Leguminosae (123), Rosaceae (102), Cyperaceae (102) and Polygonaceae (63). Over 1 720 species, accounting for 86 percent of forage plants, occur in the humid and subhumid pastures of eastern Tibet, and 540 species, or 27 percent of forages, occur in the arid and semi-arid grasslands of the northwest (Gu, 2000).

The vegetation of the Plateau and its floral elements differ strongly from the subtropical mountain forest vegetation of southeastern Tibet and adjoining regions (Chang, 1981). Plateau species have affinities with both Sino-Himalayan and Central Asiatic elements. Endemics comprise about 1 200, a quarter of all Tibetan species. Many dominants are endemics; *Stipa purpurea* is a dominant whose centre of importance is on the plateau. *Aristida triseta*, *Orinus thoroldii* and *Trikeraia hookeri* are also endemics in some of the drier valleys. Dominants of the steppe shrublands (*Sophora moorcroftiana, Caragana versicolor, Ceratostigma griffithii*) and some important companion species (*Artemisia wellbyi, Astragalus malcolmii*) are also endemics. The dominant in alpine desert vegetation, *Ceratoides compacta*, is considered to be a specialized species that was formed during the uplift of the Tibetan Plateau (Chang, 1981).

A number of plants found on the grasslands are valuable forage genetic resources. These include species such as *Brachypodium sylvaticum, Bromus himalaicus, Dactylis glomerata, Duthiea brachypodium, Elymus nutans, E. tangutorum, Festuca ovina, F. rubra, Phleum alpinum, Roegneria melanthera* and numerous species of *Medicago*. At least ten wild relatives of *Medicago sativa* are found there (Gu, 2000). Many forages from the steppe are of interest for resistance to cold, arid and saline or alkaline conditions. Collaborative collection expeditions have been carried out by the United States Department of Agriculture and the Chinese Ministry of Agriculture to identify and collect forage germplasm.

At the junction of the Palaearctic and Indo-Malayan biogeographic realms, the steppe supports diverse mammalian faunas. The northwest Steppe contains a unique assemblage of large mammals (Miller and Schaller, 1997). Ungulates, a number of which are endemic, are of special significance (Harris and Miller, 1995): species such as Tibetan wild ass (*Equus kiang*) (Plate 8.2), wild yak (*Bos grunniens*), Tibetan antelope (*Pantholops hodgsoni*) and Tibetan gazelle (*Procapra picticaudata*) are found. The mountains provide habitat for blue sheep (*Pseudois nayaur*) and Tibetan argali (*Ovis ammon hodgsoni*). In the mountains of the eastern Steppe, where forests mix with grasslands, musk deer (*Moschus sifanicus*), MacNeil's deer (*Cervus elaphus macneilli*), white-lipped deer (*Cervus albirostris*), roe deer (*Capreolus capreolus bedford*) and takin (*Budorcas taxicolor*) are found (Miller, 1998b). In southern Tibet there are still scattered populations of Tibet red deer (*Cervus elaphus wallichi*). Around Qinghai Lake there are some Przewalski's gazelle (*Procapra przewalskii*). Goitered gazelle (*Gazella subgutturosa*) are found on the northern edge of the Plateau. Predators such as brown bear (*Ursus arctos*), wolf (*Canis lupus*), snow leopard (*Uncia uncia*), lynx (*Felis lynx*), Tibetan steppe fox (*Vulpes ferrilata*) and red fox (*Vulpes vulpes*) are found on the grasslands, and smaller mammals such as marmot (*Marmota bobak*) and pika (*Ochotona* spp.) are common (Miller and Jackson, 1994).

In Tibet alone, over 500 species of bird have been recorded (Vaurie, 1970), including large predators: steppe eagles (*Aquila nipalensis*), upland buzzards (*Buteo hemilasius*), saker falcons (*Falco cherrug*), goshawks (*Accipiter gentilis*), black kites (*Milvus migrans*) and little owls (*Athene noctua*), several species of snow finches (*Montifringilla* spp.), pheasants (*Crossoptilon* spp., *Tetraogallus* spp.), Tibetan sandgrouse (*Syrrhaptes tibetanus*), as well as waterfowl such as black-necked cranes (*Grus nigricollis*), bar-headed geese (*Anser indicus*) and ruddy shelduck (*Tadorna ferruginea*).

Dominant natural vegetation

Kingdom-Ward (1948) identified six subregions: (1) the interior plateau; (2) the outer plateau; (3) the rainy gorge region; (4) the arid gorge region; (5) the Qaidam Basin; and (6) Chinese Tibet, or the northeastern part of the plateau. Scientific investigation of grassland resources began in the 1960s, with surveys (Xizang Integrated Survey Team of Chinese Academy of Sciences, 1966, and Qinghai and Gansu Integrated Survey Team of Chinese Academy of Sciences, 1963). Chang (1981) divided vegetation on the Tibetan plateau into five major regions:

- the high-cold or alpine meadow of eastern Tibet;
- xeric shrubland and steppe along the valleys of the Yarlung Tsangpo and Indus River in southern Tibet;
- high-cold or alpine steppe in northern Tibet;
- high-cold desert in northwestern Tibet; and
- temperate desert in southwestern Tibet.

Schaller (1998) followed Chang's classification, but added a sixth region: the Qaidam Basin. Within each region, there is a diverse assortment of plant communities, varying in species composition and structure, and influenced by factors such as elevation, aspect, drainage and precipitation (Chang, 1983). For example, Chang and Gauch (1986) described 26 plant communities in western Tibet, and Achuff and Petocz (1988) identified 18 communities in the Arjin Shan region of Xinjiang on the northern edge of the Tibetan Steppe. The vegetation on the plains has a broad horizontal zonation and a relatively narrow vertical zonation on the mountain slopes, both reflecting precipitation and elevation.

The country's grassland resources were surveyed and mapped in the 1980s and classified into 17 types, based on climatic zonation, humidity index, veg-

TABLE 8.1
Grassland types of the Tibetan Steppe.

Type	Area ('000 ha)	As percentage of total area
Temperate meadow-steppe	210	0.16
Temperate steppe	3 833	2.92
Temperate desert-steppe	968	0.74
Alpine meadow-steppe	5 626	4.28
Alpine steppe	37 762	28.75
Alpine desert-steppe	8 679	6.61
Temperate steppe-desert	107	0.08
Temperate desert	2 084	1.59
Alpine desert	5 967	4.54
Tropical tussock	9	–
Tropical shrub tussock	28	0.02
Temperate tussock	1	–
Temperate shrub tussock	140	0.10
Lowland meadow	1 168	0.88
Temperate mountain meadow	6 067	4.61
Alpine meadow	58 652	44.64
Marsh	21	0.01
Total	131 322	99.93

Source: Adapted from Chen and Fischer, 1998, and Ni, 2002.

etation type and importance to the livestock industry (CISNR, 1995, 1996). Within each type, a number of formations have been identified. Table 8.1 gives the seventeen types found in the steppe.

Alpine meadow

Alpine meadow, which makes up about 45 percent of the grassland is found on valley floors and mountain slopes from about 3 500 to 4 500 m with annual precipitation over 400 mm, mainly in the east. It is widespread in southwestern Gansu, western Sichuan and southeastern and southern Qinghai, and extends into Tibet to the longitude of Lhasa. Further west, alpine meadow is primarily riparian and in areas receiving melt water (Cincotta *et al.*, 1991; Schaller, 1998). The soil is an alpine meadow soil averaging 20–40 cm in depth, and rich in organic matter. The surface layer is a substantial, resilient sod (Huang, 1987). Ni (2002) concluded that high carbon storage in alpine meadows of China, as a result of the thick sod layer, could have a significant and long-term effect on global carbon cycles.

Alpine meadow is dominated by sedges of the genera *Kobresia* (Huang, 1987); dominant species are *Kobresia pygmaea*, *K. humilis*, *K. capillifolia*, *K. setschwanensis*, *K. schoenoides* and *K. littledalei. Carex atrofusca, Polygonum viviparum* and *P. macrophyllum* are the subdominant species in the alpine meadow, and numerous forbs are also found, including species in the genera *Leontopodium, Anemone, Anaphalis, Polygonum, Pedicularis, Rheum, Androsace, Gentiana, Ranunculus, Aconitum, Astragalus, Oxytropis, Primula* and *Potentilla*. Grasses include *Elymus nutans, Roegneria nutans, Koeleria*

S.G. REYNOLDS

Plate 8.4
Elymus nutans.

litwinowii, Helictotrichon tibeticum, Brachypodium sylvaticum, Stipa aliena, Festuca rubra, F. ovina and *Deschampsia cespitosa*. Large areas of productive pasture are dominated by *Elymus nutans* (Plate 8.4) in the alpine meadow, especially in northwestern Sichuan, southwestern Gansu and eastern Qinghai. In swampy depressions in the alpine meadow there is hummock vegetation dominated by *Kobresia* spp. (30-cm tall *K. royleana* and *K. schoenoides*). Shrub communities of plants such as *Salix* spp., *Caragana jubata*, *Potentilla fruticosa* and *Rhododendron* spp. are common on northern aspects in alpine meadow.

Most Tibetan pastoralists and their stock are found in the alpine meadow region. Livestock densities can be high; in eastern Qinghai, stocking rates are 28-70 animals/km^2, and heavy grazing and trampling, together with solifluction, have disturbed the sod layer, causing extensive rangeland degradation (Schaller, 1998).

Alpine steppe

The alpine steppe comprises almost 29 percent of the area and is found between 3 500 and 4 600 m in the central and western steppe. Unlike the alpine meadow, there is no sod layer, and the soil is often gravel and coarse sandy loam; it is a variant of the temperate steppe under the cold conditions of the Tibetan plateau (Huang, 1987). Grasses of the genus *Stipa* dominate, often accompanied by cushion plants, with *S. purpurea* and *S. subsessiliflora* as the dominant grasses. Associated species are mainly xeric and meso-xeric grasses: *Poa alpina* (Plate 8.5), *P. crymophila, P. dolichachyra, Roegneria nutans, R. thoroldiana, Agropyron cristatum, Stipa aliena, Orinus thoroldii, Calamagrostis* spp., *Festuca*

A. PEETERS

Plate 8.5
Poa alpina.

S.G. REYNOLDS

Plate 8.6
Stock grazing on stubble after harvest.

rubra, *Kobresia* spp. and *Carex moorcroftii*. Shrubs include *Potentilla fruticosa*, *Ajana* spp., *Artemisia* spp. and *Ceratoides compacta*. Forbs include *Potentilla bifurca*, *Dracocephalum heterophyllum*, *Heteropappus altaicus*, *Leontopodium* spp., *Pedicularis* spp., *Allium* spp., *Oxytropis* spp. and *Astragalus* spp., with the cushion plants *Androsace tapete*, *Arenaria musciformis* and *Oxytropis microphylla*.

Plate 8.7
Turnips are becoming a popular crop for winter feed.

Along the drainage of the Yarlung Tsangpo, in the rain-shadow of the Himalaya, between 3 500 to 4 000 m on valley floors and lower mountain slopes, the dominant vegetation consists of xeric grasses such as *Aristida triseta, Stipa bungeana, Pennisetum flaccidum, Elymus nutans* and *Orinus thoroldii*. Shrubs such as *Artemisia webbiana, Berberis* spp., *Sophora moorcroftiana, S. viciifolia, Lonicera spinosa, Leptodermis sauranja* and *Ceratostigma griffithii* are often mixed with grasses, or comprise distinct communities. On the upper slopes, *Juniperus* shrub communities are found. Since this central valley region is settled by farmers, most of the grasslands have been subjected to heavy, continual grazing for centuries, if not thousands of years, and are overgrazed and degraded (Meiners, 1991; Ryavec and Vergin, 1998). Desertification, with moving sand dunes, is a serious problem in many areas in the Yarlung Tsangpo valley.

Stock graze on stubble (Plate 8.6) and fodder crops like turnips (Plate 8.7) are grown for winter feed.

Many plants in the alpine steppe have distinctive adaptations to the harsh environment (Huang, 1987). Some have shiny hairs, possibly to retain humidity and reflect heat into the interior. Some have large taproots for nutrient storage, and cushion plants create their own micro-environment by accumulating windblown soil and snow. In the alpine steppe, plant canopy cover ranges from 10 to 30 percent and productivity is often low (<300 kg/DM/ha). Within the alpine steppe region, swampy depressions, fed by snow and glacial melt streams, are dominated by *Kobresia* spp. These areas are key grazing areas, since growth starts earlier than on the steppe, which depends on summer precipitation (Miller and Schaller, 1996). The alpine steppe is important for pastoral production (Miller and Bedunah, 1993). Most is still in quite good condition, although there are areas of overgrazing around settlements. Schaller (1998) estimated livestock density in the alpine steppe in northern Tibet at 8.7 animals/km² (comprising sheep, 5.71/km²; goats, 2.60/km²; yak, 0.36/km²; and horses, 0.07/km²).

Alpine desert steppe

The alpine desert steppe, which extends out of north Tibet into southern Xinjiang, is a bleak and arid landscape with large areas almost devoid of vegetation (Schaller, 1998). It makes up about 6 percent of the total grassland of the Steppe. Vegetation is similar to the alpine steppe, but plant cover is less. The dwarf shrub *Ceratoides compacta* and the sedge *Carex moorcroftii* are the dominant plants. There is little livestock in this cold, high desert, and even wild ungulates are limited in number (Miller and Schaller, 1998).

Temperate mountain meadow

The temperate mountain meadow is mainly in western Sichuan, southeastern Qinghai and east Tibet, and often found as meadows within forest between 3 330 and 4 200 m. It makes up 4.6 percent of the area. Forests are primarily of spruce (*Picea* spp.). Important grass genera include *Festuca, Ptilagrostis, Poa, Helictotrichon, Agrostis, Bromus, Elymus, Roegneria* and *Deyeuxia*. Common forbs are of the genera *Polygonum, Aconitum, Delphinium, Rheum* and *Ligularia*. Shrubs include *Rhododendron, Philadelphus, Sorbus, Salix, Spiraea, Prunus* and *Lonicera*.

Temperate desert

The temperate desert found in the Qaidam Basin is a transition zone between the Mongolian desert and the alpine steppe of the Tibetan plateau. It is orogeni-cally part of Tibet, but belongs floristically to the Mongolian province (Walter and Box, 1983). The Qaidam basin is 100–200 km wide and 600 km long, once filled by a sea, with mean elevation around 3 000 m, about 1 500 m higher than the Mongolian Plateau and about the same below the Tibetan plateau. Shrubs of the genera *Calligonum, Haloxylon, Nitraria, Reaumuria, Salsola, Artemisia, Tamarix, Ephedra, Kalidium* and *Sympegma* dominate. There are large salt flats scattered across much of the Basin, and marshy areas support communities of *Phragmites*.

Classification of grassland types and plant communities

The rangelands of the Tibetan Autonomous Region have been classified into 12 different types (Mou, Deng and Gu, 1992; Deng, 1981; Gu, 2000). Table 8.2 lists these different types and the dominant groups within each type for the Tibetan Autonomous Region.

TABLE 8.2
Grassland types and plant communities in the Tibetan Autonomous Region.

Formation	Community
Alpine meadow	*Kobresia* spp.
Alpine shrub meadow	*Rhododendron – Kobresia*
Subalpine shrub meadow	*Sabina – Kobresia bellardii*
	Picea – Kobresia bellardii
	Quercus semicarpifolia – Kobresia bellardii
	Salix – Spiraea – Berberis
Mountain shrub steppe	*Sophora viciifolia – Pennisetum flaccidum*
	Sophora viciifolia – Orinus thoroldii
Mountain steppe	*Artemisia stracheyi – Kobresia bellardii*
	Artemisia stracheyi – Stipa sp.
	Artemisia stracheyi – Orinus thoroldii
	Orinus thoroldii
	Achnatherum hookeri
	Stipa bungeana – Pennisetum flaccidum
Alpine steppe	*Stipa purpurea*
	Stipa purpurea – Kobresia sp.
	Stipa purpurea – Caragana versicolar
	Stipa purpurea – Festuca ovina
Mountain desert steppe	*Stipa glareosa*
	Stipa glareosa – Ceratoides latens
	Caragana versicolar – Stipa glareosa
	Caragana versicolar – Ceratoides latens
	Ajania fruticulosa – Stipa glareosa
Mountain desert	*Ceratoides latens – Stipa* sp.
	Ceratoides latens
Alpine desert	*Carex moorcroftii*
	Ceratoides compacta – Carex moorcroftii
	Ceratoides compacta
Alpine cushion vegetation	
Lake basin and valley meadow grassland	
Woodland meadow	

SOURCE: Adapted from Mou, Deng and Gu, 1992, and Gu, 2000.

Vegetational attributes

Vegetational attributes of the Tibetan Steppe vary greatly depending on the particular type, topography, soils, precipitation and grazing history. Some of the important vegetation characteristics that can help elucidate rangeland dynamics on the Steppe are botanical composition, productivity and nutritional content of rangeland herbage.

BOTANICAL COMPOSITION

Table 8.3 shows average botanical composition for alpine steppe and alpine desert in the Chang Tang Wildlife Reserve of northern Tibet, where the average elevation is 4 800 m and annual precipitation about 250 mm. Much of the grass is one species, *Stipa purpurea*. On mountain slopes in the alpine steppe, grasses decrease and forbs increase. In the alpine desert, sedges become more important, making up from 48 to almost 70 percent of vegetation; the primary sedge is *Carex moorcroftii*. Table 8.4 depicts average botanical composition

TABLE 8.3
Botanical composition in the Chang Tang Wildlife Reserve, northern Tibet (percentage basis).

		Alpine Steppe		Alpine Desert Steppe	
	plains	plains	mountain		
Grasses	61.9	58.8	29.8	42.7	17.5
Sedges	15.2	28.5	22.8	48.5	69.8
Forbs	17.5	10.6	35.2	6.2	9.3
Shrubs	5.4	2.1	12.2	2.6	3.4

SOURCE: Adapted from Miller and Schaller, 1997

TABLE 8.4
Botanical composition of rangeland in Hainan Prefecture, Qinghai (percentage basis).

	Alpine Meadow	Temperate Meadow-Steppe
Grasses	8.20	68.00
Sedges	40.70	3.87
Legumes	4.05	2.45
Edible forbs	29.33	18.68
Non-edible forbs	17.72	7.00
Total	100.00	100.00

SOURCE: Lang, Huang and Wang, 1997.

TABLE 8.5
Annual dry matter production and carrying capacity for different grassland types in Hainan Prefecture, Qinghai Province.

Pasture type	Dry matter (kg/ha)	Carrying capacity (ha/SU/yr)
Alpine meadow	934	0.78
Temperate meadow-steppe	623	1.17
Alpine steppe	594	1.23
Temperate desert steppe	345	2.11
Temperate desert	228	3.19
Lowland meadow	1 341	0.54

NOTES: SU = Stock Unit.
SOURCE: Lang, Huang and Wang, 1997.

in an alpine meadow and in temperate meadow-steppe in eastern Qinghai. In alpine meadow, grasses comprise only 8 percent of vegetation, while sedges comprise 40 percent, with the balance being forbs. In temperate meadow-steppe, a high proportion of vegetation (68 percent) is grasses.

GRASSLAND PRODUCTIVITY

The standing crop on the Steppe varies considerably. Alpine meadows are some of the most productive, as average annual dry matter (DM) production may reach 1 000 kg/ha. Productivity of desert pasture is low, averaging only 100–200 kg/DM/ha. Table 8.5 gives annual DM production and carrying capacity of different pasture types. Harris and Bedunah (2001), in Aksai County, Gansu Province, found average standing crop varied from 115 kg/DM/ha in desert shrub to 790 kg/DM/ha in desert sub-irrigated meadows (Table 8.6).

Nutrient content of herbage

On most of the steppe, natural forage is the only source of nutrients, except for small amounts of hay and purchased concentrates, so understanding

TABLE 8.6
Standing crop (kg/DM/ha) for different vegetation types in Aksai County, Gansu (3 100 to 4 400 m).

Vegetation type	Standing crop	Dominant species
Desert shrub	115	*Sympegma regelii, Reaumuria soongarica*
Desert steppe	167	*Oxytropis aciphylla, Leymus paboanus, Stipa glareosa*
Alpine desert shrub	141	*Ceratoides compacta, Stipa glareosa*
Alpine steppe	245	*Stipa purpurea, Poa* spp., *Festuca* spp., *Carex moorcroftii*
Desert sub-irrigated meadows	790	*Carex* spp., *Achnatherum splendens*
Meadows and sandy grasslands	423	*Carex* spp., *Leymus paboanus, Stipa* spp., *Kobresia* spp.

SOURCE: Harris and Bedunah, 2001.

TABLE 8.7
Crude Protein (CP) and Total Digestible Nutrients (TDN) of vegetation in Guoluo Prefecture, Qinghai Province (as percentage of dry matter).

Plant Form	Grasses		Forbs		Shrubs	
	CP	TDN	CP	TDN	CP	TDN
Late June	16.12	79.48	16.60	85.43	19.14	83.11
Late July	15.02	78.21	14.95	83.93	17.76	82.56
Mid-September	10.47	79.61	10.46	83.77	9.97	80.69

SOURCE: Sheehy, 2000.

the nutrient dynamics of forage in relation to animal needs is critical. Understanding temporal and spatial dynamics of forage is also important, with regard both to plant and animal needs and to demand functions in the livestock production system (Sheehy, 2000).

Investigations in an alpine meadow environment in Guoluo Prefecture, Qinghai, provide surprising information about the nutrient content of forages. Table 8.7 shows average crude protein (CP) content of three classes of forage and average percent total digestible nutrients (TDN) at three different times during the growing season. An important characteristic of the forage is the high protein and nutrient content of all growth forms at the end of the growing season. The total amount of nutrients available to livestock going into the autumn and winter is much higher than found in many other grazing ecosystems. This implies that: (1) sufficient nutrients remain available on the Tibetan Steppe to maintain livestock through normal periods when forage is not growing; (2) even degraded vegetation has relatively high nutrients; and (3) capacity of grasslands to support livestock needs to be evaluated in a nutrient context as well as a consumable biomass content (Sheehy, 2000).

Grassland degradation

About a third of the pasture of the Steppe is now considered moderately to severely degraded, calling into question its long-term sustainability under current use (Sheehy, 2001). In Tibet, the percent of degraded pasture increased from 18 to 30 percent of total area between 1980 and 1990. Degradation is a growing concern in Naqu, where degraded land makes up almost 40 percent of the total degraded rangeland in the whole of the Tibetan Autonomous Region (Ciwang, 2000).

Seriously degraded alpine meadow is often termed "black beach", since the *Kobresia*-dominated community has deteriorated to such a degree that most of the sedges and associated grasses have disappeared, leaving annuals and bare soil. The dynamics of this degradation are not well understood; it is usually blamed on overgrazing and the burrowing of pikas, but there is increasing evidence that climate change and desiccation may play a major role in vegetation changes (Miehe, 1988). Livestock may just accentuate natural ecological processes instead of being the underlying cause.

THE TIBETAN PASTORAL PRODUCTION SYSTEM

Tibetan pastoralism has evolved through long-term adaptation and persistence by herders (Ekvall, 1968; Goldstein, 1992; Goldstein and Beall, 1991; Miller, 1999b). Pastoralists kept a mix of livestock in terms of species and class and used a mosaic of grazing sites, exploiting seasonal and annual variability. Herders bartered products (Plate 8.8) for grain and supplies; quite elaborate trade linkages (Plate 8.9) developed between pastoral and agricultural areas; traditional pastoralism was more than subsistence oriented. Tibetan pastoralism is distinct ecologically from that of other semi-arid regions, except Mongolia (Ekvall, 1974), since it is separated from agricultural areas by temperature not aridity (Ekvall, 1968; Barfield, 1993; Goldstein and Beall, 1990; Miller, 1998a). The yak (Plate 8.10), which is superbly adapted to the cold Tibetan Steppe, also distinguishes Tibetan pastoralism (Cai and Wiener, 1995; Miller, 1997b).

Plate 8.8
Yaks transporting wool.

DANIEL MILLER

Plate 8.9
Yak pack train.

S.G. REYNOLDS

Plate 8.10
*The Yak (*Bos grunniens*).*

Historical and cultural aspects

Pastoralists have probably been raising stock on the Tibetan Steppe for 4 000 years (Barfield, 1989; Lattimore, 1940). As early as the Hsia dynasty (2205-1766 BC), nomadic Qiang were making fine woven woollen material in the Kunlun Mountains. In the Shang dynasty (1766-1027 BC) nomads in eastern Tibet were renowned for their horses. The development of Tibetan pastoralism was

DANIEL MILLER

Plate 8.11
Kokonor camp with the distinctive black yak-hair tents.

DANIEL MILLER

Plate 8.12
Amdo woman and tent.

shaped by nomads from Central Asia who brought sheep, goats and horses. The Tibetan black, yak-hair tent (Plates 8.11 and 8.12) is strikingly similar to the goat-hair tents of Afghanistan, Iran and Iraq (Manderscheid, 2001). The yak, domesticated on the Steppe (Miller *et al.*, 1994), enabled nomads to exploit the high grassland.

Most herders are Tibetan but there are small groups of Mongols and Kazakhs in Qinghai. Population density across much of the Steppe is less than two persons per square kilometre (Ryavec and Vergin, 1998). For a distance of almost 3 000 km, Tibetan is spoken and has been a written language for about 1 300 years. In recent decades, pastoralists across most of the Steppe have built houses and livestock shelters, on traditional winter-spring pastures where they spend up to 6–7 months of the year. The vast majority of herders have been "settled" for some time, but graze their livestock in a transhumant manner (Miller, 1998c).

Livestock management

Pastoral practices are similar across the Steppe, although the composition and size of herds differ. Herders keep milking (Plates 8.13 and 8.14) and dry herds of yak, yak-cattle crosses, sheep (Plate 8.15), goats and horses. The yak in many ways defines pastoralism across the plateau; they are preferred for riding in rough country, at extreme altitudes and in snow (Ekvall, 1974); their dung is an important fuel. The Tibetan term for yaks, *nor*, is also translated as "wealth". Sheep and goats are most important in the west where they suit the vegetation better than do yaks; there sheep and goats are milked; in the east, yaks supply all the nomads' milk needs. Mutton is the preferred meat. Goats yield cashmere, meat and milk; Tibetan cashmere is among the best in the world. Sheep, goats and camels (Plate 8.16) are also used as pack animals but, with expanding road access, their role for transport has diminished. Horses are used primarily for riding, but are also used as pack animals. Mares are not milked and Tibetans

Plate 8.13
Milking yak.

DANIEL MILLER

Plate 8.14
Milk collection.

S.G. REYNOLDS

Plate 8.15
Sheep grazing on the high plateau.

do not eat horsemeat. Livestock belong to individual families since the communes were disbanded and the 'household responsibility system' introduced in the early 1980s. Each family is responsible for its livestock and the processing and marketing of livestock products.

The proportion of species and the size of herds differs according to grassland factors and the suitability of the landscape for different animals. Table 8.8

DANIEL MILLER

Plate 8.16
Mongols and pack camels.

TABLE 8.8
Average livestock numbers per family in various Counties and Townships.

Administrative unit	Yak	Sheep	Goats	Horses
Shuanghu County, Tibet	18	282	107	4
Nyima County, Tibet	14	220	144	2
Amdo County, Tibet	45	189	25	4
Takring Township, Naqu County, Tibet	31	57	13	1.5
Tagmo Township, Naqu County, Tibet	30	54	11	1.5
Nyerong County, Tibet	27	46	8	1.4
Aba County, Sichuan	70	34	0	6
Hongyuan County, Sichuan	85	7	0	5
Maqu County, Gansu	46	48	0	6
Marma Twp, Maqu County, Gansu	51	71	0	6
Nyima Township, Maqu County, Gansu	46	81	0	1.8
Luqu County, Gansu	33	65	0	2

Sources: Interviews and Government Records.

shows herd composition for 16 counties and townships across a distance of 1 500 km from west to east. For example, in Shuanghu County of the Tibetan Autonomous Region, yaks make up only 4 percent of livestock; whereas in Hongyuan County of Sichuan, about 1 200 km to the east, yaks comprise 85 percent. Shuanghu is drier and the alpine steppe vegetation suits sheep and goats. Hongyuan is wetter and vegetation is dominated by alpine meadow. Herd compositions within a geographic area can also differ with the skills, preferences and availability of labour. Luqu County, in southwestern Gansu, is close to Aba and Hongyuan Counties in Sichuan and pastures are comparable, but in Luqu the government encouraged pastoralists to raise sheep, hence it has a much higher percentage of sheep than neighbouring counties.

The number of animals that herder households raise also varies considerably across the Steppe. In Shuanghu County in Tibet, an average-income family of five keeps about 280 sheep, 100 goats, 18 yaks and 4 horses. In Naqu County a family of five would have 60–80 sheep and goats, 30–35 yaks and two horses. A rich family in Naqu may have 200–300 sheep and goats and 100 yaks. In Hongyuan County in northwest Sichuan a typical family would have 80–100 yaks, five horses and no, or a few, sheep. Of the 80–100 yaks a family in Hongyuan has, only 30 to 40 are milking females. In Phala in northwest Shigatse Prefecture of Tibet, the richest herding family with six persons in the household had 286 sheep, 250 goats, 77 yaks and 8 horses.

Herd structure illustrates pastoralists' expertise in animal husbandry. In Phala, almost 60 percent of the adult sheep and goats are females. Adult males, at 30 percent of the flock, may seem high, but a significant portion of herders' income is from fibre from adult males and adult males for meat. In pastoral areas, livestock graze year-round. Some hay is cut for weak animals and horses in winter and spring. In recent years, however, some herders are sowing pastures for winter-spring grazing or hay.

Herds on the move

Traditional extensive grazing management was adapted to local conditions and stock were regularly moved between pastures to maintain grassland condition and animal productivity. Grazing lands were parcelled into seasonal pastures and grazed according to managerial and production objectives. Pastoralists' movements were well prescribed by complex social organizations and were highly regulated. Mobility is still vital for most herders (Plate 8.17), although

DANIEL MILLER

Plate 8.17
Herders moving on the high plain.

with escalating settlement, livestock mobility is being curtailed. The system was designed around the seasonal movement of livestock; herds rotated between pastures to use forage in summer and reserve grass for autumn and early winter to prepare animals for the long winter. The survival today of numerous, prosperous groups of Tibetan pastoralists bears witness to their extraordinary indigenous knowledge, resourcefulness and animal husbandry skills. Much of the grazing ecosystem is intact and sustains a unique flora and wild fauna, despite centuries of grazing, indicating its remarkable resilience. Now, however, traditional, proven, yet often quite sophisticated livestock and grazing management systems are being altered as modern development sweeps across the Tibetan steppes.

Land tenure

Before 1949 there was a feudal "estate" system with land controlled by religious and aristocratic elites (Goldstein and Beall, 1990:54). Wealthy, powerful monasteries controlled huge fiefdoms with numerous pastoral estates and thousands of subjects. Herders were bound to an estate and not free to leave it, but owned their animals and managed them as they wished; they paid taxes and provided corvée labour to their lord.

Traditionally, pastoral estates were divided into numerous pastures, with borders recorded in a register book (Goldstein and Beall, 1990:69). Households received pastures according to the number of livestock owned, including multiple pastures for use at different seasons. Estate officials enforced pasture boundaries. Herding households were independent of each other regarding management of their pastures and animals and there was no "common" pasture open to all. On pastoral estates the system balanced grassland resources and livestock by reallocating pastures between families according to a census conducted every three years. Herders whose stock had increased were allocated more pasture and those whose herds had declined lost land, the aim being to maintain a specified number of livestock on each pasture (Goldstein and Beall, 1990:70).

In many areas herders were organized as a confederacy of separate kin-based groups which were of different sizes and each had customary rights to land of varying extent, used at different seasons. Groups were divided into 'encampments' of five to ten households and each encampment had rights to a set of seasonal grazing areas within the wider 'tribal' territory. Natural features like ridges and streams (Levine, 1998) marked boundaries. Herders had heritable grazing rights within a group territory (Clarke, 1998).

Traditionally, in areas outside the control of large pastoral estates, grazing rights were very insecure and depended on force (Levine, 1998). While the rights of tribes to certain tracts of land were fixed – unless and until other tribes took them by force – rights of encampments were more fluid. The camping sites and grazing grounds of the various groups could be changed from one part of the tribal territory to another at the discretion of tribal leaders and in response to changing needs of the encampment (Levine, 1998). In the Golog region of the northeastern Steppe winter camps had a sense of 'ownership' by specific encampment groups. Households in the encampment had 'individual and exclusive rights over certain hayfields' near winter sites (Ekvall, 1954).

Since 1949 the state has induced profound changes in land tenure and social organization of pastoral communities. In the 1950s, when land reform was being implemented throughout China, pasture was nationalized and aristocratic and monastic lords lost their estates. State ownership of grassland was not incorporated into law until 1982 (Ho, 2000). When communes were established in the late 1950s and 1960s, ownership was vested in the production teams, which came to regard the grassland as collective property. What emerged was a *de facto* situation of state and collectively owned pasture. All livestock was the property of the communes. Herders were transformed to holders of a share in the communes' livestock. In the commune era, however, mobile pastoralism continued and no attempt was made to reduce the geographic scope of livestock production.

Decollectivization of the agricultural sector in China was authorized in 1978. Institutional rural reforms began in agricultural areas of eastern China, where communes and state farms were dismantled and their lands redistributed under the family-based Household Contract Responsibility System (Ho, 1996). In agricultural areas farmers could lease land and land use rights could be subcontracted or inherited. The contract system became the orthodox form of land tenure for agriculture and was applied to grasslands with the promulgation of the Grassland Law in 1985 (Ho, 2000), which states that the user right of state or collective pasture may be leased to households for a 'long term', although in practice lease periods extend to 30 years and in special circumstances to 50 years. In much of the pastoral area of Qinghai, southwest Gansu and northwestern Sichuan, many herders have settled and have fenced pastures contracted to them. There is evidence that the allocation of rangeland is at the community and small group level, much as in the pre-commune era (Goldstein and Beall, 1991).

Transformation of the traditional pastoral production system

The profound changes of recent decades are transforming traditional land use, altering pasture conditions and disrupting the lives of pastoralists. Often these political, social, economic and ecological transformations have altered previously stable relationships between pastoralists and the grasslands.

In the mid-1980s winter grazing lands were allocated to households and winter pastures were fenced (Plate 8.18); this began in the Qinghai Lake region, but quickly spread to herding areas in Gansu and Sichuan. Exclusive usufruct rights to specific grazing lands for herding households, valid in most cases for 30 years, have now been established. These rights can be inherited, but not

DANIEL MILLER

Plate 8.18
Fenced rangeland.

bought or sold. There is no mechanism yet in place for the readjustment of grazing land to individual families when livestock numbers fluctuate.

In the Tibetan Autonomous Region, however, grassland is not yet allocated to households, but is being allocated to groups of herders. One explanation for the difference in the privatization process in Tibet is that the grasslands are not as productive and the expense involved in fencing individual properties would be prohibitive. A new development is that summer grazing lands are also being privatized and fenced, except again in the Tibetan Autonomous Region where they are being allocated to groups instead of households. To complement the privatization a 'Four-Way Programme' is being implemented and consists of:

- fencing about 20 to 30 ha of productive winter pasture, reserved from grazing in summer and autumn, to provide grazing during the late winter and/or spring;
- construction of shelters for livestock;
- construction of homes for nomads in their winter pasture site; and
- planting small (0.5 to 2 ha) plots of oats for hay in the corrals around winter settlements (Plate 8.19).

In some areas, additional interventions include:

- fencing about 20 ha of degraded land which is rehabilitated by reseeding; and
- fencing of an additional 20 ha which is then improved with fertilizer, chemicals and improved management.

These activities are being undertaken on a large scale, with substantial government and donor investment, in almost all pastoral areas of Qinghai,

Plate 8.19
Oats for winter feed (as hay) being grown in a sheep pen, Qinghai, China.

Gansu and Sichuan. However, even in Tibet, great attention is being given to "scientific" animal husbandry and settling of herders.

The heavy livestock losses experienced on the plateau in recent years has convinced many authorities that transhumant pastoralism needs to be restructured. Programmes to settle herders, privatize and fence pasture and develop fodder for winter are seen as ways to prevent losses in severe winters and control what is perceived as widespread pasture degradation. While some of these interventions have merit, such as the growing of annual forage for hay, the long-term ecological implications of privatizing pasture and reducing the spatial movement of herds have received little analysis (Miller, 2000). The socio-economic and land-tenure ramifications of herders being settled on defined properties have also not been examined.

Foggin and Smith (2000) concluded that summer-autumn pastures may be unintentionally degraded further as artificially high winter populations of stock are forced to graze on summer-autumn pasture of reduced size. Official live-stock-management views technology as having the ability to overcome resource limitations but fails to consider that a greater proportion of winter-spring pasture means a lesser proportion of summer-autumn pasture and overgrazing becomes increasingly likely as more livestock graze on a continuously decreasing area during a short growing season (Foggin and Smith, 2000). Considerable investment may be misdirected or inappropriately divided between winter-spring and summer-autumn zones and associated projects. For example, in Dari County of Qinghai, grassland condition has continued to deteriorate despite a decrease in livestock and considerable investment in "construction" projects.

The popular government development paradigm in the Tibetan Steppe, adopts a livestock rather than a grassland management perspective (Foggin and Smith, 2000); stock numbers are of primary importance and attention to vegetation secondary. As the human pastoral population increased there was a strong tendency to rely more heavily on winter-spring grazing, the condition of which decreased as human population density – and livestock density – increased. Since winter-spring is when most livestock die from poor nutrition, an increase in the area of winter-spring grazing land or the supply of feed in winter-spring is a rational response to ensure that more stock survive. This focus on maximizing livestock production detracts from promoting sustainable grassland management.

Snowstorms and pastoral system dynamics

Across much of the Tibetan Steppe, where there is sufficient rainfall and the pastoral system appears to operate in an equilibrium manner with regards to forage production, the continental climate and periodic weather perturbations in the form of sudden and brutal snowstorms add to the complexity and dynamic nature of the ecosystem (Goldstein, Beall and Cincotta, 1990; Miller, 2000). Snowstorms are a fundamental component of the Tibetan Steppe and probably serve as an important regulatory mechanism in the pastoral system. Serious losses occur as a result of heavy snowfalls and severe cold weather (Cincotta *et al.*, 1991; Clarke, 1998; Goldstein, Beall and Cincotta, 1990; Miller, 1998a; Schaller, 1998; Prejevalsky, 1876, in Schaller, 1998). From 1955 to 1990, six severe winters with heavy snow were reported, resulting in 20 to 30 percent losses in livestock each time. Schaller (1998) reported an unusually heavy snowfall of 30 cm in October 1985, followed by temperatures that dropped to -40°C, in southwestern Qinghai that resulted in large numbers of livestock and wildlife dying. Goldstein and Beall (1990) found that all lambs and kids died in the spring of 1988 in the Phala area of Tibet. The winter of 1989–1990 in Tibet resulted in the loss of 20 percent of livestock in affected areas. The winter of 1995–1996 was severe in many parts of the plateau, with 33 percent of livestock lost in Yushu Prefecture of Qinghai. Losses in summer are not uncommon; Goldstein and Beall (1990) found that after five days of snow in the summer of 1986, a herding area lost 30 percent of its stock. Ekvall (1974) mentions the effect of hail on Tibetan herds. Much of the Steppe probably functions as a non-equilibrium system with stock numbers frequently checked by climatic factors, such as snowstorms, rather than by increasing pressure of livestock on the pastures (Miller, 1997a).

Another severe winter was in 1997–98, when usually early and severe snowfalls in September was followed by cold weather, preventing the snow from melting. More snow followed and by November, the pasture was buried under deep snow. By April 1998, more than three million head had been lost. Thousands of families, many of which had lost all their livestock, suddenly faced poverty. In Naqu prefecture, 20 percent of the pastoral population of

340 000 lived in poverty prior to the severe 1997–98 winter; in the following year the percentage had increased to 40 percent.

Officials label heavy snowfalls and severe winters as "disasters"; however, pastoralists have been herding on the Tibetan Steppe for centuries and have dealt with snowstorms and cold weather – those of the winter of 1997–1998 are natural events of the pastoral system. Herding has always been a high-risk enterprise; pastoralists adopt strategies that minimize risk and make best use of the resources (Goldstein and Beall, 1990; Miller, 1998a). In contrast to severe droughts in semi-arid pastoral areas, heavy snowfalls do not affect the vegetation negatively. Unlike droughts, where the effects on livestock are more prolonged, severe snowstorms are sudden events, with a very short or no "warning" period, and often causing livestock deaths in days or weeks.

DILEMMA ON THE TIBETAN STEPPE

With attempts to transform pastoral livestock production towards a market economy the goal has been to increase off-take. This has been promoted through privatization of herds and land, settling herders, introduction of less mobile, intensive grazing management and of rainfed forage. Many of these interventions have been responses to political or economic objectives and while they have improved the delivery of social services, in many instances, they conflict with the goal of maintaining grassland health and stability since they limit the mobile nature of pastoralism (Miller, 1999a; Goldstein and Beall, 1989; Wu, 1997a). Movements between seasonal pastures are being reduced or eliminated; herd composition is being restructured along commercial lines; herders are being compelled to become livestock farmers. The environment and the pastoral cultures are under threat where mobility has been eliminated or substantially reduced (Humphrey and Sneath, 1999; Sneath and Humphrey, 1996).

A disproportionate amount of research is oriented to maximizing livestock productivity, rather than understanding how livestock fit into the ecological system in a socially sustainable way. There is also a problem regarding the effective privatization of pastoral land tenure. Transaction costs associated with the policy are high, including high private costs relative to the benefits and high public costs of monitoring and enforcing contractual provisions related to pasture management (World Bank, 2001). As Banks (1999) has outlined, privatization policy was based on the assumption that, through the better definition of property rights and introduction of individual land tenure, security would be improved and this would prevent a "tragedy of the commons" scenario which in turn would give herders the incentive to manage their pasture better and invest in improvement. It was asserted that private ownership, by combining interest in both land and livestock, would prevent overgrazing (Banks, 1997). This model has been widely rejected by most pastoral specialists, who have found it a very poor guide to understanding transhumant pastoralism and planning development of pastoral areas.

Privatization of land in semi-arid pastoral areas often leads to lower levels of production, decreasing numbers of people supported on equivalent land and in some cases unsustainable or even destructive use of natural resources (Galaty *et al.*, 1994). Individualization of tenure leads to loss of flexibility in grazing management and consequently, a means to manage environmental risk. In Inner Mongolia (Sneath, 1998) found that that the highest levels of grassland degradation were in areas with the lowest stock mobility; mobility indices were a better guide to degradation than densities of livestock. Williams (1996a, b) noted that grassland enclosures in Inner Mongolia compound grazing problems by intensifying stocking rates on highly vulnerable land, exacerbating wind and soil erosion across large areas only to protect small isolated fields dedicated to poorly financed fodder cultivation.

The fact that many prosperous pastoral groups still populate the Tibetan plateau is evidence of their extensive knowledge about grasslands and livestock. Multi-species grazing maximizes the use of forage but requires complex management. Multiple species minimizes the risk of total loss from disease or winter storms. As McIntire (1993) found for Africa, the central characteristics of traditional pastoralism – low productivity, high variability in forage and livestock production, low production density and high market transaction costs – mean that conventional markets in land, labour and capital have not become well developed. Tibetans, nevertheless, often develop quite sophisticated arrangements for meeting their labour requirements, for managing grassland without exclusive private property rights and for allocating their livestock as capital in the absence of financial markets.

There is increasing evidence that many of current policies for Tibetan pastoral areas may be based on flawed information about herd sizes and incorrect assumptions about the destructiveness of traditional pastoral systems. Political and donor-driven pressure to develop the hinterland of Western China and to alleviate poverty among pastoralists also means that many of the underlying ecological and socio-economic issues are not adequately addressed before development programmes are undertaken. As Goldstein, Beall and Cincotta (1990) pointed out, it would be tragic if the herding way of life was gradually undermined and destroyed by modern notions of conservation and development based on faulty evidence, negative stereotypes and untested assumptions.

Mobility

Throughout the Steppe, pastoralists who, until a few decades ago, lived in tents (Plate 8.20) year-round have built houses for themselves and shelters for their livestock and have fenced private winter pastures (Plate 8.18). Does a 'home on the range', however, have to signify the demise of mobile pastoralism? Or, is there still potential to engage in mobile herding and maintain some of the best aspects of traditional management?

DANIEL MILLER

Plate 8.20
Longri summer camp.

The emphasis on settling herders in Western-style, intensive ranching type of operations and a conservative approach to stocking and fencing has led to misguided policies and projects throughout the world. The mobility paradigm does not argue for the 'good, old days', nor try to maintain pastoralists in their current conditions (Niamir-Fuller, 1999); it seeks to put in place proper policies, legal frameworks and support systems to enable pastoralism to evolve towards an economically, socially and environmentally sustainable livelihood. It presents a framework for analysing pastoral issues related to their resources, the herders, their adaptive strategies and their common property regimes and not only gives mobile livestock production systems a raison d'être, but tries to redress the imbalance caused by emphasis on intensive production (Niamir-Fuller, 1999).

The mobility paradigm would advocate that livestock mobility is an essential ingredient for sustainable development in Tibetan grasslands and that houses, shelters and privately fenced enclosures for hay and winter-spring grazing could be compatible so long as livestock are allowed opportunistic mobility. It would acknowledge the importance of "key sites", or high-value grazing patches and the need for access to them. It would make the case for pooling of household livestock into larger herds to be herded on shared pastures and seek to revitalize common property regime institutions. The mobility paradigm would seek ways to manage uncertainty and risk better through risk minimizing and risk buffering. There would also have to be a commitment to decentralization and real participatory processes.

CONCLUSION

The economic viability and environmental sustainability of pastoral production on the Tibetan Steppe is under considerable scrutiny. The Tibetan Steppe has received little research attention from grassland ecologists and specialists in pastoralism. Lack of information limits proper management and sustainable grassland development. Pastoral ecosystem dynamics are poorly understood and data on ecological processes taking place are limited. Many questions concerning how vegetation functions and the effect of grazing on the pastoral system remain unanswered. There is a critical need for more in-depth studies of the relationship between herbivores and the vegetation resource, and the relationship between domestic livestock and wild herbivores.

For the Tibetan Steppe there is need for fresh perspectives and information on ecosystem dynamics and pastoral development. Theories of plant succession leading to a single equilibrium community have been found to be inadequate for understanding the complex successional pathways of semi-arid and arid rangeland ecosystems (Stringham, Krueger and Thomas, 2001; Westoby, Walker and Noy-Meir, 1989a). This recognition has generated a search for an alternative theory that more adequately reflects the dynamics of pasture ecosystems. Theories involving multiple successional pathways, multiple steady states and state-and-transition processes are gaining in acceptance. On Tibetan Steppe pastures therefore, traditional measures for condition and carrying capacities may not be effective gauges for management. New perspectives regarding non-equilibrium ecosystem dynamics and concepts about plant succession processes in semi-arid ecosystems provide interesting frameworks for analysing Tibetan Steppe pastures (Cincotta, Zhang and Zhou, 1992; Fernandez-Gimenez and Allen-Diaz, 1999; Westoby, Walker and Noy-Meir, 1989b).

Neither are the socio-economic dimensions of Tibetan pastoral production systems well known (Clarke, 1992; Goldstein and Beall, 1989; Levine, 1998); greater efforts need to be directed towards developing a better understanding of current systems and how they are changing and adapting to development influences. Practices vary considerably across the area and need to be analysed (Clarke, 1987). Why do herders in different areas maintain different herd compositions? What are current offtake rates and how do increasing demands for livestock products in the marketplace affect livestock sales? What constraints and opportunities for improving livestock productivity are recognized by the herders? What forms of social organization exist for managing livestock and grasslands? How have these practices changed in recent years and what are the implications of these transformations? Answers to these and related questions, will help unravel many of the complexities of Tibetan pastoralism. Analyses of the socio-economic processes at work are a key challenge for researchers. It will also be important to determine which aspects of indigenous knowledge systems and traditional pastoral strategies can be used in the design of new development interventions on the Tibetan Steppe (Miller, 2002; Wu, 1998).

There is growing appreciation of the complexity and ecological and economic efficacy of traditional pastoralism (Wu, 1997b) which provides hope that the knowledge that pastoralists possess will be used in designing development interventions. It also gives a prospect that the pastoralists will be listened to and involved in the planning and implementation of pastoral development. Herders must be involved in the initial design of interventions, their needs and desires must be heard and their knowledge put to use. An important message for policy-makers is the need for active participation by the herders in all aspects of the development process and for empowered herders to manage their own development.

Given the generally poor experience with settling herders in other pastoral areas of the world, it will be interesting to watch the attempts to foster more sedentary livestock production systems on Tibetan grasslands. What effects will the privatization of the grazing lands have on pasture condition? Will herders overgraze pastures which they now view as their own property? What kinds of monitoring programmes are needed to look after the privatized pastures? What effect will private land and fences have on traditional mechanisms for pooling livestock into group herds and group herding?

There is a need to re-orient policy objectives in terms of grassland management and livestock production, and in the management of rural development. Maximizing agricultural output is not relevant to current circumstances. The need in the twenty-first century is for ecologically and economically sustainable development of pastoral areas, neither of which is consistent with output maximization (World Bank, 2001). Policies and development strategies should be based on consideration of ecological constraints, the interests and aspirations of the pastoralists themselves and alternative methods of meeting social objectives. There is a general need to invest more in grassland and livestock research in the Tibetan Steppe to guide policies and to help herders develop appropriate technologies for the range of ecological and socio-economic conditions found. Research needs to be more participatory and herders need to play a larger role in setting priorities and in determining the merits of findings.

Opportunities do exist, however, for improving the management of pastoral resources, increasing livestock productivity and bettering the livelihoods of the population. Programmes stressing multiple use, participatory development, sustainability, economics and biodiversity could be realized through complementary activities in resource management, livestock production and wildlife conservation. Sustainable land use on the Tibetan Steppe depends heavily on the local-level users of the resources – the Tibetan herders. It is at this level that pastoral resource use decisions are made on a daily basis. It is also at this local level that awareness, incentives and institutional and infrastructure conditions must be appropriate in order to secure sustainable grassland management.

Sustainable grassland management and pastoral development on the Tibetan Steppe requires: (1) greater concern about the welfare of herders; (2) increased concern about grassland degradation and ecosystem processes; and (3) the political will to address the problems. Concern and political will are not enough: there also has to be improved human resource capability to design and implement policies and actions. Lack of capacity at the local level is one of the main constraints to more sustainable pastoral development and pasture management in the Tibetan Steppe. It is necessary, therefore, to foster an enabling environment for local-level capacity building. This must take into account the local variability and site-specific conditions related to climate, soils, ecology, livestock production and socio-economic factors.

REFERENCES

Achuff, P. & Petocz, R. 1988. Preliminary resource inventory of the Arjin Mountains Nature Reserve, Xinjiang, People's Republic of China. World Wide Fund for Nature, Gland, Switzerland.

Banks, T.J. 1997. Pastoral land tenure reform and resource management in Northern Xinjiang: A new institutional economics approach. *Nomadic Peoples*, 1(2): 55–76.

Banks, T.J. 1999. State, community and common property in Xinjiang: Synergy or strife. *Development Policy Review*, 17: 293–313.

Barfield, T. 1993. *The Nomadic Alternative.* Englewood Cliffs, New Jersey, USA: Prentice-Hall.

Barfield, T. 1989. *The Perilous Frontier: Nomadic Empires and China.* Oxford, UK: Basil Blackwell.

Cai Li & Wiener, G. 1995. *The Yak.* FAO Regional Office for Asia and Pacific, Bangkok, Thailand.

Chang, D. 1983. The Tibetan plateau in relation to the vegetation of China. *Annals of the Missouri Botanical Garden*, 70: 564–570.

Chang, D. 1981. The vegetation zonation of the Tibetan Plateau. *Mountain Research and Development*, 1(1): 29–48.

Chang, D. & Gauch, H. 1986. Multivariate analysis of plant communities and environmental factors in Ngari, Tibet. *Ecology*, 67(6): 1568–1575.

Cincotta, R., Zhang, Y. & Zhou, X. 1992. Transhumant alpine pastoralism in Northeastern Qinghai Province: An evaluation of livestock population response during China's agrarian economic reform. *Nomadic Peoples*, 30: 3–25.

Cincotta, R., van Soest, P., Robertson, J., Beall, C. & Goldstein, M. 1991. Foraging ecology of livestock on the Tibetan Chang Tang: A comparison of three adjacent grazing areas. *Arctic and Alpine Research*, 23(2): 149–161.

CISNR [Commission for Integrated Survey of Natural Resources]. 1995. *Atlas of Grassland Resources of China.* Beijing, China: Map Press,

CISNR. 1996. *Map of Grassland Resources of China.* Beijing, China: Science Press.

Ciwang, D. 2000. The status and harnessing of the grassland ecological environment in Naqu, Tibetan Autonomous Region, pp. 106–112, *in:* Z. Lu and J. Springer (eds). *Tibet's Biodiversity: Conservation and Management.* Beijing, China: China Forestry Publishing House.

Clarke, G. 1998. Socio-economic change and the environment in a pastoral area of Lhasa Municipality, Tibet. pp. 1–46, *in:* G. Clarke (ed). *Development, Society and Environment in Tibet.* Papers presented at a Panel of the 7th International Association of Tibetan Studies, Graz, Austria, 1995. Verlag de Osterreichischen, Vienna, Austria.

Clarke, G. 1992. Aspects of the social organization of Tibetan pastoral communities. pp. 393–411, *in: Proceedings of the 5th Seminar of the International Association for Tibetan Studies.* Narita, Japan.

Clarke, G. 1987. China's reforms of Tibet and their effects on pastoralism. *IDS Discussion Paper,* No. 237. Institute of Development Studies, Brighton, England, UK.

Deng, L. 1981. Classification of grasslands in Xizang (Tibet) and the characteristics of their resources. pp. 2075–2083, *in:* D. Liu (ed). *Proceedings of Symposium on Qinghai-Xizang Plateau.* Beijing, China: Science Press.

Ekvall, R. 1954. Some differences in Tibetan land tenure and utilization. *Sinologica,* 4: 39–48.

Ekvall, R. 1968. *Fields on the Hoof: The Nexus of Tibetan Nomadic Pastoralism.* New York, NY, USA: Hold, Rinehart and Winston.

Ekvall, R. 1974. Tibetan nomadic pastoralists: Environment, personality and ethos. *Proceedings of the American Philosophical Society,* **113**(6): 519–537.

Ellis, J. & Swift, D. 1988. Stability of African pastoral ecosystems: alternate paradigms and implications for development. *Journal of Range Management,* **41**(6): 450–459.

Fernandez-Gimenez, M. & Allen-Diaz, B. 1999. Testing a non-equilibrium model of rangeland vegetation dynamics in Mongolia. *Journal of Applied Ecology,* **36**: 871–885.

Foggin, M. & Smith, A. 2000. Rangeland utilization and biodiversity on the alpine grasslands of Qinghai Province. pp. 120–130, *in:* Z. Lu and J. Springer (eds). *Tibet's Biodiversity: Conservation and Management.* Beijing, China: China Forestry Publishing House.

Galaty, J., Hjort af Ornas, A., Lane, C. & Ndagala, D. 1994. Introduction. *Nomadic Peoples,* **34/35**: 7–21.

Goldstein, M. 1992. Nomadic pastoralists and the traditional political economy – a rejoinder to Cox. *Himalayan Research Bulletin,* 12(1-2): 54–62.

Goldstein, M. & Beall, C. *1989.* The impact of reform policy on nomadic pastoralists in Western Tibet. *Asian Survey, 29(6): 619–624.*

Goldstein, M. & Beall, C. 1990. *Nomads of Western Tibet: Survival of a Way of Life.* Hong Kong, China: Oydessy.

Goldstein, M. & Beall, C. 1991. Change and continuity in nomadic pastoralism on the Western Tibetan Plateau. *Nomadic Peoples,* **28**: 105–122.

Goldstein, M., Beall, C. & Cincotta, R. 1990. Traditional nomadic pastoralism and ecological conservation on Tibet's Northern Plateau. *National Geographic Research,* **6**(2): 139–156.

Gu, A. 2000. Biodiversity of Tibet's rangeland resources and their protection. pp. 94–99, *in:* Z. Lu and J. Springer (eds). *Tibet's Biodiversity: Conservation and Management.* Beijing, China: China Forestry Publishing House.

Harris, R. & Bedunah, D. 2001. Sheep vs. sheep: Argali and livestock in western China. Unpublished final report to the National Geographic Society. University of Montana, Missoula, USA.

Harris, R. & Miller, D. 1995. Overlap in summer habitats and diets of Tibetan Plateau ungulates. *Mammalia,* **59**(2): 197–212.

Ho, P. 1996. Ownership and control in Chinese rangeland management since Mao: the case of free-riding in Ningxia. *ODI Pastoral Development Network Paper,* No. 39c.

Ho, P. 2000. China's rangelands under stress: A comparative study of pasture commons in the Ningxia Hui Autonomous Region. *Development and Change,* **31**: 385–412.

Huang, R. 1987. Vegetation in the northeastern part of the Qinghai-Xizang Plateau. pp. 438–489, *in:* J. Hovermann and W. Wang (eds). *Reports of the Northeastern Part of the Qinghai-Xizang (Tibet) Plateau.* Beijing, China: Science Press.

Humphrey, C. & Sneath, D. 1999. *The End of Nomadism? Society, State and the Environment in Inner Asia.* Durham, USA: Duke University Press.

Kingdom-Ward, F. 1948. Tibet as a grazing land. *Geographical Journal,* **110**: 60–75.

Lang, B., Huang, J. & Wang, H. 1997. Report on the pasture and livestock survey in IFAD Project Areas, Hainan Prefecture, Qinghai Province, China. Unpublished report. IFAD Project Office, Xining, Qinghai.

Lattimore, O. 1940. *Inner Asian Frontiers of China.* New York, New York, USA: American Geographic Society.

Laycock, W.A. 1991. State states and thresholds of range condition on North American rangelands: A viewpoint. *Journal of Range Management,* **44**(5): 427–433.

Levine, N. 1998. From nomads to ranchers: Managing pasture among ethnic Tibetans in Sichuan. pp. 69–76, *in:* G. Clarke (ed). *Development, Society and Environment in Tibet.* Papers presented at a Panel of the 7th International Association of Tibetan Studies, Graz, Austria, 1995. Verlag de Osterreichischen, Nienna, Austria.

Manderscheid, A. 2001. The black tents in its easternmost distribution: The case of the Tibetan Plateau. *Mountain Research and Development,* **21**(2): 154–160.

McIntire, J. 1993. Markets and contracts in African pastoralism. pp. 519–529, *in:* K. Hoff, A. Braverman and J. Stiglitz (eds). *The Economics of Rural Organization: Theory, Practice and Policy.* New York, NY, USA: Oxford University Press.

Meiners, S. 1991. The upper limit of alpine land use in Central, South and Southeastern Tibet. *GeoJournal,* **25**: 285–295.

Miehe, G. 1988. Geoecological reconnaissance in the alpine belt in southern Tibet. *GeoJournal,* **17**(4): 635–648.

Miller, D. 1997a. New perspectives on range management and pastoralism and their implications for Hindu Kush-Himalayan-Tibetan plateau rangelands. pp. 7–12, *in:* D. Miller and S. Craig (eds). *Rangelands and Pastoral Development in the Hindu*

Kush-Himalayas. Proceedings of a Regional Experts' Meeting, Kathmandu, Nepal, 5–7 November 1996. ICIMOD, Kathmandu, Nepal.

Miller, D. 1997b. Conserving and managing yak genetic diversity: An introduction. pp. 2–12, *in:* D. Miller, S. Craig and G. Rana (eds). *Conservation and Management of Yak Genetic Diversity.* Proceedings of a Workshop. Kathmandu, Nepal, 29–31 October 1996. ICIMOD, Kathmandu, Nepal.

Miller, D. 1998a. *Fields of Grass: Portraits of the Pastoral Landscape and Nomads of the Tibetan Plateau and Himalayas.* ICIMOD, Kathmandu, Nepal.

Miller, D. 1998b. Conserving biological diversity in Himalayan and Tibetan Plateau rangelands. pp. 291–320, *in: Ecoregional Co-operation for Biodiversity Conservation in the Himalaya,* Report of the International Meeting on Himalaya Ecoregional Co-operation, 16–18 February 1998, Kathmandu, Nepal. New York, New York, USA: UNDP and WWF.

Miller, D. 1998c. Grassland privatization and future challenges in the Tibetan Plateau of Western China. pp. 106–122, *in:* Jian Liu and Qi Lu (eds). *Proceedings of the International Workshop on Grassland Management and Livestock Production in China.* Beijing, China, 28–29 March 1998. Reports of the Sustainable Agricultural Working Group, China Council on International Cooperation on Environment and Development (CCICED). Beijing, China: China Environmental Science Press.

Miller, D. 1999a. Nomads of the Tibetan Plateau rangelands in Western China, Part Two: Pastoral Production. *Rangelands,* **21**(1): 16–19.

Miller, D. 1999b. Nomads of the Tibetan Plateau rangelands in Western China, Part Three: Pastoral Development and Future Challenges. *Rangelands,* **21**(2): 17–20.

Miller, D. 2000. Tough times for Tibetan nomads in Western China: Snowstorms, settling down, fences and the demise of traditional nomadic pastoralism. *Nomadic Peoples,* **4**(1): 83–109.

Miller, D. 2002. The importance of China's nomads. *Rangelands,* **24**(1): 22–24.

Miller, D. & Bedunah, D. 1993. High elevation rangeland in the Himalaya and Tibetan Plateau: issues, perspectives and strategies for livestock development and resource conservation. pp. 1785–1790. *Proceedings of the 17th International Grassland Congress,* New Zealand Grassland Association, Palmerston North, New Zealand.

Miller, D., Harris, R. & Cai, G. 1994. Wild yaks and their conservation on the Tibetan Plateau. pp. 27–34, *in:* R. Zhang, J. Han and J. Wu (eds). *Proceedings of the 1st International Congress on Yak.* Gansu Agricultural University, Lanzhou, China.

Miller, D. & Jackson, R. 1994. Livestock and snow leopards: making room for competing users on the Tibetan Plateau. pp. 315–328, *in:* J. Fox and Du Jizeng (eds). *Proceedings of the Seventh International Snow Leopard Symposium.* International Snow Leopard Trust, Seattle, USA.

Miller, D. & Schaller, G. 1996. Rangelands of the Chang Tang Wildlife Reserve, Tibet. *Rangelands,* **18**(3): 91–96.

Miller, D. & Schaller, G. 1997. Conservation threats to the Chang Tang Wildlife Reserve, Tibet. *Ambio*, **26**(3): 185–186.

Miller, D. & Schaller, G. 1998. Rangeland dynamics in the Chang Tang Wildlife Reserve, Tibet, pp. 125–147, *in:* I. Stellrecht (ed). *Karakorum-Hindukush-Himalaya: Dynamics of Change*. Koln, Germany: Rudiger Koppe Verlag.

Mou, X., Deng, L. & Gu, A. 1992. [*Rangelands of Xizang (Tibet)*] (In Chinese). Beijing, China: Science Press.

Ni, J. *2002.* Carbon storage in grasslands of China. *Journal of Arid Environments,* **50**: 205–218.

Niamir-Fuller, M. 1999. *Managing Mobility in African Rangelands: the Legitimization of Transhumance*. London, UK: IT Publications, on behalf of FAO and Beijer International Institute of Ecological Economics.

Olson, D. & Dinerstein, E. 1997. The Global 200: Conserving the World's Distinctive Ecoregions. Conservation Science Program, WWF-US, Washington, D.C., USA

Ryavec, K. & Vergin, H. 1998. Population and rangelands in Central Tibet: A GIS-based approach. *GeoJournal*, **48**(1): 61–72.

Schaller, G. 1998. *Wildlife of the Tibetan Steppe*. Chicago, USA: University of Chicago Press.

Sheehy, D. 2001. The rangelands, land degradation and black beach: A review of research reports and discussions. pp. 5–9, *in:* N. van Wageningen and Sa Wenjun (eds). *The Living Plateau: Changing Lives of Herders in Qinghai*. Kathmandu, Nepal: ICIMOD.

Sheehy, D. 2000. Range resource management planning on the Qinghai-Tibetan Plateau. Unpublished report, prepared for the Qinghai Livestock Development Project. ALA/CHN/9344. EU Project, Xining, Qinghai Province, China.

Sneath, D. 1998. State policy and pasture degradation in Inner Asia. *Science,* **281**: 1147–1148.

Sneath, D. & Humphrey, C. 1996. *Culture and Environment in Inner Asia: I. The Pastoral Economy and the Environment*. Cambridge, UK: White Horse Press.

Stringham, T., Krueger, W. & Thomas, D. 2001. Application of non-equilibrium ecology to rangeland riparian zones. *Journal of Range Management*, **54**(3): 210–217.

Thomas, A. 1999. Overview of the geoecology of the Gongga Shan Range, Sichuan Province, China. *Mountain Research and Development*, **19**(1): 17–30.

Vaurie, C. 1970. *Tibet and its Birds*. London, UK: Witherby.

Walter, H. & Box, E. 1983. The deserts of Central Asia. pp. 193–236, *in:* N. West (ed). *Ecosystems of the World. V: Temperate Deserts and Semi-Deserts*. New York, NY, USA: Elsevier.

Westoby, M., Walker B. & Noy-Meir, I. 1989a. Range management on the basis of a model which does not seek to establish equilibrium. *Journal of Arid Environments,* **17**: 235–239.

Westoby, M., Walker B. & Noy-Meir, I. 1989b. Opportunistic management for rangelands not at equilibrium. *Journal of Range Management*, **44**: 427–433.

Williams, D. 1996a. The barbed walls of China: A contemporary grassland drama. *Journal of Asian Studies,* **55**(3): 665–691.

Williams, D. 1996b. Grassland enclosures: Catalyst of land degradation in Inner Mongolia. *Human Organization,* **55**(3): 307–312.

World Bank. 2001. *China: Air, Land and Water. Environmental Priorities for a New Millennium.* Washington, D.C., USA: World Bank.

Wu, N. 1998. Indigenous knowledge of yak breeding and crossbreeding among nomads in western Sichuan, China. *Indigenous Knowledge and Development Monitor,* **1**(6): 7–9.

Wu, N. 1997a. Tibetan pastoral dynamics and nomads' adaptation to modernization in northwestern Sichuan, China. Unpublished research report (Grant No. 5947-97). National Geographic Society, Washington, D.C., USA.

Wu, N. 1997b. *Ecological Situation of High-Frigid Rangeland and Its Sustainability: A Case Study of the Constraints and Approaches in Pastoral Western Sichuan, China.* Berlin, Germany: Dietrich Reimer Verlag.

Chapter 9
Australian grasslands

John G. McIvor

SUMMARY

Australia has a latitudinal range of 11°S to 44°S, which, coupled with precipitation from 100 mm to 4 000 mm, generates a wide range of grassland environments. The landscape is characterized by vast plains with only limited elevated areas. Native herbage remains the basis for a significant portion of the grazing industry. Europeans settled in Australia two hundred years ago, and have had a massive impact on vegetation through agricultural development and introduction of exotic plants and animals. Most farms rely on animal products from grasslands. Grazing land tenure is a mix of freehold and leasehold from government. Family owned and operated farms remain the dominant unit. Most grassland products are exported. Arid and semi-arid tropical areas are used for extensive cattle grazing; water from artesian wells and bores is necessary. Pasture growth is very seasonal and stock lose weight in the dry season. The intermediate rainfall zone extends from southeastern Queensland through New South Wales, northern Victoria and southern South Australia, and includes part of southwestern Australia. Crops are combined with sheep rearing; ley farming systems, where a legume-based pasture phase of two to five years is alternated with crops for one to three years, were widely adopted in southern areas. This high-rainfall zone forms the greater part of the coastal belt and adjacent tablelands of the three eastern mainland states; sown pastures are widely used. Sheep and cattle dominate livestock numbers; wool sheep and beef cattle predominate, but dairying is locally important. Animals that compete for grazing include a range of macropods and feral domestic species. Sown pasture technology is well developed in the temperate zone, based on the use of selected, exotic species, with emphasis on legumes. Development of sown pastures was slower in the tropical areas and suffered a set-back when disease affected *Stylosanthes* stands.

INTRODUCTION

Grasslands and grazing have been important over much of Australia since human colonization and grazing remains the most widespread land use, covering approximately 70 percent of the continent. Grasslands support the native game hunted by the original Aboriginal colonists and the domestic grazing animals introduced by European colonists in the late eighteenth century. Native herbs (particularly grasses) and shrubs provided the initial grazing but these have been supplemented – and in some cases replaced – by exotic species.

There are a number of descriptions of Australian grasslands (e.g. McTaggart, 1936; Moore, 1970, 1993; Groves and Williams, 1981) that have been drawn on in preparing this paper. Following Moore (1970), all herbaceous communities used for livestock production are considered grasslands, and include both native communities that are grazed and pastures composed of mainly introduced plants, either sown or volunteer. This paper concentrates on dryland or rainfed pastures, but irrigated pastures are important (approximately one million hectares), particularly in some dairying areas in southern Australia (about half of all irrigation water in Australia is used on pastures).

LOCATION

Australia covers an area of 7.68 million km², from 11°S to 44°S, and this latitudinal range, coupled with annual rainfalls ranging from 100 mm to more than 4 000 mm, both coastal and inland areas, and a variety of soils, generates a wide range of grassland environments.

PHYSICAL FEATURES

The Australian landscape is characterized by vast plains and plateaux (three-quarters lie between 180 and 460 m above sea level) with only limited elevated areas. The continent can be divided into three major structural components – the stable Western Shield, the gently warped Central Basin, and the Eastern Uplands (from Tasmania to north Queensland), which are of ancient origin but have been rejuvenated to some degree. These components determine the pattern of relief and drainage. The Eastern Uplands contain the highest mountains in Australia (including Mt Kosciusko, 2 200 m) and the only area with snow. They form the divide between the steep eastern-flowing rivers and those draining west. The Central Basin has two major drainage systems – the Murray-Darling system, which includes runoff from the southeastern rim, and one draining internally to Lake Eyre. The Great Artesian Basin lies to the west of the Eastern Uplands in Queensland, New South Wales and South Australia, and water from this Basin has enabled grazing industries to establish and persist over a wide area of arid and semi-arid inland Australia.

CLIMATE
Rainfall

Total annual precipitation varies from more than 4 000 mm in the mountainous areas of northeast Queensland to approximately 100 mm in the north of South Australia. Approximately one-third of Australia receives over 500 mm of rain, one-third has 250 to 500 mm and one-third has less than 250 mm; rainfall is greatest in coastal areas and lower inland. Seasonal distribution varies markedly over the continent, from strong summer dominance in the north

TABLE 9.1
Climate data for selected stations. Rainfall periods are October–March (summer) and April–September (winter). Maximum temperature is the average daily maximum temperature during the hottest month and minimum temperature is the average daily minimum temperature during the coldest month.

Location	Lat.	Long.	Rainfall (mm)		Temperature (°C)		Evaporation (mm)
			Summer	Winter	Max.	Min.	
Daly Waters	16.26°S	133.37°E	625	43	38.5	11.7	2 508
Cairns	16.89°S	145.76°E	1 567	440	31.5	17.0	2 254
Gayndah	25.66°S	151.75°E	510	196	32.4	6.9	2 035
Charleville	26.41°S	146.26°E	326	156	34.9	4.1	2 583
Narrogin	32.94°S	118.18°E	113	391	30.9	5.6	1 646
Wagga Wagga	35.16°S	147.46°E	276	309	31.2	2.7	1 830
Hamilton	37.83°S	142.06°E	268	432	25.9	4.2	1 311

SOURCE: Data from the Bureau of Meteorology Climate Averages.

(e.g. Daly Waters in Table 9.1) to strong winter dominance in the southwest (e.g. Narrogin in Table 9.1). The total amounts and distribution reflect the continental weather systems. Monsoonal rains fall in the extreme north between November and March; tropical cyclones can affect most of northern Australia during this time but they are very erratic; and trade winds provide orographic rains to the northeast Queensland coast. In southern Australia, in contrast, the most precipitation comes from frontal rains occurring from May to September.

Erratic rainfall, disastrous droughts and occasional floods are a feature of the Australian climate. When variability is expressed in terms of the mean deviation as a percentage of the annual mean, the most reliable areas are the northwest coast near Darwin, the southwest of Western Australia, coastal areas in South Australia, Victoria and New South Wales, and Tasmania. Variability increases inland, and the great bulk of Australian rangelands have highly erratic rainfall. Maximum variability is found on the western coast near the Tropic of Capricorn and in central Australia. Much of the variation in rainfall in eastern Australia can be related to the ENSO (El Niño-Southern Oscillation) phenomenon of sea surface temperatures and atmospheric pressures over the Pacific Ocean.

Temperature and evaporation
Summers are warm to hot (Table 9.1). Maximum temperatures above 38°C are common in inland areas and, apart from the mountains of the southeast, can occur occasionally in other areas. Winters are warm in northern Australia and cold in the south, with occasional snow above 600 m. Frosts occur in all regions except the extreme north, and coastal areas in other tropical and subtropical regions. Evaporation is lowest in the Tasmanian highlands. On the mainland, evaporation is lowest in coastal areas and increases inland to maximum values exceeding 3 000 mm in central Australia. The generally mild conditions make it unnecessary to house animals during winter.

Growing seasons

Given the variation in amount and distribution of rainfall and the temperature range over the continent, it is not surprising there is a wide range in growing seasons – from no reliable season in arid inland areas, to almost year-long seasons in some coastal areas. Fitzpatrick and Nix (1970) described a method for estimating growing seasons from climatic data. They developed indices varying in value from zero to one for light, temperature and moisture. A value of zero means that the level of that factor is so low that all growth is prevented; a value of one means that there is no limitation to growth by that factor. The three indices are then combined to produce a growth index that measures the combined impact of all factors. Figure 9.1 shows the average weekly values of the temperature and moisture indices for four sites in Table 9.1 and demonstrates a range of growing seasons (the light index has been omitted as radiation is usually not limiting to growth). At Hamilton (in the high rainfall zone of the section on "pastoral and agricultural systems", below), moisture limits growth in summer but there is often sufficient for some growth. Moisture availability increases rapidly in autumn and there is a period of increased growth until low temperatures limit growth in winter, followed by a spring "flush" before water again becomes limiting in summer. At Narrogin (wheat-sheep zone)

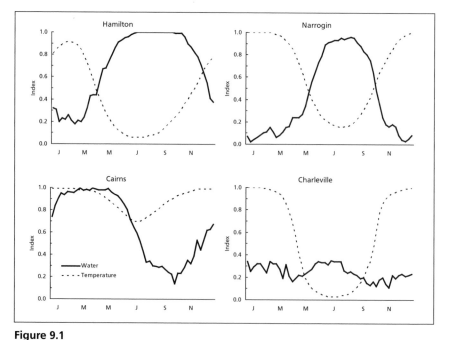

Figure 9.1

Average weekly water and temperature indices for selected Australian locations.
Source: Fitzpatrick and Nix, 1970.
Notes: Water indices were calculated using the WATBAL model (Keig and McAlpine, 1974) and temperature indices were estimated from the relationships of Fitzpatrick and Nix (1970) for tropical legumes (Cairns and Charleville) and temperate species (Hamilton and Narrogin). A value of 0 means that the level of that factor is so low that all growth is prevented, and a value of 1 means that there is no limitation to growth by that factor.

there is almost no summer moisture and growth occurs mainly in autumn and spring although the temperature limitations in winter are not as severe as those at Hamilton. At Cairns, in the wet tropics of northeast Queensland, both temperature and moisture levels are high during the wet season and the major limit to growth is moisture during the dry season. At Charleville (in the pastoral zone), average moisture levels are low throughout the whole year (although they can be high at any time of the year in a particular year) and temperatures are severely limiting for tropical species in winter.

SOILS

Hubble (1970) identified three important features of Australian soils. First, the generally low nutrient status, with widespread and severe deficiencies of nitrogen and phosphorus (and sometimes sulphur), and varying deficiencies of trace elements (copper, zinc, molybdenum, cobalt, manganese, boron). Multiple deficiencies are common and, as Morley (1961) remarked, "Australian soils are rich only in the diversity and intensity of their deficiencies." Second, the poor physical condition of surface soils, which, over large areas, are massive or weakly structured with low macroporosity, set hard on drying and tend to surface sealing. As a result, water infiltration is often poor and water storage low. Third, over large areas, the soils have strongly weathered or differentiated profiles, including those with strong texture contrast. Good soils (deep, fertile, well drained) are not common and are used for cropping if the climate is suitable, leaving the poorer soils for pastures.

LIVESTOCK

Sheep and cattle dominate the Australian livestock numbers, but there have been marked changes in their relative importance over the past 30 years. The majority of the sheep are Merinos for wool, but British breeds and their crosses with Merinos are important for lamb production. Sheep numbers peaked at 180 million in 1970, then declined, but rose again to 170 million in 1990. Market prospects for wool have been poor since then and numbers declined to 119 million in 2000. Most of the cattle are beef animals but dairying is important in wetter coastal areas and some irrigation districts, particularly in Victoria. Cattle numbers reached a peak of 33 million in 1976, then fell until the mid-1980s, but have since increased to 24 million beef cattle and 3 million dairy cattle in 2000. There are important goat herds in some inland areas, and an estimated feral goat population of 4.5 million and a small deer industry with approximately 200 000 animals.

WILDLIFE

Australia has large populations of wildlife, including both native species and feral populations of exotic animals. There are a number of important predators (dingo, fox, wild pig, raven or crow, eagle), and also a range of animals that compete for grazing. These include a range of macropods (kangaroos, wallabies) and also domestic species (rabbits, donkeys, horses, camels). Rabbits have been and continue to be large competitors with domestic stock, although their numbers have been reduced by myxoma virus since the 1950s, and more recently by rabbit calicivirus. Australia had no equivalent of the huge herds of herbivores in parts of Africa or America, and the native plants evolved under conditions of generally light grazing, which has had serious consequences for their survival under increased grazing pressures since European settlement.

SOCIAL ASPECTS AND INSTITUTIONS
People
The date of settlement of Australia by humans is debated, but there have been Aborigines in Australia for over 60 000 years; they were primarily hunters and their major influence on the grasslands would have been through widespread use of fire, to encourage feed for their prey and to assist with hunting.

In contrast to this long period of Aboriginal occupation, Europeans only settled in Australia a little over 200 years ago, but in this time they have had massive impacts on the vegetation, both intentional (tree clearing, cropping and sown pasture introductions, fertilizer application, domestic grazing animals, etc.) and accidental (weeds, pest animals). Settlement was rapid and almost all suitable lands were occupied by the end of the nineteenth century. Despite this rapid spread, the population remains concentrated in major cities and coastal urban areas, with only a sparse population in the interior. Approximately 80 percent of Australia, including all the pastoral zone (see section below), has a population density of less than 1 person/km^2. For example, the Diamantina Shire in southwest Queeensland has an area of 94 832 km^2 and had a resident population of 319 in the 2001 Census.

Political system
Until 1901, Australia consisted of six self-governing British colonies, which federated in 1901 to become states of the Commonwealth of Australia, with democratically elected governments at national, state and local levels. Specific powers were transferred to the Commonwealth government (e.g. defence, immigration, social welfare) but many important powers affecting agriculture remain State responsibilities, including land use and ownership, water supplies, and control of pests and noxious weeds.

Land tenure and ownership
Grazing land tenure in Australia is a mix of freehold and leasehold from government. Freehold is commonest in the higher rainfall areas, with leasehold most important in the extensive grazing lands in the tropics and arid inland Australia. Overall, only approximately 10 percent of land is privately owned, but the proportion varies widely between states and territories, from less than

1 percent in the Northern Territory to approximately 60 percent in Victoria. Leases vary from state to state, from annual to perpetual, although the majority are for long periods, and the conditions also vary, e.g. improvements (buildings, fences, water supplies) to be made, and stock numbers to be carried. There have been some important changes in the last decade: Aboriginal land rights have raised uncertainties concerning the rights of pastoral lessees; increasing emphasis on land condition in pastoral leases; and increasingly restrictive conditions on the use and management of freehold land in relation to vegetation management, particularly tree clearing.

Approximately 90 000 of Australia's 145 000 agricultural properties rely on animal products from pastures and grasslands (Anon., 1999). Family owned and operated farms have been, and remain, the dominant structural unit in Australian agriculture. In a 1994–95 survey by the Australian Bureau of Agricultural and Resource Economics (ABARE), 99.6 percent of all broadacre (grazing, cropping) and dairy farms were family owned and only 0.4 percent were corporately operated (i.e. at least partially owned by a publicly listed company) (Martin, 1996). Corporate ownership is most significant in the beef industry, particularly in northern Australia. However, even in the beef industry in 1996–97, only 1.1 percent of specialist beef properties were corporately owned (Martin *et al.*, 1998). The corporate properties were much larger (47 percent of the total property area) and owned more cattle (19 percent of total numbers). The majority of family-owned properties are in New South Wales (31 percent of all family-owned farms), Queensland (28 percent) and Victoria (26 percent), whereas the corporate properties are mainly in Queensland (40 percent of all corporate properties) and the Northern Territory (32 percent). Farm numbers are declining as properties amalgamate, and numbers have halved in the last forty years.

Authorities responsible for land management

Land is a State government responsibility under the Australian Constitution. All states and territories have lands departments responsible for titles and some aspects of management. During the early years of European settlement emphasis was placed on the occupation of land and establishing and maintaining agricultural production. After the gold rushes in the 1850s, there were demands for large numbers of small farms to develop the country and stimulate economic development. Closer Settlement Acts were passed in the 1860s and Government sponsored closer settlement schemes to promote rural development remained important until the 1970s, especially after both World Wars. This emphasis on agricultural production continued until recently; now increased stress has been placed on land management issues.

Market systems

Agricultural production is privately controlled, but Australia has had a variety of marketing mechanisms for agricultural products. However, with the cessation of the wool reserve price scheme in 1992, these mechanisms are no longer important for products from grasslands.

Most of the production from grasslands is exported. For the three years from 1994 to 1997 (ABARE, 1998) Australia produced an average of 1 800 000 t of beef and veal and 582 000 t of mutton and lamb – 42 percent and 56 percent, respectively, of which was exported, together with 628 000 live cattle and 5.6 million live sheep. Whole milk production averaged 8 650 million litres, and although only a small amount was exported as whole milk (71 million litres), 64 percent of the 739 000 t of dairy products (butter, cheese, whole milk powder, skim milk powder, casein) were exported. Average wool production during this period was 718 000 t and the amount exported exceeded this figure with the sell-off of accumulated supplies. This dependence on exports means that international prices have a large impact on returns to producers.

Pastoral and agricultural systems

Many factors affect the agricultural system adopted in an area – climate and growing conditions, soil type, topography, markets, distance to markets, labour availability, etc. Animal production systems can be conveniently considered in the three zones used by ABARE – the pastoral zone, the wheat-sheep zone and the high rainfall zone. These differ in the manner in which land and resources are used and the commodities produced.

Pastoral zone

This zone includes the arid and semi-arid regions and most of the northern tropical areas. Agricultural land use in this zone is characterized by extensive grazing of native vegetation. Although some cropping is undertaken, it is impractical on most properties because of inadequate rainfall. Corporate property ownership is more important than in the other two zones.

The native vegetation in the arid interior has been used since the mid-nineteenth century, with wool production most important in southern Australia and beef most important in central and northern Australia. Sown pastures are of very restricted and minor importance. The zone has no reliable growing season, droughts occur frequently and production and financial returns vary from year to year. Water supplies from artesian and sub-artesian bores are critical for continued animal production over wide areas. The beef industry is based on breeding, with some animals grown and fattened locally, but many sent elsewhere for fattening, including to the flooded natural pastures of the Channel country in western Queensland.

The wool industry is based almost entirely on grazing Merinos on native pastures for medium quality wool. Properties are large (5 000 to more than 100 000 ha, with 5 000 to 20 000 sheep) and, due to wide fluctuations in pasture yield and quality, stocking rates are low (one sheep to 2–40 ha). Wool production levels are satisfactory, but lambing percentages are often low in the harsh environment. Despite this, most operations are breeding flocks. In times of high cereal prices there is some cropping on the higher rainfall margins of the zone, but animal products are the major source of income.

The tropical grazing lands have a reliable summer growing season and winter dry season. Pasture growth is rapid during the early growing season and herbage quality is high, but later drops to low levels; animals gain weight during the growing season and lose in the dry season. Beef production is the only major land use. Initially all cattle were *Bos taurus* breeds (especially Shorthorn); now almost all are *Bos indicus* or their crosses, which are better adapted, with greater resistance to heat stress, stronger resistance to ticks, increased foraging ability and a higher forage intake (Frisch and Vercoe, 1977; Siebert, 1982), leading to superior growth, breeding performance and survival.

The zone is an important source of stores for fattening elsewhere, and production of grade beef for the United States of America market has been a major outlet. In the past decade, an important trade in live cattle to southeast Asia has developed. This has been particularly important for beef producers in north-western Australia, who are close to these markets but remote from markets in Australia and also from abattoirs.

The tropical grazing lands range from the more productive areas of coastal and central Queensland to the remote parts of the Kimberley and Cape York Peninsula. There are major differences between these regions. In coastal and central Queensland, the properties and herds are smaller (typically less than 10 000 ha and carrying 500 to 2 000 cattle), animal husbandry and management inputs are greater, animal productivity is higher and the north Asian markets are important. In the remote areas, properties and herds are much larger (200 000 to 500 000 ha, with 6 000 to 8 000 cattle), animal productivity is lower and the live export, store and American markets are most important.

Sown pastures are important in eastern and central Queensland, but, apart from limited areas in the "Top End" of the Northern Territory, they are of minor importance elsewhere, and cattle depend on native pastures. A number of introduced species are now naturalized (e.g. *Stylosanthes* spp., *Cenchrus ciliaris*). The use of feed supplements (particularly urea-based ones) is widespread. Cereal cropping is important in central and southern Queensland and is sometimes integrated with animal production in ley pasture rotations.

Wheat-sheep zone

The wheat-sheep zone has a climate and topography that generally allows regular cropping of grains in addition to the grazing of sheep and cattle on a more intensive basis than in the pastoral zone. Rainfall is generally adequate for a range of pasture species, usually in a crop-pasture rotation. Farms are much smaller than those in the pastoral zone but larger than those in the high rainfall zone.

This zone of intermediate rainfall extends from southeastern Queensland (500–750 mm annual rainfall) through the slopes and plains of New South Wales (300–600 mm), northern Victoria (300–550 mm) and southern South Australia (250–500 mm), and includes part of southwestern Australia (250–700 mm). The most important crops are wheat, barley, oats, grain legumes, pulses and oilseeds, with sorghum important in the northern areas. Merino wool growing (medium fibre diameter), fat lamb and beef production are the major animal industries. Both crop and animal products are important income sources and the balance between land uses depends largely on relative financial returns; in recent years there has been an increase in crops and a large decrease in wool. The more reliable seasonal conditions than in the pastoral zone and the flexibility of multiple income sources leads to more stable income. Family owned farms dominate in this zone.

Ley farming systems, where a pasture phase of two to five years is alternated with a crop phase of one to three years, were widely adopted in southern areas after the Second World War. The short-term pastures are important for improving soil fertility and providing disease breaks for subsequent crops, as well as animal production. Almost all pasture plants are annuals, reflecting both the length of the growing season and the ease of removing them for the cropping phase. Subterranean clover (*Trifolium subterraneum*) is widely used on the acidic soils and annual medics (*Medicago* spp.) on more alkaline soils in drier areas. These pastures provide both high quality grazing for animals and improved soil structure and increased soil nitrogen for utilization by crops. However, as discussed later, productivity of these legume pastures has declined. This has led to some farmers switching to continuous cropping using grain legumes and fertilizer to supply nitrogen, minimum tillage to maintain soil physical conditions, alternation of cereals with grain legumes, pulses and oilseeds for disease control, and herbicides for weed control.

Feedlots (where cattle are confined in yards and completely hand or mechanically fed to attain high levels of production) has become important in Australia in the last 30 years. There are about 800 accredited feedlots with a capacity of 900 000 head. They are mostly in Queensland and New South Wales and serve both the domestic and export markets (especially Japan). Cattle which previously would have been grass fed are finished on a diet of grain for 30 to 300 days (but most commonly 90–120 days) depending on the market.

High rainfall zone

This zone forms the greater part of the coastal belt and adjacent tablelands of the three eastern mainland states, small areas in southeastern South Australia and southwestern Western Australia, and the whole of Tasmania. Rainfall is summer-dominant or spread throughout the year in Queensland and northern New South Wales, and winter-dominant in southern areas. Higher rainfall, steeper topography, more adequate surface water and greater humidity make this zone less suitable than the wheat-sheep zone for grain-based cropping, but more suitable for grazing and growing other crops, but there has been an increase in cereal growing with new cultivars in recent years. These wetter areas have a longer growing season than the other zones and pasture improvement is widespread, with *Trifolium subterraneum* and, in the wetter areas, *T. repens* and *Lolium perenne* as important species.

Production of wool, prime lambs and beef are important, and all three are carried out on some properties, giving increased stability of income. Farm sizes range from small, often part-time operations, to large enterprises of more than 5 000 ha. In contrast to the pastoral and wheat belt farms, where medium quality wool dominates, fine wool production is more important in these wetter areas.

Dairying is limited to areas with a long growing season (or irrigation) for the production of high quality pastures. Victoria and New South Wales are the major dairy producing states. Although the feeding of concentrates is increasing, production is pasture-based and farms consist almost entirely of sown pastures. Income is derived from milk sales for whole milk consumption and manufacturing and sales of surplus cattle. Most dairy farms are operated by their owners, with the family providing most of the labour. There have been massive changes in the dairy industry during the past 30 years, with fewer farms and farmers and large increases in production per cow and per hectare. Average herd size has increased to 150 head, with some herds of more than 1 000 cows.

NATURAL VEGETATION
Despite the amount of pasture development, native herbage remains the base of a significant portion of the grazing industry. There have been a number of classifications and descriptions of the Australian vegetation (e.g. Leeper, 1970; Carnahan, 1989; Thackway and Cresswell, 1995). Moore (1970) classified the Australian grazing lands into 13 groups on the basis of climate, the characteristics and height of the major grasses (tall: >90 cm; mid: 45–90 cm; short: <45 cm) and important species. Three of the groups are of little value for grazing (heaths and sedgelands, mallee, forest lands). The distribution of the other ten groups is shown in Figure 9.2 and they are described below, drawing largely on Moore (1970, 1993), with additional information from the detailed descriptions of pasture lands of northern Australia in Tothill and Gillies (1992). The extent of grasslands in Australia is shown in Figure 9.3.

Tropical tall-grass
These communities are the grassy understorey of tropical woodlands which extend in an arc across northern Australia and have been further divided into monsoon, tropical and subtropical by Mott *et al.* (1985) and Tothill and Gillies (1992). Monsoon tall-grass communities occur in regions with annual rainfall greater than 750 mm and a highly reliable distribution of wet and dry seasons,

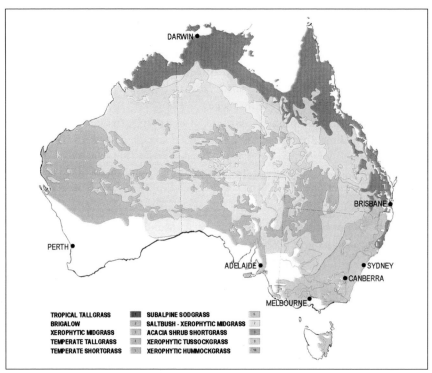

Figure 9.2
Natural vegetation zones of Australia.
Source: Adapted from Moore, 1970.

Plate 9.1
Tropical tall-grass community dominated by Themeda triandra *in northeast Queensland.*

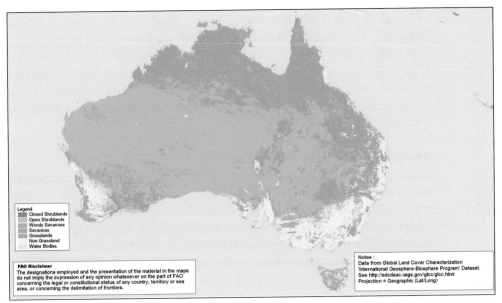

Figure 9.3
Extent of grasslands in Australia.

in the northern Kimberley region of Western Australia, the "Top End" of the Northern Territory, and northern Cape York Peninsula in Queensland. In contrast, the tropical (northeastern Queensland) and subtropical (southeastern Queensland) tall-grass communities have a less defined and more unreliable rainfall pattern, and usually less than 750 mm annual rainfall.

Within the monsoon tall-grass communities, those dominated by perennial grasses (*Themeda triandra* (Plate 9.1), *Chrysopogon fallax, Sorghum plumosum, Sehima nervosum, Heteropogon contortus* and *Aristida* spp.) occur on texture contrast and earth soils, and communities dominated by annuals (*Sorghum* spp., *Schizachyrium fragile*) grow on sands and skeletal soils. *Heteropogon contortus* is an important species in the tropical and subtropical tall-grass communities in eastern Queensland. Originally, *Themeda triandra* was commoner, and in some areas *Heteropogon contortus* is decreasing and the stoloniferous grasses *Bothriochloa pertusa* and *Digitaria didactyla* are increasing. Other important genera are *Bothriochloa, Dichanthium, Chrysopogon* and *Aristida*. Treeless grasslands dominated by *Dichanthium* and *Bothriochloa* spp. occur on cracking clays. Tree clearing to increase herbage growth has been widespread in the subtropical tall-grass, but less important in the tropical and monsoon areas, where the yield responses are less (Mott *et al.*, 1985).

Brigalow

Brigalow (*Acacia harpophylla*) forest and woodlands extend from central Queensland to northern New South Wales on medium to high fertility clays or loams. A variety of other woody species also occur (*Eucalyptus, Acacia, Casuarina, Terminalia*). The native understoreys are sparse and unproductive, with major grasses being species of *Paspalidium, Bothriochloa, Aristida* and *Chloris*. These communities have been extensively cleared for development to exploit their natural fertility by sown introduced pastures (mainly based on the grasses *Cenchrus ciliaris, Chloris gayana* and *Panicum maximum* var. *trichoglume*) and cropping.

Xerophytic mid-grass

These grasslands form the herbaceous layer of semi-arid low woodlands on a wide range of light soils of poor to moderate fertility in both northern and southern Australia. In northern Australia they occur in a subcoastal arc inland from the tropical tall-grass communities, in Western Australia, the Northern Territory and Queensland in areas with 350–750 mm annual rainfall. They have variable composition, with a range of dominant species including *Aristida* spp., *Chloris* spp., *Bothriochloa decipiens, B. ewartiana, Eriachne* spp., *Digitaria* spp. and *Chrysopogon fallax*. Annuals are also important (*Sporobolus australasicus, Aristida* spp., *Dactyloctenium radulans*). The southern component is widespread in western New South Wales, where *Danthonia* spp., *Chloris truncata, C. acicularis, Stipa variabilis, S. setacea, S. aristiglumis* and species of *Eragrostis, Aristida, Enneapogon* and *Enteropogon* are important.

These woodlands have variable tree and shrub layers. Tree clearing has been important in central and southern Queensland and New South Wales. Major increases in the density of the shrub layer (species of *Eremophila, Cassia, Dodonaea* and *Acacia*) have reduced grass production and threaten the viability of grazing in some areas.

Temperate tall-grass

Dichelachne spp., *Poa labillardieri* and *Themeda triandra* give sparse grazing in the wetter forest and heath areas of eastern New South Wales, Victoria and Tasmania, and also in the dry sclerophyllous forests, where *Danthonia pallida* is also important. These pastures are of low grazing value and animal production in these areas depends on clearing and the development of sown pastures.

Temperate short-grass

Apart from small areas of treeless grassland, these communities form the herbaceous layer of temperate woodlands growing on a range of soils extending from southern Queensland through New South Wales and Victoria to southeast South Australia, with other areas near Adelaide, in Tasmania and in the southwest of Western Australia. Annual rainfall varies from 400 to 650 mm, with summer dominance in the north and winter dominance in the south. These woodlands were among the first areas used for domestic livestock and have been extensively modified by clearing, grazing, fertilizer application and the introduction of exotic species. They were originally composed of taller, warm-season grasses (*Themeda triandra, T. avenacea, Stipa bigeniculata, S. aristiglumis, Poa labillardieri*) but with higher grazing pressures since European settlement these have been replaced by short, cool-season species (*Danthonia* spp., *Stipa variabilis, Chloris* spp.) and exotic annuals (*Hordeum leporinum, Bromus* spp., *Trifolium* spp., *Medicago* spp., *Erodium* spp. and *Arctotheca calendula*).

Sub-alpine sodgrass

Small areas of this community occur as treeless grasslands or the understorey of subalpine woodlands on acid soils with annual rainfall above 750 mm in the southeastern highlands. The principal grasses are *Poa* spp., *Danthonia nudiflora* and *Themeda triandra*. Historically, these grasslands were used for summer grazing, often after burning during early summer, but grazing has declined as emphasis is now placed on water supply, tourism and conservation.

Saltbush-xerophytic mid-grass

These communities are often treeless and are characterized by chenopod shrubs, usually less than one metre tall, from the genera *Atriplex, Maireana, Sclerolaena, Rhagodia* and *Enchylaena*. They are important in New South Wales, South Australia (Plate 9.2) and Western Australia, with smaller amounts in Queensland and the Northern Territory in areas with 125 to 400 mm rainfall. The space between the shrubs is covered with annual grasses and forbs

Plate 9.2
Saltbush community in South Australia.

after rain – in the south they are *Danthonia caespitosa, Stipa variabilis, Chloris truncata* and species of *Calandrinia, Ptilotus* and *Sclerolaena.* In the north, *Enneapogon* spp., *Eragrostis* spp., *Aristida* spp. and *Dactyloctenium radulans* are important. Grazing animals show marked preferences for different species in these communities. Studies in southern New South Wales (Leigh and Mulham, 1966a,b, 1967) showed animals prefer green grasses and forbs, then dry grass and forbs, followed by annual and short-lived perennial chenopods, with the perennial *Atriplex* and *Maireana* shrubs least preferred. The perennial saltbush plants confer stability to the soils and vegetation and serve as an important drought reserve; during droughts, saltbush may be a major part of the diet. The combination of drought and overgrazing has led to loss of saltbush, with the palatable *Atriplex* and *Maireana* species disappearing.

Acacia shrub–short-grass

Acacia shrublands are widespread in arid Australia on lighter textured infertile soils in all states except Victoria. Mulga (*Acacia aneura*) is the major shrub, but other *Acacia, Cassia* and *Eremophila* species are also important, plus chenopods in southern areas. These shrubs provide important "top feed" and mulga in particular is lopped or pushed over to provide feed for stock during droughts. The herbage layer is dominated by annual and short-lived perennial grasses and forbs. The principal grasses are *Eragrostis* spp., *Monachather paradoxus, Eriachne* spp., *Aristida contorta, Thyridolepsis mitchelliana, Stipa* spp., *Neurachne* spp. and *Enneapogon* spp. Common forbs are species of *Calotis, Helipterum* and *Ptilotus.*

Plate 9.3
Acacia nilotica *thicket and seedlings (foreground) in a Mitchell grass community.*

Animal production depends on the herbage layer, the composition of which varies widely, depending on the timing of the unreliable rainfall in these arid areas. Winter rain produces a flush of ephemerals with forbs (particularly members of the Asteraceae) prominent; summer rain favours perennial and annual grasses and is responsible for the bulk of the herbage.

Xerophytic tussockgrass

Communities dominated by Mitchell grass (*Astrebla* species) are widespread (40 million hectares) on heavy, cracking clay plains of inland northern Australia, particularly in Queensland. Many of these are true grasslands, with no trees, but large areas also have scattered trees and shrubs. Some areas have been invaded by the exotic tree *Acacia nilotica* (see Plate 9.3). The perennial *Astrebla* plants provide stability and drought reserve feed, but animal production is closely related to the growth of short-lived, nutritious inter-tussock species, mainly annual grasses (particularly *Iseilema* spp., but also *Dactyloctenium* spp. and *Brachyachne convergens*) and forbs (species of *Boerhavia*, *Sida*, *Portulaca* and *Ipomoea*). Cattle can gain weight on dry annual herbage, but lose weight when depending on dry Mitchell grass. Other perennial grasses may also be important – *Panicum decompositum*, *Aristida latifolia*, *Eragrostis* spp., *Bothriochloa* spp., *Dichanthium* spp., *Eulalia aurea* and *Chrysopogon fallax*.

The Mitchell grass lands are the most productive of the semi-arid and arid grazing lands in Australia. They have been stable, withstanding prolonged heavy grazing, although there is concern about invasion by *Aristida latifolia* in some areas.

Xerophytic hummockgrass

These communities – characterized by perennial species of *Plectrachne* and *Triodia* ("spinifex") – occupy large areas of sandy soils with annual rainfalls of 200 to 400 mm, and shallow skeletal soils in higher rainfall areas. *Plectrachne* and *Triodia* plants form hummocks or mounds from 1 to 6 m in diameter, and there are sparse populations of shrubs and small trees (*Acacia* spp. and *Eucalyptus* spp.) throughout much of the area. These areas have low and erratic rainfall and include waterless deserts of little or no value for grazing. Although the spinifex grasses are generally unpalatable to stock except after fire, and the mature herbage is very low quality, these lands provide important grazing (mainly for breeding cattle), especially if other, more palatable, perennial species (e.g. *Chrysopogon fallax*, *Eragrostis* spp.) are present. After rain, annual grasses and forbs provide valuable grazing.

SOWN PASTURES

Pasture improvement in Australia has been and continues to be, based on the use of selected, exotic species, with particular emphasis on legumes. Many

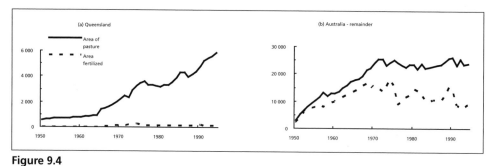

Figure 9.4

Changes since 1950 in the area of sown pastures and the area of pasture fertilized.
(a) Queensland. This area is mainly tropical pastures and includes most of the tropical
pastures sown in Australia. (b) Remainder of Australia. This area is almost all temperate
pastures and occurs mainly in Western Australia, New South Wales, Victoria and South
Australia.
SOURCE: Data from the Australian Bureau of Statistics and ABARE.

of these have been intentional introductions, but others are local strains of accidental introductions, such as many *Trifolium subterraneum* cultivars.

Although the native communities described in the section on natural vegetation still remain important, introduction of exotic pasture species commenced at or soon after European settlement. The poor quality of pastures near Sydney was soon recognized and requests for pasture legumes and grasses were made before 1800, and lucerne and clovers were among the non-indigenous plants growing in the Colony in 1803 (Davidson and Davidson, 1993). By the early twentieth century, many of the pasture plants currently used were already being exploited, although on a much smaller scale than at present (*Lolium perenne, L. multiflorum, Dactylis glomerata, Medicago sativa, Trifolium repens, T. pratense, T. fragiferum, Paspalum dilatatum, Panicum maximum*) (Davies, 1951). In addition, there had been a number of accidental introductions that were to be of great importance, although their potential had not been recognized (e.g. *Trifolium subterranean*, annual *Medicago* spp., *Cenchrus ciliaris* and *Stylosanthes humilis*).

There have been considerable differences between the development of temperate and tropical pastures and these are considered separately in the following sections.

Figure 9.4 shows the changes in the area of sown pastures from 1950 onwards for Queensland (mainly tropical pastures) and the remainder of Australia (mainly temperate pastures).

Temperate pastures

During the first 50 years of the twentieth century, much information was gathered on temperate pasture species and their growth requirements: A.W. Howard had actively promoted subterranean clover; the superphosphate responses by pastures had been documented; and the role of trace elements had been discovered. Until the 1920s, emphasis was on identifying suitable species, but thereafter the search shifted to strains and cultivars within species.

These developments provided the base for sown pastures but the depression of the 1930s and drought and war during the 1940s meant large-scale pasture improvement (the "sub and super" revolution based on widespread sowing of *Trifolium subterraneum* and the application of superphosphate) was delayed until the early 1950s (Crofts, 1997). During this period, there were high or record prices for wool, wheat, butter and beef; myxoma virus dramatically reduced the rabbit population; seasons were favourable; and a period of rapid and sustained pasture development commenced, which continued until the late 1960s (Figure 9.4).

As Figure 9.4 shows, there has been little change in the area of temperate sown pastures since 1970. This decline in pasture development has had a number of causes – periods of unprofitable prices for wool, beef and wheat; continuing cost-price pressures on farmers; major widespread droughts; rapid increase in the price of superphosphate during the oil crisis in the 1970s; removal of the superphosphate bounty; and reduced income tax deductions for pasture improvement (Crofts, 1997).

Fertilizer application has been a key component of pasture development in temperate areas and approximately 90 percent of the fertilizer used is superphosphate. Superphosphate was tested on pastures in southern Australia early in the twentieth century and its impacts on pasture and animal production documented (e.g. Trumble and Donald, 1938). Figure 9.4 shows that during the 1950s the area of pasture treated with fertilizer was similar to the total sown pasture area, but the proportion fertilized then declined to 80 percent during the 1960s, to 56 percent in the 1970s and 46 percent in the 1980s. This decline has continued since, and a recent ABARE survey of grain-producing farms found that less than 10 percent of the pastures were fertilized (Hooper and Helati, 1999).

The results of a number of surveys of commercial sown pastures were summarized by Wilson and Simpson (1993). There were numerous reports of "legume decline" covering *Trifolium subterraneum*, *Medicago* species and *Trifolium repens* in both the high-rainfall and wheat-sheep zones. Weedy annual grasses and forbs were prominent in both zones. Many reasons have been suggested for the legume decline, including reduced phosphate application; other nutrient deficiencies; soil acidity and associated nutrient imbalances; increased nitrogen levels; insect pests; diseases; and increased grazing pressure (Wilson and Simpson, 1993). These changes have had serious consequences – herbage quantity and quality have declined, reducing animal production, while in the cropping areas, where the legume-based pastures had maintained soil fertility, soil nitrogen levels have fallen and soil structure deteriorated.

Tropical pastures

Development of sown pastures was slower in the tropical areas, but the success of introduced pastures in southern Australia during the 1950s provided a model for similar development in tropical Australia. A number of species had been introduced during the late nineteenth and early twentieth centuries, either intentionally (e.g. *Panicum maximum*, *Chloris gayana* and *Brachiaria mutica*) or accidentally (e.g. *Stylosanthes humilis* and *Cenchrus ciliaris* (Plate 9.4)). Plant introduction and evaluation has continued, with initial emphasis on grasses, but increasing attention has since been paid to legumes, especially after a major expansion of research in the 1950s (Eyles and Cameron, 1985).

Most of the tropical pastures have been sown in Queensland, with smaller areas in northern New South Wales, the Northern Territory and Western Australia. Figure 9.6 shows a slow increase in the area of sown pasture in Queensland until 1960, followed by a rapid expansion in pasture sowings from the 1960s onwards, about ten years after a similar increase in temperate Australia. This expansion continued until the 1990s, apart from decreases in the late 1990s and late 1980s associated with disease outbreaks in *Stylosanthes humilis* stands, poor returns for animal products and expansion of cropping areas (Walker and Weston, 1990). About 70 percent of the area sown to pasture has been sown solely to grasses. These grass-only pastures are mainly on fertile soils, particularly those which previously supported brigalow (*Acacia harpophylla*) and gidgee (*A. cambagei*). In contrast, sown grass-

Plate 9.4
Buffel grass (Cenchrus ciliaris), the most widely planted grass in semi-arid tropical areas. Buffel grass can support high levels of animal production, but has also been listed as an environmental weed.

J.G. McIVOR

Plate 9.5
Sward of Stylosanthes hamata *growing under trees in the Northern Territory.*

legume pastures are more important on less fertile soils (Walker and Weston, 1990). A special development has been the use of shallow ponds to grow flood-tolerant grasses (*Brachiaria mutica, Hymenachne amplexicaulis* and *Echinochloa polystachya*) to provide green herbage during the dry season.

In contrast to southern Australia, fertilizer application has been much less important in tropical pasture development. This partly reflects the use of grass-only pastures on fertile soils and also the importance of the *Stylosanthes* species (see Plate 9.5) with their low phosphorus requirements and ability to grow well on soils with low available phosphorus (4–8 ppm) levels (McIvor, 1984; Jones *et al.*, 1997). As for southern Australia, superphosphate dominates fertilizer usage on pasture, comprising approximately 70 percent of the total fertilizer applied. However, nitrogen-fertilized grasses have important specialized roles, including pastures based on temperate species for winter production on some dairy farms.

There have been no surveys for sown tropical pastures equivalent to those noted above in temperate areas. However, there are problems with some sown pastures, with approximately 100 000 ha per year going out of production during the period 1986/87 to 1989/90 (Walker, 1991) due to a decline in sown species (Walker and Weston, 1990). Although grass-only pastures on fertile soils are initially very productive, this phase generally lasts only four to ten years then plant and animal productivity declines due to reductions in available nitrogen and sometimes loss of desirable species (Myers and Robbins, 1991; Jones, McDonald and Silvey, 1995).

AVAILABLE SPECIES AND CULTIVARS

There are currently nearly 500 cultivars registered or where applications for plant breeders' rights have been granted. These include fodder crops, lawn-amenity grasses and shrub legumes, but most are pasture grasses and herbaceous legumes. The cultivars come from 70 tropical and subtropical species (37 grass, 33 legume) and 60 temperate (24 grass, 36 legume) species. Not all the cultivars are still used, and only a few are important. Almost all cultivars are from introduced species, except for a few native grasses (*Astrebla* spp., *Danthonia* spp., *Themeda triandra*, *Microlaena stipoides*). In addition to the registered cultivars, there are some additional introductions that are used although not officially registered.

SEED PRODUCTION

Although pastures are grown over a wide area, seed production is restricted to much smaller areas, where there is a reliable growing season (or irrigation is available) and also a reliably dry harvesting season. Seed production of tropical and sub-tropical species is concentrated on the east coast of Queensland and northern New South Wales, with small amounts produced in the Northern Territory. South Australia, Victoria and Western Australia are the major states for the production of clovers and medics, while alfalfa and temperate perennial grasses are produced in all southern states. The average pasture seed production during the three years 1996–98 was 26 000 t, with most production in Victoria and South Australia (Anon., 1999).

CURRENT GRASSLAND ISSUES
Research

Pasture development in Australia has drawn on research and experiences elsewhere, but local research has been vitally important to solve uniquely Australian problems, and Australia has developed a strong pasture research effort. Most of this research has been publicly funded. While pasture research continues to be important, the funding and level of activity have declined in recent years. Indeed, reduced funding for pasture research (by both government and industry) was rated the most severe constraint in a recent survey of threats and limitations to the use of tropical pastures (McDonald and Clements, 1999).

Not only has the amount of pasture research changed in recent years, the research approach has also altered. Research stations now have a smaller role and a greater proportion of the research is conducted on private properties, some of it with producers participating in the design and conduct of experiments, and interpretation of the results.

A major part of the research effort has been the development of new cultivars (plant introduction, breeding, characterization and evaluation), and major national programmes were established for grasses and legumes (Pearson, 1994).

These studies have included identifying suitable species for new or difficult environments or for changed farming systems, and also the development of superior strains within existing commercial species. Although cultivar development has been predominantly publicly funded, private industry plays an important role in temperate perennial species.

While the development of new cultivars continues, there is now increased research effort on pasture management and the role of pastures in farming systems. The importance of high quality pastures for increased animal production continues, but there are a number of "new" issues (see next section) that have become important areas for research. These include increased water use by deep rooted species (e.g. *Medicago sativa, Phalaris aquatica*) to dry out soil profiles to reduce soil salinization; the role of perennial grasses for improving soil structure and organic matter levels; and the role of pastures in cereal rotations, both as sources of nitrogen and also for weed control in areas where herbicide-resistant weeds have become a problem. This research is complemented by the commercial evaluation of recently released cultivars and identification of the best ways to incorporate pastures into farming systems.

Management of grasslands

Management of grasslands aims for a desirable composition that gives both high production (including crop products as well as animal products) and maintenance of the resources. The desirable composition varies both temporally and spatially and, given the range of requirements, a mix of species is almost always needed.

There are management problems in all pasture zones. In the high rainfall and wheat-sheep zones, low nutritive value of herbage over the summer dry season and low herbage availability in the autumn and winter are important limitations to animal production (Wilson and Simpson, 1993). Productive legumes are important both to provide nitrogen for associate grasses (and following crops) and for their high herbage quality, but, as noted earlier, legume decline is a major issue.

In the pastoral zone, major limitations to animal production are herbage quality and quantity, and, in wool-growing areas, vegetable contamination of wool by seeds and fruiting structures of problem species. High grazing pressures have led to the replacement of palatable species by species that avoid high grazing pressure by their unpalatable, fibrous or ephemeral nature. This leads to low herbage quantity (particularly in southern and central Australia, where grasses are replaced by inedible shrubs) and poor quality (particularly in northern Australia, where pastures are dominated by C_4 grasses and there is a long dry season). Native shrubs (e.g. species of *Cassia, Dodonea* and *Eromophila*) are a major problem in southern and central Australia, while, in the northern areas exotic species are also important (e.g. *Acacia nilotica* (Plate 9.3), *Cryptostegia grandiflora* (Plate 9.6), *Prosopis* spp., *Parkinsonia aculeata* and

Plate 9.6
Exotic woody weeds in northern Australia. Dense stand of Cryptostegia
grandiflora, *with some climbing over trees along a watercourse.*

Ziziphus mauritiana). Tothill and Gillies (1992) made a major assessment of the
condition of native pastures in northern Australia. They divided the pastures
into three classes – sustainable (main desirable species maintaining >75 percent
dominance); deteriorating (increased presence (>25 percent) of undesirable
pasture species and/or woody weeds); and degraded (predominance of undesirable species). Overall, only 56 percent of pasturelands were rated sustainable, with 32 percent deteriorating and 12 percent degraded.

In sown tropical pastures both legume dominance and lack of legume persistence are problems in different regions. In the semi-arid tropics, where some
stylo (*Stylosanthes* spp.) pastures are now nearly 30 years old, stylo dominance
(particularly *Stylosanthes scabra*) is causing some concern. The problem is
worst on infertile soils, where stylos have been over-sown into native pastures.
In stylo-grass pastures, animal preference for grass is very strong during the
early wet season (Gardener, 1980) leading to heavy selective grazing of the
grasses, which are susceptible at this stage of their growth (Hodgkinson *et al.*,
1989; Mott *et al.*, 1992). A number of measures have been recommended to
reduce the stylo dominance – fire, pasture spelling, sowing grazing-tolerant
grasses, and raising soil phosphorus levels (McIvor, Noble and Orr, 1998).
In the drier subtropics, legume persistence remains a problem, and the success of legume-based pastures has been more variable. Weeds continue to be a
problem. During the past decade, unpalatable *Sporobolus* species (*pyramidalis,
natalensis, indicus* var. *major*) have increased and extended inland, and Siam
weed (*Chromolaena odorata*) has been recorded for the first time.

A number of approaches to pasture management have been suggested. Westoby, Walker and Noy-Meir (1989) proposed a state-and-transition model of vegetation change, where vegetation exists in a number of more-or-less stable states, and moves between these under the influence of management and climatic factors. State-and-transition models have been developed for the major native grassland communities in northern Australia (McIvor and Scanlan, 1994; Stockwell *et al.,* 1994; Orr, Paton and McIntyre, 1994; Hall *et al.,* 1994; McArthur, Chamberlain and Phelps, 1994; Jones and Burrows, 1994) and provide a basis for management by highlighting opportunities to make desirable changes, and also the risks of undesirable changes occurring if management is not proactive. Jones (1992) applied state-and-transition models to sown pastures of *Macroptilium atropurpureum* and *Setaria sphacelata*. These pastures can be converted to *Digitaria didactyla* and *Axonopus affinis* with sustained heavy grazing; resting from grazing reverses this conversion, but becomes progressively less effective the longer the heavy grazing is maintained.

Drawing on a model proposed by Spain, Pereira and Gauldron (1985) for the evaluation of tropical pastures, Kemp (1991) developed a "pasture management envelope", where management aims to maintain pastures within upper and lower limits for productive stable pastures (proportion of key species, e.g. legumes) and for animal performance (forage on offer). Legume contents below the lower limit are unlikely to make important contributions to feed supply and nitrogen fixation, while, above the upper limit, pastures are likely to be unstable and prone to invasion by nitrophilous weeds. Above the upper limit to forage on offer, much of the herbage would not be utilized, while, below the lower limit, herbage intake (and possibly animal survival) would suffer, pasture growth would be reduced and reduced ground cover would expose the soil to erosion. Where pastures are outside this envelope of limiting conditions, management needs to be altered to move the pasture into the envelope. This will often involve changing seasonal grazing pressure (e.g. resting tropical pastures during the early wet season; heavy spring grazing of clover-based pastures). Fire is also used in some areas. While there is little use of fire with sown pastures, it is important for native pastures, particularly in tropical areas to remove accumulated dry herbage, alter grazing behaviour and control woody weeds.

In Australia in recent years there has been widespread interest in grazing systems, with considerable debate over the merits of systems based on short grazing periods and long rest periods (e.g. short-duration grazing, time-control grazing, cell grazing) compared with continuous grazing. A number of producers have enthusiastically adopted these systems and report large benefits, both for financial performance and for sustainability of resources (McCosker, 1994; McArthur, 1998; Gatenby, 1999), although other producers have not had positive results (e.g. Waugh, 1997). In contrast to the positive benefits reported from these grazing systems, reviews of grazing systems research conclude that continuous grazing is no worse than rotational grazing, and may be better for animal production (Norton, 1998). Norton (1998) considered reasons for this divergence of views, and concluded that differences were related to uniformity of utilization – this was constant, even in small experimental paddocks, irrespective of grazing system, so the experiments showed no benefit for rotational grazing. However, utilization is often not uniform in large commercial paddocks, and more even utilization is achieved when they are subdivided for rotational systems, leading to production benefits.

Resource issues and rehabilitation

Despite the success of much pasture development there are major resource issues in Australian grasslands. Soil degradation is estimated to cost Australian agriculture more than one billion dollars annually in lost rural production (Williams, 1999). While soil erosion continues to be a problem, it is not as severe in many areas as during the early to mid-twentieth century, but salinity, accelerated acidification and tree dieback have emerged as important grassland problems in the last twenty years.

Whilst some soils are naturally acid, there has been accelerated acidification of soils under legume pastures, both in temperate (e.g. Williams, 1980; Ridley, Helyar and Slattery, 1990) and in tropical areas (Noble, Cannon and Muller, 1997). A number of processes contribute to this: removal of plant (particularly hay making) and animal products; net transfer of nutrients as dung and urine within paddocks; leaching of nitrate (and associated cations) below the root zone; and increases in soil organic matter and cation exchange capacity. The use of acid-tolerant species may provide a partial solution to the problem, but overcoming long-term acidification will require the use of lime.

The removal of trees and their replacement by crops and annual pastures has brought about major changes to the hydrological cycle. Dryland salinity now affects about 2.5 million hectares of land, and there is potential for this to increase to more than 12 million hectares (Williams, 1999). Western Australia and Victoria are the states most affected, but New South Wales, South Australia and Queensland also have increasing areas. Reversing these changes to the hydrological cycle will require deeper-rooted plants to reduce recharge by transpiring water before it enters the groundwater, and plants to increase discharge and lower the watertable. Deep-rooted perennial pasture species (e.g. *Medicago sativa* and *Phalaris aquatica*) have a role (e.g. Ridley *et al.*, 1997; McCallum *et al.*, 1998; Pitman, Cox and Belloti, 1998), but major tree replanting will probably be required, and has begun in some areas.

Native tree dieback (progressive, usually protracted, dying back of branches, often ending in tree death) has become important, and is most severe in long settled, intensively farmed areas, such as the New England Tableland of New South Wales. Repeated defoliation by leaf eating insects is one of many factors involved

TABLE 9.2
Impact of pasture development on the number of species recorded in experimental pastures near Charter Towers, north Queensland. The values are the means of three years (1990–92) and two sites where the treatments have been fully imposed for at least 4 years.

Pasture	% sown species	Number of species			
		Sown	Native	Exotic	Total
Lightly grazed, live trees, native pasture	0.1	1.0	27.9	1.4	30.3
Heavily grazed, live trees, fertilized over-sown legume-grass pasture	86.1	4.2	15.0	1.7	20.9
Heavily grazed, trees cleared, fertilized legume-grass pasture sown on cultivated seedbed	93.2	4.5	11.4	0.5	16.4

Source: From McIvor, 1998.

in the tree dieback syndrome, and sown pastures are implicated in the higher levels of insect defoliation. Two mechanisms are suggested. Firstly, the fertilized improved pastures improve and increase the supply of food for insect larvae and support higher populations of soil invertebrates than native pastures (King and Hutchison, 1983). Secondly, the higher soil nutrient levels also improve the feed quality and attractiveness of the tree leaves for adult insects. The combination of larger populations and attractive foliage greatly increases the grazing of trees by insects. A survey of Queensland properties found increased severity of tree dieback symptoms on properties where more than 50 percent of the area was improved pasture (Wylie *et al.*, 1993).

Biodiversity in grasslands
The impacts of pasture development on biodiversity are still being debated. While new species have been added, and become naturalized in many cases, at least some native species have been disadvantaged. However, as surveys show, many other species are present in sown pastures.

Pasture development has a number of components, all of which may influence biodiversity – tree clearing, sowing introduced species, fertilizer application, increased grazing pressures, herbicide use, and irrigation. McIvor (1998) examined some of these (tree clearing, superphosphate application, sown species, cultivation, and stocking rates), both separately and in combination, at two sites in north Queensland. The individual management treatments all affected diversity, but the responses varied with season, site and measurement scale. The density of native species decreased with pasture sowing and cultivation, but increased at high stocking rates, and with tree killing at one of the sites. When the treatments were combined, there was a decline in native species as intensity of development increased and the extra sown species were insufficient to prevent a decline in the total number of species (Table 9.2).

Environmental management
While much has been learned about the development and use of pastures, pasture management does not exist in isolation and must be combined with other aspects of property management if we are to have sustainable use of our

grasslands. Both on- and off-farm impacts and landscape- and regional-scale relationships need to be considered. McIntyre, McIvor and MacLeod (2000) have outlined a set of principles for the grazing of eucalypt woodlands that provide guidelines for achieving environmental sustainability. These need to be combined with other aspects of property and enterprise management and regional planning to give both profitability and conservation of natural resources. Such management will not be easy with a variable and changing climate and variable and often low prices for products, but will be needed for sustainable land use. The strong development of both the Landcare movement and Integrated Catchment Management groups over the last decade provides some hope. These groups of producers and other concerned people have recognized that some problems are beyond the capacity of individual producers, and have combined their resources to conduct activities that aim to improve resource management.

SUSTAINABLE PASTURE MANAGEMENT: LEARNING FROM THE PAST, MANAGING FOR THE FUTURE

Pasture management will always be complex, as we are dealing with mixed plant populations that are defoliated to varying degrees growing in a widely varying climate. There have been great increases in the understanding of the limits to pasture growth and production under Australian conditions, and continuing changes to farming systems in the past and the future will continue to throw up new challenges requiring continuing new knowledge and adaptations. Higher production levels have been a major theme for research and commercial development, but there is an increasing realization that stability and optimization of production systems within an inherently variable environment are objectives that are preferable to an exclusive emphasis on maximizing productivity.

European farming in Australia commenced with attempts to transfer European practices to the new environment. However, as the limitations of the new environment were discovered, major changes were made to farming systems as more was learned about the constraints and ways to overcome them. This can be illustrated by historical changes in the wheat industry (Donald, 1965; Malcolm, Sale and Egan, 1996). Initially, poorly adapted, late maturing English varieties were grown each year, depleting soil nutrient levels, so that by the end of the nineteenth century yields declined to half those originally achieved from virgin soils. Major changes were made early in the twentieth century: super-phosphate began to be widely used, overcoming the widespread phosphorus deficiency; long fallows (more than one year) were adopted, increasing water supply and nitrogen availability from the breakdown of organic matter; and the early maturing variety Federation was bred for Australian conditions. Yields returned to levels achieved from virgin soils. However, the long fallows meant soils were bare for long periods and erosion (by both water and wind) was a major problem and the soil organic matter levels fell, reducing both nitrogen supply and soil stability, so that there was no further yield improvement after the 1920s. After 1950, ley-farming rotations were widely used, with legume pastures improving both the soil nitrogen status and physical condition. This resulted in spectacular yield increases, but, as mentioned elsewhere, the legumes have become less effective. With the decline of legume pastures and low prices for animal products, some farmers switched from ley-pasture rotations to continuous cropping using grain legumes and nitrogen fertilizer to provide nitrogen, no- or minimum-tillage to maintain soil structure, and herbicides for weed control. Herbicide-resistant plants have developed in a number of troublesome weeds (e.g. *Avena* spp., *Lolium rigidum* and *Raphanus raphanistrum*) and there are doubts if such a system can maintain soil organic matter and physical properties (Malcolm, Sale and Egan, 1996). A pasture phase in the farming systems may be necessary to overcome these problems.

Importance of legumes

Nitrogen is a major limiting nutrient in grasslands, but nitrogen fertilizer use on grasslands has been low in Australia due to the high costs relative to the value of livestock products, and there are also problems with soil acidification and nitrate contamination of water supplies. Use of nitrogen fertilizers remains restricted to situations offering high financial returns, such as for winter feed supplies on dairy farms in the subtropics.

The productive use of legumes has been a major success story of Australian farming. Prior to the rapid period of pasture development that commenced in the 1950s (Figure 9.4) many pastures were sparse, heavily infested with rabbits, contained inferior annual species, and soils were badly eroded. In the cereal growing areas, dust storms occurred regularly, removing much of the surface soil, and soil organic matter levels had fallen, reducing soil stability and lowering soil nitrogen levels (Malcolm, Sale and Egan, 1996). Temperate pastures based on *Trifolium* and *Medicago* species, with application of superphosphate, provided greatly increased animal and crop production and improved soil fertility from the 1950s (Donald, 1965). However, as outlined above, the effectiveness of this system has declined. Despite this, legume-based pastures continue to provide production benefits, even if at a lower level than in the past.

The experiences in southern Australia provided a model for northern Australia and optimistic estimates were made of the area suitable for sown pastures in the tropics, such as 50–60 million hectares in Queensland (Davies and Eyles, 1965; Ebersohn and Lee, 1972; Weston *et al.*, 1981), although later estimates reduced this to 22 million hectares (Walker and Weston, 1990). Initial hopes for twining legumes (e.g. *Macroptilium atroprupureum* and *Desmodium* spp.) were not fulfilled, although some use of these species continues. Their elevated growing points are sensitive to grazing (Clements, 1989) and these species lack persistence under heavy grazing. There are successful developments

Plate 9.7
Leucaena leucocephala, *a high quality productive shrub legume capable of providing high levels of animal production.*

based on *Stylosanthes* species and *Leucaena leucocephala* (Plate 9.7) and the area sown to these species continues to increase. A number of other tropical legumes have smaller but still successful roles e.g. *Aeschynomene americana, Chamaecrista rotundifolia, Centrosema pascuorum* and *Vigna parkeri*. There is an increasing demand for ley legumes for cropping systems in the tropics and sub-tropics. The cropping industry is situated mainly on clay soils which previously supported grassland or brigalow. However years of continuous cropping has depleted soil fertility and yields and grain protein contents are falling. There is an urgent need to restore the fertility and legume-leys (e.g. *Clitoria ternatea*) can play a key role (Dalal *et al.*, 1991).

While there have been positive changes from the use of legumes, such as increased production and soil improvement, legumes can also have negative impacts, such as accelerated soil acidification. There will be a continuing need for research and development to overcome problems that arise, as well as continuing management – using legumes is not simply a matter of selecting and sowing a species and expecting it to survive and produce with little management.

Role of native pastures

Much of the research (and commercial) activity with pastures has concentrated on exotic rather than native species. Although the possible value of native species was realized along with the need for scientific study of their characteristics and value (Davies, 1951), the widespread conclusion was *"our native plants have neither actual or potential value as artificially sown species ... they are incapable of high production, of response to high levels of fertility. They are adapted ... to poor soils, to light grazing ...and drier climatic conditions ... "*   **Donald, 1970.**

However, few pastures contain only sown species and some native species have survived – in the strongly winter dominant rainfall areas there are few, but where there is a summer rainfall component (Wilson and Simpson, 1993), or in the tropics where rainfall is summer dominant, important native species remain in sown pastures and many areas have not been sown.

While the conclusion of Donald (1970) remains generally true for high fertility conditions, the increases in soil fertility following the widespread use of subterranean clover and superphosphate have not been sustained, and many areas have "poor soils, drier conditions" where the native species are adapted. Many early comparisons of native and introduced species were biased (Wilson and Simpson, 1993) and more recent assessments have concluded that there is a role for native species as they have valuable agronomic features and can provide good quality herbage at times of the year (Archer and Robinson, 1988; Robinson and Archer, 1988). The native pastures will generally not support the high stocking rates that fertilized, introduced pastures can support. However, at low to moderate rates, their presence and contribution can be exploited and they will have a continuing role in animal production.

Environmental weeds

Although exotic pasture species have provided large economic benefits to Australia, as a number of pasture plants have become naturalized increasing attention is being given to their impacts on the environment. A number have been listed as environmental weeds, i.e. species that invade native communities and cause changes to the vegetation structure (species composition and abundance) or the function of ecosystems, or both. Two features important in pasture species are common in these environmental weeds – the ability to invade or colonize new or unsown areas, and the ability to dominate vegetation where they occur. In a recent list of environmental weeds in Australia, 11 of the 55 major and significant ones were pasture species; of the top 18, six were pasture species – *Brachiaria mutica, Cenchrus ciliaris, Echinochloa polystachya, Glyceria maxima, Hymenachne amplexicaulis* and *Pennisetum polystachyon* (Humphries, Groves and Mitchell, 1991). Where conditions are suitable (e.g. little competing vegetation, suitable soil fertility and grazing regimes) all these species are capable of forming almost monospecific stands. Under the recently developed National Weeds Strategy, the import entry protocols for assessing the weed potential of all proposed new plant imports have been strengthened to prevent the introduction of plants with weed potential. However, there are a number of pasture species now well established or naturalized that are not currently considered weeds, but might well be in the future.

FUTURE

Products from pastures and grasslands have made great contributions to the Australian economy – during the nineteenth century the native grasslands supported the grazing industries (particularly wool) that, together with gold, made Australia prosperous. During the twentieth century, temperate pastures based on subterranean clover and other legumes, and to a lesser extent tropical pastures, raised production levels and financial returns to previously unachievable levels.

Future pasture management will involve concerns for both productivity and the environment both on- and off-property. As a recent assessment of the sustainability of Australian agriculture has shown, long-term productivity has been increasing for all broadacre and dairy industries, but resource issues – sodic and acid soils, native vegetation, salinity – have also become important and increasing problems (SCARM, 1998). Pastures, both sown and native, will continue to be important for both production and environmental impacts. As discussed earlier, rates of pasture development are closely linked to seasonal conditions and the profitability of farming enterprises, and this situation is likely to continue. Costs of pasture development and maintenance have been and remain a major concern to growers. A recent survey (Clements, 1996; McDonald and Clements, 1999) found that of 21 possible constraints to the future use of tropical pasture plants, farmers rated uncertain commodity prices, high cost of establishment and costs of maintaining improved pastures among the top four.

Agriculture is declining in relative importance in the economy and will continue to do so, but it will remain an important contributor to both the national and regional economies for many years. Grasslands and pastures will remain important – in many areas they provide the only means of producing a valuable product where there are no viable alternatives. In arable areas, grasslands will continue to have a role in crop rotations for increasing nitrogen supply, disease breaks and weed control as herbicide resistance reduces the effectiveness of herbicides.

REFERENCES

ABARE [Australian Bureau of Agricultural and Resource Economics]. 1998. *Australian Commodity Statistics 1998.* Australian Bureau of Agricultural and Resource Economics, Canberra ACT, Australia.

Anon[ymous]. 1999. Agriculture 1997–98. Australian Bureau of Statistics Catalogue No. 7113.0.

Archer, K.A. & Robinson, G.G. 1988. Agronomic potential of native grass species on the northern tablelands of New South Wales. II. Nutritive value. *Australian Journal of Agricultural Research,* **39:** 425–436.

Carnahan, J.A. 1989. *Natural Vegetation, Australia.* Department of Administrative Services, Canberra ACT, Australia.

Clements, R.J. 1989. Rates of destruction of growing points of pasture legumes by grazing cattle. pp. 1027–1028, *in: Proceedings of the 16th International Grassland Congress.*

Clements, R.J. 1996. Pastures for prosperity. 3. The future for new tropical pasture species. *Tropical Grasslands,* **30**: 31–46.

Crofts, F. 1997. Australian pasture production: the last 50 years. pp. 1–16, *in:* J.V. Lovett and J.M. Scott (eds). *Pasture Management and Production.* Melbourne, Australia: Inkata Press.

Dalal, R.C., Strong, W.M., Weston, E.J. & Gaffney, J. 1991. Sustaining multiple production systems. 2. Soil fertility decline and restoration of cropping lands of sub-tropical Queensland. *Tropical Grasslands,* **25**: 173–180.

Davidson, B.R. & Davidson, H.F. 1993. *Legumes: The Australian Experience.* Taunton, UK: Research Studies Press.

Davies, J.G. 1951. Contributions of agricultural research in pastures. *Journal of the Australian Institute of Agricultural Science,* **17**: 54–66.

Davies, J.G. & Eyles, A.G. 1965. Expansion of Australian pastoral production. *Journal of the Australian Institute of Agricultural Science,* **31**: 77–93.

Donald, C.M. 1965. The progress of Australian agriculture and the role of pastures in environmental change. *Australian Journal of Science,* **27**: 187–198.

Donald, C.M. 1970. Temperate pasture species. pp. 303–320, *in:* R.M. Moore (ed). *Australian Grasslands.* Canberra ACT, Australia: Australian National University Press.

Ebersohn, J.P. & Lee, G.R. 1972. The impact of sown pastures on cattle numbers in Queensland. *Australian Veterinary Journal,* **48**: 217–223.

Eyles, A.G. & Cameron, D.G. 1985. *Pasture Research in Northern Australia – its History, Achievements and Future Emphasis.* Brisbane, Australia: CSIRO.

Fitzpatrick, E.A. & Nix, H.A. 1970. The climatic factor in Australian grassland ecology. p. 326, *in:* R.M. Moore (ed). *Australian Grasslands.* Canberra ACT, Australia: Australian National University Press.

Frisch, J.E. & Vercoe, J.E. 1977. Food intake, eating rate, weight gains, metabolic rate and efficiency of feed utilization in *Bos taurus* and *Bos indicus* crossbred cattle. *Animal Production,* **25**: 343–358.

Gardener, C.J. 1980. Diet selection and liveweight performance of steers on *Stylosanthes hamata*-native grass pastures. *Australian Journal of Agricultural Research,* **31**: 379–392.

Gatenby, A. 1999. Rangeland management: sustainable agriculture requires sustainable profit. pp. 165–172 (Vol. 2 – Agriculture), *in: Outlook 99.* Proceedings of the National Agriculture and Resource Outlook Conference, Canberra ACT, Australia, 1999. Canberra ACT, Australia: Australian Bureau of Agricultural and Resource Economics.

Groves, R.H. & Williams, O.B. 1981. Natural grasslands. pp. 293–316, *in:* R.H. Groves (ed). *Australian Vegetation.* Cambridge, UK: Cambridge University Press.

Hall, T.J., Filet, P.G., Banks, B. & Silcock, R.G. 1994. A state and transition model of the *Aristida-Bothriochloa* pasture community of central and southern Queensland. *Tropical Grasslands,* **28:** 270–273.

Hodgkinson, K.C., Ludlow, M.M., Mott, J.J. & Baruch, Z. 1989. Comparative responses of the savanna grasses *Cenchrus ciliaris* and *Themeda triandra* to defoliation. *Oecologia,* **79:** 45–52.

Hooper, S. & Helati, S. 1999. Pasture: establishment, maintenance and expenditure on grain producing farms. pp. 47–59, *in: Australian Farm Surveys Report 1999.* Canberra ACT, Australia: Australian Bureau of Agricultural and Resource Economics.

Hubble, G.D. 1970. Soils. pp. 44–58, *in:* R.M. Moore (ed). *Australian Grasslands.* Canberra ACT, Australia: Australian National University Press.

Humphries, S.E., Groves, R.H. & Mitchell, D.S. 1991. Plant invasions: The incidence of environmental weeds in Australia. *Kowari,* **2:** 1–134.

Jones, P. & Burrows, W.H. 1994. A state and transition model for the mulga zone of south-west Queensland. *Tropical Grasslands,* **28:** 279–283.

Jones, R.J., McIvor, J.G., Middleton, C.H., Burrows, W.H., Orr, D.M. & Coates, D.B. 1997. Stability and productivity of *Stylosanthes* pastures in Australia. 1. Long-term botanical changes and their implications in grazed *Stylosanthes* pastures. *Tropical Grasslands,* **31:** 482–493.

Jones, R.M. 1992. Resting from grazing to reverse changes in sown pasture composition: application of the 'state-and-transition' model. *Tropical Grasslands,* **26:** 97–99.

Jones, R.M., McDonald, C.K. & Silvey, M.W. 1995. Permanent pastures on a brigalow soil: the effect of nitrogen fertiliser and stocking rate on pastures and liveweight gain. *Tropical Grasslands,* **29:** 193–209.

Keig, G. & McAlpine, J.R. 1974. WATBAL: A computer system for the estimation and analysis of soil moisture regimes from simple climatic data. CSIRO Division of Land Use Research Technical Memorandum, No. 74/4.

Kemp, D. 1991. Perennials in the tablelands and slopes: defining the boundaries and manipulating the system. *Proceedings of the Annual Conference of the Grassland Society of New South Wales,* **6:** 24–30.

King, K.L. & Hutchison, K.J. 1983. The effects of sheep grazing on invertebrate numbers and biomass in unfertilised natural pastures of the New England Tablelands (NSW). *Australian Journal of Ecology,* **8:** 245–255.

Leeper, G.W. (ed). 1970. *The Australian Environment.* 4th ed. Carlton, Australia: Melbourne University Press.

Leigh, J.H. & Mulham, W.E. 1966a. Selection of diet by sheep grazing semi-arid pastures of the Riverine Plain. 1. A bladder saltbush (*Atriplex vesicaria*)-cotton bush (*Kochia aphylla*) community. *Australian Journal of Experimental Agriculture and Animal Husbandry,* **6:** 460–467.

Leigh, J.H. & Mulham, W.E. 1966b. Selection of diet by sheep grazing semi-arid pastures of the Riverine Plain. 2. A cotton bush (*Kochia aphylla*)-grassland (*Stipa* *variabilis-Danthonia caespitosa*) community. *Australian Journal of Experimental Agriculture and Animal Husbandry*, **6**: 468–474.

Leigh, J.H. & Mulham, W.E. 1967. Selection of diet by sheep grazing semi-arid pastures of the Riverine Plain. 3. A bladder saltbush (*Atriplex vesicaria*)-pigface (*Disphyma australe*) community. *Australian Journal of Experimental Agriculture and Animal Husbandry*, **7**: 421–425.

McArthur, S. 1998. Practical evidence supports cell grazing benefits. *Australian Farm Journal Beef*, September 1998: 8–9.

McArthur, S.R., Chamberlain, H.J. & Phelps, D.G. 1994. A general state and transition model for the mitchell grass, bluegrass-browntop and Queensland bluegrass pasture zones of northern Australia. *Tropical Grasslands*, **28**: 274–278.

McCallum, M.H., Connor, D.J. & O'Leary, G.J. 1998. Lucerne in a Wimmera farming system: water and nitrogen relations. pp. 258–261, *in: Proceedings of the 9th Australian Agronomy Conference*. Parkville, Australia: Australian Agronomy Society.

McCosker, T. 1994 The dichotomy between research results and practical experience with time control grazing. pp. 26–31, *in: Australian Rural Science Annual 1994*. Sydney, Australia: Percival Publishing.

McDonald, C.K. & Clements, R.J. 1999. Occupational and regional differences in perceived threats and limitations to the future use of sown tropical pasture plants in Australia. *Tropical Grasslands*, **33**: 129–137.

McIntyre, S., McIvor, J.G. & MacLeod, N.D. 2000. Principles for sustainable grazing in eucalypt woodlands: landscape-scale indicators and the search for thresholds. pp. 92–100, *in*: P. Hale, A. Petrie, D. Moloney and P. Sattler (eds). *Management for Sustainable Ecosystems*. University of Queensland, Brisbane, Australia: Centre for Conservation Biology.

McIvor, J.G. 1984. Phosphorus requirements and responses of tropical pasture species: native and introduced grasses and introduced legumes. *Australian Journal of Experimental Agriculture and Animal Husbandry*, **24**: 370–378.

McIvor, J.G. 1998. Pasture management in semi-arid tropical woodlands: Effects on species diversity. *Australian Journal of Ecology*, **23**: 349–364.

McIvor, J.G., Noble, A.D. & Orr, D.M. 1998. Stability and productivity of native pastures oversown with tropical legumes. North Australia Program Occasional Publication No. 1. Meat Research Corporation, Sydney, Australia.

McIvor, J.G. & Scanlan, J.C. 1994. A state and transition model for the northern speargrass zone. *Tropical Grasslands*, **28**: 256–259.

McTaggart, A. 1936. A survey of the pastures of Australia. *CSIR Bulletin*, No. 99.

Malcolm, L.R., Sale, P. & Egan, A. 1996. *Agriculture in Australia*. Melbourne, Australia: Oxford University Press.

Martin, P. 1996. Ownership and management of broadacre and dairy farms. pp. 46–47, *in: Farm Surveys Report 1996*. Canberra ACT, Australia: Australian Bureau of Agricultural and Resource Economics.

Martin, P., Riley, D., Jennings, J., O'Rourke, C. & Toyne, C. 1998. The Australian Beef Industry 1998. *ABARE Research Report*, No. 98.7.

Moore, R.M. (ed). 1970. *Australian Grasslands*. Canberra ACT, Australia: Australian National University Press.

Moore, R.M. 1993. Grasslands of Australia. pp. 315–360, *in:* R.T. Coupland (ed). *Natural Grasslands Eastern Hemisphere and Résumé*. Amsterdam, The Netherlands: Elsevier.

Morley, F.H.W. 1961. Subterranean clover. *Advances in Agronomy*, **13:** 57–123.

Mott, J.J., Ludlow, M.M., Richards, J.H. & Parsons, A.D. 1992. Effects of moisture supply in the dry season and subsequent defoliation on persistence of the savanna grasses *Themeda triandra, Heteropogon contortus* and *Panicum maximum. Australian Journal of Agricultural Research*, **43:** 241–260.

Mott, J.J., Williams, J., Andrew, M.H. & Gillison, A.N. 1985. Australian savanna ecosystems. pp. 56–82, *in:* J.C. Tothill and J.J. Mott (eds). *Ecology and Management of the World's Savannas*. Canberra ACT, Australia: Australian Academy of Science.

Myers, R.J.K & Robbins, G.B. 1991. Sustaining productive pastures in the tropics. 5. Maintaining productive sown grass pastures. *Tropical Grasslands*, **25:** 104–110.

Noble, A.D., Cannon, M. & Muller, D. 1997. Evidence of accelerated soil acidification under *Stylosanthes* dominated pastures. *Australian Journal of Soil Research*, **35:** 1309–1322.

Norton, B.E. 1998. The application of grazing management to increase sustainable livestock production. *Animal Production in Australia*, **22:** 15–26.

Orr, D.M., Paton, C.J. & McIntyre, S. 1994. A state and transition model for the southern speargrass zone of Queensland. *Tropical Grasslands*, **28:** 266–269.

Pearson, C.J. 1994. The Australasian temperate pasture grass improvement program. *New Zealand Journal of Agricultural Research*, **37:** 265–268.

Pitman, A., Cox, J.W. & Belloti, W.D. 1998. Water usage and dry matter production of perennial pasture species down a duplex toposequence. pp. 268–269, *in: Proceedings of the 9th Australian Agronomy Conference*. Parkville, Australia: Australian Agronomy Society.

Ridley, A.M., Helyar, K.R. & Slattery, W.J. 1990. Soil acidification under subterranean clover (*Trifolium subterraneum* L.) in northeastern Victoria. *Australian Journal of Experimental Agriculture*, **30:** 195–201.

Ridley, A.M., White, R.E., Simpson, R.J. & Callinan, L. 1997. Water use and drainage under phalaris, cocksfoot and annual ryegrass pastures. *Australian Journal of Agricultural Research*, **48:** 1011–1023.

Robinson, G.G. & Archer, K.A. 1988. Agronomic potential of native grass species on the northern tablelands of New South Wales. I. Growth and herbage production. *Australian Journal of Agricultural Research*, **39:** 415–423.

SCARM [Standing Committee on Agriculture and Resource Management]. 1998. *Sustainable Agriculture: Assessing Australia's Recent Performance*. Standing

Committee on Agriculture and Resource Management Technical Report No. 70. CSIRO, Canberra ACT, Australia.

Seibert, B.D. 1982. Research findings in relation to future needs. *Proceedings of the Australian Society of Animal Production,* **14:** 191–196.

Spain, J., Pereira, J.M. & Gauldron, R. 1985. A flexible grazing management system proposed for the advanced evaluation of associations of tropical grasses and legumes. pp. 1153–1155, *in: Proceedings of the 15th International Grassland Congress.* Kyoto, Japan, 1985. Nishi-nasunu, Japan: Japanese Society of Grassland Science.

Stockwell, T.G.H., Andison, R.T., Ash, A.J., Bellamy, J.A. & Dyer, R.M. 1994. Development of state and transition models for pastoral management of the golden beard grass and limestone grass pasture lands of NW Australia. *Tropical Grasslands,* **28:** 260–265.

Thackway, R. & Cresswell, I.D. (eds). 1995. *An Interim Biogeographic Regionalisation for Australia.* Canberra ACT, Australia: Australian Nature Conservation Agency.

Tothill, J.C. & Gillies, C. 1992. The pasture lands of northern Australia. *Tropical Grassland Society of Australia Occasional Publication,* No. 5.

Trumble, H.C. & Donald, C.M. 1938. The relation of phosphate to the development of seeded pasture on a podsolised sand. *Council for Scientific and Industrial Research Bulletin 116,* **12:** 1–49.

Walker, B. 1991. Sustaining tropical pastures - summative address. *Tropical Grasslands,* **25:** 219–223.

Walker, B. & Weston, E.J. 1990. Pasture development in Queensland - A success story. *Tropical Grasslands,* **24:** 257–268.

Waugh, W. 1997. Pastures under adverse conditions – handling what you have: grazing systems in practice. pp. 91–94, *in: Proceedings of the 12th Annual Conference of the Grassland Society of New South Wales.* Dubbo, Australia, 1997. Orange, Australia: Grassland Society of New South Wales.

Westoby, M., Walker, B.H. & Noy-Meir, I. 1989. Opportunistic management for rangelands not at equilibrium. *Journal of Range Management,* **42:** 266–274.

Weston, E.J., Harbison, J., Leslie, J.K., Rosenthal, K.M. & Mayer, R.J. 1981. Assessment of the agricultural and pastoral potential of Queensland. Technical Report, No. 27. Agricultural Branch, Queensland Department of Primary Industries, Brisbane, Australia.

Williams, C.H. 1980. Soil acidification under clover pasture. *Australian Journal of Experimental Agriculture and Animal Husbandry,* **20:** 561–567.

Williams, J. 1999. Biophysical aspects of natural resource management. pp. 113 123 (Vol. 1 – Commodity Markets and Resource Management), *in: Outlook 99.* Proceedings of the National Agriculture and Resource Outlook Conference, Canberra, 1999. Canberra ACT, Australia: Australian Bureau of Agricultural and Resource Economics.

Wilson, A.D. & Simpson, R.J. 1993. The pasture resource base: status and issues. pp. 1–25, *in:* D.R. Kemp (ed). *Pasture Management Technology for the 21st Century*. Melbourne, Australia: CSIRO.

Wylie, F.R., Johnson, P.J.M. & Eisemann, R.L. 1993. A survey of native tree dieback in Queensland. Queensland Department of Primary Industries, Forest Research Institute Research Paper, No. 16.

Chapter 10
The Russian Steppe

Joseph G. Boonman and Sergey S. Mikhalev

SUMMARY

The steppe crosses the Russian plain, south of the taiga, penetrating deep into Siberia. It comprises three main types, which run in roughly parallel bands from east to west: forest steppe in the north, through steppe, to semi-desert steppe in the south. Within these belts, zones of temporary inundation on floodplains or in zones of internal drainage provide valuable hay land. The steppe was increasingly ploughed for crops during the twentieth century; initially crops were rotated with naturally regenerated grassland, but from mid-century cultivation was increasingly intensive. During the collective period, the emphasis was on industrial stock rearing, with housed cattle and high inputs; since decollectivization, intensive enterprises are closing for economic reasons, and systems have yet to stabilize. If ploughed land is left undisturbed it will return naturally to steppe vegetation in six to fifteen years. Hay is very important for winter feed, and much is made from seasonally flooded meadows. Many marginal, semi-arid areas of the steppe have been put under crops, but are not economically viable; much of the cereals so produced are fed to livestock, but grain yields are very low and yield no more livestock products than would natural grassland, but at far higher cost. Marginal cropland should return to grass.

INTRODUCTION

North of the Black and Caspian Seas, straddling both Don and Volga catchments, lies a stretch of steppe that saw some of the last horse-mounted nomadic tribes of Europe in action as late as the end of the fifteenth century. These were the Tatar of the Golden Horde. Then an equally heroic force, now of self-proclaimed free farmer-soldiers, whose mixed-farming with crop and livestock was community- and family-based, later called Cossacks, emerged to hold the newly acquired frontiers of Tsarist Russia.

Throughout history, the Russian steppe had been a natural boundary that deterred major civilizations or migrations from entering through its southern gateways. Not physical obstacles – in fact both Don and Volga are major navigable rivers and run from north to south – but the sheer size and emptiness of country that had to be traversed effectively separated the north from the south. Although in search of new granaries, ancient Greek colonization did not extend much further than the coastal rims of the Black Sea. In a similar fashion,

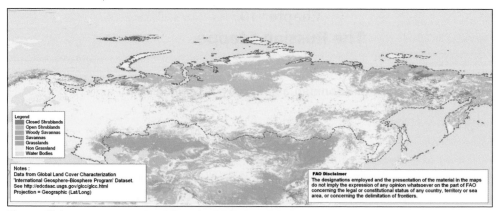

Figure 10.1
Extent of grasslands in the Russian Federation.

the empires of Rome and even nearby Byzantium made very few inroads into what would develop, at the start of this millennium, into the Russian heartland. The only, yet major, exceptions were invasions by the Huns in the fourth and by the Mongols in the thirteenth century, but these emerged from the same long stretch of steppe, near its far eastern fringe.

This vast Eurasian plain – with taiga in the north, forest in the middle and the steppe as its southern flank – stretches over 10 000 km from west to (south)east, from the Baltic Sea and crosses the Dnepr, Don and Volga rivers, deep into Siberia across the Urals, which convention has designated as the border between Europe and Asia (Figure 10.1). Most of the country's farm land is in the so-called "fertile triangle", with its base along the western border from the Baltic to the Black Sea and that tapers eastward to the southern Urals, where it narrows to a strip about 400 km wide extending across the southwestern fringes of Siberia.

This chapter discusses the steppe; an overall description of Russian pastures and ruminant production systems is given in the Country Pasture Profile for the Russian Federation (Blagoveshchenskii *et al.*, 2002), to be found on the FAO Grassland Web site <http://www.fao.org/ag/AGP/AGPC/doc/Counprof/russia.htm>.

THE STEPPE IN PERSPECTIVE

Truly virgin steppe has become a rarity, especially west of the Urals. The last major onslaught took place in the 1950s, when huge campaigns to raise agricultural production led to 43 million hectares of steppe being sacrificed to the plough, seemingly for ever (Maslov, 1999). It virtually meant the end of the virgin steppe in the Volga region, in Kazakhstan and western Siberia. The land put to the plough rivalled in size the whole of Canada's agricultural area.

As part of the collateral damage, interest in and knowledge of the steppe as a natural resource became rare in the eyes of the authorities, and faded as the experts themselves passed from the scene. Should active extensification and steppe rehabilitation, of which there is little sign at present, appear at some stage again on the agendas, it will have to draw on the old literature records, such as are being recalled in this chapter. These records are of further importance as they developed independently from scientific and managerial thinking in the West, especially in the USA, where similar vegetation types seem to have given rise to quite different approaches, both in science and in management. Recent literature from the Russian Federation on the subject is mostly related to satellite imagery and ecological modelling (Gilmanov, Parton and Ojima, 1997). To avoid confusion, and because of the reliance here on older literature, the botanical names will be quoted as originally reported. Consequently, we use *Euagrypyron* and *Agropyron repens* rather than *Elytrigia repens*.

Current tendencies in Russian agriculture are that the large-style arable units of the former Kolkhozy and Sovkhozy collective production units are retained as the central and collective core, mainly for cereal production, with only a little livestock held centrally. Livestock will be divorced further from the collective by the *kolkhozniki* themselves and become more family-based. Sooner or later, family herds will have to rely on family-run pastures, hayfields and by-products of their own arable operations. At present, communal and public grazing resources are used by privately owned livestock.

Is history repeating itself? Grazing rights shared out by or among the village community (*mir*) were typical of the pre-revolution era. While the grazing land – and often the grazing itself – was communal, livestock were family-owned. Fenced-off grazing blocks and "ranches" were rare. Although large landholdings in the more prosperous agricultural regions were the rule, landlords invariably had to cope with large resident communities of peasants and with their demands for cropland, pasture and hay for their cattle in return for labour. Does the present-style Kolkhoze fulfil the role of the pre-revolution landlord? Do peasants continue to expect to be provided for as before? Is a Russia with family-based autonomous farms still a long way off?

The Russian steppe, like many of the major natural grasslands of the world, is a formidable natural resource. With the present land-reform programmes following a new, often uncharted, course it may well be that the natural grassland and, in particular, the steppe will resume a large part of its old significance as a primary grazing resource. The Former Soviet Union (FSU)-industrial-style Kolkhozy and Sovkhozy, with livestock housed throughout the year, have proved uneconomic and unsustainable. Family-based mixed farming with paddock grazing may develop in parallel with the current tendency of grazing the kolkhozniki herds on natural grassland and steppe. Permanent or temporary pasture as a resource of grazing and fodder may regain prominence at the expense of annual fodder and grain crop. Half of the cereal crop, it was claimed, was fed to livestock. Maize used to be grown for silage on more than 10 million hectares, often in areas either too cold or too dry, whether aided or not with supplementary irrigation. The agronomic, economic and environmental implications of these new developments for outdoor grazing, though largely positive on balance, provide a formidable challenge.

SEMANTICS

Luga, senokosy i pastbishcha [meadows, hay meadows and pastures] and *Lugovodstvo* [meadow cultivation] are Russian terminology to emphasize the distinction commonly drawn between land for hay or for grazing, respectively, where the English language would simply refer to grassland. Russian terminology tends to distinguish between "meadows" as dominated by hay-type grasses and "pastures" as utilized through grazing, whereas this distinction has little meaning in contemporary English. However, in Russian terminology, the term "meadows" (composed of mesophytes) is often used in contrast to "steppe" (xerophytes), and assumes significance in dry steppe land crossed by rivers, which are bordered by extensive floodplains that harbour the meadows. Meadows have a more temperate and humid climate resonance (Shennikov, 1950). Meadow and steppe are used as descriptive terms away from the landscape or geographical zones they represent. The continued usage in Russian of terms such as meadow steppe, desert steppe and mountain steppe add to the confusion (Gilmanov, 1995). In this chapter, grassland is used in the general sense, including steppe, whereas pasture refers to a particular field or application. Maize silage is a fodder and so are Sudan grass and alfalfa, but the latter are called forages when grazed.

Emphasis on hay as the principal source of fodder to see cattle through the winter has been typical of Russian "grassland" terminology. Early mention of haymaking by the northern Slavs date back to the birth of their civilization, around 1000 A.D. Numerous are the references in the arts to "village hay-festivals" as the entire peasant community was engaged in the process of mowing and bringing in the hay. Hay, rather than fodder crops, was the rule. A high ratio of meadow to arable land was essential to sustain farming (Chayanov, 1926). Fodder beet, rape and turnips were much less grown than in more Atlantic climates further west. One reason was that most of the hay was derived from low-lying meadow land that had no other economic use. Second, the growing season for fodder crops is either too short, in the north, or too dry, in the east and south, or both. Even alfalfa is a late arrival; it is believed to have been grown in Tajikistan and Uzbekistan before the Greco-Persian wars of the sixth and fifth centuries BC; it is, however, unlikely to have reached the Volga region earlier than it did Western Europe because of the geographic north-south isolation mentioned above.

CLIMATE, VEGETATION AND SOILS

Somewhat Atlantic in climate at its start near the Baltic Sea, on its way east the Eurasian plain is met by an increasing severity and length of continental winters, precluding arable cropping at the eastern extreme. High latitudes and absence of moderating maritime influences determine the harsh continental climate prevalent in Russia. Huge mountain ranges along the southern borders and Central Asia preclude penetration of maritime tropical air masses. The Arctic Ocean acts as a snow-covered, frozen mass rather than a relatively warm ocean influence. As the territory lies in a westerly wind belt, warm influences from the Pacific Oceans do not reach far inland. In winter a large cold high-pressure cell, centred in Mongolia, spreads over much of Siberia.

In the low-pressure system of summer, warm and moist air pushes from the Atlantic Ocean well into Siberia. In many areas, however, the summer rainfall distribution is not always advantageous for agriculture. June and July are often dry, while rain may interfere with cereal harvest in August. Annual precipitation decreases from over 800 mm in western Russia to below 400 mm along the Caspian Sea.

Climate and vegetation fuse in zones that extend across the country in eastern-western belts. The tundra of the Arctic coast, with its permafrost and vegetation of mosses, lichens and low shrubs, is too cold for trees. The next (sub-Arctic) zone is the boreal (coniferous) forest, the taiga, occupying two-fifths of European Russia and most of Siberia. Much of this region also has permafrost. Large areas are devoid of trees, primarily because of poor local drainage, and the vegetation is marshy. The soils of the taiga are podsolic and infertile.

Further south stretches a belt of mixed forest from Saint Petersburg in the north to the border with Ukraine in the south. The mixed-forest grades through a narrow zone of forest-steppe before passing into the true steppe.

True steppe, as distinct from the forest-steppe further north, is predominantly a grass vegetation with a few stunted trees only in sheltered valleys. The true steppe belt begins along the Black Sea coast, encompasses the western half of the northern Caucasian plain, and extends northeast across the lower Volga, the southern Urals and the southern parts of western Siberia.

Together with the forest-steppe, the steppes form the chernozem belt, the agricultural heartland of Russia. The forest-steppe is black chernozem soil, high in organic matter (OM) and minerals, and better watered than the steppe. Steppe soils are somewhat lower in OM, but high in minerals, and many are also classified as brown-steppe (chestnut).

ECOLOGICAL CLASSIFICATION

In the Russian Federation with its vast uninterrupted plains, zones delineating the major vegetation types agree conveniently with climatic zones and, in a way, also with major soil types. Typically, these zones tend to run in semi-parallel belts in a slightly northwesterly to southeasterly direction.

Topography, watercourses and variation in soil conditions become relevant at the rayon [a small territorial administrative division] or rather at the (former) Kolkhoz or Sovkhoz level. It was at this unit level that grassland description was to be refined and effected for land management and, ultimately, grassland improvement. Both the objective and framework of the approach were pre-scribed. However, more than elsewhere in the world, classification in the coun-try lost itself in attempts to be all-USSR in compass, ending up with hundreds of codes and numbers. Colloquial terms could have summed it all up in one word (e.g. *mochazina* – non-peaty swamp; *liman* – flooded steppe in the lower reaches of rivers). Impeded drainage means swamp in the northern forest coun-try, but lush pasture in the steppe. Conversely, overgrazing can lead to bareness to an extent that the vegetation assumes the appearance of a drier climate than rainfall data suggest. Grasslands – and steppe are no exception – are an integra-tion of climate, soil, animal and man-made conditions. Vegetation may often provide a better guide to the agricultural environment than the instruments of meteorologist or geologist (Whyte, 1974). "What are the main species and what do they tell us?" is often a most relevant question.

Grasslands are subject to fluctuations in composition, but recurring pat-terns are recognized. The major features, physiognomy (the aspect in terms of height, density and cover) and species, are fairly constant or they oscillate around a certain equilibrium, both between and within woody and herbaceous species. Major changes are usually a long-term affair. Only when grassland is artificially drained permanently of excess water, or altered dramatically by repeated ploughing and cropping, can changes in the vegetation become irre-versible. As we will see, steppe is relatively quick to restore.

ECOLOGICAL (SITE) POTENTIAL

Much as early classifications were based on botanical composition, awareness was growing that ecological potential could be related to a recognizable vegetation group. To many observers, however, current vegetation is a very poor indicator of ecological potential and possible land use. The problem is then how to reconcile current vegetation with ecological potential. Classification means one thing to the specialist in phytogeography, but quite another to the planner concerned with grassland improvement. Site potential – that is, the vegetation that ecological factors indicate should dominate – is the guiding factor. A climax vegetation can be reconstructed based on natural succession towards an equilibrium with the environment. This process may be interrupted and vegetation may then be described as, say, a "fire subclimax" or a "grazing subclimax". The concept of climax should relate to site potential as determined by physical factors of the environment: climate, soil and topography. Tundra, steppe and semi-desert are then ecoclimatic zones, which can be characterized further by plant species and associations to delineate recognizable types of vegetation.

The term grassland or steppe is here used to denote a vegetation that is dominated by grasses and occasionally herbs, whatever the plant succession. The grasses used in cultivation today are those found growing in the wild

TABLE 10.1
Important species of the Russian steppe.

Maturity group[1]	Typical species and their characteristics
Very early (April/May)	*Poa bulbosa* L. Tufted <20 cm, bulb-like thickening at the base. Principal plant in semi-arid and fallow vegetations on chernozem and chestnut soils, dries off in summer but highly productive and nutritious in spring and autumn.
Early	*Festuca sulcata* Beck. Tufted <35 cm, greyish leaves. Prevalent and predominant in virgin steppe and old fallows on chernozem and chestnut soils. Highly productive; also sown.
	Stipa lessingiana Trin. & Rupr. Tufted <50 cm, prevalent on virgin steppe and old fallow, also in forest-steppe and mountain steppe belts, the best of the *Stipa* genus, comparable with *Festuca sulcata* but unpalatable after heading.
	Koeleria gracilis Pers. Tufted <25 cm, virgin steppe and old fallows, productive.
Medium	*Agropyron pectiniforme* Roem. et Schult. Tufted <90 cm (Plate 10.1); typical of clayey and loamy dark chestnut soils in semi-arid conditions and dominant in limans (near rivers); productive; also sown.
	Agropyron sibiricum (Willd.) P.B. Tufted <100 cm, typical of and predominant on light soils in steppe.
	Agropyron racemosum (Trin.) Richt. Rhizomatous <50 cm; common in steppe on old fallow and chestnut soils; more drought resistant and halophytic and coarser than *A. repens*.
	Bromus inermis Leyss. Rhizomatous <100 cm; typical of chernozem fallow soils in steppe and forest-steppe and in floodplains, often in pure stands; broad adaptation; also sown.
Late	*Agropyron repens* (L.) P.B. (syn *Elytrigia repens*). Rhizomatous, <80 cm (dryland), <170 cm (floodplains); predominant on old fallow chernozem and dark chestnut soils; tolerates flooding and salinity; sown on saline soils.
	Stipa capillata L. Tufted <60 cm, most prevalent after *S. lessingiana* but late, common in steppe, forest-steppe, semi-arid zone; palatable and desirable only prior to heading. Awned seed sticks to the wool and penetrates the skin, which can be fatal.

NOTES: (1) Based on heading dates in the steppe (beginning of growth ca mid-April).

yesterday (e.g. *Poa pratensis*). Natural and cultivated grasses are still close (Boonman, 1993). "Natural" should not be taken to mean either primitive or unproductive, nor should "natural" be equated with climax or static. In current colloquial use, "natural grass" has come to mean any of the following: 1. Grass, unsown; 2. Grass sown, but long ago and now run-down, in contrast to recently sown; 3. Local, as opposed to exotic grass species; or 4. Primitive, as opposed to improved and sown grass. It has become customary to equate natural grassland with anything that can be grazed, but that is not (known to be) sown. Often it is also meant to denote the grazing land as it was assumed to have been since time immemorial, or "as it ought to be".

Some notes on important steppe species are shown in Table 10.1.

RAMENSKII'S GRASSLAND CLASSIFICATION

In Russian literature on grassland classification, little direct reference can be found to discussions that have prevailed in the West, that is, to Clementsian succession with its climax terminology or to the more recently proposed transition-state models, nor to the Braun-Blanquet approach of characterizing vegetation. The "Markovian model" is at times referred to, but is hard to distinguish from that of Clements. By contrast, note was taken in the West of the work done in Russia by L.G. Ramenskii (Sorokina, 1955). In his standard work, Ramenskii (1938) emphasized the need to judge land in the most comprehensive manner and that all factors, biotic and abiotic, be taken into account to explain why certain variations ("modifications") in the

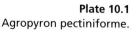

Plate 10.1
Agropyron pectiniforme.

vegetation occur. Ramenskii's classifications are known as "phytotopological" with major emphasis on the habitat. First, all natural grassland is divided into dryland or floodplain. Second, subdivisions are based on topography and moisture conditions. No less than 50 categories were formulated, each with 22 subdivisions based on moisture conditions. Within similar habitats, several plant associations occur.

For instance, on dark-chestnut loamy soil of the dry steppe plains, Ramenskii found the following associations as grazing intensity increases:

- in virgin steppe, a low-grass sward with *Stipa lessingiana* (Plate 10.2), but less *Festuca sulcata*;
- after a few years, predominantly *Festuca sulcata*;
- under intensive grazing, *Poa bulbosa* associations; and
- finally, after excessive grazing, an association with *Polygonum aviculare*.

This is typical succession-regression (see also Table 10.2). Ramenskii's analysis of the constituents of the vegetation itself was not quantitative, but estimated by so-called vertical "projection", by simply estimating the degree of cover at one particular date. No mechanical devices for ranking constituent species or for weighing samples were employed. Potential yields were estimated from empirically established standard graphs (see also section below on Botanical condition).

After ploughing and cropping steppe for several years, the following appear in the fallow:

Plate 10.2
Stipa lessingiana

TABLE 10.2
The effect of grazing intensity on grassland changes

Grazing intensity	Oka floodplain meadows	Northern Caucasus Common Chernozem	Western Kazakhstan Dark chestnut
Absent		Stipa spp., Festuca sulcata; herbs; Agropyron spp. and Bromus spp. frequent	
Weak	Phleum pratense, Agrostis alba, Geranium pratense	Stipa, Festuca sulcata; fewer herbs; Agropyron spp. and Bromus spp.	Stipa lessingiana, Festuca sulcata, Stipa capillata, Artemisia austriaca
Moderate	Festuca rubra, Carum carvi, Bromus inermis, Alopecurus pratensis, Agrostis alba	Festuca sulcata	Festuca sulcata, Koeleria gracilis, Stipa capillata, Artemisia austriaca
Intensive	Poa pratensis, Achillea millefolium, Leontodon spp., Medicago falcata, Carex schreberi, Trifolium repens, Alopecurus pratensis	Poa bulbosa, much Carex schreberi, Artemisia austriaca and Euphorbia seguieriana	Artemisia austriaca, Poa bulbosa, Euphorbia virgata
Excessive	Polygonum aviculare and a few of the above	Polygonum aviculare and Ceratocarpus arenarius	Polygonum aviculare, Agropyron spp., Ceratocarpus arenarius, Bassia spp.

SOURCE: Larin, 1956.

- First year: annuals.
- Second and third year: biennial and perennial herbs.
- Third and fourth year: *Agropyron racemosum* emerging.
- Fifth to eighth year: *Agropyron racemosum* over 80 percent of the herbage, with *Festuca sulcata* (Plate 10.3) emerging.
- *Festuca sulcata* predominant.

Plate 10.3
Festuca sulcata

- To about the fifteenth year: *Stipa lessingiana* becomes predominant (return to the initial virgin steppe).

Thus, at least five distinct associations are found. Depending on the management of the fallow and on the previous cropping history of the land, several tens of associations may be distinguished. Although each modification has significance for current utilization, habitat potential remains very much the same. Shennikov, therefore, preferred to allocate Ramenskii's virgin low-sward grass stage to "herbaceous steppe"; the *Agropyron* fallow to "(mesophilic) meadow type" and the *Polygonum* association to "herbaceous annual vegetation", all forming part of the *Herbosa* basic type of vegetation (see below). Shennikov's was a commendable effort of amalgamating the elements that unite rather than divide.

The emphasis at the time on terminology such as "phytocoenosis" and "zoocoenosis", together forming the biocoenosis and interrelating with the biogeocoenosis, is worth noting (Sukachev, 1945). Another emphasis was the division into four vegetation types: 1. *Lignosa* – tree-shrub; 2. *Herbosa* – herbaceous plants (see above); 3. *Deserta* – desert plants; and 4. *Errantia* – various.

Shennikov's hierarchy for a particular situation might be: 1. Vegetation-type group: *Herbosa*. 2. Type of vegetation: meadow (humid-grassland mainly used for hay). 3. Class of formations: true meadow (as against steppe or swamp). 4. Formation group: coarse grass, coarse sedge. 5. Formation: *Alopecurus pratensis* dominant. 6. Association group: various admixtures of *Alopecurus pratensis*. 7. Associations.

Sukachev's classification is "phytocoenological", whereas Ramenskii's is "phytotopological", and the latter's example was followed by Dmitriev (1948) and Chugunov (1951). However, the distinction is often blurred. Ramenskii's seral stages of plant succession, although not coined as such by him or his successors, are classical examples of linear Clementsian succession.

Conversely, bare ground is colonized by ruderals, which give place to seral grassland stages as organic matter accumulates and these are eventually replaced by taller bunch grasses. Clements (1916) ideas proved applicable not only in USA, but also in Canada (Coupland, 1979, whose work used to be quoted in Russia) and in East and South Africa (Phillips, 1929). It is doubtful if it ever was Clements' aim to apply the succession model to all situations liable to transition, or to claim that climax vegetation was the most desirable or most productive from the agricultural point of view in all situations. Plant succession can be studied with the aim of identifying the preferred seral stages with desirable composition. As we will see in Russia, many instances can also be found in which some of the seral stages (fallow land) are considerably more diverse and productive in herbage than the climax vegetation itself. It goes too far, however, to regard this as counter-evidence for the succession model. As in the Great Plains of USA, the climax grasses of the Russian steppe are productive and acceptable to livestock; they provide ground cover to protect soil and are effective plants in utilizing environmental growth factors to fix carbon and to cycle nutrients.

The interplay of biotic, climatic and edaphic components of the environment is relevant, as these modify the dynamics of grassland communities. Efforts at grassland improvement are directed at manipulating the botanical composition to encourage the more desirable species and suppress those less desirable. A basic thrust in current grassland improvement has been the comparison of the current site condition with what it ought to be, i.e. site potential. Acknowledgement of various stable vegetation states at a particular site widens the scope for opportunistic management that is responsive to abiotic events and that is not bound under all circumstances by doctrines that abhor fire or that only value stocking rates that are moderate.

BOTANICAL CONDITION (ECOLOGICAL MONITORING)

Few are the instances where ecological techniques can have such an impact on practical management decisions in agriculture as those developed in grassland science. Botanical assessment has proved a more reliable and efficient criterion of condition, and, therefore, of productivity of grassland, than yield measurements themselves. Given the enormous tasks of natural resource management ahead, it is appropriate here to draw attention to new techniques of botanical grassland surveys.

The FSU had "State Institutes for Land Control" in each republic, which carried out surveys about every ten years on the same (grass)land. Surveys were and are applied with strict adherence to FSU-wide methodology that has seen little change over the decades. The emphasis was primarily on maximizing production, that is, on setting animal production levels and, ultimately, the levels of grants and credits extended to the agricultural enterprises to meet these production levels regularly. For their part, Kolkhozy and Sovkhozy were required to produce grassland inventories, with a denomination of vegetation, soil type, other physical conditions as well as details of current utilization and proposed improvements for each area on the map.

The methodology in use for the measurement of yield-on-offer in quadrats (rope-frames) is quite complex and labour intensive. Components are separated by hand and analysed. The chemical analysis estimates feed units and protein of the edible portion, which is equated with the green material present in the sample. To achieve this, the technique uses a variable height of cutting, giving that portion of growth that is most likely to be grazed. Conversion of these data to animal production is not, however, flawless. True growth – not just yield-on-offer – can only be assessed by placing protective cages and moving them around at each sampling. Without reference data, carrying capacity cannot be assessed instantaneously.

Botanical analysis using the current methodology provides relative proportions, on an air-dry basis, of the species present in the quadrat, but the data are not used to full ecological potential. Since the emphasis is on measuring for setting animal production, botanical data are not applied to monitor composition or succession-regression compared with the preferred composition. In fact, the said proportions could provide more valuable information on the successional status of a pasture than any other observations made. Botanical data are more powerful predictors of pasture condition than yield data and can be assessed in a meaningful and less laborious way, e.g. by the dry weight rank (DWR) technique ('t Mannetje and Jones, 2000).

Production measurement used to be the approach in the FSU surveys. With the shift from being a part of the centrally planned production administration to agencies responsible for the resource management of the country, there has to be a reassessment of what technology is now relevant. The ultimate objective of the new-style monitoring is to rehabilitate the grasslands to acceptable preferred composition and to keep them at the preferred composition.

Decentralized development and devolved management of grazing rights – at the level of rayon, village, if not of the individual – call for a change in methodology and its ultimate application, in keeping with the requirement for natural resource management at the national level. New technologies proposed for monitoring and measurement that are accurate and cost efficient are the DWR technique for botanical composition and, when required but not essential, the comparative yield estimate (CYE) technique for yield-on-offer. Additional information to determine condition is also needed (plant size, sward density, soil condition).

Monitoring involves checking changes in the condition of grassland through monitoring the changes in composition and the changes in soil condition. With the data acquired, management and stocking rates can be adjusted to prevent or reverse degradation. Conversely, measuring involves assessing the productivity of grassland through measurement of true growth rather than of yield-on-offer. With the data acquired, stocking rates can be adjusted to maintain livestock productivity. Rather than production-oriented measurement, ecological parameters have been found to be the most valuable and cost-effective approach to monitor grassland condition. An up-to-date description of grassland monitoring methods, approaches and tools can be found in 't Mannetje and Jones (2000).

Husbandry should be directed towards maintaining a dynamic equilibrium around the preferred botanical composition that is the target pasture composition for sustainable development. The preferred composition differs from earlier, more orthodox, interpretations of Clementsian succession, which hold that the most desirable and only stable or sustainable composition is the climax. Numerous are the examples whereby climax grasses are found to be less productive than those at an intermediate position in the succession.

STEPPE DYNAMICS IN RELATION TO BOTANICAL COMPOSITION
Weather
A few examples should suffice. *Poa pratensis* in the forest zone as well as *Festuca sulcata* and *Agropyron sibiricum* in the steppe preserve their green shoots under the snow until spring and some growth may occur, even under the snow. Assimilation and growth begin in spring at temperatures of 3–5°C. Ephemerals and "ephemeroids" (Russian term denoting perennials whose vegetative parts die down annually, e.g. *Poa bulbosa*) flower in spring, the rest in early summer. Plants dry off as summer peaks, dormancy sets in, and tillering is not resumed until the rains return in autumn. Weather conditions of the preceding season have a marked effect. Without snow cover, a whole range of plants perish, including clovers and ryegrass. When the soil is not frozen but has a thick cover of 30 cm of snow for more than three months, these and other plants will die off (*vyprevanie*), probably because of continued respiration. A snowless winter followed by a cold spring and drought may prevent seed set in the surviving grasses.

From fallow to steppe
The following transitional stages from fallow onto virgin steppe used to be considered characteristic: 1. Annual weeds. 2. Perennial weeds. 3. Rhizomatous plants. 4. Bunch grasses. 5. Secondary virgin steppe. However, in more modern

thinking, the earlier of these stages are not necessarily hierarchical but often run parallel, with the rhizomatous stage at times little in evidence.

Russia's foremost early grassland improvement pioneer, V.R. Vil'yams, had repeatedly pointed out, *circa* 1920, that the interrelationships between plant and environment are such that one soil-plant complex is replaced by another. He even took this to the extreme that, in the sod-formation process, forests thin out naturally and finally give way to grassland. Shennikov (1941) repudiated this part of Vil'yams concept and argued that a forest-to-grassland conversion is not observed in nature, unless man-assisted by clearing and burning and, occasionally, under the influence of mass destruction by insects active in the forest floor.

Vil'yams had, however, rightly drawn attention to the phenomenon of organic matter accumulation in grassland soil, as well as to the ageing and subsequent decline ("depression") in productivity of (new) grassland (Mid-term depression; Soil-chemical effects of grasses). In his view, grassland that has reached the "densely-tufted phase" is degenerate, beyond rehabilitation and should be ploughed and re-sown, fertilizer at this stage not being worthwhile. However, as we will see below, attempts aimed at arresting and encouraging the fallow grass phases dominated by more desirable plants can bring about the improvement wanted.

The Steppe and its types

In 1954, of the whole territory of Russia (1 690 million hectares), some 144 million hectares were under natural grassland (hay meadow and pasture) before the crop expansion campaigns (Table 10.3). If tundra were included, another 206 million hectares should be added. Kazakhstan had a relatively small area under meadows (12 million hectares against 176 million hectares) while Ukraine, in contrast, had relatively little grassland as a whole. Fallow is usually included under arable and not under grassland.

Data for 1998, from the Russian Academy of Agricultural Sciences (RASHN), put the total for Russia at 83.6 million hectares of grassland (37 percent of agricultural land), with 21.6 million hectares and 62.0 million hectares for hay meadows and pastures, respectively. The difference from 1954, 60 million hectares, is estimated to be 17 million hectares, representing steppe that was ploughed in the 1950s (Maslov, 1999).

TABLE 10.3
Area under natural grass (millions of hectares), not including tundra, 1954.

	Land	Hay meadows		Pastures		Grassland
	Total	Total	Fallow	Total	Fallow	Total[1]
Russian Federation	1 690	49	4.6	95	4.0	144
Kazakhstan	275	12	2.2	176	2.2	188
Ukraine	60	3.2	0.03	4.7	0.2	7.9
FSU (USSR)	2 227	74	7.2	347	8.8	421

Notes: (1) Excluding fallow land.
Source: Administrativno territorialnoe delenie soyznykh respublik, 1954.

Forest steppe

Between the forest zone in the north and the semi-desert in the south stretches the steppe belt. Characteristic of forest steppe is the alternation of forest islands and large areas of more herbaceous vegetation. The European part is considerably more humid (460–560 mm) than the Asian part (315–400 mm), and warmer. Whereas, in the forest-steppe zone, the relief is hilly on the western side of the Urals, lowland plains prevail in western Siberia, with many depressions occupied by lakes and marshes.

In the European forest steppe, practically all catchment areas occupied by chernozems are under cultivation. Small areas of forests consist of birch, aspen and oak. Grasslands have remained on steep slopes and near the riverbeds (flood meadows). Because of intensive grazing, *Poa angustifolia* and *Festuca sulcata* predominate. On better preserved hayfields (Plate 10.4), a wide variety of grasses (*Calamagrostis epigeios* and species of *Agropyron, Bromus, Festuca, Phleum* and *Poa*) and legumes (*Trifolium pratense, T. repens* and *Medicago, Vicia* and *Lathyrus* spp.) and herbs are found. Hay yields of 1 000–1 500 kg/ha used to be recorded, and were considered good. In overgrazed areas, yields are only a third of that.

In the Asian part of the forest steppe, forests used to occupy up to 15 percent of the territory and consisted of birch, aspen and willow, but no oak. Groundwater levels are high, so swamps are common. Much less of the land has been ploughed than on the western side of the Urals, and then mostly on the ridges. On the plains, solonetzic soils and typical chernozems (mainly solonetzic) predominate. The predominant plant is *Calamagrostis epigeios*, which is very typical of western Siberia. Other species are *Poa pratensis, Galatella punctata* and *Peucedanum ruthenicum*. Hay yields are 600–800 kg/ha.

S.S. MIKHALEV

Plate 10.4
Haymaking in a forest-steppe floodplain.

TABLE 10.4
Climate data of the chernozem-steppe.

	Sum of mean daily temperatures over 10°C	Precipitation mm/year	January, mean temperature (°C)
Northern Caucasus	3 000-3 500	400-600	0 to -7
Central Chernozem	2 600-3 200	350-500	-5 to -12
Volga Territory	2 200-2 800	300-400	-12 to -16
Ural	2 000-2 900	300-400	-15 to -17
Western Siberia	1 800-2 100	300-350	-16 to -19
Eastern Siberia	1 600-2 000	200-400	down to -30

SOURCE: Chibilev, 1998.

Steppe

The steppe zone covers an area of 143 million hectares. The climate (Table 10.4) is more continental but becomes more humid towards the foothills of the mountain ranges (Caucasus, Urals and Altai foothills).

The principal soils of the steppe are chernozems and dark chestnut soils. However, in the Rostov (Salsk and Primanchy steppe) and Volgograd regions, as well as in Kazakhstan, solonetz and solonchaks are numerous.

Characteristic of the steppe are treeless plains with a dominance of *Stipa* spp. and *Festuca sulcata*. Trees and shrubs are confined to depressions and ravines and include *Caragana frutex*, *Spiraea* spp., *Amygdalus nana*, and *Cytisus* spp. Steppe grasses, including the xerophytic types, cease activity in summer and dry up entirely. With new rains in late August and early September, tillering recommences. In sharp contrast to the forest and forest-steppe zones, ephemerals and ephemeroids appear in spring and conclude their cycle of development in 60–70 days. From the husbandry point of view, the following subdivision seems useful: 1. Virgin steppe and old fallows. 2. Mid-term fallows of 2–3 to 7–10 years. 3. Young fallows.

Virgin steppe

Only small isolated islands of steppe were preserved in the European part of the FSU: Askaniya, Starobelsk, Khrenovskaya, Streletskaya (Olikova and Sycheva, 1996). Larger areas used to occur in Russia in the Salsk and Primanchy steppe in Rostov Oblast [region], in Volgograd Oblast and in Stavropol Kray. Closer to the Caspian Sea, in the northern parts of the Dagestan Republic, stretches the sandy, semi-arid Nogayskaya steppe. The largest areas are in Kazakhstan, but, apart from the solononetz and solonetzic soils, millions of hectares were sacrificed to cropping in the 1950s and 1960s.

As pointed out earlier, the distinguishing lines between the vegetation of virgin steppe and old abandoned fallows are blurred, so that much of the uncropped land may soon return to steppe and not bear much sign of having been cropped for so long. The underlying processes that help to facilitate this return are emphasized here, with a focus on the work done in the period when virgin steppe still formed a formidable grazing and hay resource.

In fact, the grass swards of the steppe are – also when still green and in active growth – low (<10 cm) and rich in herbs in the northern areas, and rich in xerophytic species in the southern areas. Reported hay yields are no more than 700 kg/ha in the north and 450 kg/ha in the south. In view of the inherently high soil fertility and total precipitation, a somewhat more productive sward would be expected, especially when at the same time a huge mass of vegetation (>1 m high) is found in nearby flood-meadows. This contrast, which is especially evident in early summer, is simply too large to be explained away by limitations posed by nitrogen availability (immobilization versus silt deposition), drought versus flooding, or by early grazing versus late haymaking. The hypothesis formulated here is that the lack of vigorous growth in steppe vegetation is largely because – by the time of stem elongation in April/May – insufficient moisture (in the form of rain) is available or can be drawn upon to make mineralized nitrogen available. In addition, because of severe winters, very little of the soil organic matter has decomposed by that time. Crop nutrition studies have shown that, on arable land in chernozem soils, some 75 kg/ha nitrogen is mineralized and another 75 kg P_2O_5 is made available each year. Steppe vegetation was mainly used for extensive grazing in spring and autumn. Where *Festuca sulcata* is plentiful and snow not too heavy, winter grazing can be satisfactory in southern regions.

Semi-desert

The semi-desert stretches in a crescent along the northern shores of the Caspian Sea in European Russia and then covers large parts of Kazakhstan. Western Siberia has no typical semi-desert. The crescent begins with the Nogaskaya steppe in northern Dagestan, crosses Kalmykia and south of Volgograd towards Astrakhan, on the Volga estuary, and past Guryev, into Kazakhstan. In the FSU, semi-desert totalled 127 million hectares. Snow in winter is light enough to permit winter grazing. The climate of the semi-desert is, however, more continental than that of the steppe. Low moisture and high temperatures in summer are conducive to the development of solonchaks and, especially, of solonetz, although the soils are mainly light chestnut and brown. Small variations in microrelief, with very shallow depressions, add to the heterogeneity of the vegetation. Typical of the semi-desert are large sandy stretches ("barkhan" dunes) and "liman" (flood meadows in lower reaches of semi-desert rivers). Flat areas ("plakor") east of the Volga typically consist of sub-shrub associations: *Artemisia pauciflora* + *Kochia prostrata* (Plate 10.5), interspersed with ephemerals and ephemeroids (e.g. *Poa bulbosa, Tulipa* spp. and *Allium* spp.). Near shallow depressions, grasses consist of *Festuca sulcata*, predominantly, followed by *Agropyron pectiniforme, Stipa lessingiana* and *Stipa capillata* and a mixture of herbs. Incidentally, *Festuca sulcata* together with *Stipa capillata* or *Stipa lessingiana* are also typical of "mountain steppe" at 1 000–3 000 m altitude.

Plate 10.5
Kochia prostrata

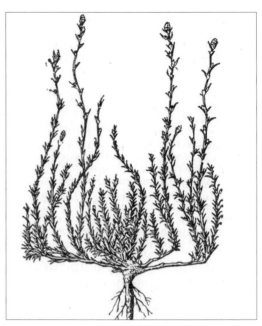

Plate 10.6
Artemisia lercheana

MEADOW TYPES
Liman
Due to the exceptional flatness of the surrounding area, semi-desert rivers that spread out over enormous areas in spring often never reach the Caspian Sea, and form the meadow areas called limans (Mamin and Savel'eva, 1986). Such areas can be 30–40 km wide, but shallow enough for wheeled transport to pass. Intense evaporation and high watertables promote the development of solonchaks and solonetz, with predominance of halophytes or tolerant plants (*Artemisia* spp. (Plate 10.6), *Puccinellia* spp., *Atriplex verrucifera* and *Agropyron repens*). Patterns of concentric rings emerge, with water receding from the perimeter towards the centre, a pattern that is reflected in the vegetation. *Artemisia monogyna* and *Atriplex verrucifera* are in the outer rings that are rarely flooded and then only for a few days. The area may be hundreds of hectares in size. Further towards the centre, the rings or strips flooded once in two to three months with water in a layer of 30–60 cm until June/July produce stands of almost pure *Agropyron* spp. that grows up to 150 cm and gives hay yields of 6 000–7 000 kg/ha. The centre and lowest parts of the liman may consist of reed thickets. In the FSU, limans used to occupy over 7 million hectares. Needless to say, limans are of great economic significance in the Saratov and Volgograd region, and may take much of the pressure off the surrounding catchment grazing areas. Only minor ditches need to be constructed to lead water to areas with the most valuable fodder plants (*Agropyron repens*, *Agropyron pectiniforme* and *Euagropyron* spp., with *Medicago sativa* ssp. *falcata*, *Bromus inermis* and *Beckmannia* spp.).

Typical plants of the favourable parts of the sandy (loam) stretches are *Artemisia arenaria*, *A. astrachanica*, *Carex colchica*, *Kochia prostrata*, *Agropyron sibericum*, *Stipa capillata* and *S. joannis*. In lower places, the water table may be at 100–200 cm. *Agropyron sibericum* is the most valuable grass in this environment, yielding up to 1 000 kg DM/ha. Heavy grazing is believed to pulverize the top soil and increase *Agropyron sibericum* at the expense of *Artemisia astrachanica*.

Floodplain meadows
The steppe is traversed (Plate 10.7), in a north-south direction, by some of Europe's largest rivers. When in spate, large areas on either side are inundated. First in early spring, with the snow melting in the region itself; second, in late spring, when the waters of snow melting in the north arrive. Flood meadows are found over the whole length of the river course. The limans, in contrast, are confined to the lower reaches and in flat semi-desert country.

In the FSU, the total area covered by floodplain meadows (Plate 10.8) was over 30 million hectares, divided equally between hay and grazing. Their value is rated higher the drier the nearby catchment. As with the limans described

Plate 10.7
Forest-steppe with a floodplain in the distance.

Plate 10.8
Forest-steppe floodplain.

earlier, vegetation is much determined by the frequency, duration and depth of flooding, as well as by the degree and quality of silt sedimentation. All sorts of classifications have been thought out. Prolonged flooding over 40 days or more is withstood by *Phalaris* spp., *Bromus inermis, Stipa pratensis* and many *Carex* spp. (Table 10.5). Prolonged flooding is the rule in the floodplains of the greater steppe rivers (Dnepr, Don, Volga, Ural). Salination (solonchaks) is common in the outer reaches (upper flood meadows).

Three major zonal strips can be distinguished:

TABLE 10.5
Distribution of flood meadow vegetation.

	Forest Zone	Steppe Zone	Desert Zone
Flooded for no more than 15–20 days	*Festuca ovina, Nardus stricta, Phalaris* spp.	*Festuca sulcata, Euagropyron* spp., often solonetzic or solonchakic with *Artemisia* spp., *Glycyrrhiza* spp. and *Puccinellia* spp. Herbs with shrubs.	Poplar and *Elaeagnus* spp. forests, thorny shrubs, *Glycyrrhiza* spp., *Alhagi* spp., Chenopodiaceae.
Flooded annually for 20–40 days	Herbs, *Agrostis alba*, white clover and other legumes. Tall gramineae with *Phleum* spp., *Alopecurus* spp., *Festuca pratensis*. Moist *Deschampsia* spp., *Agrostis* spp.	Tall gramineae with *Agropyron repens* or *Alopecurus* spp., with a small quantity of herbs, *Vicia cracca* and *Lathyrus* spp. More rarely, *Poa pratensis* with herbs.	*Aeluropus littoralis, Agropyron* spp. and *Glycyrrhiza* spp.
Flooded annually for >40 days	*Phalaris* spp., with sedges, sedge – *Bromus* spp., *Deschampsia* spp. with *Carex caespitosa* and reeds. Bogged-up alder stands, osier beds, tussocky swamps	Reeds, bulrushes, cattail, *Agropyron* spp., less often *Alopecurus* spp., *Cirsium* spp. and *Carex acuta*, boggy osier beds, a few sedge marshes.	Reeds. There are almost no sedge marshes.
Woody and shrubby vegetation	Conifers and partially deciduous forests, mainly in the central floodplains. Much willow and alder	Deciduous forests on the floodplain near a river and on the central plain. Much willow and steppe shrubs.	Poplars, tamarisks, oleaster (*Elaeagnus* spp.) forests. Few willows, many thorny shrubs and shrub-Chenopodiaceae.

1. Close to the river: *Artemisia dracunculus, A. pontica, A. campestris, Glycyrrhiza* spp. (liquorice, in floodplains – a very common but high-tannin legume), *Calamagrostis epigeios, Bromus inermis* and *Stipa capillata. Bromus inermis* dominates in the lower parts.

2. Central: *Festuca sulcata, Euagropyron* spp. and *Agropyron* spp. on the higher parts. *Agropyron* spp. dominant in the lower parts, with *Carex* spp. in the depressions.

3. Periphery, close to the watershed: *Festuca sulcata, Stipa capillata* and *Agropyron sibiricum* on the more elevated and non-saline sites, together with various herbs and steppe shrubs. In the lower, solonetzic, parts *Agropyron pectiniforme* predominates, or *Glycyrrhiza* spp. with *Agropyron* spp. and *Alopecurus* spp. On solonchaks, *Puccinellia* spp. with *Artemisia monogyna* is most prevalent.

Flood meadows are a principal source of hay. In the steppe itself, hay yields off *Euagropyron* and *Puccinellia* meadows are 1 000 kg/ha. Tall-grass associations (species of *Bromus, Agropyron, Festuca, Alopecurus* and *Phleum*) give hay yields of 5 000 kg/ha. With *Phalaris* spp., yields can be even higher. Inevitably, abuse by overexploitation occurs. Grazing hay meadows in early spring or in late fall should be discouraged. Alternative uses for early or late hay on the one hand and for grazing on the other should be encouraged. Swamps with reed, bulrush and sedge are common. When deciduous trees (aspen, poplar, elm, oak) are found in the steppe, it is mostly close to the watercourses.

FALLOW
Mid-term to old fallow
From the tenth to fifteenth years of fallow, *Stipa* spp. and *Festuca sulcata* begin to dominate and the land resembles virgin steppe.

Young fallow

In the first year, botanical composition is little different from the previous arable weed composition, which reflects preceding crops and their husbandry. The commonest plants are annuals such as *Chenopodium album, Salsola kali, Setaria* spp., *Artemisia absinthium, A. sieversiana, Brassica campestris, Sonchus arvensis, Polygonum aviculare, P. convulvulus, Avena fatua, Camelina* spp., *Thlaspi arvense, Lappula* spp., *Sisymbrium* spp., *Berteroa* spp., *Lactuca* spp., various thistles, *Erigeron canadensis, Urtica cannabina, Crepis tectorum, Bromus tectorum,* and *Cannabis sativa.* Perennials develop and begin to predominate: *Cirsium arvense, Sonchus arvensis, Artemisia campestris, A. frigida, A. austriaca, Melilotus alba, Gypsophila* spp., *Achillea millefolium, Falcaria vulgaris,* spurge (Euphorbiaceae) and *Potentilla argentea,* together with rhizomatous grasses such as *Agropyron repens, A. racemosum, Calamagrostis epigeios* and *Bromus inermis.*

Much higher herbage yields are obtained in the fallow phase. Larin (1956) speaks of 4 000–8 000 kg/ha of fresh and 1 000–2 000 kg/ha of dry matter, whereas the steppe produces no more than 800 kg/ha of hay! Low productivity of the virgin steppe itself, in comparison with high productivity of (unsown) green fallow on top of intermittent crop yields, has no doubt been a major incentive to plough virgin steppe, at least on the richer and better watered soils.

However, green fallows are heterogeneous and many of the herbaceous weeds are ignored by the grazing animal, such as *Chenopodium album, Artemisia* spp., *Thlaspi* spp., *Salsola kali* and other thistles. Herbs are grazed highly selectively, not least because of the wide range in date of flowering and maturity. This is an advantage in summer, when the virgin steppe itself has dried off. Hay is then a better alternative and many Russian authors claim that when the mixed herbage is turned into silage, the rate of utilization is higher than when grazed. Conversely, *Agropyron repens, Avena fatua, Bromus* spp. and *Setaria* spp., together with herbs such as *Sonchus arvensis, Polygonum convolvulus, Polygonum aviculare* and *Brassica campestris* provide relatively good pasture, with 2 500–3 500 kg/ha of edible fresh matter.

As the fallow period develops, rhizomatous perennials take over in about the fourth to fifth year: *Agropyron repens* on chestnut soils, *A. racemosum* on lighter soils, and *Bromus inermis* and *Calamagrostis* spp. This is the most valuable fallow phase from the herbage point of view. *Agropyron* hay is highly valued. Patches with *Achillea* spp., *Artemisia austriaca* and *A. frigida* may still be much in evidence. In the final stages of return to the virgin steppe, rhizomatous grasses and *Artemisia* spp. begin to give way to *Festuca sulcata* and *Stipa* spp.

Avenues of steppe improvement

Land and grass resources in the steppe zone are grossly underutilized. Most farms are overstocked, yet even on the better farms in favourable areas, yields of both milk and cereals are not high enough. Such farming is prodigal with land, nutrients and labour. In the continuing debate on how to preserve the environmental resource base, it is high time to point out that there can be no excuse for the deterioration of very large areas of land in order to produce crops or livestock at such low efficiency (Boonman, 1993).

Efforts towards intensification need not necessarily imply high costs. Low-input strategies must optimize results from the efforts already made. Correct timing can double the effect of a particular input, e.g. early sowing or fertilizer application. Conversely, cash inputs should not be dismissed too lightly as "uneconomic" or "outside the reach of poor farmers" because it is well known that farmers recognize and adopt an improvement (e.g. using seed of a superior new cultivar) when they see its value. Dairy production is a profitable part of mixed farming since milk, if produced throughout the year, tends to command high prices and bring in regular cash income. Great advances are often made by simple measures, especially in animal nutrition.

As for grass resources, natural grasslands may seen insignificant in their outward appearance and even less so in their response to improved husbandry. In spring their start is slow and growth ceases earlier in autumn, compared with elite sown grasses. However with the same amount of intelligent care, primary (natural or virgin) grassland often needs no replacement at all by sown pasture grasses, let alone by legumes. Secondary grassland (fallow land) is not very static as it passes through its various stages of transition or succession, which differ with different husbandry systems. If the rhizomatous or *Agropyron* stages are the most productive of all, it is advantageous to extend and maintain that phase for as long as possible. Rotational grazing shows advantage over continuous grazing in situations where the quantity of available herbage is low, and this is the case throughout the year on most of the steppe. The proportion of desirable grasses, legumes or herbs can be manipulated with the aid of the grazing animal. Cutting can be another useful tool. Many hay meadows, in well-watered if not periodically flooded areas, have developed under age-long haymaking. Apart from providing feed for winter, cutting would seem an automatic tool to control many shrubs.

MANAGEMENT INTERVENTIONS
Grazing

Grazing is the most potent of biotic factors; many palatable, annual herbs disappear forthwith. Russian authors at one time generally held that taller grasses, especially those with sizeable aftermath, maintain themselves well in hay meadows but much less under grazing only and are, consequently grazed out first. In the steppe, *Stipa capillata* is such an example, compared with *Festuca sulcata*, *Euagropyron* spp. and *Koeleria gracilis*. A note of caution needs to be sounded here. No doubt, some of the less competitive species may have long flowering culms. Between species, however, height of the vegetative sward

Plate 10.9
Poa bulbosa.

and eventual height of flowering culms are poorly correlated. *Lolium perenne* and *Festuca rubra* are obvious contrasts. Also, it is not entirely clear what the confounding effects in a sward are of growth stage, palatability and residual leaf area of any given species in competition with others. Whether plants with "lower cauline-leaved rather than upper cauline-leaved foliage" are necessarily more competitive under grazing, is therefore doubtful. Competitiveness of a genotype is also poorly related with potential herbage yield in pure stands (Boonman and van Wijk, 1973). See also the sections on Haymaking and on Sown forage, below.

Poa bulbosa (Plate 10.9) heads early in spring and is thereafter not eaten. *Artemisia austriaca* forms a rosette. As grazing intensity increases, *Polygonum* spp. and other annuals (Cruciferae, Compositae) remain and take over. The factors responsible are not necessarily the actual grazing itself but associated phenomena, such as compaction due to treading. The effects of grazing on soil compaction and soil moisture retention are recurrent themes. Hoof impact is the cause of disappearance of moss and lichen from grassland. Positive effects of scattered dung and urine are only evident when the pasture is sufficiently moist and stocked by at least 0.5 Livestock Unit (LU) per ha. In the steppe, the effects are minimal, if not negative, because grass on and around dung pats is avoided by the grazing animal. The grazing animal is also believed to assist in plant pollination and in the distribution of seed, although volunteer seedlings contribute little to the productive sward (Rabotnov, 1969), and when they do so it is mostly in the form of annuals to make up for loss of cover.

Grazing (stocking) management

Russian authors generally agree about the advantage of rotational grazing. If the ultimate aim is to match, if not to synchronize, the supply of available forage with the demands of the grazing animals or to maintain the vigour of acceptable pastures, then various scenarios are possible. Haymaking is a strong Russian tradition. A lot of the debate in other countries such as USA and Australia on the pros and cons of rotational versus continuous grazing has ignored the very role and place of grass conservation. Grass conservation is essential to carry productive dairy stock through winter or dry season, but mowing is also a convenient husbandry tool to regulate the supply of fresh grass and put a brake on grass growing too fast in the most favourable parts of the season (Boonman, 1993). It is obvious that no hay can be made under continuous grazing, so direct comparisons with rotational grazing may be meaningless. However, the lines dividing the two allegedly opposite systems are blurred. Are fields, grazed in daytime by animals that are housed elsewhere at night, grazed "continuously", or is this not rather a fixed form of "rotational" grazing of 12 hours on + 12 hours off? Is a field grazed continuously if for the greater part of the dry season it is excluded from grazing? Fields grazed only once every 15 days, however lightly, are also difficult to portray as being grazed continuously. What if animals are tethered and moved daily within the same field? The arguments are often largely academic, but the choice in practice is often one of simple convenience.

In Europe, with emphasis on dairying, which implies daily handling of the animals, rotational grazing within fenced but relatively small areas is the rule. Rotational grazing goes hand in hand with crop-pasture rotations in mixed farming, as all fields need to be protected from unwanted grazing. On large beef cattle estates, fencing, if any, may be reduced to the perimeter. Still, absence of fencing and the imposition of herding does not imply that grazing is continuous. On the free range, grazing rotations are naturally imposed by the presence or absence of water and by seasonal differences in the vegetation, so that rotation may take the form of a grazing procession rather than of a rotation. Seasonal grazing areas may develop as separate entities (Boonman, 1993).

Haymaking

Like grazing, cutting also has direct and indirect effects. The haymaking season in Russia is relatively late, in hot mid-summer (July). Soil is exposed, topsoil dries out and is compacted by subsequent rain. In mixed vegetation, shade-loving species perish and this is particularly so in secondary grassland following forest clearing. Late-heading species are also at a disadvantage. As we have seen above (in Grazing), species with upper cauline-leaved foliage were believed to be at an advantage under haymaking regimes. It should be repeated that although species differ in their reaction to either grazing or cutting and, as a result, produce a different botanical composition, it is difficult to attribute this to plant stature alone. Red clover and other herbs produced distinct types whether under cutting or grazing regimes with early and late heading types, respectively (Shennikov, 1941). Variation in cutting date also has considerable effect on species composition. Land that is continually used for haymaking becomes more and more impoverished and yields decline. In the forest zone, moss reappears. Floodplains in the Yenisei valley, after being cleared from willows and alders, changed under continuous haymaking, with dominance first by *Calamagrostis langsdorffii*, five to eight years later by *Anthriscus silvestris* and finally by *Alopecurus pratensis* (Vershinin, 1954).

Fire

Burning is an additional factor, if not a tool, in the management of steppe and semi-desert. Some even believe that the tree-less steppe is the result of burning, rather than of climate or soil. Burning is necessary to deal with "starika" – dead vegetation or standing hay of previous year(s). Burnt soil covered with ash warms up and dries out more quickly. Soil nitrogen is released. Subsequent herbage yield may not be increased, is rather decreased, but regrowth after burning is more nutritious. On the negative side, absence of cover by the onset of winter adds to reduced snow and moisture retention for subsequent spring regrowth. In *Festuca/Stipa/Artemisia* steppe, burning increases *Stipa* spp. (Plate 10.10), *Agropyron desertorum* (Plate 10.11) and *Festuca sulcata*, but decreases *Artemisia* spp.

Ploughing

Of all the husbandry measures, ploughing has the most dramatic effect on botanical composition. The effect is largely temporary, with the steppe returning to its "original" state within ten years. It is not clear whether the length of this moratorium is linearly related to the intensity and kind of cropping. Most of the steppe has seen the plough at some stage, but the last and major onslaught in terms of area came in the 1950s, when millions of hectares of the remaining virgin steppe were sacrificed to cropping. Fortunately, however, the insight that permanent cropping was impossible without disastrous effects on soil quality prevailed. Fallowing was the rule, ideally until the "transition of fallow land into virgin land", as formulated by N.G. Vysotskii in 1915, was completed. Nevertheless in more recent decades, new policies and campaigns of heavy mechanization, combined with fertilizer, herbicides and irrigation, posed as serious a threat to the fallow as the plough had earlier meant to the steppe itself.

Plate 10.10
Stipa *species.*

Plate 10.11
Agropyrum desertorum.

Uncontrolled tumble-down fallow is a nuisance to subsequent cropping as it encourages rather than suppresses some of the principal weeds. Conversely, bare fallows, however desirable from the weed control and perhaps the water conservation points of view, are not conducive to restoring soil structure.

Physical improvements

The principal step in steppe improvement is to prevent deterioration by inferior or harmful material and species. Dominance of superior constituents cannot, in many instances, be achieved by grazing with a specific or varied kind of livestock alone. Intentional elimination of less desirable species and starika is needed to complement the action of grazing, cutting or even burning. Oversowing (without adequate soil preparation) is rarely worth the effort as seedlings have great difficulty in establishing themselves in an established sward, however sparse, except perhaps in genuinely humid environments. Some effective measures are: 1. removal of tussocks, shrubs and starika; 2. removal of litter and brushwood after floods; 3. regulation of silt deposition on floodplain meadows; and 4. regulation of the water regime (drainage of stagnant surface waters; liman irrigation; temporary flooding of floodplain meadows; construction of ice dykes; protection for snow retention).

A lot of the clearing can be done with appropriate machinery and the same applies to the levelling that is needed to enable a field to be mown for hay. The removal of major deficiencies in moisture and fertility conditions contributes to the prevalence of more desirable grasses and or clovers; the same applies to regimes of alternate grazing and mowing on the one hand and of early and late mowing on the other. By assisting the correct distribution of spring waters, natural limans can be improved without great effort. Solonchaks and boggy places should not receive water.

Snow retention through windbreaks and standing vegetation is another effective measure in the forest steppe, steppe and semi-desert zones. Crop yields are greatly increased. In experiments by N.G. Andreev in the 1930s in Saratov Oblast, yields *of Agropyron racemosum* on fallow land were raised by 50–75 percent (see also Andreev, 1974a,b). Elsewhere, *Stipa-Festuca sulcata* pastures increased by 16–31 percent in yield (Larin, 1956). Snow retention can be combined with arrangement of ridges and furrows to block the flow of water from melting snow.

EXAMPLES OF THE EFFECT OF MANAGEMENT ON BOTANICAL COMPOSITION

Stipa capillata, common on virgin steppe and old fallow in the Rostov, Volgograd and Stavropol areas, is troublesome since the seed has awns which, when caught in the wool not only spoil it, but bore through the skin and when in greater numbers can cause death of goats and sheep. Burning has proved useless. Grazing with larger herbivores is recommended. Light grazing, especially when early, and early mowing increases rather than decreases this grass. Pastures should not be grazed earlier than the heading phase of *Festuca sulcata* and *Stipa lessingiana*. These grasses will then remain almost uneaten and will go to seed, while the later heading *Stipa capillata* will be eaten out selectively. Mowing of *Stipa* spp. must be conducted systematically from early head-emergence right up to the flowering stage and aftermath growth must be grazed or mown in fall. These pastures are best grazed by cattle (and horses) and, when there is little *Stipa* spp., by sheep. Stocking pressure should be increased for two to three consecutive years.

Medicago polymorpha can be abundant in the steppe of European Russia. Although it is well eaten, *M. polymorpha* can be a most harmful plant because the pods spoil the wool. It can be suppressed by hard and prolonged grazing. Herbicides are also effective.

Artemisia spp. (*A. lercheana, A. pauciflora, A. astrachanica*) are reduced by burning, and grasses such as *Festuca sulcata, Euagropyron* spp. and *Stipa* spp. are encouraged.

FERTILIZER

Fertilizing the steppe is only mentioned in passing here. The effects of nitrogen, phosphorus and potassium on yield, on quality and on botanical composition are well established (Smurygin, 1974) and differ little from what is found in similar soil conditions in the West. Unlike in steppe, phosphorus and potassium are a pre-condition in lowland marshy conditions and in acid soils in the north. The most spectacular fertilizer is nitrogen. However, land-to-capital ratios in most of Russia are such that nitrogen fertilizer is best reserved to those situations where all the limiting factors mentioned earlier have been removed and where moisture conditions are favourable to enable the grass to benefit fully from the fertilizer applied. Such circumstances are rare. However, most of all, fertilizer should be profitable in terms of the produce from the livestock fed from it. Most of the fertilizer is used on dairy farms in the forest zone in the north near the major cities. Yield increases in dry matter from 2 to 8 t/ha were reported from the Tula and Kaluga regions (Larin, 1956). In the view of the authors, grassland and grazing will soon regain their rightful place in Russia at the expense of arable fodder crops such as maize grown for silage. More and better use will also have to be made of manure and urine, one of the most neglected resources at present, especially from the storage point of view. Night grazing, through mobile camps if necessary, should be the rule, were it only to benefit by the manure and urine dropped on the spot.

Legumes should also fare better under balanced manure and fertilizer regimes. In the view of the authors, clovers should be highly appreciated where their continuous presence can be assured. Inducing clovers by sowing and other measures is often not only costly but also temporary in its effect. Savings on nitrogen fertilizers may be offset by the extra requirements for other fertilizers, especially phosphate.

As far as the steppe zone is concerned, the same development as regards fertilizer is forecast for the better-watered areas, the floodplains. P and K are usually not in short supply. Some botanical effects observed in the steppe vegetation are worth mentioning. At the Baskhir Experimental Station,

Mikheev and Musatova (1940) found that *Festuca sulcata* gave way to *Poa pratensis* as the result of manure (30 t/ha). The same manure increased hay yield by (only) 1 900 kg/ha. Sedges also tend to be reduced and *Agropyron* spp. are encouraged.

MID-TERM DEPRESSION

Newly established grasslands tend to go through a depression after a few years, and this was recognized early by Vil'yams. More persistent varieties, together with better N-nutrition, have done much to alleviate this problem. Steppe fallow land with *Agropyron repens* is highly valued. After a few years, however, it tends to give way to the less valuable *Poa angustifolia* and *Festuca sulcata*, and yields may be reduced by half. Re-ploughing the field helps to rejuvenate the *Agropyron repens*, especially when combined with N-fertilizer and when used first for hay and subsequently for grazing. The same applies to *A. racemosum* in the Volgograd area, western Siberia and Kazakhstan, where it formerly covered millions of hectares. Hay yields were often doubled. Measures to promote snow retention are essential. The introduction of machinery like the rotovator facilitated destroying the existing sward. A more recent and valuable aid is glyphosate as an effective but very safe herbicide.

SOWN FORAGE

For many engaged in increased fodder production, all the measures mentioned above are not effective enough. Refuge is sometimes sought in sowing perennial grasses, with or without legumes and with or without intermittent arable cropping. However annual fodders such as maize for silage and oats, lent themselves more easily to the industrial style agriculture sought after in the FSU. A lot of maize is grown in Russia in areas north of latitude 55°N, which are considered too cold in the West (e.g. Scotland, Denmark), and many of the areas are too dry for silage maize. Late springs with late frosts and winter frosts as early as the first half of September shorten the growing season for maize even more radically. Existing, commercial early-maturing hybrids are not early enough for large parts of Russia; the problem has still not been solved, neither agronomically nor economically, let alone from the environmental point of view.

Short of complete ploughing and reseeding, over-sowing has been recommended at times. Perhaps this was inspired by positive results obtained with over-sowing in areas that had been cleared of trees and shrubs in the more northerly forest zone. However doubtful in economic terms such advice might be for steppe conditions, the species recommended are worth mentioning: *Bromus inermis, B. erectus, Agropyron pectiniforme, A. sibiricum, A. desertorum, Euagropyron* spp., *Festuca sulcata, Medicago sativa, M. s. subsp. falcata, Melilotus alba*, sainfoin (*Onobrychis viciifolia*) and *Kochia prostrata* (Chenopodiaceae). In regions east of the Urals with abundant late-summer rainfall, annual forages such as oats, rye, *Sorghum sudanense*, vetches and peas were experimented with for over-sowing but the recommended list is considerably reduced for normal pasture sowing (after proper land cultivation): *Medicago sativa, M. s.* subsp. *falcata, Onobrychis, Bromus inermis,* and *Agropyron pectiniforme* with, in addition, for the dry steppe: *Agropyron sibiricum* and *Festuca sulcata* (Larin, 1956). No indications exist as to what extent such sowings have been experimental or commercial, nor to what extent implementation was hindered by the obvious limitations of seed availability of some of these unusual species. Remarkable in this listing is the absence of *Festuca arundinacea*. More recent experience has shown that *Agropyron cristatum* is perhaps the best grass for sowing (T. Veenstra, pers. comm.).

As was customary at the time, complex mixtures were considered superior to single-species as a matter of course, on purely theoretical grounds, such as risk aversion. More modern thinking – not shared by biodiversity adherents – has it that less competitive species, however productive, are better left out from mixtures from the start because they are doomed to disappear rapidly from the sward anyway. The aim should be the "ecological combining ability" of potential partners, an ability that does not necessarily have much to do with morphological or botanical differences. As long as alleged advantages of complex mixtures cannot be substantiated, simple mixtures are advocated, if only to reduce seed costs. A considerable amount of energy was spent in FSU days on calculating "norms" for sowing of each species in accordance with *Goststandart* (All-Union State Standards).

THE DILEMMA

Many observers regard virgin steppe as not productive enough as a grazing or fodder resource. Sown pastures have great potential but require a high level of expertise and are often too short-lived. Continuous arable cropping consists mostly of wheat, with yields of grain scarcely higher than that of the old steppe's hay. The irony is that in FSU over half of the grain was fed back to livestock. The steppe is on the one hand too fertile not to be cropped and to be left to "ranching", but on the other too dry to be cropped intensively and permanently. All three pathways – grazing, cropping and an integration of the two – have in the past been explored, both empirically and experimentally. In the view of the authors, the best alternative land use is one crop of wheat alternated with long spells under grass fallow, or sown pastures of shorter duration. Alfalfa is grown separately on the best and irrigated land. Grass hay is brought in from the floodplains. Marginal land is best returned to steppe.

CROP-PASTURE ROTATIONS

V.R. Vil'yams (1922, 1951) was one of the first scientists to publish research results on the subject ("travopol'naya") and on the special role of grasses in soil fertility. Crop rotation regimes used to be strictly preached, but in FSU practice it was lip service to the "rotation" doctrine rather than consistent application of Vil'yams' example. Much value was attached to having a fodder crop or a grain legume in the rotation, irrespective of the fact that these covered the soil for no more than six months and were harvested whole, without much residue left or returned to the soil. Maize is often harvested first for grain and in the second pass for the stalks and foliage made into silage. If a crop-rotation effect does appear it is perhaps just as likely to be due to "just another crop" than to the specific effects usually attributed to semi-permanent grasses or legumes. In actual fact, the effect may be simply one of suppression of specific weeds, pests or diseases, and may also be brought about by other arable crops.

PHYSICAL EFFECTS OF GRASSES ON THE SOIL

Soil science used to be highly developed in Russia, not only soil classification. The unique role that grass plays in restoring soil quality lost after cropping was recognized in Russia earlier than in the West. In investigations carried out by N.I. Savvinov at the Saratov Malouzenski Solonetz Station, the length of all roots in the top 40 cm soil layer was, six months after sowing, almost three times greater in *Agropyron pectiniforme* than in alfalfa of the same age (Larin, 1956). Intensity, rather than depth, of rooting was considered important.

Soil organic matter and methods of increasing it are commonly associated with high soil quality, because a soil rich in organic matter is often productive and can sustain arable cropping for long periods. Such a soil will also trap rainwater rather than let it cause erosion (Klimentyev and Tikhonov, 1995).

Cultivation, in contrast, is accompanied by a decline in organic matter and by subsequent mineralization. Under continuous cropping without inputs, little organic matter is added or returned whereas losses are much greater. In capitalized farming systems in temperate climates, with high input of fertilizers and mechanical or chemical weed control, organic matter is commonly regarded as less critical and organic matter may be left to find its own level and may be maintained by crop residues. High, albeit not the highest, yields have been obtained under continuous cropping without special attention to adding organic matter.

Evidence has been presented to indicate that a grass break in crop rotations preserves soil structure and punctuates the nutrient drain in crop removal. Improved structure may reveal itself in less erosion or in better plant establishment and, finally, in better yields. However, the immediate effects on topsoil structure are the most obvious. Erosion control also applies to conditions of grazing. Overgrazed land is not only more liable to erosion, it suffers more from drought, due to loss of snow cover and of rainwater.

MIXED FARMING BASED ON CROP-GRASS ROTATIONS

In Russia, alternatives to deal effectively with maintaining soil quality and combating soil erosion are not within easy reach of the small-scale farmer and – unless good basic husbandry is guaranteed – often not economically justified. The impression is that continuous cropping cannot be sustained on the majority of soils at the present low levels of fertilizer, biocides and mechanization. In present-day farming practice, however, improved production of grass for feeding cattle is the main motive inducing farmers to plant pastures. If stock that help to improve soil fertility are kept, they should themselves be profitable. In the same fashion it is not profitable to grow legumes for the main purpose of fixing nitrogen.

The large expansion in arable area in the 1950s and 1960s in the FSU was at the expense of the steppe. The first crops after ploughing were good. Most of the remaining grassland was soon broken and converted into arable land. Very little new grass was sown. It was perhaps not appreciated that the fertility encountered had been built up through grassland. Conversely, forage production was promoted primarily as a means of improving animal production. Efforts were directed at separate components, e.g. dairying based on maize silage or on zero-grazing, with little regard for the soil-degrading effect this practice has.

In the 1970s and 1980s in the FSU, direct grazing became rare and was sacrificed to large-scale stall-feeding and to zero-grazing operations based on fodder crops such as maize and oats. Many of these operated on the extreme edges of the mixed-farming scene, and lost sight of the crop-livestock integration perspective.

In the past decade, by contrast, village herds have increasingly began to roam the surrounding countryside. Communal or public grazing resources are increasingly threatened by livestock privately owned. Workable solutions are needed to come to the aid of vulnerable grasslands, livestock, crops and soils, especially for the small mixed-farm family. Although the former large Kolkhoz-style arable farming units may be retained as the central and collective core, livestock production will continue to become more and more family-based. Sooner or later, family herds will have to be fed from family-run pastures and from by-products of the arable operations. This should provide a sound basis for crop-pasture rotations.

CONCLUSIONS

The political and social changes of the past fifteen years have had a marked effect on grassland and livestock production systems. The great industrial livestock units based on indoor feeding are now few, and many have broken up for economic reasons. Much of the ruminant livestock is now in small family-owned herds, often too small for economic herding. A fresh approach to grazing rights and stock management is needed to ensure that the new grazing situation maintains livestock production while avoiding environmental damage through overuse of nearby grassland while neglecting more distant pastures. This will require interventions in two fields: first, facilitating the development of group herding so that families can collaborate to hire a common herder to manage their joint herds; and, second, by allocating grazing rights and responsibility for pasture maintenance to such groups.

Much marginal land has been ploughed to produce meagre crops of cereals, which has largely been used for stock feed. Such land can be returned to grassland fairly simply: steppe is relatively easy to restore when cropland is abandoned to fallow. If economic conditions are propitious, it can be reseeded – reseeding techniques and adapted ecotypes of suitable grasses are known. Sown grasses may bring temporary relief, but they should be sufficiently persistent and economically justified, compared with spontaneous fallow grasses. Sown pastures require careful husbandry and considerable expertise. Return of large areas of unprofitable cropland to grassland makes sense both environmentally and economically.

REFERENCES

Andreev, A.W. 1974a. *Kul'turnie pastbitscha w yushnich rayonach* [Cultivated pastures in southern regions]. Moscow, Russia: Rossel'chozizdat.

Andreev, N.G. 1974b. Potentialities of native haylands and pastures in the Soviet union. pp. 165–175, *in: Proceedings of the 12th International Grassland Congress.* Moscow, Russia, 11–24 June 1974.

Blagoveshchenskii, G., Popovtsev, V., Shevtsova, L., Romanenkov, V., & Komarov, L. 2002. Country Pasture/Forage Resource Profile – Russian Federation. See: http://www.fao.org/ag/AGP/AGPC/doc/Counprof/russia.htm

Boonman, J.G. 1993. *East Africa's Grasses and Fodders: Their Ecology and Husbandry.* Dordecht, The Netherlands: Kluwer Academic Publishers.

Boonman, J.G. & van Wijk, A.J.P. 1973. Breeding for improved herbage and seed productivity. *Netherlands Journal of Agricultural Science*, **21**: 12–23.

Chayanov, A.V. [1926]. *In:* D. Thorner, B. Kerblay and R.E.F. Smith (eds). 1966. *A.V. Chayanov on the Theory of Peasant Economy.* Homewood, Illinois, USA: American Economic Association.

Chibilev, A.A. 1998. *Stepi sewernoii Ewrazii* [Steppes of northern Eurasia]. Instutut stepi [Steppe Institute] of UrO RAN, Ekaterinburg, Russia.

Chugunov, L.A. 1951. *Lugovodstvo* [Grassland Husbandry]. Leningrad and Moscow, Russia: Selkhozgiz.

Clements, F.E. 1916. *Plant Succession: An Analysis of the Development of Vegetation.* Carnegie Institute Publication No. 242. Washington D.C., USA.

Coupland, R.T. 1979. Grassland Ecosystems of the World: Analysis of Grasslands and their Uses. *Int. Biol. Progr.* 18.

Dmitriev, A.M. 1948. *Lugovodstvo s osnovami lugovedeniya* [Grassland husbandry and its scientific principles]. Moscow, Russia: Selkhozgiz.

Gilmanov, T.G. 1995. The state of rangeland resources in the newly independent states of the former USSR. pp. 10–13, *in: Proceedings of the 5th International Rangeland Congress.* Salt Lake City, USA.

Gilmanov, T.G., Parton, W.J. & Ojima, D.S. 1997. Testing the "Century" ecosystem level model on data sets from eight grassland sites in the former USSR representing a wide climatic/soil gradient. *Ecological Modelling*, **96**: 191–210.

Klimentyev A.I. & Tikhonov, V. Y. 1995. Estimate of erosion losses of organic matter in soils of the steppe zone of the southern Urals. *Eurasian Soil Science*, **27**(6): 83–92.

Larin, I.V. 1956. *Lugovodstvo i pastbishchnoe khozyaistvo* [Grassland husbandry]. Leningrad and Moscow, Russia: Selkhozgiz.

Mamin, V.F. & Savel'eva, L.F. 1986. *Limani - kladowie kormow* [Limans' fodder resource]. Nizhne-Volzhskoye knizhnoye Izdatel'stwo, Volgograd, Russia.

't Mannetje, L. & Jones, R.M. (eds). 2000. *Field and laboratory methods for grassland and animal production research.* Wallingford, UK: CABI.

Maslov, B.S. 1999. *Otcherki po istorii melioratsii w Rossii* [Essays on melioration history in Russia]. Moscow, Russia: GU ZNTI "Meliowodinform".

Mikheev, V.A. & Musatova, K.M. 1940. Poverkhnostnoe uluchshenie tipchakovo-myatlikovogo pastbishcha [Surface improvement of a "tipchak" meadow grass pasture]. *Trudy Bashkir op. st. shivotn*, **1**.

Olikova, I.S. & Sycheva, S.A. 1996. Water regime of virgin chernozems in the central Russian upland and its changes. *Eurasian Soil Science*, **29**(5): 582–590.

Phillips, J.F.V. 1929. Some important vegetation communities in the Central Province of Tanganyika Territory. *South African Journal of Science*, **26**: 332–372.

Rabotnov, T.A. 1969. Plant regeneration from seed in meadows of the USSR. *Herbage Abstracts* (Review Article), **39**(4): 28.

Ramenskii, L.G. 1938. *Vvedenie v kompleksnoe pochvenno-geobotanicheskoe issledovanie zemel'* [Introduction to the Complex Soil and geobotanical Investigation of Lands]. Moscow, Russia: Selkhozgiz.

Shennikov, A.P. 1941. *Lugovedenie* [Grassland science]., Leningrad, Russia: Izd. LGU.

Shennikov, A.P. 1950. *Ekologiya Rastenii* [Plant ecology]. Moscow, Russia: Sovetskaya Nauka.

Smurygin, M.A. 1974. Basic trends of grassland research in the USSR. pp. 76-88, in: *Proceedings of the 12th International Grassland Congress*. Moscow, Russia, 11–24 June 1974.

Sorokina, V.A. 1955. Some results of applying the methods of L.G. Ramenskii. *Herbage Abstracts* (Review Article), **25**(4): 209–218.

Sukachev, V.N. 1945. Biogeotsenologiya i fitotsenologiya [Biogeocoenology and phytocoenology]. *Doklady An SSSR*, **47**.

Vershinin, L.G. 1954. *Sroki senokosheniya na zalivnykh lugakh nizov'ev Eniseya* [Times of haymaking on flood meadows of the lower reaches of the Yenisey]. Leningrad, Russia: Selkhozgiz.

Vil'yams, V.R. 1922. *Estestwenno-nauchnye osnowy lugowodstwa, ili lugowedeniye* [Natural and Historical Fundamentals of Grassland Husbandry]. Moscow, Russia: "Nowaya Derewnya".

Vil'yams, V.R. 1951. *Izbrannie sotchineniya po woprosam bor'bi c zasuchoi. "Klassiki russkoi agronomii w bor'be s zasuchoi"* [Classics of Russian agronomy in combating drought]. Moscow, Russia: Izdatel'stwo Academii Nauk SSSR.

Whyte, R.O. 1974. *Tropical Grazing Lands. Communities and Constituent Species.* The Hague, The Netherlands: W. Junk.

Chapter 11
Other grasslands

INTRODUCTION

As indicated in Chapter 1, this section attempts to cover some of the gaps in the description of grassland zones and their problems. Summaries of the grassland and grazing situation in areas not addressed in the main chapters are presented. The basis of the summaries is the series of Country Pasture Resource Profiles published by the FAO Grassland and Pasture Crops Group and which provide basic information about the pasture and forage resources of countries; these profiles provide more detailed information and extensive bibliographies (see the Web site <http://www.fao.org/ag/AGP/AGPC/doc/pasture/forage.htm> and the CD-ROM "Country Pasture Profiles" (Reynolds, Suttie and Staberg, 2005)); developing countries have been the main focus since this is FAO's major zone of interest.

AFRICA
North Africa

This section draws on Pasture Profiles for Algeria (Nedjraoui, 2001), Morocco (Berkat and Tazi, 2004) and Tunisia (Kayouli, 2000). These North African countries have large areas of grazed land and many pastoral features in common, and stretch from 13°E to 12°E and from 19°N to 37°19′N; vast areas of their southern part is desert. The relief is in two broad categories, the Atlas and the Sahara. The Atlas are a group of ranges running southwest to northeast roughly adjacent and parallel to the Mediterranean coastline. South of the Atlas, a series of steppic plateaux descend to the Sahara, which is a great barrier between the Mediterranean zone and the tropics.

The northern mountains capture most of the precipitation and agriculture lands are concentrated in the north; the highest Atlas lands are forest and summer grazing. The climate is typically Mediterranean, with hot summers and rain occurring during the cool season. Temperature is governed both by altitude and the degree of continentality. The region has all the Mediterranean bioclimates, from perhumid to perarid for bioclimatic levels, and from cold to hot for temperatures.

Livestock are important throughout the zone and in most farming systems: sheep are the most important and are the main livestock of the steppe, although small flocks are kept in most areas for domestic use; several local breeds are used according to regional adaptation. Cattle are mainly kept in the northern farming areas and are commonly fed on crop residues, by-products and concentrates; the traditional breeds were taurins of the Atlas Brown type, but there are now many crosses with exotic dairy breeds, notable black and white ones.

SARDI

Plate 11.1
Trifolium fragiferum.

Goats are widespread although much less numerous than sheep. Camels are a mainstay in the desert areas.

The mountains of the north once had a Mediterranean forest vegetation, which has been greatly reduced by clearing for agriculture or felling; in some places forest is degraded to matorral. The steppes are the great traditional grazing lands; *Artemisia* steppes (*Artemisia herba-alba*) are extremely widespread and there are large stands of *Stipa tenacissima* ('alfa) and *Lygeum spartum* (esparto). *Stipa tenacissima* and *Lygeum spartum* are mediocre fodders but are commercially important since they are harvested for papermaking and basketry on such a scale that these populations have been damaged. An unusual browse formation in western Morocco is the argan (*Argania spinosa*) zone, where this shrub is browsed by goats, which clamber into the trees to feed; argan seed yields an edible oil.

Cereals are often grown in rotation with fallow, which produces large areas of high-quality grazing. Many Mediterranean fallow plants have been domesticated in Australia and incorporated into cereal-fallow rotations; there have been many attempts to re-import these plants and the associated technology into North Africa but with very limited success, as large cereal farmers are not livestock owners and fallows are often let to passing transhumant herds, which graze them to bare ground. The rich pastoral flora of the fallows includes: *Avena* spp., *Bromus* spp., *Hordeum* spp., *Lolium rigidum*, *Hippocrepis* spp., *Lathyrus aphaca*, *Lotus* spp., *Medicago ciliaris*, *M. littoralis*,

M. orbicularis, M. polymorpha (the commonest, with many highly productive forms), *M. rugosa, M. scutellata, M. truncatula, Melilotus* spp., *Scorpiurus* spp. and *Trifolium* spp.

Sown pasture is uncommon in the region, but many valuable pasture plants native to North Africa have been widely used elsewhere. They include *Dactylis glomerata, Festuca arundinacea, Lolium multiflorum, L. rigidum, L. perenne, Phalaris aquatica, Hedysarum coronarium, Medicago sativa* and *Trifolium fragiferum* (see Plate 11.1).

Fodder is grown in specialized dairy enterprises in the farming areas; oats are a common winter fodder, as is maize in summer. Oat hay is produced by large cereal farms, mainly for sale, and demand often exceeds supply and prices are high, making it an expensive feed per unit of energy. Oat and hay production in the region are described by Chaouki *et al.* (2004).

Traditional sheep rearing was based on transhumance, with variants according to local conditions; frequently it involved moving to agricultural lands to graze stubbles and straw in summer, and to the desert fringe in winter. Recently, transhumance has been greatly reduced: much of the steppe has been cleared for rainfed cereal growing of doubtful sustainability, even down to the 300 mm isohyet in some cases; this clearing was officially encouraged and those who "developed" the steppe by clearing gained title to their holding. Many of the rural population are now agropastoralists, with a little cropland and small flocks. The human population of the steppe has exploded: in Algeria the steppe population was 925 700 in 1954; in 2003 it was about 4 000 000; during the same period, the number of nomads only rose from 595 240 to 625 000. Nomadism in Algeria is now sporadic and most only make short movements, the feed shortage being met by crop residues, stubble grazing and purchased grain; only owners of large flocks continue long migration, and they are equipped with transport.

Tunisia shows a similar pattern of disappearing transhumance. Increasing settlement of nomads, increase in sheep numbers in marginal zones, expansion of cultivation and reduction of fallow have greatly increased pressure on available land and reduced soil fertility. Grazing land is becoming scarcer and meagre as more and more land is put under crops. Sheep and goats traditionally grazed on hillsides and steppes in winter in the centre, and stubble in summer in the north during transhumance. This continues, but is much reduced. Increased purchasing power has raised the demand for livestock products so farmers are changing to intensive sheep rearing with feed supplements, based on imported cereals.

West Africa

West Africa has great grazing areas, between the humid forest in the south and the desert in the north. Rainfall decreases from south to north so the vegetation belts run east-west. In the extreme north the Saharan zone is hyper-arid with skeletal

MARZIO MARZOT

Plate 11.2
Millet, a major crop in the arid and semi-arid areas.

soils; crops are only possible under special conditions; stock-rearing, where it is possible, reigns without competition. Detailed descriptions are available in the pasture profiles for Burkina Faso (Kagoné, 2002), Mali (Coulibally, 2003) Niger (Geesing and Djibo, 2002) and Ghana (Oppong-Anane, 2001).

The Sahelian zone, from the Atlantic through Chad, is arid, with a summer rainfall of 250–500 mm and a dry season of nine to eleven months. In the northern Sahel, which belongs to the Saharan-Sindian floristic domain according to Wickens (1997), the 150 mm isohyet corresponds to the southern limit of the Saharan species *Cornulaca monacantha*, *Panicum turgidum* and *Stipagrostis pungens* and to the northern limit of such Sahelian shrubs as *Boscia senegalensis* and *Commiphora africana* and the grass *Cenchrus biflorus*.

The Sahel's southern limit adjoins the deciduous woodlands of the Sudanian domain at between 450 and 500 mm/yr precipitation. *Acacia* spp. dominate the thin scrub along with *Balanites aegyptiaca*; laterite outcrops and cuirasses are colonized by *Combretum nigricans*, *Guiera senegalensis*, *Lannea acida* and *Sclerocarya birrea*. The grass component of the northern dunes is dominated by *Cenchrus biflorus*, *Aristida mutabilis* and *Schoenfeldia gracilis*. To the south, *Schoenfeldia gracilis* is important; on flood plains of rivers, grasslands with perennials like *Echinochloa stagnina*, *Oryza barthii* and *Vossia cuspidata* provide excellent grazing when the floods have receded. Crops are grown, opportunistically, with millet (*Pennisetum* spp.) the most important – it is usually sown when rain falls, with resowing, perhaps several times, until a reasonable stand is attained.

The Sahelian grazing lands have suffered much damage in the past fifty years, through an increasing human population, excessive advance of cropping into very marginal areas and serious deforestation, mainly for firewood, all exacerbated by recurrent droughts. The great drought of 1968 was particularly serious, as were others in the early 1980s.

The Sudanian zone, with from 500 mm to 1 100 mm/yr rainfall, is mainly on ferruginous tropical soils, with colluvions in depressions. Agricultural activity is more intense and the chance of crops succeeding is much more reliable. Millet is still important on light soils in the drier parts, along with cowpea and groundnut, with sorghum on heavier soils. The range of crops widens as rainfall increases: maize is grown and cotton is a cash crop. Stock-rearing is sedentary, with some migration away from cropland in the growing season. Areas with between 800 and 1 400 mm/yr precipitation is "parkland", where much of the original forest has been cleared for cropping but trees that yield useful products have been protected; it is characterized by *Vitellaria paradoxa* (shea butter), *Parkia biglobosa*, *Lannea acida* and *Sclerocaraya birrea*. The herbaceous layer was dominated by *Andropogon gayanus*, which is becoming scarce because of clearing and in cultivated areas has been replaced by vast areas of poor, unpalatable grasses. Forage quality is generally poorer than in the Sahel.

In the subhumid Sudano-Guinean zone, the rains last five to seven months, and agriculture is oriented to tubers (yams, cassava) and fruits. This is the wooded savannah (*savane arborée* - analogous to the *miombo* of central-southern Africa) and open forest (*forêt claire*). The tree layer is dominated by *Daniella olivieri* and *Isoberlina doka,* and associated grasses are *Hyperaemia* spp., *Schizachryium rupestre, S. semi-herbe* and *Diheteropogon hagerupii.*

The southern, humid parts of West Africa are not grazing areas. Tsetse flies (*Glossina* spp.), the vectors of trypanosomiasis, are a major hindrance to the expansion of animal husbandry; ticks are also a serious problem. Root crops are important for subsistence, and many tree crops are grown, including oil-palm and cacao.

There are two main stock-rearing ethnic groups, the Tuareg and the Fulani (Peul). Tuareg live on the desert fringe, and are divided into many groups: some are still exclusively transhumant herders; others are part of a pastoral economy, staying in villages or camps close to their fields. Exclusive herders occupy land that is unsuitable for crops, to the north of the agropastoralists.

Fulani (Plate 11.3) are cattle breeders, but small ruminants (Plate 11.4) provide meat for a family while cattle are capital, investment and prestige. There are both stock-rearing and agropastoralist groups; agropastoralist Fulani occupy the southern Sahelian space. Transhumant groups sow millet near the fringe of cultivation during their migration. As tsetse fly challenge is reduced through tree and bush clearing, Fulani are increasingly settling, notably in Nigeria.

Transhumance systems traverse the land of farming communities and their herds may graze the stovers and fallows of farming groups. Many agricultural

MARZIO MARZOT

Plate 11.3
*Wodaabe man with his herd. The Wodaabe are nomads and are part of the
Fulani ethnic group.*

MARZIO MARZOT

Plate 11.4
Small ruminants on the move.

groups keep few or no cattle and the transhumant herds help by manuring
some fields. This is changing and farmers increasingly conserve their stovers
and may even sell them to passing herds.

Camels (Plate 11.5) are kept throughout the Sahelian zone but do not enter
the trypanosomiasis areas. Sheep are local breeds and may be milked; Fulani

MARZIO MARZOT

Plate 11.5
Dromedary camels are used for transporting goods across the desert, and are also good milk producers.

MARZIO MARZOT

Plate 11.6
Kouri cattle are a unique breed well adapted to the semi-aquatic environment of Lake Chad.

sheep are important north of the zone of trypanosomiasis; in forest zones the trypanotolerant *djallonke* breed is reared in small groups. Sahelian goats, a long-legged type, are kept in the main herding areas; the Red Sokoto Goat (*chèvre rouge de Maradi*), a breed of clearings in the Sudanian and Sahelosudanian zones, is renowned for the quality of its leather. In areas of high tsetse fly challenge, trypanotolerant dwarf goats are reared.

Sahelian cattle are mainly either long-horned or short-horned zebu; the Kouri, a taurin, occurs around Lake Chad (Plate 11.6); these breeds are not trypanotolerant and how far they can penetrate towards forested areas is governed by tsetse fly challenge. Cattle rearing and animal husbandry are much less important in the agricultural, well-watered zones; however, local trypanotolerant breeds of cattle, sheep and goats are raised in clearings and on fallows in the shifting cultivation system. N'Dama cattle from Guinea, Muturu from Nigeria and Baoulé from Côte D'Ivoire, which are among the better-known trypanotolerant breeds, are taurin types (*Bos taurus brachyceros*), not zebus. N'Dama have been introduced to other tsetse-infested parts of Africa, notably the Republic of the Congo (Chabeuf, 1983), to establish beef production in areas where it was not previously possible. Crosses between zebus and taurins are used in intermediate zones according to the level of tsetse challenge; some have breed status, such as the Sanga and Néré.

Madagascar

Madagascar has one of the larger cattle herds in Africa; most are raised on natural grassland; FAOSTAT gives figures of about 10 000 000 over the past twenty years, but Ministry estimates in 2000 were 7 260 000, of which 1 000 000 were draught oxen, 500 000 dairy cattle and the remainder zebu (Rasambainarivo and Ranaivoarivelo, 2003); stock counts are complicated by many stockowners letting their cattle roam in a semi-feral state because of security problems. Small stock are limited to the drier south: about a million goats and half a million sheep; only local breeds are kept in extensive systems. The highlands and the wet east coast are agricultural; rice is the staple crop. Cattle are kept for draught in farming areas but few are milked. Some exotic or grade dairy cattle are kept near towns in the highlands, but settled Malagasy are not traditional milk drinkers.

Madagascar lies between 11°57' and 25°29'S and 43°14' and 50°27'E. Highlands (above 888 m) occupy the whole north-south axis. The eastern slopes fall abruptly to the Indian Ocean; the western versant has gentler slopes occupied by great plains, which extend to the Mozambique Channel. The climate is unimodal tropical, typified by a rainy season (November–March) and a dry season (April–October). The length of seasons varies according to the region. Altitude also has its effect, especially insofar as temperature is concerned. The dry season is cold in the highlands, where frost can occur (regions of Ambatolampy and Antsirabe).

Human settlement in Madagascar is relatively recent, about 2000 years, and livestock came with them. Much of Madagascar had been covered by forest, but forest cover is decreasing rapidly and is now only about 22 percent of the land area. The area of savannah is 387 404 km², 68 percent of the island. Most savannahs (62 percent) are in the west and the south, and 76 percent are below 800 m. The grasses of Madagascar were the subject of an in-depth study by Bosser (1969). The grasslands are floristically poor and there are no wild ungulates, but nor is there tseste fly, and many of the serious livestock diseases of mainland Africa are also absent.

The main extensive grazing areas are in the northwest, mid-west and south. Bush fires occur all over the pastoral areas every year. Land tenure in the pastoral land is essentially traditional; its management depends, *grosso modo*, on whomsoever uses it. Insecurity of tenure favours the continued extensive use of the grasslands. The grazing lands are grasslands with few trees or shrubs, except in the extreme south. Poor soils and frequent fire maintain a grassy vegetation under rainfalls that should support savannah or forest.

In northern savannahs, *Heteropogon contortus* is dominant on the plateaux, but replaced by *Aristida* spp. on severely eroded areas (Plate 11.7). At the foot of slopes and on colluvions, the commonest grasses are *Hyparrhenia rufa* and *Hyperthelia dissoluta*. Bottom lands are covered by *Echinochloa* spp. and a retinue of secondary grasses. The relief is dominated by vast plains at altitudes below 300 m. Annual rainfall is 1 000 mm and the dry season lasts from mid-March to the end of November.

In the mid-west, plateaus and the gentle slopes are covered by *Heteropogon contortus* and *Hyparrhenia rufa,* but in many places serious erosion has allowed *Aristida* spp. and *Loudetia* spp. to establish. The soil cover of

J.M. SUTTIE

Plate 11.7
Madagascar plateau area with a dry season cover of Themeda triandra *on disturbed soil in the foreground and* Aristida rufescens *and* Hyparrhenia spp. *on the main area.*

perennials does not exceed 20–40 percent. Steep slopes are covered by *Aristida rufescens* and *Loudetia simplex*. The percentage of bare soil is high (90 percent), indicating serious erosion. Colluvions are covered by *Panicum maximum* and *Hyparrhenia variabilis*.

The southern savannahs are the largest of the regions. The topography is vast plains. The region has low rainfall and few rainy days. Toliary is the driest area, with 275 mm over 27 rainy days. There is great inter-year variability. The rainiest months are December to February. Water is a problem for stock between April and November. The south is renowned for its big herds of zebus and small stock. The population live in "a cattle civilization". *Heteropogon contortus* is the commonest grass on soils not subject to waterlogging. According to the topography and the degree of erosion, some species can dominate; this is the case for *Loudetia simplex* and *Aristida* spp., which occupy degraded slopes. *Hyparrhenia rufa*, *Hyperthelia dissoluta* and *Cynodon dactylon* occupy areas that may receive runoff. Cacti (*Opuntia* spp.) are characteristic fodder plants. The extreme south, on limestone, has characteristic thorn-scrub, with many endemic plants, dominated by tall Didieraceae.

Many forages have been grown successfully, but only a few dairy farmers grow them. Pasture improvement by over-sowing with *Stylosanthes guyanensis* and *S. humilis* was tested on a large scale in the mid-west in the early 1970s, but, after initial promise, the legume was wiped out by anthracnose.

SOUTH AMERICA
The Llanos

The Llanos of Venezuela (Vera, 2003) are part of the 50 million hectares of savannahs in the Orinoco River basin. The vegetation communities can be divided into four main subregions.

The **Piedmont Savannahs** consist of large alluvial areas and terraces covered originally by semi-deciduous forests and savannahs, though the latter predominates. They are southeast of the Andes and descend gradually to the plains. They are characterized by a rich tree flora, shrubs and grasses, most of which are common to the other types of savannah. These include *Andropogon selloanus*, *A. semiberbis*, *Axonopus canescens*, *A. purpusii*, *Bulbostylis* spp., *Elyonurus adustus*, *Leptocoryphium lanatum*, *Panicum olyroides*, *Paspalum plicatulum*, *P. gardnerianum*, *Trachypogon plumosus*, *T. vestitus* and *T. montufari*. On average, the maximum aboveground stand of savannah reaches 7 t/ha/yr, with about twice that amount below ground.

The savannahs of the **High Plains** or **Mesas** are north of the Orinoco, at 150–270 m, descending into the *Llanos de Monagas*. They are covered by a deciduous tree savannah where the herbaceous layer predominates and is dominated by *Trachypogon plumosus* or *T. vestitus*, with *Andropogon selloanus*, *Axonopus canescens* and *Leptocoryphium lanatum* as subdominant grasses.

The sparse tree layer is composed of *Curatella americana, Byrsonima crassifolia* and *Bowdichia virgiloides.* Aboveground production of the grass layer peaks at 3 200-4 200 kg/ha when burnt, whereas yields are 30 percent lower if protected. Fire is the only economically feasible management tool. Burning, even in mid-dry season, induces a regrowth if water reserves allow.

The **Alluvial Overflow Plains,** which occupy a depression of 3 800 000 ha in the central Llanos between the piedmont and the high plains, are very flat, with only one to two metres between the highest and lowest points. Higher land constitutes natural levees, where the soil is a sandy alluvium, whereas clay particles settle in the lower parts (basins), which have slow drainage; rain drains very slowly and the lower parts remain flooded during most of the rainy season, but have a high carrying capacity in the dry season. The area is used for extensive cattle and buffalo grazing (96 percent for cattle; 4 percent under forests), although frequently wild capybara are raised with cattle. The botanical composition of levees and basins differs, but this type of savannah has more palatable species than the others, and has been modified by human intervention, especially in an area of 250 000 ha enclosed by low dykes and floodgates to regulate water levels in sections of 3 000 to 6 000 ha each. Land permanently above water is colonized by *Axonopus purpusii, A. affinis* and *Leptocoryphium lanatum*; sections moderately flooded contain *Panicum laxum* and *Leersia hexandra* as dominants; and the strongly flooded areas are dominated by *Hymenachne amplexicaulis, Reimarochloa acuta* and *Leersia hexandra.* Cyperaceae are also abundant. Aboveground yields vary between the 5 t DM/ha of the levees to 2–3 t DM/ha in the basins. According to some estimates, regulation of water level in the *Modulos* can increase carrying capacity up to fivefold.

The **Aeolian Plains,** which extend north-east from the Colombian Andean Piedmont into southern Venezuela, are characterized by dunes covered by sparse vegetation, almost treeless, and dominated by *Trachypogon ligularis* and *Paspalum carinatum*; inter-dunal depressions are occupied by a *Mesosetum* savannah. Both formations are low yielding and of low palatability.

The Gran Chaco

This section is based on Riveros (2002) and Garbulsky and Deregibus (2004). The Gran Chaco, between 17° and 33°S and 65° and 60°W, is a vast plain in the River Plate Basin that extends through northern Argentina, southeastern Bolivia, northwestern Paraguay and a small area of southwestern Brazil. It stretches for about 1 500 km from north to south, and 700 km from east to west, without any physical barriers intervening. Its area is about 850 000 km². The Chaco, which extends into both tropical and temperate zones, is one of the major wooded grasslands in South America, but suffers from intense degradation through unrestricted forest and bush clearing, overgrazing and continuous monoculture.

V. ALEJANDRO DEREGIBUS AND MARTIN F. GARBULSKY

Plate 11.8
Park grasslands in NE Chaco, a summer view.

It slopes gradually eastwards, at 100–500 m above sea level, except for the Sierras in Cordoba, Argentina, which reach 2 800 m. The climate, of the wet-dry seasonal type, varies without sudden changes since there are no natural barriers. Temperatures rise from south to north and rainfall from west to east. The warmest months coincide with those of maximum rainfall, which favoured the evolution of herbaceous forages of the C_4 type.

Most early settlement was along the coast and major waterways. A railway and water supplies opened the Chaco to settlement. Commercial beef production developed in the nineteenth century. Large tracts were colonized and the exploitation of the Chaco began in earnest. Between 1910 and 1920, the southeast of the Paraguayan Chaco was an area for extensive cattle production and sugar cane growing. Grazing was totally unmanaged, there was uncontrolled burning, and overfelling of forest led to its replacement by undesirable thorny vegetation.

Introduction of livestock alone is not enough to explain the dramatic and rapid changes that took place in the vegetation. The most potent factor was the dispersion of watering points so that a much greater proportion of the herbage could be consumed, leaving little or none to be burnt. The demise of the fire climax led to an increased scarcity of forage through increased grazing and increased growth of unpalatable, woody species. This was the only grassland intervention introduced by the ranchers. Grazing was continuous, with mixed herds of cattle, horses, goats, asses and sheep roaming uncontrolled on the same land, with no limits but the distance to water in the dry season; small

Plate 11.9
A savannah type in SE Chaco, winter view.

stock were often penned at night. The boundaries of grazing territories were ill-defined and herds' grazing land often overlapped; this led to severe over-grazing and rapid degradation of the pastoral cover. In less than fifty years, the once-rich landscape had been almost sterilized and altered as a result of this "no management" system.

In Argentina, the main vegetation types are:

Humid to subhumid or **Oriental Chaco** is a parkland formation (Plate 11.8), where patches of *Quebracho Colorado Chaqueño* (*Schinopsis* spp.) forest alternate with open grassland. There are also areas of *Copernica alba* palm, usually under swamp conditions with accumulation of salts.

Arid and semi-arid Chaco. This is present in Argentina (Plate 11.9), in the east of Bolivia and western Paraguay, with a small area in southwest Brazil. It is a huge area of flat land, increasingly arid from east to west. Open grasslands derived from forest through bush clearing and fire occupy a lesser area than in the humid and subhumid zones. Forests are dominated by xerophytes and are more open than in the eastern Chaco. Cacti are common among trees and shrubs. Pastoral resources include a vast number of trees and shrubs, as well as forage plants that are only found in man-made clearings.

The **Montane zone** is mostly in Argentina, but extends into Bolivia and Paraguay. The landscape is broken by hills, which have a higher rainfall than the lowlands; hillsides collect moist air coming from the Atlantic. The forest vegetation contains many species found in the lower Chaco, and some trees of higher rainfall areas; the grass cover is very limited.

In Paraguay, the Chaco, referred to as the "western region", is almost flat, with 32 000 km² suitable for crops, but only a very small area is cultivated. The grazed area covers 124 000 km², mostly on natural grassland. Two main vegetation groups are recognized in Paraguay: the xeromorphic group dominates the landscape; *matorral* is the main formation in all the centre, north and west. Mesomorphic vegetation that dominates towards the south and centre-east develops on heavier, better structured soils and is covered by a mosaic of alternating forest of *Schinopsis balinese, Caesalpinia paraguariensis* and *Phyllostylon rhamnoides*; palm-savannahs of *Copernica alba*; and marshes.

Extensive livestock rearing is, and will probably remain, a major land use in the Chaco. Bush encroachment brought about by overstocking and lack of grazing management is very serious, leading to erosion, loss of wildlife habitat, and greatly reduced livestock production. The economics of herbicides and mechanical clearing are not clear. In most sub-tropical areas of extensive grazing, the strategic use of pasture resting and controlled fire is the only economic way of keeping bush in check.

Poor management in the Chaco leads to invasion by unpalatable weeds, caused by loss of soil fertility, which must be kept at high levels to assure survival of introduced forages. Proper adjustment of carrying capacity is also essential. Natural grassland is better than degraded, weed-infested, "improved pasture". Sown pastures may have an important role in the Paraguayan Chaco compared with the rest of the area.

Pampas

The Pampas (Garbulsky and Deregibus, 2004), which occupies about 50 million hectares between the 2°C and the 13°C isotherms, has a temperate climate with mild, snow-free winters. Precipitation decreases from 1 200 mm in the northeast to 500 mm/yr in the ecotonal change to the Monte region. Rain is evenly distributed through the year in the east, but is concentrated in the warm season in the west.

This Region is characterized by its lack of native trees, flat terrain, fertile soils, extended croplands and native or sown pastures. As soils are fertile and summers shorter and milder than in the north, many C_3 grasses and temperate legumes grow during the cool season. Thus a seasonal alternation occurs between C_4 and C_3 plants. Species alternation maintains green grass year-long and is ideal for resource utilization in a seasonally variable climatic environment; mild water deficits in summer are better overcome by C_4 grasses. Temperate grasses and legumes of good quality (above 20 percent protein and 70–80 percent digestibility) allow total utilization during winter of the remnant biomass of summer grasses, so there is seldom accumulation of forage in winter.

Native humid-grasslands cover the Flooding Pampa, some parts of Entre Ríos Province and most river and stream banks. Their warm season components are grasses of the Panicoideae, Chlorideae, Andropogoneae and

Oryzeae. Alternating seasonally with them, thrive grasses of the Agrosteae, Aveneae, Festuceae, Phalarideae and Stipeae. As soil fertility increases to the west of the Paraná River and south of the Río de la Plata, a myriad of herbaceous legumes grow (*Cassia* spp., *Crotalaria* spp., *Desmanthus* spp., *Phaseolus* spp., *Vicia* spp., etc.).

Flooding Pampas grasslands

The very slight slope of the plains results in a low morphogenic potential and endoreic or areic drainage, in spite of a subhumid climate. These topographical characteristics cause extensive and lengthy flooding during periods of abundant precipitation (once every decade), causing severe damage and heavy losses where human influence has been prominent. Lesser floods, which occur at the end of winter and in early spring, are the most remarkable features of this region.

The typical physiognomy of the Flooding Pampa is extended, treeless grasslands (except where trees are planted) and its community is dominated by *Paspalum dilatatum* (Plates 11.10a and b), *Bothriochloa laguroides* and *Briza subaristata. P. quadrifarium* and *Stipa trichotoma* are bunch grasses that dominate the southwestern part of the area.

Non-saline grasslands produce about 5 t DM/ha/yr, with a clear summer peak – a pattern that contrasts with the small variation in standing crop greenness. Forage productivity in winter (July) is 5 kg DM/ha/day, being

Plate 11.10a
A grassland dominated by Paspalum dilatatum. *Summer view.*

V. ALEJANDRO DEREGIBUS AND MARTIN F. GARBULSKY

V. ALEJANDRO DEREGIBUS AND MARTIN F. GARBULSKY

Plate 11.10b
A grassland dominated by Paspalum dilatatum. *Winter (flooded) view.*

30 kg DM/ha/day in December and January. Scarce winter production is caused by the depletion of cool-season grasses caused by continuous overgrazing of domestic cattle after windmills and fences were introduced 100 years ago. The dominance of warm-season grasses and loss of nitrogen fertility further prevent the establishment of cool-season grasses every autumn. Low winter productivity limits the carrying capacity and determines the production system of the area: cow-calf operations. Almost 3.5 million cattle roam the 6 million hectares of the Flooding Pampas, exporting 2 million calves annually to be raised on pastures in cropland or feed yards. Annual secondary production may be estimated at 90 kg/ha.

Winter productivity may be significantly increased by hard early autumn grazing or herbicide spraying of the warm-season grasses, followed by nitrogen fertilization. This promotes the establishment and growth of *Lolium multiflorum*, an excellent quality exotic grass that thrives well in intermediate communities. Phosphate fertilization may also increase cool-season grass production by promoting the density of herbaceous legumes *Lotus tenuifolius* and *Trifolium repens* that enrich soil nitrogen through fixation.

Cropland Pampas cultivated pastures

The most renowned Pampas is the sector extending in a circle around the Flooding Pampas. Constituting the main cropping area of Argentina, with 77 percent of the cattle stock and 70 percent of the human population, it contains the major cities and industrial development. The original tussock grasslands are now rainfed croplands producing soybeans, maize, wheat

V. ALEJANDRO DEREGIBUS AND MARTIN F. GARBULSKY

Plate 11.11
Cows on grassland in the Pampas.

and sunflower as the main crops. After several years of crops, improved pastures are sown in a four- to five-year rotation to maintain soil fertility. When pastures are grown, the seasonal forage production alternates between alfalfa, which grows in the warm season, and grasses and clovers that grow in cooler weather. Oats are also a popular forage crop.

Sown pastures (Plate 11.11) are grazed by steers, yearlings or dairy cattle. Forage legumes like *Medicago sativa*, *Trifolium repens*, *T. pratense* and *Lotus corniculatus* and grasses such as *Festuca arundinacea*, *Phalaris arundinacea*, *Bromus catharticus*, *Dactylis glomerata*, *Lolium perenne* and *L. multiflorum* or *Agropyron elongatum* are grown. When pastures are adequately fertilized (principally with P), primary production may achieve 12 to 15 t DM/ha/yr or more. This primary production allows 500 kg/ha of beef annually or 200 kg/ha of milk fat.

Nowadays, cash crop prices and the higher profits of agriculture have led to a decrease in cattle numbers in this area. To this can be added genetically modified soybeans and modern no-tillage practices, that reduce the need for pasture-cash crop rotations to maintain soil fertility.

Monte shrubland

The Monte phytogeographic province is a strip that surrounds the Calden and Semi-arid Chaco regions up to the Atlantic coast of Chubut province, covering 50 million hectares. Its physiognomy is dominated by a tall shrub stratum with *Prosopis alpataco*, *P. flexuosa* (Fabaceae), *Larrea divaricata*, *L. cuneifolia* and *L. nitida* (Zygophyllaceae). Fodder shrubs include the genus *Atriplex*. Towards the northern tip of the Monte province, *Prosopis* spp. are dominant in the shrub layer, while the southern extreme is dominated by *Larrea* spp. The grass layer, which is the most important forage source, is composed of a mixture of C_4 and C_3 species. Towards the north, the C_4 group (*Panicum urvilleanum, Chloris castilloniana, Pappophorum caespitosum* and *P. phillippianum*) dominate and to the south the C_3 (*Stipa tenuis, S. speciosa, Poa ligularis* and *P. lanuginosa*) increase in importance. *Prosopis* spp. are widely browsed by small ruminants like goats, as their shoots and pods are rich in protein.

ASIA
Central Asia
Pasture descriptions are included for Kyrgyzstan (Fitzherbert 2000) and Uzbekistan (Makhmudovich, 2001). Uzbekistan's grazing lands are described in detail by Gintzburger *et al.* (2003) and the problems of transition of all Central Asia to decollectivized farming and animal husbandry is discussed by Ryan, Vlek and Paroda (2004) and Gintzburger (2004). The Central Asian Region, which comprises Kazakhstan, Kyrgyzstan, Turkmenistan and Uzbekistan, is a vast low-altitude plain, bordered to the south by mountains that rise to the Pamirs. The Chinese Autonomous Region of Xinjiang and the northern fringe of Afghanistan are, geographically, part of the region, but their recent history and grassland management have been very different from those of countries of the former USSR. These arid to semi-arid plains had, until the twentieth century, been mainly exploited by mobile herding, with farming concentrated in oases and the valleys of the great rivers flowing to the Aral Sea.

The plains are below 500 m, with large areas below 200 m, sloping to the Aral sea, which is about 53 m above mean sea level. The Uzbekistan vegetation zones will serve to show the general banding of pastures from the grazing point of view. The territory of the republic is divided into:

A desert belt (*chul*), which is the zone of irrigated farming and Karakul sheep: annual precipitation is 100–250 mm; average annual temperature is about 15°C. Vegetation types are desert, psammophytic shrub and ephemeral-semi-shrub vegetation.

The foothill plains belt (*adyr*) is the zone of rainfed lands, with very low precipitation. The main rainfed areas and big oases of irrigated farming are concentrated in the desert (*chul*) zone. The yearly average temperature is 13°C, but in the south it is 14–16°C; annual precipitation is 200–545 mm; the prevailing soil type is light and typical sierozems, with widely spread ephemeral vegetation. The mid-mountain belt (*tau*) is rainfed land with normal precipitation of the Tashkent, Samarkand and Surkhandarya Regions. The average annual temperature is 8–11°C; annual precipitation is over 400 mm. Along with rainfed grain farming, the belt is extremely favourable for orchards and vineyards. The high-mountains belt (*yaylau*) is the zone of summer pastures.

Most of the lowlands of Central Asia have a very cold variant of the Mediterranean arid and semi-arid climate. Their latitude range (35°–46°) is similar to that of the steppes in the northern part of western Asia, the Maghreb and Spain to the west, and the Gobi and Mongolia to the east. Precipitation as rain and snow falls in the cold winter–spring period, with winter extreme minima often falling below -20°C.

Small ruminants, primarily sheep, are the main livestock of the region; fine-wool breeds were greatly encouraged during the soviet period, but these are less hardy than local breeds and the wool no longer commands interesting prices; local fat-tailed breeds are now at least as common as fine-wools; in Uzbekistan, Karakul are raised for their pelts. Camels are used for transport – the Arabian type in the south and east, with the Bactrian taking over in Kazakhstan. Horses are also very important. Cattle are raised in agricultural zones and in the mountains, and yak are locally important in Kyrgyzstan.

Before the Russian revolution, the pastures were exploited by herders who depended entirely on the grassland resources; herders and their livestock moved seasonally between lowland winter pastures and summer grazing. In the 1930s the herders were settled and collectivized; this stopped transhumant movement between different ecological zones. The system of state farms, cooperatives and state services would be similar to those for the USSR described in Chapter 10. Planned socialist systems were imposed, including breed improvement and feeding. Later, the usefulness of seasonal movement was recognized and land in different seasonal zones was allocated to cooperatives and state farms.

Heavy grazing and firewood collection have seriously reduced vegetation cover and the natural grazing has become degraded, with a loss of productivity and increasing desertification; destruction of forests and shrubs has led to wind erosion. Rehabilitation techniques were developed and have been applied on a fairly large scale; they are described by Gintzburger *et al.* (2003). After decollectivization, with fragmentation of herds and holdings and lack of clarity concerning herders' responsibility for maintaining the pasture resource, rehabilitation activities have been greatly reduced.

The impact of decollectivization on livestock production systems, grassland management and herder's livelihoods has been dramatic and negative (Aw-Hassan *et al.*, 2004). Large agrofood complexes were dismantled and cooperative farms were privatized. Marketing systems collapsed and many traditional markets were lost. Institutional changes have not kept pace with changes in production systems. One overall result has been a sharp decline in stock numbers in some of the countries, especially sheep; falls have been most marked in Kazakhstan, Kyrgyzstan and Tajikistan. Fitzherbert (2000) reports that sheep numbers in Kyrgyzstan fell from 9 500 000 in 1990 to 3 250 000 in 1999.

The reforms led to a massive shift from collective to household herds; often household stock numbers are too few to warrant independent herding and communal or family herding has not yet developed; this often leads to stock remaining, unsupervised, close to homesteads: nearby pastures are overgrazed while distant ones are hardly used (Iñguez *et al.* 2004). Previously, considerable quantities of fodder was grown and conserved for winter; this has declined very considerably as the republics concentrate on self-sufficiency in cereals, which they can no longer procure readily from elsewhere. Lack of conserved feed and reduced herd mobility exacerbate the serious problems of winter feeding.

CHINA

This section is based on the Pasture Profile for the People's Republic of China (Hu and Zhang, 2003a) and on Hu and Zhang (2003b). The Tibet-Qinghai plateau has been described in Chapter 8. Detailed description and discussion of herding in Tibet Autonomous Region is given in Nyima (2003); grazing management of alpine ecosystems on the Tibet Qinghai Plateau is discussed by Ruijun (2003a), who also provides detailed information on yak nutrition (Ruijun, 2003b). Transhumant systems in Xinjiang and the production of winter fodder by herders is described by Wang (2003). China has vast grazing lands. The pastoral areas are concentrated in six provinces and autonomous regions: Inner Mongolia (Plates 11.12, 11.13 and 11.14), Xinjiang (Plate 11.15), Tibet, Qinghai (Plates 11.16 and 11.17), Sichuan and Gansu, where extensive stock raising is the main agricultural enterprise. These six have 70 percent of sheep, all the camels, 25 percent of cattle and goats, 44 percent of horses and 39 percent of donkeys in China.

Mixed farming, on relatively small family farms, is the agricultural system of the rest of the country, where livestock are still important, but are mainly

Plate 11.12
Pastoral scene in July near Hailar City, Inner Mongolia, China.

S.G. REYNOLDS

Plate 11.13
Herder with sheep, Inner Mongolia, China.

S.G. REYNOLDS

Plate 11.14
Horse herd near Hailar City, Inner Mongolia, China.

fed on crop residues, some sown pasture and limited rough grazing if available. The pasture of family farms still belong to the state and families pay according to a Long-term Grassland Use Contract with the government; the livestock belong to the family. In the past decade, the government has put the "Long-term contract grassland use system" into force with great effort. Under this system, grassland productivity is improved by subdividing pastures and allocating long-term grazing right to individual families based on the number of family members, with fencing (Plate 11.18), homestead and barn, establishing artificial grassland and building infrastructure for water and electricity supply. In places, motorcycles are replacing horses (Plate 11.19).

S.G. REYNOLDS

Plate 11.15
Small ruminants on summer pasture, Altai, Xinjiang, China.

J.M. SUTTIE

Plate 11.16
Qinghai summer pastures.

Despite its vast territory and the effects of topography and atmosphere circumfluence, there are only three climatic zones: East Monsoon, Northwest Arid and Semi-arid, and the Qinghai-Tibet Alpine Zone. China can be divided into three natural zones, namely the monsoon zone in the east, which accounts for 45 percent of all land; the arid inland zone in the northwest, with 30 percent of all land; and Qinghai-Tibet Plateau inland zone in the southwest, with 25 percent of all land. The eastern monsoon zone is agricultural; the northwest and southwest are pastoral.

Plate 11.17
Qinghai, summer camp.

Plate 11.18
Qinghai: grass reserved for winter.

Plate 11.19
Qinghai – motorcycles are replacing horses.

Plate 11.20
Yak at 4 300 m in Linzhou County, about 70 km from Lhasa, Tibet Autonomous Region, China.

Cattle (*Bos taurus* and *Bos indicus*) are found everywhere below 2000 m. Yak (Plate 11.20) are mainly kept on the Qinghai-Tibet Plateau at 3 000 to 5 000 m. There are 15 million yaks in China (Qinghai, Tibet, Sichuan, Gansu, Xinjiang and Yunnan), around 90 percent of the world total. Buffalo of the swamp type are kept in humid tropical and subtropical areas. They are stall-fed and mainly kept for draught and meat. Sheep, the main grazing stock, are kept in temperate areas within 30° to 50°N and 75° to 135°E. Goats are the most widely distributed livestock in China, since they can adapt to many climates and pastures. Horses are the traditional draught animals below 4 000 m. Camels are important in temperate deserts. There are some single humped camels in south Xinjiang, but the great majority are Bactrian.

Feeding systems in the north differ from those in the west. Inner Mongolian grasslands are flat and the environment is simple; pastures can be grazed at any season if water is available; animals are moved rotationally following a certain range and routine. In desert areas of Xinjiang there are two seasonal grazing belts, basins and mountains. Animals graze in the basins in winter, move to mountains in spring and to high mountains in summer, returning to basins in late autumn; this is a strict seasonal grazing system and animals spend 1 or 2 months travelling from winter to summer pasture. On the Qinghai-Tibet Plateau, animals graze above 3 000 m, but pastures are still divided into seasonal belts: low cold season pasture and high warm season pasture.

China had a total grassland area of about 393 million hectares in 1994, about 12 percent of the world's grassland. Usable grassland is 331 million hectares – 35 percent of the national land area. Most grassland is in the northern arid and cold zones. The six major pastoral provinces account for 75 percent of national grassland and around 70 percent of grazing livestock. The great size of the country and its range of latitudes, altitudes and rainfall leads to a wide range of grassland types. According to the Vegetation-habitat Classification System, grassland in China can be divided into nine classes and 276 types. There are 69 types in the Temperate Steppe Class, 39 types in the Temperate Desert Class, 25 types in the Warm Shrubby Tussock Class, 39 types in the Tropical Shrubby Tussock Class, 51 types in the Temperate Meadow Class, 24 types in the Alpine Meadow Class, 17 types in the Alpine Steppe Class, 4 types in the Alpine Desert Class and 8 types in the Marshes Class.

Many plants play an important role in forming a grassland community in terms of coverage and herbage yield in large grassland areas and various grassland types. The most important species in different grassland classes are considered below.

The **Temperate Steppe class** is typically *Leymus chinensis* (Plate 11.21), *Stipa baicalensis, S. grandis, S. krylovi, S. bungeana, S. breviflora, S. glareosa, S. klemenzii, S. capillata, Festuca ovina, Cleistogenes squarrosa, Filifolium sibiricum, Artemisia frigida, A. halodendron, A. ordosica, A. intramongolica, Thymus serpyllum* var. *mongolium* and *Ajania fruticulosa*.

S.G. REYNOLDS

Plate 11.21
Leymus chinensis.

Plants of the **Alpine Steppe class** are cold-resistant, mainly from the Gramineae and Compositeae. The most important are *Stipa purpureum, S. subsessiflora, Festuca ovina* subsp. *sphagnicola, Orinus thoroldii, Carex moorcroftii, Artemisia stracheyi* and *A. wellbyi.*

Among the dominant plants of the **Temperate Desert class** are super-xerocole shrubs and sub-shrubs; the most important are *Seriphidium terrae-albae, S. borotalense, Artemisia soongarica, Salsola passerina, S. laricifolia, Sympegma regelii, Anabasis salsa, Reaumuria soongarica, Ceratoides latens, Kalidium schrenkianum, Potaninia mongolica, Nitraria sphaerocarpa, Ephedra przewalskii, Haloxylon erinaceum* and *H. persicum.*

The **Alpine Desert class** is ecologically in the harshest environment. The dominant plants have super ability to resist cold and drought. The most important are *Rhodiola algida* var. *tangutica, Seriphidium rhodanthum* and *Ceratoides compacta.*

The **Warm Shrubby Tussock class** is dominated by mainly grasses of medium height and some forbs. The most important are *Bothriochloa ischaemum, Themeda triandra* var. *japonica, Pennisetum centrasiaticum, Spodiopogon sibiricus, Imperata cylindrica* var. *major* and *Potentilla fulgens.*

Dominant plants of the **Tropical Shrubby Tussock class** are almost all hot-season grasses. The most important are *Miscanthus floridulus, M. sinensis, Imperata cylindrica* var. *major, Heteropogon contortus, Arundinella setosa, A. hirta, Eremopogon delavayi, Eragrostis pilosa, Eulalia phaeothrix, E. quadrinervis* and *Dicranopteris dichotoma.*

The **Temperate Meadow class** is dominated mainly by perennial temperate and medium-humid mesophytic grasses; some are halophytes or forbs. The most important are *Achnatherum splendens, Arundinella hirta, Agrostis* *gigantea, Calamagrostis epigeios, Bromus inermis, Deyeuxia angustifolia, D. arundinacea, Poa pratensis, P. angustifolia, Miscanthus sacchariflorus, Phragmites communis, Brachypodium sylvaticum, Festuca ovina, Carex duriuscula, Potentilla anserina, Sanguisorba officinalis, Iris lactea* var. *chinensis, Suaeda* spp. and *Sophora alopecuroides.*

Dominant plants of the **Alpine Meadow class** are mainly cold-resistant perennials. Most are *Kobresia* spp. and forbs. The most important are *Kobresia pygmaea, K. humilis, K. capillifolia, K. bellardii, K. littledalei, K. tibetica, Carex atrofusca, C. nivalis, C. stenocarpa, Blysmus sinocompressus, Poa alpina, Polygonum viviparum* and *P. macrophyllum.*

Marsh classes are dominated mainly by Cyperaceae and Gramineae. The most important are *Carex meyeriana, C. muliensis, C. appendiculata, C. stenophylla, Scirpus yagara, S. triqueter, Phragmites communis* and *Triglochin palustre.*

Grassland deterioration – a worldwide problem – is severe in China. According to data published in 1994, the area of degraded grassland was 68 million hectares at the end of the 1980s – 27.5 percent of all grassland. It has increased remarkably in the past decade. Now 90 percent of grassland shows signs of deterioration, of which moderately degraded grassland is 130 million hectares (32.5 percent of total) and it is increasing by 20 million hectares each year.

The government is taking vigorous measures to deal with grassland degradation. According to the *Planning Programme of National Ecological Environment Construction* and *Outline of Fifteenth Ten-Year Plan*, the following should be achieved by 2010:

- artificial grassland and improved grassland increased by 50 million hectares;
- 33 million hectares of degraded grassland and 20 million hectares of desertified land improved;
- of 600 000 ha of eroded land controlled; and
- 6.7 million hectares of cropland (on >25° slope) returned to forest and grass.

Improvement is being undertaken by closure, with or without reseeding, and is associated with a very large programme of returning sloping arable land to pasture.

SOUTH ASIA
Himalaya-Hindu Kush

These grasslands and associated grazing systems are discussed in detail in a recent FAO publication (Suttie and Reynolds, 2003) and in the country Pasture Profiles of the five countries: Afghanistan, Bhutan, India, Nepal and Pakistan (Thieme, 2000; Wangdi, 2002; Misri, 1999; Pariyar, 1999; Dost, 1998). The Himalayas (see Plate 11.22), which form a barrier between the Tibetan plateau and the plains of India and Pakistan, run obliquely northwest to southeast for about 2 500 km. They contain the highest mountains in the world and protect the subcontinent from cold air from the north. The grazing zone goes beyond

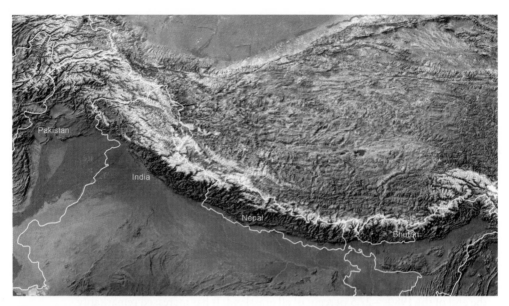

Plate 11.22
The Himalaya-Hindu Kush and Tibetan Plateau area.

the true Himalaya, through the foothills of the Karakoram to the Hindu Kush and most of Afghanistan's mountains, to the shoulder of the Pamirs; in the west of Pakistan it includes the Balochistan uplands. The grazing lands of Nepal and Bhutan are at the eastern end of the zone.

There is a wide altitudinal range, from the plains at 200–300 m, to the snow line, which may be over 5 000 m in summer. Rainfall increases southeastwards; the most northerly, semi-arid parts are in the rain-shadow of the Himalaya, but thereafter the grasslands receive the monsoon, and Nepal and Bhutan are humid. Temperatures also rise with decreasing latitude, the pastures range from about 37°N to 27°N. There are, therefore, considerable differences in vegetation, in altitudinal bands and north–south changes.

The flora of the semi-arid west shows considerable Western and Central Asian influences – the wild olive grows as far east as western Nepal. In all cases, the Himalayas abut the great alluvial plains, but at low altitude the vegetation changes as well. In Pakistan, the foothills are under *Acacia* forest; in the Nepal Terai there is dipterocarp (sal – *Shorea robusta*) forest, indicating higher rainfall and a warmer climate.

Afghanistan is at the convergence of the Mediterranean, the Tibetan and the Himalayan vegetation types, and towards the Pakistan border is influenced by the monsoon. For the vast majority of the grazing lands, low precipitation, with winter incidence, means that the main grazing vegetation type is *Artemisia* steppe. The mainstay of this vast area is *Artemisia*; the plant of the extensive grazing lands is generally referred to as *A. maritima*; the altitude range of the *Artemisia* steppe is from about 300 to 3 000 m. In neighbouring Turkmenistan and Uzbekistan, *A. herba-alba*, *A. turanica* and *A. maikara* are mentioned. Throughout most of its range, *A. maritima* is associated with *Poa bulbosa*; *Stipa* spp are frequent. There is a very short flush of annuals in spring, but these dry off quickly. Other sub-shrubs associated with *Artemisia* include species of *Acantholimon*, *Acanthophyllum*, *Astragalus*, *Cousinia* and *Ephedra*. In eastern areas close to Pakistan, where rainfall is adequate, species of *Cymbopogon*, *Chrysopogon*, *Heteropogon*, *Aristida* and other grasses of the monsoon areas occur, often associated with *Acacia modesta* and *Olea cuspidata*. By 2002, Afghanistan was in the ninth year of drought (see Plate 11.23); herds had been wiped out and the grasslands were in a sorry state. Although 2003 was better, the 2004 precipitation was below normal; however, there was good snowfall in the winter of 2004/2005 so the 2005 outlook was more promising. But the big reduction in small and large ruminants has resulted in much more of the range-lands being ploughed for crops, particularly in the north. Livestock recovery is likely to be slow.

In Nepal, at the other end of the precipitation range, tropical pasturelands are dominated by the grasses *Phragmites karka*, *Saccharum spontaneum*, *Imperata cylindrica*, *Cymbopogon jwarancusa* and *Bothriochloa intermedia*. Because of human activity, *Imperata cylindrica* is dominant throughout, and the weed *Eupatorium* sp. is gradually replacing many palatable plants. Subtropical pas-

J.M. SUTTIE

Plate 11.23
Severely degraded grassland, Faryab, Afghanistan.

J.M. SUTTIE

Plate 11.24
Transhumant Kuchi *flock after rain, near Kandahar, Afghanistan.*

tures, associated with *Pinus roxburghii* forests, are heavily grazed and infested with *Eupatorium adenophorum*, *Pteridium aquilinum*, *Urtica parviflora* and *Artemisia vulgaris*. The main forage species are *Arundinella bengalensis*, *A. nepalensis*, *Bothriochloa intermedia*, *B. pertusa*, *Chrysopogon gryllus*, *Cynodon dactylon*, *Heteropogon contortus*, *Apluda mutica*, *Brachiaria decumbens*, *Imperata cylindrica* and *Eragrostis pilosa*. Temperate pastures are associated with oak or mixed broad-leafed species or bluepine (*Pinus wallichianai*), but, due to heavy grazing, less palatable species such as *Arundinella hookeri* are found. The common forages are *Arundinella hookeri*, *Andropogon tristis*, *Poa* spp., *Chrysopogon gryllus*, *Dactylis glomerata*, *Stipa concinna*, *Festuca* spp., *Cymbopogon* spp., *Bothriochloa* spp., *Desmodium* spp. and *Agrostis micrantha*. Subalpine pastures are associated with a variety of shrubs. Common genera are *Berberis*, *Caragana*, *Hippophae*, *Juniperus*, *Lonicera*, *Potentilla*, *Rosa*, *Spiraea* and *Rhododendron*. In many areas, *Pipthantus nepalensis* has invaded productive pastures once dominated by *Danthonia* spp. The common grasses are *Elymus* spp., *Festuca* spp., *Stipa* spp., *Bromus himalaicus*, *Chrysopogon gryllus*, *Cymbopogon schoenanthus*, and *Koeleria cristata*. *Elymus nutans* is of great importance at high elevations. Alpine pastures are associated with *Rhododendron*. The main types of grazed vegetation are: *Kobresia* spp., *Cortia depressa*, and *Carex–Agrostis–Poa* associations.

The grasslands are exploited by both sedentary and transhumant groups (see Plate 11.24); the latter belong to minorities. Population pressure is very high throughout the zone and all suitable (along with much unsuitable) land is cultivated. Transhumant groups move between the plains in winter and alpine

Plate 11.25
Traditional straw storage platform and buffalo shelter in the Nepal Terai near Tarahara.

J.M. SUTTIE

pastures in summer. The upward movement to cooler areas in summer provides better fodder and makes use of seasonal alpine and subalpine pastures, but it is also almost essential for small stock because they would suffer severely from disease and parasites were they to remain on the plains during the hot and very humid monsoon season. Overwintering in or near farming areas in the warm plains has several advantages: herders can buy crop residues (see Plate 11.25), feed grain and fodder and graze stubbles; they are close to markets for stock and produce, and can often find seasonal employment. Sedentary groups may send stock to summer pastures when these are accessible. Transhumants must herd their flocks through or between farms and forest land to reach their seasonal grazing pastures. In places that receive the monsoon, designated areas are set aside through the monsoon periods and, after the rains, hay is made from over-ripe herbage; it is of very low quality but is nevertheless highly prized. The grasslands, including hayfields, are extremely steep and trekking routes are difficult.

Herders and herding ethnic groups tend to specialize in either large or small ruminants; small stock are more important in the dry areas. Camels are raised in Afghanistan and Pakistan's Balochistan, and are used as transport to highland grazing, but are not used further east. Yak are important in Ladakh in India, Nepal and Bhutan, and a few are present in the coldest parts of Afghanistan and Pakistan. In Bhutan and eastern India, some mithun (*Bos gaurus*) and their crosses with cattle are raised. Buffalo are kept in some farming areas, but are far more important on the plains. Indigenous breeds are used throughout, except in some urban areas, notably Quetta, where Afghan refugees have brought exotic black-and-white cattle and management skills.

In Nepal and Bhutan, buffalo graze the lowest pastures, cattle slightly higher, cattle × yak hybrids the high pastures, and pure yak the highest. Seasonal movements mean that the winter pastures of one group may be the summer pastures of that below.

It is generally agreed that Himalayan pastures are overstocked and degraded (Plate 11.23), although there is little historical evidence as to their former state. Regulations concerning forest grazing, stock numbers, seasons for using various pastures, as well as grazing fees, were codified in the late nineteenth century for India (including present-day Pakistan), but with increasing population and political pressure these rules are not always observed.

India

The Himalayan lands have been described above. This is based on Misri (1999). India has the largest cattle herd of any country, 226 million (FAOSTAT, 2004) and also has 97 million buffalo; these are mainly raised by sedentary groups and fed on opportunistic grazing, crop residues and, in some cases, usually irrigated, fodder. The irrigated tracts of northern India have intensive fodder production for stall-fed stock, and a similar situation is found in the irrigated tracts of Pakistan.

The grazing of animals takes place on a variety of grazing lands. Pastures and grasslands have often resulted from degradation and destruction of forests until savannahs are formed. True pastures as climax vegetation are found only in sub-alpine and alpine pastures in the higher altitudes of the Himalayas. Dabadghao and Shankaranarayan (1973) have grasslands classified into five types.

- *Sehima – Dichanthium* **grasslands** are spread over the Central Indian plateau, Chota Nagpur plateau and Aravallis. The elevation ranges between 300 and 1 200 m.
- *Dichanthium – Cenchrus – Lasiurus* **grasslands** cover northern parts of Gujarat, Rajasthan, Aravalli ranges, southwestern Uttar Pradesh, Delhi and Punjab. The elevation ranges between 150 and 300 m.
- *Phragmites – Saccharum – Imperata* **grasslands** are in the Gangetic plains, the Brahamputra Valley and the plains of Punjab. The elevation ranges between 300 and 500 m.
- *Themeda – Arundinella* **grasslands** are found in the States of Manipur, Assam, West Bengal, Uttar Pradesh, Himachal Pradesh and Jammu and Kashmir. The elevation ranges between 350 and 1 200 m.

- **Temperate – Alpine grasslands** are found above 2 100 m and include the temperate and cold arid areas of Jammu and Kashmir, Himachal Pradesh, Uttar Pradesh, West Bengal and the northeastern states.

The transhumant system is prevalent in the Himalayan region. However, this system still exists in some states situated in the plains, such as Rajasthan (which abuts on similar desert zones of Pakistan), Madhya Pradesh, Tamil Nadu, Gujrat and Uttar Pradesh.

The rural system involves free grazing on community grazing lands and forests, supplemented with green fodder cultivated in the farmer's fields. During lean periods, such as summer and autumn, tree leaf fodder is also used. These monsoon grasslands are only productive during the rainy season, and the dry season is long and severe; their feeding quality, like that of all grasslands with marked wet and dry seasons, is mediocre when they are young and poor thereafter.

Pakistan

The Himalayan lands have been described above. In the arid regions of Pakistan (Dost, 1998) complexity, variability and uncertainty characterize the grazing systems. Livestock grazing practices in the Thal, Cholistan, Kohistan and Tharparkar desert areas are similar. In early winter, people leave their villages in search of better grazing and migrate into irrigated areas. In the early monsoon season, when forage is abundant, during July–November, they return to their villages and leave their animals to graze. Private livestock are allowed to

Plate 11.26
Sheep grazing stubble, with Acacia nilotica *on field edges, in the Punjab, Pakistan.*

Plate 11.27
Delivering fodder to urban livestock, Punjab, Pakistan

Plate 11.28
Harvesting oat fodder, Punjab, Pakistan.

graze state-owned rangelands after paying nominal grazing fees. Cattle, sheep, goats and camels graze the Tharparker and Kohistan rangelands, but buffalo are not common. The great majority of large ruminants, however, are not kept on grazing lands but in the agricultural tracts, mainly on irrigated holdings, where they can graze after crops are harvested (see Plate 11.26); usually they are stall-fed on crop residues (see Plate 11.27), cultivated fodder (which is grown on a very large scale, for example fodder oats – see Plate 11.28) and, for commercial dairying, concentrates. Production systems involving intensive fodder production are described by Dost (2003). Pakistan has some 25 million buffalo (India and Pakistan combined have 71% of the world's buffalo) and 23 million cattle (FAOSTAT, 2004), largely fed on-farm.

THE NEAR EAST
Syrian Arab Republic
The country is largely pastoral, with 45 percent of its land being grazing and pasture and 20 percent desert (Masri, 2001). The climate is typically Mediterranean and precipitation is low, decreasing towards the interior. Most of the grazing land is in the semi-desert and desert (*badia*) with less than 200 mm rainfall; there is a little mountain grazing; plains with over 200 mm rainfall are now under rainfed crops. Cattle are kept in the agricultural areas but are absent from the main grazing lands.

From earliest times until the end of the Second World War, Syrian grazing lands were under tribal control, population density was low and the herders were nomadic, moving seasonally with their flocks. Pastoral communities evolved codes of laws and customs and the organization of groups and sub-groups based on family relationship. Each group used to maintain grazing rights on certain resources in its traditional land as *hema* (pasture reserved for use in drought or emergency) and negotiated when necessary with the other groups for movement of its livestock to areas of more favourable climatic conditions during periods of drought. The chief was the first among equals, and unanimously obeyed and respected by members. The social structure of the pastoral groups was close to a cooperative organization.

Large areas of grazing land were only accessible once the autumn rains had fallen, and herds had to leave them once surface supplies of water ran out, so the pastures were rested for a long period of the year. There was no external feed source so stock numbers were limited to what could be carried through the lean season on available pasture and water. There was no rainfed cropping on marginal lands.

After the war, the situation changed rapidly. The central authorities became much stronger and the tribal system was disintegrating. Motor transport, introduced during the war, allowed transport of goods, water and feed, making large areas of grazing accessible for much of the year. Grazing land was nationalized and became an open-access resource with no supervision over its use. Settlement of the Bedouin became official policy; this greatly improved their access to medical care, education, water and other services, and led on the one hand to a rapidly increasing population, and on the other a great reduction in mobile herding. Cheap cereals allowed increasing numbers of stock to be kept through the lean season.

MARZIO MARZOT

Plate 11.29
Syrian rangeland has become degraded due to overgrazing.

Marginal land was increasingly cleared for rainfed cropping. Yields are low and uncertain; if they seem too low or the crop is unlikely to mature because of drought, it will be grazed. Clearing of grazing land was encouraged by granting land rights to those who developed it.

Sheep are the main grazing livestock; the only local breed, the *Awasii*, is a milch sheep that is well adapted to harsh desert conditions, and its fat tail provides a reserve of nutrients for periods of feed shortage. They graze in the badia from late autumn till late spring, with supplements, then they migrate to the rainfed and irrigated areas, clearing all crop residues (cereal, cotton, beet and summer vegetables) before returning again to the badia. The main constraint to sheep production is degradation of grazing land (Plate 11.29), which increases dependency on supplementary feed.

The subsidized state feed policy puts pressure on the already degraded pasture through an increase in sheep numbers, which get most of their food as concentrates but continue to eat any available herbage. The sheep population was 2.9 million in 1961; it rose to 5.5 million in 1971, 10.5 million by 1981 and peaked at 15.5 million in 1991; it then fell to just over 10 million, and for the past seven years has been just over 13 million (FAOSTAT, 2004). Goats are the second most numerous livestock; their numbers rose from 439 000 in 1961 to 1 million in 1981, and have remained at that level. Two main types of goat are kept; the Shami goat is a milch breed, and they are kept around homesteads; the other is the mountain goat, which grazes in the mountain ranges.

Before the Second World War the Syrian badia was in good condition, climax plants like *Salsola vermiculata, Atriplex leucoclada, Artemisia herba-alba* and *Stipa barbata* were widespread and flocks of gazelle were present. Herders went to the badia with the onset of rains in autumn and had to leave when the water supply dried up in late Spring. Range livestock depended on grazing until 1958, when concentrate feeds were introduced. The rate of concentrate use increased to 25, 50 and 75 percent in the 1960s, 1970s and 1980s, respectively.

Jordan

About 90 percent, or 80 771 km², of the Kingdom is grazing land, 69 077 km² of which receives less than 100 mm of rainfall, and 1 000 km² of marginal grazing with 100–200 mm annual rainfall. Natural and man-made forests cover 760 km², out of 1 300 km² registered as forests (Al-Jaloudy, 2001). There are also about 500 km² of state-owned land used for grazing in mountainous areas.

The average altitude of the highlands ranges from 600 m in the north to 1 000 m in the middle and 1 500 m in the south. There is a semi-arid zone (350–500 mm annual rainfall) with a small subhumid zone (over 500 mm annual rainfall). The Arid Zone comprises the plains between the badia and the highlands. Rainfall ranges between 200 mm in the east and 350 mm in the west. Rainfed crops are mainly barley (in areas with 200–300 mm rainfall) wheat and fruit trees (in areas with between 300 and 350 mm rainfall). Badia (Eastern Desert), which covers about 8 million hectares – 90 percent of the Kingdom – has very sparse vegetation cover and an annual rainfall of less than 200 mm. In the past it was only used for grazing. In the last two decades, however, 20 000 ha have been irrigated, using underground water.

Jordan is on the eastern margins of the Mediterranean climatic zone. This climate is characterized by hot, dry summers and cool, wet winters; more than 90 percent of the country receives less than 200 mm annual precipitation.

There are four bioclimatic zones.

- **Mediterranean**: This region is restricted to the highlands from 700–1750 m above sea level. The rainfall ranges from 300–600 mm. The minimum annual temperature ranges from 5° to 10°C.
- **Irano-Turanian**: A narrow strip that surrounds all the Mediterranean ecozone except in the north; it is treeless. The vegetation is mainly small shrubs and bushes such as *Artemisia herba-alba*, and *Anabasis syriaca*. Altitudes range from 500 to 700 m, and rainfall ranges from 150 to 300 mm.
- **Saharo-Arabian**: This is the eastern desert or badia and comprises almost 80 percent of Jordan. It is flat except for a few hills or small volcanic moun-

tains. Altitude is in the 500–700 m range. The mean annual rainfall ranges from 50 to 200 mm, and mean annual minimum temperatures range from 15° to 2°C. Vegetation is dominated by small shrubs and small annuals in the wadi beds.

- **Sudanian**: It starts from the northern part of the Dead Sea and ends at the tip of the Gulf of Aqaba. The vegetation is characterized by a tropical tree element, such as *Acacia* spp. and *Ziziphus spina-christi*, in addition to some shrubs and annual herbs.

Badia (semi-desert)

The most significant use of this zone is pastoralism. Sheep and goats graze the forage produced on the desert range in the short period following rainfall; precipitation is less than 100 mm/year, which falls off towards the east and the south till it reaches 50 mm or less. Most are state lands. *Artemisia herba- alba, Retama raetam, Achillea fragrantissima* and *Poa bulbosa* are common in the wadi beds, while the unpalatable *Anabasis* sp. is present in most places. Despite its deterioration, this is the main grazing land of Jordan. The average annual dry matter production is 40 kg/ha in normal years; this can rise to 150 kg/ha in protected areas and range reserves. Steppes were used generally for grazing, but it is estimated that about 90 percent of the steppe has been privatized and ploughed for barley.

There are estimated to be 2 200 000 head of sheep and goats in Jordan. Nomadic grazing has declined to less than 10 percent of the sheep and goats, which belong to less than 5 percent of herders. The ratio of semi-settled herds has increased to more than 70 percent of sheep and goats. The remaining small ruminants (about 20 percent) follow a system that is mixed with agriculture, especially in the west of the Kingdom.

Small ruminant production systems developed gradually in the middle of the past century as a result of a number of changes: increasing settlement of the nomadic Bedouin in the marginal areas; a change to sheep and goat raising instead of camels; deterioration of traditional grazing systems (eastward and westward trips); spread of the use of vehicles for movement of flocks and equipment; and increased dependence on imported feed.

The **traditional mobile system** prevails in the arid to semi-arid east and south. Herds move from one place to another, on foot or by truck, looking for grazing or water. The sheep depend on natural herbage as their main source of feed, in addition to the feed given in winter for a period that varies with availability of herbage.

In the **semi-nomadic system,** sheep depend partially on grazing and crop by-products. They move to land adjacent to the fields and spend the winter around the houses, where they survive on the feed given to them.

In the **settled (semi-extensive) system,** stock are kept in fattening units but graze in the morning and return to their units in the afternoon. They feed on crop by-products and the adjacent natural grazing. Supplementary feed is given as required.

In the **intensive system,** sheep are kept on permanent farms with modern facilities and equipment. They are given balanced feed, and health care is provided.

Existing statistics indicate that there are 2 200 000 small ruminants, which depend for half their food requirements on imported feed. Natural grazing supplies only 25–30 percent of their requirements, as its productivity has declined to half of its potential and the area has decreased. In the past, the availability of fodder and water, and the search for them, were the limiting factors for movement of herds. Nowadays, food and water are transported to herds wherever they are, and it is possible to quickly transport the herds themselves. In 1930, the sheep herd was 229 100 and remained at a similar level until 1950; by 1970 it had doubled; and by 1990 had reached 1.5 million, where it currently stands. Goat numbers in 1930 were 289 500; they have risen in recent years, to 479 000 in 1990 and 547 500 in 2003, but to nothing like the extent of sheep, which are far better suited to intensive fattening.

Existing policies are not comprehensive and are incompatible with national needs and development plans. Feed subsidy policies from the 1980s until 1997 brought about the unusual increase in sheep and goats numbers and the deterioration in local production of feed. Also allocation of wide tracts of the best range to private ownership caused their deterioration and desertification.

Pastoral communities informally claim common tribal rights and enjoy free access and use of natural resources in their rangelands, but these claims are only recognized in settled areas. In all the unsettled areas the state asserts ownership regardless of customary tribal claims. State claims over grazing lands changed the traditional welfare system, caused the breakdown of resource allocation mechanisms and transformed secured-access rights into secured-tenure rights. Consequently, customary management rules are often no longer being enforced. State appropriation did not deny local communities access to their traditional pasture, but favoured a situation of open-access to grazing and expansion of barley cultivation.

EUROPE
Turkey
Turkey lies between 36° and 42°N and 26° and 45°E; its pasture area is 124 000 km² but it is declining (Karagöz, 2001). Pastures belong to the state and are open for common use. According to the (1998) Pasture Law, grazing will be assigned to municipalities or village communities once their boundaries are determined and certified; thereafter carrying capacity and duration of grazing will be determined for each area, then the villages will be given the right to graze the determined and certified areas for a given period with a set number of animals.

Turkey has an average altitude of 1 131 m; low (0–250 m), medium (250–1 000 m) and high altitude areas (>1 000 m) constitute 10.0, 34.5 and 55.5 percent of the country, respectively. The European section is fertile hilly land. The Asian part consists of an inner high plateau, with mountain ranges along the north and south coasts.

Average annual temperatures vary between 18° and 20°C on the south coast, fall to 14° to 15°C on the west coast, and, depending on elevation, fluctuate between 4° and 18°C in the interior. Substantial temperature variations are observed between the coast and the interior in winter. Winters are cold in the east and interior, but relatively warm on the south coast. Average temperatures in January and February are around 0°C in the east, 5° to 7°C on the north and west coasts, and 8° to 12°C on the south coast.

Heavy rainfall is general on mountains facing the sea. Towards the interior, rainfall decreases. Rains begin in autumn and continue until late spring on the Marmara, Mediterranean and Aegean coasts. In the interior and southeastern Anatolia, rainfall is mostly in spring.

Ruminant livestock consist of 11 million cattle, 29.4 million sheep and 8 060 000 goats. Cattle numbers have not changed in the last 30 years, while sheep, goat and buffalo numbers decreased steadily. Most livestock are still under traditional management relying on extensive grazing. Farms are small and fragmented, with 85 percent under 10 ha.

About 71 percent of all pure breeds are in the central-north, Aegean, Marmara and central-south regions; elsewhere extensive stock rearing is general, with local sheep and cattle breeds. The Mediterranean region is the least developed for livestock, but has 25 percent of the goats.

At the beginning of the twentieth century the population of Turkey was 12 million, livestock numbers were low and there was no serious pasture management problem. After the First World War, there were 440 000 km² of natural grazing and about 20 million livestock units. After the Second World War, animal numbers remained the same, but grazing was reduced to 430 000 km². Since then there has been a sharp increase in animal numbers and decrease in pasture. The trend continues; nowadays the number of animals grazing on Turkey's pastures is three to four times their carrying capacity (Figure 11.1 shows the changes in pasture area in Turkey).

The most productive pastures are in the east of the Black Sea region, where herders move in transhumance between lowland and alpine grasslands. East Anatolia has 37 percent of the pasture, grazing pressure is lower, so pasture condition is better; transhumance is also practiced here. Southeast Anatolia is one of the most heavily grazed zones; pastures dry out at the end of June; some of the livestock are moved to eastern Anatolia or to high mountains of the southeastern Taurus. In Mediterranean and Aegean Regions, the principal vegetation above 500 m is maquis, which is unsuitable for cattle. About a quarter of the goat population is in this region and are taken to higher elevations

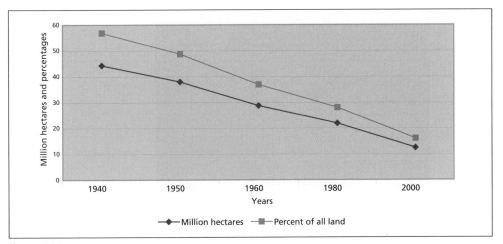

Figure 11.1
Pasture area changes over time in Turkey.

Plate 11.30
Alfalfa (Medicago sativa).

for 7–8 months. Marmara is an area of intensive animal husbandry. Central Anatolia has the least productive grazing lands; annual rainfall is between 250–500 mm; pastures dry out very quickly; grazing pressure is high; and pastures are steppic. Central Anatolia is a high plateau with few high mountains, so livestock graze fallows and stubble in summer.

S.G. REYNOLDS

Plate 11.31
*Sainfoin (*Onobrychis viciifolia*).*

The land tenure system is a major constraint to grassland management. Common areas are grazed free of charge, so are not managed properly. Boundaries of pastures are not clearly determined nor assigned to village communities.

The number of people in agriculture declined to 34 percent in 2000. Young rural people spend up to ten months annually in cities. Labour requirements are met by hiring shepherds or modifying the system to more labour-effective strategies. As the rural population declines, specialist animal producers are increasing their herd sizes. Rotational grazing is ignored because it requires extra investment. Herdsmen are well aware of its benefits, but continue to graze all parts of the grasslands from early spring until winter.

Reduction of fallow has been a major government concern over the past 25 years, and has given fruitful results in increasing forage and grain legume production. The area of fallow was 4 900 000 ha in 1998, compared with 8 400 000 ha in 1979.

Alfalfa (*Medicago sativa*) has long been grown in Turkey, which is one of the centres of genetic diversity of the crop. There are alfalfa fields up to 50 years old in the east. "Kayseri" – the oldest registered and most widely used cultivar – gives 3-4 cuts under irrigation. Average hay yield of alfalfa is about 7 t/ha. It is the major fodder crop of the irrigated areas and is also cultivated under rainfed conditions in the east of the country. Alfalfa (Plate 11.30) is replaced by sainfoin, *Onobrychis viciifolia* (Plate 11.31), under rainfed conditions, where it is more productive and seed production is much easier.

This chapter has attempted to cover some important grassland areas to complement the main chapters. For more details, reference should be made to the FAO Web site or the CD referred to in the opening paragraph.

BIBLIOGRAPHY

Al-Jaloudy, M.A. 2001. Pasture Profile for Jordan. See: http://www.fao.org/ag/AGP/AGPC/doc/Counprof/Jordan.htm

Aw-Hassan, A., Iñguez, L., Musaeva, M., Suleimenov, M., Khusanov, R., Moldashev, B., Ajibekov, A. & Yakshilikov, Y. 2004. Economic transition impact on livestock production in Central Asia: Survey results. *In:* Ryan, Vlek & Paroda, 2004, q.v.

Berkat, O. & M. Tazi. 2004. Pasture Profile for Morocco. See: http://www.fao.org/ag/AGP/AGPC/doc/Counprof/Morocco/morocco.htm

Bosser, J. 1969. Graminées des pâturages et de cultures à Madagascar. *Mémoires ORSTOM*, No. 35. 440 p.

Chabeuf, N. 1983. Trypanotolerant cattle in West and Central Africa. *Journal of the South African Veterinary Association*, 54(3): 165–170.

Chaouki, A.F., Chakroun, M., Allagui, M.B. & Sbeita, A. 2004. Fodder oats in the Maghreb. pp. 53–91, *in:* Suttie and Reynolds, 2004, q.v.

Coulibally, A. 2003. Pasture Profile for Mali. See: http://www.fao.org/ag/AGP/AGPC/doc/Counprof/Mali/mali.htm

Dabadghao, P.M. & Shankarnarayan, K.A. 1973. *The Grass Cover of India.* New Delhi, India: ICAR.

Dost, M. 1998. Pasture Profile for Pakistan. See: http://www.fao.org/ag/AGP/AGPC/doc/Counprof/Pakistan.htm

Dost, M. 2003. Fodder production for peri-urban dairies in Pakistan. Available from: http://www.fao.org/ag/AGP/AGPC/doc/pasture/dost/fodderdost.htm

FAOSTAT. 2004. Data downloaded from < http://www.fao.org/waicent/portal/statistics_en.asp >

Fitzherbert, A.R. 2000. Pastoral Profile for Kyrgyzstan. See: http://www.fao.org/ag/AGP/AGPC/doc/Counprof/kyrgi.htm

Garbulsky, M.F. & Deregibus, V.A. 2004. Pasture Profile for Argentina. See: http://www.fao.org/ag/AGP/AGPC/doc/Counprof/Argentina/argrentina.htm

Geesing, D. & Djibo, H. 2001. Pasture Profile for Niger. See: http://www.fao.org/ag/AGP/AGPC/doc/Counprof/niger.htm

Gintzburger, G. 2004. Agriculture and Rangelands in Middle Asian Countries. *In*: Ryan, Vlek & Paroda, 2004, q.v.

Gintzburger, G., Toderich, K.N., Mardonov, B.K. & Mahmudov, M.M. 2003. Rangelands of the Arid and Semi-Arid Zones in Uzbekistan. Published jointly by CIRAD, France, and ICARDA, Syria. 426 p.

Hu, Z. & Zhang, D. 2003a. Pasture Profile for China. See: http://www.fao.org/ ag/AGP/AGPC/doc/Counprof/china/china1.htm

Hu, Z. & Zhang, D. 2003b. China's pasture resources. pp. 81–113, *in:* Suttie & Reynolds, 2003, q.v.

Iñguez, L., Sulemenov, M., Yusopov, S., Ajibekov, A., Kineev, M., Kheremov, S., Abdusattarov, A. & Thomas, D. 2004. Livestock production in Central Asia: constraints, and research opportunities. *In:* Ryan, Vlek & Paroda, 2004, q.v.

Kagone, H. 2002. Pasture Profile for Burkina Faso. See: http://www.fao.org/ag/ AGP/AGPC/doc/Counprof/BurkinaFeng.htm

Karagöz, A. 2001. Pasture Profile for Turkey. See: http://www.fao.org/AGP/ AGPC/doc/Counprof/Turkey.htm

Kayouli, C. 2000. Pasture Profile for Tunisia. See: http://www.fao.org/ag/AGP/ AGPC/doc/Counprof/TUNIS.htm

Makhmudovich, M. 2001. Pasture Profile for Uzbekistan. See: http://www.fao. org/ag/AGP/AGPC/doc/Counprof/uzbekistan.htm

Masri, A. 2001. Pasture Profile for Syria. See: http://www.fao.org/ag/AGP/ AGPC/doc/Counprof/syria.htm

Misri, B.K. 1999. Pasture Profile for India. See: http://www.fao.org/ag/AGP/ AGPC/doc/Counprof/India.htm

Nedjraoui, D. 2001. Pasture Profile for Algeria. See: http://www.fao.org/ag/ AGP/AGPC/doc/Counprof/Algeria.htm

Nyima, T. 2003. Pastoral systems, change and the future of the grazing lands in Tibet. pp. 151–187, *in:* Suttie & Reynolds, 2003, q.v.

Oppong-Anane, K. 2001. Pasture Profile for Ghana. See: http://www.fao.org/ag/ AGP/AGPC/doc/Counprof/Ghana.htm

Pariyar, D. 1999. Pasture Profile for Nepal. See: http://www.fao.org/ag/AGP/ AGPC/doc/Counprof/Nepal.htm

Rasambainarivo, J.H. & Ranaivoarivelo, N. 2003. Pasture Profile for Madagascar. See: http://www.fao.org/ag/AGP/AGPC/doc/Counprof/Madagascar/mada-gascareng.htm

Reynolds, S.G., Suttie, J.M. & Staberg, P. 2005. Country Pasture Profiles, CD-ROM, FAO, Rome, Italy.

Riveros, F. 2002. The Gran Chaco. Available at: http://www.fao.org/ag/AGP/ AGPC/doc/Bulletin/GranChaco.htm

Ruijun, L. 2003a. Alpine rangeland ecosystems and their management in the Qinghai Tibetan plateau. Chapter 13. *In:* Wiener, Jianlin & Ruijun, 2003, q.v.

Ruijun, L. 2003b. Yak nutrition – a scientific basis. *In:* Wiener, Jianlin & Ruijun, 2003, q.v.

Ryan, J., Vlek, P. & Paroda, R. 2004. *Agriculture in Central Asia: Research and Development.* Proceedings of a Symposium held at the American Society for Agronomy Annual Meetings, 10–14 November 2002. ICARDA: Aleppo, Syria.

Suttie, J.M. & Reynolds, S.G. (eds). 2003. *Transhumant Grazing Systems in Temperate Asia. FAO Plant Production and Protection Series*, No. 31. 331 p.

Suttie, J.M. & Reynolds, S.G. (eds). 2004. *Fodder oats: a world overview. FAO Plant Production and Protection Series*, No. 33. 251 p.

Thieme, O. 2000. Pasture Profile for Afghanistan. See: http://www.fao.org/ag/AGP/AGPC/doc/Counprof/AFGAN.htm

Vera, R.R. 2003 Pasture Profile for Venezuela. See: http://www.fao.org/ag/AGP/AGPC/doc/Counprof/venezuela.htm

Wang, W.L. 2003. Studies on traditional transhumance and a system where herders return to settled winter bases in Burjin county, Altay prefecture, Xinjiang, China.. *In:* Suttie & Reynolds, 2003, q.v.

Wangdi, K. 2002. Pasture Profile for Bhutan. See: *http://www.fao.org/ag/AGP/AGPC/doc/Counprof/Bhutan.htm*

Wickens, G.E. 1997. Has the Sahel a future? *Journal of Arid Environments*, **37**: 649–663.

Wiener, G., Jianlin, H. & Ruijun, L. 2003. *The yak.* 2nd edition. FAO/RAOP publication 2003/06. FAO Regional Office for Asia and the Pacific, Bangkok, Thailand. See: http://www.fao.org/documents/show_cdr.asp?url_file=/DOCREP/006/AD347E/AD347E00.htm

Chapter 12
Grassland perspectives

INTRODUCTION

Most high quality grassland is now converted to crops, mixed farming or artificial pastures, so extensive grazing is a way of making economic use of grassland that is not suited to more intensive agricultural enterprises. It follows that investment in such grasslands should be kept to the minimum necessary for their profitable and sustainable exploitation by livestock, whether they be managed commercially or traditionally.

GRASSLAND SYSTEMS

The main chapters have reviewed a wide and representative variety of grasslands in a range of climates, from cold continental to the Equator. Five – eastern Africa, southern Africa, Mongolia, the Tibetan Steppe and the Russian Steppe – are ancient grazing lands. The remaining four have been settled and stocked in relatively recent times: Patagonia, the Campos, central North America and Australia. Some are used by traditional, partly subsistence systems; eastern Africa and part of southern Africa are managed traditionally; and Mongolia has reverted to subsistence herding. Patagonia, the Campos, the Great Plains and Australia are managed commercially. Three areas, Mongolia, the Tibetan Plateau and Russia, have undergone collectivization and decollectivization during the past century. Most of the systems described have some interaction with crop production and fodder production or agropastoralism, for, at farm or regional level, grazing lands and crop production are often mutually dependent, but Mongolia, Tibet Autonomous Region, China and, to a lesser degree, Patagonia are purely pastoral.

Of the systems described briefly in Chapter 11, West Africa and Madagascar are tropical, traditional systems; North Africa, the Syrian Arab Republic and Jordan are subtropical semi-arid areas where transhumant herding had been traditional but where breakdown of traditional authority and grazing systems, aggravated by sedentarization, cheap cereals and motor transport, has led to very severe pasture degradation. The South American systems – the Gran Chaco, the Pampas and the Llanos – are commercial systems of relatively recent settlement. Central Asia and China (at least its northern and western grazing lands), which are contiguous, were areas of transhumant herding, but systems have been disturbed, first by collectivization and then by decollectivization, which has followed very different paths in the two areas. The Hindu Kush-Himalaya zone, which has both sedentary and transhumant systems on the same grasslands, is under severe stress due to population increase. Turkey was a pastoral country, but much of the grasslands have been developed for increasingly commercial crop production, without a concomitant reduction in livestock numbers.

THE STATE OF THE GRASSLANDS

The condition of the world's grasslands is very varied but, in many cases, it is far from satisfactory. Long-term historical data on pasture is scarce in most areas, so the degree of change or degradation has to be inferred from present condition.

In all but the coldest and driest zones, large areas of the better land have been cleared for crops, leaving the poorer pasture to extensive stock rearing; in traditional areas of subsistence farming this is due to increasing human population among agricultural groups; elsewhere expansion of crops into marginal lands has been in the hope of profit, which has often not been realized. Most of the world's grasslands are on poor quality land: according to Buringh and Dudal (1987), only about one-sixth of the world's grasslands are on high and medium category land, while the remaining five-sixths are on low to zero classes, so the potential for further clearing of grassland for sustainable cropping seems low.

Cultivation of grassland has led to problems of access to water for stock and wildlife, loss of lean season grazing, obstruction of migration routes and fragmentation of wildlife habitat. Increasing population pressure and poverty, especially in the savannah zones of Africa, has driven subsistence cultivators further into the drylands; it is usually the best soils and areas along watercourses and other water sources that are developed first; these have usually been lean-season or emergency grazing lands of pastoral groups and their clearing can upset grazing systems, and leads to degradation of the remaining grassland.

Crop production is not the sole invasive use of grasslands: forestation can bar migration routes as can fencing for game exclusion (or protection); declaration of game reserves in pastoral areas can affect herding, and mining and oil extraction also cause damage.

In **eastern Africa,** pastoral systems are contracting through the expansion of cropping, and grassland is increasingly being integrated into farming systems. National land tenure legislation is not related to traditional grazing rights and puts pastoralism at a disadvantage compared with crops. The pastoral vegetation, however, is resilient, and recovers well after drought.

In **South Africa** also, much of the better grassland in commercial areas has been cleared for annual cropping, and in communal areas the better watered land has been converted into a patchwork of crops and thicket. The grassland vegetation is generally resilient, although there is some degradation in the driest areas. Bush encroachment is a problem in many vegetation types. Low returns from extensive commercial stock rearing in dry areas is leading to depopulation, and in some cases enterprises are changing to game ranching.

The human population of **West Africa** has increased greatly so the grassland has decreased and nearly all the cultivable grassland in the better watered areas, as well as vast tracts of semi-arid marginal land, are now under subsistence crops. Tribal authority, which had regulated grazing practice, broke down in many countries once they gained their independence, leaving grassland as an open-access resource.

In **North Africa,** human population has increased greatly and traditional authorities and grazing rights have broken down. Much semi-arid land has been ploughed for unsustainable annual cropping. Livestock numbers have risen and more can be carried through the lean season through the use of purchased – at one time subsidized – cereals and concentrates. Transhumance cycles are mostly greatly curtailed or herds have become sedentary. Uprooting of shrubs for fuel causes severe damage. All the grazing land is overstocked and degraded, often seriously so.

The situation in **Patagonia** contrasts sharply with that of East and South Africa. In a little over a century from the introduction of sheep ranching, the vegetation has been severely modified by overgrazing, mainly in the past fifty years. Ranching is on private land with vast paddocks and little grazing control within them. Guidelines for pasture management were only developed in the 1980s and have yet to make a strong impact.

The **Campos** is relatively well watered, and all stock rearing is commercial. Pasture technology is well developed. Introduced forages are used to palliate seasonal fluctuations in fodder availability and quality, either as sown pasture or by over-seeding. The value of properly managed native pasture is increasingly appreciated. Grasslands are generally in good condition.

The well drained parts of the **Pampas** are now farmland, where field crops are often in rotation with sown pasture. The flooding pampas is still exploited as grazing land, producing stock for fattening elsewhere.

Many of the pastures of the **Gran Chaco** deteriorated seriously during the twentieth century; before 1920 it had been almost unmanaged extensive grazing. Provision of watering points allowed far more of the vegetation to be consumed, leaving little to carry fire. This, together with uncontrolled felling of forest led to invasion by undesirable thorny vegetation. Bush encroachment brought about by overstocking and lack of grazing management is very serious, leading to erosion, loss of wildlife habitat, and greatly reduced livestock production. The economics of herbicides and mechanical clearing are not clear. In most subtropical areas of extensive grazing, the strategic use of pasture resting and controlled fire is the only economic way of keeping bush in check.

In the grasslands of **Central North America** the better-watered tall-grass prairie is now mostly under crops. Vast areas of drier land have also been cleared for cropping; much was marginal for crop production and suffers from periodic drought, which led to the "dust bowl" of the 1930s. Much of the marginal cropland has been reseeded or forested, with considerable government support. Low returns from farming and the isolation of many rural communities is resulting in urban drift. The modern trend is towards larger-scale landscape management, now that information collection and manipulation technology are available.

Central Asia was traditional transhumant herding country until the early twentieth century but, with collectivization, mobile herding ceased in the 1930s. Fine-wool sheep were encouraged during the soviet era but these are much less hardy than local breeds. Later the usefulness of seasonal movement was recognized and land in different seasonal zones was allocated to cooperatives and state farms. Heavy grazing and firewood collection have seriously reduced vegetation cover and the natural grazing has become degraded, with a loss of productivity and desertification; destruction of forests and shrubs has led to wind erosion. The impact of decollectivization on livestock production systems, grassland management and herder's livelihoods has been dramatic and negative. Large agro-food complexes were dismantled and cooperative farms were privatized. Marketing systems collapsed and many traditional markets were lost. There has been a sharp decline in stock numbers in some of the countries. The reforms led to a massive shift from collective to household herds; often household stock numbers are too few to warrant independent herding and communal or family herding has not yet developed; this often leads to stock remaining, unsupervised, close to homesteads: nearby pastures are overgrazed while distant ones are hardly used.

Mongolia is almost entirely pastoral; small areas that were cleared for cropping during the collective period have mostly been abandoned for economic reasons. Decollectivization distributed the livestock to cooperative members without clarifying grazing rights, which led to considerable confusion and lack of overall management of the pastoral resource. The people returned to mobile herding – as hardy local breeds had been maintained throughout

S.G. REYNOLDS

Plate 12.1
Pastoral scene near Arkhangai, Mongolia.

Plate 12.2
Watering camels in Mongolia.

Plate 12.3
Mongolia, land largely used by wildlife, with salt lake in the distance.

the collective period. As rural infrastructure deteriorated there has been considerable migration of people and their herds towards the central provinces, especially from the west. There is localized overgrazing near main roads and settlements, while more distant pastures are often underutilized. Overall pasture condition is satisfactory (Plate 12.1) and the vegetation resilient, even after the consecutive droughts of recent years. Pumped water supplies (Plate 12.2) have fallen into disrepair over large areas so these tracts are less used by herders, to the benefit of wildlife (Plate 12.3).

The livestock industry in **China,** including extensive grazing, was collectivized in the 1950s, but herds were still managed in transhumant systems. After decollectivization, livestock was allocated to families and grazing land has also been distributed according to the 1985 law. The allocation of relatively small areas of semi-arid grassland to families has greatly reduced herd mobility. This may have been a contributing factor in the serious deterioration of the country's grazing lands. Currently, 90 percent of grassland shows signs of deterioration, of which moderately degraded grassland is 32.5 percent. The government is taking vigorous measures to deal with grassland degradation through its *Planning Programme of National Ecological Environment Construction* and *Outline of Fifteenth Ten-Year Plan.* Like elsewhere in China, **Tibet's** grasslands suffered from a very sharp increase in stock numbers at the onset of collectivization in the mid-twentieth century. Numbers stabilized, but pasture condition is mediocre. The grasslands have been allocated to families in relatively small units and it remains to be seen how effective management will be of small areas of semi-arid risk-prone grassland.

In the **Hindu Kush-Himalaya** region there is extreme pressure on such extensive grazing lands as remain. The alpine pastures do get a seasonal rest during snow cover, but elsewhere there is constant grazing (except on seasonally closed hay land) from sedentary stock owners, and periodic grazing by transhumants. Because of the very high human population, all possible land has been cleared for crop production.

The situation in the **Near East** is similar to that in North Africa. Breakdown of tribal authority led to the disruption of traditional grazing rights and migration patterns. Purchased feed and availability of transport and water supplies enabled much larger numbers of stock to be kept through the lean season, and pastures were no longer rested once surface water supplies ran out. The human population and livestock numbers have multiplied. Much semi-arid pasture has been ploughed for unproductive cropping. Uprooting of bushes for fuel is very damaging to the pastoral vegetation.

Turkey has changed in the past century from a mainly pastoral country to one where crop production is very important. This meant a great reduction in the area of grassland, but there was no concomitant reduction in livestock, which increased in numbers. Later intensification of cropping systems replaced grazed fallow with pulses and other cash crops, further reducing grazing resources. Turkey's pastures are now stocked well above their carrying capacity. The land tenure system is a major constraint to grassland management. Common areas are grazed free of charge, so are not managed properly. Boundaries of pastures are not clearly determined nor assigned to village communities. Labour is becoming scarce in pastoral areas as people move to towns, so flocks are not well herded.

The grasslands of the **Russian steppe** were increasingly cleared for crops during the twentieth century; initially crops rotated with tumble-down fallow, but later the cropping cycle became more intensive. Meadows in floodplains and depressions remained an important source of hay. Stock were mainly housed during the collective period. The system has yet to stabilize following decollectivization, but herds are fragmented and are left to graze at will, leading to overgrazing close to homesteads while distant pastures are neglected.

The studies concentrate on domestic livestock, but most mention the other grazers, which are important in natural grassland ecosystems – ranging from large ruminants and marsupials to the rodents and lagomorphs that are major herbivores in many cool, semi-arid situations. Wildlife plays an important role in maintaining some grasslands, such as in eastern Africa, where the presence of elephants and fire are important.

GRASSLAND DEVELOPMENT, IMPROVEMENT AND REHABILITATION

Most grasslands, whether commercially or traditionally managed, have required some development inputs to make stock-rearing possible or more efficient. All grazing resources have to be taken into account and these cover much more than the herbaceous stratum.

Grassland resources
Water
Water is the major determining factor in stock management in most extensive grazing lands; in areas dependent on seasonal surface water, stock must move out once sources have dried. Improvement of water supply by creating water points or improving existing ones, and clearing of undesirable vegetation to allow free access for stock and better grass growth, are common to both systems, and provision of minerals or traditional salt licks is frequent. Water availability is a factor in determining many migration patterns in mobile systems. In both East and West Africa, traditional rules govern pastoral water use, and in very dry areas water is a more important resource than is grazing. In areas with very cold winters, as noted in the Mongolia study, surface water freezes; wells provide water, but, in their absence, herders may have to extract water from below ice, melt snow or have stock eat snow to find water – in severe winter weather events, dehydration may be as damaging to stock as lack of food.

Without water development, stock would be limited to areas close to permanent sources of water throughout the dry season, and large areas of grassland would not be useable for livestock production. From ancient times, stock watering points have been developed to assure year-round water supply within a group's grazing area or to make grazing land accessible. Access to water is mentioned as a limiting factor to use of some grazing areas in South Africa. According to the South American studies, creation of water supplies has made stock rearing possible in large areas of Patagonia and the Gran Chaco, and the importance of water development is stressed in Australia. Conversely, the breakdown of mechanized wells after decollectivization has rendered large tracts of Mongolia inaccessible to domestic livestock. The type of livestock affects the frequency of water; camels are by far the hardiest, whereas most cattle and small stock can only graze for about two days away from water in hot, dry climates.

Techniques in commercial systems vary according to available water supplies and include: wells and boreholes (artesian or pumped); dams and ponds; and pumping and piping from water bodies. Traditional systems include wells, which are important in the Sahel and parts of East Africa – those of the Borana are particularly well developed. Various methods of water harvesting and storage are used in semi-arid areas, including *birka* (cisterns) in Somalia and *hafir* (dug tanks) in several Arabic countries.

Creation of water points has been widely used, especially in Africa, as a means of making new pastures available to traditional herders, often with the intention of reducing pressure on existing grassland. Even if rules for water use and grazing management are drawn up, it is difficult to enforce them, especially in times of stress. Concentration of stock around permanent water points is given as a cause of pasture degradation in many of the studies – in both commercial and traditional systems.

Water is sometimes transported by truck, which is expensive, but if, as is the case in Syria and Jordan, the pasture is being used as hard standing for herds fattened on bought feed, it can be profitable, whatever the effect on any remaining vegetation.

In a few cases (Mongolia, Russia) water-spreading is sometimes used to improve grass growth, especially for haymaking. Irrigation is frequently used, mainly in commercial systems, to grow fodder, usually for conservation.

Natural salt-licks

Natural salt-lick (deposits or salt springs that animals lick) are valued in many zones of extensive grassland and are used by both livestock and grazing wildlife. Herders in, for example, sub-Saharan Africa and Mongolia take their herds long distances for periodic access to licks. Salt is, of course, commonly given to livestock, either alone or in proprietary blocks that may contain other minerals. Where herbage is deficient in minerals, which are essential to animal growth, their well-being and productivity suffers. Phosphorus deficiency is widespread and is especially acute in sub-Saharan Africa. Several minor elements may be deficient in localized areas: the pastures of the Kenya Rift Valley between Nakuru and Naivasha were notorious for poor livestock performance; this "Nakuritis" was diagnosed as cobalt deficiency and has since been found on many other grasslands.

Trees and shrubs

Trees and shrubs are important features of many grasslands, especially of savannahs. Some are very useful, others are invasive weeds. Trees provide valuable shade in hot climates and seasons and they give shelter in winter. Some trees are browsed and may be lopped for fodder – their fruits can also provide valuable feed. A wide range of genera is involved and their management is still poorly understood; the tolerance of most woody species to stock-feeding regimes and lopping still needs study, although a good deal of work has been done on *Leucaena*. Woody vegetation provides branches and poles for building and making corrals and firewood. Where firewood is scarce, excessive cutting causes serious environmental damage, as in steppic conditions, where much damage is due to uprooting sub-shrubs for fuel. Some trees provide fruit which is valued by local people – such trees may be retained selectively and given some protection. Woody vegetation is, however, often invasive, especially in tropical and sub-tropical conditions; bush encroachment is generally taken as a sign of poor management and overgrazing; this is dealt with below.

Pasture development methods

Clearing

After water supply, clearing is a common part of developing extensive grassland for grazing. Where land is being developed for crops or sown pasture, clearing may involve some removal of stones, termite hills and other obstructions, but, for extensive grazing, clearing usually involves removing or thinning woody vegetation to improve access and grass growth or to reduce tsetse fly habitat. In traditional systems, fire is the commonest agent for clearing or controlling trees and shrubs. Specialized equipment is used for large-scale commercial clearing – tree-pushers, drag chains, bulldozers, root ploughs and root rakes, and, for shrubs, various rollers and shredders; the debris may be burnt. The degree of clearing or thinning will depend on the original vegetation and the use to which it is put, but it is usually partial and selective, leaving useful trees, shade and shelter. Selective clearing has been used to reduce tsetse habitat. Woodland destruction for pasture development is now recognized as environmentally undesirable, although it continues on a fairly large scale in the Amazon basin. Strategic thinning of woody vegetation has a role in pasture development and improvement, but it must be done within the context of the ecosystem involved. The Australian study indicates that some leases now restrict tree clearing; it also highlights the fact that the removal of trees and their replacement by crops and annual pastures has made major changes to the hydrological cycle and can lead to serious salination of soils.

Bush control

Bush control is necessary in many grassland types; it is a maintenance activity, while bush clearing is development. Bush encroachment usually indicates faults in the management system and is associated with high grazing pressures; several mechanisms are involved according to vegetation type and management system. Unpalatable shrubs may increase when the more palatable ones are overgrazed; if little dry herbage remains in the non-growing season there may not be hot enough fires to control the bush. Goats browse much more than cattle and mixed grazing is probably less favourable to bush establishment than cattle alone; goats may be used to browse regrowth after fire. Herbicides are used in some commercial systems; they are favoured in South Africa and used to prepare land for over-seeding in the Campos. Bush encroachment is mentioned in many of the studies. Indigenous plants are usually involved but alien shrubs and trees can be very invasive: the Australian study mentions *Acacia nilotica*, which is a highly respected source of browse and pods in Africa, Pakistan and India; *Opuntia* spp. are pasture weeds in many areas outside their homeland; *Prosopis velutina*, which has been widely used for revegetation of degraded dry areas in parts of Africa, northern India and Pakistan, invades grazing land and forms dense thickets; in wetter areas, *Lantana camara* is a widespread pest; and in high-rainfall zones, guava (*Psidium* spp.) colonizes grazing land.

Fire

Controlled fire is a major factor in determining the composition of grasslands and a widespread and powerful tool in grassland management. Its effect depends on its intensity, seasonality, frequency and type. The intensity depends on the type, structure and abundance of fuel. It is mentioned in most of the studies, except in those with more arid climates. Fire is used to remove unpalatable grass and enable regrowth and access to the young herbage by grazing stock. It often stimulates regrowth and supplies a green bite when most needed. Fire is also used, as discussed above, to control woody vegetation. Burning of grassland must be carefully controlled and timed, otherwise it can cause serious damage; this is not discussed in any of the studies, although planning burning and controlling fire is difficult and labour-consuming. Since fire has so severe an effect, burning must take the whole ecosystem into account, not only the grass and the grazing livestock. Ill-timed fire can have a devastating effect on wildlife, including nesting and young birds. Most developed countries have regulations governing burning of natural vegetation. For example periodic burning is necessary to maintain the *Calluna*-dominated pastures of the United Kingdom; strips are burnt in different years to produce a mosaic of heather of different ages. Burning is regulated by law and the season is defined to minimize damage to wildlife according to a "Muirburn Code" (The Scottish Executive 2003). Uncontrolled fire is, of course, a risk in many areas. It may occur spontaneously through lightning strike, but very often it is due to careless grassland burning, through fires lit to drive out game or through arson. The Mongolia study mentions the care taken by herders to avoid grassland fire – in Mongolia's cold winter there would be no regrowth and burnt herbage is lost. While too frequent burning is undesirable, long periods between fires may in some cases, lead to a build up of combustible material which, if ignited, will give a very fierce and destructive fire.

Fencing

Fencing is widely used in the development of commercial grazing enterprises to delimit properties and subdivide them for ease of management. Block size is generally large on low-yielding grasslands since fencing and fence maintenance are costly; this can lead to uneven stock distribution. Fences are also used to protect forages and hay land within properties. The Patagonia study gives an example of protecting high-quality meadows for individual management. Fences are not used by traditional herders, but authorities sometimes erect fences within traditional grazing lands for disease control.

Grassland improvement

"Improvement" of extensive natural grassland by introduction of selected local or exotic grasses and legumes has been done experimentally in most of the better-watered zones, and is used by some commercial systems; it is, of course, along with sown pasture, common in commercial mixed farming and more intensively managed grassland. Techniques usually involve at least temporary suppression of the existing vegetation (by fire, hard grazing, herbicides or mechanically, alone or in combination) and differing degrees of disturbance of the soil surface; fertilizer is often used, and when legumes are introduced to an area for the first time inoculation of their seed with the appropriate *Rhizobium* is a wise precaution.

Choice of species and cultivar to suit climate, soil and ultimate use is very important and, while there is a very wide range of genetic material of pasture crops available, it may be difficult to match them to new areas. Finding commercial quantities of seed of locally adapted cultivars and ecotypes is often difficult. Care in management is often needed to assure the longevity of the introduced species, and maintenance fertilizer may be required. The success of, and in part the need for, over-seeding depends not only on climate and soil but also the vigour and aggressiveness of the native vegetation. The studies dealing with commercial systems all mention over-seeding. It has been successful in Patagonia on an experimental scale, using both indigenous and exotic material, but, in such dry conditions, was unlikely to be economically viable. In the Campos, over-seeding, especially with exotic temperate species, mainly legumes, is successful and the introduction of temperate legumes has a very beneficial effect on winter pastures. Pasture improvement is widely used in Australia and self-reseeding annuals (especially *Medicago* spp. and *Trifolium* spp.) have become important in the Mediterranean climatic zone; the self-reseeding *Stylosanthes humilis* was very important in tropical pastures until it was wiped out by disease. The South African and North American studies mention over-seeding for the revegetation of abandoned cropland – a subject discussed below.

Attitudes to over-seeding and the introduction of exotic pasture plants to natural grassland ecosystems are changing. The ability to spread and colonize in a grazing situation used to be a desirable characteristic of plants for pasture improvement – now such plants may be regarded as invasive aliens.

Fertilizer may be used, with or without reseeding if the botanical composition of the sward is appropriate and economics warrant it, and slashing is sometimes used to reduce coarse vegetation.

Grassland rehabilitation

Degraded grassland is a symptom of weakness in the pastoral production system and these weaknesses have to be identified and dealt with before further action can be taken. Where rehabilitation of grassland is desirable it should be through management methods, with or without water-spreading. Over-seeding degraded rangeland is rarely an attractive option and reliance has to be put on making the most of the recovery of the natural vegetation. Assuring even grazing over an area, keeping stock numbers within reasonable limits, and avoiding localized overgrazing can all help.

Degradation of pasture can have effects more serious than reduction of available grazing; increased runoff can lead to flooding and siltation of more valuable land and infrastructure lower in the catchment. In such cases action may have to be taken to reduce runoff; in severe cases grassland that is a focus for runoff and erosion may have to be closed, temporarily or permanently, with or without forestation – this is being done on a large scale in China, notable in the Yellow River and Yangtze catchments. Many grasslands are very resilient and will recover from serious misuse through resting; if, however, change and degradation has been very serious, the grassland may have passed the point of recovery, and while rest will allow some sort of vegetative cover to develop, it will not be as the original grassland.

Two situations closely allied to grassland rehabilitation are old mining and industrial sites and cropland that is being removed from cultivation. Treatment of mining sites is a specialized matter. Marginal cropland going out of cultivation is mentioned in East and South Africa, North America and Russia. Where adapted grasses are available, reseeding may be a better option than relying on tumble-down fallow since old crop land may not turn spontaneously to a grassland but to weeds or thicket.

HERD MANAGEMENT

In commercial systems management generally aims at improving animal status and usually concentrates on one, or at the most two, species. Common management practices to that end include: dividing herds into categories so that they get the appropriate treatment, avoiding underage and unseasonable breeding; controlling parasites and predators; providing veterinary care; and using and maintaining breeds that suit their land and potential markets. Commercial properties are often ring-fenced and divided into paddocks to allow herd division and, in some cases, rotational grazing or resting of part of the grassland.

Choice of species and breed is in part determined by the pasture and the climate, but, in commercial systems, market requirements are central and, on extensive grazing, beef cattle and sheep predominate. In warmer climates, zebus or cattle with some zebu blood, often developed locally, are becomingly increasingly popular. Cattle are usually specialized breeds, not dual or multipurpose. Sheep breeds commonly raised in Australasia dominate the other commercial areas studied.

Traditional systems, while selling livestock and livestock products, are designed primarily to provide subsistence and security to the herders. Livestock are usually multipurpose, producing meat, milk, fibre, hides, transport, draught and manure, which is also used as fuel in treeless lands. They often keep several species, which may be herded separately; this assists in providing a wider range of products. In sub-Saharan Africa, many herders keep cattle, sheep and goats, but in the drier areas small stock, or in northeast Africa, camels and small stock, are kept. In North Africa and western Asia, small stock, especially sheep and camels, were general in extensive herding but with the increasing popularity of motor transport camels have become much less common. In India and Pakistan, buffalo are also herded, but herding groups tend to keep a narrow range of stock and specialize in either small or large ruminants. In much of Central Asia and Mongolia, herding involves "the five animals" – horses, camels, cattle, sheep and goats. There are a number of reasons, in addition to widening the range of products, for keeping several species: they may make more efficient use of grazing resources than monospecific grazing, for example, goats, horses and camels make better use of shrubs than do cattle or sheep; pasture condition may be better maintained if several species are involved; and multiple species may also reduce risk.

Traditional systems use local, hardy, often multi-purpose breeds, which can survive and produce under harsh conditions without many external inputs. Introduction of blood of "more productive" breeds to herding systems has had little effect since such animals are soon weeded out under herding conditions: the massive reduction in sheep numbers after decollectivization in those countries of the former USSR where "improved" breeds were kept, contrasts with the rise of stock numbers in Mongolia, which had maintained local breeds, during the same period. Market demand affects traditional systems also, although less so than commercial ones: the main livestock of the Jordanian badia was camels, but over the years these have been replaced by sheep fed on bought feed; decollectivization in Mongolia coincided with high prices for cashmere and goat numbers rose much more sharply than those of other stock.

Plate 12.4
Fenced areas (exclosures) in Inner Mongolia demonstrate the impact of excessive grazing on pasture condition.

Stocking rates and stock distribution

Regulation of the stocking rate and managing the spatial and temporal distribution of livestock are the basis of grazing management (Plate 12.4). The amount of livestock that a particular area of grassland can carry is not dependent on its botanical composition alone, since it has to take into account the management objectives of the graziers and the availability and siting of other grassland resources, notably water. Extensive grasslands are not homogeneous but usually show spatial heterogeneity according to moisture and fertility gradients. Stock may tend to concentrate on the better grassland and ignore poorer sites or those farther from water. Some pastures may be suited to grazing at certain seasons or, as in alpine grasslands, only available seasonally. Stocking must be seen in the context of the whole area available and management decisions made in the light of local knowledge, be it the rancher who knows his property well or the herding group with traditional knowledge of their grazing grounds: extensive grazing is managed at the landscape rather than at the local scale.

Since the productivity of natural pasture, especially in drier climates, varies widely from year to year, the maximum amount of livestock that can be raised thereon also varies. Commercial systems usually have stock in paddocks, whereas traditional herders move their livestock daily to follow changes in the quantity and quality of pasture. Emergency feeding or destocking is expensive: commercial enterprises usually have more conservative stocking rates than traditional, mobile ones; the latter accept more risk and may be able to move to avoid severe forage or water shortages.

The studies show that there are wide ranges of stocking rates used or advocated within areas. With up-to-date technology, most of the commercial areas are now able to make more accurate assessment of forage availability and grassland condition over wide areas and better estimate safe stocking rates and monitor their effect. The Patagonia study shows that early stocking rates were far too high and led to serious resource degradation. The Australian study shows a surprisingly high estimate of degradation, with over half the pastures of northern Australia either degraded or deteriorating. In other studies on commercial systems, overstocking has not been a serious problem. The eastern African study quotes many conflicting estimates of carrying capacity and grassland degradation. However, these have not been based on as detailed work as those in commercial areas. In Mongolia, the traditional herding system follows a four-season pattern, grazing different pastures at each season, thus distributing the grazing load, with strategic short-distance moves, *otor*, to other pasture with different categories of animals as part of the routine and also helping to spread grazing and make best use of resources.

Political changes have affected the movement and management of livestock in many herding lands. Decollectivization has affected vast areas of the grazing lands of Central Asia and Russia. In Mongolia, collapse of rural infrastructure and pumped water supplies have led to many areas remaining ungrazed, and lack of security for winter grazing areas can restrict long migrations. In Central Asia and the Russian steppe, family herds are now too small to warrant herding, so livestock remain close to homesteads, while more distant pastures are unused. In Turkey, urban drift has led to a scarcity of people willing to work as shepherds – again, distant grasslands are underused. In Africa, civil security and stock theft are problems.

The lean season

Feed availability is very unevenly distributed throughout the year in areas of extensive grasslands, since these generally have a restricted growing season due to rainfall or temperature. Managing stock through the lean season is a major concern in all the systems described and both traditional and commercial stock owners exercise skill and ingenuity in palliating seasonal feed scarcity. Situations and strategies vary, as do the causes of the deficit and the types of production.

In warm and tropical climates, the dry season is the main time of feed deficit. The problem is not always a lack of standing vegetation, but that many tropical grasslands, once mature, provide herbage of very low nutritive value. In traditional systems, fodder conservation is almost unknown; stock graze as best they can and lose weight through the dry season. In eastern and southern Africa, pastoral groups usually remain within their own territory, although there may be some seasonal movement – they usually have little access to crop residues. In West Africa, however, pastoral groups are transhumant, moving between the desert edge and the forest fringe; they frequently have access to crop residues. Browse is important in dry-season feeding although this is not dealt with in detail in the African chapters. Water is often scarce during the dry season and in traditional systems it may be as important as feed. Fodder conservation is not part of the feeding strategies of these pastoralists.

Crop residues, however, are important in many traditional grassland systems, especially in agropastoral systems; they are also widely used (with or without treatment) in many commercial systems and feedlots. Hay and straw conservation and use is discussed in another publication in this series (Suttie, 2000) and silage making in the tropics by t'Mannetje (2000).

Lean-season strategies in cold areas depend partly on whether the winters are dry or not, and on the depth of snow cover. In areas of summer precipitation, such as Mongolia, the grasslands of northern China and the Tibet-Qinghai plateau, livestock can graze throughout the winter, although unusual weather events can cause severe losses. The herding strategy is to get stock into the best possible condition during summer and autumn so that they can survive the winter. Transhumance between three or four seasonal pastures is still practised in Mongolia; the winter pastures are the key to the annual system; mobility gives herders some opportunity to escape adverse weather events. Seasonal de-stocking, which includes both sale of excess stock and slaughter and freezing of the stock that will be consumed domestically before the spring thaw, reduces

J.M. SUTTIE

Plate 12.5
*Alfalfa (*Medicago sativa*) hay being collected for winter feeding of stock in Altai Prefecture, Xinjiang, China.*

the number of animals that have to overwinter. A little meadow hay is made, but its use is limited to a few weak stock; Wang (2003) describes a case where herding has been combined with irrigated fodder growing (Plate 12.5), with very positive results. Stock may be housed or sheltered at night and during severe weather. Such systems are probably inevitable in a subsistence economy in situations where complementary fodder is inaccessible and very expensive, but it does mean that stock must be bred for hardiness rather than high productivity and also that animals are old by the time they reach slaughter weight. The Patagonian sheep industry, also in a cold, semi-arid zone, relies on natural grazing without supplementation, with set stocking throughout the year.

In the cattle-raising systems of the northern parts of central North America, the common approach is very different from that of traditional systems, and winter feeding is widely used, not only because inclement weather may preclude grazing but also because the feeding value of natural pasture drops off sharply after the growing season. In many cases, natural grassland is used in conjunction with arable, and fodder for winter will be produced on-farm; large amounts of alfalfa hay and some cereal hay are used.

In Mediterranean-type climates, the lean season is the hot, dry summer; in many cases, transhumant systems were used to palliate its effects. These have become severely modified and in much of North Africa and Western Asia cultivation of semi-arid lands has reduced the available pastures. Many countries in this region had subsidized grain sales to herders; meat prices are high and purchased grain is still widely used, with stocking rates far in excess of anything the grazing lands could support. The use of large quantities of feed along with improved water supplies, or trucked water, has had disastrous results for the pastoral vegetation. When discussing sustainable development of drylands, FAO (1993) points out that improperly managed feeding can be very detrimental to pasture condition:

"Drought and dry-season feeding reserves are a priority in terms of livestock production, but can cause overstocking and destruction of rangeland if purchased feed is used to maintain excessive grazing pressure on rangeland. Reserves are therefore best organized within the one management unit. Government subsidies on feed brought into drylands are especially destructive and are best avoided."

Stratification

Stratification of livestock production – generally fattening stock under more favourable conditions than those in which they were raised – is widespread in commercial systems, and can be a means of reducing the numbers carried on pastures through the lean season. It also speeds up the production cycle since, if stock are moved to better pastures and feedlots, they avoid the growth checks and weight loss associated with extensive grasslands due to scarce, low-quality fodder during the lean season. Markets increasingly require meat from quickly grown stock. Stratified production systems are generally associated with the commercial livestock sector; traditional herders have usually less access to fattening facilities and many native breeds are less responsive to intensive feeding than improved ones. Various systems of stratification and/or feedlots are mentioned in the chapters on South Africa, the Campos (where much finishing is on better pastures), North America, and Australia. In Russia, indoor feeding was the rule. Feedlot fattening of cattle from extensive systems has been carried out in Kenya in the past. Small-scale fattening is, of course, common in many agropastoral and agricultural systems. In China, where there is an increasing demand for meat in the increasingly prosperous urban areas, intensive fattening of stock from extensive grasslands has developed. Fattening is done in farming areas relatively close to cities where rice straw (fermented with ammonia or urea) forms the base of the ration, and cereals and agro-industrial by-products are readily available (see Dolberg and Finlayson, 1995; Simpson and Ou, 1996). Fattening stock is either local or from the great northern and western grazing lands. China has both an expanding market for beef and a sound transport system between the grasslands and the fattening areas.

Stratification of sheep production, although little discussed in the text, is common in parts of Europe and probably elsewhere; sheep from the Scottish hills are traditionally fattened in the lowlands, and hill ewes are crossed with other breeds for lowland meat production. Sheep fattening is widespread in the Near East, sometimes with imported lambs, usually using cereals and concentrates – this has nothing to do with reducing grazing pressure. In many Islamic countries, there is seasonal specialized sheep and goat fattening for religious festivals.

SOWN PASTURE AND FODDER

Sown pasture is often complementary to natural grassland in commercial systems as, for example, strategic feed for specific seasons, for fattening or conservation. In many places under favourable conditions of soil and climate, sown pasture, often in rotation with crops, has replaced natural grassland, but that is not the subject under discussion here. It is used by medium to large farms in commercial systems. Pasture improvement, which can involve clearing, over-seeding, etc., is discussed later, although the dividing line between "improved grassland" and sown pasture is not a clear one. Traditional systems with small holdings and unfenced cropland are unsuited to grazed artificial pasture – although they may use cut-and-carry fodder. Sown pastures were well developed in the commercial sector in Kenya before structural changes in agriculture led to a vast reduction in the number of large dairy farms; the technology is described in Bogdan's (1977) classic *Tropical pasture and fodder plants.* In the commercial sector in South Africa, artificial pastures are widely used in the better watered areas; elsewhere in Africa, including Madagascar and the North, sown pasture is not used, nor is it used in the Middle East or in Asia ("artificial grassland" is a term much used in China, but is usually either alfalfa for hay or annual forage for cut-and-carry). Patagonia is unsuited climatically to sown pasture, as are Mongolia and Tibet. The Campos, which is relatively well watered, has developed sown pastures using both summer- and winter-growing species, and sown pasture is important in the Pampas. In central North America, sown pasture, often in rotation with crops, plays an important role in livestock production. It is, of course, very important in other areas of North America, Western Europe and, notably, New Zealand.

Sown pasture is widely used in the better-watered parts of Australia, especially in the Mediterranean and temperate parts, although also used in the tropics. In areas of Mediterranean climate, self-reseeding annual forages are widely used in rotation with annual crops, most of the forages used are of Mediterranean origin, and the system is very similar to the ancient cereal-grazed-fallow rotation of that zone, except that, after initial seeding and establishment, fertilizer and grazing management is aimed at allowing the annuals to seed and regenerate: the area under annual rotational pastures ("leys" locally) is declining as rotation of cereals with other annual cash crops, including pulses, becomes more profitable. Much work has been carried out on tropical pastures, and these are of some importance, but there is need for legumes better adapted to grazing since *Stylosanthes* spp., once a mainstay of sown and improved tropical pastures, were seen to be susceptible to attack by *Colletotrichum* spp. in the 1980s. Pasture improvement through over-seeding is also important. Sown pasture was not important on the Russian steppe during the period immediately prior to decollectivization, but the authors of Chapter 10 argue that it should become so.

Sown fodder

Fodder in this context is forages grown as whole-crop feed for livestock, whether fed green or conserved. Such crops are often used to supplement grazing or for fattening or dairy production in many systems. Fodder is little used in the traditional pastoral systems of sub-Saharan Africa, but is becoming increasingly used in agropastoral and crop producing areas as available free grazing disappears. In eastern and southern Africa, fodders were widely grown on large-scale dairy farms (Plate 12.6), but changes in farm size and farming systems have led to a great reduction in the range of fodders now grown; *Pennisetum purpureum* is widely used for cut-and-carry feeding by smallholders (Plates 12.7 and 12.8). Commercial grazing systems in South Africa use some fodder, including some for "exceptional circumstances", but most others require irrigation, which can usually be used more profitably for other crops. Some fodder is grown in North Africa, a little irrigated alfalfa and, more important, oats for hay, which is often produced for sale to herders from drier areas (Chaouki *et al.*, 2004). Little fodder is grown in the desert grazing lands of the Near East. Egypt is unusual in North Africa as nearly all its livestock are stall fed, and cultivated fodder is important to supplement crop residues – the production system is very similar to that of the irrigated tracts of Punjab, and Alexandrian clover,

Plate 12.6
Irrigated ryegrass pastures (Lolium multiflorum) *near Fort Nottingham, KwaZulu-Natal, South Africa.*

Plate 12.7
Pennisetum purpureum.

Trifolium alexandrinum (Plate 12.9), is the major winter fodder, with coarse cereals in summer.

Cold, semi-arid Patagonia has little land suited to fodder production, and irrigated lands are reserved for cash crops. The main production systems of the Campos also rely on year-round grazing. In the Gran Chaco, alfalfa is grown

S.G. REYNOLDS

Plate 12.8
Smallholder cut-and-carry dairy operation using Napier grass, near Embu, Kenya.

SARDI

Plate 12.9
*Egyptian clover or berseem (*Trifolium alexandrinum*).*

for hay, and, in some areas, smallholders produce hay for sale – this is described in Suttie (2000).

Fodders are widely grown in Central North America and in commercial mixed farming systems throughout Europe and North America. A method of making oat fodder accessible to cattle even under snow cover is described

DUANE McCARTNEY

Plate 12.10
Cattle grazing oats through snow in Canada, where the oats were swathed at dough stage in September.

from Canada by Fraser and McCartney (2004); "swath grazing" provides late autumn and early winter grazing for beef cows (Plate 12.10). Late-sown cereals are swathed in the early autumn from heading until dough stage. The livestock then graze the swaths through the snow. The emphasis on fodder rather than grazing in the former USSR is mentioned above. Fodder growing and conservation are an ancient tradition in Turkey.

Fodders are widely used in the better watered areas of Australia, for on-farm use, local sale and export (Armstrong *et al.*, 2004) and are also widely grown in New Zealand. As discussed in Chapter 10, fodder was a mainstay of livestock production in the collective period, with much less interest in grazing, but this is changing under economic pressure.

In Central Asia during collective times, fodder, especially alfalfa, was widely grown for winter reserves; the area has fallen sharply since decollectivization, since there is now a need to use irrigated land to assure local cereal needs, and livestock numbers have fallen. Great areas of fodder are grown in China. Hu and Zhang (2003) give the area under alfalfa as 1 804 700 ha, forage maize at 570 500 ha and fodder oats at 274 400 ha. The climate of the Tibetan steppe and Mongolia is not suitable for fodder; a little oats is grown by Tibetan herders with subsidized seed from elsewhere; Mongolia grew fodder oats during the collective period, but that ceased for economic reasons – only in the far west is some irrigated alfalfa grown for hay.

Plate 12.11
*Alfalfa or lucerne (*Medicago sativa*).*

Plate 12.12
*Persian clover or shaftal (*Trifolium resupinatum*).*

In the Hindu Kush-Himalaya region, fodders are grown, especially in Afghanistan and Pakistan; alfalfa (Plate 12.11) and shaftal (*Trifolium resupinatum*) (Plate 12.12) are important, but the areas are restricted by lack of land. Vast areas of fodder are produced in the irrigated tracts of the plains

J.M. SUTTIE

Plate 12.13
Oat seed production in Nepal.

of Pakistan, India and, to a lesser degree, Nepal to supplement crop residues in the feeding of vast numbers of stall-fed cattle and buffaloes: *Trifolium alexandrinum* and oats (Plate 12.13) are major winter crops, and coarse cereals predominate in summer.

SOCIAL AND ECONOMIC FACTORS

Often the problems of grasslands and their users are more socio-economic than technical. Better management and improved livelihoods can only be attained if the legal, social and economic problems associated with pastoralism, especially traditional herding, are dealt with. "Training herders" used to be recommended in many projects, but it is futile to try to transfer technical ideas, probably developed elsewhere, when the herders have no security of tenure, the techniques have not been convincingly tested locally and poverty and population pressure mean that herders will not take extra risks.

Tenure

Secure tenure of land or grazing rights is essential if stock-raisers and pastoralists are to have secure livelihoods and can invest in and manage grassland in a sustainable fashion. Where grassland production systems are purely commercial (as in the studies on the commercial sector in South Africa, Patagonia, the Campos and Central North America) the land is held in either freehold or long-term leasehold. Commercial stock raisers can, therefore, invest in infrastructure, notably water and fencing – a major use of fencing may be to delimit properties. Since commercial enterprises hold valid land titles their land can be used as collateral for loans.

In the extensive, pastoral subsistence sector, grazing rights are much less clear. In the distant past these lands would have been managed under traditional authorities and disputes over encroachment by other herding groups or cultivators probably settled in battle. Changing times and régimes have left many pastoral groups in a state of uncertainty, and they are often relatively neglected minorities, except in countries that are mainly pastoral – these are few: Mongolia and Somalia are examples. In the traditional sector, grazing rights means pastoral resources in their wider sense, including access to water and to mineral licks where these are used. The land rights of settled farmers are recognized in most countries since they are resident on their farms and obviously use them; the rights of pastoral groups, however, who are usually mobile, are usually less well defined since they only use a piece of grassland at a particular season. If others clear such grassland for crops, however unsustainable, it may be viewed as "development" and pastoralists are at a disadvantage in claiming their rights. In addition, traditional pastoral tenure is not usually strong enough to prevent confiscation by the state, probably without compensation, for mineral prospection, infrastructure, building or nature reserves. While cropland can conveniently be allocated to individual smallholders, the large areas of low-yielding grassland involved in mobile herding and the desirability of managing such pasture at the landscape scale make the allocation of grassland to individual families problematic (although such allocation has been done in China). Allocation to groups seems preferable, but at what scale and how to decide to whom grazing should be allocated is problematic.

Markets and trade

Commercial systems are, of course, market oriented, and nowadays most traditional systems sell their surplus production; the East African study indicates that even conservative ethnic groups which formerly did not sell stock now market their surplus. Most of the studies report poor prices for grassland produce; wool is probably most severely affected. The break-up of the USSR disrupted markets in Central Asia and Mongolia, and these countries have yet to find new outlets. The effect of freer world trade on produce from extensive grasslands has still to be seen, but meat produced by traditional herders who are far from consumers may be at a disadvantage – especially as urban consumers increasingly demand meat from cattle that have been finished in feedlots or off good pasture.

Herder organization and community participation

Regime and political change have disrupted old herder groupings and hierarchies, and decollectivization has left large areas with a disorganized pastoral sector.

Often herds are too small for it to be profitable for a family to spare labour to take them to pasture, and herding communities are fragmented. If semi-arid grasslands are to be managed sustainably, some planning is necessary at the landscape scale. It is now widely accepted that rural development, including grassland development, should be led by the ultimate users. Community participation is essential, but if it is to be effective, rather than token talking, a high priority should be developing some means of having herders organize themselves into larger groups for deciding local herding policy, discussing with regional authorities and sharing herding tasks.

Demotic factors

Population pressure and rising populations on decreasing pastoral resources are mentioned in many traditional areas. The number of livestock that any area of extensive grassland can carry sustainably is finite. If pastoral populations grow larger than their resource base can stand it is unlikely that technical solutions will be found.

Diversification

Because of poor returns from animal husbandry a number of commercial enterprises in most of the countries studied are looking at alternative and potentially more profitable uses for their grasslands. Raising game and wildlife is already practised in eastern and South Africa and is probably expanding – this may be for specialist meats, tourism, hunting of a combination. Some mention organic meat.

Tourism and eco-tourism is another use of grasslands; in commercial areas its benefits will go to the landowner; the extent to which it will become important is unclear except where noteworthy scenery or wildlife is involved since many grassland areas are remote and have little infrastructure. Tourism is encouraged by many governments since it brings them revenue. However, in areas of traditional herding, tourism must be seen as beneficial by the graziers involved; the owners of large private establishments may negotiate fees, but in traditional systems tourists may be regarded as a nuisance if they make no contribution to local livelihoods. A quotation from an article in the travel section of the *Times* (2004) is a good example of this:

> "*Mongolia's reindeer people say that tourism is threatening their way of life. 207 people from Tsaganuur say that the small but growing numbers of tourists are disrupting the peace of the taiga where their reindeer roam*"

GRASSLAND IN THE ENVIRONMENT

Although grasslands are of primary environmental importance, not least as catchment areas and sites for *in situ* conservation of biodiversity, their preservation and proper management are given relatively little attention by environmentalists and governments, which often see the traditional livestock

MARZIO MARZOT

Plate 12.14
Kreb, a mixture of grains from wild grasses, is still used for human food in the Lake Chad area.

sector more as a problem than an essential part of maintaining grasslands and their biodiversity. Reserves and national parks are many and increasing; they often reduce traditional grazing lands, with little or no attention to their traditional users. Such reserves are for wildlife, biodiversity and often the consequent tourism, but the grassland biome of such reserves requires properly managed grazing for its survival. Grassland reserves as such are rarely mentioned: China (Hu and Zhang 2003) has eleven, covering two million hectares.

Non-livestock grassland products get little attention, but are important to local communities. Many wild plants are harvested as fruit and vegetables. Wild grass seeds are used as cereals (Plates 12.14 and 12.15). Many medicinal plants for both local use and sale are gathered from grasslands, as is wood and fuel. An interesting case study from the Lake Chad area is provided by Batello, Marzot and Touré (2004).

In places such as in Nepal (see Plate 1.15) or in the Tibet Autonomous Region, China, near Lake Namtso (Plates 12.16a, b), grassland sites can have a special religious significance. At Lake Namtso the nearby grasslands are

Plate 12.15
Nomads agree that some areas should be protected from grazing so that grasses can produce seed for Kreb harvesting.

Plate 12.16a
Near Lake Namtso, Tibet Autonomous Region, China.

S.G. REYNOLDS

Plate 12.16b
Pilgrims at Lake Namtso.

subject to heavy tourist and pilgrim traffic on certain occasions and tented encampments can spread out from the focal point to surrounding areas.

SOME CONCLUSIONS

The preceding chapters cover a very wide range of grassland types and production systems. They demonstrate clearly that extensive grassland exists in many forms and is exploited in many ways, and that each great group requires its own way of management. This chapter does not attempt to summarize all the conclusions that can be drawn from them, but some important ones are:

- Many grasslands are in poor condition. Most communally or traditionally managed grasslands show some degree of degradation, and many are seriously damaged.
- Modern technology allows relatively rapid assessment of herbage availability and pasture cover, as well as the processing of this information. This can be applied to commercially managed grasslands, but there are many problems – logistical, social and economic – in getting such information to traditional pastoralists and in their making use of it.
- Grasslands cover a very large proportion of the globe and are of primary environmental importance, so their sustainable management is a matter of widespread interest and is not limited to those who gain their livelihoods therefrom. The general public benefits from the proper management of catchments, landscapes for wildlife, tourism, conservation of biodiversity, recreation and hunting, but the management costs fall on the pastoralists be

they traditional or commercial. In many areas, commercial stock-rearing off extensive grassland is in economic difficulties and the peoples of traditional systems are mostly poor to very poor. How can those who manage the grasslands be encouraged to do so for the general good, and how can they be recompensed for adjusting management to even more environmentally friendly ways?

- The management of communally held grasslands is generally in great difficulties. Clarification of grazing rights, the putting in place of an appropriate legal framework, which should take into account existing perceived rights, and allocation of some form of long-term security is necessary before herders can begin to indulge in medium- to long-term modifications to their existing systems. Technical grassland interventions (apart from veterinary care) can only be useful once the tenure situation is clarified.

- The overall management of extensive grazing lands should be done within a wide framework on a very large, landscape scale so that it is effective in dealing with the whole range of pastoral resources and products, covers the migration territories of transhumant groups as well as conserving wildlife and catchments. In traditional areas, pastoralists are often in small, poorly organized groups. Better planning and management is only likely to succeed if the pastoral population is assisted to organize itself into large groups that can enter into dialogue with one another and the authorities, not only to participate but to play a leading role in the planning and management processes.

- High, and often increasing, livestock numbers, often associated with reduction of the area available for grazing, is usually associated with reported grassland degradation. In pastoral systems, rising animal numbers are often associated with rises in the human population. The remaining extensive grasslands are mainly in situations where intensification and increase of herbage production is unlikely to be practical or economic. Rarely can more pasture land be made available so, when population numbers obviously exceed the carrying capacity of the land, thought must be given to alternative sources of livelihood.

- Localized overgrazing with neglect of distant pasture is reported in several studies (this includes poor distribution of stock in big paddocks) and is a new but serious problem in countries that have undergone decollectivization and where there are vast areas of steppic and mountain pasture. Again, there is a strong case for organization of the pastoral population to adopt community herders, allocate ex-collective grazing rights and rehabilitate pastoral infrastructure.

- Provision of lean-season feed is an important part of many extensive systems, this is excellent in farming systems and where stock are housed off the pasture in the lean season. Maintaining numbers of stock far in excess of the grassland carrying capacity with purchased feed is, however, extremely destructive, and subsidizing concentrates and cereals for herders is undesirable for sustainable grassland use.

- Improvement of the pastoral vegetation in extensive grasslands should mainly be through manipulation of grazing pressure and the use of controlled fire. Over-seeding is not usually successful on poor soils with unreliable rainfall and is now often regarded as undesirable for the environment; it can, of course, be very useful in agropastoral systems in more favourable conditions.

- A very wide range of genetic material of species, cultivars and ecotypes of pasture grasses and legumes have been collected and screened, but only a very restricted range is readily available commercially.

- Sown pasture, for grazing and mowing, plays a very important role in large- and medium-scale commercial mixed farming, and the use of perennial pastures is to be encouraged wherever possible and profitable since they are often more environmentally desirable than annual cut-and-carry fodders.

- Fodder crops can be useful for strategic use on favoured areas in extensive systems, especially for conservation or supplementing vulnerable classes of stock. They are suitable for both smallholder and large-scale mixed farming enterprises and are becoming increasingly popular with smallholders who have access to markets for milk or fattened stock. While fodder technology is well developed generally, there is still a lot to be done in identifying locally adapted material for smallholder areas, assuring seed supplies and training farmers.

- What is the potential for diversifying the use of grasslands? Commercial producers are experimenting with, for example, tourism and game-ranching. Will such management maintain the grassland biome?

- The area of grassland being put into reserves to conserve wildlife and biodiversity, as well as to encourage tourism, is increasing, often without regard to existing pastoral use. It is desirable that the creation of such reserves should take into account their effect on migration routes, access to essential grassland resources and to what extent grazing livestock and controlled fire will be permitted or encouraged.

- Grasslands are sources of many products other than food for grazing livestock, but grassland scientists have tended to limit their interests to grazing resources. Greater attention to wider ethnobotanical matters is desirable.

REFERENCES

Armstrong, K., de Ruiter, J. & Bezar, H. 2004. Fodder oats in New Zealand and Australia – history, production and potential. pp. 153–177, *in:* Suttie & Reynolds, 2004, q.v.

Batello, C., Marzot, M. & Touré, A.H. 2004. *The Future is an Ancient Lake: Traditional knowledge, biodiversity and genetic resources for food and agriculture in Lake Chad Basin ecosystems.* FAO, Rome, Italy.

Bogdan, A.V. 1977. *Tropical pasture and fodder plants.* London, UK: Longmans. 474 p.

Buringh, P. & Dudal, R. 1987. Agricultural land use in space and time. *In:* M.G. Wolman and F.G.A. Fournier (eds). SCOPE vol. 32. Chichester, UK: John Wiley and Sons.

Chaouki, A.F., Chakroun, M., Allagui, M.B. & Sbeita, A. 2004. Fodder oats in the Maghreb. pp. 53–91, *in:* Suttie & Reynolds, 2004, q.v.

Dolberg, F. & Finlayson, P. 1995. Better feed for animals: more food for people. *World Animal Review,* No.82.

FAO. 1993. Key aspects of strategies for sustainable development of drylands. FAO, Rome, Italy. 60 p.

Fraser, J. & McCartney, D. 2004. Fodder Oats in North America. pp. 19–36, *in:* Suttie & Reynolds, 2004, q.v.

Hu, Z. & Zhang, D. 2003. China's pasture resources. pp. 81–113, *in:* Suttie & Reynolds, 2003, q.v.

t'Mannetje, L. 2000. Silage making in the tropics with particular emphasis on smallholders. *FAO Plant Production and Protection Paper,* No. 161. 180 p.

Shu, W. 2003. Fodder oats in China: an overview. pp. 123–144, *in:* Suttie & Reynolds, 2004, q.v.

Simpson, J. R. & Ou Li. 1996. Feasibility analysis for development of Northern China's beef industry and grazing lands. *Journal of Range Management,* **49**: 560–564.

Suttie, J.M. 2000. *Hay and straw conservation for small-scale farming and pastoral conditions. FAO Plant Production and Protection Series,* No. 29. 303 p.

Suttie, J.M. & Reynolds, S.G. (eds). 2003. Transhumant grazing systems in temperate Asia. *FAO Plant Production and Protection Series,* No. 31. 251 p.

Suttie, J.M. & Reynolds, S.G. (eds). 2004. Fodder oats: a world overview. *FAO Plant Production and Protection Series,* No. 33. 251 p.

Scottish Executive. 2003. The Muirburn Code. See: http://www.scotland.gov.uk/library3/environment/mbcd-00.asp

The Times. 2004. No tourists say nomads. Travel Section, The Times (London). p. 2. 20 November 2004.

Wang, W.L. 2003. Studies on traditional transhumance and a system where herders return to settled winter bases in Burjin county, Altai Prefecture, Xinjiang, China. pp. 115–141, *in:* Suttie & Reynolds, 2003, q.v.

Index